CROSSWORD
SOLVER

CROSSWORD SOLVER

Compiled by

*Nancy E. M. Bailey, Jeanne Brady, Jane Horwood,
Huw Jones and Simon Tomlin*

MARKS &
SPENCER

Marks and Spencer p.l.c.
Baker Street, London W1U 8EP
www.marksandspencer.com

Copyright © Exclusive Editions 2001

This book was created by Magpie Books,
an imprint of Constable & Robinson Ltd

ISBN 1-84273-037-1

A copy of the British Library Cataloguing-in-Publication Data
is available from the British Library

CONTENTS

Science and Technology

Sports, Games and Hobbies

Trade, Commerce and Professions

Transport

INTRODUCTION

The Marks & Spencer *Crossword Solver* is the ideal guide for any crossword enthusiast, presenting over 70,000 carefully selected and classified words in a user-friendly format that will prove invaluable in solving even the most cryptic of crosswords.

The aim of the *Crossword Solver* is to enable you to find the word you want quickly and with the minimum of fuss. Once you have deduced the subject area from the clue, simply look up the relevant category and then scan down to the required number of letters – it really is that simple.

The extensive range of subjects covers everything from literature and the arts to computing and the Internet, all listed in clear and easy to use sections. Most sections are subdivided by numbers of letters in words, with the words then following in alphabetical order; short sections appear in alphabetical order, with the number of letters following.

The *Crossword Solver* is completely up-to-date, covering twenty-first century terminology while retaining the more archaic and arcane words that so often crop up in crosswords. Its wide coverage of subjects means that it can also be used as a first point of general encyclopaedic reference.

ABBREVIATIONS

Abbreviations

1

b. born
C Celsius, Centigrade, Conservative
c cent(s)
c. circa (around, about)
d old penny, old pence (denarius)
d. died
E east, Ecstasy
F Fahrenheit
f feminine, franc(s), forte
g gram(s)
h hour(s)
J Joule
K kelvin, kilobyte
L large, Latin, Liberal, learner
l litre(s)
M monsieur, medium
m masculine, metre(s), minute(s)
m. married, minute(s)
N newton, north
n neuter
p penny, pence, piano
p. page
q. query, question
R Royal, Rex (King), Regina (Queen)
S small, south
s second(s)
V volt(s)
v verse, versus (against), very
W watt(s), west

2

AA Alcoholics Anonymous, Automobile Association
AC air conditioning, alternating current
A/C air conditioning
a/c account
AD Anno Domini (in the year of our Lord)
AI Amnesty International, artificial insemination, artificial intelligence
a.m. ante meridiem (before noon)
AS Anglo-Saxon
BA Bachelor of Arts
BC Before Christ
BD Bachelor of Divinity

BS Bachelor of Science
BT British Telecom
Bt Baronet
ca circa (around, about)
cc carbon copy, cubic centimetre(s)
CD compact disc
cf. compare
ch. chapter
cl centilitre(s)
cl. class, clause
cm centimetre(s)
CO commanding officer
Co. company, county
c/o care of
CV curriculum vitae
DA District Attorney (US)
DC direct current
DD Doctor of Divinity
DJ disc jockey, dinner jacket
DM Deutschmark
do ditto
Dr doctor
ea. each
Ed. editor
e.g. exempli gratia (for example)
eq. equal
ER Elizabeth Regina (Queen)
EU European Union
ex. example, without, from
FA Football Association
FC football club
ff fortissimo
FM frequency modulation
Fr. French, Friday
ft foot, feet
GB Great Britain, gigabyte(s)
GC George Cross
GI general issue (US)
Gk Greek
gm gramme(s)
GM George Medal, genetically modified
GP General Practitioner
GR Georgius Rex (King George)
Gr. Greek
Gt great
HM His/Her Majesty
HP hire purchase
hp horsepower

Abbreviations

HQ headquarters
hr hour
Hz Hertz
ID identification
i.e. id est (that is)
in inch(es)
IQ intelligence quotient
JP Justice of the Peace
Jr junior
KC King's Counsel
kg kilogram(s)
km kilometre(s)
Kt knight
lb libra (pound)
Lt Lieutenant
MA Master of Arts
MB Bachelor of Medicine, megabyte(s)
MC Master of Ceremonies, Military Cross
MD Doctor of Medicine
ME Middle English, myalgic encephalomyelitis
mf mezzo forte
mg milligram(s)
mm millimetre(s)
MO medical officer
MP Member of Parliament, military police
Mr mister
MS manuscript, multiple sclerosis
Mt mount
NB nota bene (note well)
NE north-east
no number (numero)
nr near
NT New Testament
NW north-west
NY New York
NZ New Zealand
OE Old English
OM Order of Merit
Op. opus (work)
OT Old Testament
oz ounce(s)
PA personal assistant, public-address system
PC personal computer, police constable, politically correct
pd paid
PE physical education
pf pianoforte
pl plural
PM Prime Minister
p.m. post meridiem, post mortem

PO post office
pp pianissimo
pp. pages
p.p. per procuration (by proxy)
PR proportional representation, public relations
PS postscript
pt pint
QC Queen's Counsel
qr quarter
qt quart
q.v. quod vide (which see)
RA Royal Academy
RC Roman Catholic
Rd road
RE Religious Education
SE south-east
SF science fiction
SJ Society of Jesus
SM sadomasochism, Sergeant-Major
sq. square
Sr senior
SS steamship
St Saint, street
SW south-west
TA Territorial Army
TB tuberculosis
TV television
UK United Kingdom
UN United Nations
US United States
VC Victoria Cross
VD venereal disease
v.g. very good
VR Victoria Regina (Queen)
vs versus
vv verses
WC water closet
wt weight
XL extra large
yd yard
yr your

3

AAA Amateur Athletic Association, American Automobile Association
ABC alphabet, American Broadcasting Company
ADC aide-de-camp
Adm. Admiral
AGM annual general meeting
aka also known as
AOB any other business

AOR	adult-oriented rock	DSc	Doctor of Science
APR	annual percentage rate	DSM	Distinguished Service Medal
Apr.	April	DSO	Distinguished Service Order
arr.	arrive(s, ed)	DSS	Department of Social Security
ATM	automated or automatic teller machine	DTI	Department of Trade and Industry
ATS	Auxiliary Territorial Service	EEC	European Economic Community
Aug.	August	ENE	east-north-east
aux.	auxiliary	ESE	east-south-east
Ave	avenue	Esq.	Esquire
BBC	British Broadcasting Corporation	etc.	etcetera
BDS	Bachelor of Dental Surgery	FBI	Federal Bureau of Investigation (US)
bhp	brake horsepower	FDA	Food and Drug Administration (US)
BMA	British Medical Association		
BNP	British National Party	Feb.	February
Bro.	brother	fem.	feminine
BSc	Bachelor of Science	fig.	figure
BSE	bovine spongiform encephalopathy	f.o.b.	free on board
		FRS	Fellow of the Royal Society
BST	British Summer Time	gal.	gallon(s)
Btu	British Thermal Unit(s)	GBE	Knight Grand Cross of the British Empire
BVM	Blessed Virgin Mary		
cap.	capital	Gen.	General
CBE	Commander of the British Empire (Order)	GHQ	General Headquarters
		GHz	gigahertz
CBI	Confederation of British Industry	Gib.	Gibraltar
		GMO	genetically modified organism
CBS	Columbia Broadcasting System (US)	GMT	Greenwich Mean Time
		HIV	Human Immunodeficiency Virus
CFC	chlorofluorocarbon	HMS	His/Her Majesty's Ship
CIA	Central Intelligence Agency	Hon.	honorary, Honourable
CID	Criminal Investigation Department	HRH	His/Her Royal Highness
		hrs	hours
c.i.f.	cost, insurance, freight	IBA	Independent Broadcasting Authority
CIO	Congress of Industrial Organizations (U.S.)		
		ILO	International Labour Organization
CJD	Creutzfeldt-Jakob disease	Inc.	incorporated
CNN	Cable News Network (US)	INS	Immigration and Naturalization Service (US)
COD	cash or collect on delivery		
cwt	hundredweight	ins	inches
DBE	Dame Commander of the British Empire (Order)	IOU	(acknowledgment of debt)
		IRA	Irish Republican Army
DDT	dichlorodiphenyl trichlorocethane	IRS	Internal Revenue Service (US)
		ITV	Independent Television
DEA	Drug Enforcement Agency (US)	IUD	intrauterine device
Dec.	December	Jan.	January
DFC	Distinguished Flying Cross	Jun.	junior
DFM	Distinguished Flying Medal	KBE	Knight Commander of the British Empire (Order)
DIY	do it yourself		
DNA	deoxyribonucleic acid	KGB	Komitet Gosudarstvennoi Bezopasnosti (Committee of State Security)
DOS	disc operating system		
doz.	dozen		
DSC	Distinguished Service Cross		

KKK	Ku Klux Klan	OBE	Officer of the British Empire (Order)
kph	kilometres per hour		
Lab.	Labour	Oct.	October
lbw	leg before wicket	OTC	Officer Training Corps
LCD	liquid crystal display	PBS	Public Broadcasting Service (US)
LLB	Bachelor of Laws		
LLD	Doctor of Laws	PhD	Doctor of Philosophy
loq.	loquitur (speaks)	PLO	Palestine Liberation Organization
LSD	Lysergic acid diethylamide		
L.S.D.	Librae (pounds), solidi (shillings), denarii (pence)	PMS	premenstrual syndrome
		PMT	premenstrual tension
LSE	London School of Economics	pop.	population
Ltd	Limited	POW	prisoner of war
Maj.	Major	pro	professional
Mar.	March	PTO	please turn over
MBA	Master of Business Administration	PVC	polyvinyl chloride
		QED	quod erat demonstrandum (which was to be demonstrated)
MBE	Member of the British Empire (Order)		
MCC	Marylebone Cricket Club	RAC	Royal Automobile Club
MCP	male chauvinist pig	RAF	Royal Air Force
MEP	Member of the European Parliament	RAM	random access memory
		ref	referee, reference
MHz	megahertz	rep	repertory, representative
Mme	Madame	Rev.	Reverend
MOD	Ministry of Defence	RIP	requiescat in pace (may he/she rest in peace)
MOT	Ministry of Transport		
mph	miles per hour	RMS	Royal Mail steamer
MSc	Master of Science	RNA	ribonucleic acid
MSF	Manufacturing, Science and Finance (trade union)	ROM	read-only memory
		RSI	repetitive strain injury
MSS	Manuscripts	RUC	Royal Ulster Constabulary
MTV	Music Television	SAS	Special Air Service
NBC	National Broadcasting Company (US)	Sec.	secretary
		Sen.	senator
NCO	non-commissioned officer	SNP	Scottish National Party
NFU	National Farmers' Union	Soc.	society
NHS	National Health Service	SOS	(distress signal)
NNE	north-north-east	SSE	south-south-east
NNR	National Nature Reserve	SSW	south-south-west
NNW	north-north-west	STD	sexually transmitted disease, subscriber trunk dialling
Nos	numbers		
Nov.	November	tbs	tablespoon(s)
NRA	National Rifle Association (US)	TNT	trinitrotoluene (explosive)
NSW	New South Wales	TUC	Trades Union Congress
NUJ	National Union of Journalists	UDA	Ulster Defence Association
NUM	National Union of Mineworkers	UDI	unilateral declaration of independence
NUS	National Union of Seamen, National Union of Students		
		UFO	unidentified flying object
NUT	National Union of Teachers	UHF	ultra-high frequency
NVQ	National Vocational Qualification	UHT	ultra heat treated
		UNO	United Nations Organization
NYC	New York City	USA	United States of America, United States Army
OAP	old age pensioner		

USN	United States Navy
USS	United States Ship
VAT	value-added tax
VDU	visual display unit
VHF	very high frequency
VIP	very important person
viz	videlicet (namely)
vol	volume
VSO	Voluntary Service Overseas
WNW	west-north-west
WPC	Woman Police Constable
WSW	west-south-west
WTO	World Trade Organization

4

AIDS	Acquired Immune Deficiency Syndrome
asst	assistant
Bart	baronet
Beds	Bedfordshire
Brit	British
Bros	brothers
BUPA	British United Provident Association
Capt.	Captain
chap.	chapter
C of E	Church of England
Corp.	Corporal, corporation
dept	department
DETR	Department for the Environment, Transport and the Regions
DfEE	Department for Education and Employment
DLit	Doctor of Literature
GATT	General Agreement on Tariffs and Trade
GCSE	General Certificate of Secondary Education
Glos	Gloucestershire
GNVQ	General National Vocational Qualification
ibid.	ibidem (in the same source)
inst.	instant (in the present month)
ISBN	International Standard Book Number
MAFF	Ministry of Agriculture, Fisheries and Food
Mlle	Mademoiselle
MusB	Bachelor of Music
MusD	Doctor of Music
NASA	National Aeronautics and Space Administration

NATO	North Atlantic Treaty Organization
OECD	Organization for Economic Co-operation and Development
OHMS	On His/Her Majesty's Service
OPEC	Organization of Petroleum Exporting Countries
Oxon	Oxfordshire, of Oxford
PAYE	pay as you earn
PDSA	People's Dispensary for Sick Animals
Prof.	professor
recd	received
Regt	regiment
RIBA	Royal Institute of British Architects
RSPB	Royal Society for the Protection of Birds
RSVP	répondez s'il vous plaît (please reply)
Sept.	September
Serg.	Sergeant
tbsp	tablespoon(s)
TEFL	teaching English as a foreign language
TGWU	Transport and General Workers' Union
USAF	United States Air Force
USSR	Union of Soviet Socialist Republics
WASP	white Anglo-Saxon Protestant
YMCA	Young Men's Christian Association
YWCA	Young Women's Christian Association

5

ad lib	ad libitum (as much as desired)
ANZAC	Australian and New Zealand Army Corps
ASCII	American standard code for information interchange
assoc.	associate, association
B&B	bed and breakfast
Berks	Berkshire
Bucks	Buckinghamshire
Cambs	Cambridgeshire
CD-ROM	compact disc read-only memory
CITES	Convention on International Trade in Endangered Species

DLitt	Doctor of Letters	Yorks	Yorkshire
et seq.	et sequens (and what follows)		
Hants	Hampshire	**6**	
Herts	Hertfordshire	Cantab.	of Cambridge
Lancs	Lancashire	Messrs	Messieurs
Lieut.	Lieutenant	Ofsted	Office for Standards in Education
NAAFI	Navy, Army and Air Force Institutes	per pro	per procurationem (by proxy)
NSPCC	National Society for the Prevention of Cruelty to Children	Staffs	Staffordshire
		UNESCO	United Nations Educational, Scientific and Cultural Organization
op. cit.	opere citato (in the work cited)	UNICEF	United Nations International Children's Emergency Fund
P and O	Peninsular and Oriental		
RSPCA	Royal Society for the Prevention of Cruelty to Animals	**7**	
		E. and OE.	errors and omissions excepted
Rt Hon.	Right Honourable	mod cons	modern conveniences
Rt Rev.	Right Reverend		
Salop	Shropshire	**8**	
UNHCR	United Nations High Commission for Refugees	UNPROFOR	United Nations Protection Force
Wilts	Wiltshire		

States of the USA

Alabama	AL, Ala	Missouri	MO, Mo
Alaska	AK, Alas	Montana	MT, Mont
Arizona	AZ, Ariz	Nebraska	NE, Neb
Arkansas	AR, Ark	Nevada	NV, Nev
California	CA, Cal, Calif	New Hampshire	NH
Colorado	CO, Colo	New Jersey	NJ
Connecticut	CT, Conn	New Mexico	NM
District of		New York	NY
Columbia	DC	North Carolina	NC
Delaware	DE, Del	North Dakota	ND, N Dak
Florida	FL, Fla	Ohio	OH, O.
Georgia	GA, Ga	Oklahoma	OK, Okla
Hawaii	HA	Oregon	OR, Or.,Oreg
Idaho	ID, Id, Ida	Pennsylvania	PA, Penn
Illinois	IL, Ill	Rhode Island	RI
Indiana	IN, Ina	South Carolina	SC
Iowa	IA, Ia	South Dakota	SD, S Dak
Kansas	KS, Kan	Tennessee	TN, Tenn
Kentucky	KY, Ky, Ken	Texas	TX, Tex
Louisiana	LA, La	Utah	UT
Maine	ME	Vermont	VT
Maryland	MD, Md	Virginia	VA
Massachusetts	MA, Mass	Washington	WA, Wash
Michigan	MI, Mich	West Virginia	WV, W Va
Minnesota	MN, Minn	Wisconsin	WI, Wis
Mississippi	MS, Miss	Wyoming	WY, Wyo

ANIMALS

Mammals, including Sea Mammals

2	atok	oxen	capul	otter	auroch	guenon
ai	axis	paca	civet	ounce	aye-aye	hacker
ox	bear	paco	coati	panda	baboon	heifer
zo	boar	pard	coney	pekan	badger	hogget
	buck	peba	coypu	pongo	bandar	howler
3	bull	pika	crone	potto	bandog	impala
ape	calf	pony	cuddy	punch	bayard	inyala
ass	cavy	prad	daman	ratel	beaver	jackal
bat	colt	puma	dhole	rhino	beluga	jaguar
bok	cony	quey	dingo	sable	bharal	jennet
cat	coon	rusa	dogie	saiga	bobcat	jerboa
cow	deer	saki	drill	sajou	boomer	kalong
cub	dieb	seal	dsomo	sasin	bovine	kennet
cur	dogy	skug	eland	serow	burhel	koodoo
doe	douc	stag	fitch	sheep	cabrie	langur
dog	eyra	stot	fossa	shrew	caprid	lechwe
dso	fawn	stud	gayal	skunk	castor	llama
dzo	foal	tahr	genet	sloth	catalo	malkin
elk	gaur	tegg	goral	sorex	cattle	malmag
ewe	girl	tehr	grice	spado	cayuse	margay
fox	goat	titi	harpy	steer	chacma	marmot
gib	gyal	topi	hinny	stoat	coaita	marten
gnu	hack	unau	hippo	swine	colugo	mawkin
goa	hare	urus	horse	takin	cosset	messan
hog	hart	urva	hound	talpa	cougar	monkey
kid	hind	vole	human	tapir	coyote	morkin
kob	ibex	wolf	hutia	tatoo	cuscus	musk ox
man	jade	yale	hyena	tayra	dassie	nilgai
mog	jomo	zati	hyrax	tiger	desman	nilgau
nag	kine	zebu	indri	tigon	dickey	numbat
pig	kudu	zobo	izard	urial	dik-dik	ocelot
ram	lamb		jocko	urson	donkey	onager
rat	lion	**5**	jumbo	vison	dugong	oorial
roc	lynx	addax	kaama	vixen	duiker	ourebi
roe	mara	aguti	koala	waler	dzeren	ovibos
sai	mare	ammon	kulan	whale	ermine	pallah
sow	mice	baloo	kyloe	whelp	fennec	possum
teg	mico	beast	lemur	yapok	ferret	pygarg
tod	mink	bidet	loris	zibet	foussa	quokka
tup	mohr	biped	manis	zizel	fox bat	rabbit
ure	moke	bison	manul	zoril	galago	racoon
wat	mole	bongo	mhoor	zorra	garran	red fox
yak	mona	brach	moose	zorro	garron	reebok
zho	mule	brock	mouse		gelada	renard
	musk	bruin	nagor	**6**	gerbil	rhebok
4	neat	bunny	nyala	agouti	gibbon	rhesus
anoa	oont	burro	okapi	aliped	gopher	ridgil
arna	orca	camel	oribi	alpaca	grison	rodent
atoc	oryx	caple	otary	argali	grivet	rouncy

Animals

sagoin	dolphin	noctule	brown rat	sewellel
sambar	draft ox	nylghau	bushbaby	sewer rat
sea ape	eanling	opossum	bushbuck	sika deer
sea cow	echidna	panther	cachalot	sirenian
serval	ermelin	peccary	capuchin	squirrel
simian	fatling	polecat	capucine	staggard
sorrel	fitchet	potoroo	capybara	steambok
spayad	fitchew	pricket	carcajou	stinkard
suslik	foumart	primate	cariacou	suilline
taguan	fur seal	procyon	cave bear	suricate
tapeti	galla ox	raccoon	cavicorn	talapoin
tarand	gazelle	red deer	chipmunk	tamandua
tarpan	gelding	reed rat	civet cat	tamanoir
tauric	gemsbok	rietbok	creodont	tetrapod
teledu	genette	rock doe	cricetus	ungulata
tenrec	gerenuk	roe buck	cunjevoi	viscacha
theave	giraffe	roe deer	dormouse	wanderoo
tupaia	gorilla	rorqual	duckbill	warrigal
tusker	grampus	sambhur	earthhog	water-hog
urchin	guanaco	sapajou	elephant	water-rat
vermin	guereza	sassaby	entellus	weanling
vervet	gumnura	sciurus	grey wolf	wild boar
vicuna	hamster	sea-bear	grysbock	wild goat
walrus	hircine	sea-calf	hair seal	yearling
wapiti	huanaco	sealion	harp seal	zorrillo
weasel	jacchus	souslik	hartbees	
wombat	jackass	sumpter	hedgehog	**9**
wow-wow	jumbuck	sunbear	hedgepig	arctic fox
	keitloa	tamarin	hoggerel	armadillo
7	kidling	tarsier	hylobate	babacoote
acouchy	klipdas	thiller	kangaroo	babirussa
ant bear	lemming	tigress	kinkajou	bamboo rat
aurochs	leopard	twinter	kiwikiwi	bandicoot
bantung	libbard	vicuana	lamantin	barbastel
bearcat	linsang	viverra	mandrill	binturong
bighorn	lioness	warthog	mangabey	black bear
blesbok	macaque	wild ass	marmoset	black buck
bonasus	madoqua	wildcat	mastodon	blue whale
boshbok	mammoth	wild dog	mongoose	brown bear
bosvark	manatee	wistiti	musk deer	carnivore
brocket	markhor	wolf dog	musquash	catamount
buffalo	marmose	zamouse	noctilio	chickaree
bullock	meerkat		pacarana	deermouse
bush cat	miniver	**8**	pangolin	delundung
bushpig	mole rat	aardvark	platypus	didelphid
caracal	mormops	aardwolf	porpoise	draught ox
caribou	mouflon	anteater	red panda	dray horse
cattalo	muntjak	antelope	reedbuck	dromedary
chamois	musimon	babirusa	reindeer	dziggetai
cheetah	musk rat	behemoth	riverhog	eared seal
chikara	mustela	black fox	ruminant	flying fox
colobus	mycetes	black rat	schimmel	grey whale
dasypod	mylodon	bontebok	sea otter	groundhog
dasyure	narwhal	brant fox	serotine	guinea pig

honey bear
ichneumon
jungle cat
lagomorph
leviathan
livestock
monoceros
monotreme
mouse deer
orangutan
pachyderm
packhorse
pademelon
palm civet
pipistrel
polar bear
porcupine
prongbuck
pronghorn
quadruman
quadruped
rearmouse
reermouse
rock hyrax
rosmarine
shrew mole
silver fox
sitatunga
springbok
steinbock
stonebuck
thylacine
tragelaph
tree hyrax
tree shrew
viverrine
water mole
water vole
waterbuck
white bear
wild horse
wolverene
wolverine
woodchuck
zoophagon

10

angora goat
angwantibo
animalcule
anthropoid
babiroussa
Barbary ape
birch mouse

black rhino
black whale
bottlenose
brown hyena
buckjumper
camelopard
catterhine
chevrotain
chimpanzee
chinchilla
coatimundi
common seal
cottontail
diphyodont
draft horse
fallow deer
fieldmouse
giant panda
hartebeest
hippogryff
house mouse
human being
jackrabbit
Kodiak bear
Malay tapir
minke whale
musk beaver
paddymelon
pichiciago
pilot whale
pine marten
prairie dog
pygmy shrew
quadrumana
raccoon dog
rhinoceros
right whale
river horse
rock badger
rock rabbit
saki monkey
sea-leopard
sea-unicorn
shrew mouse
sperm whale
springhaas
timber wolf
vampire bat
white rhino
wildebeest

11

American elk
barbastelle

digitigrade
douroucouli
flying lemur
flying mouse
fox squirrel
Grevy's zebra
grizzly bear
jumping deer
kangaroo rat
killer whale
mountain cat
muntjac deer
orang-outang
pipistrelle
rat kangaroo
red squirrel
rock wallaby
Scilly shrew
sea elephant
snow leopard
wildebeeste
wishtonwish
woolly lemur

12

Arabian camel
Barbary sheep
Bengal monkey
catamountain
Dall porpoise
draught horse
elephant seal
ferae naturae
flittermouse
grey squirrel
harvest mouse
hippopotamus
horseshoe bat
klipspringer
mountain hare
mountain lion
pouched mouse
rhesus monkey
roan antelope
rock squirrel
Shetland pony
spider monkey
spotted hyena
striped hyena
tree kangaroo
water opossum
woolly monkey

13

Asian elephant
Bactrian camel
Chapman's zebra
European bison
golden hamster
humpback whale
Indian buffalo
laughing hyena
mountain zebra
Parry's wallaby
ring-tail coati
sable antelope
spiny anteater
spiny dormouse
Tasmanian wolf
tree porcupine

14

Australian bear
bridled wallaby
Burchell's zebra
crab-eating seal
dormouse possum
edible dormouse
fin-backed whale
flying squirrel
Greenland whale
ground squirrel
Indian elephant
Indian pangolin
Isabelline bear
marmoset monkey
Patagonian cavy
snowshoe rabbit
Tasmanian devil

15

African elephant
American buffalo
Bennett's wallaby
black rhinoceros
finless porpoise
harbour porpoise
humpbacked whale
rabbit bandicoot
ring-tailed lemur
sabretooth tiger
Tasmanian possum
Thomson's gazelle

18

duck-billed platypus

CATS

3	queen	Burmese	sealpoint	**12**
mog	smoke	Persian	Tonkinese	brown Burmese
red	tabby	ragdoll		Scottish Fold
Rex		red self	**10**	
tom	**6**	Siamese	Abyssinian	**13**
	Birman	Turkish	chinchilla	tortoiseshell
4	feline		Cornish Rex	Turkish Angora
Abby	Havana	**8**	lilac-point	
blue	kitten	Balinese	longhaired	**14 and over**
Manx	moggie	Devon Rex	Turkish Van	chocolate-point (14)
	mouser			domestic shorthair
5	ratter	**9**	**11**	(17)
cream	Somali	blue-point	Russian Blue	Japanese Bobtail (15)
felis	tomcat	chinchilla	shorthaired	Norwegian Forest (15)
kitty		ginger tom	silver tabby	Scottish wildcat (15)
Korat	**7**	grimalkin		
pussy	British	Maine Coon		

CATTLE, SHEEP AND PIGS

(C) = cow; (S) = sheep; (P) = pig

3	6	8	Icelandic (S)	**13**
cow	beeves	Ayrshire (C)	Rough Fell (S)	Aberdeen Angus (C)
ewe	bovine	Cotswold (S)	shearling	Beef Shorthorn (C)
hog	Dexter (C)	Dartmoor (S)	Shorthorn (C)	Texas Longhorn (C)
ram	Dorset (S)	Drysdale (S)	Southdown (S)	Welsh Mountain (S)
sow	Galway (S)	Friesian (C)	White Park (C)	
	gimmer	Galloway (C)		**14 and over**
4	heifer	Guernsey (C)	**10**	Bluefaced Leicester
boar	hogget	Herdwick (S)	British Lop (P)	(S) (18)
bull	Jersey (C)	Hereford (C,	Exmoor Horn (S)	British Milk Sheep
calf	Merino (S)	P)	Gloucester (C)	(16)
gilt	Orkney (S)	Highland (C)	Hill Radnor (S)	Dairy Shorthorn (C)
herd	Oxford (S)	Holstein (C)	Large Black (P)	(14)
lamb	porker	Landrace (P)	Large White (P)	Gloucester Old Spot
Manx (S)	Romney (S)	Limousin (C)	Saddleback (P)	(P) (17)
runt	Sussex (C)	Longhorn (C)	Shropshire (S)	Large Black-white
Soay (S)	Vaynol (C)	milch cow	South Devon (C)	(P) (15)
	wether	Mulefoot (P)		Oxford Sandy and
5		Pietrain (P)	**11**	Black (P) (19)
Angus (C)	**7**	Shetland (C,	Belgian blue (C)	Scottish Blackface
Devon (C)	Brahman (C)	S)	Irish moiled (C)	(S) (17)
dogie	bullock	Tamworth	Middle White	Vietnamese
Duroc (P)	Cheviot (S)	(P)	(P)	Potbelly (P) (18)
flock	Iberian (P)		Wensleydale (S)	
Jacob (S)	jumbuck	**9**		
Kerry (C)	lambkin	Berkshire (P)	**12**	
steer	Lincoln (S)	Charolais (C)	Barbary sheep	
stirk	mouflon	Guinea Hog	fighting bull	
swine	Red Poll (C)	Hampshire	Manx Loaghtan	
Welsh (P)	Suffolk (S)	(P)	(S)	

DOGS

3
cur
dam
lab
lym
pug
pup

4
chow
dogo
mutt
Peke
puli
Skye
tike
Tosa
tyke

5
akita
bitch
boxer
brach
Cairn
canis
corgi
dingo
hound
husky
pi-dog
pooch
puppy
spitz
whelp

6
Afghan
barbet
basset
beagle
borzoi
briard
canine
cocker
collie
Eskimo
gundog
Kuvasz
lap dog
Lassie
limmer

pariah
poodle
pug dog
pye-dog
pyrame
ranger
ratter
saluki
setter
toy dog

7
basenji
beardie
bird dog
bulldog
clumber
deer-dog
dry-foot
griffon
harrier
lion dog
longdog
lurcher
Maltese
mastiff
mongrel
pointer
samoyed
sharpei
Sheltie
sloughi
snap dog
spaniel
Staffie
starter
terrier
whippet
wolf dog

8
Airedale
Alsatian
Blenheim
chow-chow
coachdog
demi-wolf
Derby dog
Doberman
elkhound
foxhound
guide dog

hound dog
house dog
keeshond
komondor
Labrador
malemute
papillon
Pekinese
pinscher
sealyharn
sheepdog
springer
St Hubert
turnspit
watchdog
water-dog

9
badger dog
Bed Gelert
boarhound
buckhound
chihuahua
dachshund
Dalmatian
deerhound
Eskimo dog
Great Dane
greyhound
Kerry blue
Llasa apso
papillion
Pekingese
police dog
red setter
retriever
Rin Tin Tin
schipperke
schnauzer
St Bernard
staghound
wolfhound

10
Bedlington
Beth Gelert
bloodhound
fox terrier
hearing dog
Maltese dog
otterhound
Pomeranian

Rottweiler
scent hound
schipperke
sighthound
sniffer dog
Welsh corgi
Welsh hound
wirehaired
working dog

11
Afghan hound
basset hound
bichon frise
Bruxelloise
bull mastiff
bull terrier
carriage dog
Fell terrier
Irish setter
Jack Russell
Kerry beagle
rough collie
Skye terrier
Talbot hound

12
Belvoir hound
border collie
Cairn terrier
Dandy
  Dinmont
gazelle hound
German collie
Gordon setter
Irish spaniel
Irish terrier
Japanese Chin
Newfoundland
Saint Bernard
Saintongeois
seeing-eye dog
smooth collie
smooth-haired
water spaniel
Welsh terrier

13
affenpinscher
Alpine spaniel
bearded collie
border terrier

Boston terrier
cocker spaniel
Dandie
  Dinmont
English setter
French bulldog
Scotch terrier
Sussex spaniel

14
clumber spaniel
German
  shepherd
Irish wolfhound
Norfolk spaniel
Norfolk terrier
Norwich terrier
Tibetan mastiff

15
Aberdeen
  terrier
Airedale terrier
Alaskan
  malamute
Belgian
  sheepdog
blue Gascon
  hound
Brussels griffon
Cuban
  bloodhound
Egyptian
  bassett
English
  springer
golden retriever
Greyfriars
  Bobby
Highland
  terrier
Japanese
  spaniel
Lakeland
  terrier
Norfolk
  springer
Scottish terrier
Sealyham
  terrier
springer
  spaniel

23

16	17	18
Doberman pinscher	Bedlington terrier	King Charles spaniel
Italian greyhound	English toy spaniel	Old English sheepdog
Shetland sheepdog	Manchester terrier	Rhodesian ridgeback
	Parson Jack Russell	
	Scottish deerhound	

HORSES, PONIES, ETC.

3	mount	mustang	Falabella	quarter horse
ass	Neddy	palfrey	packhorse	Shetland pony
bay	Pinto	piebald	Percheron	Suffolk Punch
cob	steed		racehorse	thoroughbred
dun	Welsh	**8**	stud horse	
nag	zebra	chestnut	wild horse	**13**
		Friesian		carriage horse
4	**6**	gin horse	**10**	Chapman's zebra
Arab	bronco	Holstein	Clydesdale	Connemara pony
hack	brumby	packmule	coach horse	Haflinger pony
mule	dobbin	palomino	draft horse	New Forest pony
pony	donkey	polo pony	Exmoor pony	
roan	equine	skewbald	Lippizaner	**14**
	hinney		Shire horse	Burchell's zebra
5	quagga	**9**		Icelandic horse
burro		brood mare	**12**	
equus	**7**	carthorse	Cleveland Bay	**16**
filly	Arabian	Dales pony	Dartmoor pony	Przewalski's horse
hinny	jackass	dray horse	hackney horse	Welsh mountain pony

MARSUPIALS

3	**6**	opossum	planigale	rock wallaby	Tasmanian
roo	boomer	wallaby	thylacine	sminthopsis	wolf
	cuscus				
4	numbat	**8**	**10**	**12**	**14**
joey	possum	kangaroo	honey mouse	marsupial rat	marsupial
	quokka	wallaroo	rat opossum	mouse opossum	mouse
5	wombat			tree kangaroo	Tasmanian
koala		**9**	**11**		devil
quoll	**7**	bandicoot	hare wallaby	**13**	
yapok	dasyure	pademelon	rat kangaroo	marsupial mole	

BIRDS

3		owl	tit	aves	coot	erne	gull	kaka
auk	hen	pen	tui	barb	crax	eyas	hawk	kite
cob	jay	pie		baya	crow	fowl	hern	kiwi
daw	kae	poe	**4**	bird	dodo	fung	huia	knot
emu	kea	ree	alca	bubo	dove	gawk	huma	koel
fop	kia	roc	anas	chat	duck	gier	ibis	kora
fum	mew	ruc	arco	cock	dupe	guan	iunx	kuku
	moa							

lark	amzel	ornis	veery	gentoo	pouter
loom	ardea	ortyx	virgo	godurt	powter
loon	ariel	ousel	wader	godwit	puffin
lory	biddy	ouzel	wagel	gooney	pullet
mina	bongo	owlet	whaup	gorhen	pygarg
myna	booby	pewee	wonga	goslet	queest
naff	bowet	pewit		grakle	quelea
nene	brant	picus	**6**	grouse	racama
nias	bucco	pipit	aiglet	hacket	ratite
nyas	capon	pitta	aigret	hagden	redcap
otis	chick	poaka	alcedo	hareld	reeler
pauw	chirm	poult	alcyon	hoazin	roberd
pavo	claik	prion	ancona	hoopoe	roller
pern	colin	purre	argala	hoopoo	rotche
pica	crake	quail	auklet	howlet	ruddoc
piet	crane	radge	avocet	jabiru	runner
poll	creak	raven	bantam	jacana	scamel
pope	daker	reeve	barbet	jaeger	scobby
pout	didus	robin	bonxie	jerkin	scoter
rail	diver	rodge	bowess	kakapo	sea-bar
rhea	drake	sacre	brolga	kiddow	sea-cob
rixy	dunny	saker	buffel	lanner	sea-mew
roch	eagle	sally	bulbul	leipoa	sea-pie
rock	egret	sasia	cagmag	linnet	shrike
rook	eider	saury	canary	loriot	shrite
ruff	finch	scape	chewet	magpie	sicsac
rukh	galah	scarf	chough	marrot	simurg
runt	ganza	scaup	chukar	martin	siskin
rype	geese	scops	citril	menura	smeath
shag	glede	scray	condor	merlin	strich
skua	goose	senex	corbie	merops	strick
smee	goura	serin	corvus	merula	sultan
smew	grebe	shama	coucal	missel	takahe
sora	gripe	sitta	cuckoo	monaul	tarsel
sord	harpy	skite	culver	mopoke	tercel
sore	heron	snipe	curlew	mot-mot	thrush
spot	hobby	solan	cushat	musket	tirwit
swan	Jager	soree	cygnet	nandow	tomtit
taha	junco	spink	cygnus	nestor	toucan
teal	larus	squab	darter	oriole	towhee
tern	lowan	stare	dipper	osprey	tringa
tody	lyrie	stilt	drongo	oxbird	trogon
wavy	macaw	stint	ducker	parrot	turaco
wren	madge	stork	dunlin	paster	turbit
xema	maneh	strix	eaglet	pavone	Turdus
yaup	mavis	swift	einack	peahen	turkey
yite	merle	tarin	elanet	pecker	turner
yunx	minah	terek	falcon	peewee	turtle
zati	miner	topau	fulmar	peewit	waggel
	monal	topet	galeen	pernis	weaver
5	murre	tucan	gambet	petrel	whidah
agami	mynah	twite	gander	pigeon	whydah
ajuru	nandu	umbre	gannet	plover	wigeon
amsel	noddy	urubu	garrot	poulet	willet

Animals

witwal	dum-bird	limpkin	scammel	witwall
woosel	dunnock	lorilet	scooper	wood owl
yaffle	egg-bird	mallard	sea-crow	wrybill
ynambu	emu-wren	manakin	sea-duck	wryneck
zivola	fantail	manikin	sea-fowl	yeldrin
zoozoo	fen duck	marabou	seagull	
	fern owl	maracan	sea-hawk	**8**
7	fig-bird	martlet	senegal	aasvogel
antbird	finfoot	megamys	seriema	accentor
apteryx	fish owl	mew gull	serinus	adjutant
attagas	flicker	migrant	shirley	aigrette
attagen	flusher	minivet	simargh	alcatras
awlbird	gadwall	modwall	sirgang	amadavat
babbler	gavilan	moorhen	skimmer	arapunga
barn owl	gobbler	motacil	skylark	avadavat
bee-bird	gorcock	moth-owl	snow-owl	barnacle
bittern	gorcrow	mudlark	spadger	bateleur
blue-cap	goshawk	muggent	sparrow	beam-bird
bluetit	gosling	oilbird	squacco	becafico
buceros	grackle	ortolan	staniel	bee-eater
bullbat	grallae	oscines	stannel	bell-bird
bummalo	greyhen	ostrich	stanyel	blackcap
bunting	greylag	oven tit	stumpie	bluebill
buphaga	griffin	pandion	sturnus	bluebird
bushtit	haggard	partlet	sunbird	blue-wren
bustard	halcyon	peacock	swallow	boat-bill
buzzard	harfang	peafowl	swimmer	boat-tail
cackler	harnmer	pelican	tadorna	bobolink
caponet	harrier	penguin	tanager	bobwhite
cariama	hawk owl	percher	tarrock	bockelet
carvist	hen-harm	peterel	tattler	bockeret
catbird	hickway	phaeton	tiercel	brancher
cheeper	hoatzin	phoenix	tinamou	brevipen
chewink	hoot owl	pinnock	tinamus	bush chat
chicken	horn owl	pintado	titlark	bush lark
ciconia	ice-bird	pintail	titling	bush wren
coal tit	impeyan	pochard	titmice	calandra
cobswan	jacamar	poe-bird	touraco	calangay
colibri	jackass	poultry	tree tit	caneroma
columba	jackdaw	puttock	trochil	caracara
corella	jacksaw	quabird	tumbler	cardinal
cotinga	jacobin	quetzal	turakoo	cargoose
courlan	jashawk	raddock	vulture	cheewink
courser	jedcock	rantock	vulturn	clot-bird
cowbird	kamichi	redhead	wagtail	cockatoo
creeper	kestrel	redpoll	wapacut	cockerel
cropper	killdee	redwing	warbler	coquimbo
Cuculus	kinglet	robinet	waxbill	corn bird
dorhawk	lagopus	rooster	waxwing	curassow
dorking	lapwing	rosella	weebill	cursores
dottrel	lavrock	rotchie	whooper	cutwater
doucher	Leghorn	ruddock	widgeon	dabchick
dovekie	lentner	sakeret	widock	daker-hen
dovelet	lich-owl	sawbill	wimbrel	dandy-hen

didapper
dinornis
dipchick
dorr-hawk
dotterel
duck-hawk
duckling
dun-diver
eagle-owl
estridge
fauvette
fig-eater
finnikin
firetail
fish-hawk
flamingo
gairfowl
gamecock
gang-gang
garefowl
garganey
great tit
greenlet
grey teal
grosbeak
guachero
hackbolt
hamburgh
hawfinch
hazel-hen
hemipode
hernshaw
hickwall
hornbill
hula-bird
keskidee
killdeer
kingbird
landrail
langshan
lanneret
laverock
lorikeet
love-bird
lyrebird
mandarin
mannikin
marabout
marsh tit
megapode
mina bird
mire crow
mire drum
moorcock

moorfowl
moorgame
morillon
musk duck
mute swan
mynabird
nestling
nightjar
notornis
nuthatch
oldsquaw
oxpecker
paitrick
parakeet
paroquet
peachick
percolin
petchary
pheasant
plungeon
podargus
popinjay
prunella
puff-bird
pygmy owl
redshank
redstart
reedling
ricebird
ring dove
ringtail
rock dove
sagecock
sandpeep
screamer
scrub tit
sea eagle
shelduck
shoebill
shoveler
sittella
snowbird
snowy owl
songbird
songlark
songster
starling
struthio
swamphen
tanagers
tantalus
tawny owl
terntero
thrasher

thresher
throstle
titmouse
tomnoddy
tragopan
tube-nose
umbrette
waterhen
wheatear
whimbrel
whinchat
whip-bird
whistler
white-ear
white-eye
wildfowl
wood duck
woodchat
woodcock
woodlark
xanthura
yeldring
yeldrock
yoldring
zopilote

9

accipiter
aepyornis
albatross
andorinha
ant-thrush
autophagi
baltimore
bean goose
beccafico
beefeater
bellminah
bergander
birgander
black cock
black duck
black swan
black tern
blackbird
blacktail
blue crane
bottletit
bower-bird
brambling
broadbill
brown hawk
bullfinch
buzzardet

campanero
cassowary
cereopsis
chaffinch
chatterer
chevalier
chickling
church owl
coalmouse
cockatiel
colemouse
columbine
cormorant
corncrake
crossbill
currawong
dandy-cock
deinornis
dowitcher
eagle-hawk
eider duck
fallochat
field wren
field-duck
fieldfare
fig parrot
figpecker
firecrest
francolin
French pie
friar-bird
fringilla
frogmouth
gallinazo
gallinule
gerfalcon
gier-eagle
glaucopis
goldcrest
golden-eye
goldfinch
goldspink
goosander
grass wren
grassbird
great skua
grenadier
grey heron
grossbeak
guillemot
guinea-hen
gyrfalcon
hammerkop
heathbird

heathcock
heronshaw
horned owl
Jenny-wren
jerfalcon
kittiwake
lint-white
log-runner
macartney
mallemuck
mango bird
marshbird
merganser
merulidan
miresnipe
mollymauk
mouse-hawk
mud-sucker
muscicapa
natatores
night hawk
ossifrage
paradisea
paraquito
pardalote
parrakeet
parroquet
partridge
passerine
peregrine
phalarope
pied-goose
pinefinch
ptarmigan
quachilto
razorbill
red grouse
redbreast
rhynchops
rifle-bird
ring ousel
ring ouzel
rosefinch
rossignol
salangale
sandpiper
scratcher
scrub-bird
scrub-fowl
scrub-wren
seaparrot
shearbill
sheldrake
shitepoke

shoveller	blue-throat	love-parrot	wood-shrike	mulga parrot
shrike-tit	boobook owl	magpie-lark	yaffingale	Muscovy duck
silver-eye	brent goose	mallee-fowl	yellow-bird	nightingale
skunk-bird	budgerigar	maned goose	yellowlegs	Pacific gull
snake-bird	budgerygah	meadowlark	zebra finch	plain turkey
snow goose	burrow-duck	muttonbird		powerful-fowl
soareagle	butter-bird	night heron	**11**	procellaria
sooty tern	butterbump	night raven	apostle-bird	pterodactyl
sore eagle	canary bird	noisy-minah	banded stilt	punchinello
spinebill	canvasback	nutcracker	barn swallow	quail-thrush
spoonbill	chiffchaff	parson-bird	black falcon	querguedule
stick-bird	chittagong	peewee-lark	black martin	rainbow-bird
stilt-bird	coddy-moddy	petty-chaps	bonebreaker	reed bunting
stock dove	cow-buntung	prairie hen	bristle-bird	reed sparrow
stonechat	crested tit	pratincole	brush-turkey	reed warbler
stone-hawk	crow-shrike	ramphastos	bush-creeper	rhamphastos
storm-bird	demoiselle	regent-bird	butcherbird	rock warbler
strigidae	didunculus	rock parrot	button quail	scarlet ibis
swamp-hawk	dishwasher	rock pigeon	Canada goose	scissor-bill
swine-pipe	dollar bird	sacred ibis	carrion crow	sea-pheasant
talegalla	dusky minah	sagegrouse	cattle egret	shell-parrot
tetraonid	dusky robin	salpinctes	chanticleer	shrike-robun
thickhead	ember goose	sand grouse	cochinchina	singing-bird
thornbill	eurylaimus	sand martin	cock-sparrow	snow bunting
tiercelet	eyas-musket	sanderling	conirostres	snow ortolan
tragopan	fledgeling	sassorolla	corn bunting	soldierbird
trochilus	flycatcher	screech-owl	diamondbird	song sparrow
trumpeter	fratercula	sea-swallow	Dorking fowl	sparrowhawk
turnstone	goatmilker	shearwater	dragoon-bird	stone curlew
waterbird	goatsucker	silver-gull	fairy martin	stone plover
waterfowl	goldhammer	solan goose	fallow finch	storm petrel
water-rail	gooneybird	song shrike	flock pigeon	tree sparrow
wedgebill	grassfinch	song thrush	frigate bird	tree swallow
wheat-bird	greenfinch	summer duck	fruit pigeon	treecreeper
whiteface	greenshank	tailorbird	gallows-bird	wallcreeper
whitetail	grey falcon	talegallus	gnat-snapper	whitethroat
widow-bird	grey parrot	tanagridae	golden eagle	whooper swan
wild goose	grey plover	tit-warbler	grallatores	wood warbler
willow tit	ground dove	tree-runner	grey wagtail	woodcreeper
windhover	ground lark	tropic-bird	harrier-hawk	wood-swallow
woodspite	ground robin	turkey cock	herring gull	yellow robin
wyandotte	guinea-fowl	turtle dove	hooded robun	
	gymnocitta	water ouzel	house martin	**12**
10	hammerhead	weaver-bird	hummingbird	Adele penguin
aberdevine	harpy eagle	whidah-bird	kestrel-hawk	adjutant bird
ant-catcher	hen-harrier	white brant	king penguin	bronze pigeon
Arctic skua	honeyeater	white egret	king vulture	burrowing-owl
Arctic tern	honey-guide	white stork	lammergeier	capercaillie
bearded tit	hooded crow	whydah-bird	leatherhead	capercailzie
bell-magpie	hoodie crow	willow wren	leptodactyl	cardinalbird
bird of prey	jungle-fowl	wonga-wonga	lily-trotter	collared dove
blight-bird	king parrot	wood pigeon	magpie-goose	crested grebe
blue-bonnet	kingfisher	woodgrouse	meadow-pipit	cuckoo-shrike
blue-breast	kookaburra	woodpecker	mockingbird	curvirostral

dentirostres	sage-thrasher	carrier pigeon	**14**
fairy penguin	sedge warbler	coachwhip-bird	babbling thrush
falcon-gentle	serpent eater	crested pigeon	bird of paradise
golden oriole	shrike-thrush	fantail pigeon	canvasback duck
golden plover	stone-chatter	long-tailed tit	diamond sparrow
grass warbler	stone's-mickle	mistletoe-bird	double-bar finch
ground thrush	stormy petrel	owlet-nightjar	golden pheasant
harvest goose	stubble goose	oystercatcher	horned screamer
hedge sparrow	stubble quail	plain-wanderer	king-lory parrot
honeybuzzard	swamp harrier	recurviroster	Manx shearwater
house sparrow	tiger bittern	red-wattle bird	mountain thrush
marsh harrier	turbit pigeon	rosella parrot	nankeen kestrel
marsh warbler	turner pigeon	secretary bird	prairie chicken
missel thrush	water wagtail	shining parrot	rhinoceros bird
mistel thrush	wattle turkey	spider-catcher	robin-redbreast
mourning dove	whip-poor-will	stink-pheasant	silver pheasant
musk parakeet	white goshawk	swallow-shrike	spotted harrier
nutmeg pigeon	yellowhammer	tumbler pigeon	tawny frogmouth
painted quail		turkey vulture	welcome swallow
pallid cuckoo	**13**	turkey-buzzard	whistling eagle
peaceful dove	Adelie penguin	white cockatoo	
punk cockatoo	Baltimore bird	willow warbler	
razor-grinder	barnacle goose	yellow bunting	
red-head finch	black cockatoo	yellow wagtail	

Marine Fauna

FISH, INCLUDING CRUSTACEA

For whales, dolphins etc., see **Mammals.**

2	tau	dart	mort	tuna	cisco	minim
id		dorn	newt	tusk	cobia	moray
	4	dory	opah	woof	cohoe	morse
3	amia	elva	orca	zant	cuddy	mugil
bib	bass	esox	orfe		cudle	muray
cod	blay	fash	parr	**5**	danio	murry
dab	bley	file	peal	ablen	doree	mysis
dar	bret	goby	pike	ablet	dorse	myxon
eel	brit	grig	pope	allis	elops	nacre
eft	burt	hake	pout	angel	elver	nurse
fin	cale	huck	quab	apode	fleck	perai
gar	carp	huso	raun	banny	fusus	perca
ged	chad	jack	rudd	beroe	gadus	perch
hag	char	kelt	ruff	binny	gibel	phoca
ide	chub	keta	sapo	blain	gummy	piper
lob	chum	ling	scad	bleak	guppy	pogge
lox	clam	lipp	scar	bleck	hilsa	porgy
ray	coho	lomp	scup	bogue	julis	poulp
roe	crab	luce	shad	boops	laker	powan
sar	cusk	mako	snig	bream	loach	prawn
sei	dace	masu	sole	brill	loche	reeve
tai	dare	moki	tope	charr	maray	roach

29

roker	burbot	plaice	teredo	echinus	pandore
ruffe	caplin	pollan	tiburo	eel-fare	pegasus
saith	caranx	porgie	tomcord	eelpout	pen-fish
salmo	cepola	poulpe	trygon	escolar	piddock
sargo	cheven	puffer	turbot	fiddler	pig-fish
saury	chevin	puller	twaite	finback	pointer
scrod	clupea	redcap	ulican	fin-fish	pollack
scurf	cockle	red-cod	urchin	finnock	pollard
sepia	comber	red-eye	vendis	garfish	pollock
sewin	conger	remora	wapper	garpike	polypus
shark	conner	robalo	weever	garvock	pomfret
skate	cultch	rochet	whaler	girrock	quinnet
smelt	cuttle	romero	wirrah	gladius	rat-tail
smolt	dagoba	roughy	wrasse	goldney	red-fish
smout	dentex	ruffin	zander	gourami	reef-eel
smowt	diodon	runner	zeidae	gournet	ripsack
snook	doctor	sabalo	zingel	grouper	rock-cod
solen	dorado	sadina		grundel	ronchil
sprag	dugong	saithe	**7**	grunter	ronquil
sprat	dun-cow	salmon	acaleph	gudgeon	rorqual
sprod	ellops	samlet	actinia	gurnard	rotifer
squid	espada	sander	ale-wife	gwiniad	sand-eel
sudak	finnan	sardel	anchovy	gwyniad	sardine
sweep	gadoid	sargus	asterid	haddock	sawfish
tench	ganoid	sauger	batfish	hagbolt	schelly
toado	gardon	saurel	bergylt	haireel	scomber
togue	ginkin	saynay	bloater	halibut	sculpin
torsk	goramy	scampi	blue cap	herling	sea-bass
troll	grilse	scarus	blue-eye	herring	sea-fish
trout	groper	scurff	bocking	homelyn	sea-hare
tunny	gunnel	sea-ape	bonetta	houting	sea-pike
twait	gurami	sea-bat	box-fish	jewfish	sea-wolf
umber	gurnet	sea-cat	brassie	keeling	shadine
whelk	hermit	sea-dog	bubbler	lampern	sillock
whiff	hilsah	sea-eel	bummalo	lamprey	silurus
witch	hussar	sea-egg	calamar	latchet	skegger
	isopod	sea-fox	capelin	lobster	smerlin
6	jerkin	sea-hog	cat-fish	long-tom	snapper
alburn	keltie	sea-owl	catodon	mahseer	sock-eye
alevin	kipper	sea-pad	chimera	manatee	spawner
allice	launce	sea-pig	cichlid	manchet	sphyrna
anabas	loligo	sephen	cidaris	merling	squalus
angler	maigre	shanny	cod-fish	monodon	sterlet
barbel	margot	shiner	codling	moon-eye	stripey
beakie	meagre	shrimp	copepod	morwong	sun-fish
belone	megrim	snacol	cow-fish	mud-fish	thwaite
beluga	milter	soosoo	crabite	muraena	tiddler
blenny	minnow	sparid	croaker	murexes	top-knot
blower	morgay	sucker	crucian	murices	torgoch
bonito	mud-eel	tailor	crusien	oar-fish	torpedo
bounce	mullet	tarpon	cyprine	octopod	tub-fish
bowfin	otaria	tarpum	dog-fish	octopus	ulichon
braise	partan	tautog	drummer	old-wife	umbrine
buckie	pholas	tawtog	dun-fish	osseter	vendace

whiting	goldfish	salt-fish	blue shark	sea-mullet
worm-eel	graining	sand-fish	blue sprat	sea-needle
xippias	grayling	sardelle	bony bream	sea-spirit
	green eel	saw-shark	brandling	sea-urchin
8	grub-fish	scopelus	bulltrout	sheat-fish
acalepha	gymnotus	sea-acorn	bummaloti	silver-eel
albacore	hair-tail	sea-devil	calamarys	spatangus
albicore	halicore	sea-horse	ceratodus	spear-fish
ammodyte	hand-fish	sea-lemon	chaetodon	stargazer
anableps	horn-beak	sea-louse	cling-fish	stingaree
anguilla	horn-fish	sea-perch	cole-perch	sting-fish
arapauma	jentling	sea-robin	conger eel	stink-fish
arapunga	John Dory	sea-snipe	coral fish	stockfish
argonaut	jugulars	shore eel	coryphene	stomapoda
asterias	kelp-fish	siskiwit	cover-clip	suctorian
band-fish	king crab	skipjack	crustacea	surmullet
bill fish	king-fish	snake eel	devil fish	sweetlips
blue fish	lady-fish	sparling	dimyarian	swordfish
boarfish	lancelet	spelding	echinidan	thorn-back
buckling	land crab	speldrin	engraulis	threadfin
bullhead	lump-fish	speldron	finny-scad	tiffenbat
cachalot	lung-fish	spirling	fire-flair	tittlebat
cackerel	mackerel	springer	fish-louse	troutling
calamory	malarmat	spurling	fishroyal	trumpeter
chimaera	melanure	starfish	fortesque	trunk fish
coalfish	menhaden	sting-ray	frost-fish	tunny fish
corkwing	monkfish	sturgeon	globe-fish	whitebait
corystes	moon-fish	sun-bream	goldsinny	whitefish
crawfish	moray eel	surf-fish	golomynka	wobbegong
crayfish	mormyrus	tarwhine	grenadier	
dapedium	nannygai	teraglin	grey nurse	**10**
dapedius	numbfish	testacea	hard-belly	angel shark
dealfish	ophidion	thornbut	hardyhead	angler fish
dragonet	pennydog	thrasher	hippodame	archerfish
drum-fish	phinnock	thresher	houndfish	banstickle
eagle-ray	physalia	toad-fish	hybodonts	barracoota
earshell	physeter	trevally	jaculator	barracouta
errantes	pickerel	troutlet	jollytail	basket fish
eulachon	pigmy-eel	tusk-fish	kingstone	black bream
exocetus	pilchard	water-fox	lampshell	blind shark
file-fish	pipe-fish	weedfish	mango fish	blue groper
fin-scale	piraruck	wolf-fish	menominee	blue puller
fire-fish	polyneme		murray cod	bottlefish
flagtail	Poor John	**9**	ostracian	brown trout
flatfish	raft-fish	acalephae	pilot fish	butterfish
flathead	red perch	acipenser	porbeagle	canolefish
flounder	redbelly	angelfish	pyllopodame	cestracion
forktail	rhizopod	Argentine	razor fish	clouded eel
fox-shark	rock cale	ascidians	red mullet	clypeaster
frog-fish	rock-bass	asteroida	river crab	cock-paddle
gillaroo	rock-fish	barracuda	roundhead	coelacanth
gilt-head	rockling	black sole	sand-lance	cowanyoung
glass-eel	roncador	blackfish	saury-pike	ctenoidans
goatfish	sailfish	blue nurse	schnapper	demoiselle

dragonfish
echinoderm
fiddle-fish
fingerling
flute-mouth
flying fish
ganoidians
garter fish
ghost-shark
giant toado
goblin fish
great skate
grey mullet
groundling
hammerfish
hammerhead
hermit crab
holothuria
horseleech
knight-fish
loggerhead
lumpsucker
maskanonge
maskinonge
mirror dory
morris pike
Moses perch
parrot-fish
pearl perch
periwinkle
pigmy perch
purplefish
pycnodonts
rapier fish
red gurnard
red morwong
red rockcod
ribbon worm
ribbon-fish
robbercrab
rudder-fish
Samsonfish
sand-hopper
sand-mullet
sandy sprat
scopelidae
sea poacher
sea-garfish
sea-leopard
sea-unicorn
silver dory
silverfish
silverside
square-tail

squeteague
sturionian
sucker-fish
tailor-fish
tassel-fish
tiger shark
tongue-sole
triple-tail
turret-fish
velvet fish
weaver fish
whale-shark
white shark
yellow-tail
zebra shark

11

balance fish
banded toado
bellows fish
black angler
blue-pointer
bridled goby
brineshrimp
brown groper
calling crab
carpet shark
carp-gudgeon
chanda perch
chondrostei
common skate
common toado
crested goby
cycloidians
electric eel
electric ray
five-fingers
flying squid
golden perch
gurnet perch
herring cale
hippocampus
jackass fish
javelin fish
Jumping Joey
kingsnapper
leatherskin
leopard fish
lepidosiren
little tunny
man-o'-war fish
Moorish idol
orange perch
papersailor

peacock fish
peacock sole
pennant fish
prickleback
pterichthys
rainbow fish
red bullseye
red firefish
rock whiting
salmon-trout
sand whiting
schoolshark
sea-elephant
sea-hedgehog
sea-scorpion
serpentfish
silver perch
silver toado
silver-belly
smooth toado
soldier-crab
soldier-fish
statry toado
stickleback
stonelifter
suckingfish
surgeon fish
swallow fish
tallegalane
trumpet fish
wheelanimal
whistle fish
wolf herring

12

basking shark
black drummer
black rock-cod
blue trevally
coachwhip ray
cucumber fish
dipterygians
dusky morwong
fan-tailed ray
fatherlasher
fighting fish
forehead fish
gargoyle fish
giant herring
gray tuskfish
oyster-blenny
painted saury
piked dogfish
plectognathi

Plesiosaurus
rainbow trout
rat-tailed ray
river garfish
rock flathead
scarlet bream
sea-porcupine
sentinel crab
silver mullet
smooth angler
Stout Long-Tom

13

allports perch
banded pigfish
barred garfish
Barred Long-
   Tom
black king fish
black trevally
branchiostoma
climbing perch
dactylopterus
dusky flathead
entomostracan
finnan haddock
flying gurnard
giant boarfish
horse mackerel
horseshoe crab
leafy seahorse
leatherjacket
long-finned eel
magpie-morwong
marbled angler
mermaid's purse
mountain trout
ox-eyed herring
porcupine fish
Red-lndian fish
salmon catfish
saltwater fish
sandpaper fish
scarlet angler
Sergeant Baker
silver batfish
silver drummer
snub-nosed dart
southern tunny
spiny flathead
spiny seahorse
striped angler
thresher shark
tiger-flathead

14
banded sea-perch
black stingaree
branchiostegan
brown-sweetlips
butterfly bream
enaliosaurians
estuary catfish
Greenland shark
Greenland-whale
king barracouta
king parrotfish
little numbfish
Macquarie perch

many-banded sole
marine annelida
one-finned shark
painted gurnard
purple sea-perch
red gurnet-perch
river blackfish
short-finned eel
shovel-nosed ray
Slender Long-Tom
smooth flathead
spotted whiting
striped catfish
striped gudgeon

striped sea-pike
white horsefish
15
Australian perch
Australian smelt
beaked coral-fish
bottlenose shark
common stingaree
crusted flounder
crusted weed-fish
edriophthalmata
frigate mackerel
hairback herring
little cling-fish

little conger eel
long-finned perch
marbled flathead
painted dragonet
short suckerfish
small-headed sole
smooth stingaree
spangled grunter
Spanish mackerel
spotted cat-shark
spotted eagle-ray
spotted pipefish
white-spotted ray

MOLLUSCS, INCLUDING FOSSIL SHELLS

f.s. = fossil shell

3
ark
ear
fig
mya
pen
top

4
clam
clio
cone
file
foot
frog
lima
moon
slip
slit
slug
spat
star
unio
worm

5
agate
amber
auger
baler
bulla
canoe
chama

chank
conch
donax
drill
ensis
fusus
galea
gaper
helix
mitre
murex
nacre
naiad
olive
ormer
peuce
razor
sepia
snail
solen
squid
tooth
tulip
turde
venus
whelk

6
basket
bonnet
buckie
carpet
chiton

cockle
cowrie
crinoid
cuttle
dodman
dolium
fornix
furrow
helmet
isopod
jingle
limpet
loligo
macoma
mantle
margin
matrix
mohair
mussel
natica
needle
nerite
ogygia
olenus
ostrea
oyster
pecten
quahog
sea ear
sunset
tellin
teredo
triton

trivea
trough
turban
volute
winkle

7
abalone
acerans
actaeon
aplysia
artemis
ascidia
astarte
Babylon
balanus
bivalve
brocade
crabite
crinoid
diceras
discoid
eschera
etheria
fungite
geoduck
glaucus
lantern
mollusc
muscite
mytilis
nauplii
neptune

octopod
octopus
ovulite
pandora
patella
piddock
polyzoa
purpura
quahaug
scallop
sea hare
sea slug
slipper
spindle
spirula
spondyl
sundial
taccata
tellina
toheroa
trumpet
zoolite

8
ammonite (f.s.)
anodonta
argonaut
balanite
blue-nose
buccinum
capstone
ceratite
choanite

cololite
conchite (f.s.)
decapoda
dendrite
dog whelk
echinite
epiornis
escallop
favosite
galerite
janthina
mangelia
muricite
mytilite
nautilus
necklace
ostracea
pagurian
pedireme
phyllite
porphyry
ram's horn (f.s.)
retinite
scaphite (f.s.)
sea lemon
sea snail
seashell
shipworm
solenite (f.s.)
spirifer
strombus
teredine
testacel

tridacna
trochite
tunicary
tunshell
volulite (f.s.)
volutite (f.s.)
woodcock

9
acephalan
aepiornis
alasmodon
alcyonite
amphipoda
belemnite (f.s.)
buccinite (f.s.)
cancerite
carpolite
clausilia
conularia
copralite
corallite
crow stone
dentalium
dicynodon
dolabella
ecardines
encrinite
fan mussel
gastropod
giant clam
hippurite
hodmandod
lithocarp
lithodome
lithophyl
marsupite
miliolite (f.s.)
moon snail
muscalite (f.s.)
nautilite

nummulite
ostracian
ostracite (f.s.)
palmacite
patellite (f.s.)
pond snail
pteropods
reliquiae
rock-borer
scaphopod
serpulite (f.s.)
staircase
stone lily
strombite (f.s.)
tellinite (f.s.)
trilobite (f.s.)
turbinite (f.s.)
turrilite (f.s.)
venus clam

10
amphineura
amphitrite
batrachite
brachiopod
cephalopod
conchifera
confervite
cuttlefish
date mussel
dendrolite
entomolite
entrochite
euomphalus
  (f.s.)
gyrogonite
haliotidae
heteropoda
odontolite
palmacites
periwinkle

polymorphe
snake stone (f.s.)
stone borer
stone eater
tubiporite
ulodendron
wentletrap
wing oyster
xanthidium

11
asterialite
asterolepis
cetotolites
cheirolepis
dinotherium
fairy stones
fasciolaria
finger stone
globigerina
gongiatites (f.s.)
holoptychis
ichthyolite
madreporite
milleporite
needle whelk
ornitholite
oyster drill
pearl oyster
rhyncholite
river oyster
siphonifers
sting winkle
strobolites
terabratula
tiger cowrie
trachelipod

12
amphibiolite
boring mussel

Chinaman's hat
cornu-ammonis (f.s.)
deinotherium
figured stone
Hungarian cap
macrotherium
megalichthys
pelican's foot
pentacrinite
saddle oyster
sea butterfly
serpentstone
zamiostrobus

13
acorn barnacle
bleeding tooth
bothrodendron
carboniferous
dolichosaurus
elephant's tusk
entomostomata
goose barnacle
hard-shell clam
keyhole limpet
lamellibranch
lepidodendron
paper nautilus
soft-shell clam

14
conchyliaceous (f.s.)
pearly nautilus
syringodendron

15
cyclobranchiata
tectibranchiata

OTHER MARINE ANIMALS

5
coral
naiad
polyp

6
fungia

medusa
sea-mat
sea-oak
sponge

7
actinia

anemone
eschara
hydroid
polypus
polyzoa
sea-slug
trepang

8
alcyonic
anthozoa
flatworm
polypary
porifera
red coral

sea-squirt
tubipore
zoophyte

9
alcyoneae
alcyonite

bathybius
comb-jelly
ecardines
jellyfish
madrepore
pink coral
scaur-cock

10
abrotanoid
alva marina

ctenophore
sea anemone
tubiporite

11
sea cucumber

12
ulotrichales

13
sea gooseberry

Reptiles and Amphibians

3
asp
boa
bom
eft
kaa
olm

4
apod
emys
evet
frog
kufi
naga
naia
newt
pama
pipa
rana
seps
toad
worm

5
aboma
adder
agama
anole
anura
aspic
cobra
draco
elaps
gecko
guana
hydra
jiboa
krait
mamba
racer
siren
skink
snake
tokay
varan

viper
waral

6
agamid
anolis
caiman
cayman
daboia
dipsas
dragon
gavial
hassar
hydrus
iguana
jacare
lizard
moloch
mugger
python
Sauria
taipan
triton
turtle
uraeus
vipera
worral
worrel

7
axolotl
caudate
chelone
coluber
gharial
ghavial
hicatee
labarri
lacerta
langaha
monitor
ophidia
paddock
rattler
saurian
scincus

serpent
snapper
tadpole
testudo
tuatara
urodela
varanus
zonurus

8
acontias
allosaur
amphibia
anaconda
asp viper
basilisk
bull frog
cat snake
cerastes
chelonia
Congo eel
dinosaur
dragonet
fox snake
hatteria
hiccatee
horn toad
jararaca
keelback
lachesis
matamata
menopome
moccasin
mudpuppy
ophidian
pit viper
platanna
pliosaur
pollywog
rat snake
red snake
ringhals
sand fish
sand toad
sea snake
slow-worm

terrapin
tortoise
tree frog
typhlops

9
alligator
batrachia
blindworm
blue krait
boomslang
box turtle
bull snake
caelilian
chameleon
chelonian
corn snake
crocodile
dart snake
eyed skink
galliwasp
giant frog
giant toad
green toad
hairy frog
hamadryad
horned asp
hylaesaur
iguanodon
king cobra
king snake
marsh frog
milk snake
ophiosaur
pine snake
pterosaur
puff adder
ring snake
salamander
sphenodon
stegosaur
terrapeen
tree snake
vine snake
wart snake
water newt

whip snake
wolf snake
worm lizard

10
amphibians
batrachian
black mambo
black snake
brontosaur
bushmaster
clawed frog
cockatrice
copperhead
coral snake
cotylosaur
dabb lizard
death adder
dendrophis
Diplodocus
edible frog
eyed lizard
false viper
fer-de-lance
glass snake
grass snake
green mamba
green racer
green snake
hellbender
homorelaps
horned frog
horned toad
hylaesaur
loggerhead
megalosaur
natterjack
night adder
plesiosaur
pond turtle
Pteranodon
river snake
rock python
sand lizard
sea serpent
sidewinder

smooth newt	ichthyosaur	green tree boa	**14**
tic polonga	Indian cobra	herpetofauna	boa constrictor
tiger snake	lace monitor	horned iguana	brown tree snake
wall lizard	leopard frog	horned lizard	coach-whip snake
water pilot	midwife toad	Komodo dragon	cobra de capello
water snake	Pterodactyl	leopard snake	fire salamander
11	rattlesnake	pond tortoise	four-lined snake
banded krait	royal python		golden tree frog
black cayman	smooth snake	**13**	Himalayan viper
carpet viper	Stegosaurus	aquatic lizard	horn-nosed viper
cottonmouth	Surinam toad	bearded lizard	long-nosed viper
crested newt	thorn lizard	frilled lizard	poikilothermic
dolichosaur	thorny devil	giant tortoise	rat-tailed snake
flying snake	Triceratops	green pit	saw-scaled viper
Gaboon viper	tyrannosaur	viper	snake-eyed skink
gartersnake	water lizard	green tree frog	snapping turtle
gila monster	water python	Nile crocodile	
goliath frog		Russell's viper	**15**
green lizard	**12**	schaapsticker	egg-eating snakes
green turtle	chained snake	spade-foot toad	golden tree snake
horned viper	chicken snake	spotted lizard	painted terrapin
	flying lizard	water moccasin	

Insects, Arachnids, Worms, etc.

3	mite	eruca	blatta	evania	tsetse	cricket
ant	moth	fluke	bot fly	gadfly	veneer	culicid
bee	pium	imago	breese	hop-fly	weevil	cyclica
bot	pupa	julus	breeze	hopper	woubit	daphnia
bug	puss	larva	buzzer	hornet		deer-fly
cob	puxi	limax	caddis	jigger	**7**	diopsis
dor	slug	louse	capsid	lappet	acerans	diptera
fly	tant	midge	chafer	larvae	agrilus	duck-ant
nit	tick	musca	chigoe	locust	annelid	epeirid
pug	wasp	ox-fly	chigre	maggot	antenna	epizoon
sow	worm	pulex	chinch	mantis	anthill	fig gnat
tau	zimb	satyr	cicada	maybug	antlion	firefly
		sauba	cicala	mayfly	aphides	fish-fly
4	**5**	snail	cimbex	midget	athalia	frog-fly
boud	acera	splex	cimiss	motuca	bean-fly	fulgora
cleg	aphid	tinea	coccus	mutuca	beehive	gall-fly
dart	aphis	vespa	cocoon	mygale	blowfly	globard
flea	atlas		crabro	saw-fly	boat-fly	gray-fly
frit	borer	**6**	cynips	scarab	bruchus	hexapod
gnat	brize	acarid	day-fly	sow-bug	bull fly	hine-bee
goat	cimex	acarus	diurna	sphinx	bull-bee	horn-bug
grig	comma	ant cow	dog-bee	spider	carabus	horn-fly
grub	culex	aptera	dog-fly	squill	cat flea	June
lema	dorny	ash-fly	earwig	termes	cestoid	bug
lice	drake	bedbug	elater	Thecla	cheslip	katydid
mawk	drone	bee-fly	epeira	Thrips	coronet	lady-cow
mida	emmet	beetle	eupoda	tipula	crambus	lampfly

lobworm	fleshfly	**9**	sheep tick	froghopper
lugworm	fossores	Amazon ant	spider-fly	goatchafer
lycaena	fruit fly	anopheles	squashbug	greendrake
mawworm	gall-gnat	aphid pest	sugar-mite	hairstreak
microbe	gall-wasp	arachnida	tanystoma	harvest bug
papilio	gammarus	book louse	tarantula	harvestman
path-fly	glow worm	breeze-fly	tarentula	hessian-fly
pismire	greenfly	bumblebee	thysamura	horse-emmet
puceron	honey-bee	burrelfly	tree louse	jigger flea
rose-bug	horse-bot	buzzardet	tsetse fly	lantern-fly
rotifer	horsefly	caddis-fly	tumblebug	leaf insect
salamis	housefly	canker-fly	turnip-fly	leafroller
sandfly	Isoptera	centipede	warble-fly	musk beetle
sawback	itchmite	cheese-fly	water-flea	neuroptera
shad-fly	lace-leap	chrysalis	wax-insect	orthoptera
skipper	ladybird	churrworm	waxworker	palnerworm
snow-fly	lecanium	cicindela	whirlygig	phylloxera
stylops	longhorn	clavicorn	woodborer	pine weevil
termite	mealy-bug	cochineal	woodlouse	plant-louse
tin-worm	milleped	cockroach	worker ant	ribbonworm
tortynx	mosquito	coffeebug	worker bee	rice weevil
wasp-fly	mucivora	coleopter	xylophaga	ringbarker
wood ant	multiped	corn aphis		rosechafer
	myriapod	corn borer	**10**	saltigrade
8	natantes	crab-louse	armropods	sandhopper
acaridan	night-fly	cynipides	bark weevil	scaraebeus
adder-fly	nocturna	dermestes	bird spider	seed weevil
antennae	paropsis	dipterans	blisterfly	sheep louse
arachnid	pedipalp	dorbeetle	bluebotte	silverfish
attercop	phyllium	dragonfly	boll weevil	soldier ant
black ant	pupipara	driver-ant	bombardier	stag beetle
black-fly	queen ant	dumbledor	cabbage fly	star psylla
bookworm	queen bee	earthworm	caddicefly	turnip flea
braconid	rotifera	eumenidae	cankerworm	twig-psylla
bullhead	sand flea	fig-psylla	cheese-mite	voetganger
calandra	sand wasp	flying ant	chrysomela	vorticella
calandre	scolytus	forest-fly	coccinella	wheatmidge
calomela	scorpion	forficula	cockchafer	wolf spider
case-worm	shipworm	gall-midge	coleoptera	xylophagan
cerambyx	sparkler	hemiptera	corn beetle	
chelifer	stonefly	hornet-fly	corn weevil	**11**
cocktail	tapeworm	humblebee	digger wasp	ametabolian
Colorado	tenebrio	ichneumon	dolphin-fly	apple-sucker
crane fly	tetrapod	lac-insect	dorr-beetle	arachnidans
dog-louse	tung-tung	leaflouse	drosophila	auger beetle
drake-fly	waterbug	longicorn	drumbledor	balm-cricket
drone-bee	water-fly	membracid	dumbledore	black beetle
drone-fly	wheat-fly	millipede	dung beetle	bloodsucker
dybiscus	whirlwig	orange-bug	dynastidan	cantharides
ephemera	white ant	pine-aphis	entomolite	capharis bug
erotylus	whitefly	plant-lice	ephemerans	caterpillar
erycinia	wireworm	pyralidae	fan cricket	chalcia wasp
ettercap	woodlice	rugweevil	fen cricket	coprophagan
flatworm	woodmite	sheep lice	flea beetle	cryptophago

entomophaga	vinefretter	saprophagans	purple emperor
Ephemeridae	water beetle	scarab beetle	shot-hole borer
flour weevil	water skater	sexton beetle	slender weevil
gallinipper	wheel animal	spring beetle	
grain beetle	woodfretter	spruce sawfly	**14**
grasshopper		walking stick	bimia longicorn
greenbottle	**12**	water boatman	cabbage-root fly
horsemarten	book scorpion	wattle-psylla	Colorado beetle
Hymenoptera	buzzard clock		elephant beetle
Lepidoptera	carpenter ant	**13**	figbranch borer
mole cricket	carpenter bee	black lecanium	Hercules beetle
pine girdler	clerid beetle	blister beetle	ironbark sawfly
scolopendra	diadem spider	carpenter's bee	
scorpion fly	dimerosomata	daddy-long-legs	**15**
snout beetle	flower beetle	diamond beetle	furniture beetle
stick insect	ground beetle	fig-leaf beetle	serricorn beetle
subulicorns	horned clerid	goliath beetle	thickset chalcid
terebrantia	horse stinger	ichneumon wasp	wheel animalcule
tetrapteran	milk-white ant	jumping spider	yellow longicorn
thysanurans	moneyspinner	leatherjacket	
tiger beetle	nightcrawler	lime-tree borer	**16**
timberborer	pinhole borer	mangold beetle	deathwatch beetle
Trichoptera	Rhynchophera	praying mantis	

Butterflies and Moths

4	goat moth	fritillary	tussock moth
goat	hawk moth	gatekeeper	
moth	puss moth	hairstreak	**12**
puss	vapourer	herald moth	bent-wing moth
	wood moth	lappet moth	cabbage white
5		looper moth	cecropia moth
atlas	**9**	magpie moth	cinnabar moth
comma	brimstone	red admiral	oak eggar moth
	butterfly	small heath	peppered moth
6	cedar moth	timber moth	red cedar moth
burnet	chrysalis	veneer moth	speckled wood
lappet	clearwing	willow moth	white admiral
	ghost moth	winter moth	
7	holly blue		**13**
bee moth	large blue	**11**	chalk hill blue
buff tip	orange tip	beehawk moth	clouded yellow
monarch	small blue	cabbage moth	purple emperor
peacock	tiger moth	caterpillar	tortoiseshell
pug moth		clothes moth	
ringlet	**10**	codling moth	**14** *and over*
skipper	acacia moth	drinker moth	death's head hawk moth (18)
	Adonis blue	Emperor moth	elephant hawk moth (16)
8	brown argus	leaf bag moth	hummingbird hawk moth (19)
case moth	burnet moth	meadow brown	privet hawk moth (14)
cinnabar	carpet moth	painted lady	seedling gum moth (15)
corn moth	common blue	small copper	
forester	ermine moth	swallowtail	

Males, Females and Young of Animals

(M) = male; (F) = female; (Y) = young

3

cob (M swan)
cow (F cow, elephant, whale)
cub (Y bear, fox, lion, wolf, tiger)
doe (F deer, hare, rabbit)
dog (M dog, fox)
ewe (F sheep)
fry (Y fish)
hen (F most birds, lobster, salmon)
hob (M ferret)
kid (Y goat)
kit (Y ferret)
pen (F swan)
pup (Y dog, seal)
ram (M sheep)
sow (F badger, pig)
tom (M cat)
tup (M sheep)

4

boar (M badger, pig)
buck (M deer, rabbit)
bull (M cow, elephant, whale)
calf (Y cow, elephant, whale)
cock (M most birds, lobster, salmon)

colt (Y horse)
duck (F duck)
eyas (Y hawk)
fawn (Y deer)
foal (Y horse, zebra)
gilt (F pig)
hind (F deer)
jill (F ferret)
joey (Y kangaroo)
lamb (Y sheep)
mare (F horse)
parr (Y fish)
stag (M deer)

5

billy (M goat)
bitch (F dog, wolf)
chick (Y most birds)
drake (M duck)
elver (Y eel)
goose (F goose)
nanny (F goat)
poult (Y pheasant, turkey)
puppy (Y dog)
queen (F cat)
shoat (Y pig)
steer (M cow)
vixen (F fox)
whelp (Y dog, wolf)

6

cygnet (Y swan)
eaglet (Y eagle)
gander (M goose)
heifer (F cow)
kitten (Y cat)
peahen (F peafowl)
piglet (Y pig)

7

bullock (M cow)
gosling (Y goose)
jackass (M donkey)
leveret (Y hare)
lioness (F lion)
peacock (M peafowl)
rooster (M chicken)
tadpole (Y frog, toad)
tigress (F tiger)

8

cockerel (M chicken)
jennyass (F donkey)
stallion (M horse)
yearling (Y horse)

10

leopardess (F leopard)
pantheress (F panther)

ARCHITECTURE AND CONSTRUCTION

Architectural and Construction Terms

3
bar
bay
cob
dpc
hip
hut
inn
key
mew
pub
spa
sty

4
anta
apse
arch
area
bank
barn
bead
byre
café
cage
cell
club
cowl
crib
dado
dais
dike
dome
door
exit
flag
flat
flue
fort
gaol
gate
grot
haha
hall
jail
jamb
keep

kiln
kirk
lath
lift
lock
loft
mart
maze
mews
mill
mint
moat
mole
nave
nook
oast
ogee
oven
pale
pane
pave
pier
pile
plan
post
quay
rail
ramp
rink
roof
room
ruin
sash
seat
semi
shed
shop
sill
sink
site
slat
stay
step
stoa
stud
tige
tile

tomb
town
trap
turf
vane
vill
vyse
wair
wall
wing
wood
yard

5
abbey
abode
aisle
alley
annex
arris
attic
bayed
block
booth
bower
brace
brest
brick
build
built
cabin
choir
court
crypt
dairy
depot
domed
Doric
drain
eaves
entry
erect
fence
flats
floor
forum
gable

glass
glaze
grate
grout
gully
harem
hotel
house
hovel
hydro
igloo
ionic
jetty
joint
joist
jutty
kiosk
kraal
latch
ledge
lobby
lodge
manse
mitre
newel
niche
ogive
order
oriel
paned
panel
patio
plank
pound
putty
quoin
rails
ranch
range
Roman
scape
sewer
shaft
shelf
shell
slate
slatt

socle
solar
spire
stack
stage
stair
stake
stall
stand
steps
stile
stone
store
stove
strut
study
suite
tabby
thorp
tiled
tourn
trone
truss
Tudor
vault
villa
wharf
works

6
abacus
access
alcove
alette
annexe
arbour
arcade
ashlar
asylum
atrium
aviary
bakery
batten
belfry
bourse
bricks
canopy

casino
castle
cellar
cement
chalet
chapel
chevet
chunam
church
cilery
cinema
cintre
circus
closet
coffer
coigne
column
coping
corbel
corona
coving
creche
cupola
dagger
debris
design
donjon
drains
dugout
estate
exedra
facade
fascia
fillet
finial
fresco
friary
frieze
gablet
garage
garret
gazebo
girder
glazed
godown
Gothic
grange

grille
grotto
gutter
hangar
hearth
hog pen
hostel
impost
inwall
Ionian
kennel
ladder
lanary
larder
lean-to
lierne
linhay
lintel
locker
lock-up
loggia
log hut
louver
louvre
lyceum
mantel
market
mihrab
mitred
morgue
mortar
mosaic
mosque
mud hut
museum
mutule
niched
Norman
office
outlet
pagoda
palace
paling
pantry
parget
paving
perron

pharos
piazza
pig pen
pigsty
pillar
pinery
plinth
poling
portal
priory
prison
pulpit
putlog
quarry
rafter
rancho
recess
refuge
rococo
ropery
rosery
rubble
rustic
saloon
saw pit
school
scroll
shanty
smithy
soffit
spence
square
stable
stairs
stores
stucco
studio
subway
tarsia
tavern
temple
tender
thatch
thorpe
tilery
tiling
timber

tolsey	cassino	herbary	pugging	varnish	corridor
torsel	castlet	hip roof	pug mill	vaulted	cow house
trench	ceiling	hogcote	pyramid	veranda	cradling
trough	cesspit	hospice	quarrel	viaduct	crescent
turret	chamber	hot wall	railing	village	cromlech
unroof	chancel	hydrant	rebuild	voluted	cross tie
untile	chantry	jib door	rectory		cupboard
veneer	chateau	joinery	re-edify	**8**	curb roof
vestry	chevron	kennels	reeding	abat-jour	cutchery
vihara	chimney	keyhole	rejoint	abattoir	darkroom
vinery	choltry	kitchen	repaurs	abutment	dead wall
vintry	cistern	knocker	reredos	acanthus	decorate
vivary	cob wall	kremlin	rockery	air brick	detached
volute	college	landing	roofing	air drain	doghouse
wattle	compost	lantern	rostrum	airtight	domicile
wicket	conduit	lattice	rotunda	anteroom	door case
wigwam	convent	laundry	sanctum	apophyge	door nail
window	cornice	lazaret	sawmill	approach	doorpost
xystus	cortile	library	scallop	aquarium	doorsill
zaccho	cottage	lunette	seabank	arboured	doorstep
zenana	crocket	mansard	seawall	astragal	dovecote
zigzag	cubicle	mansion	section	atheneum	dovetail
	culvert	masonry	shebeen	backdoor	dowel pin
7	curtain	megaron	shelter	backroom	drainage
academy	dashing	mill dam	shelves	ballroom	draughty
acroter	deanery	minaret	shingle	baluster	dry store
air duct	demesne	minster	shutter	banister	dry stove
air flue	domical	moellon	slating	basement	dust hole
alcazar	dooring	mud wall	Spanish	basilica	dwelling
almonry	doorway	mullion	spicery	bathroom	elevator
ambitus	doucine	munnion	stadium	building	emporium
ancones	dovecot	nailery	staging	bungalow	entrance
annulet	dungeon	narthex	station	buttress	entresol
anticum	edifice	nogging	steeple	caliduct	epistyle
arcaded	embassy	nunnery	storied	capstone	erection
archway	entasis	nursery	sun room	caryatid	espalier
armoury	eustyle	obelisk	surgery	casement	estimate
atelier	factory	oratory	systyle	causeway	excavate
balcony	farmery	ossuary	tambour	cavation	fanlight
ballium	fernery	out gate	tannery	cenotaph	fireclay
baroque	fixture	paddock	taproom	cesspool	fish weir
bastion	fluting	pantile	tegular	chaptrel	flatting
bedroom	foundry	parapet	terrace	chatelet	flooring
bossage	fullery	parlour	theatre	cincture	freehold
boudoir	gallery	passage	tie beam	cloister	fretwork
brewery	gateway	pension	tracery	clubroom	frontage
builder	granary	pentice	tracing	coal hole	fusarole
butlery	granite	pentile	transom	coal shed	gargoyle
butment	grapery	pergola	trellis	cockloft	geodesic
buttery	grating	piggery	turncap	coliseum	grillage
cabinet	groined	pillbox	unbuilt	comptoir	grouting
cafenet	grounds	plaster	unpaved	concrete	handrail
canteen	hallway	portico	untiled	contract	hen house
capitol	hay loft	postern	vachery	corn loft	hoarding

41

hoistway	rood loft	alarm bell	decorated	labyrinth
home farm	roof tree	alignment	distemper	lazaretto
hospital	ropewalk	almshouse	doorplate	leasehold
hostelry	sacristy	apartment	doorstead	letterbox
hothouse	sailloft	apex stone	doorstone	lift shaft
ice house	sale room	arabesque	dormitory	linenfold
intrados	scaffold	arch brick	dowelling	mausoleum
jalousie	seminary	architect	drain trap	metalling
keel arch	seraglio	archivolt	dripstone	mezzanine
keystone	showroom	archstone	dust stove	mock-Tudor
kingpost	skirting	aerostyle	earthbank	modillion
kingwood	skylight	art school	elevation	monastery
lathwork	slop shop	ashlaring	embrasure	music hall
lavatory	smeltery	athenaeum	episenium	music room
legation	soil pipe	bakehouse	eremitage	octastyle
lichgate	solarium	bay window	escalator	octostyle
lift well	spanroof	bede house	esplanade	orphanage
limewash	stabling	bell gable	estaminet	oubliette
log cabin	stuccoed	bell tower	excavator	outer door
loghouse	sudatory	belvedere	farmhouse	outer gate
lych gate	sunproof	bivaulted	ferestral	palladian
madhouse	taphouse	boathouse	firebrick	pargeting
magazine	tectonic	bow window	fireplace	parquetry
memorial	tenement	brick clay	fir-framed	parsonage
mill pond	terminus	brick kiln	fishgarth	parthenon
monolith	thatched	brick dust	flagstone	partition
monument	tollgate	Byzantine	flashings	party wall
mortuary	town hall	campanile	floriated	pay office
moulding	transept	cartouche	framework	penthouse
newsroom	trapdoor	cathedral	frontdoor	peristyle
openwork	triglyph	ceilinged	frontroom	pillarbox
orangery	turf roof	cellarage	garreting	playhouse
outhouse	tympanum	chop house	gatehouse	pleasance
overhang	underpin	claustral	gravel pit	pontifice
palisade	upstairs	clay slate	grotesque	poorhouse
panelled	vicarage	clay stone	guardroom	pressroom
pantheon	wainscot	cloakroom	guestroom	prize ring
pavement	wardroom	cloisters	guildhall	promenade
pavilion	waxworks	clubhouse	gullyhole	quicklime
pedestal	well hole	coalhouse	gymnasium	race stand
pediment	well room	coal store	headstone	rail fence
pentroof	windmill	cocoonery	hermitage	rainproof
pilaster	windowed	coffer dam	hexastyle	raintight
pinnacle	wood shed	colonnade	homestall	refectory
plashing	woodwork	colosseum	homestead	rendering
platform	workroom	composite	hypocaust	reservoir
plumbing	workshop	construct	infirmary	residence
pointing	ziggurat	consulate	ingle nook	residency
pothouse	zikkurat	cooperage	interaxal	rest house
propylon		copestone	interaxis	ring fence
red brick	**9**	courtyard	ironworks	roughcast
refinery	acropolis	cross beam	jettyhead	sallyport
registry	acroteria	crown post	jut window	scantling
rockwork	aerodrome	day school	kerbstone	scrimshaw

sectional
spareroom
staircase
stillroom
stockroom
stonewall
stonework
storeroom
stretcher
structure
stylobate
swinecote
synagogue
tablature
tenements
threshold
tile drain
tollbooth
tollhouse
tower room
townhouse
treillage
triforium
turf house
turnstile
undermine
underprop
undrained
vestibule
wallpaper
wallplate
warehouse
waste pipe
water tank
whitewash
windproof
windtight
winevault
wiregauze
workhouse

10
antechapel
araeostyle
arc-boutant
architrave
archivault
backstairs
ball flower
balustered
balustrade
bargeboard
bedchamber
bell turret

brick-built
brick earth
cantilever
catafalque
chapellany
cavity wall
chimney cap
chimney pot
clerestory
clock tower
coachhouse
coalcellar
common room
conversion
Corinthian
court house
covered way
crenulated
cripplings
cross-aisle
crown glass
culver tail
damp course
decoration
decorative
depository
dining hall
dining room
dispensary
distillery
ditriglyph
dome-shaped
doorhandle
doricorder
double hung
double lock
dowel joint
drawbridge
drying room
Dutch tiles
earth house
embankment
enrockment
engine room
excavation
facia panel
fir-wrought
first floor
fives court
flint glass
flock paper
forcing pit
foundation
garden city

glasshouse
grandstand
Greek cross
greenhouse
ground plan
ground sill
guardhouse
habitation
hipped roof
hippodrome
hunting box
hypaethral
insulation
intramural
ionic order
ionic style
jerry-built
knot garden
laboratory
lady chapel
lancet arch
Latin cross
lazar house
lighthouse
lumber room
maisonette
manor house
market town
necropolis
Norman arch
overmantel
panopticon
pebbledash
persiennes
plastering
plate glass
portcullis
post office
power house
propylaeum
proscenium
pycnostyle
quadrangle
repointing
repository
robing room
rock temple
Romanesque
roof garden
rose garden
rose window
roundhouse
roundtower
rubblework

sanatorium
sanitarium
septic tank
settlement
skew bridge
skyscraper
slaked lime
solar panel
smokestack
space frame
state house
stillatory
storehouse
street door
structural
tetrastyle
tiring room
Tudor style
undercroft
university
unoccupied
untenanted
varnishing
ventilator
vestry room
watch house
watchtower
water tower
way station
white-limed
wicket gate
window sash
windscreen
wine cellar

11
antechamber
caravansary
castellated
cementation
cementatory
chain bridge
columbarium
compartment
concert hall
contabulate
coping stone
corbel steps
cornerstone
counterfort
curtail step
distempered
door knocker
dovetailing

drawing room
dress circle
entablature
fan vaulting
finger plate
florid style
foundations
frieze panel
glass mosaic
ground floor
hearthstone
latticework
leaded light
load-bearing
louvre board
machicoulis
mantelpiece
mantelshelf
manufactory
market cross
morning room
observatory
office block
oriel window
outbuilding
picture rail
plasterwork
postern gate
postscenium
public house
purpose-built
reading room
reconstruct
rectilinear
renaissance
reservatory
residential
reticulated
Roman cement
rustication
sarcophagus
scaffolding
shooting box
staddle roof
stringboard
subcontract
summer house
superstruct
tessellated
tiled hearth
timber frame
trelliswork
Turkish bath
Tuscan order

undercoated
unfurnished
uninhabited
ventilation
wainscoting
war memorial
water supply
weathercock
whitewashed
window frame
window glass
window ledge
wire grating
wooden house
wrought iron

12
amphitheatre
araeosystyle
archbuttress
architecture
assembly room
auction rooms
building site
caravanserai
chapel of ease
chapel of rest
chimneypiece
chimney shaft
cockle stairs
conservatory
construction
constructure
country house
covered court
culver-tailed
dormer window
draughtproof
dressing room
entrance hall
floor timbers
folding doors

garden suburb
geodesic dome
guest chamber
half-timbered
Ionian column
kitchen range
labour-saving
lake dwelling
lightning rod
lock-up garage
louvre window
machicolated
mansion house
meeting house
mission house
outer gateway
pantechnicon
parquet floor
penitentiary
power station
purbeck stone
retiring room
semi-detached
spiral stairs
substruction
substructure
subterranean
sweating room
three-ply wood
timber-framed
tower bastion
town planning
tracing cloth
tracing linen
tracing paper
unmodernized
unornamental
unornamented
untenantable
unventilated
urban renewal
valance board

venetian door
wainscotting
weatherproof
winter garden

13
amphiprostyle
ancient lights
architectonic
architectural
assembly rooms
back staircase
breakfast room
butler's pantry
camera obscura
chimney corner
compass window
contabulation
coursing joint
double glazing
Dutch clinkers
dwelling house
dwelling place
encaustic tile
entrance lobby
establishment
ferro-concrete
Grecian temple
lattice window
machicolation
martello tower
master builder
Norman doorway
Perpendicular
portland stone
satellite town
skirting board
specification
subcontractor
sweating house
transom window
triumphal arch

uninhabitable
vaulting shaft
venetian blind
vinyl emulsion
wattle and daub

14
airing cupboard
architectonics
central heating
drying cupboard
filling station
flying buttress
lath and plaster
mezzanine floor
office building
picture gallery
portland cement
powder magazine
reconstruction
superstructure
threshing floor
venetian window
wayside station
whispering dome

15
air conditioning
dampproof course
discharging arch
electric heating
feather boarding
foundation stone
hydraulic cement
pleasure gardens
pleasure grounds
refreshment room
spiral staircase
vitruvian scroll
weather boarding
withdrawing room

Famous Buildings and Constructions

6
Sphinx

7
Red Fort (Delhi)

8
Alhambra (Granada)

Escorial
Taj Mahal

9
Acropolis
Colosseum
Hermitage
Hill House (Helensburgh)

London Eye
Notre Dame
Parc Güell (Barcelona)
Parthenon

10
Jama Masjid (Delhi)
Sacré Coeur

Sears Tower (Chicago)
Stonehenge
Versailles

11
Doge's Palace (Venice)
Eiffel Tower
Hagia Sophia
   (Istanbul)
Machu Picchu
Musée d'Orsay
Soane Museum
   (London)
York Minster

12
Fallingwater
Great Pyramid
Hadrian's Wall

13
Dome of the Rock

Fatehpur Sikri (Agra)
Sistine Chapel
Tower of London

14
Blenheim Palace
Brooklyn Bridge
Centre Pompidou
Le Petit Trianon
Lloyd's Building
Millennium Dome
Piazza San Marco
   (Venice)
Sagrada Familia
   (Barcelona)
Wells Cathedral

15
Angel of the North
Radcliffe Camera
   (Oxford)
Statue of Liberty

16
Buckingham Palace
Canary Wharf Tower
Golden Gate Bridge
Guggenheim Museum
   (Bilbao)
Lincoln Cathedral
Palace of the Winds
   (Jaipur)
Pyramide du Louvre
St Paul's Cathedral

17
Centre le Corbusier (Zurich)

18
Glasgow School of Art
King's College Chapel
   (Cambridge)

19
Empire State Building

The Seven Wonders of the Ancient World

Colossus of Rhodes (16)
Hanging Gardens of Babylon (23)
Pharos of Alexandria (18)
Pyramids of Egypt (15)

Statue of Jupiter at Olympia (24)
Temple of Diana at Ephesus (22)
Tomb of Mausolus (14)

CULTURE AND THE MEDIA
Art

3
air
art
hue
key
mat
oil
pen
pop
sit

4
airy
arts
base
body
bust
chic
copy
dada
daub
draw
etch
flat
form
gild
gilt
halo
icon
ikon
limn
line
mark
mask
nude
oils
pose
show
tint
wash
work

5
batik
block
board
brush
cameo
chalk
craft

curio
draft
drawn
easel
frame
genre
glaze
gloss
grave
hatch
image
inlay
japan
lines
lumia
model
motif
mount
mural
Op Art
paint
photo
piece
pin-up
print
salon
scape
scene
shade
smear
stamp
still
study
stump
tinge
torso
trace
turps
virtu

6
artist
bedaub
blow up
camera
canvas
colour
crayon
cubism
depict

design
doodle
drawer
enamel
engild
etcher
figure
fresco
garret
graven
gothic
ground
incise
limner
master
medium
mock-up
mosaic
opaque
pastel
patina
plaque
pop art
poster
purism
relief
school
sculpt
shadow
sitter
sketch
statue
studio
symbol
tripod

7
academy
acrylic
aniline
archaic
art deco
art form
artwork
atelier
aureole
baroque
Bauhaus
biscuit
camaieu

cartoon
carving
ceramic
chasing
classic
close-up
collage
contour
copyist
Dadaism
daubing
develop
diagram
diptych
draught
drawing
engrave
etching
faience
fast dye
Fauvism
felt tip
folk art
gallery
gilding
glazing
gouache
graphic
high art
hot tone
imagism
impasto
lacquer
lino-cut
lunette
montage
mordant
moulded
outline
painter
palette
pattern
picture
pigment
plaster
plastic
portray
profile
realism
relievo

remodel
replica
rococco
scenist
scratch
scumble
shading
sketchy
spatula
stencil
stipple
support
tableau
tempera
texture
thinner
touch up
tracery
tracing
T-square
varnish
vehicle
woodcut

8
abstract
academic
aesthete
anaglyph
aquatint
art class
art paper
artistic
Barbizon
bohemian
ceramics
charcoal
chromism
cool tone
creation
dark room
depicter
designer
eggshell
emulsion
engraver
exposure
exterior
fair copy
figurine

fine arts
fixative
freehand
fretwork
Futurism
graffiti
graphics
grouping
half-tone
handling
hatching
idealism
inscribe
interior
likeness
luminist
majolica
monotype
monument
mounting
negative
oil paint
original
ornament
painting
panorama
pastiche
penumbra
portrait
printing
repousse
sculptor
seascape
sketcher
skyscape
statuary
symmetry
tachisme
tapestry
tectonic
throwing
tincture
trecento
triptych
vignette
warm tone
zoom lens

9
aesthetic

aggregate
applique
aquarelle
aquatinta
art school
asymmetry
ballpoint
bas-relief
blackware
blueprint
bric-a-brac
brushwork
cartridge
cartouche
cerograph
chinaware
cityscape
cloisonne
colourful
colourist
crayonist
damascene
decorator
distemper
emblemata
embossing
enameller
engraving
facsimile
geometric
glassware
gradation
grisaille
grotesque
highlight
hot colour
indelible
indian ink
inscriber
japanning
landscape
lay figure
lithotint
low relief
mannerism
marquetry
maulstick
mezzotint
miniature
modelling
modern art
modernism
objet d'art
oil colour

old master
oleograph
painterly
pictorial
portrayal
portrayer
primitive
ready made
represent
rough copy
sculpture
scumbling
sketch pad
sketching
statuette
still life
stippling
strapwork
symbolism
Symbolist
tailpiece
tattooing
technique
tenebrism
townscape
treatment
woodblock
work of art

10
achromatic
aesthetics
anaglyphic
anaglyptic
art gallery
Art Nouveau
atmosphere
automatism
avant-garde
background
biomorphic
block print
body colour
caricature
cartoonist
ceramicist
cerography
classicism
cloudscape
coloration
cool colour
dead colour
decoration
embossment

embroidery
enamelling
enamelware
exhibition
fitch brush
flat colour
foreground
full-length
graphic art
hair pencil
half-length
illuminate
impression
India paper
kinetic art
linseed oil
lithograph
masterwork
mezzotinto
monochrome
naturalism
night piece
organic art
oil colours
paintbrush
pastellist
pen and wash
pencilling
photograph
pietra dura
pigmentary
plasticine
plasticity
portcrayon
Raphaelite
rich colour
Romanesque
sculptress
serigraphy
silhouette
silk screen
sketchbook
Surrealism
synthesism
terracotta
tessellate
turpentine
warm colour
waterscape

11
abstract art
academician
alto-relievo

aquatinting
calligraphy
charcoalist
chiaroscuro
chinoiserie
coat of paint
colour cycle
colour print
composition
concrete art
connoisseur
copperplate
draughtsman
eclecticism
electrotype
engravement
enlargement
french chalk
graphic arts
ground plane
heliochrome
iconography
illuminator
illusionism
imprimatura
life drawing
lithography
marqueterie
masterpiece
neo-romantic
oil painting
pavement art
perspective
photography
picturesque
plastic arts
pointillism
pointillist
portraiture
poster paint
potter's clay
primitivism
proportions
renaissance
restoration
rough sketch
scenography
solid colour
watercolour
wood carving

12
alkyd colours

artist's model
cave painting
caricaturist
colour circle
drawing board
drawing paper
illumination
illustration
lithographer
palette knife
photographer
photomontage
picture frame
potter's wheel
reproduction
scraper board
stained glass
tessellation
tracing paper

13
black and white
complementary
daguerreotype
decorative art
expressionism
glass painting
Impressionism
Neo-Classicism
Pre-Raphaelite
primary colour
social realism
underpainting

14 *and over*
action painting (14)
cabinet picture (14)
chromatography (14)
constructivism (14)
conversation piece (17)
draughtsman-ship (15)
Neo-Impressionism (16)
Neo-Romanticism (14)

pavement artist (14)
picture gallery (14)
plaster of paris (14)

portrait painter (15)
Post-Impressionism (17)
representational (16)

steel engraving (14)
vanishing point (14)

Fictional Characters

DICKENS

2

Jo (Bleak House)

3

Bet (Oliver Twist)
Gay (Dombey and Son)
Jip (David Copperfield)
Joe (Pickwick Papers)
Kit (Old Curiosity Shop)
Pip (Great Expectations)
Tim (A Christmas Carol)
Tox (Dombey and Son)

4

Aged, the (Great
  Expectations)
Bray (Nicholas Nickleby)
Dick (Oliver Twist)
Fang (Oliver Twist)
Fips (Martin Chuzzlewit)
Fogg (Pickwick Papers)
Gamp (Martin
  Chuzzlewit)
Grip (Barnaby Rudge)
Grub (Pickwick Papers)
Hawk (Nicholas
  Nickleby)
Heep (David Copperfield)
Hugh (Barnaby Rudge)
Jupe (Hard Times)
Knag (Nicholas
  Nickleby)
Mary (Pickwick Papers)
Mell (David Copperfield)
"Nemo" (Bleak House)
Peel (Pickwick Papers)
Pell (Pickwick Papers)
Peps (Dombey and Son)
Pott (Pickwick Papers)
Prig (Martin Chuzzlewit)
Pyke (Nicholas Nickleby)
Riah (Our Mutual
  Friend)
Rosa (Bleak House)
Rugg (Little Dorrit)
Slum (Old Curiosity
  Shop)
Tigg (Martin Chuzzlewit)
Wade (Little Dorrit)
Wegg (Our Mutual Friend)

5

Agnes (David Copperfield)
Bates (Oliver Twist)
Betsy (Oliver Twist)
Bevan (Martin
  Chuzzlewit)
Biddy (Great
  Expectations)
Brass (Old Curiosity Shop)
Brick (Martin Chuzzlewit)
Brown (Dombey and Son)
Casby (Little Dorrit)
Chick (Dombey and Son)
Choke (Martin
  Chuzzlewit)
Clare (Bleak House)
Crupp (David Copperfield)
Daisy (Barnaby Rudge)
Diver (Martin Chuzzlewit)
Drood (Edwin Drood)
Emily (David Copperfield)
Fagin (Oliver Twist)
Flite (Bleak House)
Giles (Oliver Twist)
Gills (Dombey and Son)
Gowan (Little Dorrit)
Gride (Nicholas Nickleby)
Grove (Old Curiosity Shop)
Guppy (Bleak House)
Gwynn (Pickwick Papers)
Janet (David Copperfield)
Jerry (Old Curiosity Shop)
Kenge (Bleak House)
Krook (Bleak House)
Lobbs (Pickwick Papers)
Lorry (Tale of Two Cities)
Lupin (Martin Chuzzlewit)
Maggy (Little Dorrit)
Miggs (Barnaby Rudge)
Mills (David Copperfield)
Molly (Great Expectations)

Monks (Oliver Twist)
Mould (Martin
  Chuzzlewit)
Nancy (Oliver Twist)
Neddy (Pickwick Papers)
Noggs (Nicholas
  Nickleby)
Perch (Dombey and Son)
Pinch (Martin
  Chuzzlewit)
Pluck (Nicholas
  Nickleby)
Price (Nicholas Nickleby)
Pross (Tale of Two Cities)
Quale (Bleak House)
Quilp (Old Curiosity
  Shop)
Rudge (Barnaby Rudge)
Short (Old Curiosity
  Shop)
Sikes (Oliver Twist)
Slyme (Martin
  Chuzzlewit)
Smart (Pickwick Papers)
Smike (Nicholas
  Nickleby)
Sophy (David
  Copperfield)
Squod (Bleak House)
Stagg (Barnaby Rudge)
Toots (Dombey and Son)
Tozer (Dombey and Son)
Trabb (Great
  Expectations)
Trent (Old Curiosity
  Shop)
Twist (Oliver Twist)
Venus (Our Mutual
  Friend)

6

Babley (David
  Copperfield)
Badger (Bleak House)
Bagman, the (Pickwick
  Papers)

Bailey (Martin Chuzzlewit)
Bamber (Pickwick Papers)
Bantam (Pickwick Papers)
Barkis (David Copperfield)
Barley (Great Expectations)
Barney (Oliver Twist)
Beadle (Little Dorrit)
Bedwin (Oliver Twist)
Bitzer (Hard Times)
Boffin (Our Mutual Friend)
Briggs (Dombey and Son)
Bucket (Bleak House)
Budger (Pickwick Papers)
Bumble (Oliver Twist)
Bunsby (Dombey and Son)
Buzfuz (Pickwick Papers)
Carker (Dombey and Son)
Carton (Tale of Two Cities)
Codlin (Old Curiosity Shop)
Corney (Oliver Twist)
Cousin (Dombey and Son)
Cuttle (Dombey and Son)
Darnay (Tale of Two Cities)
Dartle (David Copperfield)
Dennis (Barnaby Rudge)
Dodson (Pickwick Papers)
Dombey (Dombey and Son)
Dorrit (Little Dorrit)
Dowler (Pickwick Papers)
Dr Peps (Dombey and Son)
Durden (Bleak House)
Feeder (Dombey and Son)
Folair (Nicholas Nickleby)
George (Bleak House)
Gordon (Barnaby Rudge)
Graham (Martin Chuzzlewit)
Guster (Bleak House)
Harmon (Our Mutual Friend)
Harris (Martin Chuzzlewit)
Hawdon (Bleak House)
Hexham (Our Mutual Friend)
Higden (Our Mutual Friend)
Hubble (Great Expectations)
Hunter (Pickwick Papers)
Hutley (Pickwick Papers)
Jarley (Old Curiosity Shop)
Jasper (Edwin Drood)
Jingle (Pickwick Papers)
Johnny (Our Mutual Friend)
Lammle (Our Mutual Friend)
Lumbey (Nicholas Nickleby)
Magnus (Pickwick Papers)
Marley (A Christmas Carol)
Martón (Old Curiosity Shop)
Maylie (Oliver Twist)
Merdle (Little Dorrit)
Milvey (Our Mutual Friend)
Mivins (Pickwick Papers)
Moddle (Martin Chuzzlewit)
Morfin (Dombey and Son)
Mullet (Martin Chuzzlewit)
Muzzle (Pickwick Papers)
Nipper (Dombey and Son)
Orlick (Great Expectations)
Pancks (Little Dorrit)
Pegler (Hard Times)
Perker (Pickwick Papers)
Phunky (Pickwick Papers)
Pipkin (Pickwick Papers)
Pirrip (Great Expectations)
Pocket (Great Expectations)
Pogram (Martin Chuzzlewit)
Rachel (Hard Times)
Raddle (Pickwick Papers)
Rigaud (Little Dorrit)
Sapsea (Edwin Drood)
Sawyer (Pickwick Papers)
Sleary (Hard Times)
Sloppy (Our Mutual Friend)
Strong (David Copperfield)
Tapley (Martin Chuzzlewit)
Toodle (Dombey and Son)
Tupman (Pickwick Papers)
Varden (Barnaby Rudge)
Wardle (Pickwick Papers)
Weller (Pickwick Papers)
Wilfer (Our Mutual Friend)
Willet (Barnaby Rudge)
Winkle (Pickwick Papers)

7

Barbara (Old Curiosity Shop)
Bardell (Pickwick Papers)
Bazzard (Edwin Drood)
Blimber (Dombey and Son)
Blotton (Pickwick Papers)
Bobster (Nicholas Nickleby)
Boldwig (Pickwick Papers)
Brooker (Nicholas Nickleby)
Browdie (Nicholas Nickleby)
Bullamy (Martin Chuzzlewit)

Charley (David Copperfield)

Chester (Barnaby Rudge)

Chillip (David Copperfield)

Chivery (Little Dorrit)

Chuffey (Martin Chuzzlewit)

Cleaver (Our Mutual Friend)

Clenham (Hard Times)

Crackit (Oliver Twist)

Creakle (David Copperfield)

Crewler (David Copperfield)

Dawking (Oliver Twist)

Dedlock (Bleak House)

Defarge (Tale of Two Cities)

Drummle (Great Expectations)

Edmunds (Pickwick Papers)

Estella (Great Expectations)

Fleming (Oliver Twist)

Gargery (Great Expectations)

Garland (Old Curiosity Shop)

Gazingi (Nicholas Nickleby)

General (Little Dorrit)

Granger (Dombey and Son)

Gridley (Bleak House)

Grimwig (Oliver Twist)

Grinder (Old Curiosity Shop)

Groffin (Pickwick Papers)

Heyling (Pickwick Papers)

Hopkins (Pickwick Papers)

Jackson (Pickwick Papers)

Jaggers (Great Expectations)

Jellyby (Bleak House)

Jiniwin (Old Curiosity Shop)

Jinkins (Pickwick Papers)

Jobling (Bleak House, Martin Chuzzlewit)

Jorkins (David Copperfield)

Kenwigs (Nicholas Nickleby)

Larkins (David Copperfield)

Lewsome (Martin Chuzzlewit)

Manette (Tale of Two Cities)

Meagles (Little Dorrit)

Mowcher (David Copperfield)

Mrs Heep (David Copperfield)

Mrs Pott (Pickwick Papers)

Nadgeth (Martin Chuzzlewit)

Neckett (Bleak House)

Nubbles (Old Curiosity Shop)

Nupkins (Pickwick Papers)

Pawkins (Martin Chuzzlewit)

Peecher (Our Mutual Friend)

Pipchin (Dombey and Son)

Podsnap (Our Mutual Friend)

Sampson (Our Mutual Friend)

Scadder (Martin Chuzzlewit)

Scrooge (A Christmas Carol)

Skewton (Dombey and Son)

Slammer (Pickwick Papers)

Slunkey (Pickwick Papers)

Smangle (Pickwick Papers)

Smauker (Pickwick Papers)

Snagsby (Bleak House)

Snawley (Nicholas Nickleby)

Snubbin (Pickwick Papers)

Snuffin (Nicholas Nickleby)

Sparsit (Hard Times)

Spenlow (David Copperfield)

Squeers (Nicholas Nickleby)

Stryver (Tale of Two Cities)

Tiny Tim (A Christmas Carol)

Tippins (Our Mutual Friend)

Todgers (Martin Chuzzlewit)

Trotter (Pickwick Papers)

Trundle (Pickwick Papers)

Wackles (Old Curiosity Shop)

Wemmuck (Great Expectations)

Whimple (Great Expectations)

Whisker (Old Curiosity Shop)

Wickham (Dombey and Son)

Wobbler (Little Dorrit)

8

Ada Clare (Bleak House)

Alphonse (Nicholas Nickleby)

Bagstock (David Copperfield)

Barnacle (Little Dorrit)

Blathers (Oliver Twist)

Brandley (Great Expectations)

Bravassa (Nicholas Nickleby)

Brittles (Oliver Twist)

Brownlow (Oliver Twist)

Bullseye (Oliver Twist)

Carstone (Bleak House)

Chadband (Bleak House)

Chitling (Oliver Twist)

Claypole (Oliver Twist)

Cleriker (Great Expectations)

Cluppins (Pickwick Papers)

Cratchit (A Christmas Carol)

Crummles (Nicholas Nickleby)

Cruncher (Tale of Two Cities)

Crushton (Pickwick Papers)
Dr Lumbey (Nicholas Nickleby)
Dr Strong (David Copperfield)
Evremond (Tale of Two Cities)
Finching (Little Dorrit)
Fladdock (Martin Chuzzlewit)
Fledgeby (Our Mutual Friend)
Gashford (Barnaby Rudge)
Haredale (Barnaby Rudge)
Havisham (Great Expectations)
Hortense (Bleak House)
Jarndyce (Bleak House)
Jem Grove (Old Curiosity Shop)
La Creevy (Nicholas Nickleby)
Ledbrook (Nicholas Nickleby)
Lenville (Nicholas Nickleby)
Littimer (David Copperfield)
Losberne (Oliver Twist)
Magwitch (Great Expectations)
Micawber (David Copperfield)
Miss Knag (Nicholas Nickleby)
Miss Wade (Little Dorrit)
Mrs Crupp (David Copperfield)
Mrs Gowan (Little Dorrit)
Mrs Lupin (Martin Chuzzlewit)
Mrs Perch (Dombey and Son)
Mrs Rudge (Barnaby Rudge)
Nickleby (Nicholas Nickleby)
Old Lobbs (Pickwick Papers)

Peggotty (David Copperfield)
Petowker (Nicholas Nickleby)
Pickwick (Pickwick Papers)
Plornish (Little Dorrit)
Skettles (Dombey and Son)
Skiffins (Great Expectations)
Skimpole (Bleak House)
Slinkton (Great Expectations)
Sparkler (Little Dorrit)
Stiggins (Pickwick Papers)
Tom Pinch (Martin Chuzzlewit)
Tom Scott (Old Curiosity Shop)
Tom Smart (Pickwick Papers)
Traddles (David Copperfield)
Trotwood (David Copperfield)
Westdock (Martin Chuzzlewit)
Whiffers (Pickwick Papers)

9

Amy Dorrit (Little Dorrit)
Belvawney (David Copperfield)
Betsy Prig (Martin Chuzzlewit)
Bill Sikes (Oliver Twist)
Blackpool (Hard Times)
Bob Sawyer (Pickwick Papers)
Bounderby (Hard Times)
Boythorne (Bleak House)
Charlotte (Oliver Twist)
Cherryble (Nicholas Nickleby)
Chickweed (Oliver Twist)
Cleopatra (Dombey and Son)
Compeyson (Great Expectations)

Dr Blimber (Dombey and Son)
Dr Jobling (Martin Chuzzlewit)
Dr Manette (Tale of Two Cities)
Dr Slammer (Pickwick Papers)
Gradrind (Hard Times)
Gregsbury (Nicholas Nickleby)
Grewgious (Edwin Drood)
Harthouse (Hard Times)
Headstone (Our Mutual Friend)
Jem Hutley (Pickwick Papers)
Joe Willet (Barnaby Rudge)
Leo Hunter (Pickwick Papers)
Lightwood (Our Mutual Friend)
Lillyvick (Nicholas Nickleby)
Mantalini (Nicholas Nickleby)
Markleham (David Copperfield)
Miss Flite (Bleak House)
Miss Gwynn (Pickwick Papers)
Miss Miggs (Barnaby Rudge)
Miss Mills (David Copperfield)
Miss Pross (Tale of Two Cities)
Mrs Bedwin (Oliver Twist)
Mrs Budger (Pickwick Papers)
Mrs Corney (Oliver Twist)
Mrs Dowler (Pickwick Papers)
Mrs Harris (Martin Chuzzlewit)
Mrs Hubble (Great Expectations)
Mrs Hunter (Pickwick Papers)
Mrs Jarley (Old Curiosity Shop)
Mrs Lammle (Our Mutual Friend)

Mrs Maylie (Oliver Twist)
Mrs Merdle (Little Dorrit)
Mrs Milvey (Our Mutual Friend)
Mrs Pegler (Hard Times)
Mrs Raddle (Pickwick Papers)
Mrs Varden (Barnaby Rudge)
Mrs Wilfer (Our Mutual Friend)
Murdstone (David Copperfield)
Ned Dennis (Barnaby Rudge)
Nell Trent (Old Curiosity Shop)
Old Orlick (Great Expectations)
Pardiggle (Bleak House)
Pecksniff (Martin Chuzzlewit)
Phil Squod (Bleak House)
Potterson (Our Mutual Friend)
Riderhood (Our Mutual Friend)
Ruth Pinch (Martin Chuzzlewit)
Sam Weller (Pickwick Papers)
Sarah Gamp (Martin Chuzzlewit)
Silas Wegg (Our Mutual Friend)
Smallweed (Bleak House)
Smorltork (Pickwick Papers)
Snodgrass (Pickwick Papers)
Swiveller (Old Curiosity Shop)
Tappertit (Barnaby Rudge)
Tom Codlin (Old Curiosity Shop)
Towlinson (Dombey and Son)
Uriah Heep (David Copperfield)

Veneering (Our Mutual Friend)
Verisopht (Nicholas Nickleby)
Walter Gay (Dombey and Son)
Wickfield (David Copperfield)
Witherden (Old Curiosity Shop)
Woodcourt (Bleak House)
Wrayburne (Our Mutual Friend)

10

Alice Brown (Dombey and Son)
Ayresleigh (Pickwick Papers)
Bill Barley (Great Expectations)
Bitherston (Dombey and Son)
Chevy Slyme (Martin Chuzzlewit)
Chuzzlewit (Martin Chuzzlewit)
Dame Durden (Bleak House)
Edwin Drood (Edwin Drood)
Flintwinch (Little Dorrit)
Henry Gowan (Little Dorrit)
Jack Bamber (Pickwick Papers)
Jack Bunsby (Dombey and Son)
Job Trotter (Pickwick Papers)
Joe Gargery (Great Expectations)
John Carker (Dombey and Son)
John Grueby (Dombey and Son)
John Harman (Our Mutual Friend)
John Willet (Barnaby Rudge)
Kit Nubbles (Old Curiosity Shop)
Little Dick (Oliver Twist)
Little Nell (Old Curiosity Shop)
Little Paul (Dombey and Son)
MacStinger (Dombey and Son)
Mark Tapley (Martin Chuzzlewit)
Mary Graham (Martin Chuzzlewit)
Mrs Bardell (Pickwick Papers)
Mrs Clenham (Little Dorrit)
Mrs Crewler (David Copperfield)
Mrs Gargery (Great Expectations)
Mrs Garland (Old Curiosity Shop)
Mrs General (Little Dorrit)
Mrs Grudden (Nicholas Nickleby)
Mrs Jellyby (Bleak House)
Mrs Jiniwin (Old Curiosity Shop)
Mrs Kenwigs (Nicholas Nickleby)
Mrs Meagles (Little Dorrit)
Mrs Nubbles (Old Curiosity Shop)
Mrs Pipchin (Dombey and Son)
Mrs Skewton (Dombey and Son)
Mrs Sparsit (Hard Times)
Mrs Squeers (Nicholas Nickleby)
Mrs Todgers (Martin Chuzzlewit)
Mrs Wackles (Old Curiosity Shop)
Mrs Whimple (Great Expectations)
Mrs Wickham (Dombey and Son)
Paul Dombey (Dombey and Son)
Rosa Dartle (David Copperfield)
Rose Maylie (Oliver Twist)

Rouncewell (Bleak House)
Sally Brass (Old Curiosity Shop)
Signor Jupe (Hard Times)
Sliderskew (Nicholas Nickleby)
Smallweed (Bleak House)
Sowerberry (Oliver Twist)
Stareleigh (Pickwick Papers)
Steerforth (David Copperfield)
Tattycoram (Little Dorrit)
Tony Weller (Pickwick Papers)
Turveydrop (Bleak House)
Wititterly (Nicholas Nickleby)

11

Abel Garland (Old Curiosity Shop)
Arthur Gride (Nicholas Nickleby)
Bella Wilfer (Our Mutual Friend)
Betsey Quilp (Old Curiosity Shop)
Betty Higden (Our Mutual Friend)
Bob Cratchit (A Christmas Carol)
Cecilia Jupe (Hard Times)
Copperfield (David Copperfield)
Daniel Quilp (Old Curiosity Shop)
Dolge Orlick (Great Expectations)
Dora Spenlow (David Copperfield)
Edith Dombey (Dombey and Son)
Emily Wardle (Pickwick Papers)
Emma Peecher (Our Mutual Friend)

Fanny Dombey (Dombey and Son)
Fanny Dorrit (Little Dorrit)
Frank Milvie (Our Mutual Friend)
Gabriel Grub (Pickwick Papers)
"Game Chicken", the (Dombey and Son)
Ham Peggotty (David Copperfield)
Harry Maylie (Oliver Twist)
Jack Hopkins (Pickwick Papers)
James Carker (Dombey and Son)
Jarvis Lorry (Tale of Two Cities)
Jesse Hexham (Our Mutual Friend)
John Browdie (Nicholas Nickleby)
John Chivery (David Copperfield)
John Dawkins (Oliver Twist)
John Edmunds (Pickwick Papers)
John Jobling (Martin Chuzzlewit)
John Podsnap (Our Mutual Friend)
John Smauker (Pickwick Papers)
John Wemmock (Great Expectations)
Lady Dedlock (Bleak House)
Linkinwater (Nicholas Nickleby)
Little Emily (David Copperfield)
Louisa Chick (Dombey and Son)
Lucretia Tox (Dombey and Son)
Miss Gazingi (Nicholas Nickleby)
Miss Larkins (David Copperfield)
Miss Mowcher (David Copperfield)

Monflathers (Old Curiosity Shop)
Mrs Brandley (Great Expectations)
Mrs Clupping (Pickwick Papers)
Mrs Crummles (Nicholas Nickleby)
Mrs Finching (Little Dorrit)
Mrs Gummidge (David Copperfield)
Mrs Micawber (David Copperfield)
Mrs Nickleby (David Copperfield)
Mrs Plornish (Little Dorrit)
Mrs Sparkler (Little Dorrit)
Newman Noggs (Nicholas Nickleby)
Oliver Twist (Oliver Twist)
Peter Magnus (Pickwick Papers)
PollyToodle (Dombey and Son)
Pumblechook (Great Expectations)
Robin Toodle (Dombey and Son)
Slackbridge (Hard Times)
Snevellicci (Nicholas Nickleby)
Solomon Peel (Pickwick Papers)
Solomon Pell (Pickwick Papers)
Susan Nipper (Dombey and Son)
Susan Weller (Pickwick Papers)
Sweedlepipe (Martin Chuzzlewit)
Tim Cratchit (A Christmas Carol)
Toby Crackit (Oliver Twist)
Tom Chitling (Oliver Twist)
Tony Jobling (Bleak House)

Tracy Tupman (Pickwick Papers)

Tulkinhorn (Bleak House)

12

Abel Magwitch (Great Expectations)

Agnes Fleming (Oliver Twist)

Alfred Jingle (Pickwick Papers)

Allred Lammle (Our Mutual Friend)

Artful Dodger, the (Oliver Twist)

Barnaby Rudge (Barnaby Rudge)

Bayham Badger (Bleak House)

Bully Stryver (Tale of Two Cities)

Charley Bates (Oliver Twist)

Colonel Diver (Martin Chuzzlewit)

Edith Granger (Dombey and Son)

Edward Cuttle (Dombey and Son)

Edward Dorrit (Little Dorrit)

Elijah Pogram (Martin Chuzzlewit)

Emma Haredale (Barnaby Rudge)

Emma Micawber (David Copperfield)

Esther Hawdon (Bleak House)

Fanny Cleaver (Our Mutual Friend)

Fanny Squeers (Nicholas Nickleby)

Feenix Cousin (Dombey and Son)

George Gordon (Barnaby Rudge)

Honeythunder (Edwin Drood)

John Jarndyce (Bleak House)

John Westlock (Martin Chuzzlewit)

Kate Nickleby (Nicholas Nickleby)

Koeldwethout (Nicholas Nickleby)

Little Dorrit (Little Dorrit)

Lizzie Hexham (Our Mutual Friend)

Lord Barnacle (Little Dorrit)

Lucie Manette (Tale of Two Cities)

Madeline Bray (Nicholas Nickleby)

Major Pawkins (Martin Chuzzlewit)

Martha Endell (David Copperfield)

Matilda Price (Nicholas Nickleby)

Miss Bravassa (Nicholas Nickleby)

Miss Havisham (Great Expectations)

Miss La Creevy (Nicholas Nickleby)

Miss Ledbrook (Nicholas Nickleby)

Miss Skiffins (Great Expectations)

Montague Tigg (Martin Chuzzlewit)

Mrs Gradgrind (Hard Times)

Mrs Markleham (David Copperfield)

Mrs Pardiggle (Bleak House)

Mrs Veneering (Our Mutual Friend)

Mulberry Hawk (Nicholas Nickleby)

Noah Claypole (Oliver Twist)

Peepy Jellyby (Bleak House)

Phillip Pirrip (Great Expectations)

Sampson Brass (Old Curiosity Shop)

Samuel Weller (Pickwick Papers)

Solomon Daisy (Barnaby Rudge)

Solomon Gills (Dombey and Son)

Sophy Crewler (David Copperfield)

Stoney Briggs (Dombey and Son)

Sydney Carton (Tale of Two Cities)

Thomas Sapsea (Edwin Drood)

Tite Barnacle (Little Dorrit)

Tom Gradgrind (Hard Times)

William Guppy (Bleak House)

William Sikes (Oliver Twist)

13

Anabella Allen (Pickwick Papers)

Arthur Clenham (Little Dorrit)

Belinda Pocket (Great Expectations)

Benjamin Stagg (Barnaby Rudge)

Captain Bunsby (Dombey and Son)

Captain Cuttle (Dombey and Son)

Captain Dowler (Pickwick Papers)

Captain George (Bleak House)

Captain Hawdon (Bleak House)

Charles Darnay (Tale of Two Cities)

Charley Hexham (Tale of Two Cities)

Clara Peggotty (David Copperfield)

Dick Swiveller (Old Curiosity Shop)

Dodson and Fogg (Pickwick Papers)

Dr John Jobling (Martin Chuzzlewit)

Edward Chester (Barnaby Rudge)

Emily Peggotty (David Copperfield)

Ernest Defarge (Tale of Two Cities)

Flora Finching (Little Dorrit)

Gabriel Varden (Barnaby Rudge)

George Heyling (Pickwick Papers)

George Nupkins (Pickwick Papers)

George Sampson (Our Mutual Friend)

Harriet Beadle (Little Dorrit)

Harriet Carker (Dombey and Son)

Herbert Pocket (Great Expectations)

Jane Murdstone (David Copperfield)

Jerry Cruncher (Tale of Two Cities)

Lavinia Wilfer (Our Mutual Friend)

Lord Verisopht (Nicholas Nickleby)

Madame Defarge (Tale of Two Cities)

Mary Ann Raddle (Pickwick Papers)

Matthew Pocket (Great Expectations)

Mealy Potatoes (David Copperfield)

Minnie Meagles (Little Dorrit)

Miss Belvawney (Nicholas Nickleby)

Miss Potterson (Our Mutual Friend)

Misses Kenwigs, the (Nicholas Nickleby)

Misses Wackles, the (Old Curiosity Shop)

Mrs Macstinger (Dombey and Son)

Mrs Rouncewell (Bleak House)

Mrs Sowerberry (Oliver Twist)

Peg Sliderskew (Nicholas Nickleby)

Rachael Warclle (Pickwick Papers)

Ralph Nickleby (Nicholas Nickleby)

Richard Babley (David Copperfield)

Samuel Slumkey (Pickwick Papers)

Seth Pecksniff (Martin Chuzzlewit)

Thomas Groffin (Pickwick Papers)

Tumley Snuffim (Nicholas Nickleby)

William Dorrit (Little Dorrit)

14

Abbey Potterson (Our Mutual Friend)

Agnes Wickfield (David Copperfield)

Allen Woodcourt (Bleak House)

Augustus Moddle (Martin Chuzzlewit)

Barnet Skettles (Dombey and Son)

Bentley Drummle (Great Expectations)

Betsey Cluppins (Pickwick Papers)

Betsey Trotwood (David Copperfield)

Captain Boldwig (Pickwick Papers)

Cecilia Bobster (Nicholas Nickleby)

Daniel Peggotty (David Copperfield)

Edward Sparkler (Little Dorrit)

Edwin Cherryble (Nicholas Nickleby)

Florence Dombey (Dombey and Son)

Francis Spenlow (David Copperfield)

Frank Cheeryble (Nicholas Nickleby)

Frederick Trent (Old Curiosity Shop)

General Scadder (Martin Chuzzlewit)

Harold Skimpole (Bleak House)

Hiram Grewgious (Edwin Drood)

Honoria Dedlock (Bleak House)

Isabella Wardle (Pickwick Papers)

Jefferson Brick (Martin Chuzzlewit)

Lavinia Spenlow (David Copperfield)

Mercy Pecksniff (Martin Chuzzlewit)

Monsieur Rigaud (Little Dorrit)

Mrs Betty Higden (Our Mutual Friend)

Mrs Copperfield (David Copperfield)

Mrs Polly Toodle (Dombey and Son)

Mrs Snevellicci (Nicholas Nickleby)

Reginald Wilfer (Our Mutual Friend)

Reuben Haredale (Barnaby Rudge)

Rev. Frank Milvey (Our Mutual Friend)

Roger Riderhood (Our Mutual Friend)

Samuel Pickwick (Pickwick Papers)

Serjeant Buzfuz (Pickwick Papers)

Simon Tappertit (Barnaby Rudge)

Sir John Chester (Barnaby Rudge)

Therese Defarge (Tale of Two Cities)

Thomas Traddles (David Copperfield)

Tim Linkinwater (Nicholas Nickleby)

15

Alfred Mantalini (Nicholas Nickleby)

Caroline Jellyby (Bleak House)

Clarissa Spenlow (David Copperfield)

Conkey Chickweed (Oliver Twist)

Cornelia Blimber
(Dombey and Son)
Dora Copperfield
(David Copperfield)
Edward Murdstone
(David Copperfield)
Estella Havisham
(Great Expectations)
Eugene Wrayburne
(Our Mutual Friend)
Ferdinand Barnacle
(Little Dorrit)
Frederick Dorrit
(Little Dorrit)
General Fladdock
(Martin Chuzzlewit)
Georgina Podsnap
(Our Mutual Friend)
Godfrey Nickleby
(Nicholas Nickleby)
Henrietta Boffin (Our
Mutual Friend)

Henry Wititterly (Nicholas
Nickleby)
Hon. Elijah Pogram (Martin
Chuzzlewit)
James Steerforth (David
Copperfield)
Jonas Chuzzlewit (Martin
Chuzzlewit)
Josephine Sleary (Hard
Times)
Josiah Bounderby (Hard
Times)
Julia Wititterly (Nicholas
Nickleby)
Louisa Gradgrind (Hard
Times)
MacChoakumchild (Hard
Times)
Madame Mantalini (Nicholas
Nickleby)
Miss Snevellicci (Nicholas
Nickleby)

Monsieur Defarge (Tale of
Two Cities)
Nathaniel Pipkin
(Pickwick Papers)
Nathaniel Winkle
(Pickwick Papers)
Nicodemus Boffin (Our
Mutual Friend)
Ninetta Crummles
(Nicholas Nickleby)
Paul Sweedlepipe (Martin
Chuzzlewit)
Professor Mullet (Martin
Chuzzlewit)
Richard Carstone (Bleak
House)
Serjeant Snubbin
(Pickwick Papers)
Sir Mulberry Hawk
(Nicholas Nickleby)
Smallweed Family (Bleak
House)

THOMAS HARDY

5
David (The Trumpet
Major)
Meggs (Wessex Poems)
Molly (The Trumpet
Major)
Unity (A Pair of Blue
Eyes)

6
Dr Bath (Mayor of
Casterbridge)
Marion (Tess of the
d'Urbervilles)
Michel (Wessex Poems)

7
Barbree (Wessex Poems)
Cawtree (The
Woodlanders)
Charlie (Return of the
Native)
Cockton (A Laodicean)
Dr Chant (Tess of the
d'Urbervilles)
Dr Jones (The
Woodlanders)
Knowles (A Laodicean)
Mr Hewby (A Pair of

Blue Eyes)
Rev. Glin (A Pair of Blue
Eyes)
Vilbert (Jude the
Obscure)

8
Boldwood (Mayor of
Casterbridge)
Buzzford (Mayor of
Casterbridge)
Cain Ball (Far from the
Madding Crowd)
Car Darch (Tess of the
d'Urbervilles)
Dr Breeve (The Hand of
Ethelberta)
Humphrey (Return of the
Native)
Izz Huett (Tess of the
d'Urbervilles)
Maitland (Wessex
Poems)
Matt Grey (Wessex
Tales)
Mr Grower (Mayor of
Casterbridge)
Mrs Edlin (Jude the
Obscure)

Mrs Hurst (Far from the
Madding Crowd)
Uncle Joe (Jude the
Obscure)

9
Amos Graye (Desperate
Remedies)
Bannister (The Trumpet
Major)
Battersby (Wessex
Poems)
Elijah New (Wessex
Tales)
Henry Fray (Far from
the Madding
Crowd)
Jan Coggan (Far from
the Madding Crowd)
Jane Smith (A Pair of
Blue Eyes)
Jim Clarke (Wessex
Tales)
Jim Owlett (Wessex
Tales)
John Green (Wessex
Tales)
John Power (A
Laodicean)

John Smith (A Pair of Blue Eyes)
John South (The Woodlanders)
Laban Tall (Far from the Madding Crowd)
Mark Clark (Far from the Madding Crowd)
Mr Bollens (Desperate Remedies)
Mr Wilkins (A Laodicean)
Mrs Brooks (Tess of the d'Urbervilles)
Mrs Morris (Desperate Remedies)
Owen Graye (Desperate Remedies)
Sarah Hall (Wessex Tales)

10
Abner Power (A Laodicean)
Angel Clare (Tess of the d'Urbervilles)
Anne Seaway (Desperate Remedies)
Beck Knibbs (Tess of the d'Urbervilles)
Bob Loveday (The Trumpet Major)
Captain Vye (Return of the Native)
Chalkfield (Return of the Native)
Dr Charlson (Wessex Tales)
Fanny Robin (Far from the Madding Crowd)
Felix Clare (Tess of the d'Urbervilles)
Gabriel Oak (Far from the Madding Crowd)
Helena Hall (Wessex Tales)
Jack Dollop (Tess of the d'Urbervilles)
James Clare (Tess of the d'Urbervilles)
J. Appleseed (Tess of the d'Urbervilles)
John Upjohn (The Woodlanders)

Jude Fawley (Jude the Obscure)
Lucy Savile (Wessex Tales)
Marty South (The Woodlanders)
Mercy Chant (Tess of the d'Urbervilles)
Milly Birds (A Laodicean)
Mr Cartlett (Jude the Obscure)
Mrs Dollery (The Woodlanders)
Mrs Goodman (A Laodicean)
Nancy Darch (Tess of the d'Urbervilles)
Olly Dowden (Return of the Native)
Paula Power (A Laodicean)
Philip Hall (Wessex Tales)
Rev. Melrose (Wessex Tales)
Rhoda Brook (Tess of the d'Urbervilles, Wessex Tales)
Tim Tankens (Wessex Poems)

11
Abel Whittle (Mayor of Casterbridge)
Alfred Neigh (The Hand of Ethelberta)
Andrew Jones (Wessex Tales)
Anne Garland (The Trumpet Major)
Diggory Venn (Return of the Native)
Esther Beach (The Trumpet Major)
Eustacia Vye (Return of the Native)
Faith Julian (The Hand of Ethelberta)
Farmer Groby (Tess of the d'Urbervilles)
Farmer Lodge (Wessex Tales)
Henry Knight (The

Woodlanders)
Jacob Noakes (The Trumpet Major)
Job Mitchell (The Trumpet Major)
Lucy Melbury (The Woodlanders)
Martha Sarah (Wessex Tales)
Matthew Moon (Far from the Madding Crowd)
Mr Gradfield (Desperate Remedies)
Mrs Rolliver (Tess of the d'Urbervilles)
Oliver Giles (Wessex Tales)
Rev. Woodwell (A Laodicean)
Robert Trewe (Wessex Tales)
Simon Burden (The Trumpet Major)
Wilf Latimer (Wessex Tales)
William Dare (A Laodicean)
William Worm (A Pair of Blue Eyes)

12
Abraham Brown (Desperate Remedies)
Arabella Donn (Jude the Obscure)
Charles Downe (Wessex Tales)
Conjurer Fall (Tess of the d'Urbervilles, Mayor of Casterbridge)
Damon Wildere (Return of the Native)
Dr E. Fitzpiers (The Woodlanders)
Felix Jethway (A Pair of Blue Eyes)
Fred Beancock (The Woodlanders)
George Barnet (Wessex Tales)
Grace Melbury (The Woodlanders)
James Comfort (The Trumpet Major)

Jonathan Kale (Tess of
the d'Urbervilles)
Levi Everdene (Far from
the Madding Crowd)
Mary Ann Money (Far
from the Madding
Crowd)
Miss Bicknell (A Pair of
Blue Eyes)
Miss Fontover (Jude the
Obscure)
Mother Cuxsom (Mayor
of Casterbridge)
Retty Priddle (Tess of the
d'Urbervilles)
Richard Crick (Tess of
the d'Urbervilles)
Sue Bridehead (Jude the
Obscure)
Susan Nonsuch (Return
of the Native)
Thomas Ballam (Wessex
Tales)
Timothy Tanfs (The
Woodlanders)
Win. Marchmill (Wessex
Tales)

13
Aeneas Manston
(Desperate Remedies)
Captain Flower (The
Hand of Ethelberta)
Captain T. Hardy (The
Trumpet Major)
Charles Darton (Wessex
Tales)
Clyn Yeobright (Return
of the Native)
Cuthbert Clare (Tess of
the d'Urbervilles)
Cytherea Graye
(Desperate Remedies)
Dan Chickerell (The
Hand of Ethelberta)
Donald Farfree (Mayor of
Casterbridge)
Elizabeth Leat
(Desperate Remedies)
Ella Marchmill (Wessex
Tales)
Eunice Manston
(Desperate Remedies)
George Melbury (The

Woodlanders)
Gertrude Lodge (Wessex
Tales)
Grammer Oliver (The
Woodlanders)
James Everdene (Far
from the Madding
Crowd)
Johnny Nonsuch (Return
of the Native)
Joseph Lickpan (A Pair
of Blue Eyes)
Lady Petherwin (The
Hand of Ethelberta)
Lizzy Newberry (Wessex
Tales)
Lord Luxellian (A Pair of
Blue Eyes)
Louisa Menlove (The
Hand of Ethelberta)
Martha Garland (The
Trumpet Major)
Miller Loveday (The
Trumpet Major)
Mrs Goodenough (Mayor
of Casterbridge)
Parson Thirdly (Far
from the Madding
Crowd)
Robert Creedle (The
Woodlanders)
Robert Lickpan (A Pair
of Blue Eyes)
Robert Loveday (The
Trumpet Major)
Sergeant Brett (The
Trumpet Major)
Stephen F. Smith (A Pair
of Blue Eyes)
Susan Henchard (Mayor
of Casterbridge)
Trumpeter Buck (The
Trumpet Major)

14
Adelaide Hinton
(Desperate Remedies)
Arabella Fawley (Jude
the Obscure)
Billy Smallbury (Far
from the Madding
Crowd)
Christina Crick (Tess of
the d'Urbervilles)

Cuningham Haze (A
Laodicean)
Drusilla Fawley (Jude
the Obscure)
Felice Charmond (The
Woodlanders)
Festus Derriman (The
Trumpet Major)
George Somerset (A
Laodicean)
Grandfer Cantle (Return
of the Native)
Jacob Smallbury (Far
from the Madding
Crowd)
Jean Bernadotte (Wessex
Poems)
Joey Chickerell (The
Hand of Ethelberta)
John Springrove
(Desperate Remedies)
Joseph Chinnery
(Desperate Remedies)
Lady E. Luxellian (A
Pair of Blue Eyes)
Liddy Smallbury (Far
from the Madding
Crowd)
Lieutenant Mild (A
Laodicean)
Lord Mountclere (The
Hand of Ethelberta)
Lucetta Le Sueur (Mayor
of Casterbridge)
Matilda Johnson (The
Trumpet Major)
Mayor Camperton (A
Laodicean)
Parson Tringham (Tess
of the d'Urbervilles)
Rev. John Raunham
(Desperate Remedies)
Timothy Fairway
(Return of the Native)
Timothy Summers
(Wessex Tales)

15
Alec D'Urberville (Tess
of the d'Urbervilles)
Arthur Kingsmore (A
Pair of Blue Eyes)
Captain de Stancy (A
Laodicean)

Charlotte Moulin (The Hand of Ethelberta)

Christian Cantle (Return of the Native)

Edgar Mountclere (The Hand of Ethelberta)

Eustace Ladywell (The Hand of Ethelberta)

General Angerean (Wessex Poems)

Gertrude Jethway (A Pair of Blue Eyes)

Hayomont Goumont (Wessex Poems)

Joan Durbeyfield (Tess of the d'Urbervilles)

John Durbeyfield (Tess of the d'Urbervilles)

Joseph Poorgrass (Far from the Madding Crowd)

Martin Cannister (A Pair of Blue Eyes)

Michael Henchard (Mayor of Casterbridge)

Richard Crickett (Desperate Remedies)

Sergeant Stanner (The Trumpet Major)

Sir P. D'Urberville (Tess of the d'Urbervilles)

Tess Durbeyfield (Tess of the d'Urbervilles)

Tranter Sweatley (Wessex Poems)

William Boldwood (Far from the Madding Crowd)

William Tremlett (The Trumpet Major)

16

Benjamin Derriman (The Trumpet Major)

Captain Aldclyfte (Desperate Remedies)

Christopher Coney (Mayor of Casterbridge)

Edward Springrove (Desperate Remedies)

Elfride Swancourt (A Pair of Blue Eyes)

George Gillingham (Jude the Obscure)

John Winterbourne (The Woodlanders)

Little Father Time (Jude the Obscure)

Marshal Macdonald (Wessex Poems)

Mr and Mrs Belmaine (The Hand of Ethelberta)

Richard Stockdale (Wessex Tales)

17

Bathsheba Everdene (Far from the Madding Crowd)

Charlotte de Stancy (A Laodicean)

Christopher Julian (The Hand of Ethelberta)

Corporal Tullridge (The Trumpet Major)

Cytherea Aldclyfte (Desperate Remedies)

Eliza L. Durbeyfield (Tess of the d'Urbervilles)

Giles Winterbourne (The Woodlanders)

J. Stoke D'Urberville (Tess of the d'Urbervilles)

Mr and Mrs Doncastle (The Hand of Ethelberta)

Myrtyle Chickerell (The Hand of Ethelberta)

Picotee Chickerell (The Hand of Ethelberta)

Richard Phillstson (Jude the Obscure)

Sir Ralph Petherwin (The Hand of Ethelberta)

Thomasin Yeobright (Return of the Native)

18

Cornelia Chickerell (The Hand of Ethelberta)

Georgina Chickerell (The Hand of Ethelberta)

Mr and Mrs Chickerell (The Hand of Ethelberta)

Sir William de Stancy (A Laodicean)

19

Anthony Cripplestran (The Trumpet Major)

Ethelberta Petherwin (The Hand of Ethelberta)

Jones Saddle-Sergeant (The Trumpet Major)

Mrs Charlotte Troyton (A Pair of Blue Eyes)

Sergeant Francis Troy (Far from the Madding Crowd)

SHAKESPEARE

3

Nym (King Henry V, Merry Wives of Windsor)

Say, Lord (King Henry VI, Part 2, Antony and Cleopatra)

4

Adam (As You Like It)

Ajax (Troilus and Cressida)

Anne, Lady (King Richard III)

Bona (King Henry VI, Part 3, As You Like It)

Cade (King Henry VI, Part 2, Antony and Cleopatra)

Cato (Julius Caesar)

Davy (King Henry IV, Part 2, Antony and Cleopatra)

Dick (King Henry VI,
Part 2, Antony and
Cleopatra)
Dion (Winter's Tale)
Dull (Love's Labour's
Lost)
Eros (Antony and
Cleopatra)
Fang (King Henry IV,
Part 2, Antony and
Cleopatra)
Ford (Merry Wives of
Windsor)
Ford, Mrs (Merry Wives
of Windsor)
Grey (King Henry V)
Grey, Lady (King Henry
VI, Part 3, As You Like
It)
Grey, Lord (King Richard
III)
Hero (Much Ado About
Nothing)
Hume (King Henry VI,
Part 2, Antony and
Cleopatra)
Iago (Othello)
Iden (King Henry VI,
Part 2, Antony and
Cleopatra)
Iris (The Tempest)
Jamy (King Henry V)
John (King Henry IV,
Part 2, Antony and
Cleopatra)
John, Don (Much Ado
About Nothing)
John, King (King John)
Juno (The Tempest)
Kent, Earl of (King Lear)
Lear, King (King Lear)
Lion (Midsummer
Night's Dream)
Luce (Comedy of Errors)
Lucy (King Henry VI,
Part 1, All's Well That
Ends Well)
Moth (Love's Labour's
Lost, Midsummer
Night's Dream)
Page (Merry Wives of
Windsor)
Page, Mrs (Merry Wives
of Windsor)

Peto (King Henry IV,
Part 1, All's Well That
Ends Well, King Henry
IV, Part 2, Antony and
Cleopatra)
Puck (Midsummer
Night's Dream)
Ross, Lord (King Richard
II)
Ross (Macbeth)
Snug (Midsummer
Night's Dream)
Time (Winter's Tale)
Vaux (King Henry VI,
Part 2, Antony and
Cleopatra, King Henry
VIII)
Wart (King Henry IV,
Part 2, Antony and
Cleopatra)
York, Archbishop of
(King Henry IV, Parts 1
and 2, All's Well That
Ends Well, Antony and
Cleopatra, King
Richard III)
York, Duchess of (King
Richard II, King
Richard III)
York, Duke of (King
Henry V, King Richard
II, King Richard III)

5
Aaron (Titus Andronicus)
Abram (Romeo and
Juliet)
Alice (King Henry V)
Angus (Macbeth)
Ariel (The Tempest)
Bagot (King Richard II)
Bates (King Henry V)
Belch (Twelfth Night)
Bigot (King John)
Biron (Love's Labour's
Lost)
Blunt (King Henry IV,
Parts 1 and 2, All's Well
That Ends Well,
Antony and Cleopatra)
Boult (Pericles)
Boyet (Love's Labour's
Lost)
Bushy (King Richard II)

Butts (King Henry VIII)
Caius (Cymbeline, Merry
Wives of Windsor)
Casca (Julius Caesar)
Celia (As You Like It)
Ceres (The Tempest)
Cinna (Julius Caesar)
Cleon (Pericles)
Clown (Measure for
Measure, Twelfth
Night)
Corin (As You Like It)
Court (King Henry V)
Curan (King Lear)
Curio (Twelfth Night)
Denny (King Henry
VIII)
Diana (All's Well That
Ends Well, Pericles)
Edgar (King Lear)
Egeus (Midsummer
Night's Dream)
Elbow (Measure for
Measure)
Essex, Earl of (King
John)
Evans (Merry Wives of
Windsor)
Flute (Midsummer
Night's Dream)
Froth (Measure for
Measure)
Ghost (Hamlet)
Gobbo (Merchant of
Venice)
Gower (King Henry IV,
Part 2, Antony and
Cleopatra, King Henry
V, Pericles)
Green (King Richard II)
Helen (Cymbeline,
Troilus and Cressida)
Henry (King Richard III)
Henry (K.) (King Henry
IV, Parts 1 and 2, All's
Well That Ends Well,
Antony and Cleopatra,
King Henry V, King
Henry VI, Parts 1, 2
and 3, King Henry
VIII)
Henry (P.) (King John)
Julia (Two Gentlemen of
Verona)

Lafeu (All's Well That Ends Well)

Louis Dauphin (King Henry V, King John)

Louis, King (King Henry VI, Part 3, As You Like It)

Louis, Lord (King Richard III)

Lucio (Measure for Measure)

March, Earl of (King Henry IV, Part 1, All's Well That Ends Well)

Maria (Love's Labour's Lost)

Melun (King John)

Menas (Antony and Cleopatra)

Milan, Duke of (Two Gentlemen of Verona)

Mopsa (Winter's Tale)

Osric (Hamlet)

Paris (Romeo and Juliet, Troilus and Cressida)

Pedro, Don (Much Ado About Nothing)

Percy (King Henry IV, Parts 1 and 2, All's Well That Ends Well, Antony and Cleopatra, King Richard II)

Percy, Lady (King Henry IV, Part 1, All's Well That Ends Well)

Peter (King Henry VI, Part 2, Antony and Cleopatra, Measure for Measure)

Phebe (As You Like It)

Philo (Antony and Cleopatra)

Pinch (Comedy of Errors)

Poins (King Henry IV, Parts 1 and 2, All's Well That Ends Well, Antony and Cleopatra)

Priam (Troilus and Cressida)

Queen (Cymbeline)

Regan (King Lear)

Robin (Merry Wives of Windsor)

Romeo (Romeo and Juliet)

Rugby (Merry Wives of Windsor)

Sands, Lord (King Henry VIII)

Snare (King Henry IV, Part 2, Antony and Cleopatra)

Snout (Midsummer Night's Dream)

Speed (Two Gentlemen of Verona)

Timon (Timon of Athens)

Tubal (Merchant of Venice)

Varro (Julius Caesar)

Viola (Twelfth Night)

Wales, Prince of (King Henry IV, Parts 1 and 2, All's Well That Ends Well, Antony and Cleopatra, King Richard III)

6

Adrian (The Tempest)

Aegeon (Comedy of Errors)

Aeneas (Troilus and Cressida)

Albany, Duke of (King Lear)

Alexas (Antony and Cleopatra)

Alonso (The Tempest)

Amiens (As You Like It)

Angelo (Comedy of Errors, Measure for Measure)

Antony (Antony and Cleopatra)

Armado (Love's Labour's Lost)

Arthur (King John)

Audrey (As You Like It)

Banquo (Macbeth)

Basset (King Henry VI, Part 1, All's Well That Ends Well)

Bianca (Othello, Taming of the Shrew)

Blanch (King John)

Blount (King Richard III)

Bottom (Midsummer Night's Dream)

Brutus (Coriolanus, Julius Caesar)

Bullen (King Henry VIII)

Cadwal (Cymbeline)

Caesar (Antony and Cleopatra)

Caphis (Timon of Athens)

Cassio (Othello)

Chiron (Titus Andronicus)

Cicero (Julius Caesar)

Clitus (Julius Caesar)

Cloten (Measure for Measure)

Cobweb (Midsummer Night's Dream)

Curtis (Taming of the Shrew)

Dennis (As You Like It)

Dorcas (Winter's Tale)

Dorset, Marquis of (King Richard III)

Dromio (Comedy of Errors)

Dumain (Love's Labour's Lost)

Duncan (K.) (Macbeth)

Edmund (King Henry VI, Part 3, As You Like It, King Lear)

Edward (King Henry VI, Part 2, Antony and Cleopatra)

Edward (K.) (King Richard III)

Edward (P. of Wales) (King Henry VI, Part 3, As You Like It, King Richard III)

Elinor (King John)

Emilia (Othello, Winter's Tale)

Exeter, Duke of (King Henry V, King Henry VI, Part 3, As You Like It)

Fabian (Twelfth Night)

Feeble (King Henry IV, Part 2, Antony and Cleopatra)

Culture and the Media

Fenton (Merry Wives of Windsor)

France, King of (All's Well That Ends Well, King Lear)

France, Princess of (Love's Labour's Lost)

Gallus (Antony and Cleopatra)

George (King Henry VI, Parts 2 and 3, Antony and Cleopatra, As You Like It, King Richard III)

Grumio (Taming of the Shrew)

Gurney (King John)

Hamlet (Hamlet)

Hecate (Macbeth)

Hector (Troilus and Cressida)

Helena (All's Well That Ends Well, Midsummer Night's Dream)

Henry V, King (King Henry V)

Hermia (Midsummer Night's Dream)

Horner (King Henry VI, Part 2, Antony and Cleopatra)

Imogen (Cymbeline)

Isabel (King Henry V)

Jaques (As You Like It)

Juliet (Measure for Measure, Romeo and Juliet)

Launce (Two Gentlemen of Verona)

Le Beau (As You Like It)

Lennox (Macbeth)

Lovell (King Henry VIII)

Lucius (Julius Caesar, Timon of Athens, Titus Andronicus)

Marina (Pericles)

Morgan (Cymbeline)

Morton (King Henry IV, Part 2, Antony and Cleopatra King Richard III)

Mouldy (King Henry IV,

Part 2, Antony and Cleopatra)

Mr Ford (Merry Wives of Windsor)

Mr Page (Merry Wives of Windsor)

Mutius (Titus Andronicus)

Nestor (Troilus and Cressida)

Oberon (Midsummer Night's Dream)

Oliver (As You Like It)

Olivia (Twelfth Night)

Orsino (Twelfth Night)

Oswald (King Lear)

Oxford, Duke of (King Henry VI, Part 3, As You Like It)

Oxford, Earl of (King Richard III)

Pedant (Taming of the Shrew)

Philip, King (King John)

Pierce (King Richard II)

Pistol (King Henry IV, Part 2, Antony and Cleopatra, King Henry V, Merry Wives of Windsor)

Portia (Julius Caesar, Merchant of Venice)

Quince (Midsummer Night's Dream)

Rivers (Earl) (King Richard III)

Rivers, Lord (King Henry VI, Part 3, As You Like It)

Rogero (Winter's Tale)

Rumour (King Henry IV, Part 2, Antony and Cleopatra)

Scales, Lord (King Henry VI, Part 2, Antony and Cleopatra)

Scarus (Antony and Cleopatra)

Scroop (King Henry IV, Parts 1 and 2, All's Well That Ends Well, Antony and Cleopatra, King Richard II)

Scroop, Lord (King Henry V)

Seyton (Macbeth)

Shadow (King Henry IV, Part 2, Antony and Cleopatra)

Silius (Antony and Cleopatra)

Silvia (Two Gentlemen of Verona)

Simple (Merry Wives of Windsor)

Siward (Macbeth)

Strato (Julius Caesar)

Surrey, Duke of (King Richard II)

Surrey, Earl of (King Henry VIII, King Richard III)

Talbot (King Henry VI, Part 1, All's Well That Ends Well)

Tamora (Titus Andronicus)

Taurus (Antony and Cleopatra)

Thaisa Pericles)

Thisbe (Midsummer Night's Dream)

Thomas (Measure for Measure)

Thurio (Two Gentlemen of Verona)

Tranio (Taming of the Shrew)

Tybalt (Romeo and Juliet)

Tyrrel (King Richard III)

Ursula (Much Ado About Nothing)

Venice, Duke of (Merchant of Venice, Othello)

Verges (Much Ado About Nothing)

Vernon (King Henry IV, Part 1, All's Well That Ends Well, King Henry VI, Part 1, All's Well That Ends Well)

Wolsey, Lord (King Henry VIII)

7

Adriana (Comedy of
Errors)
Aemilia (Comedy of
Errors)
Agrippa (Antony and
Cleopatra)
Alarbus (Titus
Andronicus)
Alencon, Duke of (King
Henry VI, Part 1, All's
Well That Ends Well)
Antenor (Troilus and
Cressida)
Antonio (Merchant of
Venice, Much Ado
About Nothing, The
Tempest, Twelfth
Night, Two Gentlemen
of Verona)
Arragon, Prince of
(Merchant of Venice)
Aumerle, Duke of (King
Richard II)
Bedford, Duke of (King
Henry V, King Henry
VI, Part 1, All's Well
That Ends Well)
Berkley (Earl) (King
Richard II)
Bertram (All's Well That
Ends Well)
Bourbon, Duke of (King
Henry V)
Brandon (King Henry
VIII)
Calchas (Troilus and
Cressida)
Caliban (The Tempest)
Camillo (Winter's Tale)
Capulet (Romeo and
Juliet)
Capulet, Lady (Romeo
and Juliet)
Cassius (Julius Caesar)
Catesby (King Richard
III)
Cerimon (Pericles)
Charles (As You Like It)
Charles Dauphin (King
Henry V)
Charles (K.) (King Henry
V)
Claudio (Measure for

Measure, Much Ado
About Nothing)
Conrade (Much Ado
About Nothing)
Costard (Love's Labour's
Lost)
Cranmer (A.-B.) (King
Henry VIII)
Dauphin, The (King
Henry VI, Part 1, All's
Well That Ends Well,
King John)
Dionyza (Pericles)
Don John (Much Ado
About Nothing)
Douglas, Earl of (King
Henry IV, Part 1, All's
Well That Ends Well)
Eleanor (King Henry VI,
Part 2, Antony and
Cleopatra)
Escalus (Measure for
Measure, Romeo and
Juliet)
Escanes (Pericles)
Flavius (Julius Caesar,
Timon of Athens)
Fleance (Macbeth)
Gloster, Duchess of (King
Richard II)
Gloster, Duke of (King
Henry V, King Henry
VI, Part 3, As You Like
It, King Richard III)
Gloster, Earl of (King
Henry VI, Part 1, All's
Well That Ends Well)
Gloster, Prince of (King
Henry IV, Part 2,
Antony and Cleopatra)
Goneril (King Lear)
Gonzalo (The Tempest)
Gregory (Romeo and
Juliet)
Helenus (Troilus and
Cressida)
Henry IV (K.) (King
Henry IV, Parts 1 and
2, All's Well That Ends
Well, Antony and
Cleopatra)
Henry VI (K.) (King
Henry VI, Parts 1, 2
and 3, All's Well That

Ends Well, Antony and
Cleopatra, As You Like
It)
Herbert (King Richard
III)
Horatio (Hamlet)
Hostess (Taming of the
Shrew)
Hotspur (King Henry IV,
Parts 1 and 2, All's Well
That Ends Well,
Antony and
Cleopatra)
Iachimo (Cymbeline)
Jessica (Merchant of
Venice)
Laertes (Hamlet)
Lavinia (Titus
Andronicus)
Leonato (Much Ado
About Nothing)
Leonine (Pericles)
Leontes (Winter's Tale)
Lepidus (Antony and
Cleopatra)
Lincoln (Bishop of) (King
Henry VIII)
Lorenzo (Merchant of
Venice)
Lucetta (Two Gentlemen
of Verona)
Luciana (Comedy of
Errors)
Macbeth (Macbeth)
Macbeth, Lady
(Macbeth)
Macduff (Macbeth)
Macduff, Lady (Macbeth)
Malcolm (Macbeth)
Marcius (Coriolanus)
Mardian (Antony and
Cleopatra)
Mariana (All's Well That
Ends Well, Measure for
Measure)
Martext (As You Like It)
Martius (Titus
Andronicus)
Mercade (Love's Labour's
Lost)
Messala (Julius Caesar)
Michael (King Henry VI,
Part 2, Antony and
Cleopatra)

Michael (Sir) (King
Henry IV, Parts 2 and
3, All's Well That Ends
Well, Antony and
Cleopatra)
Miranda (The Tempest)
Montano (Othello)
Morocco, Prince of
(Merchant of Venice)
Mowbray (King Richard
II)
Mowbray, Lord (King
Henry IV, Part 2,
Antony and Cleopatra)
Mrs Ford (Merry Wives of
Windsor)
Mrs Page (Merry Wives of
Windsor)
Nerissa (Merchant of
Venice)
Norfolk, Duke of (King
Henry VI, Part 3, As
You Like It, King
Henry VIII, King
Richard II, King
Richard III)
Octavia (Antony and
Cleopatra)
Old Gobo (Merchant of
Venice)
Ophelia (Hamlet)
Orlando (As You Like It)
Orleans, Duke of (King
Henry V)
Othello (Othello)
Paulina (Winter's Tale)
Perdita (Winter's Tale)
Phrynia (Timon of
Athens)
Pisanio (Cymbeline)
Proteus (Two Gentlemen
of Verona)
Publius (Julius Caesar,
Titus Andronicus)
Pucelle (King Henry VI,
Part 1, All's Well That
Ends Well)
Pyramus (Midsummer
Night's Dream)
Quickly, Mrs (King
Henry IV, Parts 1 and
2, All's Well That Ends
Well, Antony and
Cleopatra, King Henry

V, Merry Wives of
Windsor)
Quintus (Titus
Andronicus)
Richard (King Henry VI,
Parts 2 and 3, Antony
and Cleopatra, As You
Like It, King Richard
III)
Richard (K.) (King
Richard II, King
Richard III)
Salanio (Merchant of
Venice)
Salerio (Merchant of
Venice)
Sampson (Romeo and
Juliet)
Setebos (The Tempest)
Shallow (King Henry IV,
Part 2, Antony and
Cleopatra, Merry
Wives of Windsor)
Shylock (Merchant of
Venice)
Silence (King Henry IV,
Part 2, Antony and
Cleopatra)
Silvius (As You Like It)
Simpcox (King Henry VI,
Part 2, Antony and
Cleopatra)
Slender (Merry Wives of
Windsor)
Solinus (Comedy of
Errors)
Stanley (King Henry VI,
Parts 2 and 3, Antony
and Cleopatra, As You
Like It)
Stanley, Lord (King
Richard III)
Suffolk, Duke of (King
Henry VI, Part 2,
Antony and Cleopatra,
King Henry VIII)
Suffolk, Earl of (King
Henry VI, Part 1,
All's Well That Ends
Well)
Theseus (Midsummer
Night's Dream)
Thryeus (Antony and
Cleopatra)

Titania (Midsummer
Night's Dream)
Travers (King Henry IV,
Part 2, Antony and
Cleopatra)
Troilus (Troilus and
Cressida)
Ulysses (Troilus and
Cressida)
Urswick (King Richard
III)
Valeria (Coriolanus)
Varrius (Antony and
Cleopatra, Measure for
Measure)
Vaughan (King Richard
III)
Velutus (Coriolanus)
Warwick, Earl of (King
Henry IV, Part 2,
Antony and Cleopatra,
King Henry V, King
Henry VI, Parts 1, 2
and 3, All's Well That
Ends Well, As You Like
It)
William (As You Like It)

8
Abhorson (Measure for
Measure)
Achilles (Troilus and
Cressida)
Aemilius (Titus
Andronicus)
Aufidius (Coriolanus)
Auvergne, Countess of
(King Henry VI, Part 1,
All's Well That Ends
Well)
Baptista (Taming of the
Shrew)
Bardolph (King Henry
IV, Parts 1 and 2, All's
Well That Ends
Well, Antony and
Cleopatra, King Henry
V, Merry Wives of
Windsor)
Bardolph, Lord (King
Henry IV, Part 2,
Antony and Cleopatra)
Bassanio (Merchant of
Venice)

Beatrice (Much Ado About Nothing)

Beaufort (King Henry VI, Part 1, All's Well That Ends Well)

Beaufort, Cardinal (King Henry VI, Part 2, Antony and Cleopatra)

Belarius (Cymbeline)

Benedick (Much Ado About Nothing)

Benvolio (Romeo and Juliet)

Bernardo (Hamlet)

Borachio (Much Ado About Nothing)

Bouchier, Cardinal (King Richard III)

Bullcalf (King Henry IV, Part 2, Antony and Cleopatra)

Burgundy, Duke of (King Henry V, King Henry VI, Part 2, All's Well That Ends Well, King Lear)

Campeius, Cardinal (King Henry VIII)

Canidius (Antony and Cleopatra)

Capucius (King Henry VIII)

Charmian (Antony and Cleopatra)

Clarence, Duke of (King Henry IV, Part 2, Antony and Cleopatra, King Richard III)

Claudius (Julius Caesar)

Claudius (K.) (Hamlet)

Clifford (King Henry VI, Part 2, Antony and Cleopatra)

Clifford, Lord (King Henry VI, Parts 2 and 3, Antony and Cleopatra, As You Like It)

Colville (King Henry IV, Part 2, Antony and Cleopatra)

Cominius (Coriolanus)

Cordelia (King Lear)

Cornwall, Duke of (King Lear)

Cressida (Troilus and Cressida)

Cromwell (King Henry VIII)

Dercetas (Antony and Cleopatra)

Diomedes (Antony and Cleopatra, Troilus and Cressida)

Dogberry (Much Ado About Nothing)

Don Pedro (Much Ado About Nothing)

Edward Vl (K.) (King Richard III)

Eglamour (Two Gentlemen of Verona)

Falstaff (King Henry IV, Parts 1 and 2, All's Well That Ends Well, Antony and Cleopatra, Merry Wives of Windsor)

Fastolfe (King Henry VI, Part 1, All's Well That Ends Well)

Florence, Duke of (All's Well That Ends Well)

Florizel (Winter's Tale)

Fluellen (King Henry V)

Gadshill (King Henry IV, Part 1, All's Well That Ends Well)

Gardiner (King Henry VIII)

Gargrave (King Henry VI, Part 2, Antony and Cleopatra)

Gertrude (Q.) (Hamlet)

Gratiano (Merchant of Venice, Othello)

Griffith (King Henry VIII)

Harcourt (King Henry IV, Part 2, Antony and Cleopatra)

Hastings, Lord (King Henry IV, Part 2, Antony and Cleopatra, King Henry VI, Part 3, As You Like It, King Richard III)

Hermione (Winter's Tale)

Humphrey (King Henry IV, Part 2, Antony and Cleopatra, King Henry VI, Part 2, Antony and Cleopatra)

Isabella (Measure for Measure)

Jack Cade (King Henry VI, Part 2, Antony and Cleopatra)

Jourdain (King Henry VI, Part 2, Antony and Cleopatra)

King John (King John)

King Lear (King Lear)

Lady Anne (King Richard III)

Lady Grey (King Henry VI, Part 3, As You Like It)

Lawrence (Romeo and Juliet)

Leonardo (Merchant of Venice)

Leonatus (Cymbeline)

Ligarius (Julius Caesar)

Lodovico (Othello)

Lord Grey (King Richard III)

Lord Ross (King Richard II)

Lucentio (Taming of the Shrew)

Lucilius (Julius Caesar, Timon of Athens)

Lucullus (Timon of Athens)

Lysander (Midsummer Night's Dream)

Malvolio (Twelfth Night)

Margaret (King Henry VI, Parts 1 and 2, All's Well That Ends Well, Antony and Cleopatra, King Richard III, Much Ado About Nothing)

Margaret (Q.) (King Henry VI, Part 3, As You Like It)

Marullus (Julius Caesar)

Mecaenas (Antony and Cleopatra)

Menelaus (Troilus and Cressida)

Francisca (Measure for Measure)

Francisco (Hamlet, The Tempest)

Frederick (As You Like It)

Friar John (Romeo and Juliet)

Glansdale (King Henry VI, Part 1, All's Well That Ends Well)

Glendower (King Henry IV, Part 1, All's Well That Ends Well)

Grandpree (King Henry V)

Guiderius (Cymbeline)

Guildford (King Henry VIII)

Helicanus (Pericles)

Henry VIII (K.) (King Henry VIII)

Hippolyta (Midsummer Night's Dream)

Hortensio (Taming of the Shrew)

Katharina (Taming of the Shrew)

Katharine (King Henry VIII, Love's Labour's Lost)

Katharine (P'ess) (King Henry V)

Lady Percy (King Henry IV, Part 1, All's Well That Ends Well)

Lancaster, Duke of (King Richard II)

Lancaster, Prince of (King Henry IV, Parts 1 and 2, All's Well That Ends Well, Antony and Cleopatra)

Longsword (King John)

Lord Lovel (King Richard III)

Lord Sands (King Henry VIII)

Lychorida (Pericles)

Macmorris (King Henry V)

Mamillius (Winter's Tale)

Marcellus (Hamlet)

Mareshall (King John)

Moonshine (Midsummer Night's Dream)

Nathaniel (Love's Labour's Lost)

Patroclus (Troilus and Cressida)

Petruchio (Taming of the Shrew)

Polixenes (Winter's Tale)

Richard II (K.) (King Richard II)

Rousillon, Count of (All's Well That Ends Well)

Rousillon, Countess of (All's Well That Ends Well)

Salisbury, Earl of (King Henry V, King Henry VI, Parts 1 and 2, All's Well That Ends Well, Antony and Cleopatra, King John, King Richard II)

Sebastian (The Tempest, Twelfth Night)

Servilius (Timon of Athens)

Simonides (Pericles)

Southwell (King Henry VI, Part 2, Antony and Cleopatra)

Tearsheet (King Henry IV, Part 2, Antony and Cleopatra)

Thersites (Troilus and Cressida)

Trebonius (Julius Caesar)

Valentine (Twelfth Night, Two Gentlemen of Verona)

Ventidius (Antony and Cleopatra, Timon of Athens)

Vincentio (Taming of the Shrew)

Voltimand (Hamlet)

Volumnius (Julius Caesar)

Woodville (King Henry VI, Part 1, All's Well That Ends Well)

Worcester, Earl of (King Henry IV, Parts 1 and

2, All's Well That Ends Well, Antony and Cleopatra)

Young Cato (Julius Caesar)

10

Alcibiades (Timon of Athens)

Andromache (Troilus and Cressida)

Andronicus (Titus Andronicus)

Anne Bullen (King Henry VIII)

Antipholus (Comedy of Errors)

Archidamus (Winter's Tale)

Barnardine (Measure for Measure)

Brakenbury (King Richard III)

Buckingham, Duke of (King Henry VI, Part 2, Antony and Cleopatra, King Henry VIII, King Richard III)

Calphurnia (Julius Caesar)

Canterbury (A-Bishop of) (King Henry V, King Henry VIII, King Richard III)

Coriolanus (Coriolanus)

Duke of York (King Henry V, King Richard II, King Richard III)

Earl of Kent (King Lear)

Earl Rivers (King Richard III)

Euphronius (Antony and Cleopatra)

Fortinbras (Hamlet)

Henry Percy (King Henry IV, Parts 1 and 2, All's Well That Ends Well, Antony and Cleopatra, King Richard II)

Holofernes (Love's Labour's Lost)

Hortensius (Timon of Athens)

John Talbot (King Henry VI, Part All's Well That Ends Well)

King Henry V (King Henry IV, Part 2, Antony and Cleopatra)

Longaville (Love's Labour's Lost)

Lord Rivers (King Henry VI, Part 3, As You Like It)

Lord Scales (King Henry VI, Part 2, Antony and Cleopatra)

Lord Scroop (King Henry V)

Lord Talbot (King Henry VI, Part 1, All's Well That Ends Well)

Lysimachus (Pericles)

Marc Antony (Antony and Cleopatra)

Margarelon (Troilus and Cressida)

Menecrates (Antony and Cleopatra)

Montgomery (King Henry VI, Part 3, As You Like It)

Prince John (King Henry IV, Part 2, Antony and Cleopatra)

Proculeius (Antony and Cleopatra)

Richard III (K.) (King Richard III)

Saturninus (Titus Andronicus)

Sempronius (Timon of Athens)

Sir Michael (King Henry IV, Parts 1 and 2, All's Well That Ends Well, Antony and Cleopatra)

Somerville (King Henry VI, Part 3, As You Like It)

Starveling (Midsummer Night's Dream)

Touchstone (As You Like It)

Willoughby, Lord (King Richard II)

Winchester (Bishop of) (King Henry VIII)

11

Abergavenny, Lord (King Henry VIII)

Artimidorus (Julius Caesar)

Bishop of Ely (King Henry V, King Richard III)

Bolingbroke (King Henry VI, Part 2, Antony and Cleopatra, King Richard II)

Dame Quickly (King Henry IV, Parts 1 and 2, All's Well That Ends Well, Antony and Cleopatra)

Doctor Butts (King Henry VIII)

Doctor Caius (Merry Wives of Windsor)

Duke of Milan (Two Gentlemen of Verona)

Earl Berkley (King Richard II)

Earl of Essex (King John)

Earl of March (King Henry IV, Part 1, All's Well That Ends Well, King Henry VI, Part 3, As You Like It)

James Gurney (King John)

John of Gaunt (King Richard II)

King Henry IV (King Henry IV, Parts 1 and 2, All's Well That Ends Well, Antony and Cleopatra)

King Henry VI (King Henry VI, Parts 1, 2 and 3, All's Well That Ends Well, Antony and Cleopatra, As You Like It)

Lady Capulet (Romeo and Juliet)

Lady Macbeth (Macbeth)

Lady Macduff (Macbeth)

Lord Mowbray (King Henry IV, Part 2, Antony and Cleopatra)

Lord Stanley (King Richard III)

Mrs Anne Page (Merry Wives of Windsor)

Mrs Overdone (Measure for Measure)

Mustardseed (Midsummer Night's Dream)

Peasblossom (Midsummer Night's Dream)

Philostrate (Midsummer Night's Dream)

Plantagenet (King Henry VI, Parts 1, 2 and 3, All's Well That Ends Well, Antony and Cleopatra, As You Like It)

Prince Henry (King John)

Robert Bigot (King John)

Rosencrantz (Hamlet)

Westminster (Archbishop of) (King Richard II)

William Page (Merry Wives of Windsor)

Young Siward (Macbeth)

12

Decius Brutus (Julius Caesar)

Duke of Albany (King Lear)

Duke of Exeter (King Henry V, King Henry VI, Part 3, As You Like It)

Duke of Oxford (King Henry VI, Part 3, As You Like It)

Duke of Surrey (King Richard II)

Duke of Venice (Merchant of Venice, Othello)

Earl of Oxford (King Richard III)

Earl of Surrey (King Henry VIII, King Richard III)

Cleopatra, As You Like It)

Earl of Pembroke (King Henry VI, Part 3, As You Like It, King John)

Earl of Richmond (King Richard III)

Edmund Mortimer (King Henry IV, Part 1, All's Well That Ends Well, King Henry VI, Part 1, All's Well That Ends Well)

Hostess Quickly (King Henry IV, Parts 1 and 2, All's Well That Ends Well, Antony and Cleopatra)

Justice Shallow (King Henry IV, Part 2, Antony and Cleopatra)

King Richard III (King Richard III)

Launcelot Gobbo (Merchant of Venice)

Lord Willoughby (King Richard II)

Marcus Antonius (Julius Caesar)

Metellus Cimber (Julius Caesar)

Northumberland, Ear of (King Henry IV, Parts 1 and 2, All's Well That Ends Well, Antony and Cleopatra, King Henry VI, Part 3, As You Like It, King Richard II)

Northumberland, Lady (King Henry IV, Part 2, Antony and Cleopatra)

Octavius Caesar (Antony and Cleopatra, Julius Caesar)

Peter of Pomfret (King John)

Pompeius Sextus (Antony and Cleopatra)

Prince Humphrey (King Henry IV, Part 2, Antony and Cleopatra)

Queen Elizabeth (King Richard III)

Queen Katharine (King Henry VIII)

Sextus Pompeius (Antony and Cleopatra)

Sir James Blount (King Richard III)

Sir James Tyrrel (King Richard III)

Sir John Stanley (King Henry VI, Part 2, Antony and Cleopatra)

Sir Walter Blunt (King Henry IV, Parts 1 and 2, All's Well That Ends Well, Antony and Cleopatra)

Sir William Lucy (King Henry VI, Part 1, All's Well That Ends Well)

Smith the Weaver (King Henry VI, Part 2, Antony and Cleopatra)

Tullus Aufidius (Coriolanus)

Walter Whilmore (King Henry VI, Part 2, Antony and Cleopatra)

15

Aemilius Lepidus (Julius Caesar)

Bishop of Lincoln (King Henry VIII)

Dromio of Ephesus (Comedy of Errors)

Duke of Lancaster (King Richard II)

Earl of Cambridge (King Henry V)

Earl of Salisbury (King Henry V, King Henry VI, Parts 1 and 2, All's Well That Ends Well, Antony and Cleopatra,

King John, King Richard II)

Earl of Worcester (King Henry IV, Parts 1 and 2, All's Well That Ends Well, Antony and Cleopatra)

Edmund of Langley (King Richard II)

Lord Abergavenny (King Henry VIII)

Margery Jourdain (King Henry VI, Part 2, Antony and Cleopatra)

Marquis of Dorset (King Richard III)

Menenius Agrippa (Coriolanus)

Prince of Arragon (Merchant of Venice)

Prince of Morocco (Merchant of Venice)

Robin Goodfellow (Midsummer Night's Dream)

Sicinius Volutus (Coriolanus)

Sir Anthony Denny (King John)

Sir Hugh Mortimer (King Henry VI, Part 3, As You Like It)

Sir John Falstaff (King Henry IV, Parts 1 and 2, All's Well That Ends Well, Antony and Cleopatra, Merry Wives of Windsor)

Sir John Fastolfe (King Henry VI, Part 1, All's Well That Ends Well)

Sir John Mortimer (King Henry VI, Part 3, As You Like It)

Sir Nicholas Vaux (King Henry VIII)

Sir Thomas Lovell (King Henry VIII)

Titus Andronicus (Titus Andronicus)

OTHER FICTIONAL CHARACTERS

NB: Names are ordered by first letter of first names; no following title indicates an eponymous character, or one who appears in a series of books, etc.

3
Kaa (The Jungle Book)
Kim

4
Abel (Middlemarch)
Ahab (Moby Dick)

5
Akela (The Jungle Book)
Alice (Alice's Adventures in Wonderland)
Aslan (The Lion, the Witch and the Wardrobe)
Baloo (The Jungle Book)
Boxer (Animal Farm)
Topsy (Uncle Tom's Cabin)

6
Ayesha (She)
Dr Aziz (A Passage to India)
Jeeves
Laurie (Little Women)
Marmee (Little Women)
Mowgli (The Jungle Book)
Pinkie (Brighton Rock)
Square (Tom Jones)

7
Ben Gunn (Treasure Island)
Candide
Dracula
Ishmael (Moby Dick)
Jo March (Little Women)
Lord Jim
Mellors (Lady Chatterley's Lover)
Orlando

8
Amy March (Little Women)
Bagheera (The Jungle Book)

Dr Watson
Faithful (The Pilgrim's Progress)
Fielding (A Passage to India)
Flashman (Tom Brown's Schooldays)
Gunga Din
Jane Eyre
Lockwood (Wuthering Heights)
Meg March (Little Women)
Moby Dick
Moriarty (Sherlock Holmes)
Napoleon (Animal Farm)
Peter Pan
Queequeg (Moby Dick)
Snowball (Animal Farm)
Squealer (Animal Farm)
Thwackum (Tom Jones)
Tom Brown (Tom Brown's Schooldays)
Tom Jones

9
Beau Geste
Beth March (Little Women)
Christian (The Pilgrim's Progress)
Ellen Dean (Wuthering Heights)
Flora Post (Cold Comfort Farm)
Indian Joe (The Adventures of Tom Sawyer)
James Bond
Mad Hatter (Alice's Adventures in Wonderland)
March Hare (Alice's Adventures in Wonderland)
Mrs Ramsay (To the

Lighthouse)
Tom Sawyer (The Adventures of Tom Sawyer)
Shere Khan (The Jungle Book)
Yossarian (Catch-22)

10
Alf Garnett (TV, Till Death Us Do Part)
Becky Sharp (Vanity Fair)
Big Brother (1984)
Dr Dolittle
Dorian Gray (The Picture of Dorian Gray)
Edward Hyde (Dr Jekyll and Mr Hyde)
Emma Bovary (Madame Bovary)
Heathcliff (Wuthering Heights)
Jane Bennet (Pride and Prejudice)
Jean Brodie (The Prime of Miss Jean Brodie)
Jim Hawkins (Treasure Island)
Jon Forsyte (The Forsyte Saga)
Lorelei Lee (Gentlemen Prefer Blondes)
Major Major (Catch 22)
Mary Bennet (Pride and Prejudice)
Molly Bloom (Ulysses)
Perry Mason
Tinker Bell (Peter Pan)
Wife of Bath (Canterbury Tales)

11
Black Beauty
Cheshire Cat (Alice's Adventures in Wonderland)

Edgar Linton (Wuthering Heights)
Henry Jekyll (Dr Jekyll and Mr Hyde)
Lydia Bennet (Pride and Prejudice)
Mary Poppins
Mr Rochester (Jane Eyre)
Phineas Finn
Phineas Fogg (Around the World in 80 Days)
Rhett Butler (Gone with the Wind)
Silas Marner
Walter Mitty (The Secret Life of Walter Mitty)
White Rabbit (Alice's Adventures in Wonderland)

12
Adela Quested (A Passage to India)
Ashley Wilkes (Gone with the Wind)
Captain Flint (Treasure Island)
Fleur Forsyte (The Forsyte Saga)
Irene Forsyte (The Forsyte Saga)
Leopold Bloom (Ulysses)
Moll Flanders
Scheherazade (Arabian Nights)
Wendy Darling (Peter Pan)
Winston Smith (1984)

13
Bertie Wooster
Eliza Dolittle (Pygmalion)
Emma Woodhouse (Emma)
Jolyon Forsyte (The Forsyte Saga)
Joseph Andrews
Lady Bracknell (The Importance of Being Earnest)
Richard Hannay (The 39 Steps)
Robin McGregor (Rob Roy)
Scarlett O'Hara (Gone with the Wind)
Victor Meldrew (TV, One Foot in the Grave)

14
Charles Bingley (Pride and Prejudice)
George Knightly (Emma)
Gudrun Brangwen (Women in Love)
Jonathan Harker (Dracula)
Long John Silver (Treasure Island)
Maggie Tulliver (The Mill on the Floss)
Sherlock Holmes
Ursula Brangwen (Women in Love)

15
Allan Quatermain (King Solomon's Mines)
Catherine Bennet (Pride and Prejudice)
Elizabeth Bennet (Pride and Prejudice)
Huckleberry Finn
Lord Peter Wimsey
Squire Allworthy (Tom Jones)

16 *and over*
Catherine Earnshaw (Wuthering Heights) (17)
Constance Chatterley (Lady Chatterley's Lover) (19)
Fitzwilliam Darcy (Pride and Prejudice) (16)
Horatio Hornblower (17)
Judith Starkadder (Cold Comfort Farm) (16)
Nicholas Bulstrode (Middlemarch) (17)
Phantom of the Opera (17)
Professor Higgins (Pygmalion) (16)
Victor Frankenstein (18)

Films

2	Gigi	Klute	Harvey	Vertigo	The Piano
ET	Jaws	Rocky	Henry V	Witness	
If	Rope	Shane	Mad Max		**9**
		Shoah	Psycho	**8**	Betty Blue
3	**5**	Yanks	The Fly	Body Heat	Dr Zhivago
Big	Alfie	Yentl	The Kid	Duck Soup	Genevieve
JFK	Alien		Top Hat	Fantasia	Get Carter
Kes	Bambi	**6**		High Noon	Local Hero
Ran	Birdy	Batman	**7**	King Kong	Nosferatu
	Dumbo	Ben Hur	Amadeus	Mona Lisa	Snow White
4	Evita	Carmen	Cabaret	Oklahoma	
Babe	Fargo	Gandhi	Platoon	Star Wars	**10**
Diva	Ghost	Grease	Titanic	The Field	Blue Velvet

Brassed Off
Casablanca
Eraserhead
Goodfellas
Moonstruck
My Fair Lady
Peeping Tom
Taxi Driver
The Misfits
The Servant
Videodrome
Wall Street

11
Bladerunner
Citizen Kane
Deliverance
Don't Look Now
Forrest Gump
The Evil Dead
The Exorcist
Mean Streets
Performance
Pulp Fiction
The Big Sleep
The Cruel Sea
The Red Shoes
The Third Man
True Romance
Wild at Heart

12
Calamity Jane
Gregory's Girl
Hope and Glory
Mrs Doubtfire
South Pacific
The Blue Angel
The Go-Between
The Godfather
The Wicker Man
Withnail and I

13
Apocalypse Now
Cathy Come Home
Death in Venice
Dr Strangelove
Reservoir Dogs
Some Like It Hot
The Dambusters
The Deer Hunter
The Wizard of Oz
Trainspotting

14
American Beauty
Black Narcissus
Brief Encounter
Chariots of Fire
Cinema Paradiso

Land and Freedom
Lassie Come Home
Paint Your Wagon
Secrets and Lies
The Commitments
The Great Escape
The Ladykillers
The Seventh Seal

15
Double Indemnity
Gone with the Wind
She's Got to Have It
The Sound of Music
Thelma and Louise

16 *and over*
A Night to Remember (16)
Battleship Potemkin (18)
Buena Vista Social Club (20)
Four Weddings and a Funeral (23)
It's a Wonderful Life (17)
Lawrence of Arabia (16)
Passport to Pimlico (17)
Saturday Night Fever (18)
The League of Gentlemen (20)

Literary, Poetic and Grammatical Terms

2	epic	poet	caret	haiku	psalm	vowel
do	epos	quip	carol	humor	quote	
	foot	rime	casal	ictus	rhyme	**6**
3	form	root	codex	idiom	rondo	accent
ego	gest	rule	colon	idyll	runic	active
lay	glee	rune	comma	iliad	scald	adonic
ode	hymn	saga	dirge	image	scene	adverb
pun	iamb	scan	ditty	index	shift	Aeneid
	idyl	song	drama	infix	slang	alcaic
4	mime	tone	elegy	irony	stich	annals
agon	mood	verb	elide	lyric	style	anthem
bard	myth	weak	epode	maxim	sylva	aorist
case	noun	word	essay	metre	tense	aptote
coda	past		fable	motif	theme	ballad
copy	pean	**5**	farce	novel	tilde	bathos
dual	play	affix	folio	paean	triad	chanty
duan	plot	blurb	geste	poesy	Vedas	chorus
Edda	poem	canto	gloss	prose	verse	clause

cliche
climax
comedy
crisis
critic
dactyl
dative
define
derive
digram
dipody
ending
epodic
epopee
finite
future
gender
genius
gerund
gnomic
govern
heroic
hiatus
homily
hubris
humour
hybris
hymnal
hyphen
iambic
iambus
jargon
kabuki
lacuna
legend
lyrist
macron
mantra
memoir
monody
neuter
number
object
parody
pathos
period
person
phrase
pidgin
plural
poetic
poetry
prefix
review

rhythm
riddle
rondle
satire
simile
sketch
slogan
sonnet
stanza
stress
strong
suffix
symbol
syntax
thesis
umlaut
verbal
zeugma

7

adjunct
anagram
analogy
analyse
anapest
antonym
apocope
apology
article
ballade
berhyme
bucolic
cadence
caesura
cantata
cedilla
chanson
choreus
collate
content
context
couplet
decline
descant
diction
digraph
distich
eclogue
edition
elegiac
elision
epicene
epigram
epistle

epitaph
fantasy
fiction
Georgic
harmony
Homeric
homonym
idyllic
imagery
inflect
introit
journal
lampoon
leonine
lexicon
litotes
lyrical
meiosis
mimesis
nemesis
novella
Odyssey
paradox
parsing
passive
peanism
perfect
persona
phoneme
poetics
polemic
present
pronoun
prosaic
prosody
proverb
psalter
refrain
regular
requiem
Sapphic
sarcasm
scaldic
semiped
servile
setting
sextain
spondee
stichic
strophe
subject
syncope
synonym
systole

tiercet
tragedy
trilogy
triolet
triplet
trochee
villain
virelay
Vulgate
war song
western

8

ablative
absolute
acrostic
allusion
alphabet
amoebean
analysis
anapaest
anaphora
anti-hero
antiphon
apodosis
archaism
assonant
asterisk
bacchius
balladry
caesural
canticle
chiasmus
choliamb
choriamb
clerihew
contrast
critique
dactylic
definite
dieresis
dialogue
discrete
doggerel
dramatic
ellipsis
enclitic
epic poem
epigraph
epilogue
epitrite
euphuism
feminine
folk tale

footnote
full stop
generate
genitive
glossary
guttural
horation
language
laureate
libretto
limerick
logogram
lyricism
madrigal
metaphor
metrical
mispoint
mock epic
morpheme
negative
nonsense
optative
Ossianic
oxymoron
paradigm
particle
partsong
pastoral
personal
phonetic
Pindaric
poetical
positive
prologue
quantity
quatrain
relative
rhapsody
rhetoric
romantic
scanning
scansion
scenario
sentence
singular
solecism
stanzaic
suspense
swan song
syntaxis
systolic
temporal
threnody
thriller

tribrach
trimeter
triptote
unpoetic
versicle
vignette
vocative
whodunit
word play

9

accidence
adjective
ampersand
anapestic
Anglicism
anonymous
anthology
antispast
apocopate
archetype
Asclepiad
assonance
biography
birthsong
broadside
burlesque
cacophony
catharsis
classical
conjugate
consonant
criticism
decastich
diaeresis
dipthong
dithyramb
ditrochee
elegiacal
enclitics
etymology
euphemism
facsimile
flashback
formative
free verse
Gallicism
gerundive
grammatic
hemistich
hendiadys
hexameter
hexastich
hypallage

Literary, Poetic and Grammatical Terms

hyperbole
idiomatic
imperfect
inflexion
inversion
irregular
leitmotiv
lyric poem
masculine
metaplasm
minor poet
monometer
monorhyme
nonostich
neologism
objective
parataxis
partitive
past tense
phillipic
philology
Pindarism
platitude
poetaster
pot boiler
potential
preterite
pricksong
principal
privative
prose poem
prosodian
prosodist
quartette
quotation
recension
reddition
reflexive
roundelay
sea chanty
semantics
semicolon
semivowel
soliloquy
syllepsis
symbolism
symposium
symptosis
synalepha
syntactic
telestich
terza rima
trisagion
Virgilian

10
accusative
amphibrach
amphimacer
anapaestic
anarthrous
anastrophe
anastrophy
antagonist
antepenult
anticlimax
antiphonal
antiphonic
apostrophe
apposition
atmosphere
avant-garde
bestseller
blank verse
bowdlerize
caricature
choliambic
choriambic
choriambus
circumflex
colloquial
comparison
declension
definition
definitive
denouement
derivation
derivative
dissonance
dolichorus
epenthesis
epenthetic
generative
government
grammarian
hexametric
hyperbaton
hyphenated
imperative
impersonal
indefinite
infinitive
inflection
intonation
involution
linguistic
lyric verse
manuscript
metathesis

mock heroic
morphology
neuter verb
nom de plume
nominative
ottava rima
palindrome
paraphrase
participle
passion play
pentameter
Petrarchan
picaresque
plagiarism
pluperfect
pronominal
provection
reciprocal
short story
similitude
spoonerism
subjective
synaeresis
tetracolon
tetrameter
tetrastich
transitive
unpoetical
vernacular

11
alexandrine
amphibology
anacoluthon
antispastic
antiphrasis
antistrophe
aposiopesis
association
ballad style
bibliomancy
catastrophe
chansonette
comic relief
comparative
concordance
conjunction
conjunctive
constituent
declination
descriptive
disjunctive
dissyllabic
dissyllable

dithyrambic
dithyrambus
future tense
ghost writer
grammatical
hemistichal
heteroclite
hudibrastic
linguistics
lyric poetry
miracle play
oblique case
parenthesis
portmanteau
preposition
proposition
punctuation
regular verb
reiterative
subjunctive
subordinate
substantive
superlative
suppression
syntactical
tragicomedy
trimetrical

12
alliteration
alliterative
alphabetical
anteposition
antibacchius
antimetrical
antiphonical
antiphrastic
antistrophic
archilochian
bibliography
deponent verb
dissyllabify
distributive
epigrammatic
episodically
epithalamium
etymological
grammaticism
grammaticize
heteroclitic
hexametrical
indeclinable
intransitive
metaphorical

minnesingers
nursery rhyme
onomatopoeia
perfect tense
poet laureate
postposition
prescriptive
present tense
prothalamium

13 and over
antepenultimate
(15)
definite article
(15)
epigrammatical
(14)
frequentative
(13)
future perfect
(13)
historic present
(15)
hysteron
  proteron (16)
indicative mood
(14)
interrogative
(13)
inverted commas
(14)
irregular verb
(13)
lyrical poetry
(13)
objective case
(13)
personification
(15)
poetic licence
(13)
positive degree
(14)
possessive case
(14)
science fiction
(14)
split infinitive
(15)
transformation
(14)
ungrammatical
(13)

Music and Musical Instruments

2	beat	song	crook	pitch	twang	eighth
do	bell	stop	croon	polka	valse	encore
fa	brio	tace	crowd	primo	vibes	euphon
ff	clef	time	dance	quill	viola	fading
gu	coda	toll	dirge	rebec	vocal	fiddle
la	drum	tone	ditty	reeds	voice	figure
mi	duet	trio	dolce	regal	volta	finale
pp	echo	tuba	drone	resin	volti	fluter
re	fife	tune	duple	rondo	waits	follia
si	fine	turr	elegy	round	waltz	fugato
ut	flat	vamp	etude	sanko	wrest	gallop
va	fret	vina	flute	sansa	yodel	giusto
	glee	viol	forte	scale	zinke	graces
3	gong	vivo	fugal	scena		ground
air	harp	voce	fugue	score	**6**	guitar
alt	high	vola	galop	segno	accent	hammer
bar	hold	wind	gamba	segue	adagio	intone
bis	horn	wood	gamut	senza	anthem	Ionian
bow	hymn		gigue	shake	arioso	jingle
cue	jazz	**5**	grace	shalm	atabal	kettle
doh	kent	acuta	grave	sharp	atonal	legato
duo	koto	adapt	knell	shawn	attune	Lieder
fah	lead	album	kyrie	sitar	aubade	litany
gue	Lied	arsis	largo	sixth	ballad	lutist
hum	lilt	assai	lento	slide	ballet	lydian
jig	lute	atone	lyric	snare	beemol	lyrist
key	lyre	banjo	major	soave	bolero	manual
kit	mass	basso	march	sol-fa	bridge	medley
lah	mode	basta	metre	sound	bugler	melody
lay	mood	baton	mezzo	stave	cadent	minuet
Piu	mort	bebop	minim	strad	cantor	monody
pop	mute	bells	minor	strum	catgut	motive
rag	neum	blare	molto	suite	chaunt	nobile
ray	node	blues	mosso	swell	chimes	oboist
run	note	bones	motet	swing	choral	octave
sax	oboe	brass	motif	tabor	choric	off-key
soh	opus	breve	naker	tacet	chorus	pavane
sol	part	bugle	nebel	tardo	citole	phrase
tie	peal	canon	neume	tempo	contra	plagal
vox	pean	canto	nodal	tenor	corona	player
zel	pipe	carol	nonet	theme	cornet	presto
	poco	cello	notes	third	crooks	quaver
4	port	cento	octet	thrum	cymbal	rattan
alla	reed	chant	opera	tonic	da capo	rattle
alto	reel	cheng	organ	tonus	damper	rebeck
arco	rest	chime	paean	tosto	design	record
aria	root	choir	pause	triad	diesis	revert
ayre	sang	chord	pavan	trill	ditone	rhythm
band	sign	clang	pedal	trite	divoto	rounds
bard	sing	clank	piano	trope	drones	rubato
base	slur	corno	pieno	tuner	duetto	sacbut
bass	solo	croma	piper	tutti	dulcet	sancho

scales	andante	descend	pianola	syncope
sennet	angelot	descent	pibroch	taborer
septet	animato	diagram	piccolo	taboret
serial	apotome	dichord	piffero	tambour
sestet	apotomy	discord	pomposo	tambura
sextet	arghool	distune	posaune	theorbo
shanty	arietta	dittied	prelude	tibicen
shofar	ariette	drummer	ragtime	timbrel
singer	ars nova	epicede	quartet	timpani
sonata	attuned	euphony	quintet	timpano
sop sax	bagpipe	eutonia	recital	tipping
spinet	ballade	fagotto	refrain	toccata
stanza	bandore	fanfare	reprise	tone row
string	baryton	fermata	requiem	tremolo
subito	bassist	fiddler	rescore	triplet
tabour	bassoon	fistula	ripieno	trumpet
tabret	bazooka	flatten	romance	tubicen
tam-tam	bellows	flutina	rondeau	tuneful
tenuto	bitonal	flutist	rondino	ukelele
tercet	bodhran	fuguist	rosalia	upright
tierce	bravura	furioso	roulade	up-tempo
timbal	cadence	gavotte	sackbut	vespers
timbre	cadency	gittern	sambuca	vibrato
tirade	cadenza	gravita	sambuke	vihuela
tom-tom	calando	gravity	samisen	violist
treble	calypso	G-string	sarangi	violone
trigon	cantata	harmony	saxhorn	warbler
tucket	canzona	harpist	scherzo	whistle
tune up	canzone	hautboy	schisma	zithern
tuning	caprice	jukebox	sciolto	zuffolo
tymbal	celesta	karaoke	scoring	
tzetze	cellist	keynote	secondo	**8**
unison	cembalo	locrian	septole	absonant
up-beat	chamade	lullaby	serpent	absonous
vamper	chanson	maestro	settina	addition
veloce	chanter	marimba	settino	alto clef
ventil	chikara	mazurka	seventh	antiphon
vielle	chorale	measure	shophar	arch lute
violin	cithara	mediant	singing	arpeggio
vivace	cithern	melisma	sistrum	autoharp
volata	clapper	melodic	sithara	bagpipes
volume	clarion	mistune	skiffle	baritone
warble	clavier	musette	slurred	barytone
zambra	con brio	musical	soloist	bass clef
zincke	concert	natural	soprano	bassetto
zither	conduct	ocarina	sordine	bass drum
	cornett	octette	sordono	bass horn
7	counter	offbeat	sosplro	bass note
aeolian	cremona	organum	spinnet	bass oboe
aeolist	crooner	pandora	stopped	bass viol
agitato	crotalo	pan pipe	stretto	beat time
allegro	cymbals	phonica	strophe	bell harp
alt horn	czardas	pianino	sub-bass	berceuse
amoroso	descant	pianist	subject	canticle

canzonet	grazioso	pastoral	trombone	decachord
carillon	guimbard	phantasy	tympanon	deep-toned
castanet	half-note	phrasing	tympanum	dissonant
castrato	harmonic	Phrygian	vigoroso	dithyramb
cavatina	harp lute	pianette	virginal	drone pipe
chaconne	hawk bell	plectrum	virtuosi	drumstick
cheville	high note	post horn	virtuoso	dulcitone
clappers	hornpipe	psaltery	vocalion	elbow pipe
clarinet	infinito	quantity	vocalist	elevation
clarsach	interval	recorder	voce colo	euphonism
clavecin	intonate	reed pipe	warbling	euphonium
claviary	isotonic	register	woodwind	euphonize
composer	Jew's harp	resonant	zambomba	extempore
composto	jongleur	response		fiddle-bow
con amore	keyboard	rhapsody	**9**	flageolet
con anima	key bugle	rigadoon	accordion	flute stop
concerto	knackers	saraband	acoustics	folk music
confusco	lentando	semitone	allemande	furibondo
conjusto	libretto	septette	alto viola	gallopade
continuo	ligature	sequence	andamento	generator
couranto	lutanist	serenade	andantino	glissando
cromorna	lutenist	serenata	antiphony	grace note
crotchet	madrigal	sestetto	arabesque	gradation
deep tone	maestoso	sextette	archilute	grandioso
demi-tone	major key	sforzato	atonality	Gregorian
diapason	mandolin	shamisen	bagatelle	guitarist
diatonic	martenot	side drum	balalaika	half shift
diminish	melodeon	smorzato	banjoline	hand organ
ding-dong	melodics	sonatina	barcarole	harmonica
distance	melodist	songster	bass flute	harmonics
doloroso	melodize	spiccato	bird organ	harmonium
dominant	minor key	spinette	bombardon	harmonize
down beat	minstrel	staccato	bow string	hexachord
drumbeat	mirliton	sticcado	brass band	high-pitch
drumhead	miserere	subtonic	brillante	hightoned
duettist	moderato	symmetry	bugle horn	homophony
dulcimer	modulate	symphony	cacophony	imbroglio
eleventh	monotone	syntonic	cantabile	immusical
energico	monotony	tabourer	capriccio	impromptu
ensemble	movement	tabouret	castanets	improvise
entr'acte	musicale	tamboura	celestina	in harmony
euphonic	musician	tell-tale	charivari	interlude
euphonon	nocturne	tenoroon	chromatic	inversion
exercise	notation	terzetto	clarionet	irregular
falsetto	notturno	threnody	claviharp	jazz music
fandango	obligato	timoroso	coach horn	lagrimoso
fantasia	operatic	tonalist	conductor	languente
fantasie	operetta	tonality	consonate	larghetto
flautist	oratorio	tone down	contralto	leger-line
folk song	organist	tone poem	cornopean	leitmotif
forzando	ostinato	trap drum	crescendo	mandolute
galement	overture	tremando	cymbalist	melodious
galliard	pan pipes	triangle	dead march	metronome
gemshorn	part song	trichord	death bell	mezzo-voce

modulator
monochord
monophony
monotonic
mouth harp
music book
nose flute
obbligato
octachord
orchestra
part music
pastorale
phonetics
pianolist
pitchpipe
pizzicato
plainsong
polonaise
polychord
polyphony
polytonal
quadrille
quailpipe
quartette
quintette
recording
reed organ
rehearsal
resonance
rhythmics
ricercare
roundelay
saxophone
semibreve
semitonic
septimole
seraphine
sforzando
siciliana
siciliano
signature
slow march
snare drum
soft pedal
solfeggio
sollecito
sopranist
sostenuto
sotto voce
sound post
spiritosa
spiritual
strascino
succentor

symphonic
syncopate
tablature
tabourine
tailpiece
tambourin
tenor bass
tenor clef
tenor horn
tenor tuba
tenor viol
tessitura
theorbist
timetable
timpanist
trillando
troubador
trumpeter
tubophone
tympanist
union pipe
unmusical
untunable
variation
viola alto
violinist
voluntary
vox humana
whistling
xylophone

10
accidental
adaptation
affettuoso
allegretto
appoggiato
attunement
background
bandmaster
barcarolle
base spring
basset horn
bassoonist
binotonous
bull fiddle
cantillate
canzonetta
chiroplast
chitlarone
chorus girl
clarichord
clavichord
colorature

concertina
con spirito
continuato
contrabass
cor anglais
cornettist
dance music
demiditone
diastaltic
diminuendo
discordant
disharmony
dissonance
dissonancy
dolcemente
double bass
double time
dulcet tone
embouchure
enharmonic
Eolian harp
Eolian lyre
euphonicon
euphonious
extraneous
flugelhorn
folk-singer
fortissimo
French harp
French horn
gramophone
grand piano
grand opera
ground bass
harmonicon
harp-string
homophonic
hurdy-gurdy
incidental
instrument
intermezzo
intonation
kettle drum
lentamente
light opera
major chord
major scale
minor chord
minor scale
minstrelsy
mixolydian
modulation
monotonous
mouth organ

mouthpiece
musica viva
musicology
opera buffa
opera music
ophicleide
orchestral
orpheoreon
pentachord
percussion
pianissimo
pianoforte
polyphonic
prima donna
recitative
recitativo
ritardando
ritornello
semiquaver
soprano sax
sourdeline
sousaphone
staphyline
Stradivari
Strathspey
strepitoso
string band
stringendo
submediant
supertonic
suspension
symphonion
symphonist
syncopated
syncopator
tamboureen
tambourine
tarantella
tersanetus
tetrachord
tin whistle
tonic chord
tonic major
tonic minor
tonic solfa
triple time
trombonist
tuning fork
twelve tone
undulation
variamento
vibraphone
vistomente
vocal music

zumpé piano

11
accelerando
Aeolian harp
Aeolian lyre
alla capella
alto-ripieno
arrangement
ballad opera
barrel-organ
bene-placito
broken chord
canned music
capriccioso
church music
clairschach
clarion note
composition
concertante
contra basso
contrapunto
contra-tenor
counterpart
decrescendo
demi-cadence
diatessaron
discordance
discordancy
equisonance
extemporize
fiddlestick
figured bass
fingerboard
first violin
graphophone
Guido's scale
harmoniphon
harmonizing
harpsichord
highpitched
hunting-horn
hydraulicon
incantation
madrigalist
mandolinist
minnesinger
music master
natural note
nickelodeon
opera bouffe
orchestrate
passing bell
passing note

piano player	bass baritone	polytonality	**14 *and over***
piano violin	boogie-woogie	pralltriller	Ambrosian chant (14)
polyphonism	cembal d'ambre	repercussion	banjo mandoline (14)
polyphonist	chamber music	sesqualtera	brass instrument(s)
prestissimo	chromaticism	sounding-post	(15, 16)
progression	clarinettist	spheremelody	chromatic scale (14)
quarter note	clavicembalo	Stradivarius	demisemiquaver (14)
quarter tone	comedy ballet	thorough bass	direct interval (14)
rallentando	concert grand	tuning hammer	double-tongueing (15)
rock and roll	concert pitch	ukulele banjo	electric guitar (14)
sacred music	contrapuntal	viola da gamba	electronic music (15)
saxophonist	cottage piano	vocalization	fife-and-drum band
senza rigore	counterpoint		(15)
solmization	counter-tenor	**13**	Gregorian chant (14)
string music	divertimento	accompaniment	Highland bagpipe
subsemitone	double octave	bagpipe player	(15)
symphonious	extravaganza	choral singing	instrumentalist (15)
syncopation	false cadence	conservatoire	instrumentation (15)
transposing	funeral march	cornet-a-piston	Lowland bagpipe (14)
tridiapason	glockenspiel	disharmonious	mandolin player (14)
unaccordant	guitar string	harmonic chord	musical director (15)
viola d'amore	inharmonious	musical comedy	musical festival (15)
viol da gamba	instrumental	music festival	musique concrete (15)
violoncello	marcatissimo	operatic music	regimental band (14)
vivacissimo	mezzo-relievo	orchestration	string quartette (15)
voce-di-petto	mezzo-soprano	ranz-des-vaches	symphony concert
voce-di-testa	military band	sacred concert	(15)
volti-subito	musicologist	sol-fa notation	tintinnabulary (14)
	opera comique	staff notation	tintinnabulate (14)
12	orchestrator	string octette	tintinnabulation (16)
accordionist	organ grinder	string quartet	triple tongueing (15)
acoustic bass	organ recital	superdominant	wind instrument(s)
allegrissimo	pandean pipes	swanee whistle	(14,15)
appassionata	passion music	terpsichorean	
appoggiatura	penny whistle	tetradiapason	
assai allegro	philharmonic	transposition	
augmentation	philomusical	violoncellist	

Novels

3	Kipps	Molloy	Lord Jim	Cranford	The Spire
Kim	Money	Murphy	Maurice	Flashman	The Trial
She	Scoop	Nausea	Orlando	Germinal	The Waves
	Sybil	Pamela	Rebecca	High Rise	The Years
4	Zadig		The Bell	Jane Eyre	Tom Jones
Clea		**7**	The Fall	Lucky Jim	Waverley
Dr No	**6**	Candide	Ulysses	Moby Dick	Villette
Emma	Amelia	Cat's Eye		Nostromo	
Nana	Ben Hur	Dracula	**8**	Pale Fire	**9**
	Herzog	Ivanhoe	Adam Bede	The Beach	Agnes Grey
5	Junkie	Jo's Boys	Antic Hay	The Idiot	Balthazar
Crash	Lolita	Justine	Clarissa	The Magus	Cloud Howe

Dead Souls
Dubliners
Fanny Hill
Hard Times
Hawksmoor
I, Claudius
Kidnapped
Little Men
Moon Tiger
On the Road
The Castle
The Devils
The Hobbit
The Plague
Waterland
White Fang

10
Animal Farm
Bleak House
Cannery Row
Clayhanger
Don Quixote
East of Eden
Edwin Drood
Goldfinger
Hotel du Lac
Howards End
Lorna Doone
Malone Dies
Mountolive
Persuasion
Possession
Sunset Song
The Bell Jar
The Rainbow
Time's Arrow
Titus Alone
Titus Groan
Vanity Fair
Vile Bodies
Young Adolf

11
Black Beauty
Burmese Days
Cakes and Ale
Crome Yellow
Daisy Miller
Elmer Gantry
Gormenghast
Grey Granite
Heat and Dust
Little Women

Martha Quest
Middlemarch
Mrs Dalloway
Oliver Twist
Silas Marner
The Big Sleep
The Green Hat
The Loved One
The Outsider
Untouchable
War and Peace
What Katy Did
Women in Love

12
Anna Karenina
Arabian Nights
A Suitable Boy
Bend Sinister
Brighton Rock
Casino Royale
Fear of Flying
Frankenstein
The Ginger Man
Little Dorrit
London Fields
Madame Bovary
Mapp and Lucia
Moll Flanders
Of Mice and Men
Room at the Top
The Ghost Road
The Moonstone
The Old Devils
The Sea, The Sea
The Unnamable
Whisky Galore

13
A Kind of Loving
Black Mischief
Brave New World
Daniel Deronda
Earthly Powers
Finnegan's Wake
Live and Let Die
Love on the Dole
Mansfield Park
North and South
Pincher Martin
Schindler's Ark
Sons and Lovers
Tarka the Otter
The History Man

The Last Tycoon
The Jungle Book
The Naked Lunch
Under Milk Wood
Winnie the Pooh

14
A Handful of Dust
Absalom! Absalom!
A Room with a View
Black Narcissus
Castle Rackrent
Cider with Rosie
Darkness at Noon
Death on the Nile
Decline and Fall
Empire of the Sun
Jude the Obscure
Lord of the Flies
National Velvet
Of Human Bondage
Our Man in Havana
Rites of Passage
Robinson Crusoe
Tales of the City
The Ambassadors
The Color Purple
The Great Gatsby
The Information
The L-shaped Room
The Wasp Factory
The Water-Babies
Treasure Island
Tristram Shandy
Uncle Tom's Cabin

15
A Christmas Carol
A Dry White Season
A Passage to India
Cold Comfort Farm
Darkness Visible
Flaubert's Parrot
Heart of Darkness
Northanger Abbey
Our Mutual Friend
Portrait of a Lady
Puck of Pook's Hill
The Country Girls
The Old Wives' Tale
The Secret Garden
The Sun Also Rises
The Woman in White
Things Fall Apart

Three Men in a Boat
To the Lighthouse

Wide Sargasso Sea
Wuthering Heights

16
A Clockwork Orange
A Tale of Two Cities
David Copperfield
Gulliver's Travels
Martin Chuzzlewit
Myra Breckinridge
Nicholas Nickleby
The Call of the Wild
The Grapes of Wrath
The Handmaid's Tale
The Maltese Falcon
The Satanic Verses
The Scarlet Letter
The Way of all Flesh
The Young Visiters
Under the Volcano

17 *and over*
Crime and Punishment (18)
Dr Jekyll and Mr Hyde
Great Expectations (17)
How Green Was My Valley (19)
King Solomon's Mines (17)
Midnight's Children (17)
Nineteen Eighty-Four (18)
Pride and Prejudice (17)
The Lord of the Rings (17)
The Railway Children (18)
The Remains of the Day (18)
The Sound and the Fury (18)
The Sword in the Stone (18)
The War of the Worlds (17)
Travels with my Aunt (17)

Plays of Shakespeare

6
Hamlet
Henry V

7
Henry IV (Parts 1 and 2)
Henry VI (Parts 1, 2 and 3)
Macbeth
Othello

8
King John
King Lear
Pericles

9
Cymbeline
Henry VIII
Richard II

10
Coriolanus
King Henry V
Richard III
The Tempest

11
As You Like It
King Henry IV (Parts 1 and 2)
King Henry VI (Parts 1, 2 and 3)

12
Julius Caesar
Twelfth Night

13
King Henry VIII
King Richard II
Timon of Athens

14
King Richard III
Romeo and Juliet
The Winter's Tale

15 *and over*
A Comedy of Errors (15)
All's Well That Ends Well (20)
Hamlet, Prince of Denmark (21)
Love's Labour's Lost (16)
Measure for Measure (17)
The Merry Wives of Windsor (22)
A Midsummer Night's Dream (21)
Much Ado About Nothing (19)
Othello, the Moor of Venice (22)
Pericles, Prince of Tyre (20)
The Taming of the Shrew (19)
The Two Noble Kinsmen (19)
Troilus and Cressida (18)
Two Gentlemen of Verona (20)

Publishing, Printing and Journalism

2
ad
em
en
o.p.
pi
s.c.
w.f.

3
ads
bed
box
cub
cut
die
dtp
imp
mat
out
pie
pot
run
set
sub
web

4
back
body
bold
bulk
caps
comp
copy
cyan
dash
demy
edit
etch
face
film
flap
font
grid
lead
limp
news
open
page
pica
puff

pull
quad
ream
ruby
rule
sewn
sink
slug
stet
take
trim
type

5
beard
black
bleed
block
blurb
cameo
canon
caret
cased
chase
chill
cloth
clump
crown
daily
Didot
draft
dummy
flong
folio
fount
gloss
index
leads
libel
linen
litho
metal
pearl
plate
point
print
proof
punch
quire
quote
Ralph
recto

reset
roman
rough
royal
run-on
scoop
serif
sigla
solid
sorts
spine
stone
story
tilde
title
verso
xerox

6
back-up
banner
boards
ceriph
cliche
coated
cock-up
column
delete
editor
flimsy
format
galley
indent
italic
jacket
keep up
layout
leader
linage
lock up
makeup
marked
masked
matrix
minion
morgue
offset
ozalid
punch
quotes
random
redtop

review
revise
rotary
screen
serial
series
set-off
sketch
spiked
splash
umlaut
weekly
weight

7
article
artwork
binding
bled off
brevier
bromide
bumping
capital
caption
cast off
cedilla
clicker
diamond
display
edition
English
engrave
etching
feature
Fraktur
full out
gravure
gripper
imprint
justify
leading
literal
masking
measure
monthly
mortice
net sale
overrun
overset
preface
prelims
printer

publish
release
reprint
rewrite
sits vac
subedit
tabloid
typeset
woodcut

8
art board
ascender
bleeding
boldface
colophon
cut flush
dateline
deadline
designer
endpaper
footnote
fudge box
hairline
halftone
hardback
headband
headline
hot metal
imperial
intaglio
keyboard
linotype
monotype
obituary
paginate
photoset
print run
register
reporter
slipcase
streamer
tailband
turnover
type area
verbatim
vignette
woodpulp

9
art editor
bookplate

bourgeois
box number
brilliant
broadside
casebound
co-edition
collating
columnist
copypaper
copyright
crossword
descender
editorial
exclusive
facsimile
freelance
furniture
idiot tape
laminated
lineblock
lower case
make ready
newpaper
newsprint
nonpareil
overprint
pageproof
paperback
paragraph
photocopy
photostat
pseudonym
publisher
quarterly
sans serif
signature
small pica
stonehand
subeditor
symposium
tear sheet
the morgue
upper case
watermark
web-offset
woodblock
wrong font

10
assembling
annotation
blockmaker

body matter
broadsheet
casting box
casting-off
catch title
city editor
compositor
copyholder
copytaster
copywriter
dead matter
dirty proof
feuilleton
film critic
four colour
imposition
impression
imprimatur
interleave
journalese
journalism
journalist
lamination
leader page
lithograph
long primer
monochrome
news agency
news editor
nom-de-plume
overmatter

pagination
paraphrase
periodical
plagiarism
press agent
reverse out
separation
short story
stereotype
supplement
syndication
title verso
trade paper
typesetter
typography
vignetting
wrong fount
xerography

11
advance copy
advertising
agony column
circulation
copyfitting
crown octavo
cub reporter
direct input
display type
galley proof
great primer

gutter press
half measure
letterpress
line drawing
lithography
night editor
platemaking
proofreader
running head
section-sewn
unjustified

12
block letters
book reviewer
cross heading
facing matter
feature story
illustration
keep standing
leader writer
London editor
magazine page
perfect bound
photogravure
sports editor
telegraphese
works manager

13
advertisement

composing room
editor-in-chief
foreign editor
justification
literary agent
spiral binding
stop press news
wire stitching

14
banner headline
dramatic critic
features editor
literary editor
managing editor
offset printing
perfect binding
personal column

15
calendered paper
running headline

16
colour separation
photolithography

17
desktop publishing

Theatre, Cinema and Broadcasting

2
no

3
act
arc
bit
bow
box
cue
dub
fan
gag
ham
hit
mug
pan
pit

rag
rep
run
set
tag
TV
wig

4
bill
book
boom
busk
cast
clap
clip
crew
dais

diva
duet
Emmy
epic
exit
film
flop
foil
gaff
gala
gods
grid
hero
idol
joke
lead
line
live

mask
mike
mime
mute
part
play
prop
role
rush
shot
show
skit
solo
spot
star
take
team
turn

wing

5
actor
ad lib
agent
angel
apron
aside
baton
break
clown
comic
debut
decor
drama
dry up
enact

exode
extra
farce
flies
focus
foyer
heavy
hokum
house
lines
mimer
mimic
movie
on cue
opera
Oscar
piece
props

radio
revue
scene
stage
stall
stunt
telly
usher
wings

6
acting
action
appear
backer
ballet
barker
big top

boards
buskin
camera
chorus
cinema
circle
circus
claque
comedy
critic
dancer
direct
dubbed
effect
encore
finale
flyman
kabuki
lights
make-up
masque
method
motley
movies
mummer
nautch
number
on tour
one act
parody
patron
patter
player
podium
prompt
puppet
recite
repeat
ring up
rushes
satire
screen
script
season
serial
series
singer
sitcom
sketch
speech
stalls
stooge
studio
talent

talkie
ticket
tights
timing
tinsel
troupe
TV show
viewer
walk-on
warm-up
writer

7

acrobat
actress
allstar
amateur
balcony
benefit
bit part
booking
buffoon
cabaret
callboy
cartoon
casting
catcall
catwalk
channel
charade
chorine
circuit
clapper
close-up
commere
company
compère
concert
console
costume
curtain
dancing
danseur
deadpan
dress up
drive in
dubbing
fan club
farceur
fantasy
feature
film set
gallery
heroine

ingenue
juggler
leg show
leotard
long run
matinee
mimicry
mummery
musical
mystery
new wave
on stage
overact
pageant
perform
phone-in
Pierrot
players
playing
playlet
pop star
portray
prelude
present
preview
produce
program
recital
reciter
re-enact
resting
revival
rostrum
scenery
showbiz
showman
sponsor
stadium
stagery
staging
stand-in
stardom
starlet
support
tableau
talkies
theatre
the gods
tragedy
trailer
trilogy
trouper
tumbler
upstage

variety
vehicle
viewing
western

8

applause
artistry
audience
audition
backdrop
bioscope
burletta
carnival
chat show
Cinerama
clapping
clowning
coliseum
comedian
conjurer
coryphee
costumer
coulisse
danseuse
dialogue
director
disguise
dramatic
dumb show
duologue
entr'acte
entrance
epilogue
exit line
farceuse
fauteuil
festival
figurant
film crew
film star
film unit
filmgoer
first act
funny man
ham actor
interval
juggling
libretto
live show
location
magician
male lead
morality

newsreel
offstage
operatic
operetta
overture
parterre
pastoral
peep show
pictures
pit stall
platform
playbill
playgoer
premiere
producer
prologue
prompter
protasis
quiz show
rehearse
ring down
scenario
set piece
showbill
side show
smash hit
stagebox
star turn
straight
stripper
subtitle
telecast
thespian
third act
tragical
travesty
typecast
wardrobe
wigmaker

9

animation
announcer
arabesque
backcloth
backstage
ballerina
bandstand
barnstorm
bit player
box office
broadcast
burlesque
cameraman

character
chorus boy
cinematic
clip joint
cloakroom
Columbine
conjuring
costumier
coulisses
criticism
cyclorama
discovery
double act
down stage
dramatics
dramatist
dramatize
drop scene
entertain
entrechat
exhibiter
figurante
film actor
film extra
film house
filmstrip
first lead
flashback
floorshow
folk dance
full house
gala night
guest star
Harlequin
impromptu
interlude
limelight
love scene
low comedy
major role
melodrama
minor role
monodrama
monologue
movie-goer
movie star
music hall
night club
orchestra
panel game
pantaloon
pantomime
pas de deux
performer

photoplay
Pierrette
pirouette
pit-stalls
play-actor
playhouse
portrayal
programme
prompt-box
publicity
punch-line
quartette
rehearsal
repertory
represent
second act
slapstick
soap opera
soliloquy
soubrette
spectacle
spectator
spotlight
stage door
stagehand
stage left
stage-name
stage play
take a part
tap dancer
the boards
title role
tragedian
usherette
wisecrack

10
afterpiece
appearance
auditorium
chorus girl
clapper-boy
comedienne
comedietta
comic opera
commercial
continuity
coryphaeus
crowd scene
denouement
disc jockey
drama group
dramaturge
dramaturgy

fantoccini
filmscript
first night
footlights
get the bird
high comedy
hippodrome
histrionic
horror film
horse opera
impresario
intermezzo
in the round
in the wings
junior lead
leading man
legitimate
librettist
marionette
masquerade
microphone
movie actor
music drama
newscaster
newsreader
on location
opera buffa
opera house
performing
play-acting
playwright
prima donna
production
prompt-book
properties
proscenium
Pulcinella
puppet show
rave notice
rave review
recitation
repertoire
repetiteur
ringmaster
screenplay
silent film
sound track
stagecraft
stage fever
stage right
star player
striptease
substitute
sword dance

tap dancing
tearjerker
television
theatre box
theatrical
torchdance
travelogue
understudy
variety act
vaudeville
walk-on part
wide screen

11
accompanist
all-star cast
art director
balletomane
barnstormer
black comedy
broadcaster
cap and bells
Cinemascope
circus-rider
cliff-hanger
comedy drama
comic relief
commentator
concert hall
credit title
cuffing room
dance troupe
documentary
drama critic
drama school
dramatic art
dress circle
electrician
entertainer
equilibrist
exeunt omnes
feature film
film theatre
fire curtain
folkdancing
funambulist
greasepaint
Greek chorus
histrionics
illusionist
impersonate
kitchen-sink
leading lady
legerdemain

light comedy
matinee idol
method actor
miracle play
opera bouffe
opera singer
pantomimist
Passion play
performance
picture show
problem play
protagonist
psychodrama
Punchinello
scene change
set designer
set the scene
showmanship
show-stopper
sound effect
spectacular
stage design
stage effect
stage fright
stage player
stage school
stage-struck
star billing
star quality
star-studded
talent scout
Technicolor
terpsichore
thaumaturgy
theatregoer
theatre land
theatricals
Thespian art
tragedienne
tragicomedy
trick-riding
unrehearsed
upper circle
variety show
ventriloquy
word-perfect

12
Academy Award
actor-manager
amphitheatre
ballet dancer
balletomania
choreography

cinema studio
clapperboard
concert party
credit titles
dramaturgist
dressing room
exotic dancer
extravaganza
film director
film festival
film producer
first-nighter
Grand Guignol
harlequinade
impersonator
introduction
juvenile lead
make-up artist
melodramatic
method acting
minstrel show
modern ballet
morality play
name in lights
natural break
opera glasses

orchestra pit
principal boy
Punch and Judy
puppet player
scene painter
scene shifter
scene stealer
screenwriter
scriptwriter
show business
silver screen
song and dance
sound effects
stage manager
stage whisper
starring role
steal the show
stock company
straight part
top of the bill

13
ballet dancing
burlesque show
cinematograph
contortionist

curtain-raiser
dance festival
deus ex machina
emergency exit
entertainment
musical comedy
projectionist
Russian ballet
safety curtain
sleight-of-hand
sound engineer
studio manager
thaumaturgics
theatre school
ventriloquist

14
ballet mistress
cinematography
continuity girl
dancing academy
domestic comedy
dramatic critic
prima ballerina
property master
school of acting

shooting script
slide projector
smoking concert
sound projector
stage carpenter
touring company
variety theatre

15
acrobatic troupe
cinematographer
classical ballet
comedy of manners
dramatic society
school of dancing
situation comedy
stage properties
strolling player
tableaux-vivants
talking pictures
tightrope walker

16
repertory theatre

EDUCATION

Educational Terminology

2
BA
KS
MA
PE
PT
RE

3
BEd
cap
CSE
DEE
don
EFL
ELT
fag
GCE
gyp
HND
ICT
LEA
MBA
NUS
NVQ
OND
PhD
Pop
SEN

4
coed
crib
dean
demy
DfEE
digs
exam
fees
form
gate
GCSE
GNVQ
gown
hall
head
hons
hood
poly

PSHE
quad
swot
TEFL
term
TESL
test

5
backs
bedel
board
break
chair
class
coach
Dip.Ed
Dphil
expel
grant
house
lines
mixed
motto
MPhil
pupil
scout
SENCO
study
tawse
tutor

6
A-level
beadle
bodley
bursar
course
day boy
degree
eights
fellow
Hilary
incept
locals
locker
master
matron
Ofsted

O-level
optime
reader
rector
regent
school
sconce
senate
supply
thesis
tripos
warden

7
academy
boarder
bulldog
burgess
bursary
captain
college
crammer
diploma
dominie
exclude
faculty
fresher
gestalt
grammar
head boy
honours
lecture
mid-term
monitor
nursery
post-doc
prefect
proctor
project
provost
reading
scholar
science
seminar
student
suspend
teacher
teach-in
torpids

Trinity
tuition
writing

8
academic
backward
baseline
ceremony
doctoral
emeritus
examinee
examiner
freshman
graduate
guidance
head girl
holidays
homework
key stage
learning
lecturer
literacy
manciple
mistress
numeracy
red-brick
remedial
research
roll call
semester
send down
statutes
textbook
tuck shop
tutorial
vacation
viva voce
wrangler

9
ancillary
art school
bilateral
classroom
collegian
day school
detention
doctorate

dormitory
exclusion
expulsion
great hall
pedagogue
playgroup
preceptor
prelector
president
principal
professor
refectory
registrar
scale post
scholarly
schoolboy
selection
single-sex
sophomore
speech day
staff room
streaming
sub-rector
trimester

10
access fund
assessment
attainment
blackboard
chancellor
collegiate
common room
coursework
day release
dining hall
eleven-plus
exhibition
extra-mural
fellowship
foundation
graduation
headmaster
illiteracy
imposition
instructor
laboratory
Michaelmas
philosophy

playground
sabbatical
schooldays
schoolgirl
schoolmate
schoolroom
school year
Sheldonian
suspension
university
vicegerent

11
certificate
co-education
convocation
examination
form teacher
headteacher
holiday task
housemaster
league table
matriculate
mortarboard
polytechnic
scholarship
school hours
student loan
tuition fees

12
academic year
aptitude test
congregation
dissertation
evening class
headmistress
kindergarten
literacy hour
master of arts
night classes
postgraduate
public orator
pupil-teacher
regent master
schoolfellow
schoolmaster
special needs
Sunday school

13	undergraduate	vice-chancellor
adult learning	vice-principal	
co-educational		**15** *and over*
comprehension	**14**	continuous assessment (20)
comprehensive	bachelor of arts	doctor of science (15)
doctor of music	boarding school	higher education (15)
grammar school	common entrance	further education (16)
matriculation	junior wrangler	hall of residence (15)
mature student	Open University	master of science (15)
schoolteacher	schoolmistress	school inspector (15)
supply teacher	senior wrangler	secondary modern (15)

Oxford and Cambridge Colleges

NB: *St* can also be spelled as *Saint*, which may affect letter counts.
(C.) = Cambridge; (O.) = Oxford; (w.) = women only

3
BNC (Brasenose, O.)
New (O.)

4
Hall (Trinity Hall, C.)

5
Caius (Gonville and) (C.)
Clare (C.)
Green (O.)
House (Christ Church, O.)
Jesus (C. and O.)
Keble (O.)
King's (C.)
Oriel (O.)

6
Darwin (C.)
Exeter (O.)
Girton (C.) (w.)
Merton (O.)
Queens' (C. and O.)
Selwyn (C.)
Wadham (O.)

7
Balliol (O.)
Christ's (C.)
Downing (C.)
Linacre (O.)
Lincoln (O.)

New Hall (C.) (w.)
Newnham (C.) (w.)
St Anne's (O.)
St Cross (O.)
St Hugh's (O.) (w.)
St John's (C. and O.)
Trinity (C. and O.)
Wolfson (C. and O.)

8
All Souls (O.)
Emmanuel (C.)
Hertford (O.)
Magdalen (O.)
Nuffield (O.)
Pembroke (C. and O.)
Robinson (C.)
St Hilda's (O.) (w.)
St Peter's (O.)

9
Brasenose (O.)
Churchill (C.)
Clare Hall (C.)
Magdalene (C.)
Mansfield (O.)
St Antony's (O.)
Templeton (O.)
Worcester (O.)

10
Greyfriars (O.)

Hughes Hall (C.) (w.)
Osler House (O.)
Peterhouse (C.)
Somerville (O.)
University (O.)

11
Campion Hall (O.)
Fitzwilliam (C.)
Regent's Park (O.)
Rewley House (O.)
Trinity Hall (C.)

12
Christ Church (O.)
St Benet's Hall (O.)
St Catharine's (C.)
St Catherine's (O.)
St Edmund Hall (O.)
Sidney Sussex (C.)

13 *and over*
Corpus Christi (C. and O.)
  (13)
Gonville and Caius (C.)
  (16)
Lady Margaret Hall (O.)
  (w.) (16)
Lucy Cavendish (C.) (w.)
  (13)
St Edmund's House (C.)
  (14)

FAMOUS PEOPLE

Artists, Architects, Cartoonists and Sculptors

3	Gere	Sant	Buell	Haden	Penny	Wylie
Arp	Gill	Shaw	Bundy	Haghe	Piper	Yeats
Cox	Gogh	Sime	Burra	Hanna	Plaas	Young
Dix	Good	Sims	Carra	Hatio	Platt	Zoppo
Dou	Gore	Spee	Chast	Hayes	Ponte	
Egg	Goya	Swan	Clark	Hurst	Ponti	**6**
Fox	Gray	Todd	Clint	Innes	Poole	Abbott
Gow	Gris	Toft	Cohen	Johns	Price	Addams
Key	Gros	Tuke	Cooke	Jones	Prout	Albers
Lam	Guys	Wade	Corad	Keane	Pugin	Allori
Lee	Hals	Wain	Corot	Keene	Redon	Archer
Low	Hand	Ward	Cossa	Kelly	Rodin	Arnold
May	Hart	Watt	Costa	Kirby	Rooke	Ashton
Pei	Held	Webb	Cotes	Klein	Rossi	Barker
Poy	Hemy	West	Craig	Klimt	Sands	Barton
Puy	Herp	Wood	Crane	Koren	Scott	Baskin
Ryn	Holl	Wren	Crane	Lance	Segar	Behnes
	Home		Credi	Lantz	Segna	Benson
4	Hone	**5**	Crome	Le Vau	Short	Benton
Adam	Hook	Aalto	Cross	Leech	Sitko	Berman
Arno	Hunt	Abbey	Crumb	Leger	Sleap	Bettes
Beck	Jack	Adams	Danby	Lemon	Small	Bewick
Bell	Kahn	Adler	David	Lewis	Smith	Birley
Bird	Kane	Allan	Davie	Lippi	Soane	Bodley
Bone	Kerr	Allen	Davis	Lotto	Soest	Boxall
Both	King	Amiet	Degas	Lowry	Speed	Braque
Burn	Klee	André	Devis	Lucas	Stael	Breuer
Capp	Lamb	Appel	Dirks	Manet	Stark	Briggs
Caro	Lane	Avery	Dixon	Maris	Steen	Brough
Cima	Lear	Bacon	Drury	Mason	Steer	Browne
Cole	Lely	Baily	Durer	Mauve	Steig	Brunel
Cuyp	Lion	Baker	Ensor	McCay	Stone	Buchel
Dadd	Loos	Balla	Ernst	Mingo	Stott	Burnet
Dali	Maes	Banks	Flagg	Moira	Studd	Burton
Dick	Marc	Barry	Foley	Monet	Terry	Butler
Dine	Miro	Barye	Freud	Moore	Tobey	Calder
Dodd	Mola	Bates	Frink	Munch	Tonks	Callow
Dore	Nash	Beale	Frith	Myers	Unwin	Campin
Dufy	Nast	Berry	Furse	Nebot	Uwins	Caniff
Dyce	Neer	Bezzi	Gaddi	Nervi	Velde	Carter
Dyck	Opie	Blake	Gaudi	Nicol	Vicky	Casson
Emin	Owen	Block	Gaunt	Noble	Vonet	Claude
Etty	Pyne	Boehm	Gibbs	Nolde	Watts	Clouet
Eves	Reid	Booth	Giles	North	Wells	Colton
Eyck	Reni	Bosch	Gotch	Opper	White	Conder
Faed	Rich	Bough	Gould	Orpen	Wiens	Cooper
Fehr	Rohe	Brett	Goyen	Palma	Woods	Copley
Ford	Rosa	Brock	Grant	Pater	Wyatt	Corbet
Gabo	Ross	Brown	Grosz	Payne	Wyeth	Cotman

Cowper
Cozens
Currie
Dahmen
Dawson
De Wint
DeBeck
Derain
Disney
Dobson
Draper
Duccio
Dunbar
Elwell
Ferber
Fildes
Fisher
Forbes
Foster
Fraser
Fuller
Fuseli
Geddes
Gibson
Gilman
Ginner
Giotto
Girtin
Glover
Gordon
Graham
Greuze
Guardi
Gulich
Hacker
Harral
Haydon
Heckel
Hilton
Holmes
Howard
Hudson
Hughes
Hunter
Ingres
Jagger
Joseph
Kaprow
Kettle
Keyser
Kilban
Knight
Krauze
Laroon

Larson
Laszlo
Lavery
Lawson
Le Nain
Leader
Lebrun
Ledoux
Legros
Leslie
Levine
Linton
Mabuse
Manson
Marini
Martin
Massys
McEvoy
Mesdac
Millet
Monaco
Moores
Morley
Morone
Morris
Muller
Mullin
Murray
Newton
Nisbet
Noland
O'Neill
Oliver
Olsson
Palmer
Panini
Parker
Parton
Paxton
Pegram
Penley
Perret
Peters
Pettie
Piombo
Pisano
Potter
Ramsay
Renoir
Ribera
Ridley
Rivera
Rivers
Robbia

Robert
Romano
Romney
Rothko
Rubens
Ruskin
Sadler
Sandby
Sandys
Sansom
Seddon
Serres
Seurat
Siegel
Sisley
Smirke
Smythe
Soglow
Spence
Stokes
Storck
Storey
Strang
Strube
Stuart
Stubbs
Tadema
Tanguy
Tayler
Taylor
Thaves
Thomas
Titian
Turner
Vacher
Van Ryn
Varley
Vernet
Walker
Waller
Wallis
Walton
Wardle
Warhol
Watson
Weekes
Weenix
Weyden
Wilkie
Wilson
Windus
Wright
Wyllie
Yeames

7
Alberti
Aretino
Baldung
Barbera
Barlach
Bassano
Bateman
Beechey
Behrens
Belcher
Bellini
Bennett
Berchem
Bernini
Blondel
Bomberg
Bonnard
Boucher
Boullee
Bramley
Bridell
Brouwer
Calvert
Cameron
Campion
Cellini
Cerceau
Cezanne
Chagall
Chardin
Charles
Cheston
Chirico
Christo
Cimabue
Clausen
Cockram
Collier
Collins
Connard
Corinth
Cortona
Courbet
Cranach
Crucker
Cundell
Da Vinci
Dalziel
Daniell
Darling
Daumier
De Hooch
De Lazlo

Delorme
Dicksee
Dighton
Douglas
Downman
Duchamp
Edridge
Edwards
El Greco
Emanuel
Epstein
Feiffer
Flaxman
Fouquet
Fox-Pitt
Francia
Freieng
Gabriel
Garnier
Garstin
Gauguin
Gertler
Gibbons
Gilbert
Gillray
Goodall
Goodwin
Greaves
Gregory
Gropius
Guarini
Guevara
Guthrie
Harding
Hartung
Hayward
Herbert
Herring
Hobbema
Hockney
Hofland
Hogarth
Hokusai
Holbein
Holroyd
Hoppner
Hopwood
Horsley
Housman
Indiana
Israels
Jackson
Jaggers
Johnson

Ketcham	Picasso	Anderson	Hilliard	Rirchner
Kneller	Pickard	Angelico	Hodgkins	Robinson
Knights	Pinwell	Armitage	Hokinson	Rossetti
Kooning	Pomeroy	Armstead	Holloway	Rousseau
Lambert	Poussin	Aumonier	Houghton	Rugendas
Lancret	Poynter	Beaumont	Ibbetson	Rushbury
Lanteri	Prinsep	Beckmann	Inchbold	Saarinen
Latrobe	Rackham	Beerbohm	Jacobsen	Sassetta
Lazarus	Raeburn	Boccioni	Jan Steen	Scamozzi
Lessore	Raphael	Boffrand	John Opie	Schinkel
Linnell	Raymond	Boughton	Johnston	Segonzac
Llander	Riviere	Brabazon	Jordaens	Severini
Lucidel	Roberts	Bramante	Kaufmann	Simmonds
Lutyens	Rouault	Brancusi	Kokoshka	Solimena
Macbeth	Roussel	Brangwyn	Kollwitz	Stanhope
Maccoll	Russell	Brearley	Kurtzman	Stothard
Maclise	Sargent	Breathed	Lambardo	Stringer
Maillol	Schetky	Brooking	Landseer	Sullivan
Mansart	Schiele	Brueghel	Lawrence	Terbosch
Maratti	Schultz	Bulfinch	Leighton	Tinguely
Martini	Shannon	Caldecot	Leonardo	Topolski
Matisse	Sickert	Calderon	Logsdail	Van Goyen
Mauldin	Siddall	Callcott	Macallum	Van Steen
McManus	Simpson	Calthorp	MacNelly	Vanbrugh
Memlinc	Smetham	Carracci	Macquoid	Vasarely
Merritt	Solomon	Chambers	Magritte	Verbeeck
Messick	Spencer	Chantrey	Maitland	Veronese
Meunier	Stanley	Crawhall	Mantegna	Vlaminck
Michaux	Stevens	Creswick	Mariette	Waterlow
Millais	Teniers	Daubigny	Marshall	Westover
Montana	Tenniel	De Keyser	Masaccio	Wheatley
Morandi	Thirtle	De Laszlo	Melville	Whistler
Morisot	Thomson	Del Prete	Mondrian	Willcock
Morland	Thurber	Delaunay	Montalba	Williams
Morrice	Tiepolo	Deverell	Montegna	Woodward
Murillo	Trudeau	Dietrich	Muirhead	Zakharov
Nasmith	Uccello	Dressler	Mulready	Zurbaran
Nattier	Ugolino	Dubuffet	Munnings	
Neumann	Utrillo	Eastlake	Naviasky	**9**
Orcagna	Van Dyck	Fielding	Nevinson	Ackermann
Orchard	Van Eyck	Fleisher	Niemeyer	Alexander
Osborne	Van Gogh	Fontaine	Oliphant	Appleyard
Pacchia	Vermeer	Frampton	Outcault	Aston Webb
Parrish	Watteau	Garofalo	Palladio	Bakhinzen
Parsons	Webster	Ghiberti	Paolozzi	Beardsley
Pasmore	Westall	Giovanni	Paul Nash	Biederman
Peacock	Whiting	Goldberg	Perugino	Bonington
Peruzzi	Willard	Gottlieb	Phillips	Borromini
Phidias	Woolner	Groening	Pissarro	Botticini
Phil May	Wynants	Hartwell	Pontormo	Branwhite
Philips	Zoffany	Hepworth	Redgrave	Canaletto
Phillip		Herkomer	Reynolds	Carpaccio
Philpot	**8**	Herriman	Richmond	Collinson
Picabia	Allinson	Highmore	Ricketts	Constable

Correggio
d'Erlanger
Delacroix
Donaldson
Donatello
Farington
Feininger
Fragonard
Franz Hals
Friedrich
Gastineau
Giorgione
Griffiths
Grunewald
Guido Reni
Guisewite
Halswelle
Hatherell
Hawksmoor
Henderson
Hollander
Honthorst
Hurlstone
Jawlensky
Kandinsky
Kemp-Welch
Kokoschka
La Thangue
Lancaster
Lanfranco
Lee-Hankey
Lightfoot
Louis Wain
MacGregor
MacKennal
Martineau
Maundrell
Mazzolino
McLachlan
McWhirter
Mestrovic
Mondriaan
Nicholson
Nollekens
Northcote

Pisanello
Rembrandt
Salisbury
Sansovino
Schalcken
Singleton
Stanfield
Steenwyck
Stevenson
Strudwick
Thornhill
Velázquez
Verrochio
von Erlach
Waterford
Watterson
Whitcombe

10
Alma-Tadema
Archipenko
Botticelli
Breenbergh
Brockhurst
Burne-Jones
Bushmiller
Caravaggio
Cattermole
Cruikshank
Del Pacchia
di Giovanni
Fiddes-Watt
Friedenson
Fulleylove
Giacometti
Glendening
Hershfield
Hirschfeld
Holman-Hunt
Jan van Eyck
Kennington
La Fresnaye
Lethbridge
Liebermann
Lorenzetti

Mackintosh
McCutcheon
Meissonier
Michelozzo
Modigliani
Onslow Ford
Orchardson
Peppercorn
Pollaiuolo
Richardson
Rowlandson
Saint-Aubin
Sanmicheli
Shackleton
Simon Vonet
Somerville
Spiegelman
Sutherland
Tintoretto
Van de Velde
Van der Goes
Van der Meer
Waterhouse
Winstanley

11
Apollodorus
Butterfield
Churriguera
Copley Heath
Della Robbia
Farquharson
Fra Angelico
Ghirlandaio
Hondecoeter
Le Corbusier
Lloyd Wright
Margaritone
Pickersgill
Poelenburgh
Rippingille
San Severino
Somerscales
Thornycroft
Van der Plaas

Van Ruisdael

12
Brunelleschi
Fantin-Latour
Gainsborough
Grandma Moses
Huchtenburgh
Lichtenstein
Loutherbourg
Michelangelo
Muirhead-Bone
Rauschenberg
Sassoferrato
Sidney Cooper
Spencer Pryse
Van der Weyden
Winterhalter
Witherington

13
de Hondecoeter
Heath Robinson
Hughes-Stanton
Van Ochtervelt

14
de Loutherbourg
Della Francesca
Ford Madox Brown
Gaudier-Brzeska
Haynes-Williams

15 and over
Gilbert and George
(16)
Leonardo da Vinci (15)
Puvis de Chavannes
(16)
Rembrandt van Ryn
(15)
Toulouse-Lautrec (15)
Van Huchtenburgh (15)

Business and Finance

4
Hill, Sir Rowland
Luce, Henry Robinson

5
Astor, John Jacob
Gates, Bill
Getty, Jean Paul
Soros, George

6
Baruch, Bernard Mannes
Caxton, William
George, Sir Edward
Hearst, William Randolph
Keynes, John Maynard
Morgan, John Pierpont

7
Branson, Sir Richard
Murdoch, Rupert

8
Carnegie, Andrew
Friedman, Milton
Nuffield, William Richard Morris, Viscount

Sheraton, Thomas
Wedgwood, Josiah

9
Arbuthnot, Alexander
Arkwright, Sir Richard
Courtauld, Samuel
Galbraith, John Kenneth
Greenspan, Alan
Gutenberg, Johannes

10
Guggenheim, Meyer
Rothermere, Harold Sidney
 Harmsworth, Viscount
Rothschild, Meyer Amschel
Vanderbilt, Cornelius

11 *and over*
Beaverbrook, William (11)
Maxwell Aitken, 1st Baron (13)
Chippendale, Thomas (11)
Northcliffe, Alfred Harmsworth,
 Viscount (11)
Rockefeller, John D. (11)

Composers

EARLY AND RENAISSANCE

4	6	7	Zarlino	Gesualdo	9 *and over*
Bull	Carver	Dowland		Glazunov	Dunstable (9)
Byrd	Lassus	Gibbons	8	Marenzio	Gabrielli (9)
	Morley	Joachim	Binchois	Ockeghem	Josquin des Pres
5	Tallis	Machaut	Dohnanyi	Taverner	(14)
Dufay		Perotin	Gabrieli	Victoria	Palestrina (10)

BAROQUE

4	6	7	Weelkes	Telemann	Scarlatti
Bach	Handel	Corelli			
	Rameau	Purcell	8	9	10
5	Schutz	Tartini	Albinoni	Buxtehude	Monteverdi
Lully		Vivaldi	Couperin	Pachelbel	

CLASSICAL AND ROMANTIC

3	Lehar	Hummel	Strauss	**9**	Sammartini
Cui	Liszt	Mahler		Balakirev	
	Sousa	Mozart	**8**	Beethoven	**11 and over**
4	Spohr	Pleyel	Bruckner	Cherubini	Dittersdorf (11)
Arne	Verdi	Wagner	Cimarosa	Donizetti	Mendelssohn
Lalo			Kreisler	MacDowell	(11)
Wolf	**6**	**7**	Massenet	Meyerbeer	Tchaikovsky (11)
	Brahms	Bellini	Paganini	Offenbach	Moussorgsky
5	Busoni	Berlioz	Respighi	Paisiello	(11)
Bizet	Chopin	Borodin	Schubert		Charpentier (11)
Boyce	Dvorak	Delibes	Schumann	**10**	Humperdinck
Falla	Foster	Puccini	Sibelius	Boccherini	(11)
Gluck	Franck	Rossini	von Weber	Kabalevsky	Leoncavallo (11)
Grieg	Glinka	Smetana		Ponchielli	Rimsky Korsakov
Haydn	Gounod	Stamitz		Saint Saens	(14)

TWENTIETH-CENTURY

3	Elgar	Carter	Janacek	Messiaen	**11 and over**
Bax	Fauré	Delius	Martinu	Scriabin	Birtwhistle (11)
Suk	Glass	Kodaly	Menotti	Sibelius	Dallapiccola (12)
	Henze	Piston	Milhaud	Thompson	Khachaturian
4	Holst	Walton	Nielsen		(12)
Berg	Ibert	Webern	Novello	**9**	Lennox Berkeley
Bush	Nyman		Poulenc	Bernstein	(14)
Cage	Parry	**7**	Quilter	Hindemith	Lutoslawski (11)
Ives	Ravel /	Albeniz	Tavener	Macmillan	Maxwell Davies
Nono	Reich	Arriaga	Tippett	Prokofiev	(13)
Orff	Riley	Babbitt	Warlock		Rachmaninov (11)
	Satie	Bantock	Xenakis	**10**	Racine Fricker
5	Weill	Beamish		Penderecki	(13)
Berio	Ysaye	Bennett	**8**	Rubinstein	Richard Strauss
Bliss		Britten	Gershwin	Schoenberg	(14)
Bloch	**6**	Copland	Grainger	Skalkottas	Shostakovich (12)
Brian	Barber	Debussy	Granados	Stravinsky	Stockhausen (11)
Carse	Bartok	Gorecki	Honegger	Villa-Lobos	Vaughan
Dukas	Boulez	Ireland	Mascagni		Williams (15)

Entertainment

FILM, THEATRE, TELEVISION AND RADIO

3	Cage, Nicholas	Hill, Benny	More, Kenneth
Day, Doris	Cher	Hope, Bob	Muir, Frank
Fry, Stephen	Cook, Peter	Hurt, John	Nunn, Trevor
Lee, Christopher	Dean, James	Kerr, Deborah	Peck, Gregory
Sim, Alistair	Depp, Johnny	Lean, David	Peel, John
	Ford, John	Lunt, Alfred	Pitt, Brad
4	Gish, Lillian	Marx Brothers	Rigg, Diana
Bron, Eleanor	Hall, Sir Peter	(the)	Swan, Donald

Tati, Jacques
Wise, Ernie

5
Adler, Larry
Allen, Dave
Allen, Woody
Bates, Alan
Benny, Jack
Brice, Fanny
Brook, Peter
Bruce, Lenny
Burke, Kathy
Burns, George
Caine, Michael
Clark, Lord
Close, Glenn
Cooke, Alistair
Cukor, George
Davis, Bette
Davis, Sammy
Dench, Dame Judi
Elton, Ben
Evans, Dame Edith
Finch, Peter
Flynn, Errol
Fonda, Henry
Fonda, Jane
Fosse, Bob
Frost, Sir David
Gable, Clark
Gabor, Zsa Zsa
Garbo, Greta
Gould, Elliot
Grade, Lord
Grant, Cary
Grant, Hugh
Greco, Juliette
Hanks, Tom
Hardy, Oliver
James, Clive
James, Sid
Kazan, Elia
Kelly, Grace
Korda, Alexander
La Rue, Danny
Leigh, Vivien
Magee, Patrick
Mason, James
Moore, Dudley
Niven, David
Quinn, Anthony
Reith, Lord
Smith, Dame Maggie

Stone, Oliver
Sykes, Eric
Terry, Dame Ellen
Tynan, Kenneth
Wayne, John
Welch, Raquel
Wogan, Terry

6
Bacall, Lauren
Bardot, Brigitte
Barnum, P.T.
Bogart, Humphrey
Brando, Marlon
Burton, Richard
Cagney, James
Chaney, Lon
Cleese, John
Cooper, Gary
de Niro, Robert
Disney, Walt
Divine
Fields, Gracie
Fields, W. C.
Finney, Albert
Garson, Greer
Godard, Jean-Luc
Harlow, Jean
Heston, Charlton
Howard, Trevor
Irving, Sir Henry
Jacobi, Derek
Keaton, Buster
Keitel, Harvey
Lauder, Sir Harry
Laurel, Stan
Monroe, Marilyn
Moreau, Jeanne
Morley, Robert
Mostel, Zero
Neeson, Liam
Newman, Paul
Norden, Dennis
O'Toole, Peter
Paxman, Jeremy
Quayle, Sir Anthony
Reiner, Rob
Renoir, Jean
Rogers, Ginger
Rooney, Mickey
Savile, Sir Jimmy
Sinden, Donald
Streep, Meryl
Taylor, Elizabeth

Temple, Shirley
Warner Brothers
Warner, David
Welles, Orson
Wilder, Billy
Wilder, Gene
Wolfit, Sir Donald

7
Andrews, Julie
Astaire, Fred
Bennett, Alan
Bentine, Michael
Bergman, Ingmar
Bergman, Ingrid
Blondin, Charles
Bogarde, Dirk
Branagh, Kenneth
Brynner, Yul
Campion, Jane
Chaplin, Sir Charles
Chester, Charlie
Cocteau, Jean
Collins, Joan
Connery, Sean
Coppola, Francis
Ford
Cushing, Peter
De Palma, Brian
Douglas, Kirk
Douglas, Michael
Feldman, Marty
Fellini, Federico
Garland, Judy
Garrick, David
Gielgud, Sir John
Goldwyn, Sam
Guthrie, Sir Tyrone
Hancock, Sheila
Hancock, Tony
Handley, Tommy
Harding, Gilbert
Hawkins, Jack
Hepburn, Audrey
Hepburn, Katherine
Hoffman, Dustin
Hopkins, Sir Antony
Houdini, Harry
Jackson, Glenda
Jacques, Hattie
Karloff, Boris
Kennedy, Ludovic
Kubrick, Stanley
Langtry, Lillie

McQueen, Steve
Montand, Yves
Monteux, Pierre
Nichols, Mike
Olivier, Lord
Rantzen, Esther
Redford, Robert
Roberts, Julia
Roberts, Rachel
Rushton, William
Russell, Jane
Russell, Ken
Secombe, Sir Harry
Sellers, Peter
Seymour, Lynn
Shearer, Moira
Sherrin, Ned
Siddons, Mrs Sarah
Simmons, Jean
Stewart, James
Swanson, Gloria
Ustinov, Sir Peter
Wheldon, Sir Huw
Winfrey, Oprah
Winters, Shelley

8
Ashcroft, Dame Peggy
Brambell, Wilfred
Bygraves, Max
Campbell, Mrs Pat
Christie, Julie
Connolly, Billy

Crawford, Joan
Dietrich, Marlene
Dimbleby, Richard
Eastwood, Clint
Grenfell, Joyce
Grimaldi, Joseph
Guinness, Sir Alec
Harrison, Sir Rex
Laughton, Charles
Lawrence, Gertrude
Levinson, Barry
Limbaugh, Rush
McGregor, Ewan
Milligan, Spike
Pickford, Mary
Polanski, Roman
Redgrave, Sir Michael
Redgrave, Vanessa
Robinson, Edward G.
Robinson, Eric
Scofield, Paul
Scorsese, Martin
Stephens, Robert
Truffaut, François
Williams, Kenneth

9
Antonioni, Michelangelo
Barrymore, John
Bernhardt, Sarah
Cardinale, Claudia
Chevalier, Maurice
Courtenay, Tom

Davenport, Bob
Depardieu, Gérard
Fairbanks, Douglas
Hampshire, Susan
Hitchcock, Alfred
Humphries, Barry
Lyttelton, Humphrey
Monkhouse, Bob
Morecambe, Eric
Nicholson, Jack
Pleasence, Donald
Plowright, Joan
Preminger, Otto
Spielberg, Steven
Streisand, Barbra
Tarantino, Quentin
Thorndike, Dame Sybil

10
Bertolucci, Bernardo
Eisenstein, Sergei
Littlewood, Joan
Muggeridge, Malcolm
Richardson, Sir Ralph
Rutherford, Dame
    Margaret
Sutherland, Donald
Whitehouse, Paul

12
Attenborough, Sir David
Attenborough, Sir Richard
Stanislavsky, Constantin

MODERN POPULAR MUSIC

3
Lee, Peggy

4
Baez, Joan
Bilk, Acker
Cash, Johnny
Cole, Nat King
Gaye, Marvin
Getz, Stan
John, Elton
Kern, Jerome
Lynn, Dame Vera
Monk, Thelonious
Piaf, Edith

Ross, Diana

5
Basie, Count
Berry, Chuck
Black, Cilla
Bowie, David
Clark, Petula
Davis, Miles
Dylan, Bob
Haley, Bill
Holly, Buddy
Horne, Lena
Jones, Tom
Melba, Dame Nellie

Melly, George
Smith, Bessie
Starr, Ringo
Swann, Sir Michael

6
Bassey, Shirley
Berlin, Irving
Coward, Sir Noel
Crosby, Bing
Jagger, Mick
Joplin, Janis
Joplin, Scott
Lennon, John
Miller, Glenn

Mingus, Charlie
Morton, Jelly Roll
Parker, Charlie
Parton, Dolly
Porter, Cole
Seegar, Peggy
Seegar, Pete
Waller, Fats
Waters, Muddy

7
Beatles, the
Brubeck, Dave
Clapton, Eric
Collins, Judy
Garland, Judy
Gilbert, William S.
Goodman, Benny
Guthrie, Woody
Hendrix, Jimi
Holiday, Billie

Jackson, Mahalia
Jackson, Michael
MacColl, Ewan
Madonna
Novello, Ivor
Richard, Sir Cliff
Rodgers, Richard
Sinatra, Frank
Stevens, Cat
Vaughan, Sarah
Warwick, Dionne

8
Coltrane, John
Flanders, Michael
Harrison, George
Liberace
MacGowan, Shane
Mitchell, Joni
Morrison, Van
Sondheim, Stephen

Sullivan, Arthur S.
Williams, Andy
Williams, Hank

9
Armstrong, Louis
Beach Boys, the
Belafonte, Harry
Ellington, Duke
Gillespie, Dizzy
Leadbelly
McCartney, Paul
Reinhardt, Django

10 *and over*
Fitzgerald, Ella (10)
Hammerstein, Oscar (11)
Led Zeppelin (11)
Lloyd-Webber, Andrew (11)
Sex Pistols, the (10)

OPERA, BALLET AND CLASSICAL MUSIC

4
Lind, Jennie

5
Baker, Dame Janet
Boult, Sir Adrian
Brain, Dennis
Bream, Julian
Davis, Sir Colin
du Pré, Jacqueline
Gigli, Beniamino
Ogdon, John
Pears, Sir Peter
Sills, Beverly
Solti, Sir George
Stern, Isaac
Wood, Sir Henry

6
Ashton, Sir Frederick
Callas, Maria
Caruso, Enrico
Casals, Pablo
Duncan, Isadora

Groves, Sir Charles
Irving, Sir Henry
Miller, Jonathan
Previn, Andre
Rattle, Sir Simon

7
Beecham, Sir Thomas
Domingo, Placido
Ferrier, Kathleen
Fiedler, Arthur
Fonteyn, Dame Margot
Karajan, Herbert von
Markova, Dame Alicia
Menuhin, Sir Yehudi
Nilsson, Birgit
Nureyev, Rudolf
Pavlova, Anna
Rambert, Dame Marie
Sargent, Sir Malcolm
Shankar, Ravi

8
Carerras, José

de Valois, Dame Ninette
Hoffnung, Gerard
Horowitz, Vladimir
Nijinski, Vaslav
Paganini, Niccolo
Te Kanawa, Dame Kiri
Williams, John

9
Ashkenazy, Vladimir
Barenboim, Daniel
Diaghilev, Serge
Pavarotti, Luciano
Toscanini, Arturo

10
Barbirolli, Sir John
Rubinstein, Artur
Soderstrom, Elizabeth
Sutherland, Dame Joan

11
Schwarzkopf, Elisabeth

Explorers

3
Cam, Diego
Rae, John

4
Back, Sir George
Byrd, Richard Evelyn
Cook, James
Diaz, Bartolomeu
Eyre, Edward John
Gann, Thomas
Park, Mungo
Polo, Marco
Ross, Sir James Clark
Soto, Hernando de

5
Anson, Lord George
Baker, Sir Samuel
White
Brown, William
Bruce, James
Burke, Robert O'Hara
Cabot, John
Cabot, Sebastian
Clark, William
Davis, John
Drake, Sir Francis
Eanes, Gil
Evans, Edgar
Evans, George William
Forbe, Rosita
Fuchs, Sir Vivian
Ernest
Gomes, Diogo
Hanno
Hedin, Sven Anders
Lewis, Meriwether
Nares, Sir George
Nuyts, Pieter
Oates, Lawrence
Ojeda, Alonso de
Parry (Admiral)
Peary, Robert Edwin
Scott, Robert Falcon
Smith, John
Speke, John Hanning
Welzl, Jan
Wills, William John

6
Baffin, William

Balboa, Vasco
Núñez de
Barrow, Sir John
Bering, Vitus
Burton, Sir Richard
Cabral, Pedro Alvares
Carson, Kit
Conway, Sir Martin
Cortés, Hernando
Cortez, Hernando
Da Gama, Vasco
Duluth, Daniel
Greysolon
Fraser, Simon
Hartog, Dirk
Hobson, William
Hudson, Henry
Landor, Savage
Larsen, Kohl
Mawson, Sir Douglas
Nansen, Fridtjof
Philby, H. St John
Pocock, Roger
Selous, Frederick
Courteney
Siemel, Sascha
Tasman, Abel
Thomas, Bertram

7
Almeida, Lourenço de
Cameron, Verney
Lovett
Cartier, Jacques
Charcot, Jean
Dampier, William
de Prado, Albert
Doughty, Charles
Montagu
Fawcett (Col.)
Fiennes, Sir Ranulph
Fremont, John Charles
Gilbert, Sir Humphrey
Hawkins, Sir John
Hillary, Sir Edmund
Houtman, Cornelis de
Houtman, Frederik de
Jolliet, Louis
Kearton, Cherry
Kennedy, William
La Salle, Robert
Cavelier

McClure, Sir Robert
Markham, Albert
Pizzaro, Francisco
Raleigh, Sir Walter
Shippee, Robert
Stanley, Sir Henry
Morton
Tristam, Nuno
Wilkins, Sir George
Hubert
William, Sir Hubert
Workman, Hunter

8
Amundsen, Roald
Columbus, Christopher
Coronado, Francisco
Vázquez de
de Brazza, Pierre
de Torres, Louis
Filchner, Wilhelm
Flinders, Matthew
Franklin, Sir John
Humboldt, Alexander
von
Johnston, Sir Harry
Hamilton
Kingsley, Mary
Magellan, Ferdinand
Radisson, Pierre Esprit
Standish, Miles
Sverdrup, Otto
Thesiger, Wilfred
Thompson, David
Vespucci, Amerigo

9
Africanus
Cadamosto, Alvise
Champlain, Samuel de
Emin Pasha
Frobisher, Sir Martin
Gonsalvez, Antam
Heyerdahl, Thor
Jenkinson, Anthony
Mackenzie, Sir
Alexander
Vancouver, George
Velasquez, Diego

10
Bransfield, Edward

Chancellor, Richard
Clapperton, Hugh
Erik the Red
Leichhardt, Friedrich
  Wilhelm Ludwig
Oglethorpe, James
  Edward
Richardson, Sir
  James
Shackleton, Sir Ernest
  Henry
Stefansson, Vzilhjalmur
Willoughby, Sir Hugh

11
La Vérendrye
Leif Ericson
Livingstone, Dr David

12
Bougainville, Louis-
  Antoine de
Cabeza de Vaca, Alvar
  Núñez
Leif Eriksson
Nordenskjold, Nils Adolf
  Erik

Younghusband, Sir
  Francis

14 and over
Bellingshausen, Fabian
  Gottlieb von (14)
Giovanni da Pian del
  Carpini (24)
Hanbury-Tenison, Robin
  Airling (14)
Oderic of Pordenone (17)
Prince Henry the
  Navigator (23)

Military and Naval Leaders

3
Lee
May
Nye

4
Adam
Bock
Bols
Byng
Duff
Dyer
Foch
Giap
Gort
Haig
Hart
Hood (Lord)
Hope
Jodl
Kerr
Peck
Pile
Robb
Saxe
Shea
Sims
Slim
Togo
Tojo
Wood

5
Anson (Lord)
Bacon
Baird
Blake
Blood
Botha
Boyce
Boyle
Brand
Brock
Broke
Bruce
Clark
Clive
Conde
Cowan
Craig
Dawes
Dayan
de Wet
Dewar
Dewey
Drake
Field
Gough
Grant
Hawke
Horne
Howes
  (Lord)
Ismay
Jacob
James
Jones
Junot
Keith
Keyes
  (Lord)
Kluge
Leese
Mahan
Maude
Milne
Model
Monro
Moore
Munro
Murat
Neill
Noble
Paget
Parma
Patch
Raban
Rooke
Scott
Smuts
Soult
Stark
Sulla
Tovey
Tromp
Tryon
Tully
Weeks
White
Wolfe

6
Abbott
Barrow
Beatty
  (Lord)
Bridge
Brueys
Buller
Butler
Caesar
Calder
Capper
Colomb
Creagh
Crerar
Cronje
Darlan
Daxout
Donitz
Duncan
Dundas
Eugene
Fisher
  (Lord)
Fraser
French
Giraud
Gordon
Goring
Graham
Halsey
Harris
Horton
Howard
  (Lord)
Hunter
Jerram
Jervis
Joffre
Keitel
Keppel
Kleist
Koniev
Madden
Mangin
Marius
Moltke
Murray
Napier
Nelson
  (Lord)
Newall
Nimitz
Oliver
Outram
Parker
Patton
Petain
Plumer
Powell
Pompey
Popham
Portal
Porter
Raeder
Raglan
Ramsay
Rawson
Rodney
  (Lord)
Rommel
Rundle
Rupert
  (Prince)
Ruyter
Scheel
Scheer
Scipio
Shovel
Spaatz
Squire
Tedder
Trajan
Walker
Wilson
Zhukov

7
Allenby
Blucher
Bradley
Burnaby
Burnett
Cadorna
Capello
Dampier
de Chair
Dempsey
Doenitz
Douglas
Exmouth
  (Lord)

Fairfax
Gamelin
Gaselee
Gatacre
Gonzalo
Gourand
Haldane
Hopkins
Jackson
Joubert
Kutuzov
Leclerc
Lyautey
MacMunn
Markham
Massena
Maurice
Maxwell
McMahon
Methuen
Mortier
Nivelle
O'Connor
Rainier
Raleigh
Roberts
Ronarch
Salmond
Seymour
Sherman
Simpson
Stewart
Sturdee
Tirpitz
Turenne
von Spee
Watkins
Weygand
Wingate

8

Berkeley
Birdwood
Boscawen
Brancker
Browning
Burgoyne
Caldwell
Campbell
Chetwode

Cochrane (Lord)
Cockburn
Colville
Craddock
Cromwell
Custance
De Gaulle
de Robeck
de Ruyter
Fanshawe
Farragut
Freyberg
Gallieni
Geronimo
Gleichen
Guderian
Hamilton
Hannibal
Havelock
Ironside
Jellicoe (Lord)
Lockhart
Manstein
Mark Kerr
Muselier
Napoleon
Pershing
Radetsky
Richmond
Saumarez
Saunders
Skobelev
Townsend
Tyrwhitt
Urquhart
van Tromp
Villaret
von Bulow
von Kluck
Wolseley
Yamamoto

9

Albemarle
Alexander
Arbuthnot
Beresford (Lord)
Berthelot
Boulanger
Callaghan

Cambridge
Chatfield (Lord)
Chermside
Connaught
Duckworth
Dundonald
Effingham
Essenhigh
Fremantle
Frobisher
Garibaldi
Harington
Higginson
Kitchener
Ludendorf
Lyttelton
Macarthur
Macdonald
Miltiades
Nicholson
Rawlinson
Robertson
Rundstedt
St. Vincent (Lord)
Trenchard
von Hipper
Warrender
Wellesley
Willcocks

10

Alanbrooke
Auchinleck
Beauregard
Bernadotte
Chelmsford
Clausewitz
Codrington
Cornwallis
Crazy Horse
Cunningham
Eisenhower
Evan-Thomas
Falkenhayn
Hindenburg
Kempenfelt
Kesselring
Kuropatkin
Longstreet
Montgomery

Mountevans (Lord)
Somerville
Timoshenko
Troubridge
Villeneuve
von Tirpitz
Voroshilov
Wellington

11

Abercrombie
Baden-Powell
Brackenbury
Collingwood
de Castelnau
Elphinstone
Marlborough
Mountbatten
(Lord)
Ochterlonie
Strathnairn
Wallenstein

12

Culme Seymour
Hunter-Weston
Schwartzkopf
Smith-Dorrien
von Mackensen
von Rundstedt
Wester-Wemyss
(Lord)
Younghusband

13 *and over*

Cork and Orrery
(Lord) (13)
Forestier-Walker
(15)
Garnet-Wolseley
(14)
Napier of Magdala
(15)
Rozhdestvensky
(14)
Frederick the
Great (17)

Philosophers and Religionists

3
Fox, George
Hus, Jan
Lee, Ann

4
Ayer, A.J.
Eddy, Mary Baker
Hume, David
Kant, Immanuel
Knox, John
Marx, Karl
Mill, John Stuart
More, Thomas
Weil, Simone

5
Bacon, Francis
Bacon, Roger
Barth, Karl
Booth, William
Burke, Edmund
Dewey, John
Hegel, Georg Willhelm
  Friedrich
Keble, John
Plato

6
Boehme, Jakob
Berlin, Sir Isaiah
Calvin, John
Engels, Friedrich
Graham, Billy
Hobbes, Thomas
Luther, Martin
Popper, Sir Karl
Sartre, Jean-Paul
Tagore, Rabindranath
Wesley, John
Wyclif, John

7
Abelard, Peter
Aquinas, St Thomas
Bentham, Jeremy
Buchman, Frank
Diderot, Denis
Erasmus, Desiderius
Leibniz, Gottfried
  Wilhelm
Russell, Bertrand
Spinoza, Benedict
Steiner, Rudolf
Tyndale, William

8
Avicenna
Berkeley, George
Foucault, Michel
Rousseau, Jean Jacques
Socrates

9
Aristotle
Blavatsky, Madame
  Helena
Confucius
Descartes, René
Heidegger, Martin
Nietzsche, Friedrich

10
Macpherson, Aimee Semple
Swedenborg, Emanuel

11
Wilberforce, Samuel

12
Krishnamurti, Jiddu
Schopenhauer Arthur
Wittgenstein, Ludwig

Politicians and Revolutionaries

3	Root	Marat	Castro	Marcos	Giscard
Kun	Tito	Nehru	Cavour	Mobuto	Goldman
Mao		Paine	Chiang	Mosley	Gomulka
Pym	**5**	Peron	Chirac	Mugabe	Himmler
Zia	Banda	Putin	Cicero	Nasser	Kennedy
	Benes	Sadat	Cobden	Pearse	Kosygin
4	Bevan	Sands	Corday	Petain	Kreisky
Amin	Bevin	Simon	Cripps	Powell	Lumumba
Biko	Blair	Smith	Cromer	Rhodes	Mandela
Blum	Burke	Smuts	Curzon	Somoza	Masaryk
Burr	Ciano	Solon	Danton	Stalin	Menzies
Bush	Desai	Tyler	Dubcek	Zapata	Mintoff
Chou	Hague	Villa	Dulles		Molotov
Clay	Hiero		Engels	**7**	Nkrumah
Foot	Hoxha	**6**	Franco	Allende	Nyerere
Gore	Husak	Aquino	Gadafy	Bakunin	Parnell
Grey	Jagan	Arafat	Gandhi	Batista	Pearson
Hess	Kadar	Bhutto	Hitler	Bolivar	Ptolemy
Marx	Laval	Brandt	Horthy	Bormann	Redmond
Meir	Lenin	Bright	Kaunda	Clinton	Reynaud

Salazar	Dollfuss	Chou En-Lai	Talleyrand
Sandino	Duvalier	Churchill	
Sukarno	Goebbels	Garibaldi	**11**
Trotsky	Hamilton	Gorbachev	Castlereagh
Trudeau	Kenyatta	Ho Chi Minh	Chamberlain
Vorster	Lycurgus	Kropotkin	Robespierre
Wallace	Makarios	Luxemburg	Shaftesbury
Webster	Morrison	Milosevic	
Yeltsin	Napoleon	Mussolini	**12**
	Pinochet	Spartacus	Bandaranaike
8	Podgorny		Hammarskjold
Abu Nidal	Poincare	**10**	Kemal Ataturk
Adenauer	Pompidou	Che Guevara	
Ayub Khan	Proudhon	Clemenceau	**13 and over**
Bismarck	Verwoerd	Hindenburg	Aung San Suu Kyi
Brezhnev	Williams	Khrushchev	(13)
Bukharin		Lee Kuan-Yew	Chiang Kai-Shek
Bulganin	**9**	Mao Tse Tung	(13)
Daladier	Ben Gurion	Metternich	Giscard d'Estaing
De Gaulle	Bonaparte	Ribbentrop	(15)
De Valera	Bruntland	Stroessner	Haile Selassie (13)

Presidents of the United States

4
Bush, George
Bush, George W.
Ford, Gerald
Polk, James K.
Taft, William

5
Adams, John
Adams, John Quincy
Grant, Ulysses S.
Hayes, Rutherford B.
Nixon, Richard M.
Tyler, John

6
Arthur, Chester A.
Carter, Jimmy
Hoover, Herbert

Munroe, James
Pierce, Franklin
Reagan, Ronald
Taylor, Zachary
Truman, Harry
Wilson, Woodrow

7
Clinton, Bill
Harding, Warren G.
Jackson, Andrew
Johnson, Andrew
Johnson, Lyndon B.
Kennedy, John F.
Lincoln, Abraham
Madison, James

8
Buchanan, James

Coolidge, Calvin
Fillmore, Millard
Garfield, James A.
Harrison, Benjamin
Harrison, William
McKinley, William
Van Buren, Martin

9
Cleveland, Grover
Jefferson, Thomas
Roosevelt, Franklin D.
Roosevelt, Theodore

10
Eisenhower, Dwight
Washington, George

Prime Ministers of Great Britain

4
Bute, Lord
Eden, Sir Anthony
Grey, Lord
Peel, Sir Robert
Pitt, William (Pitt the Younger)

5
Blair, Tony
Derby, Lord
Heath, Edward
Major, John
North, Lord

6
Attlee, Clement
Pelham, Henry
Wilson, Sir Harold

7
Asquith, Herbert
Baldwin, Stanley
Balfour, Arthur

Canning, George
Chatham, Lord (Pitt the Elder)
Grafton, Duke of
Russell, Lord John
Walpole, Sir Robert

8
Aberdeen, Lord
Bonar Law, Andrew
Disraeli, Benjamin
Goderich, Lord
Perceval, Spencer
Portland, Duke of
Rosebery, Lord
Thatcher, Margaret

9
Addington, Henry
Callaghan, James
Churchill, Sir Winston
Gladstone, William
Grenville, George
Grenville, Lord

Liverpool, Lord
MacDonald, Ramsay
Macmillan, Harold
Melbourne, Lord
Newcastle, Duke of
Salisbury, Marquis of
Shelburne, Lord

10
Devonshire, Duke of
Palmerston, Lord
Rockingham, Marquis of
Wellington, Duke of
Wilmington, Lord

11 and over
Beaconsfield, Lord (12)
Campbell-Bannerman, Sir Henry (17)
Chamberlain, Neville (11)
Douglas-Home, Sir Alec (11)
Lloyd George, David (11)

Roman Emperors

4
Geta
Nero
Otho

5
Carus
Galba
Nerva
Titus

6
Decius
Gallus
Probus
Trajan

7
Carinus

Hadrian
Tacitus

8
Balbinus
Caligula (Gaius Caesar)
Claudius
Commodus
Domitian
Floranus
Galerius
Jovianus
Julianus
Macrinus
Pertinax
Pupienus
Tiberius

9
Ballienus
Caracalla
Gordianus
Lincinius
Maxentius
Maximinus
Philippus
Vespasian
Vitellius

10
Aemilianus
Aurelianus
Diocletian
Elagabalus (Heliogabalus)
Maximianus
Numerianus

Quintillus
Valerianus
Volusianus

11 and over
Alexander Severus (16)
Antoninus Pius (13)
Constantine (11)
Constantius (11)
Glaudius Gothicus (16)
Lucius Verus (11)
Marcus Aurelius (14)
Septimius Severus (16)

Scientists, Mathematicians and Engineers

3
Ohm
Ray

4
Bell
Bohr
Born
Bose
Davy
Ford
Gold
Hahn
Hall
Hess
Howe
Jung
Koch
Mond
Pare
Reed
Salk
Swan
Watt
Wren

5
Bacon
Banks
Barry
Bondi
Boole
Boyle
Bragg
Brahe
Crick
Curie
Debye
Euler
Ewing
Fermi
Freud
Galen
Galle
Gamov
Gauss

Gibbs
Haber
Henry
Hertz
Hooke
Hoyle
Jacob
Jeans
Joule
Klein
Krebs
Lodge
Maxim
Monod
Morse
Pauli
Pliny
Raman
Segrè
Smith
Tesla
Volta
White

6
Ampère
Brunel
Bunsen
Calvin
Cantor
Dalton
Darwin
Diesel
Edison
Euclid
Froude
Fulton
Galois
Halley
Harden
Harvey
Hubble
Hughes
Hutton
Huxley
Jenner

Kekule
Kelvin
Kepler
Kuiper
Liebig
Lister
Mendel
Morgan
Napier
Nernst
Newton
Pascal
Pavlov
Perutz
Planck
Ramsay
Stokes
Thales
Turing
Watson

7
Andrews
Babbage
Banting
Cassini
Charles
Compton
Crookes
Da Vinci
Daimler
Doppler
Ehrlich
Faraday
Fleming
Galileo
Galvani
Haldane
Hawking
Hilbert
Huggins
Huygens
Kapitsa
Kendrew
Lamarck
Leblanc

Leibniz
Lesseps
Lockyer
Lorentz
Marconi
Maxwell
Medawar
Moseley
Pasteur
Pauling
Piccard
Ptolemy
Rontgen
Rumford
Seaborg
Siemens
Spinoza
Thomson
Tyndall
Virchow
Wallace
Whitney

8
Agricola
Avogadro
Bessemer
Blackett
Chadwick
de Fermat
De Forest
Einstein
Foucault
Franklin
Goodyear
Harrison
Herschel
Humboldt
Lawrence
Linnaeus
Malpighi
Mercator
Millikan
Poincare
Rayleigh
Thompson

Van Allen
Van't Hoff
Zeppelin

9
Aristotle
Armstrong
Arrhenius
Becquerel
Bernoulli
Cavendish
De Broglie
de Coulomb
Descartes
Eddington
Fibonacci
Heaviside
Kirchhoff
Lankester
Michelson

10
Archimedes
Cannizzaro
Copernicus
Fahrenheit
Flammarion
Heisenberg
Hipparchus
Mendeleyev
Paracelsus
Pythagoras
Rutherford
Stephenson
Torricelli
Trevithick

11
Grosseteste
Le Chatelier
Leeuwenhoek
Oppenheimer
Schrodinger
Van der
    Waals

Sports Personalities

ATHLETICS

3
Coe, Sebastian

4
Cram, Steve

5
Flo-Jo
Keino, Kip

Lewis, Carl
Lewis, Denise
Ovett, Steve
Owens, Jesse
Pirie, Gordon

6
Foster, Brendan
Peters, Mary

7
Elliott, Herb
Hopkins, Thelma
Johnson, Ben

8
Christie, Linford
Redgrave, Sir Steve

9 and over
Bannister, Sir
  Roger (9)
Grey-Thompson,
  Tanni (12)
Griffith-Joyner,
  Florence (14)
Whitbread, Fatima
  (9)

BOXING

3
Ali, Muhammad

4
Clay, Cassius
King, Don

5
Bruno, Frank

Hamad, Naseem
  ("Prince")
Lewis, Lennox
Louis, Joe
Tyson, Mike

6
Bugner, Joe
Cooper, Henry

Eubank, Chris
Liston, Sonny

7
Dempsey, Jack
Foreman, George
Frazier, Joe

8
Marciano, Rocky
Robinson, Sugar Ray

11
Fitzsimmons, Bob

CHESS

6
Karpov, Anatoly

7
Fischer, Bobby
Spassky, Boris

8
Alekhine, Alexander
Kasparov, Gary

10
Capablanca, José

CRICKET

4
Amis, Dennis
Bird, Dickie
Khan, Imran
Lock, Tony
Snow, John

5
Close, Brian
Evans, Godfrey
Grace, Dr W.G.
Greig, Tony
Hobbs, Sir John
Knott, Alan

Laker, Jim
Lloyd, Clive

6
Bedser, Alec
Benaud, Richard
Botham, Ian
Dexter, Ted
Edrich, John
Hadlee, Sir
  Richard
Hutton, Sir Len
Kanhai, Rohan
Lillee, Dennis

Sobers, Sir Gary
Titmus, Fred
Willis, Bob

7
Boycott, Geoffrey
Bradman, Sir Don
Compton, Denis
Cowdrey, Colin
Thomson, Jeff
Trueman, Freddie
Worrell, Sir Frank

8
Chappell, Greg
Chappell, Ian
Graveney, Tom

9 and over
Constantine, Sir
  Leary (11)
D'Oliveira, Basil (9)
Fredericks, Roy (10)
Illingworth, Ray
  (11)
Underwood, Derek
  (9)

FOOTBALL

3
Law, Denis

4
Best, George
Owen, Michael
Pele

5
Banks, Gordon
Busby, Sir Matt

Moore, Bobby
Revie, Don
Stein, Jock

6
Clough, Brian
Keegan, Kevin
Ramsey, Sir Alf

7
Beckham, David

Cantona, Eric
Greaves, Jimmy
Lineker, Gary
Ronaldo

8
Charlton, Bobby
Charlton, Jack
Dalglish, Kenny
Docherty, Tommy
Ferguson, Sir Alex

Maradona, Diego
Matthews, Sir
  Stanley

9 *and over*
Beckenbauer,
  Franz (11)
Blancheflower,
  Danny (13)
Gascoigne, Paul
  (9)

GOLF

5
Hogan, Ben
Irwin, Hale
Woods, Tiger

6
Palmer, Arnold
Player, Gary

7
Jacklin, Tony

Trevino, Lee

8
Nicklaus, Jack
Weiskopf, Tom

10 *and over*
Ballesteros,
  Severiano (11)
Oosterhuis, Peter
  (10)

MOTOR RACING

4
Hill, Graham
Hunt, James
Moss,
  Stirling

5
Clark, Jim
Lauda, Niki
Senna,
  Ayrton

6
Fangio, Juan
Piquet,
  Nelson

7
Brabham,
  Jack
Ferrari, Enzo
Stewart,
  Jackie

10
Fittipaldi, Emerson
Schumacher,
  Michael
Villeneuve, Jacques

SWIMMING

4
Webb, Captain
  Matthew

5
Spitz, Mark

6
Fraser, Dawn
Wilkie, David

7
Goodhew, Duncan

10 *and over*
Lonsbrough, Anita (10)
Weissmuller, Johnny (11)

TENNIS

4
Ashe, Arthur
Borg, Bjorn
Cash, Pat
Graf, Steffi
King, Billie Jean
Wade, Virginia

5
Court, Margaret
Evert, Chris
Jones, Ann
Laver, Rod

Lendl, Ivan
Lloyd, Chris
Perry, Fred
Seles, Monica
Wills, Helen

6
Barker, Sue
Becker, Boris
Casals, Rosemary
Cawley, Yvonne
Edberg, Stefan
Henman, Tim

Taylor, Roger

7
Connors, Jimmy
Emerson, Roy
McEnroe, John
Mottram, Buster
Nastase, Ilie
Novotna, Jana
Sampras, Pete

8
Connolly, Maureen

Little Mo
Newcombe, John
Rosewall, Ken
Williams, Venus
Williams, Serena

9
Goolagong,
  Evonne

11
Navratilova,
  Martina

OTHER SPORTS

3
Fox, Uffa (yachting)
Kim, Nellie (gymnastics)

4
Cobb, Ty (baseball)
John, Barry (rugby)
Read, Phil (motorcycling)
Ruth, "Babe" (baseball)

5
Curry, John (skating)
Davis, Joe (billiards)
Davis, Steve (snooker)
Moore, Ann
  (showjumping)
Scott, Sheila (aviation)
Smith, Harvey
  (showjumping)

6
Broome, David
  (showjumping)
Carson, Willie
  (horseracing)
Hendry, Steven (snooker)

Korbut, Olga (gymnastics)
Smythe, Pat (showjumping)
Wilson, Jocky (darts)

7
Bristow, Eric (darts)
Carling, Will (rugby)
Higgins, Alex "Hurricane"
  (snooker)
Hillary, Sir Edmund
  (mountaineering)
Johnson, Amy (aviation)
Piggott, Lester
  (horseracing)
Tabarly, Eric (yachting)
Tensing, Sherpa
  (mountaineering)

8
Comaneci, Nadia
  (gymnastics)
Cordobés, El (bullfighting)
Cousteau, Jacques-Yves
  (diving)
Latynina, Larissa
  (gymnastics)

Richards, Sir Gordon
  (horseracing)

9
Bonington, Sir Chris
  (mountaineering)
Lindbergh, Charles
  (aviation)
Pattisson, Rodney
  (yachting)

10 and over
Barrington, Jonah
  (squash) (10)
Chichester, Sir Francis
  (yachting) (10)
"Eddie the Eagle"
  (skiing) (13)
Schockemohle, Alwin
  (showjumping) (12)
Torvill and Dean
  (skating) (14)
Turischeva, Ludmila
  (gymnastics) (10)

Writers, Poets and Dramatists

NB: Authors are listed under the century in which they were born.

ANCIENT

4	Pliny	Sappho	**8**	Herodotus	**11 and over**
Du Fu		Seneca	Catullus	Lucretius	Aristophanes
Livy	**6**	Virgil	Kalidasa	Sophocles	(12)
Ovid	Cicero		Menander	Suetonius	Lucius Apuleius
	Hesiod	**7**			(14)
5	Horace	Juvenal	**9**	**10**	Omar Khayyam
Aesop	Lao-Tse	Tacitus	Aeschulus	Propertius	(11)
Homer	Lucian	Terence	Aristotle	Quintilian	Valerius Flaccus
Plato	Pindar		Euripides	Thucydides	(15)

MEDIEVAL

4	Sachs	**7**	**8**	**9**	Christine de
Bede		Abelard	Langland	Boccaccio	Pisan (16)
	6	Aquinas	Petrarch	Froissart	Duns Scotus (10)
5	Malory	Ariosto	Rabelais		Machiavelli (11)
Dante	Villon	Chaucer		**10 and over**	
Gower		Erasmus		Chrétien de	
				Troyes (16)	

1500–1600

3	Donne	Sidney	**8**	Montaigne
Gay	Pepys		Calderón	Wu Chengen
Kyd	Swift	**7**	Congreve	
	Tasso	Addison	Farquhar	**10 *and over***
4		Cellini	Perrault	Bradstreet (10)
Behn	**6**	Marlowe	Voltaire	Cyrano de Bergerac (16)
Pope	Bunyan	Marvell		Juana Inés De la Cruz
	Dryden	Molière	**9**	(17)
5	Jonson	Spenser	Cervantes	La Fontaine (10)
Basho	Milton	Webster	Corneille	Richardson (10)
Defoe	Racine		La Fayette	Shakespeare (11)

1700

3	Keats	Irving	Shelley	**9**
Key	Moore	Laclos	Southey	Coleridge
	Paine	Rowson	Walpole	Goldsmith
4	Scott	Sterne		Lomonosov
Gray	Staël		**8**	Radcliffe
Lamb		**7**	De Quincy	
Sade	**6**	Addison	Fielding	**10 *and over***
Wyss	Austen	Boswell	Hoffmann	Beaumarchais
	Balzac	Carlyle	Rousseau	(12)
5	Bryant	Freneau	Schiller	Brothers Grimm
Blake	Burney	Hazlitt	Sheridan	(the) (13)
Burns	Cooper	Johnson	Smollett	Chateaubriand
Byron	Cowper	Lessing	Stendhal	(13)
Clare	Goethe	Manzoni	Wheatley	
Heine	Hammon	Pushkin		

1800

2	Howe	Aiken	Gogol	Milne	Wells
Fo	Hugo	Akins	Gorky	Moore	White
	Kant	Alger	Green	O'Dell	Wilde
3	Lear	Babel	Hardy	Perse	Woolf
Poe	Loos	Benet	Harte	Poole	Yeats
	Mann	Brown	Hasek	Pound	Zweig
4	Owen	Bunin	Henry	Rilke	
Baum	Rhys	Busch	Hesse	Sachs	**6**
Bely	Rice	Capek	Heyse	Scott	Alcott
Blok	Saki	Chase	Ibsen	Shute	Alvaro
Buck	Sand	Crane	James	Smith	Andric
Cain	Shaw	Dario	Joyce	Stein	Arnold
Ford	West	Davis	Kafka	Stout	Balzac
Gale	Zola	Doyle	Kelly	Stowe	Barnes
Gide		Dumas	Lewis	Svevo	Barrie
Gray	**5**	Eliot	Marsh	Synge	Belloc
Grey	Adams	Field	Marti	Twain	Bierce
Hall	Agnon	Frost	McKay	Verne	Blyton

Famous People

Bolton	Proust	Kaufman	Kingsley	Mansfield
Borges	Runyon	Kipling	Lagerlof	Marinetti
Brecht	Ruskin	Lardner	Lawrence	Masefield
Breton	Sayers	Lazarus	Macaulay	Nietzsche
Brontë	Sewell	Lofting	Macleish	Pasternak
Brooke	Stoker	Masters	Mallarme	Priestley
Bryant	Tagore	Maugham	Marquand	Schreiner
Buchan	Toklas	Mauriac	Melville	Shimazaki
Butler	Toomer	Mistral	Meredith	Sillanpää
Cather	Traven	Montale	Nelligan	Spitteler
Chopin	Undset	Nabokov	Peterkin	Stapledon
Coffin	Valery	Quiroga	Plaatjie	Stevenson
Conrad	Wiggin	Ransome	Rawlings	Swinburne
Coward	Wilder	Reymont	Remarque	Thackeray
Cronin	Wilson	Richter	Rinehart	Wodehouse
Dubois		Rimbaud	Robinson	
Dunbar	**7**	Rolland	Rossetti	**10**
Fauset	Bagnold	Russell	Sandburg	Baudelaire
Ferber	Bennett	Sassoon	Sherwood	Chesterton
Flavin	Burnett	Sitwell	Sinclair	Fitzgerald
France	Carroll	Stevens	Tanizaki	Galsworthy
Fuller	Chekhov	Thoreau	Teasdale	Lagerkvist
Gibran	Cocteau	Thurber	Tennyson	Longfellow
Gilman	Colette	Tolkien	Trollope	MacDiarmid
Graves	Collins	Tolstoy	Turgenev	Mandelstam
Hamsun	Collodi	Travers	Van Doren	Maupassant
Harper	Delaney	Wallace	Verlaine	Mayakovsky
Harris	Deledda	Wharton	Wheatley	McGonagall
Holmes	Dickens	Whitman	Whittier	Montgomery
Howard	Dinesen	Woolsey	Williams	Pirandello
Hughes	Dreiser		Zamyatin	Strindberg
Huxley	Dunsany	**8**		Tarkington
Jerome	Emerson	Andersen	**9**	Washington
Jewett	Falkner	Anderson	Akhmatova	
Junger	Farjeon	Asturias	Benavente	**11 and over**
Kilmer	Forster	Bjornson	Blackmore	Apollinaire (11)
Larsen	Gallico	Browning	Bromfield	Dostoyevsky (11)
Le Fanu	Gaskell	Brunhoff	Burroughs	García Lorca
London	Grahame	Bulgakov	D'Annunzio	(11)
Lowell	Gregory	Carducci	De la Roche	Kazantzakis (11)
Machen	Haggard	Chandler	Dickinson	Machado de
Miller	Hammett	Chesnutt	Doolittle	Assis (14)
Mofolo	Hartley	Christie	Dos Passos	Maeterlinck (11)
Morris	Hillyer	Connelly	Echegaray	Martin du Gard
Mqhayi	Hodgson	Cummings	Gjellerup	(12)
Nesbit	Hopkins	De la Mare	Goncharov	Sackville-West
Norris	Housman	Douglass	Hauptmann	(13)
O'Casey	Howells	Faulkner	Hawthorne	Sienkiewicz (11)
O'Neill	Jackson	Flaubert	Hemingway	Sully-
Parker	Jeffers	Fletcher	Karlfeldt	Prudmomme
Pessoa	Jiménez	Forester	Lampedusa	(14)
Porter	Johnson	Glaspell	Lermontov	Wittgenstein
Potter	Kästner	Kawabata	Lovecraft	(12)

MODERN

2	**5**	Nixon	Brutus	Merwin	Andrews
Ba	Adams	Nwapa	Butler	Miller	Angelou
Oe	Aidoo	O'Hara	Capote	Milosz	Anouilh
Oz	Aiken	Oates	Carter	Mosley	Ashbery
	Albee	Odets	Carver	Naylor	Awoonor
3	Allen	Olsen	Clancy	Neruda	Baldwin
Abe	Auden	Oppen	Clarke	Norman	Ballard
Eco	Banks	Orton	Cooper	O'Brian	Bambara
Fry	Barth	Oyono	Cullen	O'Brien	Beckett
Lee	Bates	Paley	Delany	Okigbo	Bennett
Lem	Behan	Paton	Dhlomo	Oliver	Brodsky
Nin	Blish	Percy	Didion	Onetti	Buckler
Paz	Block	Petry	Duncan	Orwell	Buckley
Roy	Blume	Plath	Ellroy	Parker	Bullins
Tan	Brink	Potok	Elytis	Piercy	Burgess
	Burke	Queen	Erdich	Pilger	Calvino
4	Byatt	Ribas	Farmer	Pinter	Canetti
Agee	Camus	Rulfo	Faulks	Powell	Cheever
Amis	Carey	Sagan	Fowles	Proust	Clavell
Beti	Carle	Scott	Fugard	Robert	Clifton
Boll	Chase	Seuss	Fuller	Rylant	Coetzee
Cela	Clark	Silko	Gaines	Sarton	Cookson
Dahl	Cohen	Simak	George	Sartre	Cormier
Dick	Cunne	Simic	Gibson	Scarry	Cozzens
Diop	Desai	Simon	Harris	Sendak	DeLillo
Dove	Doyle	Smith	Hayden	Sexton	Drabble
Fine	Drury	Spark	Heaney	Shange	Durrell
Grau	Dugan	Stead	Heller	Singer	Dworkin
Gunn	Duras	Tlali	Henley	Smiley	Ekwensi
Head	Evans	Tyler	Hersey	Snyder	Ellison
Inge	Farah	Ulasi	Hinton	Sofala	Farrell
Jong	Foote	Vidal	Howard	Sontag	Fleming
Kerr	Frank	Waugh	Hughes	Styron	Forsyth
King	Genet	Weiss	Irving	Susann	Francis
Laye	Gluck	Welty	Jordan	Taylor	Friedan
Levi	Grass	White	Junitz	Thomas	Fuentes
Nash	Green	Wolfe	Kantor	Updike	Gallant
Neto	Haley		Kelman	Walker	Gardner
Ogot	Havel	**6**	Kogawa	Warren	Golding
Okri	Heath	Achebe	Koontz	Weldon	Gordone
Page	Himes	Aldiss	L'Amour	Wilbur	Grafton
Puzo	Hulme	Algren	Larkin	Wilson	Grisham
Rand	James	Ambler	Le Fanu	Wright	Guthrie
Reed	Jones	Asimov	Le Guin	Zindel	Hayashi
Rice	Kesey	Atwood	Leiber		Hazzard
Rich	Kizer	Baraka	Levine	**7**	Hellman
Roth	Kumin	Barker	Lively	Ackroyd	Herbert
Seth	Lorde	Barnes	Lowell	Aickman	Herriot
Uris	Lowry	Bellow	Ludlum	Aksenov	Hurston
West	Lurie	Birney	Mailer	Alegria	Ionesco
Wolf	Mamet	Bishop	McBain	Allende	Jackson
Wouk	Munro	Brooks	McEwan	Amichai	Jarrell

Johnson
Justice
Kennedy
Kerouac
Kincaid
Kinnell
Kundera
Kushner
La Farge
Laxness
Le Carre
Leonard
Lessing
Maclean
Mahfous
Malamud
Malraux
Merrill
Mishima
Mitford
Momaday
Moravia
Murdoch
Naipaul
Narayan
Nemerov
Ngugi wa
Nichols
O'Connor
Osborne
P'Bitek
Pynchon
Renault
Rendell
Richler
Rodgers
Roethke
Rossner
Rowling
Rushdie
Saadawi
Sanchez
Saroyan

Seferis
Seghers
Seifert
Sembene
Senghor
Serling
Shapiro
Sheldon
Shepard
Shields
Sholomo
Simenon
Simpson
Soyinka
Spender
Stegner
Theroux
Thiong'o
Tutuola
Van Duyn
Van Vogt
Walcott
Wyndham
Zelazny

8

Abrahams
Anderson
Atkinson
Berryman
Betjeman
Bontemps
Bowering
Bradbury
Brookner
Caldwell
Cardenal
Clampitt
Cornwell
Cortázar
Crichton
Day-Lewis
Deighton

Ding Ling
Doctorow
Eberhart
Emecheta
Esquivel
Freeling
Gellhorn
Ginsberg
Giovanni
Gordimer
Hardwick
Harrison
Heinlein
Hijuelos
Ishiguro
Jhabvala
Keneally
Kingston
Kinsella
Kosinski
Laurence
Levertov
Lindgren
MacNeice
Marshall
Matheson
McCarthy
McGinley
McMillan
McMurtry
Meredith
Michener
Mitchell
Moorcock
Morrison
O'Faolain
Ondaatje
Paretsky
Perelman
Rattigan
Ringgold
Rukeyser
Salinger

Saro-Wiwa
Schwartz
Sillitoe
Southern
Spillane
Stafford
Stoppard
Sturgeon
Sutcliff
Thompson
Tsushima
Unsworth
Vonnegut
Wambaugh
Williams

9

Allingham
Ayckbourn
Barthelme
Benedetti
Burroughs
Chayefsky
Childress
Cristofer
Du Maurier
Hansberry
Highsmith
Hillerman
Isherwood
Lispector
Llewellyn
MacDonald
Macdonald
McCaffrey
McCullers
McPherson
Mphahlele
Pratchett
Prelutsky
Quasimodo
Reid Banks
Roa Bastos

Sholokhov
Snodgrass
Steinbeck
Vittorini

10

Bainbridge
Carpentier
de Beauvoir
Durrenmatt
MacLachlan
Silverberg
Sutherland

11

Auchincloss
Breytenbach
Matthiessen
Rabearivelo
Vargas Llosa
Voznesensky
Wasserstein
Yevtushenko

12 and over

Ashton-Warner
  (12)
Cabrera Infante
  (14)
Clarke-
  Bekederemo
  (16)
Ferlinghetti (12)
García Márquez
  (13)
Ratushinskaya
  (13)
Saint-Exupery
  (12)
Solzhenitsyn (12)

Other Prominent People

3

Cid, El (Spanish hero)
Fry, Elizabeth (social
  reformer)
Ray, Man (photographer)

4

Hill, Octavia (social
  reformer)
Jung, Carl Gustav
  (psychoanalyst)

Kidd, Captain Williaim
  (pirate)
Penn, William (founder
  of Pennsylvania)

5

Acton, John Dalberg, Lord (historian)
Adams, Henry (historian)
Adler, Alfred (psychologist)
Amati, Nicolo (violin maker)
Astor, Nancy, Viscountess (first woman elected to British House of Commons)
Baird, John Logie (TV pioneer)
Banks, Sir Joseph (naturalist)
Brown, Sir Arthur Whitten (pioneer aviator)
Freud, Sigmund (pioneer psychoanalyst)
"Grock" (Adrien Wettach) (clown)
Herzl, Theodor (founder of Zionism)
Clive, Robert (Indian Empire pioneer)
Smith, Delia (cookery writer)
Zeiss, Carl (optical instrument maker)

6

Alcock, Sir John William (pioneer aviator)
Attila (the Hun)
Bailey, David (photographer)
Beeton, Isabella (cookery writer)
Butler, Mrs Josephine (social reformer)
Capone, Al (gangster)
Cavell, Edith (nurse and English patriot)
Dunant, Henri (founder of International Red Cross)
Fawkes, Guy (conspirator)

Fokker, Anton (aviation pioneer)
Mesmer, Friedrich Franz (hypnotist)
Petrie, William Flinders (archaeologist)
Pitman, Sir Isaac (inventor of shorthand)
Stopes, Dr Marie (family planning pioneer)
Turpin, Dick (highwayman)
Wright, Orville (pioneer aviator)
Wright, Wilbur (pioneer aviator)

7

Aga Khan (Ismaili leader)
Ataturk, Kemal (Turkish soldier and statesmen)
Blériot, Louis (aviator)
Blondin, Charles (acrobat)
Boyd-Orr, John, Baron (nutritionist)
Cameron, Julia Margaret (photographer)
Celsius, Anders (inventor of Centigrade thermometer)
Haeckel, Ernest Heinrich (naturalist)
Houdini, Harry (Erich Weiss) (escapologist and conjurer)
Linacre, Thomas (founder of Royal College of Physicians)
Lumière, August and Louis (cinema pioneers)
Tussaud, Mme Marie (modeller in wax)

8

Bancroft, George (historian)

Earheart, Amelia (aviator)
Larousse, Pierre Athanase (encyclopaedist)
Mercator, Geradus (geographer)
Negretti, Enrico (instrument maker)

9

Blackwell, Dr Elisabeth (first Englishwoman registered as a doctor)
Macgregor, Robert ("Rob Roy") (Scottish rebel)
Max-Muller, Friedrich (philologist and orientalist)
Pankhurst, Mrs Emmeline (suffragette leader)

10

Cagliostro, Alessandro (Guiseppe Balsamo) (alchemist)
Stradivari, Antonio (violin maker)

11

Machiavelli, Niccolo (Italian writer and political reformer)
Hippocrates (physician)
Montessori, Maria (founder of Montessori educational method)
Nightingale, Florence (pioneer in training nurses)
Schweitzer, Dr Albert (musician and medical missionary)
Shaftesbury, Anthony Ashley Cooper, 7th Earl (philanthropist)
Wilberforce, William (abolitionist)

GEOGRAPHY

NB: *St* can also be spelled as *Saint*, which may affect letter counts.

Bays and Harbours

NB: letter counts do not include the words *bay* or *harbour*.
B. = Bay; H = Harbour

Australia
Botany B. (6)
Broken B. (6)
Broughton B. (9)
Bustard B. (7)
Denial B. (6)
Discovery B. (9)
Encounter B. (9)
Geographe B. (9)
Halifax B. (7)
Hermitage B. (9)
Hervey B. (6)
Moreton B. (7)
Port Jackson B. (11)
Portland B. (8)
Port Philip B. (10)
Princess Charlotte B. (17)
Sharks B. (6)
Sydney H. (6)

Baltic Sea
Pomeranian B. (10)

Canada
Baffin B. (6)
Chaleur B. (7)
Conception B. (10)
Fortune B. (7)
Frobisher B. (9)
Fundy B. (5)
Georgian B. (8)
Hudson B. (6)
Mackenzie B. (9)
Notre Dame B. (9)
Placentia B. (9)
St George's B. (9)
Trinity B. (7)

China
Hang-Chow B. (8)

England
Barnstaple B. (10)

Bridgwater B. (10)
Lyme B. (4)
Morecambe B. (9)
Mounts B. (6)
Plymouth H. (8)
Portland H. (8)
Portsmouth H. (10)
Robin Hood's B. (10)
Tees B. (4)
Tor B. (3)
Weymouth B. (8)

France
Biscay, B. of (6)
Quiberon B. (8)

Germany
Heligoland B. (10)
Kiel B. (4)
Lubeck B. (6)

India
Bengal, B. of (6)

Ireland (Republic of)
Bantry B. (6)
Clew B. (4)
Dingle B. (6)
Donegal B. (7)
Dublin B. (6)
Galway B. (6)

Israel
Acre, B. of (4)

Italy
Naples, B. of (6)

Japan
Volcano B. (7)

Mexico
Campeche, B. of (8)

New Zealand
Admiralty (9)
Blind (5)
Cloudy (6)
Evans B. (5)
Hawke B. (5)
Kaipara H. (7)
Otago H. (5)
Pegasus B. (7)
Plenty, B. of (6)
Tasman B. (6)

Scotland
Dundalk B. (7)
Enard B. (5)
Luce B. (4)

South Africa
Algoa B. (5)
Delagoa B. (7)
False B. (5)
Table B. (5)
Walvis B. (6)

South America
St George's B. (9)

USA
Buzzard's B. (8)
Chesapeake B. (10)
Delaware B. (8)
Drake's B. (6)
Galveston B. (9)
San Francisco B. (12)
San Pablo B. (8)

Wales
Cardigan B. (8)
Carmarthen B. (10)
Colwyn B. (6)
St Bride's B. (8)
Tremadoc B. (8)

Bights, Estuaries, Fiords, Firths and Gulfs

NB: letter counts do not include the words *bight, firth*, etc.
Bt = Bight; E. = Estuary; F. = Firth; Fd = Fiord; G. = Gulf

Adriatic Sea
Trieste, G of (7)

Arabian Sea
Arabian G. (7)
Persian G. (7)

Australia
Cambridge G. (9)
Carpentaria, G. of (11)
Great Australian Bt (15)
Spencer's G. (8)
St Vincent G. (9)
Van Diemen G. (9)

Baltic Sea
Finland, G. of (7)

Burma
Martaban, G. of (8)

Canada
Boothia, G. of (6)
St Lawrence, G. of (10)

Central America
Honduras, G. of (8)
Panama, G. of (6)

China
Chi-Li, G. of (5)
Liau-Tung, G. of (8)
Pe-Chi-Li, G. of (7)

Denmark
Ringkøbing Fd (10)

England
Severn E. (6)
Thames E. (6)
Wash (the) (4)

France
St Malo, G. of (6)

Greece
Aegina, G. of (6)
Argolis, G. of (7)
Lepanto, G. of (7)
Salonika, G. of (8)

India
Cambay, G. of (6)
Cutch, G. of (5)
Manaar, G. of (6)

Italy
Cagliari, G. of (8)
Genoa, G. of (5)
Salerno, G. of (7)
Taranto, G. of (7)
Venice, G. of (6)

Latvia
Riga, G. of (4)

Mediterranean
Lions, G. of (5)

Mexico
California, G. of (10)
Mexico, G. of (6)
Tehuantepec, G. of (11)

New Guinea
Papua, G. of (5)

New Zealand
Canterbury Bt (10)

North Africa
Hammamet, G. of (8)
Tunis, G. of (5)

Norway
Christiania Fd (11)

Poland
Danzig, G. of (6)

Red Sea
Aqaba, G. of (5)
Suez, G. of (4)

Russia
Ob, G. of (2)

Scotland
Clyde, F. of (5)
Cromarty F. (8)
Dornoch F. (7)
Forth, F. of (5)
Inverness F. (9)
Lorne, F. of (5)
Moray F. (5)
Pentland F. (8)
Solway F. (6)
Tay, F. of (3)

South America
Darien, G. of (6)
Paria, G. of (5)
San Jorge, G. of (8)
San Matias, G. of (9)
Venezuela, G. of (9)

South China Sea
Siam, G. of (4)
Thailand, G. of (8)
Tongking, G. of (8)
Tonkin, G. of (6)

Sweden
Bothnia, G. of (7)

Turkey
Izmir, G. of (5)
Smyrna, G. of (6)

West Africa
Benin, Bt of (5)
Biafra, Bt of (6)
Guinea, G. of (6)

Capes, Points, Headlands and Peninsulas

NB: letter counts do not include the words *cape, head*, etc.
C. = Cape; Hd = Head; Pen. = Peninsula; Pt = Point

Antarctic
Antarctic Pen. (9)

Arctic
Thorsden, C. (8)
Washington, C. (10)

Asia
Arabia (6)
Arabian Pen. (7)
Indo-China (9)

Australia
Adieu, C. (5)
Barren, C. (6)
Bauer, C. (5)
Blanche C. (6)
Bridewater, C. (10)
Byron, C. (5)
Catastrophe, C. (11)
Claremont Pt (10)
Coffin Bay Pen. (9)
Cuvier, C. (6)
Eyre Pen. (4)
Howe, C. (4)
Leeuwin, C. (7)
Melville, C. (Austral.) (8)
Northumberland, C. (14)
Otway, C. (5)
Palmerston, C. (10)
Sand Patch Pt (9)
Sandy C. (5)
Sidmouth, C. (8)
Slade Pt (5)
Sorell, C. (6)
Tribulation, C. (11)
Upstart, C. (7)
Wiles, C. (5)
York, C. (4)
Yorke Pen. (5)

Brazil
Frio, C. (4)
Maranhão, C. (8)
São Roque, C. (8)
São Tome, C. (7)

Bulgaria
Kaliakra, C. (8)

Burma
Negrais, C. (7)
Tavoy Pt (5)

Canada
Bathurst, C. (8)
Bonavista, C. (9)
Breton, C. (6)
Breakheart Pt (10)
Clark Pt (5)
East Pt (4)
Esquimaux, C. (9)
Fogo, C. (4)
Gaspé C. (5)
Gaspé Pen. (5)
Gregory, C. (7)
Icy C. (3)
Labrador (8)
Murchison C . (8)
Race, C. (4)
Roxo, C. (4)
Sable, C. (5)
St Francis, C. (9)
St George, C. (8)
St Margaret Pt (10)
St Mary, C. (6)
Sambro, C. (6)
Snettisham Pt (10)
Walsingham, C. (10)

Central America
Blanco, C. (6)
Gracias a Dios, C. (12)

China
South C. (5)
Yang-tsi, C. (7)

Corsica
Corso, C. (5)

Crete
Busa, C. (4)
Krio, C. (4)
Sidero, C. (6)

Croatia
Istria (6)
Istrian Pen. (7)

East Africa
Amber, C. (5)
Cayenne Pt (7)

Egypt
Sinai Pen. (5)

England
Ayre Pt (4)
Beachy Hd (6)
Cornwall, C. (8)
Dodman Pt (6)
Dungeness (9)
Flamborough Hd (11)
Foreland (the) (8)
Formby Hd (6)
Hartland Pt (8)
Land's End (8)
Lizard (the) (6)
Lizard Pen. (6)
Lizard Pt (6)
Naze (the) (4)
Needles (the) (7)
North Foreland (13)
Orford Ness (10)
Portland Bill (12)
Prawle Pt (6)
St Albans Hd (8)
St Bees Hd (6)
Selsey Bill (10)
Spurn Hd (5)
Start Pt (5)
Wirral (6)

Europe
Balkan Pen. (6)
Iberian Pen. (7)
Scandinavia (11)

France
De Talbert Pt (9)
Gris-Nez, C. (7)
La Hague, C. (7)
St Gilda's Pt (8)
St Matthieu Pt (10)

Greece
Colonna, C. (7)
Gallo, C. (5)

Malia, C. (5)
Matapan, C. (7)
Peloponnese (11)

Greenland
Bismark, C. (7)
Farewell, C. (8)

Haiti
Haitien, C. (7)

India
Comorin, C. (7)
Palmyras Pt. (8)

Indonesia
Bantam, C. (6)

Ireland (Republic of)
Béara Pen. (5)
Clare, C. (5)
Clogher Hd (7)
Dingle Pen. (6)
Galley Hd (6)
Greenore Pt (8)
Inishowen Hd (9)
Loop Hd (4)
Sheep Hd (5)
Slea Hd (4)
Slyne Hd (5)
Streedagh Pt (9)

Israel
Carmel, C. (6)

Italy
Bizzuto, C. (7)
Nao, C. (3)
Vaticano, C. (8)

Japan
Kataska, C. (7)
King, C. (4)
Patience, C. (8)
Sima, C. (4)
Soya, C. (4)
Yerimo, C. (6)

Malaysia
Romania, C. (7)

Mexico
San Antonio Pt (10)
San Lucas, C. (8)

Tegupan Pt (7)
Yucatán Pen. (7)

New Zealand
Castle Pt (6)
East C. (4)
Egmont, C. (6)
Farewell, C. (8)
North C. (5)
Palliser, C. (8)
Runaway C. (7)

North Africa
Blanco, C. (6)
Bon, C. (3)
Spartel, C. (7)
Wad Nun, C. (6)

Northern Ireland
Bengore Hd (7)
Downpatrick Hd (11)
Fairhead, C. (8)

Norway
Naze (the) (4)
Nord, C. (4)
North C. (5)

Philippines
Bataan Pen. (6)

Portugal
Carvoeira, C. (9)
De Roca, C. (6)
De Sines C. (7)
Espicher, C. (8)
Mondego, C. (7)
St Vincent, C. (9)
Santa Maria, C. (10)

Russia
Aniva, C. (5)
Kola Pen. (4)
Yakan, C. (5)

Sardinia
Comino, C. (6)
Teulada, C. (7)

Scotland
Aird Pt (4)
Arisaig Pt (7)
Ardnamurchan Pen. (12)
Ardnamurchan Pt (12)

Brims Ness (9)
Buddon Ness (10)
Burrow Hd (6)
Burrow Pt (6)
Duncansbay Hd (10)
Dunnet Hd (6)
Farr Pt (4)
Fife Ness (8)
Gallon Hd (6)
Greenstone Pt (10)
Hoe Pt (3)
Kinnaird Hd (8)
Noss Hd (4)
Rattray Hd (7)
Rhynns Pt (6)
Roray Hd (5)
St Abb's Hd (6)
Sanaig Pt (6)
Sleat Pt (5)
Strathy Pt (7)
Sumburgh Hd (8)
Tarbat Ness (10)
Toe Hd (3)
Tolsta Hd (6)
Troup Hd (5)
Turn Ness (8)
Vaternish Pt (9)
Whiten Hd (6)
Wrath, C. (5)

Sicily
Granitola, C. (9)
Milazzo, C. (7)
Orlando, C. (7)
Santo Vito, C. (9)

South Africa
Agulhas, C. (7)
Good Hope, C. of (8)
Hangklip, C. (8)
Murraysburg, C. (11)
Quoin Pt (5)
Recife, C. (6)
St Lucia, C. (7)
Sordwana Pt (8)

South America
Andres Pt (6)
Cruz, C. (4)
Gallinas Pt (8)
Horn, C. (4)
Rayes Pt (5)
San Diego, C. (8)
San Francisco, C. (12)

San Lorenzo, C. (10)
Sur Pt (3)

Spain
Creus, C. (5)
De Gata, C. (6)
De Palos, C. (7)
De Penas, C. (7)
De San Adrian, C. (11)
Finisterre, C. (10)
Ortegal, C. (7)
Tarifa, C. (6)
Trafalgar, C. (9)

Tasmania
Sandy C. (5)

Thailand
Cambodia Pt (8)

Turkey
Baba, C. (4)
Glossa, C. (6)

Ukraine
Crimea (6)

USA
Ann, C. (3)
Canaveral, C. (9)
Charles C. (7)
Cod, C. (5)
Conception Pt (10)
Fear, C. (4)
Flattery, C. (8)
Florida (7)
Friars Pt (6)
Girardeau, C. (9)
Hatteras, C. (8)
Kennedy, C. (7)
May, C. (3)
Mendocino C. (9)
Sable, C. (5)
San Blas, C. (7)
Vincent, C. (7)
Sur Pt (3)

Vietnam
San Ho, C. (5)

Wales
Great Ormes Hd (10)
Gower Pen. (5)

Little Ormes Hd (11)
Lleyn Pen. (5)
Mumbles Hd (7)
Nash Pt (4)
Orme's Hd (5)
St David's Hd (8)
St Gowan's Hd (8)
Strumble Hd (8)
Worms Hd (5)

West Africa
Formosa C. (7)
Frio, C. (4)
Lopez C. (5)
Mirik, C. (5)
Negro, C. (5)
Nun, C. (3)
Palmas, C. (6)
St Paul, C. (6)
Three Points, C. (11)
Verde, C. (5)

Capital Cities

* = former; Is. = Islands

4
Aden (Yemen)
Apia (Samoa)
Baku (Azerbaijan)
Bern (Switzerland)
Bonn* (Germany)
Doha (Qatar)
Kiev (Ukraine)
Lima (Peru)
Lomé (Togo)
Malé (Maldives)
Nuuk (Greenland)
Oslo (Norway)
Riga (Latvia)
Rome (Italy)
San'a (Yemen)
Suva (Fiji)
Vila (Vanuatu)

5
Abuja (Nigeria)
Accra (Ghana)

Agaña (Guam)
Ajman (Ajman)
Amman (Jordan)
Berne (Switzerland)
Cairo (Egypt)
Dacca (Bangladesh)
Dakar (Senegal)
Delhi (India)
Dubai (Dubai)
Hanoi (Vietnam)
Kabul (Afghanistan)
Koror (Belau)
Lagos* (Nigeria)
La Paz (Bolivia)
Minsk (Belarus)
Paris (France)
Praia (Cape Verde Is.)
Quito (Ecuador)
Rabat (Morocco)
Sanaa (Yemen)
Seoul (South Korea)
Sofia (Bulgaria)

Sucre (Bolivia)
Tokyo (Japan)
Tunis (Tunisia)
Vaduz (Liechtenstein)
Yaren (Nauru)

6
Akmola (Kazakhstan)
Almaty* (Kazakhstan)
Ankara (Turkey)
Aqmola (Kazakhstan)
Asmara (Eritrea)
Astana* (Kazakhstan)
Athens (Greece)
Bagdad (Iraq)
Bamako (Mali)
Bangui (Central African
  Republic)
Banjul (Gambia)
Beirut (Lebanon)
Berlin (Germany)
Bissau (Guinea-Bissau)

Bogotá (Colombia)
Brunei (Brunei)
Dodoma (Tanzania)
Dublin (Republic of
   Ireland)
Havana (Cuba)
Harare (Zimbabwe)
Hobart (Tasmania)
Kigali (Rwanda)
Lisbon (Portugal)
London (England, UK)
Luanda (Angola)
Lusaka (Zambia)
Madrid (Spain)
Majuro (Marsall Is.)
Malabo (Equatorial
   Guinea)
Manama (Bahrain)
Manila (Philippines)
Maputo (Mozambique)
Maseru (Lesotho)
Masqat (Oman)
Moroni (Comoros)
Moscow (Russia)
Muscat (Oman)
Nassau (Bahamas)
Niamey (Niger)
Ottawa (Canada)
Peking (China)
Prague (Czech Republic)
Riyadh (Saudi Arabia)
Roseau (Dominica)
Saigon* (Vietnam)
Skopje (Macedonia)
Taipei (Taiwan)
Tarawa (Kiribati)
Tehran (Iran)
Tirana (Albania)
Valley (Anguilla)
Vienna (Austria)
Warsaw (Poland)
Zagreb (Croatia)

7

Abidjan* (Ivory Coast)
Algiers (Algeria)
Alma-Ata* (Kazakhstan)
Baghdad (Iraq)
Bangkok (Thailand)
Beijing (China)
Belfast (Northern
   Ireland)
Bishkek (Kyrgystan)
Caracas (Venezuela)

Chisnau (Moldova)
Colombo (Sri Lanka)
Conakry (Guinea)
Cotonou (Benin)
Douglas (Isle of Man)
El Aaiun (Western
   Sahara)
Honiara (Solomon Is.)
Jakarta (Indonesia)
Kampala (Uganda)
Managua (Nicaragua)
Mbabane (Swaziland)
Nairobi (Kenya)
Nicosia (Cyprus)
Palermo (Sicily)
Rangoon (Burma)
St John's (Antigua)
San José (Costa Rica)
São Tomé (São Tomé and
   Principe)
Sharjah (Sharjah)
Stanley (Falkland Is.)
Tallinn (Estonia)
Teheran (Iran)
Tbilisi (Georgia)
Thimphu (Bhutan)
Tripoli (Libya)
Valetta (Malta)
Vatican (Vatican)
Vilnius (Lithuania)
Yaoundé (Cameroun)
Yerevan (Armenia)

8

Abu Dhabi (UAE)
Ashgabat
   (Turkmenistan)
Asunción (Paraguay)
Belmopan (Belize)
Belgrade (Serbia)
Brasilia (Brazil)
Brussels (Belgium)
Budapest (Hungary)
Canberra (Australia)
Cape Town (South
   Africa)
Castries (St Lucia)
Damascus (Syria)
Djakarta (Indonesia)
Djibouti (Djibouti)
Dushanbe (Tajikistan)
Freetown (Sierra Leone)
Fujairah (Fujairah)
Funafuti (Tuvalu)

Gaborone (Botswana)
Hamilton (Bermuda)
Helsinki (Finland)
Honolulu (Hawaii)
Istanbul* (Turkey)
Katmandu (Nepal)
Khartoum (Sudan)
Kingston (Jamaica)
Kinshasa (Democratic
   Republic of the Congo)
Kishinev (Moldova)
La Habana (Cuba)
Lilongwe (Malawi)
Monrovia (Liberia)
N'Djamena (Chad)
New Delhi (India)
Plymouth (Montserrat)
Pretoria (South Africa)
St Helier (Jersey)
Santiago (Chile)
Tashkent (Uzbekistan)
Titograd* (Montenegro)
Tórshavn (Faroe Is.)
Valletta (Malta)
Victoria (Seychelles)
Windhoek (Namibia)

9

Amsterdam
   (Netherlands)
Ashkhabad
   (Turkmenistan)
Bucharest (Romania)
Bujumbura (Burundi)
Edinburgh (Scotland)
Gaberones (Botswana)
Grand Turk (Turks and
   Caicos Is.)
Islamabad (Pakistan)
Jamestown (St Helena)
Jerusalem (Israel)
Kathmandu (Nepal)
Kingstown (St. Vincent)
Ljubliana (Slovenia)
Macao City (Macao)
Mogadishu (Somalia)
Nuku'alofa (Tonga)
Phnom Penh (Cambodia)
Podgorica (Montenegro)
Port Louis (Mauritius)
Porto Novo (Benin)
Pyongyang (North
   Korea)
Reykjavik (Iceland)

119

St George's (Grenada)
San Marino (San Marino)
Sarajevo (Bosnia and Herzegovina)
Singapore (Singapore)
Stockholm (Sweden)
Thorshavn (Faroe Is.)
Ulan Bator (Mongolia)
Vientiane (Laos)

10
Addis Ababa (Ethiopia)
Basseterre (St Kitts and Nevis)
Belize City* (Belize)
Basseterre (St Christopher-Nevis-Anguilla)
Bratislava (Slovakia)
Bridgetown (Barbados)
Brunei City* (Brunei)
Copenhagen (Denmark)
Georgetown (Cayman Is., Guyana)
Kuwait City (Kuwait)
Libreville (Gabon)
Luxembourg (Luxembourg)
Mexico City (Mexico)
Montevideo (Uruguay)
Nouakchott (Mauritania)

Ougadougou (Burkina)
Panama City (Panama)
Paramaribo (Surinam)
Quezon City* (Philippines)
Tananarive* (Madagascar)
Wellington (New Zealand)

11
Brazzaville (Congo)
Buenos Aires (Argentina)
Dar es Salaam* (Tanzania)
Kuala Lumpur (Malaysia)
Monaco-Ville (Monaco)
Port Moresby (Papua New Guinea)
Port of Spain (Trinidad and Tobago)
St Peter Port (Guernsey)
San Salvador (El Salvador)
Tegucigalpa (Honduras)
Ulaanbaatar (Mongolia)
Vatican City (Vatican City)

12
Antananarivo (Madagascar)
Bloemfontein (South Africa)
Cockburn Town (Turks and Caicos Is.)
Port-au-Prince (Haiti)
Ras al-Khaimah (Ras al-Khaimah)
Santo Domingo (Dominican Republic)
Umm al-Qaiwain (Umm al-Qaiwain)
Washington DC (USA)
Yamoussoukro (Ivory Coast)

13
Guatemala City (Guatemala)
Yaren District (Nauru)

14 *and over*
Andorra la Vella (Andorra) (14)
Bandar Seri Begawan (Brunei) (17)
Lourenço Marques* (Mozambique) (15)

Cities and Towns

See also **Capital Cities**.

Afghanistan
Herat (5)
Jalalabad (9)
Kandahar (8)

Algeria
Oran (4)

Argentina
Bahia Blanca (11)
Cordoba (7)
La Plata (7)

Australia
Adelaide (8)
Alice Springs (12)

Brisbane (8)
Darwin (6)
Melbourne (9)
Newcastle (9)
Perth (5)
Sydney (6)

Austria
Innsbruck (9)
Salzburg (8)

Bangladesh
Chittagong (10)

Belgium
Antwerp (7)

Bruges (6)
Ghent (5)
Liège (5)
Ostend (6)
Ypres (5)

Brazil
Bahia (5)
Belo Horizonte (13)
Recife (6)
Rio de Janeiro (12)
São Paulo (8)

Bulgaria
Varna (5)

Burma
Mandalay (8)

Canada
Calgary (7)
Edmonton (8)
Fredericton (11)
Halifax (7)
Hamilton (8)
Kingston (8)
Montreal (8)
Niagara Falls (12)

Quebec (6)
Regina (6)
St John's (7)
Toronto (7)
Vancouver
  (9)
Victoria (8)
Winnipeg (8)

China
Anshan (6)
Canton (6)
Changchun
  (9)
Dairen (6)
Fushun (6)
Harbin (6)
Kunming (7)
Nanking (7)
Shanghai (8)
Shenyang (8)
Sian (4)
Taiyuan (7)
Tientsin (8)
Tsinan (6)
Wuhan (5)

Colombia
Cartagena
  (9)
Medellín (8)

**Congo,
Democratic
Republic of
the**
Lubumbashi
  (10)

Croatia
Split (5)

**Czech
  Republic**
Brno (4)

Egypt
Alexandria
  (10)
Aswan (4)
Giza (4)
Luxor (5)
Mansura (7)
Memphis (7)

Ismailia (8)
Port Said (4)

England

3
Ely
Eye
Rye
Usk

4
Bath
Bray
Bude
Bury
Clun
Deal
Diss
Eton
Holt
Hove
Hull
Hyde
Ince
Leek
Looe
Lydd
Ross
Ryde
Shap
Ware
Wark
Wern
Yarm
York

5
Acton
Alton
Bacup
Blyth
Bourn
Calne
Chard
Cheam
Colne
Cowes
Crewe
Derby
Dover
Egham
Epsom
Filey

Fowey
Frome
Goole
Grays
Hawes
Hedon
Hurst
Hythe
Leeds
Leigh
Lewes
Louth
Luton
March
Olney
Otley
Poole
Reeth
Ripon
Risca
Rugby
Sarum
Selby
Stoke
Stone
Tebay
Thame
Tring
Truro
Wells
Wigan

6
Alston
Alford
Ashton
Barnet
Barrow
Barton
Batley
Battle
Bawtry
Bedale
Belper
Bodmin
Bognor
Bolton
Bootle
Boston
Bruton
Bungay
Burton
Buxton
Castor

Cobham
Cromer
Darwen
Dudley
Durham
Ealing
Eccles
Epping
Exeter
Goring
Hanley
Harlow
Harrow
Havant
Henley
Hexham
Howden
Ilford
Ilkley
Ilsley
Jarrow
Kendal
Leyton
London
Ludlow
Lynton
Lytham
Maldon
Malton
Marlow
Masham
Morley
Naseby
Nelson
Neston
Newark
Newent
Newlyn
Newton
Norham
Oakham
Oldham
Ormsby
Ossett
Oundle
Oxford
Penryn
Pewsey
Pinner
Pudsey
Putney
Ramsey
Redcar
Ripley

Romney
Romsey
Rugely
St Ives
Seaham
Seaton
Selsey
Settle
Snaith
Strood
Stroud
Sutton
Thirsk
Thorne
Totnes
Walmer
Walton
Watton
Welwyn .
Weston
Whitby
Widnes
Wigton
Wilton
Witham
Witney
Wooler
Yeovil

7
Alnwick
Andover
Appleby
Arundel
Ashford
Aylsham
Bampton
Banbury
Barking
Beccles
Bedford
Belford
Berwick
Bewdley
Bexhill
Bickley
Bilston
Bourton
Bowfell
Brandon
Bristol
Brixham
Bromley
Burnham

Burnley	Malvern	Ventnor	Egremont	Sedbergh
Burslem	Margate	Walsall	Eversley	Shanklin
Caistor	Matlock	Waltham	Fakenham	Shelford
Cafford	Molesey	Wantage	Falmouth	Shipston
Cawston	Moreton	Wareham	Foulness	Sidmouth
Charing	Morpeth	Warwick	Grantham	Skegness
Chatham	Mossley	Watchet	Grantown	Sleaford
Cheadle	Newbury	Watford	Hadleigh	Southend
Cheddar	Newport	Wembley	Hailsham	Spalding
Chesham	Norwich	Wickwar	Halstead	Stafford
Chester	Oldbury	Windsor	Hastings	Stamford
Chorley	Overton	Winslow	Hatfield	Stanhope
Clacton	Padstow	Winster	Helmsley	Stanwell
Clifton	Penrith	Wisbeck	Hereford	Stockton
Crawley	Poulton	Worksop	Herne Bay	Stratton
Croydon	Prescot		Hertford	Swaffham
Darsley	Preston	**8**	Hinckley	Surbiton
Datchet	Rainham	Abingdon	Holbeach	Tamworth
Dawlish	Reading	Alfreton	Hunmanby	Thetford
Devizes	Redhill	Alnmouth	Ilkeston	Thornaby
Dorking	Redruth	Amesbury	Keighley	Tiverton
Douglas	Reigate	Ampthill	Kingston	Tunstall
Dunster	Retford	Axbridge	Lavenham	Uckfield
Elstree	Romford	Aycliffe	Lechlade	Uxbridge
Enfield	Rossall	Bakewell	Liskeard	Wallasey
Everton	Royston	Barnsley	Longtown	Wallsend
Evesham	Runcorn	Berkeley	Lynmouth	Wanstead
Exmouth	St Neots	Beverley	Maryport	Westbury
Fareham	Salford	Bicester	Midhurst	Wetheral
Farnham	Saltash	Bideford	Minehead	Wetherby
Feltham	Sandown	Bolsover	Monmouth	Weymouth
Glossop	Saxelby	Brackley	Nantwich	Woodford
Gosport	Seaford	Bradford	Newhaven	Woolwich
Grimsby	Shifnal	Brampton	Nuneaton	Worthing
Halifax	Shipley	Bridport	Ormskirk	Yarmouth
Hampton	Shipton	Brighton	Oswestry	
Harwich	Silloth	Bromyard	Penzance	**9**
Haworth	Skipton	Broseley	Pershore	Aldeburgh
Helston	Spilsby	Caerleon	Peterlee	Aldershot
Heywood	Staines	Camborne	Petworth	Allendale
Hitchin	Stilton	Carlisle	Pevensey	Alresford
Honiton	Sudbury	Caterham	Plaistow	Ambleside
Hornsea	Sunbury	Chepstow	Plymouth	Ashbourne
Hornsey	Swanage	Chertsey	Ramsgate	Ashburton
Horsham	Swindon	Clevedon	Redditch	Avonmouth
Ipswich	Swinton	Clovelly	Richmond	Aylesbury
Ixworth	Taunton	Coventry	Ringwood	Blackburn
Keswick	Telford	Crediton	Rochdale	Blackpool
Kington	Tenbury	Dartford	Rothbury	Blandford
Lancing	Tetbury	Daventry	St Albans	Blisworth
Langton	Thaxted	Debenham	St Helens	Bracknell
Ledbury	Tilbury	Dedworth	Saltburn	Braintree
Leyburn	Torquay	Deptford	Sandgate	Brentford
Lincoln	Twyford	Dewsbury	Sandwich	Brentwood

Brighouse	Newmarket	Aldborough	Mexborough
Broughton	New Romney	Altrincham	Micheldean
Cambridge	Northwich	Barnstaple	Middlewich
Carnforth	Otterburn	Beaminster	Mildenhall
Castleton	Pembridge	Bedlington	Nailsworth
Chesilton	Penistone	Bellingham	Nottingham
Chingford	Penkridge	Billericay	Okehampton
Clitheroe	Penyghent	Birkenhead	Orfordness
Congleton	Pickering	Birmingham	Pangbourne
Cranborne	Rochester	Bridgnorth	Patrington
Cranbrook	Rotherham	Bridgwater	Peacehaven
Crewkerne	St Austell	Bromsgrove	Pontefract
Cricklade	Salisbury	Broxbourne	Portishead
Cuckfield	Saltfleet	Buckingham	Portsmouth
Dartmouth	Sevenoaks	Canterbury	Potter's Bar
Devonport	Sheerness	Carshalton	Ravenglass
Doncaster	Sheffield	Chelmsford	Rockingham
Donington	Sherborne	Cheltenham	St Leonards
Droitwich	Smethwick	Chichester	Saxmundham
Dronfield	Southgate	Chippenham	Shepperton
Dungeness	Southport	Chulmleigh	Sheringham
Dunstable	Southwell	Coggeshall	Shrewsbury
Ellesmere	Southwold	Colchester	Stalbridge
Faversham	Starcross	Cullompton	Stowmarket
Fleetwood	Stevenage	Darlington	Sunderland
Gateshead	Stockport	Dorchester	Teddington
Godalming	Stokesley	Dukinfield	Teignmouth
Gravesend	Stourport	Eastbourne	Tewkesbury
Greenwich	Stratford	Eccleshall	Thamesmead
Grinstead	Tarporley	Farningham	Torrington
Guildford	Tavistock	Folkestone	Trowbridge
Harrogate	Tenterden	Freshwater	Twickenham
Haslemere	Todmorden	Gloucester	Warminster
Haverhill	Tonbridge	Halesworth	Warrington
Hawkhurst	Towcester	Hartlepool	Washington
Holmfirth	Tynemouth	Haslingdon	Wednesbury
Ilchester	Ulverston	Heathfield	Wellington
Immingham	Upminster	Horncastle	Westward Ho!
Kettering	Uppingham	Hornchurch	Whitchurch
King's Lynn	Uttoxeter	Hungerford	Whithaven
Kingswear	Wainfleet	Hunstanton	Whitstable
Lambourne	Wakefield	Huntingdon	Whittlesey
Lancaster	Warkworth	Ilfracombe	Willenhall
Leicester	Weybridge	Gillingham	Winchelsea
Lichfield	Whernside	Kenilworth	Winchester
Liverpool	Wimbledon	Kingsclere	Windermere
Longridge	Wincanton	Kirkoswald	Windlesham
Lowestoft	Wokingham	Launceston	Wirksworth
Lyme Regis	Woodstock	Leamington	Withernsea
Lymington	Worcester	Leominster	Wolsingham
Maidstone	Wymondham	Littleport	Woodbridge
Mansfield		Maidenhead	Workington
Middleton	**10**	Malmesbury	
Newcastle	Accrington	Manchester	

11
Basingstoke
Berkhamsted
Bognor Regis
Bournemouth
Bridlington
Buntingford
Cleethorpes
Cockermouth
East Retford
Glastonbury
Great Marlow
Guisborough
Haltwhistle
Hampton Wick
Hatherleigh
High Wycombe
Ingatestone
Leytonstone
Littlestone
Lostwithiel
Ludgershall
Lutterworth
Mablethorpe
Manningtree
Market Rasen
Marlborough
Much Wenlock
New Brighton
Newton Abbot
Northampton
Petersfield
Pocklington
Rawtenstall
St. Margaret's
Scarborough
Shaftesbury
Southampton
South Molton
Stalybridge
Stourbridge
Tattershall
Wallingford
Walthamstow
Westminster
Whitechurch
Woodhall Spa

12
Attleborough
Bexhill-on-Sea
Castle Rising
Chesterfield
Christchurch

Gainsborough
Great Grimsby
Great Malvern
Huddersfield
Ingleborough
Long Stratton
Loughborough
Macclesfield
Milton Keynes
Morecambe Bay
North Shields
North Walsham
Peterborough
Shoeburyness
Shottesbrook
South Shields
Stoke-on-Trent

13
Barnard Castle
Bishop's Castle
Boroughbridge
Brightlingsea
Burton-on-Trent
Bury St Edmunds
Chipping Ongar
Finchampstead
Godmanchester
Great Yarmouth
Higham Ferrers
Kidderminster
Kirkby Stephen
Knaresborough
Littlehampton
Lytham St Annes
Market Deeping
Market Drayton
Melcombe Regis
Melton Mowbray
Middlesbrough
Northallerton
Saffron Walden
Shepton Mallet
Wolverhampton
Wootton Basset

14
Berwick-on-
   Tweed
Bishop Auckland
Bishops Waltham
Chipping Barnet
Chipping Norton
Hemel

Hempstead
Kirkby Lonsdale
Market Bosworth
Mortimer's Cross
Stockton-on-Tees
Stony Stratford
Sutton Courtney
Tunbridge Wells
Wellingborough
West Hartlepool

15
Ashton-under-
   Lyne
Barrow-in-
   Furness
Burnham-on-
   Crouch
Castle Donington
Leighton Buzzard
Newcastle-on-
   Tyne
St Leonards-on-
   Sea
Stratford-on-
   Avon
Sutton Coldfield
Weston-super-
   Mare

16
Bishop's Stortford
Welwyn Garden
   City

France
Abbeville (9)
Aix (3)
Ajaccio (7)
Albi (4)
Alencon (7)
Amiens (6)
Arles (5)
Armentières (11)
Arras (5)
Avignon (7)
Bayonne (7)
Besancon (8)
Bordeaux (8)
Boulogne (8)
Brest (5)
Caen (4)
Calais (6)
Cherbourg (9)

Clermont-
   Ferrand (15)
Dieppe (6)
Dijon (5)
Dunkirk (7)
Grenoble (8)
Laon (4)
Le Havre (7)
Le Mans (6)
Lille (5)
Lourdes (7)
Lyon (4)
Marseille (9)
Marseilles (10)
Metz (4)
Montelimar (10)
Nancy (5)
Nantes (6)
Nice (4)
Nimes (5)
Orange (6)
Orléans (7)
Reims (5)
Rheims (6)
Rouen (5)
St Malo (6)
Soissons (8)
Strasbourg (10)
Toulon (6)
Toulouse (8)
Tour (4)
Verdun (6)
Versailles (10)

Germany
Aachen (6)
Aix-la-Chapelle
   (13)
Augsburg (8)
Baden Baden (10)
Bad Homburg
   (10)
Bochum (6)
Bremen (6)
Brunswick (9)
Cassel (6)
Chemnitz (8)
Coblenz (7)
Cologne (7)
Cottbus (7)
Darmstadt (10)
Dortmund (8)
Dresden (7)
Dusseldorf (10)

Erfurt (6)
Essen (5)
Frankfurt (9)
Gera (4)
Halle (5)
Hamburg (7)
Hannover (8)
Hanover (7)
Heidelberg (10)
Homburg (7)
Kassel (6)
Kiel (4)
Koblenz (7)
Koln (4)
Leipzig (7)
Magdeburg (9)
Mainz (5)
Mannheim (8)
Munich (6)
Munchen (7)
Nuremberg (9)
Nurnberg (8)
Potsdam (7)
Rostock (7)
Saarbrucken (11)
Schwerin (8)
Stuttgart (9)
Suhl (4)
Treves (6)
Trier (5)
Wiesbaden (9)
Wuppertal (9)

Greece
Corinth (7)
Mycenae (7)
Piraeus (7)
Salonika (8)
Sparta (6)

India
Agra (4)
Agartala (8)
Ahmedabad (9)
Ajmer (5)
Allahabad (9)
Alwar (5)
Amritsar (8)
Bangalore (9)
Baroda (6)
Benares (7)
Bhopal (6)
Bhubaneswar
  (11)

Bombay (6)
Calcutta (7)
Cawnpore (8)
Chandigarh (10)
Darjeeling (10)
Delhi (5)
Gwalior (7)
Howrah (6)
Hyderabad (9)
Imphal (6)
Indore (6)
Jaipur (6)
Jamalpur (8)
Jamshedpur (10)
Jhansi (6)
Jodhpur (7)
Kanpur (6)
Kohima (6)
Kotah (5)
Lucknow (7)
Madras (6)
Meerut (6)
Mumbai (6)
Mysore (6)
Nagpur (6)
Patna (5)
Poona (5)
Pune (4)
Rampur (6)
Shillong (8)
Simla (5)
Srinagar (8)
Trivandrum (10)
Varanasi (8)

Indonesia
Bandung (7)
Surabaya (8)

Iran
Abadan (6)
Isfahan (7)
Mashhad (7)
Shiraz (6)
Tabriz (6)

Iraq
Basra (5)
Mosul (5)

Ireland
  (Republic of)
Arklow (6)
Athlone (7)

Balla (5)
Ballymurphy (11)
Bantry (6)
Blarney (7)
Boyle (5)
Bray (4)
Carlow (6)
Cashel (6)
Clonmel (7)
Clontarf (8)
Cobh (4)
Cork (4)
Drogheda (8)
Dundalk (7)
Ennis (5)
Galway (6)
Kildare (7)
Kilkenny (8)
Killarney (9)
Limerick (8)
Listowel (8)
Maynouth (8)
Rathdrum (8)
Roscommon (9)
Shillelagh (10)
Sligo (5)
Tipperary (9)
Waterford (9)
Wexford (7)
Youghal (7)

Israel
Beersheba (9)
Gaza (4)
Haifa (5)
Jaffa (5)
Tel Aviv (7)

Italy
Agrigento (9)
Bari (4)
Bologna (7)
Genoa (5)
Messina (7)
Milan (5)
Naples (6)
Ostia (5)
Padua (5)
Palermo (7)
Parma (5)
Pisa (4)
Ravenna (7)
Reggio (6)
Rieti (5)

Salerno (7)
San Remo (7)
Siena (5)
Syracuse (8)
Trent (5)
Turin (5)
Trieste (7)
Vatican (7)
Venice (6)
Verona (6)

Japan
Hiroshima (9)
Kobe (4)
Kyoto (5)
Nagasaki (8)
Nagoya (6)
Osaka (5)
Sapporo (7)
Yokohama (8)

Kenya
Mombasa (7)

Lebanon
Sidon (5)
Tyre (4)

Libya
Tobruk (6)

Mali
Timbuktu (8)

Mexico
Acapulco (8)
Guadalajara (11)
Juárez (6)
Monterrey (9)
Puebla (6)

Morocco
Casablanca (10)
Fez (3)
Marrakech (9)
Marrakesh (9)
Tangier (7)
Tangiers (8)

Netherlands
Arnhem (6)
Dordrecht (9)
Eindhoven (9)
The Hague (8)

Leiden (6)
Leyden (6)
Rotterdam (9)
Utrecht (7)

New Zealand
Auckland (8)
Christchurch (12)
Dunedin (7)
Napier (6)
Nelson (6)

Northern Ireland

5
Derry
Doagh
Glynn
Keady
Larne
Newry
Omagh
Toome

6
Antrim
Augher
Bangor
Belcoo
Beragh
Comber
Lurgan

7
Belfast
Belleek
Caledon
Carrick
Clogher
Dervock
Dundrum
Dunmore
Fintona
Gilford
Glenarm
Lisburn

8
Ahoghill
Dungiven
Hilltown
Portrush
Strabane

Trillick

9
Ballintra
Ballymena
Banbridge
Bushmills
Coleraine
Cookstown
Dungannon
Kircubbin
Moneymore
Newcastle
Portadown
Rasharkin
Rostrevor
Tobermore
Tovermore

10
Ballyclare
Ballymoney
Ballyroney
Castlederg
Cushendall
Donaghadee
Glengariff
Markethill
Portaferry
Saintfield
Strangford
Tanderagee

11
Ballycastle
Ballygawley
Carrickmore
Crossmaglen
Downpatrick
Draperstown
Enniskillen
Londonderry
Magherafelt
Portglenone
Randalstown
Rathfriland

12
Castle Dawson
Castlewellan
Five Mile Town
Hillsborough
Inishtrahull
Stewartstown

13
Brookeborough
Carrickfergus
Derrygonnelly

14
Newtown Stewart

Norway
Bergen (6)
Trondheim (9)

Pakistan
Hyderabad (9)
Karachi (7)
Lahore (6)
Peshawar (8)
Quetta (6)
Rawalpindi (10

Peru
Ayacucho (8)
Cuzco (5)

Poland
Breslau (7)
Danzig (6)
Gdansk (6)
Krakow (6)
Lodz (4)
Lublin (6)
Posen (5)
Przemysl (8)

Portugal
Coimbra (7)
Faro (4)
Oporto (6)
Porto (5)

Russia
Archangel (9)
Astrakhan (9)
Cherkessk (9)
Gorky (5)
Irkutsk (7)
Kalinin (7)
Kaliningrad (11)
Kazan (5)
Konigsberg (10)
Kuibyshev (9)
Leningrad (9)
Novgorod (8)
Novosibirsk (11)

Omsk (4)
Petrograd (9)
Pskov (5)
Rostov (6)
St Petersburg (12)
Smolensk (8)
Stalingrad (10)
Sverdlovsk (10)
Ufa (3)
Vladivostok (11)
Volgograd (9)
Yakutsk (7)

Saudi Arabia
Jeddah (6)
Jidda (5)
Mecca (5)
Medina (6)

Scotland

3
Ayr
Uig

4
Alva
Barr
Duns
Elie
Kirn
Luss
Nigg
Oban
Reay
Rona
Stow
Wick

5
Alloa
Annan
Appin
Avoch
Ayton
Banff
Beith
Brora
Bunaw
Busby
Ceres
Clova
Clune

Crail
Cupar
Denny
Downe
Elgin
Ellon
Errol
Fyvie
Govan
Insch
Islay
Keiss
Keith
Kelso
Lairg
Largs
Leith
Nairn
Perth
Salen
Troon

6

Aboyne
Alford
Barvas
Beauly
Bervie
Biggar
Bo'ness
Buckie
Carron
Cawdor
Comrie
Crieff
Cullen
Culter
Dollar
Drymen
Dunbar
Dundee
Dunlop
Dunnet
Dunoon
Dysart
Edzell
Findon
Forfar
Forres
Girvan
Glamis
Hawick
Huntdy
Irvine

Killin
Lanark
Lauder
Leslie
Kilmun
Linton
Lochee
Meigle
Moffat
Pladda
Reston
Rhynie
Rosyth
Rothes
Shotts
Thurso
Tongue
Wishaw
Yarrow

7

Airdrie
Balfron
Balloch
Banavie
Bowmore
Braemar
Brechin
Brodick
Canobie
Cantyre
Carbost
Cargill
Carluke
Crathie
Culross
Cumnock
Denholm
Douglas
Dunkeld
Dunning
Evanton
Fairlie
Falkirk
Galston
Gifford
Glasgow
Glencoe
Golspie
Gourock
Granton
Guthrie
Halkirk
Kenmore

Kessock
Kilmory
Kilmuir
Kilsyth
Kinross
Kintore
Lamlash
Larbert
Lybster
Macduff
Maybole
Meldrum
Melrose
Melvich
Methven
Monikie
Muthill
Newport
Paisley
Peebles
Polmont
Poolewe
Portree
Portsoy
Renfrew
Saddell
Sarclet
Scourie
Selkirk
Stanley
Strathy
Tarbert
Tarland
Tayport
Tranent
Turriff
Tundrum
Ullster
Yetholm

8

Aberdeen
Aberlady
Abington
Annadale
Arbroath
Arrochar
Auldearn
Ballater
Banchory
Barrhill
Beattock
Blantyre
Burghead

Canisbay
Carnwath
Creetown
Cromarty
Dalkeith
Dalmally
Dingwall
Dirleton
Dufftown
Dumfries
Dunbeath
Dunblane
Dunscore
Earlston
Eyemouth
Findhorn
Fortrose
Glenluce
Greenlaw
Greenock
Hamilton
Inverary
Inverury
Jeantown
Jedburgh
Kilbride
Kilniver
Kilrenny
Kinghorn
Kirkwall
Langholm
Latheron
Leuchars
Loanhead
Markinch
Marykirk
Moniaive
Montrose
Monymusk
Muirkirk
Neilston
Newburgh
Newmilns
Penicuik
Pitsligo
Pooltiel
Quiraing
Rothesay
St Fergus
Stirling
Strichen
Talisker
Taransay
Traquair

Whithorn	Thornhill	**11**	Grahamstown
Ullapool	Tomintoul	Aberchirder	(11)
Woodside		Balquhidder	Johannesburg
	10	Bannockburn	(12)
9	Abbotsford	Blairgowrie	Kimberley (9)
Aberfeldy	Achnasheen	Campbeltown	Ladysmith (9)
Aberfoyle	Anstruther	Charlestown	Mafeking (8)
Ardrossan	Applecross	Cumbernauld	Pietermaritzburg
Berridale	Ardrishaig	Drummelzier	(16)
Bettyhill	Auchinleck	Dunfermline	Port Elizabeth
Blacklarg	Ballantrae	Ecclefechan	(13)
Bracadale	Blackadder	Fettercairn	Sharpeville (11)
Braeriach	Carnoustie	Fort William	Simonstown (10)
Broadford	Carsphairn	Fraserburgh	Soweto (6)
Broughton	Castletown	Helensburgh	
Buckhaven	Coatbridge	Invergordon	**Spain**
Cairntoul	Coldstream	Kirkmichael	Alicante (8)
Callander	Coldingham	Lossiemouth	Badajoz (7)
Carstairs	Dalbeattie	Maxwelltown	Barcelona (9)
Dumbarton	Drumlithie	Musselburgh	Bilbao (6)
Edinburgh	East Linton	Port Glasgow	Cadiz (5)
Ferintosh	Galashiels	Port Patrick	Cartagena (9)
Fochabers	Glenrothes	Prestonpans	Cordoba (7)
Inchkeith	Johnshaven	Pultneytown	Ferrol (6)
Inveraray	Kilcreggan	Strathblane	Granada (7)
Inverness	Killenaule		Las Palmas (9)
Johnstone	Kilmainham	**12**	Pamplona (8)
Kildrummy	Kilmalcolm	Auchterarder	Salamanca
Kingussie	Kilmarnock	Ballachulish	San Sebastián
Kirkcaldy	Kilwinning	East Kilbride	(12)
Leadhills	Kincardine	Fort Augustus	Santander (9)
Lochgelly	Kingsbarns	Garelochhead	Santiago de
Lochinvar	Kirkmaiden	Innerleithen	Compostela
Lochnagar	Kirkoswald	Lawrencekirk	(20)
Lockerbie	Kirriemuir	North Berwick	Saragossa (9)
Logierait	Lennoxtown	Portmahomack	Seville (7)
Mauchline	Lesmahagow	Strathpeffer	Valencia (8)
Milngavie	Linlithgow	Tillicoultry	Vigo (4)
Peterhead	Livingston		Zaragoza (8)
Pitlochry	Milnathort	**13**	
Port Ellen	Motherwell	Auchtermuchty	**Sri Lanka**
Prestwick	Pittenweem	Castle Douglas	Galle (5)
Riccarton	Portobello	Cockburnspath	Kandy (5)
Rothiemay	Ronaldsay	Dalmellington	
St Andrews	Rutherglen	Inverkeithing	**Sudan**
St Fillans	Stonehaven	Inverkeithnie	Berber (6)
Saltcoats	Stonehouse	Kirkcudbright	Dongola (7)
Shieldaig	Stoneykirk	Kirkintilloch	Omdurman (8)
Slamannan	Strathaven	Newton Stewart	
Stewarton	Strathearn	Rothiemurchus	**Sweden**
Stranraer	Strathmore		Goteborg (8)
Strathdon	Tweedmouth	**South Africa**	Gothenburg (10)
Strontian	West Calder	Bloemfontein (12)	Helsingborg (11)
Tobermory	Wilsontown	Durban (6)	Malmö (5)

Uppsala (7)

Switzerland
Basel (5)
Basle (5)
Geneva (6)
Lausanne (8)
Lucerne (7)
Zurich (6)

Syria
Aleppo (6)
Palmyra (7)

Turkey
Erzerum (7)
Istanbul (8)
Izmir (5)
Smyrna (6)

Ukraine
Dnepropetrovsk
  (14)
Donetsk (7)
Kharkov (7)
Krivoi Rog (9)
Lemberg (7)
Lvov (4)
Odessa (6)
Sevastopol
  (10)
Yalta (5)

USA

4
Gary
Lima
Reno
Troy
York
Waco

5
Akron
Miami
Omaha
Salem
Selma
Tulsa

6
Albany
Austin

Bangor
Biloxi
Boston
Dallas
Dayton
Denver
El Paso
Fresno
Irvine
Mobile
Nassau
Newark
Peoria
St Paul
Topeka
Tucson

7
Anaheim
Atlanta
Boulder
Buffalo
Chicago
Concord
Detroit
Hampton
Houston
Jackson
Lincoln
Madison
Memphis
Modesto
New York
Oakland
Orlando
Phoenix
St Louis
San Jose
Seattle

8
Berkeley
Columbus
Honolulu
Las Vegas
New Haven
Palo Alto
Pasadena
Portland
Richmond
San Diego
Santa Ana
Stamford
Syracuse

9
Anchorage
Arlington
Baltimore
Cambridge
Cleveland
Des Moines
Fairbanks
Fort Worth
Galveston
Lexington
Long Beach
Manhattan
Milwaukee
Nashville
Princeton
Rochester
Tombstone

10
Baton Rouge
Birmingham
Charleston
Cincinnati
Harrisburg
Jersey City
Kansas City
Little Rock
Los Angeles
Louisville
Miami Beach
Montgomery
New Bedford
New Orleans
Pittsburgh
Providence
Sacramento
San Antonio

11
Albuquerque
Chattanooga
Grand Rapids
Minneapolis
Palm Springs
Springfield

12 *and over*
Atlantic City (12)
Colorado Springs
  (15)
Fort Lauderdale
  (14)
Indianapolis (12)

New Brunswick
  (12)
Niagara Falls
  (12)
Oklahoma City
  (12)
Philadelphia (12)
Salt Lake City
  (12)
San Francisco
  (12)
Santa Barbara
  (12)
Washington DC
  (12)

Uzbekistan
Samarkand (9)
Tashkent (8)

Vietnam
Danang (6)
Haiphong (8)
Hue (3)

Wales

4
Bala
Holt
Mold
Pyle
Rhyl

5
Chirk
Flint
Neath
Nevin
Tenby
Towyn

6
Amlwch
Bangor
Brecon
Builth
Conway
Ruabon
Ruthin

7
Carbury
Cardiff

Cwmbran	Lampeter	Llanberis	Porth Nigel
Denbigh	Llanelly	Llandudno	Presteigne
Maesteg	Llanrwst	New Radnor	
Newport	Pembroke	Pontypool	**11**
Newtown	Pwllheli	Porthcawl	Aberystwyth
St Asaph	Rhayader	Portmadoc	Abergavenny
Swansea	Skerries	Welshpool	Braich-y-Pwll
Wrexham	Skifness		Llantrisant
Barmouth	Talgarth	**10**	Machynlleth
	Tredegar	Cader Idris	Oystermouth
8	Tregaron	Caernarvon	
Aberavon		Carmarthen	**12**
Aberdare	**9**	Crickhowel	Llandilofawr
Abergele	Aberaeron	Ffestiniog	
Bridgend	Aberdovey	Llandovery	**13**
Cardigan	Aberffraw	Llanfyllin	Merthyr Tydfil
Dolgelly	Beaumaris	Llangadock	Haverfordwest
Hawarden	Carnarvon	Llangollen	
Holyhead	Criccieth	Llanidloes	**Zimbabwe**
Kidwelly	Festiniog	Montgomery	Bulawayo (8)
Knighton	Fishguard	Plinlimmon	

Continents

Africa (6)	Australasia (11)	Europe (6)	North America (12)
Asia (4)	Australia (9)	Antarctica (10)	South America (12)

Counties of the United Kingdom and Republic of Ireland

See also **Abbreviations**.
NB: also includes county names that are no longer officially used.

England	Devon (5)	Huntingdon (10)	Northampton-
Avon (4)	Dorset (6)	Huntingdonshire	shire (16)
Bedford (7)	Dorsetshire (11)	(15)	Northumberland
Bedfordshire (12)	Durham (6)	Isle of Wight (11)	(14)
Berkshire (9)	Devonshire (10)	Lancashire (10)	North Yorkshire
Buckingham (10)	East Sussex (10)	Leicester (9)	(14)
Buckinghamshire	Essex (5)	Leicestershire	Nottingham (10)
(15)	Gloucester (10)	(14)	Nottinghamshire
Cambridge (9)	Gloucestershire	Lincoln (7)	(15)
Cambridgeshire	(15)	Lincolnshire (12)	Oxford (6)
(14)	Hampshire (9)	London (6)	Oxfordshire (11)
Cheshire (8)	Hereford (8)	Merseyside (10)	Rutland (7)
Cleveland (9)	Herefordshire	Middlesex (9)	Rutlandshire
Cornwall (8)	(13)	Monmouth (8)	(12)
Cumberland (10)	Hertford (8)	Monmouthshire	Shropshire (10)
Cumbria (7)	Hertfordshire	(13)	Somerset (8)
Derby (5)	(13)	Norfolk (7)	Somersetshire
Derbyshire (10)	Humberside (10)	Northampton (11)	(13)

Counties of the United Kingdom and Republic of Ireland

South Yorkshire (14)
Stafford (8)
Staffordshire (13)
Suffolk (7)
Surrey (6)
Sussex (6)
Tyne and Wear (11)
Warwick (7)
Warwickshire (12)
West Midlands (12)
Westmorland (11)
West Sussex (10)
West Yorkshire (13)
Wiltshire (9)
Worcester (9)
Worcestershire (14)
Yorkshire (9)

Ireland (Republic of)
Carlow (6)
Cavan (5)
Clare (5)
Connaught (9)
Cork (4)
Donegal (7)
Dublin (6)
Galway (6)
Kerry (5)
Kildare (7)
Kilkenny (8)
King's County (11)
Laois (5)
Leitrim (7)
Leix (4)
Limerick (8)

Longford (8)
Louth (5)
Mayo (4)
Meath (5)
Monaghan (8)
Offaly (6)
Queen's County (12)
Roscommon (9)
Sligo (5)
Tipperary (9)
Waterford (9)
Westmeath (9)
Wexford (7)
Wicklow (8)

Northern Ireland
Antrim (6)
Armagh (6)
Down (4)
Fermanagh (9)
Londonderry (11)
Tyrone (6)

Scotland
Aberdeen (8)
Aberdeenshire (13)
Angus (5)
Argyll (6)
Argyllshire (11)
Ayr (3)
Ayrshire (8)
Banff (5)
Banffshire (10)
Berwick (7)
Berwickshire (12)
Bute (4)
Caithness (9)
Clackmannan (11)

Cromarty (8)
Dumfries (8)
Dumfriesshire (13)
Dunbarton (9)
Dunbartonshire (14)
East Lothian (11)
Edinburgh (9)
Elgin (5)
Fife (4)
Forfar (6)
Forfarshire (11)
Haddington (10)
Inverness (9)
Inverness-shire (14)
Kincardine (10)
Kinross (7)
Kircudbright (13)
Lanark (6)
Lanarkshire (11)
Linlithgow (10)
Midlothian (10)
Moray (5)
Nairn (5)
Orkney (6)
Peebles (7)
Perth (5)
Perthshire (10)
Renfrew (7)
Renfrewshire (12)
Ross (4)
Ross and Cromarty (15)
Roxburgh (8)
Selkirk (7)
Stirling (8)
Sutherland (10)
West Lothian (11)
Wigtown (7)
Wigtownshire (12)

Wales
Anglesey (8)
Brecon (6)
Brecknockshire (14)
Caernarvon (10)
Caenarvonshire (15)
Cardigan (8)
Cardiganshire (13)
Carmarthen (10)
Carmarthenshire (15)
Clwyd (5)
Denbigh (7)
Denbighshire (12)
Dyfed (5)
Flint (5)
Flintshire (10)
Glamorgan (9)
Glamorganshire (14)
Gwent (5)
Gwynedd (7)
Merioneth (9)
Merionethshire (14)
Mid Glamorgan (12)
Montgomery (10)
Montgomeryshire (15)
Pembroke (8)
Pembrokeshire (13)
Powys (5)
Radnor (6)
Radnorshire (11)
South Glamorgan (14)
West Glamorgan (13)

Countries

*: former countries, or former names of countries

2	Malta	Persia*	Holy See	Moldavia*
UK	Natal*	Poland	Hungary	Mongolia
	Nauru	Russia	Iceland	Pakistan
3	Nepal	Rwanda	Ireland	Paraguay
CIS	Niger	Serbia	Jamaica	Portugal
DDR*	Palau*	Sicily	Lebanon	Rhodesia*
GDR*	Qatar	Sweden	Lesotho	Roumania
UAE	Samoa	Taiwan	Liberia	St Helena
USA	Spain	Tobago	Livonia	Sardinia
	Sudan	Turkey	Macedon*	Scotland
4	Syria	Tuvalu	Moldova	Slovakia
Bali	Tchad	Uganda	Morocco	Slovenia
Chad	Tibet	Zambia	Myanmar	Sri Lanka
Cuba	Timor		Namibia	St Helena
Eire	Tonga	**7**	Nigeria	Suriname
Fiji	Wales	Albania	Prussia*	Tanzania
Guam	Yemen	Algeria	Romania	Tasmania
Iran	Zaire*	Andorra	Rumania	Thailand
Iraq		Antigua	St Kitts	Togoland*
Java	**6**	Armenia	St Lucia	Trinidad
Laos	Angola	Ashanti*	São Tomé	Zanzibar
Mali	Arabia*	Assyria *	Senegal	Zimbabwe
Nejd	Azores	Austria	Somalia	
Oman	Belize	Bahamas	Sumatra	**9**
Peru	Bhutan	(the)	Surinam	Abyssinia*
Siam*	Brazil	Bahrain	Tunisia	Argentina
Togo	Brunei	Bavaria*	Ukraine	Argentine
USSR*	Canada	Belarus	Uruguay	(the)
	Cathay*	Belgium	Vanuatu	Australia
5	Ceylon*	Bermuda	Vatican	Babylonia*
Belau	Cyprus	Bohemia*	Vietnam	Caledonia*
Benin	Epirus*	Bolivia		Costa Rica
Burma	Faroes	Britain	**8**	East Timor
Chile	France	Burkina	Barbados	Gibraltar
China	Gambia	Burundi	Botswana	Greenland
Congo	(the)	Comoros	Bulgaria	Guatemala
Egypt	Greece	Croatia	Burgundy*	Indonesia
Gabon	Guinea	Dahomey*	Byelarus	Irian Jaya
Ghana	Guyana	Denmark	Cambodia*	Kampuchea*
Haiti	Hawaii	Ecuador	Cameroon	Kirghizia*
India	Israel	England	Colombia	Lithuania
Italy	Jordan	Eritrea	Djibouti	Macedonia
Japan	Kuwait	Estonia	Dominica	Manchuria*
Kandy*	Latvia	Faeroes	Ethiopia	Mauritius
Kenya	Malawi	Finland	Honduras	New Guinea
Khmer*	Malaya*	Formosa*	Hong Kong	Nicaragua
Korea	Mexico	Georgia	Kiribati	Nyasaland*
Libya	Monaco	Germany	Malaysia	Palestine
Lydia*	Norway	Grenada	Maldives	San Marino
Macao	Panama	Holland	Malvinas	Singapore

Swaziland
Transvaal*
Venezuela
West Irian

10
Azerbaijan
Bangladesh
Basutoland*
Belorussia
El Salvador
Ivory Coast
Kazakhstan
Kyrgyzstan
Luxembourg
Madagascar
Martinique
Mauretania*
Mauritania
Micronesia
Montenegro
Montserrat
Mozambique
New Zealand
North Korea
Seychelles
Somaliland
South Korea
South Yemen*
Tajikistan
Tanganyika*
Upper Volta*
Uzbekistan
Yugoslavia*

11
Afghanistan
Burkina Faso
Byelorussia
Cook Islands
Côte d'Ivoire

Dutch Guiana*
East Germany*
Mesopotamia*
Netherlands (the)
New Hebrides
Philippines
Saudi Arabia
Sierra Leone
South Africa
Soviet Union*
Switzerland
Transjordan*
Vatican City
West Germany*
White Russia*

12
Bechuanaland*
Belgian Congo*
Cocos Islands
Faero Islands
Faroe Islands
French Guiana
Great Britain
Guinea-Bissau
North Vietnam*
South Vietnam*
Tadzhikistan
Turkmenistan
United States

13
Afars and Issas*
British Guiana*
Cayman Islands*
Khmer Republic*
Liechtenstein
Norfolk Island
Trucial States*
United Kingdom
Virgin Islands

14
Czechoslovakia*
Gilbert Islands*
Irish Free State*
Mariana Islands
Papua New Guinea
Pitcairn Island
Slovak Republic
Society Islands
Solomon Islands

15
British Honduras*
Caroline Islands
Christmas Island
Falkland Islands
French Indo-China* (15)
Northern Ireland
Orange Free State*
Southwest Africa*
St Kitts and Nevis

16 and over
Antigua and Barbuda (17)
Bosnia and Herzegovina (20)
Cape Verde Islands (16)
Central African Republic (22)
Democratic Republic of the Congo (28)
Dominican Republic (17)
Equatorial Guinea (16)
Malagasy Republic* (16)
Marshall Islands (15)
Republic of the Congo (the) (18)
St Vincent and the Grenadines (25)
São Tomé and Principe (18)
Trinidad and Tobago (17)
Turks and Caicos Islands (21)
United Arab Emirates (18)
Vatican City State (16)

Deserts

NB: letter count does not include the word *desert*.

4	Sinai	Syrian	Simpson	**9**	**11**
Gobi	Sturt		Sonoran	Dasht-e-Lut	Death Valley
Thar		**7**			
	6	Alashan	**8**	**10**	**13**
5	Gibson	An Nafud	Colorado	Great Sandy	Great Victoria
Namib	Mojave	Arabian	Kalahari	Rub al-Khali	
Negev	Nubian	Atacama	Kyzyl Kum	Takla Makan	
Ordos	Sahara	Kara Kum			

Districts, Cantons, Provinces, Regions, Dependent States, etc.

Afghanistan
Herat (5)
Kandahar (8)

Africa
East Africa (10)
North Africa
 (11)
Sahara (6)
Sahel (5)
Senegambia
 (10)
Slave Coast (10)
Soudan (6)
Southern Africa
 (14)
West Africa (10)

Argentina
Entre Rios (9)
Jujuy (5)
Mendoza (7)
Salta (5)
Santa Fe (7)
Tucuman (7)

Asia
Asia Minor (9)
Bashan (6)
Bokhara (7)
Caucasia (8)
Hadramaut (9)
Hindustan (9)
Indo-China (9)
Judaea (6)
Judea (5)
Khiva (5)
Kurdistan (9)
Levant (6)
Palestine (9)
Samaria (7)
Tartary (7)
Tongking (8)
Turkestan (9)
Turkistan (9)
Turkmenia (9)

Australia
New South Wales
 (13)

Queensland (10)
South Australia
 (14)
Victoria (8)
Western
 Australia (16)
Wimmeria (8)

Austria
Burgenland
 (10)
Carinthia (9)
Carniola (8)
Lower Austria
 (12)
Salzburg (8)
Styria (6)
Tyrol (5)
Upper Austria
 (12)
Vorarlberg (10)

Azerbaijan
Caucasia (8)
Nagorno-
 Karabakh (15)

Bangladesh
Sylhet (6)

Belgium
Antwerp (7)
Brabant (7)
Eupen (5)
Flanders (8)
Hainault (8)
Liège (5)
Namur (5)
Wallonia (8)

Bolivia
La Paz (5)
Oruro (5)
Potosi (6)

Brazil
Alagoas (7)
Amazonas (8)
Bahia (5)
Ceara (5)

Espirito Santo
 (13)
Goias (5)
Maranhão (8)
Matto Grosso (11)
Minas Gerais (11)
Para (4)
Parahiba (8)
Paraiba (7)
Parana (6)
Pernambuco
 (10)
Rio de Janeiro
 (12)
Rio Grande do
 Sul (14)
Santa Catarina
 (13)
Santa Catharina
 (14)
Sergipe (7)

Burma
Mergui (6)
Shan State (9)
Tavoy (5)
Tenasserim (10)
Thayetmyo (9)

Canada
Alberta (7)
Baffinland (10)
British Columbia
 (15)
Labrador (8)
Manitoba (8)
New Brunswick
 (12)
Newfoundland
 (12)
Nova Scotia (10)
Ontario (7)
Quebec (6)
Saskatchewan
 (12)
Yukon (5)

Caribbean
West Indies (the)
 (10)

**Central
 America**
Latin America
 (12)

Chile
Iquique (7)
Linares (7)
Tacna (5)
Tarapaca (8)
Valdivia (8)
Valparaiso (10)

China
Anhwei (6)
Chekiang (8)
Fukien (6)
Heilungkiang
 (12)
Honan (5)
Hong Kong (8)
Hopeh (5)
Hunan (5)
Hupeh (5)
Inner Mongolia
 (13)
Kansu (5)
Kiangsi (6)
Kirin (5)
Kwangtung (9)
Kweichow (8)
Liaoning (8)
Macao (5)
Shansi (6)
Shantung (8)
Shensi (6)
Sinkiang (8)
Szechwan (8)
Tibet (5)
Tsinghai (8)
Yunnan (6)

Croatia
Dalmatia (8)
Slavonia (8)

Czech Republic
Bohemia (7)
Moravia (7)
Sudetenland (11)

Denmark
Jutland (7)
Viborg (6)

Egypt
Dakahlieh (9)
Fayum (5)

England
East Anglia (10)
Mercia (6)
New Forest (the)
(9)
Northumbria (11)
Potteries (the) (9)
Romney Marshes
(13)
Weald (the) (5)
Wessex (6)

Ethiopia
Tigre (5)

Europe
Banat (5)
British Isles (12)
Bukovina (8)
Gibraltar (9)
Lapland (7)
Ruthenia (8)

Finland
Tavastehus (10)

France
Ain (3)
Aisne (5)
Allier (6)
Alpes-Maritimes
(14)
Alsace-Lorraine
(14)
Alsace (6)
Anjou (5)
Aquitaine (9)
Ardennes (8)
Ariège (6)
Artois (6)
Aube (4)
Aude (4)
Aveyron (7)
Basque Country
(13)
Bearn (5)

Berry (5)
Bourbonnais (11)
Brittany (8)
Burgundy (8)
Calvados (8)
Champagne (9)
Charente (8)
Cher (4)
Correze (7)
Côte-d'Or (7)
Côtes-du-Nord
(11)
Creuse (6)
Dauphine (8)
Dordogne (8)
Doubs (5)
Drome (5)
Eure (4)
Eure-et-Loir (10)
Franche-Comte
(11)
Gard (4)
Gascony (7)
Gers (4)
Guienne (7)
Haute-Garonne
(12)
Haute-Loire (10)
Haute-Marne (10)
Haute-Saône (10)
Hautes-Alpes (11)
Haute-Savoie (11)
Hautes-Pyrenees
(Fr.) (14)
Haute-Vienne
(11)
Haut Rhin (8)
Herault (7)
Ile-de-France (11)
Ile-et-Vilaine (12)
Indre (5)
Indre-et-Loire
(12)
Isère (5)
Jura (4)
Landes (6)
Languedoc (9)
Limousin (8)
Loire (5)
Loire-Atlantique
(15)
Loiret (6)
Loir-et-Cher (10)
Lorraine (8)

Lot (3)
Lot-et-Garonne
(12)
Lozère (6)
Lyonnais (8)
Maine (5)
Manche (6)
Marne (5)
Mayenne (7)
Meuse (5)
Morbihan (8)
Nièvre (6)
Nivernais (9)
Nord (4)
Normandy (8)
Oise (4)
Orléans (7)
Orne (4)
Pas de Calais (11)
Picardy (7)
Poitou (6)
Provence (8)
Rhône (5)
Riviera (the) (7)
Roussillon (10)
Sarthe (6)
Seine (6)
Seine-et-Marne
(12)
Somme (5)
Tarn (4)
Tarn-et-Garonne
(13)
Var (3)
Vaucluse (8)
Vendée (6)
Vienne (6)
Vosges (6)
Yonne (5)

Georgia
Caucasia (8)

Germany
Baden (5)
Baden-
Württemberg
(16)
Bavaria (7)
Brandenburg (11)
Eifel (5)
Franconia (9)
Hannover (8)
Hanover (7)

Hesse (5)
Hesse-Nassau
(11)
Hohenzollern (12)
Holstein (8)
Lower Saxony
(11)
Mecklenburg (11)
North Rhine-
Westphalia (20)
Oldenburg (9)
Palatinate (10)
Pomerania (9)
Prussia (7)
Rhenish Prussia
(14)
Rhineland (9)
Saar (4)
Saarland (8)
Saxe-Altenberg
(13)
Saxe-Coburg-
Gotha (15)
Saxe-Meiningen
(13)
Saxony (6)
Schwarzwald (11)
Schaumberg-
Lippe (15)
Schleswig (9)
Schleswig-
Holstein (17)
Swabia (6)
Thuringia (9)
Waldeck (7)
Westphalia (10)
Württemberg (11)

Greece
Epirus (6)
Macedonia (9)
Morea (5)
Peloponnese (11)
Salonika (8)
Thessaly (8)
Thrace (6)

Hungary
Oedenburg (9)
Tokay (5)

India
Andhra Pradesh
(13)

Assam (5)
Bengal (6)
Bihar (5)
Bihar and Orissa
  (14)
Bombay (6)
Cachar (6)
Diu (3)
Goa (3)
Gujarat (7)
Haryana (7)
Himachal
  Pradesh (15)
Johore (6)
Karnataka (9)
Kashmir (7)
Kerala (6)
Ladakh (6)
Madhya Pradesh
  (13)
Madras (6)
Maharashtra (11)
Manipur (7)
Meghalaya (9)
Mysore (6)
Nagaland (8)
Orissa (6)
Oudh (4)
Punjab (6)
Rajasthan (9)
Rajputana (9)
Rohilkhand (9)
Simla (5)
Surat (5)
Tamil Nadu (9)
Tanjore (7)
Terai (5)
Tripura (7)
United Provinces
  (15)
Uttar Pradesh
  (12)
West Bengal (10)

Indonesia
Achin (5)

Iran
Fars (4)
Ghilan (6)
Kaspan (6)
Kerman (6)
Kermanshah (10)
Khuzestan (9)

Korassan (8)
Kum (3)
Luristan (8)
Mazandaran (10)
Teheran (7)
Tehran (6)

**Ireland
  (Republic of)**
Connaught (9)
Leinster (8)
Munster (7)
Pale (the) (4)
Ulster (6)

Israel
Galilee (7)
Gaza (4)

Italy
Abruzzi (7)
Alto Adige (9)
Apulia (6)
Bari (4)
Basilicata (10)
Calabria (8)
Campania (8)
Emilia (6)
Emilia-Romagna
  (13)
Faenza (6)
Ferrara (7)
Florence (8)
Genoa (5)
Girgenti (8)
Latium (6)
Lecce (5)
Leghorn (7)
Liguria (7)
Lombardy (8)
Lucca (5)
Macerata (8)
Mantua (6)
Marches (7)
Milan (5)
Modena (6)
Molise (6)
Novara (6)
Padua (5)
Parma (5)
Pavia (5)
Perugia (7)
Piacenza (8)
Piedmont (8)

Pisa (4)
Potenza (7)
Ravenna (7)
Riviera (the) (7)
Rome (4)
Sardinia (8)
Savoy (5)
Sicily (6)
Sondrio (7)
Syracuse (8)
Trentino (8)
Tuscany (7)
Umbria (6)
Valle d'Aosta (11)
Venetia (8)
Veneto (6)

Malaysia
Johor (5)
Johore (6)
Malacca (7)
Pahang (6)
Perak (5)
Sabah (5)
Sarawak (7)
Selangor (8)

Mexico
Alisco (6)
Baja California
  (14)
Campeche (8)
Chiapas (7)
Chihuahua (9)
Coahuila (8)
Durango (7)
Guanajuato (10)
Guerrero (8)
Hidalgo (7)
Lower California
  (15)
Jalisco (7)
Michoacan (9)
Nuevo Leon (9)
Oaxaca (6)
Ojaca (5)
Queretaro (9)
Quintana Roo
  (11)
San Luis Potosi
  (13)
Simaloa (7)
Sonora (6)
Tabasco (7)

Tamaulipas
  (10)
Tepic (5)
Tiaxcala (8)
Vera Cruz (8)
Yucatan (7)
Zacatecas (9)

Moldova
Bessarabia (10)

Morocco
Ceuta (5)
Melilla (7)
Sus (3)
Tafilet (7)

Namibia
Damaraland
  (10)
Namaqualand
  (11)

Netherlands
Drenthe (7)
Friesland (9)
Gelderland (10)
Groningen (9)
Guelderland
  (11)
Holland (7)
Limburg (7)
North Brabant
  (12)
North Holland
  (12)
Overijssel (10)
Overyssel (9)
South Holland
  (12)
Utrecht (7)
Zealand (7)
Zeeland (7)

New Zealand
Auckland (8)
Canterbury
  (10)
Hawke Bay (8)
Nelson (6)
Otago (5)
Southland (9)
Taranaki (8)
Westland (8)

Nigeria
Benue-Plateau
  (12)
East-Central
  (11)
Kano (4)
Kwara (5)
Lagos (5)
Mid-Western (10)
North-Central
  (12)
North-Eastern
  (12)
North-Western
  (12)
Rivers (6)
Sokoto (6)
South-Eastern
  (12)
Western (7)

Northern
Ireland
Ulster (6)

Norway
Bergen (6)
Christiansand
  (13)
Finmark (7)
Hamar (5)
Tromsø (6)
Trondheim (9)

Pacific
Melanesia (9)
Micronesia (10)
Polynesia (9)

Pakistan
Baluchistan (11)
Kashmir (11)
North-West
  Frontier (17)
Punjab (6)
Rawalpindi (10)
Sind (4)
Waziristan (10)

Peru
Ica (3)
Huancavelica (12)
Huanuco (7)
Lambayeque (10)

Lima (4)

Philippines
Iloilo (6)

Poland
Galicia (7)
Kielce (6)
Lublin (6)
Pomerania (9)
Posen (5)
Silesia (7)
West Prussia (11)

Portugal
Alentejo (8)
Algarve (7)
Beira (5)
Entre-Douro-e-
  Minho (16)
Estremadura (11)
Loreto (6)
Trás-os-Montes
  (12)
Villareal (9)
Vizeu (5)

Romania
Moldavia (8)
Transylvania (12)
Wallachia (9)

Russia
Astrakhan (9)
Caucasia (8)
Kamchatka (9)
Karelia (7)
Siberia (7)
Tomsk (5)
Transbaikalia
  (13)

Saudi Arabia
Hedjaz (6)
Hejaz (5)

Scotland
Highlands (9)
Lothian (7)
Lowlands (5)

Serbia
Kosovo (6)
Montenegro (10)

South Africa
Great Karroo (11)
Griqualand West
  (14)
Griqualand (10)
Karroo (6)
Marico (6)
Namaqualand
  (11)
Orange Free
  State (15)
Transvaal (9)
Witwatersrand
  (13)

South America
Guiana (6)
Latin America
  (12)
Pampas (6)
Patagonia (9)

Spain
Alicante (8)
Almeria (7)
Andalusia (9)
Aragon (6)
Asturias (8)
Basque Country
  (13)
Basque Provinces
  (15)
Biscay (6)
Caceres (7)
Cadiz (5)
Canary Islands
  (13)
Castile (7)
Catalonia (9)
Ceuta (5)
Estremadura (11)
Galicia (7)
Gerona (6)
Granada (7)
Guadalajara (11)
Guipuzcoa (9)
Huelva (6)
Huesca (6)
Jaen (4)
Leon (4)
Lerida (6)
Logroño (7)
Lugo (4)
Malaga (6)

Melilla (7)
Murcia (6)
Navarre (7)
New Castile (10)
Old Castile (10)
Orense (6)
Oviedo (6)
Palencia (8)
Pontevedra (10)
Salamanca (9)
Saragossa (9)
Segovia (7)
Seville (7)
Tarragona (9)
Toledo (6)
Valencia (8)
Valladolid (10)
Zamora (6)

Sudan
Darfur (6)
Kordofan (8)
Nubia (5)
Sennaar (7)

Sweden
Gothland (8)
Linkoping (9)
Norrland (8)
Scania (6)
Upsala (6)

Switzerland
Aargau (6)
Appenzell (9)
Basel (5)
Basle (5)
Bern (4)
Berne (5)
Fribourg (8)
Geneva (6)
Glarus (6)
Grisons (7)
Lucerne (7)
Neuchatel (9)
Oberland (8)
St Gall (6)
Schaffhausen (12)
Schwyz (6)
Thurgau (7)
Ticino (6)
Unterwalden (11)
Uri (3)
Valais (6)

Vaud (4)
Zug (3)
Zurich (6)

Turkey
Adana (5)
Adrianople (10)
Anatolia (8)
Ferghana (8)
Roumelia (8)
Sivas (5)
Trebizond (9)

Ukraine
Bessarabia (10)
Crimea (6)

USA
Alabama (7)
Alaska (6)
Arizona (7)
Arkansas (8)
California (10)
Colorado (8)

Connecticut (11)
Delaware (8)
District of Columbia (18)
Florida (7)
Georgia (7)
Hawaii (6)
Idaho (5)
Illinois (8)
Indiana (7)
Iowa (4)
Kansas (6)
Kentucky (8)
Louisiana (9)
Maine (5)
Maryland (8)
Massachusetts (13)
Michigan (8)
Minnesota (9)
Mississippi (11)
Missouri (8)
Montana (7)
Nebraska (8)
Nevada (6)
New Hampshire (12)

New Jersey (9)
New Mexico (9)
New York (7)
North Carolina (13)
North Dakota (11)
Ohio (4)
Oklahoma (8)
Oregon (6)
Pennsylvania (12)
Rhode Island (11)
South Carolina (13)
South Dakota (11)
Tennessee (9)
Texas (5)
Utah (4)
Vermont (7)
Virginia (8)
Washington (10)
West Virginia (12)
Wisconsin (9)
Wyoming (7)

Wales
Rhondda Valley (13)

Environment and Conservation

3
CFC
GMO

4
dump
haze
smog

5
biome
bloom
green
ozone
reuse
toxic

6
dioxin
energy
litter
run-off
sprawl

7
aerosol
biomass

cleanup
ecology
extinct
habitat
land use
logging
organic
recycle
species
wetland

8
acid rain
effluent
emission
landfill
oil spill
toxicity
wildlife
wind farm

9
biosphere
carbon tax
ecologist
ecosphere
ecosystem

greenwash
grey water
low-impact
old growth
ozone hole
pollutant
pollution
recycling
renewable
windpower

10
adsorption
air quality
atmosphere
biodegrade
endangered
fossil fuel
management
ozone layer
rainforest
recyclable
threatened
wave energy

11
contaminant

degradation
development
extinction
landfill tax
overfishing
over-grazing
particulate
solar energy
strip mining
sustainable
wind turbine

12
biodiversity
tidal barrage
urbanization
virgin forest
water quality
zero emission

13
ancient forest
biodegradable
biotechnology
carbon dioxide
climate change
contamination

environmental
global warming
greenhouse gas
nature reserve
sustainability
waste disposal

14
brownfield site
greenfield site
light pollution
noise pollution

15 and over
alternative fuel
(15)
desertification (15)
emissions trading
(16)
energy-efficient
(15)
environment
friendly (19)
genetic
engineering (18)
greenhouse effect
(16)

Geographical Terms

3
alp
bay
ben
bog
cay
col
cwm
dam
fen
key
lea
map
pap
ria
sea
tor
voe

4
aber
adit
arch
arid
bank
beck
bill
burn
cape
cave
city
cone
cove
crag
croy
dale
dell
dike
dune
dyke
east
eyot
ford
glen
gulf
hill
holm
holt
inch
isle
lake
land

lane
loch
lock
mere
mesa
moor
mull
naze
ness
pass
peak
pole
pond
port
race
reef
rill
road
rock
spit
spur
tarn
town
tump
vale
wadi
weir
west
wold
wood
wynd
zone

5
abyss
atlas
atoll
basin
bayou
beach
bight
bluff
broad
brook
butte
cairn
canal
chasm
cliff
coast
combe
copse

creek
crest
delta
downs
drift
duchy
esker
fault
field
fiord
firth
fjord
fleet
glade
globe
gorge
grove
heath
hurst
inlet
islet
knoll
lande
llano
lough
marsh
monte
mound
mount
mouth
north
oasis
ocean
orient
plain
point
polar
range
ridge
river
sands
scale
scarp
shelf
shire
shoal
shore
sound
south
stack
state
swamp

sward
taiga
veldt
weald

6
alpine
arctic
arroyo
bourne
canton
canyon
cirque
clough
common
corrie
county
crater
defile
desert
dingle
divide
domain
forest
geyser
hamlet
inland
island
jungle
lagoon
maidan
meadow
morass
nullah
pampas
parish
polder
rapids
ravine
region
runnel
seaway
sierra
skerry
spinny
steppe
strait
strath
stream
street
summit
tropic

tundra
upland
valley
warren

7
bogland
caldera
channel
compass
contour
country
current
cutting
deltaic
deposit
eastern
equator
erosion
estuary
glacial
glacier
habitat
harbour
highway
hillock
hilltop
hummock
iceberg
ice-floe
isthmus
lakelet
lowland
montane
new town
oceanic
oriental
plateau
prairie
rivulet
savanna
seaport
seaside
straits
thicket
torrent
tropics
village
volcano
western

8
affluent
alluvial
blowhole
brooklet
cataract
crevasse
district
downland
easterly
eastward
environs
foreland
frontier
headland
highland
hillside
interior
isthmian
landmark
land mass
landslip
latitude
littoral
lowlands
mainland
meridian
moorland
mountain
neap tide
northern
occident
quagmire
republic
salt lake
seaboard
sea level
seashore
snowline
southern
sub-polar
tropical
volcanic
westerly
westward
woodland

9
antarctic
antipodal
antipodes
avalanche

bench mark	tributary	spring tide	magnetic pole
coastline	true north	tidal creek	northeastern
continent	waterfall	topography	northwestern
coral reef	watershed	torrid zone	principality
foothills		water table	protectorate
grid north	**10**	wilderness	southeastern
heathland	confluence		southwestern
highlands	coordinate	**11**	
landslide	county town	aggradation	**13**
longitude	demography	archipelago	magnetic north
marshland	equatorial	cartography	Mediterranean
northeast	escarpment	continental	northeasterly
northerly	frigid zone	conurbation	northeastward
northward	geographer	coral island	northwesterly
northwest	glaciation	countryside	northwestward
peninsula	Gulf Stream	demographic	southeasterly
precipice	hemisphere	mountainous	southeastward
salt marsh	landlocked	polar circle	southwesterly
sandbanks	market town	polar region	southwestward
shoreline	occidental	river course	temperate zone
southeast	peninsular	subtropical	
southerly	plantation	tidal waters	**14** *and over*
southward	population	watercourse	continental drift (16)
southwest	projection		irrigation canal (15)
streamlet	promontory	**12**	plate tectonics (14)
sub-alpine	quicksands	artesian well	Tropic of Cancer (14)
tableland	rainforest	contour lines	Tropic of Capricorn (17)

Islands

NB: letter counts do not include the words *island, archipelago*, etc.
Arch.= Archipelago. I. = Island; Is. = Islands; (v.) = volcanic

Adriatic Sea
Brazza (6)
Bua (3)
Curzola (7)
Isola Grossa (11)
Lesina (6)
Lissa (5)

Aegean Sea
Euboea (6)
Imbros (6)
Lemnos (6)
Lesbos (6)
Limmos (6)

Africa
Bissagos Is. (8)
Comoros (7)
Corisco (7)
Fernando Po (10)

Ichaboe (7)
Johanna (7)
Madagascar (10)
Mayotte (7)
Nossi Be (v.) (7)
Pemba (5)
Perim (5)
St Marie (7)
St Thomas (8)
São Tomé (7)
Sherbro (7)
Zanzibar (8)

Antarctic
Balleny Is. (7)

Arabian Sea
Bahrain (7)
Kuria Muria Is.
  (10)

Laccadives (19)
Socotra (7)

Arctic
Diomede Is. (7)
Disco (5)
Disko (5)
Greenland (9)
Jan Mayen (8)
Liakhov Is. (7)
Mageroe (7)
Melville Land
  (11)
New Siberia (10)
North Devon (10)
North Somerset
  (13)
Novaya Zemlya
  (12)
Nova Zembla (10)

Parry Is. (5)
Spitsbergen (11)
West Spitsbergen
  (15)

Asia
Philippine Is. (10)
Philippines (11)
Singapore (9)
Sri Lanka (8)

Atlantic
Ascension (9)
Azores (6)
Banana Is. (6)
Bermuda (7)
Bermudas (Is.)
  (8)
Bissao (6)
Canaries (8)

Canary Is. (6)
Cape Verde Is. (9)
Corvo (5)
Desertas (8)
Faeroes (7)
Falkland Is. (8)
Falklands (9)
Faroes (6)
Fayal (5)
Ferro (5)
Flores (6)
Gomera (6)
Goree (5)
Gran Canaria (11)
Iceland (v.) (7)
Inaccessible I. (12)
Lanzarote (9)
Madeira (7)
Malvinas (8)
Rockall (7)
St Helena (8)
St Michael (9)
St Nicolas (9)
South Georgia (12
South Shetlands (14)
Tenerife (8)
Tristan da Cunha (14)
Watling I. (13)
West Indies (10)

Australia
Alban (5)
Buccaneer Arch. (9)
Cape Barren I. (10)
Christmas I. (9)
Dampier Is. (7)
D'Entrecastreaux Is. (15)
Dirk Hartog (10)
Flinders (8)
Furneaux Is. (8)
Kangaroo Is. (8)
Lord Howe Is. (8)
Melville I. (8)
Norfolk I. (7)

Tasmania (8)
Thursday I. (8)
Wellesley Is. (9)

Baltic
Aland Is. (5)
Bornholm (8)
Falster (7)
Faro (4)
Fehmeru (7)
Gotland (7)
Oesel (5)

Canada
Anticosti (9)
Baffin I. (6)
Cape Breton I. (10)
Ellesmere (9)
Fortune Bay I. (10)
Gomera (6)
Magdalen Is. (8)
Miquelon (8)
Newfoundland (12)
Prince Albert (12)
Prince Edward I. (12)
Queen Charlotte I. (14)
Sable I. (5)
Southampton (11)
Thousand Is. (8)
Vancouver (9)
Victoria (8)

Central America
Bay Is. (3)

Channel Islands
Alderney (8)
Herm (4)
Guernsey (8)
Jersey (6)
Jethou (6)
Sark (4)

Chile
Tierra del Fuego (14)

China
Amoy (4)
Chusan (6)
Hainan (6)
Hong Kong (8)
Loo Choo Is. (7)
Matsu (5)
Quemoy (6)
Taiwan (6)

Denmark
Funen (5)
Laaland (7)
Langeland (9)
Moen (4)
Samsoe (6)

England
Channel Is. (7)
Dogs, I. of (4)
Farn Is. (4)
Farne Is. (5)
Hayling I. (7)
Holy I. (4)
Lindisfarne (11)
Lundy I. (5)
Man, I. of (3)
Portland, I. of (8)
Portsea I. (7)
Purbeck, I. of (7)
St Agnes (7)
Scillies (8)
Scilly, Is. of (6)
Sheppey, I. of (7)
Thanet, I. of (6)
Wight, I. of (5)

Europe
British Isles (12)
Great Britain (12)
Ireland (7)

Fiji
Vanua Levu (9)
Viti-Levu (8)

Finland
Dago (4)

France
Belle Isle (9)
Crozet Is. (6)
Lerins Is. (6)
Miquelon (8)

Oleron (6)
Re (2)
Ushant (6)

Germany
Borkum (6)
Fohr (4)
Norderney (9)
Rugen (5)
Sylt (4)
Usedom (6)

Greece
Aegina (6)
Andros (6)
Calamo (6)
Ceos (4)
Cephalonia (10)
Chios (5)
Corfu (5)
Cos (3)
Crete (5)
Cyclades Is. (8)
Delos (5)
Dodecanese (10)
Hydra (5)
Idra (4)
Ionian Is. (6)
Ithaca (6)
Leros (5)
Lesbos (6)
Melos (5)
Milo (4)
Milos (5)
Mitylene (8)
Mykonos (7)
Naxos (5)
Negropont (9)
Patmos (6)
Paxo (4)
Rhodes (6)
Salamis (7)
Samos (5)
Santorini (v.) (9)
Scio (4)
Serifos (7)
Seriphos (8)
Skopelos (8)
Skyro (5)
Skyros (6)
Syra (4)
Thera (5)
Zante (5)
Zea (3)

India
Andaman Is. (7)
Andamans (8)
Amindivi Is. (8)
Elephanta (9)
Lakshadweep Is. (11)
Nicobar Is. (7)
Salsette (8)

Indian Ocean
Amirante Is. (8)
Christmas I. (9)
Cocos Is. (5)
Hatia (5)
Keeling Is. (7)
Maldives (8)
Mascarene Is. (9)
Mauritius (9)
Réunion (7)
Rodrigues (9)
Seychelles (10)
Sri Lanka (8)

Indonesia
Albay (5)
Amboina (7)
Anamba Is. (6)
Arru Is. (4)
Bali (4)
Banda (5)
Billiton (8)
Borneo (6)
Buru (4)
Calamianes (10)
Celebes (7)
Ceram (5)
Flores (6)
Gilolo (6)
Halmahera (9)
Java (4)
Kei Is. (3)
Krakatoa (v.) (8)
Molucca Is. (7)
Moluccas (8)
Negros (6)
Sangir Is. (6)
Spice Is. (5)
Sulu Is. (4)
Sumatra (7)
Sumbawa (7)
Sunda Is. (5)
Ternate (7)
Timor (5)

Vaigen (6)
Zebu (4)

Iran
Kishni (4)
Ormuz (5)

Ireland (Republic of)
Achill (6)
Aran (4)
Arranmore (9)
Bere I. (4)
Clare (5)
Clear (5)
Copeland Is. (8)
Dursey (6)
Eagle I. (5)
Great Blasket (12)
High I. (4)
Inishbofin (10)
Inishshark (10)
Inishturk (9)
Lambay (6)
Tory (4)
Valentia (8)

Isles of Scilly
Bryher (6)
Gugh (4)
St Agnes (7)
St Martin (8)
St Mary's (7)
Samson (6)
Tresco (6)

Italy
Capri (5)
Cherso (6)
Ischia (6)
Monte Cristo (11)
Sicily (6)

Japan
Hokkaido (8)
Hondo (5)
Honshu (6)
Iturup (6)
Kyushu (6)
Shikoka (7)
Yezo (4)

Korea
Cheja (5)

Dinding Is. (7)
Labuan (6)
Lombok (6)
Penang (5)
Prince of Wales I. (13)
Quelpart (5)
Sandlewood I. (10)
Tlmor (5)

Malaysia
Banca (5)

Mediterranean
Aegades Is. (7)
Aeolian Is. (v.) (7)
Balearic Is. (8)
Cabrera (7)
Candia (6)
Capraja (7)
Caprera (7)
Cerigo (6)
Cerigotto (9)
Corsica (7)
Cyprus (6)
Elba (4)
Formentera (10)
Gozo (4)
Ibiza (5)
Ivica (5)
Lampedusa (9)
Leucadia (8)
Lipari Is. (6)
Malta (5)
Majorca (7)
Mallorca (8)
Minorca (7)
Pantellaria (11)
Sardinia (8)
Scarpanto (9)
Sicily (6)
Stromboli (v.) (9)
Tenedos (7)

Netherlands
Ameland (7)
Beverland (9)
Dordrecht (9)
Frisian Is. (7)
Marken (6)
Rottum (6)
Texel (5)
Tholen (6)

Vlieland (8)
Voorn (5)
Walcheren (9)

New Zealand
Auckland Is. (8)
Bounty Is. (6)
Campbell (8)
North I. (5)
South I. (5)
Stewart I. (7)

Northern Ireland
Rathlin (7)

North Sea
Heligoland (10)

Norway
Lofoten Is. (7)
Tromso (6)

Pacific
Adi (3)
Admiralty Is. (9)
Aleutian Is. (8)
Banks (5)
Behring Is. (7)
Bismark Arch. (7)
Bonin Is. (5)
Bougainville (11)
Caroline Is. (8)
Chatham Is. (7)
Christmas I. (9)
Cook Is. (4)
Easter I. (6)
Ellice Is. (6)
Fanning (7)
Fiji Is. (4)
Friendlies (10)
Friendly Is. (8)
Galapagos Is. (v.) (9)
Gambier Is. (7)
Gilbert Is. (7)
Guadalcanal (11)
Guam (4)
Hall Is. (4)
Hawaii (6)
Isle of Pines (11)
Jaluit (6)
Juan Fernandez (13)

Kandava (7)
Kerguelen Land (13)
Kermadec Is. (8)
Kodiak (6)
Kurile Is. (6)
Ladrones (8)
Louisiade Arch. (9)
Low Arch. (3)
Loyalty Is. (7)
Malicolo (8)
Manihiki Is. (8)
Manitoulin Is. (10)
Marianne Is. (8)
Marquesas Is. (9)
Marshall Is. (8)
Melanesia (9)
Micronesia (10)
Molokai (7)
Nauru (5)
Navigators' I. (10)
New Britain (10)
New Hebrides (10)
New Zealand (10)
New Caledonia (12)
New Guinea (9)
Norfolk Island (13)
Oahu (4)
Oceania (7)
Otaheite (8)
Papua (5)
Pearl Is. (5)
Pelew Is. (5)
Phoenix Is. (7)
Pitcairn Is. (8)
Polynesia (9)
Pribilof Is. (8)
Pribylov Is. (8)
Raratonga (9)
Rat Is. (3)
Rotumah (7)
Samoa (5)
Sandwich Is. (8)
Savage I. (8)
Society Is. (7)
Solomon Is. (7)
Starbuck (8)
Tahiti (6)

Timor Laut Is. (9)
Tonga (5)
Tuamotu (7)
Tubugi Is. (6)
Yap (3)

Philippines
Leyte (5)
Luzon (5)
Mindanao (8)

Red Sea
Kamaran (7)
Massowa (7)

Russia
Kolonev (7)
Saghalien (9)
Sakhalin (8)

Scotland
Ailsa Craig (10)
Arran (5)
Barra (5)
Benbecula (9)
Bernera (7)
Berneray (8)
Burray (6)
Bute (4)
Canna (5)
Coll (4)
Colonsay (8)
Cumbrae (7)
Dabaz (5)
Eigg (4)
Eriskay (7)
Ewe (3)
Fair Isle (8)
Flannan Is. (7)
Foula (5)
Great Cumbrae (12)
Harris (6)
Hebrides (8)
Hoy (3)
Inchcolm (8)
Inchgarvie (10)
Inchkeith (9)
Iona (4)
Islay (5)
Isle of May (9)
Jura (4)
Lewis (5)

Little Cumbrae (13)
May, I. of (3)
Muck (4)
Mull, I. of (4)
North Uist (9)
Orkney Is. (6)
Orkneys (7)
Pomona (6)
Rhum (4)
Ronaldsay (9)
Rothesay (8)
Rum (3)
St Kilda (7)
Scarba (6)
Shetland Is. (8)
Shetlands (9)
Skerryvore (10)
Skye, I. of (4)
Soay (4)
South Uist (9)
Staffa (6)
Stroma (6)
Uist (4)
Ulva (4)
Unst (4)
Tiree (5)
Whalsay (7)
Yell (4)

South Africa
Inyak (5)
Robben I. (5)

South America
Chiloe (6)
Chincha Is. (7)
Lobos Is. (5)
Marajo (6)
Pinos (5)

Spain
Balearic Is. (8)
Balearics (9)
Canaries (8)
Canary Is. (6)
Gomera (6)
Gran Canaria (11)
Ibiza (5)
Lanzarote (9)
Majorca (7)
Mallorca (8)
Minorca (7)

Tenerife (8)

Turkey
Princes Is. (7)

USA
Ellis (5)
Hart's I. (5)
Long l. (4)
Manhattan (9)
Martha's Vineyard (15)
Nantucket (9)
Prince of Wales I. (13)
Rhode I. (5)
Roanoke (7)
Staten I. (6)
Thousand Is. (8)
Tortugas Is. (8)
Unalaska (8)

Wales
Anglesey (8)
Caldy (5)
Puffin I. (6)

West Indies
Abaco (5)
Antigua (7)
Antilles Is. (8)
Aruba (5)
Bahama Is. (6)
Bahamas (7)
Barbados (Is.) (8)
Caicos I. (6)
Caribbee Is. (8.)
Cayman Is. (6)
Cuba (4)
Curacao (7)
Desirade (8.)
Domingo (7)
Dominica (8)
Eleuthera (9)
Grenada (7)
Grenadines (10)
Guadeloupe (10)
Haiti (5)
Inagua (6)
Isle of Pines (11)
Jamaica (7)
Leeward Is. (7)

Margarita (8)	Puerto Rico (10)	St Kitts (7)	Tortuga (7)
Mariagalante	Saba (4)	St Lucia (7)	Trinidad (8)
(12)	St Bartholomew	St Martin (8)	Turks and Caicos
Martinique (10)	(13)	St Thomas (8)	Is. (14)
Montserrat (10)	St Christopher	St Vincent (9)	Virgin Is. (6)
Nevis (5)	(13)	Tobago (6)	Watling I. (7)
Porto Rico (9)	St John (6)	Tortola (7)	Windward Is. (8)

Lakes, Inland Lochs, Loughs and Sea Lochs

NB: letter counts do not include the words *lake, loch*, etc.
L. = Loch; Lou. = Lough

Afghanistan
Hamun (5)
Seistan (7)

Africa
Akamyara (8)
Albert (6)
Albert Edward
  Nyanza (18)
Albert Nyanza
  (12)
Bangweolo (9)
Cabora Bassa
  (11)
Chad (4)
Edward (6)
George (6)
Idi Amin (7)
Idi Amin Dada
  (11)
Kariba (6)
Kivu (4)
Kossu (5)
Leopold (7)
Malawi (6)
Mobuto Sésé Seko
  (14)
Moero (5)
Mweru (5)
Nyanza (6)
Nyasa (5)
Rudolf (6)
Shirwa (6)
Stefanie (8)
Tanganyika (10)
Tchad (5)
Tumba (5)
Victoria (8)
Victoria Nyanza
  (14)

Argentina
Argentino (9)
Viedma (6)

Armenia
Sevan (5)

Asia
Caspian Sea
  (10)
Dead Sea (7)
Issyk-Kul (8)
Khanka (6)

Australia
Austin (6)
Blanche (6)
Buloke (6)
Chowilla (8)
Cooroong (the)
  (8)
Eucumbene (9)
Eyre (4)
Frome (5)
Gairdner (8)
George (6)
Hindmarsh (9)
Humboldt (8)
Moore (5)
Torrens (7)
Tyrrell (7)

Bolivia
Roguaguado (10)

Burundi
Nyanza (6)

Cambodia
Sap (3)

Canada
Abitibi (7)
Athabaska (10)
Baker (5)
Camm (4)
Champlain (9)
Diefenbaker (11)
Dore (4)
Erie (4)
Etawney (7)
Garry (5)
Ghana (5)
Great Bear (9)
Great Slave (10)
Ha Ha (4)
Huron (5)
Kawarthi (8)
Kootenay (8)
Lachine (7)
Lake of the
  Woods (14)
Lesser Slave (10)
Mahood (6)
Manitoba (8)
Michikamau (10)
Minto (5)
Mistassini (10)
Muskoka (7)
Nipigon (7)
Nipissing (9)
Ontario (7)
Payne (5)
Playgreen (9)
Quesnal (7)
Rainy (5)
Reindeer (8)
Rideau (6)
Rosseau (7)
Simcoe (6)
St John (6)

Stuart (6)
Talka (5)
Timiskaming (11)
Winnipeg (8)
Winnipegosis (12)
Wollaston (9)

China
Dongting (8)
Koko Nor (7)
Tengri-Nor (9)
Tungting (8)

**Congo,
Democratic
Republic of the**
Mai-Ndombe

Egypt
Bitter Lakes (11)
Mareotis (8)
Menzaleh (8)
Nasser (6)

England
Buttermere (10)
Coniston Water
  (13)
Derwentwater
  (12)
Ennerdale (9)
Grasmere (8)
Hawes Water
  (10)
Rydal Water (10)
Serpentine (10)
Thirlmere (9)
Ullswater (9)
Virginia Water
  (13)

Wastwater (9)
Windermere (10)

Estonia
Peipus (6)

Ethiopia
Abaya (5)
Tana (4)
Tsano (5)

Europe
Scutari (7)

Finland
Enara (5)

Ghana
Volta (5)

Hungary
Balaton (7)

India
Chilka (6)
Hirakud (7)

Indonesia
Toba (4)

Iran
Urmia (5)

Ireland
(Republic of)
Allen, Lou. (5)
Derg, Lou. (4)
Ennell, Lou. (6)
Foyle, Lou. (5)
Key, Lou. (3)
Killarney, Lakes
  of (9)
Ree, Lou. (3)
Sheelin, Lou. (7)

Israel
Tiberias (8)
Sea of Galilee (12)

Italy
Como (4)
Garda (5)
Iseo (4)
Maggiore (8)

Perugia (7)
Trasimeno (9)

Japan
Biwa (4)

Kazakhstan
Aaköl (5)
Aral Sea (7)
Balqash (7)

Kyrgyzstan
Ysyk (4)

Mexico
Chapala (7)
Texcoco (7)
Tezcuco (7)
Xaltocan (8)
Xochimilco (10)

Netherlands
Ijssel Sea (9)
Ijsselmeer (10)
Yssel (5)
Zuider Zee (9)

New Zealand
Benmore (7)
Manipuri (8)
Oahu (4)
Rotomahana (10)
Tarawera (8)
Taupo (5)
Te Anau (6)
Wakatipu (8)
Wanaka (6)

Nicaragua
Nicaragua (9)

Northern
  Ireland
Belfast, Lou. (7)
Neagh, Lou. (5)

Norway
Mjøsa (5)

Peru
Titicaca (8)

Russia
Baikal (6)

Elton (5)
Ilmen (5)
Kuibyshev (9)
Ladoga (6)
Onega (5)
Peipus (6)
Rybinsk (7)

Scotland
Affric, L. (6)
Ard, L. (3)
Arkaig, L. (6)
Assynt, L. (6)
Awe, L. (3)
Broom, L. (Scot.)
Buie, L. (4)
Coille-Bharr, L.
  (11)
Earn, L. (4)
Eck, L. (3)
Ericht, L. (6)
Etive, L. (5)
Ewe, L. (3)
Fannich, L. (7)
Fyne, L. (4)
Gilp, L. (4)
Goil, L. (4)
Katrine, L. (7)
Leven L. (5)
Linnhe, L. (6)
Lochy, L. (5)
Lomond, L. (6)
Long, L. (4)
Loyal, L. (5)
Luichart, L. (8)
Maree, L. (5)
Morar, L. (5)
Moy, L. (3)
Ness, L. (4)
Quoich, L. (6)
Rannoch, L. (7)
Ryan, L. (4)
Seaforth, L. (8)
Shiel, L. (5)
Shin, L. (5)
Spey, L. (4)
Strathy, L. (7)
Sween, L. (5)
Tarbert, L. (7)
Tay, L. (3)
Tromlee, L. (7)
Torridon, L. (8)
Tummel, L. (6)
Urr, L. (3)

Voil, L. (4)

Sweden
Hjelmar (7)
Malar (5)
Wener (5)
Wetter (6)
Vänern (6)

Switzerland
Constance (9)
Geneva (6)
Lucerne (7)
Lugano (6)
Neuchatel (9)
Sempach (7)
Thun (4)
Zug (3)
Zurich (6)

Tibet
Tengri-Nor (9)

Turkey
Hirfanli (8)
Okhrida (7)
Tuz Gol (6)
Van (3)

Ukraine
Kakhovka (8)

USA
Bear (4)
Caillou (7)
Champlain (9)
Drummond (8)
Erie (4)
Grand Coulee
  (11)
Great Salt (9)
Honey (9)
Huron (5)
Indian (6)
Itasca (6)
La Crosse (8)
Lackawanna
  (10)
Lake of the
  Woods (14)
Mead (4)
Michigan (8)
Oneida (6)
Ontario (7)

Placid (6)
Pontchatrain (12)
Shasta (6)
Superior (8)
Utah (4)

Wenham (6)
Yellowstone (11)

Uzbekistan
Aral Sea (7)

Venezuela
Maracaibo (9)
Valencia (8)

Wales
Bala (4)
Vyrnwy (6)

Mountains, Mountain Ranges and Volcanoes

NB: letter counts do not include the words *hill, mountain, range*, etc.
H. = Hill; Hs. = Hills; M. = Mountain; Ms. = Mountains; Mt = Mount; Rge = Range;
(v.) = volcanic

Afghanistan
Koh-i-Baba (8)
Khyber Pass (10)

Africa
Atlas Ms. (7)
Kong Ms. (4)
Milanji, Mt (7)
Miltsin, Mt (7)
Livingstone Ms.
  (11)

Alps
Bernima, Mt (7)
Breithorn (9)
Cenis, Mt (5)
Grossglockner
  (13)
Matterhorn (the)
  (10)
Mont Blanc (9)
Monte Rosa (10)

Antarctic
Erebus, Mt (v.)
  (6)
Terror (v.) (6)

Argentina
Aconcagua, Mt
  (v.) (9)
Maipu (v.) (5)

Asia
Hermon, Mt (6)
Himalaya Rge (8)
Himalayas (9)
Hindu Kush (9)
Karakoram Rge
  (9)
Kuenluiv Ms. (8)

Pamirs (6)
Tian Ms. (4)
Tien Shan Ms. (8)
Yablonoi Ms. (8)

Australia
Barry Ms. (5)
Blue Ms. (5)
Bogong, Mt (6)
Darling, Mt (7)
Flinders Ms. (8)
Koseiusko, Mt (9)
Liverpool Rge (9)
Townsend, Mt (8)

Austria
Ortler Spitz (11)

Bolivia
Illampa, Mt (7)
Illimani, Mt (7)

Borneo
Kinabalu, Mt (v.)
  (8)

Canada
Hooker M. (6)
Laurentian Ms.
  (10)
Logan, Mt (5)
St Elias, Mt (7)
Wrangell, Mt (8)
Robson (6)

Chile
Descapezado (v.)
  (11)
Las Yeguas (v.)
  (9)
Licancaur, Mt (9)

Llullaillaco (v.)
  (12)
Tinguiririca (v.)
  (12)

China
Wenchow, Mt (7)

**Congo,
  Democratic
  Republic of
  the**
Ruwenzori Ms.
  (9)

Crete
Ida, Mt (3)

Ecuador
Chimborazo (v.)
  (10)
Cotopaxi (v.) (8)

Egypt
Sinai, Mt (5)

England
Blencathra (10)
Bow Fell (7)
Cheviot Hs. (7)
Cheviots (8)
Chiltern Hs. (8)
Chilterns (9)
Cotswold Hs. (8)
Cotswolds (9)
Cross Fell (9)
Downs (the) (5)
Edgehill (8)
Helvellyn (9)
Ingleborough (12)
Malvern Hs. (7)

Mendip Hs. (6)
Mendips (7)
Peak District
  (the) (12)
Pennine Chain
  (12)
Pennines (8)
Quantock Hs. (8)
Quantocks (9)
Scafell Pike (11)
Scafell Rge (7)
Scaw Fell Rge (8)
Skiddaw (7)
Wolds (the) (5)

Europe
Alps (4)
Balkan Ms. (6)
Balkans (7)
Carpathian Ms.
  (10)
Carpathians (11)
Caucasus Ms. (8)
Dinaric Alps (8)
Graian Alps (10)
Jura Ms. (4)
Pennine Alps (11)
Pyrenees (8)
Riesengebirge
  Ms. (13)
Sudetes Ms. (7)

France
Auvergne Ms. (8)
Faucilles Ms. (9)
Maritime Alps
  (12)
Vosges Ms. (6)

Georgia
Elbrus, Mt (6)

Kazbek, Mt (6)

Germany
Brocken, Mt (7)
Drachenfels, Mt
(10)
Erzgebirge (10)
Fichtelgebirge
(14)
Harz Ms. (4)
Swabian Alps
(11)
Taunus Ms. (6)
Zug M. (3)

Greece
Athos, Mt (5)
Olympus, Mt (7)
Ossa, Mt (4)
Parnassus, Mt (9)
Pelion, Ms. (6)
Pindus Ms. (6)
St Elias, Mt (7)

Hawaii
Hualalai (v.) (8)
Kilauea (v.) (7)
Mauna Kea (v.)
(8)
Mauna Loa (v.)
(8)

Himalayas
Altai Ms. (5)
Annapurna (9)
Dapsang, Mt (7)
Everest, Mt (7)
Dhaulagiri, Mt
(9)
Godwin Austen,
Mt (12)
Haramokh, Mt (8)
Jonsong, Mt (7)
K2 (2)
Kamet, Mt (5)
Kanchenjunga,
Mt (12)
Lhotse, Mt (6)
Makalu, Mt (6)
Nanga Parbat
(11)
Nanga-Devi (9)
Nuptse, Mt (6)
Rakaposhi (9)

Iceland
Hecla (v.) (7)
Skaptarjokull (v.)
(13)
Vatnajokull (11)

India
Abu, Mt (3)
Aravalli Ms. (8)
Dardistan, Mt (9)
Eastern Ghats
(12)
Jaintia Hs. (7)
Ghats (5)
Naga Hs. (4)
Nilgiri Hs. (7)
Nilgiris (8)
Rajmahal Hs. (8)
Siwalik Hs. (7)
Sulaiman Ms. (8)
Vindhya Ms. (7)
Western Ghats
(12)

Indonesia
Carstensz, Mt (9)
Djaja, Mt (5)
Jaya, Mt (4)
Krakatoa (v.) (8)

Iran
Demavend, Mt
8)
Elburz Ms. (6)
Kuhi-Taftan (v.)
(10)

**Ireland
(Republic of)**
Caha Ms. (4)
Carrantuohill, Mt
(13)
Galtee Ms. (6)
Knockmealdown,
Ms. (13)
Mamturk Ms. (7)

Isle of Man
Snaefell, Mt (8)

Israel
Carmel, Mt (6)
Olives, Mt of (6)
Tabor, Mt (6)

Italy
Apennines (9)
Averno, Mt (v.)
(6)
Maritime Alps
(12)
Monte Corno (10)
Solfatara (v.) (9)
Stelvio Pass (10)
Stromboli (v.) (9)
Vesuvius, Mt (8)
Vulcano (v.) (7)

Japan
Fuji, Mt (v.) (4)
Fujiyama (v.) (8)
Tomboro (v.) (8)

Jordan
Ebal, Mt (4)

Kenya
Kenya, Mt (5)

Kyrgyzstan
Lenin Peak (9)

Lebanon
Lebanon, Mt (7)

Lesotho
Mont Aux
Sources (14)

Malaysia
Ophir, Mt (5)

Mexico
Citlaltepec, Mt
(11)
Jorullo (v.) (7)
Orizaba (7)
Pico de Orizaba
(13)
Popocatepetl (v.)
(12)
Sierra Madre Ms.
(11)

New Zealand
Cook M. (4)
Hochstetter, Mt
(11)
Tarawera, Mt (8)

Tongariro (v.) (9)
Ruahine, Mt (7)

Nicaragua
Masaya (v.) (6)

North America
Cascade Ms. (7)
Rockies (7)
Rocky Ms. (5)

**Northern
Ireland**
Mourne Ms. (6)

Oman
Akhdar Ms (6)
Sham, Mt (4)

Pakistan
Khyber Pass (10)

**Papua New
Guinea**
Bougainville, Mt
(12)
Owen Stanley
Ms. (11)

Portugal
Estrelle, Mt (7)

Pyrenees
Maladetta, Mt (9)
Mont Perdu (9)
Pic du Midi (8)
Roncesvalles (v)
(12)

Russia
Elbrus, Mt (6)
Koshtan Tau (10)
Belukha (7)
Ural Ms. (4)
Urals (5)

Scotland
Ben Lawers (9)
Ben Lomond (9)
Ben Macdhui (10)
Ben More (7)
Ben Nevis (8)
Ben Venue (8)
Ben Wyvis (8)

Ben-y-Gloe (8)
Cairngorms (10)
Cairntoul (9)
Goatfell (8)
Grampians (9)
Lammermuir Hs. (10)
Lennox Hs. (6)
Moorfoot Hs. (8)
Ochil Hs. (5)
Pentland Hs. (8)
Schiehallion, Mt (12)
Sidlaw Hs. (6)

Sicily
Etna, Mt (v.) (4)

Skye
Cuillin Hs. (7

South Africa
Cedar Berge, Mt (10)
Drakensberg Ms. (11)
Drakenstein, Mt (11)
Kwathlamba, Mt (10)
Table M. (5)
Zoutpansberg, Mt (12)

South America
Andes (5)
Cazambe, Mt (7)
El Potra, Mt (7)
Darwin, Mt (6)
Itaculomi, Mt (9)
Juncal (v.) (6)

Overo (v.) (5)
Peteroa (v.) (7)
Quizapu (v.) (7)
Roraima, Mt (7)
Sahama (v.) (6)
San José (v.) (7)
Sangay (v.) (6)
Sorata (6)
Tolima (v.) (6)
Tupungato (v.) (9)

Spain
Cantabrian Ms. (10)
Mulhacen, Mt (8)
Sierra Morena (12)
Sierra Nevada (12)

Sri Lanka
Adam's Peak (9)
Pidurutalagala (14)

Switzerland
Bernese Alps (11)
Dent du Midi (10)
Diablerets, Mt (10)
Eiger (5)
Finsteraahorn, Mt (13)
Jungfrau, Mt (8)
Mönch (5)
Pilatus, Mt (7)
Rigi, Mt (4)
St Bernard (Pass) (13)
St Gothard, Mt (9)

Simplon, Mt (7)
Splugen Pass (11)
Schreckhorn (11)
Wetterhorn (the) (10)

Tajikistan
Communism (9)
Lenin Peak (9)

Tanzania
Kibo, Mt (4)
Kilimanjaro, Mt (11)

Tasmania
Nelson, Mt (6)
Ossa, Mt (4)
Wellington, Mt (10)

Trinidad
Aripo M. (5)

Turkey
Ararat, Mt (6)
Rhodope, Mt (7)

Uganda
Ruwenzori Ms. (9)

USA
Adams M. (5)
Adirondack Ms. (10)
Allegheny Ms. (9)
Appalachian Ms. (11)
Baker (v.) (5)
Big Horn Ms. (7)

Black Ms. (5)
Black Dome Peak (13)
Blue Ms. (4)
Blue Ridge Ms. (9)
Brown M. (5)
Catskill Ms. (8)
Elk Ms. (3)
Green Ms. (5)
Hayden, Mt (6)
Hoffman, Mt (7)
Hoosac Ms. (6)
Iron M. (4)
Katahdin, Mt (8)
Lafayette, Mt (9)
Lookout M. (7)
McKinley, Mt (8)
Pike's Peak (5)
Rainier, Mt (7)
Rushmore, Mt (8)
San Juan Ms. (7)
Vinta, Mt (5)
White Ms. (5)
Whitney, Mt (7)
Wind River Ms. (9)

Wales
Black Ms. (5)
Moel Fammau, Mt (10)
Pinlimmon, Mt (9)
Preseley Ms. (8)
Snowdon, Mt (8)

West Indies
La Sonfrière (v.) (11)
Pelée (v) (5)

Ports

Algeria
Algiers (7)
Oran (4)
Port Arzew (9)
Skidda (6)

Angola
Lobito (6)

Argentina
Buenos Aires (11)
La Plata (7)
Rosario (7)

Asia
Hong Kong (8)
Singapore (9)

Australia
Adelaide (8)
Brisbane (8)
Dampier (7)
Darwin (6)
Fremantle (9)
Geelong (7)
Melbourne (9)

Newcastle (9)
Port Adelaide (12)
Port Jackson (11)
Sydney (6)

Azerbaijan
Baku (4)

Bangladesh
Chittagong (10)

Belgium
Antwerp (7)
Ostend (6)
Zeebrugge (9)

Benin
Cotonou (7)
Porto Novo (9)

Brazil
Belem (5)
Para (4)
Pernambuco (10)
Recife (6)
Rio de Janeiro (12)
Santos (10)
Tobarao (7)

Bulgaria
Varna (5)

Burma
Akyab (5)
Moulmein (8)
Rangoon (7)
Sittwe (6)

Cameroon
Douala (6)

Canada
Churchill (9)
Esquimault (10)
Halifax (7)
Kitimat (7)
Montreal (8)
Owen Sound (9)
Three Rivers (11)
Vancouver (9)

Canary Islands
Las Palmas (9)

**Channel
  Islands**
St Helier (8)
St Peter Port (11)

Chile
Arica (5)
Coquimbo (8)

Valparaiso (10)

China
Amoy (4)
Chefoo (6)
Dairen (6)
Foochow (7)
Hankow (6)
Hong Kong (8)
Port Arthur (10)
Shanghai (8)
Swatow (6)
Tientsin (8)
Weihai (6)
Yingkow (7)

Colombia
Barranquilla (12)
Buenaventura
  (12)
Cartagena (9)

**Congo,
  Democratic
  Republic of
  the**
Mahdi (5)
Mbuji-Mayi (9)

Corsica
Ajaccio (7)
Bastia (6)

Croatia
Dubrovnik (9)
Pula (4)
Rijeka (6)
Split (5)

Cuba
Santiago de Cuba
  (14)

Cyprus
Larnaca (7)

Denmark
Aalborg (7)
Copenhagen (10)
Elsinore (8)
Frederikshavn
  (13)
Helsingor (8)
Horsens (7)

Odense (6)

Djibouti
Djibouti (8)

Dubai
Dubai (5)

Ecuador
Guayaquil (9)

Egypt
Alexandria (10)
Damieth (7)
Port Said (8)
Suez (4)

England
Avonmouth (9)
Barnstaple (10)
Chatham (7)
Cinque Ports (11)
Colchester (10)
Deal (4)
Devonport (9)
Dover (5)
Falmouth (8)
Felixstowe (10)
Folkestone (10)
Gravesend (9)
Grimsby (7)
Hartlepool (10)
Harwich (7)
Hull (4)
King's Lynn (9)
Liverpool (9)
London (6)
Middlesbrough
  (13)
Newcastle (9)
Newhaven (8)
North Shields
  (12)
Penzance (8)
Plymouth (8)
Poole (5)
Portland (8)
Port Sunlight (12)
Portsmouth (10)
Rye (3)
Sandwich (8)
Sheerness (9)
Southampton (11)
Sunderland (10)

Teignmouth (10)
Tilbury (7)
Weymouth (8)
Whitstable (10)

Estonia
Reval (5)
Tallinn (7)

Finland
Helsinki (8)
Turku (5)

France
Bordeaux (8)
Boulogne (8)
Brest (5)
Calais (6)
Cannes (6)
Cherbourg (9)
Dieppe (6)
Dunkirk (7)
Fos-sur-Mer (9)
Honfleur (8)
La Rochelle (10)
Le Havre (10)
Marseilles (10)
Toulon (6)

French Guiana
Cayenne (7)

Germany
Bremen (6)
Bremerhaven
  (11)
Cuxhaven (8)
Emden (5)
Flensburg (9)
Hamburg (7)
Kiel (4)
Rostock (7)
Travemunde
  (10)
Wilhelmshaven
  (13)
Wismar (6)

Ghana
Takoradi (8)
Tema (5)

Greece
Canea (5)

Corfu (5)
Hermopolis (10)
Hermoupolis (11)
Navarino (8)
Patras (6)
Piraeus (7)
Rhodes (6)

Hawaii
Honolulu (8)
Pearl Harbor (11)

Hong Kong
Kowloon (7)

Hungary
Budapest (8)

India
Bombay (6)
Calcutta (8)
Cocanada (8)
Cochin (6)
Haldia (6)
Kakinada (8)
Kandla (6)
Madras (6)
Pondicherry (11)
Trincomalee
(11)

Indonesia
Jakarta (7)
Macassar (8)
Makassar (8)
Padang (6)
Paradeep (8)

Iran
Bushire (7)

Iraq
Basra (5)

**Ireland
(Republic of)**
Cobh (4)
Cork (4)
Donegal (7)
Dundalk (7)
Dun Laoghaire
(12)
Rosslare (8)
Youghal (7)

Isle of Man
Ramsey (6)

Israel
Acre (4)
Akko (4)
Ashdod (6)
Eilat (5)
Elat (4)
Haifa (5)

Italy
Ancona (6)
Bari (4)
Brindisi (8)
Gaeta (5)
Genoa (5)
Leghorn (7)
Marsala (7)
Messina (7)
Naples (6)
Ostia (5)
Palermo (7)
Salerno (7)
Trani (5)
Trapani (7)
Trieste (7)
Venice (6)

Ivory Coast
Abidjan (7)

Jamaica
Kingston (8)
Montego Bay
(10)
Port Royal (9)

Japan
Hakodate (8)
Hiroshima (9)
Kagoshima (9)
Kobe (4)
Kochi (5
Nagasaki (8)
Osaka (5)
Shimonoseki (11)
Yokohama (8)

Kenya
Mombasa (7)

Kuwait
Kuwait (6)

Mina al-Ahmadi
(12)

Latvia
Riga (4)

Lebanon
Beirut (7)

Libya
Benghazi (8)
Tripoli (7)

Madagascar
Tamatave (8)

Majorca
Palma (5)

Malaysia
George Town (10)
Kotakinabalu
(12)
Penang (6)
Port Klang (9)

Mauritania
F'derik (6)
Nouadhibou (10)

Mauritius
Port Louis (9)

Mediterranean
Gibraltar (9)

Mexico
Guaymas (7)
Vera Cruz (8)

Minorca
Mahon (5)
Port Mahon (9)

Montenegro
Bar (3)
Kotor (5)

Morocco
Agadir (6)
Casablanca (10)
Ceuta (5)
Essaouira (9)
Melilla (7)

Mina Hassan
Tani (14)
Mogador (7)
Rabat (5)
Safi (4)
Tangier (7)
Tetuan (6)

Mozambique
Beira (5)

Netherlands
Amsterdam (9)
Delft (5)
Europoort (8)
Flushing (8)
Rotterdam (9)
Vlissingen (10)

New Zealand
Auckland (8)
Gisborne (8)
Lyttelton (9)
Nelson (6)

Nigeria
Lagos (5)
Port Harcourt
(12)

**Northern
Ireland**
Belfast (7)
Larne (5)

Norway
Bergen (6)
Christiana (10)
Christiansund
(13)
Larvik (6)
Narvik (6)
Oslo (4)
Stavangar (9)
Tromsø (6)
Trondheim (9)

Pakistan
Chalna (6)
Karachi (7)

Panama
Balboa (6)
Colón (6)

Cristobal (9)

**Papua New
 Guinea**
Port Moresby
 (11)

Peru
Callao (6)
Ilo (3)
Matarini (8)
San Juan Bay
 (10)

Philippines
Cebu (4)
Manila (6)

Poland
Danzig (6)
Gdansk (6)
Gdynia (6)
Kolobrzeg (9)
Szczecin (8)
Stettin (7)

Portugal
Lisbon (6)
Oporto (6)
Porto (5)

Puerto Rico
San Juan (7)

Romania
Constantsa (10)

Russia
Archangel (9)
Murmansk (8)
Nakhodka (8)
Okha (4)
Okhotsk (7)
Pechenga (8)
Petropavlovsk
 (13)
St Petersburg
 (12)
Taganrog (8)
Tiksi Bay (8)
Vladivostok (11)

Saudi Arabia
Jeddah (6)

Scotland
Ardrossan (9)
Dunbar (6)
Dundee (6)
Grangemouth
 (11)
Greenock (8)
Leith (5)
Port Glasgow (11)
Scapa (5)
Scapa Flow (9)
Stornaway (9)
Tain (4)
Wick (4)

Senegal
Dakar (5)

Sierra Leone
Freetown (8)

South Africa
Cape Town (8)
Durban (6)
East London (10)
Mossel Bay (9)
Port Elizabeth
 (13)
Port Natal (9)
Richard's Bay
 (11)
Simonstown (10)

South Korea
Pusan (5)

Spain
Algeciras (9)
Alicante (8)
Arrecife (8)
Barcelona (9)
Bilbao (6)
Cadiz (5)
Cartagena (9)
Corunna (7)
Ferrol (6)
Funchal (7)
La Coruña (8)
Malaga (6)
Palos (5)

Sri Lanka
Colombo (7)
Galle (5)

Lulea (5)
Malmo (5)

Sudan
Port Sudan (5)
Suakin (6)

Sweden
Goteborg (8)
Gothenburg (10)
Halmstad (8)
Helsingborg (11)
Kalmar (6)
Nykoping (8)
Stockholm (9)
Wisby (5)
Ystad (5)

Taiwan
Keelung (7)
Kaohsiung (9)
Tainan (6)

Tanzania
Dar es Salaam
 (11)
Mtwara (6)

Tasmania
Hobart (6)

Thailand
Bangkok (7)

Trinidad
Port of Spain (11)

Tunisia
Tunis (5)

Turkey
Istanbul (8)
Izmir (5)
Smyrna (6)

Ukraine
Izmail (6)
Kerch (5)
Odessa (6)
Yalta (5)

**United Arab
 Emirates**
Abu Dhabi (8)

Uruguay
Montevideo (10)

USA
Baltimore (9)
Boston (6)
Bridgeport (10)
Charleston (10)
Detroit (7)
Erie (4)
Galveston (9)
Houston (7)
Jersey City (10)
Los Angeles (10)
Nantucket (9)
New Bedford (10)
New Haven (8)
New Orleans
 (10)
New York (7)
Norfolk (7)
Pensacola (9)
Perth Amboy (10)
Portsmouth (10)
Rock Harbour
 (11)
San Francisco
 (12)
Seattle (7)

Venezuela
La Guiara (8)
Puerto Cabello
 (13)
Puerto Hierro
 (12)

Wales
Barry (5)
Cardiff (7)
Fishguard (9)
Holyhead (8)
Llanelli (8)
Milford Haven
 (12)
Pembroke (8)
Portmadoc (9)
Swansea (7)

Yemen
Aden (4)
Ahmedi (5)
Hodeida (7)
Mocha (5)

Rivers

R.= River (appears where this usually follows the name)

Afghanistan
Heri Rud (7)
Kabul R. (5)
Kuram (5)
Murghab (7)

Africa
Atbara (6)
Blue Nile (8)
Calabar (7)
Chambezi (8)
Congo (5)
Gambia (6)
Itimbiri (8)
Kafue (5)
Kagera (6)
Kubango (7)
Kwa (3)
Lomami (6)
Lualaba (7)
Luangwa (7)
Lugendi (7)
Niger (5)
Ogowai (6)
Prah (4)
Sankuru (7)
Semliki (7)
Senegal (7)
Shire (5)
Ubangi (6)
Welle (5)
White Nile (9)
Zaire (5)
Zambezi (7)

Asia
Amu Darya (8)
Amur (4)
Dnieper (7)
Hue (3)
Ili (3)
Mekong (6)
Oxus (4)
Selenga (7)
Shat-el-Arab
  (10)
Sungari (7)
Usuri (5)
Yarkand (7)
Zaratshan (9)

Australia
Albert (6)
Alice (5)
Avoca (5)
Barwon (6)
Brisbane R. (8)
Campaspe (8)
Clarence (8)
Darling (7)
Fitzroy (7)
Georgina (8)
Gilbert (7)
Glenelg (7)
Goulburn (8)
Hawkesbury (10)
Lachlan (7)
Loddon (6)
Lynd (4)
Macquarrie (10)
Mitchell (8)
Murray R. (6)
Murray-Darling
  (13)
Parramatta (10)
Peel (4)
Richmond (8)
Swan (4)
Thomson (7)
Warrego (7)
Yarra Yarra (10)

Austria
Enns (4)
Inn (3)
Traun (5)

Balkans
Stroma (Balkans)

Belarus
Beresina (8)
Dnieper (7)
Niemen (6)

Belgium
Lys (3)
Meuse (5)
Sambre (6)
Schelde (7)
Scheldt (7)

Bosnia
Drina (5)

Brazil
Japura (6)
Paraná (6)
Parima (6)
Rio Grande (9)
São Francisco
  (12)

Burma
Chindwin (8)
Irrawaddy (9)
Salween (7)
Salwin (6)

Canada
Abbitibee (9)
Abitibi (7)
Albany (6)
Bonaventure (11)
Churchill (9)
Fraser (6)
French (6)
Gatineau (8)
Great Slave R.
  (10)
Ha Ha (4)
Klondyke R. (8)
Liard (5)
Mackenzie (9)
Mallagami (9)
Mattawa (7)
Mirimichi (9)
Missimabi (9)
Moose (5)
Nelson (6)
Nipisquit (9)
Ottawa (6)
Parsnip (7)
Peace R. (5)
Peel (4)
Restigouche (11)
Rimouski (8)
Saguenay (8)
St Claire (8)
St John (6)
St Lawrence (10)
Saskatchewan
  (12)

Severn (6)
Shubenacadia
  (12)
Thames (6)
Tobique (7)
Trent (5)
Winnipeg (8)
Yukon (5)

China
Canton R. (6)
Hankiang (8)
Hoang Ho (7)
Hsi (3)
Huang (5)
Hwangho (7)
Menam (5)
Pei Ho (5)
Tarim (5)
Yangtse (7)
Yangtse Kiang
  (12)
Yellow R. (6)

Czech Republic
Moldau (6)
Morava (6)
Oder (4)

East Africa
Hawash (6)
Ikopa (5)
Juba (4)
Komati (6)
Pungwe (6)
Rovuma (6)
Rufiji (6)
Shari (5)
Tana (4)

England
Adur (4)
Aire (4)
Aln (3)
Arun (4)
Avon (4)
Axe (3)
Beaulieu (8)
Blackwater (10)
Brent (5)
Bure (4)

Calder (6)
Cam (3)
Camel (5)
Chelmer (7)
Cherwell (8)
Cole (4)
Coln (4)
Colne (5)
Coquet (6)
Crouch (6)
Dart (4)
Deben (5)
Dee (3)
Derwent (7)
Dove (4)
Eden (4)
Evenlode (8)
Exe (3)
Fal (3)
Fleet (5)
Frome (5)
Great Ouse (9)
Hamble (6)
Humber (6)
Irwell (6)
Isis (4)
Itchen (6)
Kennet (6)
Lea (3)
Loddon (6)
Lune (4)
Medina (6)
Medway (6)
Mersey (6)
Mole (4)
Monnow (6)
Naze (4)
Nen (3)
Orwell (6)
Otter (5)
Ouse (4)
Parret (6)
Rede R. (4)
Ribble (6)
Roding (6)
Rother (6)
Rye (3)
Severn (6)
Sheaf (5)
Sid (3)
Sow (3)
Stour (5)
Swale (5)
Tamar (5)

Taw (3)
Tees (4)
Teign (5)
Test (4)
Thames (6)
Torridge (8)
Trent (5)
Tyne (4)
Ure (3)
Wandle (6)
Wansbeck (8)
Wash (4)
Waveney (7)
Wear (4)
Weaver (6)
Welland (7)
Wensum (6)
Wey (3)
Wharfe (6)
Windrush (8)
Witham (6)
Wye (3)
Yare (4)
Yeo (3)

Europe
Danube (6)
Moselle (7)
Roer (4)
Rur (3)

Finland
Tornio (6)

France
Adour (5)
Agout (5)
Ain (3)
Aisne (5)
Allier (6)
Cher (3)
Durance (7)
Garonne (7)
Ill (3)
Isère (5)
Loir (4)
Loire (5)
Lot (3)
Lys (3)
Marne (5)
Mayenne (7)
Oise (4)
Rance (5)
Rhône (5)

Saar (4)
Sambre (6)
Saone (5)
Sarthe (6)
Save (4)
Seine (5)
Somme (5)
Tarn (4)
Var (3)
Vienne (6)
Vire (4)
Yonne (5)

Germany
Aller (5)
Bober (5)
Eider (5)
Elbe (4)
Elster (6)
Ems (3)
Havel (5)
Isar (4)
Lahn (4)
Lech (4)
Main (4)
Memel (5)
Neckar (6)
Neisse (6)
Oder (4)
Rhine (5)
Ruhr (4)
Saale (5)
Saar (4)
Spree (5)
Werra (5)
Weser (5)
Wipper (5)

Greece
Maritza (7)

Hungary
Draava (6)
Drave (5)
Koros (5)
Leitha (6)
Neutra (6)
Temes (5)
Theiss (6)
Tisza (5)
Waag (4)
Zenta (5)

India
Beas (4)
Brahmaputra
   (11)
Cauvery (7)
Chambal (7)
Chenab (6)
Chumbal (7)
Dihong (6)
Gandak (6)
Ganges (6)
Godavari (8)
Gogra (8)
Gumti (5)
Hooghli (7)
Hugli (5)
Hunza (5)
Indus (5)
Jumna (5)
Kanawha (7)
Kaveri (6)
Kusi (4)
Mahanadi (8)
Narbuda (7)
Porali (6)
Ravi (6)
Sutlej (6)
Sutluj (6)
Tapti (5)
Tons (4)
Toombudra (9)

Iran
Karun (5)
Kizil Uzen (9)
Zarang (6)

Iraq
Euphrates (9)
Tigris (6)

**Ireland
   (Republic of)**
Barrow (6)
Blackwater (10)
Boyne (5)
Bride (5)
Erne (4)
Feale (5)
Foyle (5)
Lee (3)
Liffey (6)
Main (4)
Shannon (7)

Slaney (6)
Suck (4)
Suir (4)
Swilly (6)
Israel
Jordan (6)

Italy
Adda (4)
Adige (5)
Agogno (6)
Anio (4)
Arno (4)
Dora (4)
Mincio (6)
Oglio (5)
Po (2)
Rubicon (7)
Tanaro (6)
Tiber (5)

Jordan
Jordan (6)

Kazakhstan
Ishim (5)
Syr (3)
Syr Daria (8)
Ural (4)

Lithuania
Niemen (6)

Malaysia
Kelantan (8)
Perak (5)

Mexico
Bolsas (6)
Grande (6)
Rio del Norte (11)
Rio Grande (9)
Tampico (7)

Moldova
Dniester (8)

Netherlands
Lek (3)
Maas (4)
Rhine (5)
Schelde (7)
Scheldt (7)
Waal (4)

Yssel (5)

New Zealand
Buller (6)
Thames (6)
Waihou (6)
Walkato (7)
Wanganui (8)

North Africa
Habra (5)
Muluyar (7)

North America
Columbia (8)
Kootenay (8)
Niagara (7)

Northern Ireland
Bann (4)
Lagan (5)

Norway
Glommen (7)

Pakistan
Jelum (5)
Jhelum (6)

Papua New Guinea
Fly (5)

Poland
Bug (3)
Dunajec (7)
Nida (4)
Oder (4)
Vistula (7)
Warta (5)
Warthe (6)

Portugal
Douro (5)
Minho (5)
Tagus (5)
Tamega (6)

Romania
Maroo (5)
Pruth (5)
Sereth (6)

Russia
Angara (6)
Desna (5)
Dnieper (7)
Dunay (5)
Indigirka (9)
Irtish (6)
Kama (4)
Katun (5)
Ket (3)
Kur (3)
Lena (4)
Moskva (6)
Neva (4)
Ob (3)
Ob Irtish (7)
Oka (3)
Onega (5)
Pechora (7)
Tara (4)
Tom (3)
Tunguska (8)
Ural (4)
Usa (3)
Viatka (3)
Volga (5)
Yana (4)
Yenesei (7)

Scotland
Aire (4)
Allan (5)
Allen (5)
Allenwater (10)
Annan (5)
Beauly (6)
Bogie (5)
Carron (6)
Cart (4)
Clyde (5)
Deveron (7)
Devon (5)
Don (3)
Doon (4)
Earn (4)
Eden (4)
Esk (3)
Etive (5)
Ettrick (7)
Ettrickwater (12)
Forth (5)
Foyers (6)
Gala Water (9)
Leven (5)

Nith (4)
Shiel (5)
Spey (4)
Tay (3)
Teith (5)
Teviot (6)
Tummel (6)
Tweed (5)
Yarrow (6)
Yarrowwater (11)

South Africa
Blood R. (5)
Buffalo (7)
Crocodile R. (8)
Gamtoos (7)
Gauritz (7)
Great Fish R. (9)
Great Kei (8)
Hex R. (3)
Kowie (5)
Limpopo (7)
Modder R. (6)
Mooi (4)
Olifant (7)
Orange (6)
Pungwe (6)
Sunday (6)
Tugela (6)
Umsimkulu (9)
Umsimvubu (9)
Umvolosi (8)
Vaal (4)
Zontag (6)

South America
Amazon (6)
Arinos (6)
Caroni (6)
Demerara (8)
Desaguadero (11)
Esmeralda (9)
Essequibo (9)
Grande (6)
Guapore (7)
Huallaga (8)
La Plata (7)
Madeira (7)
Marañón (7)
Mazaruni (8)
Orinoco (7)
Paraguay (8)
Parahiba (8)
Paraíba (7)

Paraná (6)
Paranahiba (10)
Paranaíba (9)
Pilcomayo (9)
Plate (5)
Purus (5)
Putumayo (8)
Rio Branco (9)
Rio Negro (8)
San Juan (7)
Santiago (8)
Suriname (8)
Tapajos (7)
Teffe (5)
Tocantins (9)
Ucayali (7)
Upper Paraná
(11)
Uruguay (7)
Xiugo (5)
Yavari (6)
Yuruari (7)

Spain
Aguada (6)
Alagon (6)
Douro (5)
Ebro (4)
Guadalete (9)
Guadalquivir (12)
Guadiana (8)
Manzanares (10)
Minho (5)
Rio Tinto (8)
Tormes (6)

Sweden
Gota (4)
Umea (4)

Switzerland
Aar (3)
Reuss (5)

Rhine (5)
Rhône (5)
Sulir (5)
Thur (4)
Ticino (6)

Syria
Abana (5)
Euphrates (9)
Jordan (5)
Orontes (5)

Thailand
Kwai (4)
Meklong (7)

Turkey
Euphrates (9)
Kizil Irmak (10)
Tigris (6)
Zab (3)

Ukraine
Alma (4)
Bug (3)
Dnieper (7)
Dniester (8)
Styr (4)

USA
Alabama (7)
Arkansas (8)
Big Black R. (8)
Big Blue R. (7)
Big Horn R. (7)
Big Sandy R. (8)
Big Sioux R. (8)
Black R. (5)
Brazos (6)
Cape Fear R. (8)
Catawba (7)
Colorado R. (8)
Delaware (8)

East R. (4)
Fall (4)
Feather (7)
Gila (4)
Genesee (7)
Grande (6)
Great Kanawka
(12)
Green R. (5)
Hudson (6)
Humboldt (8)
James R. (5)
Juniata (7)
Kalamazoo (9)
Kankakee (8)
Kennebec (8)
Lackawanna (10)
Lehigh (6)
Merrimac (8)
Miami (5)
Mississippi (11)
Missouri (8)
Mobile (6)
Mohawk (6)
Monagahela (10)
Nebraska (8)
Neuse (5)
Niagara (7)
Ohio (4)
Oneida (6)
Passaic (7)
Pecos (5)
Penobscot (9)
Platte (6)
Potomac (7)
Racket (6)
Rappahannock
(12)
Red R. (3)
Rio Grande (9)
Sabine (6)
Sacramento (10)
St John's (7)

Salt R. (4)
San Joaquin
(10)
Santee (6)
Savannah (8)
Scioto (6)
Seneca (6)
Shenandoah
(10)
Snake R. (5)
Spokane (7)
Sugar (5)
Susquehanna
(11)
Suwanee (7)
Tennessee (9)
Trinity (7)
Wabash (6)
White R. (5)
Wichita (7)
Wisconsin (9)

Wales
Dovey (5)
Neath (5
Severn (6)
Taff (4)
Tawe (4)
Teiti (5)
Towy (4)
Usk (3)
Wye (3)
Ystwith (7)

West Africa
Benue (5)
Gallinas (8)
Geba (4)
Grande (6)
Kwanza (6)
Rio Grande (9)
St Paul (6)
Volta (5)

Seas and Oceans

3
Red S.

4
Aral S.
Azov, S. of
Dead S.
Java S.
Kara S.
Ross S.
Sava S.
Sulu S.

5
Banda S.
Black S.
Ceram S.

China S.
Coral S.
Irish S.
Japan, S. of
Malay S.
North S.
Timor S.
White S.

6
Aegean S.
Arctic O.
Baltic S.
Bering S.
Celtic S.
Flores S.
Gaelic S.

Indian O.
Ionian S.
Laptev S.
Scotia S.
Tasman S.
Yellow S.

7
Andaman S.
Arabian S.
Arafura S.
Barents S.
Behring S.
Caspian S.
Celebes S.
Marmora, S. of
Molucca S.

Okhotsk, S. of
Pacific O.
Weddell S.

8
Adriatic S.
Amundsen S.
Atlantic O.
Beaufort S.
Ligurian S.
Macassar S.
McKinley S.
Sargasso S.

9
Antarctic O.
Caribbean S.

East China S.
Greenland S.
Norwegian S.
Zuider Zee

10 *and over*
Bellingshausen S.
  (14)
East Siberian S.
  (12)
King Haakon VIII
  S. (14)
Mediterranean S.
  (13)
South China S.
  (10)
Tyrrhenian S. (10)

Straits, Channels, etc.

NB: letter counts do not include the words *strait*, *channel*, etc.; place references
are given as a general guideline on location.

Ch. = Channel; P. = Passage; Sd = Sound; St.(s) = Strait(s)

Australia
Bass St. (4)
Queen's Ch. (6)
Torres St. (6)

Canada
Barrow St. (6)
Cabot St. (5)
Davis St. (5)
Dolphin St. (6)
Fox Ch. (3)
Georgia, St. of (7)
Hecate St. (6)
Hudson St. (6)
King George Sd
  (10)
Lancaster Sd (6)
Nootka Sd (6)
Northumberland
  St. (14)
Queen Charlotte
  Sd (14)
Smith Sd (5)

**Central
  America**
Panama Canal
  (11)

China
Formosa St. (7)

Denmark
Cattegat (the)
  (8)
Great Belt (the)
  (9)
Kattegat (the) (8)
Little Belt (the)
  (10)
Skagerrak (9)

East Africa
Mozambique Ch.
  (10)

East Indies
Malacca St. (7)
Molucca P. (7)

Sunda St. (5)

England
Bristol Ch. (7)
Dover, Sts of (5)
Downs (the) (5)
English Ch. (7)
Goodwin Sands
  (12)
Nore (the) (4)
Plymouth Sd (8)
St George's Ch.
  (9)
Solent (the) (6)
Spithead (8)

France
Biscay (6)
Pas de Calais (11)

Greenland
Denmark St. (7)

India
Palk St. (4)

Iran
Ormuz, St. of (5)

**Ireland
  (Republic of)**
Achill Sd (6)

Italy
Messina, St. of (7)
Otranto, St. of (7)

Japan
Korea St. (5)
Van Diemen St.
  (9)

Mediterranean
Bonifacio, St. of
  (9)
Suez Canal (9)

Mexico
Yucatan Ch. (7)

New Zealand
Cook St. (4)

Foveaux St. (7)	**Scotland**	**South America**	**USA**
	Caledonian Canal	Le Maire St. (7)	Florida St. (7)
North Sea	(15)	Magellan St.	Golden Gate
Dogger Bank (10)	Coll, P. of (4)	(8)	(10)
	Colonsay, P. of		Pamlico Sd (7)
Norway	(8)	**Spain**	Puget Sd (5)
Skagerrak (9)	Cuillin Sd (7.)	Gibraltar, Sts of	Hampton Roads
Tromsø Sd (6)	Harris, St. of (6)	(9)	(12)
	Jura Sd (4)		
Pacific	Kilbrennan Sd	**Sweden**	**Wales**
Bering St. (6)	(10)	Sound (the) (4)	Menai Sts (5)
	Little Minch (the)		
Red Sea	(11)	**Turkey**	**West Indies**
Bab-el-Mandeb	Minch (the) (5)	Bosphorus (the)	Mona P. (4)
St. (11)	Minches (the)	(9)	Windward P.
Suez Canal (9)	(7)	Dardanelles (the)	(8)
	North Ch. (5)	(11)	
Russia	Scapa Flow (9)	Golden Horn	
Behring St. (7)	Sleat, Sd of (5)	(10)	

Waterfalls

Angel (5)	Hamilton (8)	Roraima (7)	Trummelbach (11)
Churchill (9)	Krimmler (8)	Salto Ángel (10)	Vettisfos (9)
Gavarnie (8)	Multnomah (9)	Sete Quedas (10)	Victoria (8)
Giessbach (9)	Niagara (7)	Stanley (7)	Upper Yosemite
Guaira (6)	Ribbon (6)	Sutherland (10)	(13)

Weather

3	high	frost	chilly	trades	freshen
dry	mild	gusty	cirrus	trough	hailing
eye	mist	heavy	cloudy	warmer	icy cold
fog	pour	light	colder	winter	insular
icy	rain	misty	deluge	wintry	monsoon
low	smog	muggy	el Niño	zephyr	pouring
sun	snow	north	freeze		rainbow
wet	veer	rainy	frosty	**7**	raining
	warm	shine	hotter	air mass	settled
4	west	sleet	isobar	aurorae	showery
calm	wind	snowy	mizzle	backing	sirocco
cool		south	nimbus	blowing	snowing
damp	**5**	storm	normal	Celsius	squally
dull	below	sunny	shower	climate	stratus
east	clear	windy	simoom	cumulus	summery
gale	close		simoon	cyclone	tempest
gust	cloud	**6**	squall	degrees	thermal
hail	devil	arctic	stormy	drizzle	thunder
haze	flood	auster	sultry	drought	tornado
heat	foggy	bright	torrid	fogbank	tsunami

typhoon
veering
warmish
wintery

8
autumnal
black ice
blizzard
cold snap
cyclonic
doldrums
downpour
easterly
east wind
fogbound
freezing
heat haze
heatwave
maritime
meteoric
offshore
overcast
pour down
raindrop
rainfall
scirocco
snowfall
sunshine
thundery
tropical
westerly
west wind

9
barometer
cloudless

drift wind
drizzling
dry season
dust devil
hailstorm
hard frost
hoarfrost
hurricane
lightning
north-east
northerly
north-west
north wind
rain cloud
sea breeze
snowbound
snowstorm
south-east
southerly
south-west
south wind
tidal wave
trade wind
updraught
whirlwind

10
anemometer
centigrade
changeable
convection
depression
fahrenheit
freshening
frostbound
Gulf Stream
hot climate

land breeze
monsoonish
Scotch mist
storm cloud
waterspout

11
anticyclone
cats and dogs
cold climate
freezing fog
hard weather
lowering sky
mackerel sky
rainy season
stiff breeze
summer cloud
temperature
tempestuous
thunderbolt
thunderclap
troposphere
turbulence
wind backing
wind veering

12
anticyclonic
April showers
atmospherics
cirrocumulus
cirrostratus
condensation
currocumulus
currostratus
equinoctials
freezing rain

meteorology
storm brewing
stratosphere
thundercloud
thunderstorm
tropical heat

13
ball lightning
Beaufort scale
cumulostratus
fork lightning
freezing point
meteorologist
tropical storm
thunder shower
weather report

14
aurora borealis
meteorological
sheet lightning
torrential rain

15 *and over*
forked lightning (15)
offshore breezes (15)
prevailing winds (15)
rain cats and dogs (15)
weather forecast (15)
wind chill factor (15)
ridge of high pressure
(19)
summer lightning (15)
tropical climate (15)

GEOLOGY, ROCKS AND MINERALS

Geological Terms

2
aa

3
alp
era
gas
ore
puy
ria
vei

4
cone
culm
cusp
dune
dyke
kame
lava
Lias
lode
marl
oder
plug
sial
sill
sima
spit
till
tuff
vent
zone

5
arête
chert
crest
crust
delta
epoch
erode
esker
fault
flank
hexad
horst
leveé
loess
magma
nappe
phula
ridge
spitz
swarm
Trias

6
alpine
arkose
bourne
cirque
corrie
crater
diapir
durain
facies
firrow
fusain
gangue
geyser
gneous
graben
in situ
inlier
klippe
mantle
matrix
misfit
oolith
placer
podsol
schist
scoria
spring
striae
top-set
trough
valley

7
abyssal
aquifer
arcuate
barchan
bathyal
bedrock
bone bed
breccia
caldera
cap rock
corrode
crystal
cuvette
deltaic
drumlin
erosion
fissure
fore-set
glacier
hardpan
horizon
lapilli
litoral
meander
Miocene
molasse
moraine
Neogene
neritic
ophitic
outlier
paralic
Permian
procast
sea cave
upthrow
vesicle
vitrain
wind gap

8
abrasion
alluvial
Bajocian
biserial
blowhole
Cambrian
Charnian
cleavage
crevasse
Devonian
foliated
foreland
fracture
fumarole
ganister
granular
ice sheet
Jurassic
lopolith
Mesozoic
Orcadian
pavement
pinacoid
pisolith
Pliocene
plucking
porosity
ring dyke
ropy lava
sediment
syncline
Tertiary
trachyte
xenolith

9
amorphous
amygdales
anticline
attrition
batholith
Bathonian
block lava
clinodome
composite
cone sheet
Corallian
corrasion
corrosion
dent fault
downthrow
dripstone
dry valley
epicentre
evaporite
extrusion
flagstone
formation
freestone
fucoid bed
hercynian
insequent
intercept
isoclinal
isostatic
isotropic
laccolith
laminated
macrodome
meltwater
Oligocene
oxbow lake
Oxfordian
peneplain
pericline
phacolith
rudaceous
saltation
seat earth
striation
sub-aerial
subhedral
supergene
tectonics
triad axis
truncated
unit plane
Uriconian
ventifact

10
asymptotic
axial plane
axial ratio
calcareous
calc-sinter
caledonoid
Cenomanian
compaction
Cretacious
denudation
depression
diagenetic
Downtonian
earthquake
epigenetic
extinction
fault scarp
feeder dyke
feruginous
flocculate
fluviatile
glaciation
liquid core
Ordovician
orogenesis
outwash fan
overthrust
Palaeogene
Palaeozoic
pillow lava
plain tract
Purbeckian
Quaternary
ribbon lake
rift valley
sole thrust
stalactite
stalagmite
storm beach
strandflat
syngenetic
water table
weathering
welded tuff

11
agglomerate
Archaeozoic
arenaceaous
cementation
cementstone
coal measure
crystalline

degradation
dune-bedding
exfoliation
geosyncline
groundwater
imbrication
isomorphous
leucocratic
Longmyndian
meander belt
percolation
porphyritic
Portlandian
Pre-Cambrian
precipitate
Proterozoic
raised beach
reaction rim
sedimentary
soil profile
start thrust
thick-bedded
thrust plane
Torridonian
Tournaisian
valley tract
waste mantle
Westphalian

12
argillaceous
artesian well
bedding plane
conglomerate
cross-bedding
distributary
false-bedding
flow cleavage
glacial phase
glacial snout
hydrothermal
interglacial
interstadial
marginal lake
metamorphism
permeability
petrogenesis
plutonic rock
polymorphism
river capture
river terrace
rock pinnacle
space lattice
volcanic bomb
volcanic plug

13
braided rivers

Carboniferous
carbonization
catastrophism
catchment area
chilled margin
disconformity
mountain tract
parasitic cone
petrification
sandstone dyke
shield volcano
silicious ooze
slaty cleavage
solid solution
symmetry class
tectonic plate

14
axes of symmetry
bird's foot delta
calcareous ooze
crystal lattice
current bedding
deltidial plate
desert pavement
hydrolic action
incised meander
intrusive rocks
longshore drift

major intrusion
minor intrusion
plate tectonics
recrystallized
ripple-drifting

15
calcareous shale
cross-lamination
crystallization
frost shattering
glacial stairway
impure limestone
metamorphic rock
onion weathering
overflow channel
Radiolarian ooze

16
centre of
  symmetry
cone of depression
continental drift
Forsterite marble
secondary deposit

Rocks and Minerals

3
jet
mud
tin
wad

4
alum
bort
calx
cauk
clay
coal
gold
grit
iron
jade
lead
marl
mawl
mica

onyx
opal
ruby
sand
spar
talc
tufa
ural
zinc

5
agate
albin
amber
argil
argon
baria
beryl
borax
boron
chalk

emery
erbia
flint
fluor
glass
invar
macle
nitre
ochre
pitch
shale
silex
slate
spalt
topaz
yeode

6
barium
basalt
cobalt

copper
davina
dipyre
doggar
erbium
gabbro
galena
garnet
glance
gneiss
gypsu
m
indium
kaolin
kunkur
marble
mesole
mundic
nappal
nickel
nosean

ormolu
pumice
pyrope
quartz
radium
rutile
schorl
silica
silver
sinter
speiss
sphene
spinel
thoria
zircon

7
abraxas
alumina
amianth
arsenic

asteria
barytes
bauxite
biotime
bismuth
bitumen
breccia
cadmium
calcium
caliche
calomel
cyprine
desmine
diamond
emerald
epigene
euclase
felspar
fuscite
glucina
granite

greisen
helvine
ice spar
iridium
jacinth
jargoon
lithium
mercury
olivine
peridot
pyrites
realgar
red clay
romeine
rubicel
sardine
sardius
sinoper
thorium
uranium
wolfram

yu-stone
yttrium

8
adularia
amethyst
antimony
asbestos
blue John
calamine
calc-spar
chromium
cinnabar
corundum
diallage
diopside
dolomite
feldspar
felstone
fireclay
graphite
hyacinth
jasponyx
maganese
magnesia
massicot
mesotype
mudstone
pea stone
platinum
porphyry
pyroxene
ragstone
red earth
rock cork
rock ruby
rock salt
rock soap
rock wood
rock wool
sapphire
sardonyx
smaltine
spinelle
star ruby
sunstone
thallium
tin stone
titanium

topazine
trachyte
triphane
tungsten
turmalin
vesuvian
wood opal
wood rock
zirconia

9
alabaster
allophane
almandine
alum shale
alum slate
aluminium
amianthus
amphibole
arquifoux
asphaltum
balas ruby
basaltine
black onyx
black opal
brick-clay
brown coal
brown-spur
carbonado
carnelian
casholong
cat-silver
cobaltine
cornelian
corn stone
earth flax
erythrine
firestone
fluorspar
graystone
greensand
greystone
haematite
heavy spar
horn slate
hornstone
ironstone
jadestone
limestone

lodestone
magnesium
magnetite
malachite
manganese
marl slate
melaphyre
mica slate
mispickel
moonstone
moorstone
moss agate
muscovite
needletin
nepheline
pearl spar
periclase
pleonaste
potassium
pyrophane
rhombspar
sandstone
satin spar
siltstone
soapstone
strontium
tellurium
toadstone
turquoise
veinstone
water opal
woodstone
xanthocon

10
anthracite
aquamarine
aventurine
azure stone
bloodstone
chalcedony
chalybeate
clinkstone
eagle stone
false topaz
floatstone
greenstone
hornblende
hornsilver

iron glance
Kentish rag
lead glance
London clay
meerschaum
mica schist
Mocha stone
molybdenum
orthoclase
osmiridium
paranthine
parrot coal
picrosmine
pyrochlore
rock butter
rose quartz
sandy shale
sapphirine
seggar clay
serpentine
sismondine
sparry iron
talc schist
tourmaline
travertine

11
augen gneiss
black silver
boulder clay
chalcedonyx
chlorophane
chondrodite
chrysoberyl
dendrachate
diving stone
figure stone
Iceland spar
iron pyrites
lapis lazuli
milky quartz
Moine schist
Muller glass
muschel kalk
needlestone
pitchblende
rock crystal
smoky quartz
Speeton clay

thumerstone
titanic iron

12
Bowland shale
chrysophrase
forest marble
fuller's earth
garnet schist
greyweathers
mountain cork
mountain flax
mountain milk
mountain soap
puddingstone
quartz schist
silver glance
specular iron
sprig crystal

13
brucite marble
cinnamon stone
copper pyrites
emerald copper
fell sandstone
kerosene shale
millstone grit
plateau basalt

14
antimony glance
bituminous coal
britannia metal
brown haematite
Cairngorm stone
chlorite schist
elastic bitumen
graphic granite
Lewisian gneiss

15
hydromica schist
mountain leather
Muscovite schist

HOME LIFE

Clothing and Accessories

3
bag
bib
boa
bra
cap
fez
hat
hem
kid
kit
lap
mac
rag
tam
tie
tux
wig
zip

4
band
belt
body
boot
brim
cape
clog
coat
coif
cuff
daps
duds
garb
gear
gown
hood
hose
kilt
mitt
muff
mule
pump
robe
ruff
sari
sash
shoe
slip

sock
spur
stud
suit
toga
togs
vamp
veil
vest
wrap

5
apron
beret
boots
chaps
choli
cloak
clogs
clout
fichu
frill
frock
get-up
gilet
glove
heels
hejab
hijab
jeans
lapel
liner
lungi
mitts
pants
parka
pleat
plume
pumps
quoif
teddy
thong
topee
train
trews
tunic
vamps
V-neck
weeds

welly

6
afghan
anorak
basque
bikini
blazer
blouse
boater
bob wig
bodice
bolero
bonnet
boucle
bow tie
bowler
braces
briefs
brogue
buckle
burnet
bustle
button
caftan
capote
chador
chinos
cloche
coatee
collar
collet
corset
cravat
diaper
dickey
dirndl
ear cap
edging
fedora
flares
fleece
gaiter
garter
girdle
gusset
hankie
helmet
insole

jacket
jerkin
jersey
jumper
kaftan
khurta
kimono
kirtle
lining
mantle
mitten
mob cap
muumuu
nylons
panama
pleats
pompon
poncho
puttee
PVC mac
raglan
riband
ribbon
ruffle
samfoo
sandal
sarong
sequin
serape
sheath
shorts
slacks
sleeve
smalls
sun hat
tabard
thongs
tights
tippet
top hat
toupee
trilby
trunks
T-shirt
turban
tuxedo
tweeds
waders
whites

woolly

7
alepine
apparel
bandana
bandeau
batiste
blanket
blucher
brogans
burnous
cagoule
calotte
cantoon
capuche
cassock
casuals
challis
chapeau
chemise
chimere
chlamys
chopine
chrisom
civvies
clobber
cockade
coronet
corsage
costume
cut-away
djibbah
dollman
dornock
doublet
drawers
dupatta
egrette
fallals
falsies
flounce
fur coat
gaiters
garment
glasses
G-string
gymslip
handbag

hat-band
hoggers
homburg
hosiery
layette
leotard
loafers
Mae West
mantlet
muffler
necktie
nightie
overall
panties
parasol
pea coat
periwig
puttees
pyjamas
rain hat
rompers
shalwar
singlet
ski boot
slip-ons
slipper
soutane
sporran
stetson
sun suit
surcoat
surtout
sweater
top coat
topknot
turn-ups
twinset
uniform
wellies
wetsuit
wiggery
woollen
yashmak

8
bathrobe
bath wrap
bedsocks
bifocals

bloomers
boat-neck
body belt
boob tube
breeches
Burberry
burnoose
camisole
cardigan
cloth cap
codpiece
coiffure
corselet
culottes
dentures
dress tie
dungaree
earmuffs
ensemble
flannels
footwear
frontlet
gabarage
galoshes
gauntlet
glad rags
guernsey
gumboots
gymshoes
half-hose
headband
hipsters
jackboot
jump suit
kerchief
knickers
knitwear
leggings
lingerie
mantelet
mantilla
menswear
moccasin
neckband
negligee
nightcap
opera hat
overalls
overcoat
overshoe
pinafore
playsuit
polo-neck
pullover

raincoat
sandshoe
sherwani
shoelace
ski boots
ski pants
slippers
sneakers
snowshoe
sombrero
stocking
straw hat
sun dress
sunshade
swimsuit
tailcoat
trainers
trimming
trousers
two-piece
umbrella
wardrobe
woollens
wristlet
yarmulka
yarmulke

9
Alice band
ankle boot
baby linen
balaclava
bandolier
beachwear
bedjacket
billycock
blue jeans
bowler hat
brassiere
bush shirt
cheongsam
clump boot
cocked hat
comforter
crinoline
Cuban heel
dress coat
dress suit
duffle bag
dungarees
flip-flops
forage cap
frock coat
full dress

full skirt
fur collar
galoshes
gauntlets
glengarry
greatcoat
hairpiece
headdress
headscarf
high heels
hoop skirt
housecoat
jackboots
jockey cap
kid gloves
knee socks
loincloth
long dress
long skirt
long socks
macintosh
maxi skirt
midi skirt
millinery
mini skirt
neckcloth
nightgown
nightwear
off-the-peg
overdress
overshoes
panama hat
pantaloon
patchwork
pea jacket
peaked cap
petticoat
pixie hood
plimsolls
plus-fours
press stud
quoiffure
round-neck
sack dress
safety pin
sailor cap
sailor hat
school cap
scoop-neck
separates
shell suit
shovel hat
shower cap
sloppy joe

slouch hat
sou'wester
stilettos
stockings
stomacher
strapless
suede coat
sun bonnet
sweatband
tracksuit
trilby hat
trousseau
underwear
waistband
waistcoat
wedge heel
wristband

10
ankle socks
Aran jumper
ballet shoe
bathing cap
bobbysocks
boiler suit
bush jacket
buttonhole
chemisette
court dress
court shoes
coverchief
crêpe soles
cricket cap
cummerbund
diving suit
drainpipes
dress shoes
duffle coat
embroidery
Eton collar
Eton jacket
false nails
fancy dress
feather boa
grass skirt
halter-neck
hearing aid
kitten heel
legwarmers
lounge suit
mess jacket
monkey suit
nightdress
nightshirt

nylon shirt
opera cloak
Oxford bags
pantaloons
party dress
pinstripes
pith helmet
plastic mac
print dress
sailor suit
scratch wig
shoe buckle
shoestring
slingbacks
spectacles
sports coat
string vest
suede shoes
sunglasses
suspenders
sweatshirt
table linen
tablecloth
terry nappy
trench coat
turtleneck
underpants
waterproof
windjammer
wing collar
wrap-around

11
Aran sweater
bell bottoms
best clothes
canvas shoes
cotton shirt
crash helmet
dark glasses
deerstalker
dental plate
flared skirt
football cap
hand-me-downs
kitten heels
lace-up boots
leather coat
morning coat
neckerchief
netherlings
panty girdle
pilot jacket
prêt-à-porter

ready-to-wear
regimentals
riding habit
shoulderbag
slip-on shoes
slumberwear
stiff collar
suede jacket
tam-o'-shanter
tennis dress
tennis skirt
thermal vest
trencher cap
trouser suit
V-neck jumper
wellingtons
widow's weeds
windcheater
yachting cap

12
asbestos suit
bathing dress
billycock hat
body stocking
business suit
collar and tie
college scarf
combinations
dinner jacket
divided skirt
donkey jacket
dress clothes

dressing gown
drip-dry shirt
Easter bonnet
evening dress
handkerchief
knee breeches
leather skirt
lumber jacket
monkey jacket
morning dress
plain clothes
pleated skirt
reefer jacket
service dress
shirtwaister
sleeping suit
sports jacket
underclothes
V-neck sweater
walking boots
walking stick
wedding dress

13
Bermuda shorts
cashmere shawl
contact lenses
elevator shoes
Fair Isle shawl
fishnet tights
football boots
football scarf
hacking jacket

leather jacket
liberty bodice
long underwear
made-to-measure
mourning dress
pinafore dress
platform shoes
platform soles
shalwar kameez
shoulder strap
snorkel jacket
stiletto heels
suspender belt
underclothing

14
bathing costume
bifocal glasses
blue suede shoes
Fair Isle jumper
false eyelashes
hair extensions
horn-rim glasses
knickerbockers
nail extensions
nether garments
partial denture
reading glasses
riding breeches
Shetland jumper
starched collar
thigh-high boots
top hat and tails

winter overcoat

15
daily-wear lenses
disposable nappy
Fair Isle sweater
high-heeled shoes
knee-length boots
knee-length socks
long-tailed shirt
mourning clothes
plastic raincoat
soft contact lens
summer
  underwear
winter underwear

16
disposable lenses
fishnet stockings
little black dress
long combinations
long underclothes
long-sleeved dress
long-sleeved shirt
support stockings
thermal underwear
thigh-length boots
turtleneck jumper
twinset and pearls
varifocal glasses
white tie and tails

Cookery

3
fry
ice
mix
rub

4
bake
beat
boil
bone
coat
chop
dice
dust
fold

lard
mash
pare
peel
rare
roll
sear
sift
soak
stew

5
broil
brush
carve
chill

chine
cream
flake
grate
knead
mince
paner
roast
sauté
scald
score
steam
stuff
sweat
truss
whisk

6
blanch
braise
flambé
freeze
infuse
medium
pan-fry
paunch
pickle
piquer
reduce
render
scrape
simmer

7
al dente
clarify
parboil
deep-fry
drizzle
garnish
refresh
stir-fry

8
au gratin
barbecue
marinade
marinate
pot-roast

preserve
well done

9
bake blind
microwave
spit-roast

10
caramelize
cut and fold
medium-rare
shallow-fry

Drink

3	**tent**	**staws**	porter	sangria	rum punch
ale	wine	stout	posset	sherbet	rum shrub
ara		swats	poteen	sidecar	sangaree
bub	**5**	tafia	potion	sloe gin	schnapps
cha	arack	toddy	ptisan	snifter	sillabub
dop	assai	tonic	pulque	spirits	small ale
gin	ayala	vodka	rickey	spunkie	souchong
IPA	biddy	water	saloop	stinger	sour milk
jar	bohea	winox	scotch	tequila	spritzer
kat	bowle		shandy	tintara	syllabub
kir	broth	**6**	sherry	whiskey	tincture
nip	bumbo	alegar	simkin		verjuice
nog	byrrh	amrita	spingo	**8**	vermouth
rum	chica	apozem	spirit	absinthe	vin blanc
rye	cider	arrack	squash	Adam's ale	wish-wash
tea	cocoa	bishop	stingo	alkermes	
tot	congo	bitter	strunt	anisette	**9**
vat	cream	brandy	swipes	aperitif	applejack
vin	cuppa	bubbly	tipple	Assam tea	barley pop
	daisy	bumper	tisane	beverage	birch wine
4	haoma	canary	treble	block tea	bitter ale
arak	heavy	cassis	wallop	brick tea	black beer
beer	hogan	caudle	wherry	champers	brut wines
bock	hogen	chicha	whisky	China tea	buck's fizz
brut	hooch	claret		cider cup	Ceylon tea
cafe	hyson	coffee	**7**	ciderkin	champagne
char	irroy	congou	amoroso	cocktail	chocolate
dram	joram	crusta	bitters	dog's nose	claret cup
fine	julep	double	bourbon	dry wines	demitasse
fino	kefir	eggnog	catawba	eau-de-vie	elder wine
fizz	kvass	elixir	chianti	espresso	firewater
flip	lager	entire	cobbler	gin sling	ginger ale
grog	mobby	geneva	cordial	green tea	ginger pop
hock	mocha	gimlet	curaçao	herb beer	grenadine
lush	morat	gloria	draught	highball	heavy beer
maté	nantz	grappa	egg flip	hockclip	iced water
mead	negus	hootch	gin fizz	hydromel	Indian tea
mild	noyau	junora	gin sour	lemon top	lager beer
milk	pekoe	kephir	limeade	lemonade	lamb's wool
ouzo	perry	kirsch	liqueur	montilla	lime juice
port	pinta	kummel	low wine	near beer	lollshrob
raki	plonk	liquor	mace ale	nightcap	Manhattan
reid	punch	lotion	mineral	oopak tea	Margarita
rose	purre	nectar	oloroso	padra tea	metheglin
sack	quass	noggin	pale ale	pekoe tea	milk punch
sake	rumbo	oolong	pink gin	pouchong	milk stout
saki	salep	oulong	plottie	prasites	milkshake
slug	shrub	pastis	pulchra	ramboose	mint julep
soda	sirop	pimint	ratafia	red biddy	moonshine
stum	sling	plotly	red wine	red wines	mulled ale
swig	smash	poison	retsina	root beer	oolong tea
tape	snort	pontac	samshoo	ruby port	orange gin

orangeade
small beer
snakebite
sodawater
soft drink
sundowner
tawny port
vodkatini
white lady
white port
white wine

10
bitter beer
bloody Mary
buttermilk
café au lait
cappuccino
clary water
ginger beer
ginger wine
horse's neck
iced drinks
Jamaica rum
lime squash
malt liquor
malt whisky
malted milk
maraschino
mickey finn
mulled wine
nettle beer
pale sherry
premier cru
raisin wine
Rhine wines
Rhone wines
rye whiskey
sack posset
shandygaff

soft drinks
spruce beer
still wines
sweet wines
tonic water
twankay tea
usquebaugh
white capri
white wines

11
aguardiente
amontillado
apollinaris
apple brandy
barley broth
barley water
black and tan
black velvet
cider brandy
citron water
coconut milk
cowslip wine
depth charge
doch-an-doris
dry monopole
Earl Grey tea
gin and tonic
Irish coffee
John Collins
lemon squash
orange pekoe
peach brandy
potash water
pouchong tea
rum and black
screwdriver
scuppernong
soda and milk
souchong tea

spring water
tomato juice
vintage wine

12
champagne cup
cherry brandy
crême de cacao
crême de menthe
Cyprus sherry
ginger brandy
hair of the dog
humpty dumpty
ice-cream soda
iced lemon tea
India pale ale
Irish whiskey
kirschwasser
lager and lime
mulled claret
old-fashioned
orange brandy
orange squash
peach bitters
red wine punch
Rhenish wines
sarsaparilla
Scotch whisky
seltzer water
supernaculum
treacle water
vin ordinaire
vodka and lime

13
aerated waters
aperitif wines
apricot brandy
bijou cocktail
blended whisky

Bronx cocktail
dandelion wine
Darjeeling tea
ginger cordial
liqueur brandy
liqueur whisky
mineral waters
one for the road
orange bitters
pink champagne
planters' punch
prairie oyster
sherry cobbler
sparkling hock
sparkling wine
vodka and tonic

14
bamboo cocktail
champagne cider
champagne punch
French vermouth
Rob Roy cocktail
Singapore sling
sparkling water
sparkling wines
tequila slammer
vermouth cassis
vodka and orange
white wine punch

15
carbonated water
cascade cocktail
champagne cognac
duchess cocktail
Italian vermouth
lapsang souchong
sparkling waters

Fabrics, Fibres and Materials

3	down	shag	beige	gauze	plaid	twill
aba	felt	silk	braid	kapok	plush	voile
abb	hide	warp	capoc	khaki	rayon	
fur	jute	weft	chino	linen	sable	**6**
net	lace	wool	cloth	Lurex	satin	alpaca
PVC	lamé	yarn	crape	Lycra	serge	angora
	lawn		crêpe	moiré	suede	beaver
4	mesh	**5**	denim	nylon	terry	burlap
abba	mink	baize	drill	Orlon	tulle	calico
coir	pelt	batik	floss	piqué	tweed	canvas

chintz
cotton
Dacron
damask
fleece
marmot
merino
mohair
muslin
poplin
rattan
samite
sateen
shoddy
tartan
velour
velure
velvet
wincey

7
abb wool
acetate
Acrilan
acrylic
art silk
bay yarn
brocade
buckram
byssine
cambric
chamois
chiffon
cowhide
crochet
delaine
doeskin
drabbet
ermelin
façonne
felting
flannel
foulard
fustian
gingham

hessian
hogskin
holland
hopsack
layette
leather
leghorn
lockram
maribou
matting
oilskin
organza
paisley
pigskin
plastic
raw silk
sacking
suiting
taffeta
taffety
tatting
ticking
webbing
worsted

8
appliqué
asbestos
bonelace
buckskin
cashmere
chenille
computer
cordovan
corduroy
cordwain
cretonne
deerskin
drilling
Fair Isle
gold lace
gold lamé
gold wire
gossamer
homespun

jacquard
lambskin
moleskin
moquette
musquash
oilcloth
organdie
sarsenet
sealskin
shagreen
shalloon
shantung
sheeting
shirring
shirting
shot silk
smocking
tapestry
Terylene
Thai silk
whipcord

9
astrakhan
blond lace
bombazine
calamanco
camelhair
cassimere
cerecloth
chantilly
Courtelle
Crimplene
floss silk
gaberdine
georgette
goosedown
haircloth
horsehair
lambswool
linen mesh
moiré silk
organzine
pina cloth
point lace

polyester
sackcloth
sailcloth
satinette
shark skin
sheepskin
silk serge
spun rayon
stockinet
swansdown
tarpaulin
towelling
velveteen

10
angora wool
Berlin wool
blanketing
bobbin lace
broadcloth
brocatelle
candlewick
chinchilla
gold thread
grass cloth
Irish linen
jersey silk
jersey wool
khaki drill
mock velvet
mousseline
needlecord
pillow lace
pilot cloth
rabbit skin
seersucker
thrown silk
tussah silk

11
black patent
candystripe
cheesecloth
cloth-of-gold
flannelette

hammer cloth
Harris tweed
herringbone
Honiton lace
Leatherette
leopardskin
mechlin lace
nettlecloth
shoe leather
stockinette
torchon lace
tussore silk
watered silk

12
acetate rayon
bolting cloth
brushed denim
cavalry twill
crêpe-de-chine
Indian cotton
ripstop nylon
Shetland wool
stockingette
Welsh flannel

13
Chantilly lace
patent leather
Russia leather

14
artificial silk
chamois leather
Morocco leather
Spanish leather

15
maribou feathers
mousseline de soie
ostrich feathers

Food

3

bap	ham	pie
bun	ice	poi
egg	jam	rob
fat	nan	roe
	oxo	soy

4

bean	cake	Edam	fowl	herb
beef	cate	fare	ghee	jowl
beef	chop	fish	grub	junk
bran	chou	flan	hare	kale
brie	curd	fool	hash	lamb

lard	filet	syrup	haggis	titbit	game pie
lean	flour	table	hot dog	toffee	gelatin
loaf	fruit	taffy	hotpot	tongue	giblets
loin	fudge	tansy	humbug	trifle	gnocchi
meal	garne	toast	hummus	viands	goulash
meat	gigot	tripe	jujube	waffle	gristle
milk	glaze	viand	jumble	walnut	gruyere
mint	Gouda	wafer	junket	yogurt	haricot
mush	gravy	yeast	kelkel		haslets
naan	gruel		kidney	**7**	houmous
pâté	gumbo	**6**	leaven	aliment	jam roll
pork	heart	almond	lights	bannock	jam tart
puff	honey	batter	mousse	banquet	ketchup
roll	icing	biffin	muffin	Bath bun	lasagne
roti	jelly	blintz	mutton	beef tea	madzoon
rôti	joint	bonbon	noodle	biltong	matzoon
roux	juice	borsch	nougat	biscuit	meat pie
rusk	kebab	brains	noyeau	bloater	mustard
sago	liver	bridie	nut oil	blossom	oatcake
snow	lolly	brunch	oliver	borscht	oatmeal
soup	lunch	burger	omelet	botargo	olycook
stew	manna	butter	oxtail	bouilli	pancake
suet	matzo	canapé	paella	brisket	papmeat
tart	melba	casein	panada	broiler	paprika
veal	melts	catsup	parlein	brownie	pickles
whey	mince	caviar	pastry	bull's eye	plum jam
yolk	mocha	cereal	pepper	cabbage	plum pie
	pasta	cheese	pickle	calipee	polenta
5	paste	collop	pilaff	caramel	popcorn
aioli	pasty	congee	pillau	catchup	potargo
aspic	patty	cookie	polony	caviare	pottage
bacon	pilaf	course	posset	Cheddar	poultry
balti	pilau	crowdy	potage	chicken	praline
blini	pilaw	crumbs	potato	chicory	pretzel
blood	pitta	cutlet	quiche	chowder	pudding
board	pizza	dainty	rabbit	chutney	ramekin
bombe	prune	dinner	ragout	cob loaf	rarebit
borsh	pulse	éclair	raisin	compôte	ratafia
brawn	roast	eggnog	rasher	confect	ravioli
bread	salad	entrée	relish	corn cob	rhubarb
brose	salmi	faggot	salami	cracker	rice bun
broth	sauce	fillet	samosa	crowdie	ricotta
cakes	scoff	flitch	sea pie	crumble	risotto
candy	scone	fodder	simnel	crumpet	rissole
cheer	shape	fondue	sinker	currant	sapsago
chili	snack	fumado	sorbet	custard	sausage
clove	spice	gammon	sowens	dariole	savarin
cream	split	garlic	sponge	dessert	saveloy
crêpe	St Agur	gâteau	squash	faggots	savoury
crust	steak	gelato	staple	falafel	seafood
curds	stock	ginger	sundae	fig cake	sherbet
curry	sugar	grease	supper	fish pie	sirloin
dough	sushi	greens	sweets	fritter	soufflé
dulse	sweet	grouse	tiffin	galette	Stilton

strudel	julienne	whitepot	mincemeat	cheese flan
succado	kedgeree	yoghourt	mint sauce	cheesecake
sucrose	kickshaw		mousetrap	Chelsea bun
tapioca	lamb chop	**9**	mutton ham	comestible
tartlet	loblolly	appetizer	mutton pie	confection
teacake	lollipop	arrowroot	nutriment	corned beef
treacle	luncheon	beef steak	picalilli	cornflakes
truffle	macaroni	breakfast	pigeon pie	cottage pie
venison	macaroon	bride cake	potato pie	currant bun
vinegar	marzipan	bubblegum	potpourri	delicacies
windsor	meatball	Camembert	pound cake	dog biscuit
yoghurt	meatloaf	cassareep	provelone	estouffade
	meringue	casserole	provender	fig pudding
8	mince pie	cassonade	puff paste	flesh broth
allspice	mishmash	chipolata	raised pie	frangipane
ambrosia	molasses	chocolate	rillettes	French loaf
aperitif	moussaka	chump chop	Roquefort	fricandeau
apple jam	mushroom	comfiture	rump steak	fruit salad
apple pie	napoleon	condiment	schnitzel	giblet soup
Bath chap	olive oil	confiture	scotch egg	ginger cake
biscotin	omelette	corn bread	seasoning	girdle cake
bouillon	parmesan	corn salad	shellfish	Gloucester
chapatti	pastrami	crackling	shortcake	gorgonzola
chestnut	pemmican	cream cake	sour cream	grape sugar
chop suey	peperoni	croquette	sour dough	ground rice
chow mein	poppadum	drop scone	spaghetti	guava jelly
coleslaw	porridge	Easter egg	stir-about	ham and eggs
confetti	preserve	enchilada	succotash	hodge-podge
conserve	racahout	entremets	sugar loaf	hotchpotch
consommé	raisinee	forcemeat	sugar plum	ice pudding
couscous	ramequin	fricassee	sweetmeat	Indian corn
cracknel	rice cake	fried eggs	Swiss roll	jugged hare
cream bun	rollmops	fried fish	tipsy cake	lamb cutlet
cross bun	roly-poly	fruit cake	vegetable	maple sugar
dainties	rye bread	fruit tart	white meat	marrowbone
date roll	salad oil	galantine	wholemeal	mayonnaise
delicacy	salpicon	Genoa cake	wild honey	minced meat
dog's meat	salt fish	giblet pie		minestrone
doughnut	salt junk	gravy soup	**10**	mock turtle
dripping	salt pork	gustation	apple sauce	Montelimar
dumpling	sandwich	hamburger	apricot jam	mutton chop
escalope	scrag end	hard sauce	bath oliver	pepper cake
fish meal	seedcake	heavy cake	bêche-de-mer	peppermint
flapjack	sillabub	honeycomb	beefburger	poached egg
flummery	slapjack	Irish stew	blancmange	Pontefract
frosting	soda cake	lardy cake	blanquette	potted fish
fruit pie	sparerib	lemon curd	Bombay duck	potted meat
frumenty	squab pie	loaf sugar	bosh butter	provisions
hardbake	steak pie	lobscouse	breadstuff	pudding pie
hazelnut	stuffing	lump sugar	bridescake	puff pastry
hotchpot	tortilla	maçedoine	brown bread	raisin loaf
hung beef	turnover	madeleine	Caerphilly	rhubarb pie
ice cream	undercut	margarine	cannelloni	rolled oats
iced cake	victuals	marmalade	capillaire	saccharine

salmagundi
salmagundy
salt butter
sauerkraut
shortbread
shortcrust
simnel cake
sponge cake
stale bread
stewed meat
sugar candy
sustenance
sweetbread
tea biscuit
temse bread
tenderloin
tinned food
tortellini
turtle soup
vermicelli
water gruel
white bread
white sauce

11
baked Alaska
Banbury cake
barley sugar
bonne bouche
captain's pie
cassava cake
chiffon cake
comestibles
coulommiers
cream cheese
cullen skink
curry powder
frankfurter
French bread
gingerbread
golden syrup
green turtle
griddle cake
ham sandwich
hors d'oeuvre
hot cross bun

imam bayaldi
iron rations
jam sandwich
meat biscuit
meat pudding
medlar jelly
milk pudding
olla podrida
oyster patty
peppermints
plum pudding
raisin bread
refreshment
rice biscuit
rice pudding
saffron cake
sago pudding
sausage roll
short pastry
stewed fruit
suet pudding
tagliatelle
vinaigrette
wedding cake
Welsh mutton
Welsh rabbit
Wensleydale
wheaten loaf
wine biscuit

12
apfel strudel
apple fritter
Bakewell tart
birthday cake
bouquet garni
burnt almonds
butterscotch
cheese fondue
chip potatoes
clotted cream
Cornish pasty
corn-on-the-cob
curds and whey
Danish pastry
Dunmow flitch

eggs and bacon
Finnan haddie
foul mesdames
garlic butter
guarana bread
hasty pudding
julienne soup
liver sausage
lobster patty
maid of honour
marshmallows
merry thought
mullagatawny
nutmeg butter
peanut butter
pease pudding
plum porridge
pumpernickel
quartern loaf
refreshments
shepherd's pie
ship's biscuit
steak pudding
sweet and sour
taramasalata
tripe de roche
Welsh rarebit

13
apple dumpling
bêchamel sauce
bouillabaisse
cheddar cheese
chili con carne
Christmas cake
confectionery
cottage cheese
custard coffin
flitch of bacon
German sausage
gigot de mouton
ginger pudding
Gruyère cheese
Oxford sausage
roll and butter
salad dressing

Scotch collops
sirloin of beef
sponge pudding
Stilton cheese
toad-in-the-hole
veal-and-ham pie

14
apple Charlotte
Bologna sausage
bread and butter
bread and cheese
caramel custard
Charlotte Russe
Cheshire cheese
croque monsieur
haunch of mutton
household bread
mashed potatoes
mock turtle soup
parmesan cheese
Pontefract cake
saddle of mutton
toasted teacake
Turkish delight
wholemeal bread

15
Bakewell pudding
black-cap pudding
bubble and squeak
chocolate éclair
chocolate fondue
Devonshire cream
haunch of venison
mousetrap cheese

16 *and over*
angels on horseback
  (17)
bread and dripping (16)
Caerphilly cheese (16)
chicken tikka masala
  (18)
devils on horseback
  (17)

Household Items, including Furniture

2
CD, PC, TV

3
bag, bar, bed, bin, can, cot, cup, fan, hob, hod, ink, jar, jug, lid, mat, mop, mug, nib, nog, pad, pan, ped, pen, pew, pot, rug, tap, tin, tub, urn, vat, wok

4
ambo, bath, bowl, bunk, butt, case, cask, cist, coal, comb, cosy, cott, crib, desk, dish, door, etui, ewer, fork, form, gong, grid, hi-fi, hook, iron, lamp, lard, mull, oven, pail, peel, poke, rack, sack, safe, salt, seal, seat, sink, soap, sofa, spit, suet, tank, tape, till, trap, tray, trug, vase, wick

5
airer, apron, arras, basin, bench, besom, bidet, blind, board, broom, broth, brush, caddy, chair, chest, china, cigar, clock, cloth, coign, coppy, couch, cover, crate, creel, crock, cruet, cruse, darts, diota, divan, doily, dosel, doser, dough, drier, duvet, flask, flour, glass, globe, grate, grill, gruel, guard, hatch, herbs, jelly, jesse, joint, joram, jorum, knife, label, ladle, laver, leash, light, linen, match, mixer, mould, mural, paper, paste, paten, patin, piano, plate, poker, pouch, purse, quill, quilt, radio, range, razor, sauce, scoop, scrip, shade, shelf, sieve, skeel, slate, spice, spill, spoon, stand, steel, stock, stool, stoup, stove, strop, sugar, suite, swing, table, tache, tapis, timer, tongs, tools, torch, towel, traps, trunk, twine, vesta, video, watch, whisk, wiper, yeast

6
air bed, ash bin, ash can, ash pan, awning, basket, beaker, beater, bicker, boiler, bottle, bucket, budgie, bunker, bureau, burner, butter, camera, candle, carafe, carboy, carpet, carver, casket, caster, castor, cat bed, CD rack, cheval, coffer, consol, cooker, cradle, cupful, day bed, dishes, dog bed, drapet, drawer, duster, eggbox, eggcup, fender, filter, flagon, fly net, forfex, fridge, funnel, gas jet, geyser, goblet, goglet, grater, grease, hamper, hat box, haybox, hearth, heater, hookah, hoppet, hussif, icebox, inkpot, jugful, juicer, keeler, kettle, kitbag, kurkee, ladder, larder, locker, log bin, loofah, lowboy, mangle, mincer, mirror, mobile, napery, napkin, needle, noggin, oilcan, pallet, pantry, pastry, patera, patine, pelmet, pencil, pepper, pickle, piggin, pillow, plaque, polish, pomade, posnet, pot lid, pottle, pouffé, punkah, punnet, reamer, recipe, red ink, rocker, saddle, salver, saucer, scales, sconce, scovel, screen, settee, settle, shovel, shower, sifter, siphon, skewer, slicer, sponge, starch, string, syphon, tablet, tea set, tea urn, teacup, teapot, thread, throne, tiller, tin box, tinder, toilet, toy box, trevet, tripod, trivet, trophy, tureen, valise, vessel, wallet, window, wisket, zip bag

7
adaptor

aerator
almirah
amphora
andiron
armoire
ashtray
baggage
bath mat
bathtub
beanbag
bedding
bedpin case
beeswax
bellows
blanket
blender
blotter
bluebag
bolster
brasier
brazier
broiler
butlery
cabinet
cake tin
cambrel
canteen
cat bowl
cat food
catflap
chalice
chamois
chopper
cistern
coal bin
coal box
cobiron
coir mat
commode
compact
costrel
counter
cue rack
cuisine
curtain
cushion
cutlery
dishmat
dishmop
dog bowl
dog food
dogflap
doormat
down bed

drainer
drapery
dresser
drugget
dustbin
dustpan
dustpan
epergne
flacket
flasket
fly rail
freezer
fusebox
gas fire
gas ring
goggles
griddle
griller
grinder
hair oil
hammock
hassock
hip bath
holdall
horn cup
infuser
ink horn
kneader
kneeler
knocker
lagging
lantern
lectern
lighter
matches
matting
milk jug
monocle
netsuke
oil lamp
ottoman
padlock
panikin
pannier
percher
pianino
pianola
picture
pie dish
pillion
pitcher
platter
playpen
pomatum

pool cue
pot hook
potager
roaster
rundlet
rush mat
saccule
sadiron
salt box
samovar
sampler
sandbox
sapples
satchel
scraper
scuttle
seether
shelves
shoebox
skillet
skimmer
soapbox
sofa bed
spatula
steamer
stew pan
stopper
stopple
tallboy
tambour
tankard
tea cosy
tea tray
tent bed
terrine
thimble
tin case
toaster
tobacco
tool kit
trammel
trolley
truckle
tumbler
tun dish
TV guide
valance
vinegar
wardian
washtub
whatnot
whisket
wine bag
woodcut

work bag
work ox
wringer
yule log

8
ale bench
angel bed
armchair
baby bath
baluster
banister
barbecue
bassinet
bed cover
bed linen
bed quilt
bedstead
bedstraw
bird bath
birdcage
bookcase
bookends
bread bin
camp bath
canister
card case
cashbook
cathedra
cauldron
causeuse
CD player
cellaret
chair bed
chattels
clapdish
clay pipe
coat hook
colander
covercle
coverlet
cream jug
credenza
crockery
cupboard
curtains
cuspidor
deadlock
decanter
demijohn
dish rack
ditty box
dog chain
doorbell

doorknob
doorstep
egg slice
egg spoon
egg timer
egg whisk
endirons
eyeglass
fauteuil
field bed
firewood
fish fork
flan ring
flat-iron
flock bed
fly paper
footbath
fuse wire
gallipot
gas stove
gasalier
gridiron
handbell
hangings
hat brush
hatstand
heirloom
hipflask
holdfast
hotplate
inkstand
jalousie
knapsack
lamp wick
lanthorn
latchkey
linoleum
lipstick
loo table
love seat
matchbox
mattress
meatsafe
muffneer
nailfile
notebook
oak chest
oilcloth
oilstove
ornament
patty pan
penknife
pianette
pipe rack

postcard	wax cloth	dust sheet	newspaper	timetable
pottager	wax light	Dutch oven	nipperkin	tin opener
press bed	wineskin	DVD player	notepaper	tinderbox
quillpen	wireless	easy chair	ornaments	toothpick
radiator		egg beater	paillasse	underfelt
reticule	**9**	egg boiler	palliasse	uplighter
road book	bain-marie	eiderdown	paper rack	vanity box
saddlery	barometer	equipment	paperclip	wall clock
saucepan	bath towel	face towel	parchment	wall light
scissors	bed settee	faldstool	pepperpot	wallpaper
sea chest	bedspread	fire alarm	perdonium	washbasin
shoehorn	blackjack	fire board	pewter pot	washboard
shoelace	book stand	fire brush	pier glass	washstand
showcase	bookshelf	fire grate	pier table	water butt
sink unit	boot brush	fire guard	piggybank	water tank
sitz bath	bric-a-brac	fire irons	plate rack	wax candle
slop bowl	cake stand	fireplace	pool table	wax polish
slop pail	camp chair	fish knife	porringer	windowbox
snuffbox	camp stool	fish plate	port glass	wineglass
snuffers	can opener	fish slice	portfolio	work table
soapdish	cane chair	flowerpot	pot hanger	
spittoon	cantharus	flue brush	pot-pourri	**10**
stair rod	card table	food mixer	powder box	air cushion
standish	carpet bag	foot board	punchbowl	alarm clock
steel pen	carpeting	footstool	radiogram	alarm watch
stockpot	case knife	frying pan	rushlight	apple corer
strainer	casserole	gas burner	safety pin	bedclothes
suitcase	cat basket	gas cooker	secretary	biscuit box
sunblind	china bowl	gas geyser	serviette	biscuit tin
table mat	chinaware	gravy boat	shakedown	boot polish
tabouret	cigarette	hair tonic	shoe brush	bread board
tantalus	clack dish	hairbrush	shower cap	bread crock
tape line	clasp lock	hall table	side table	bread knife
tapestry	club chair	hand towel	sideboard	broomstick
tea board	coffee cup	haversack	sidelight	brown paper
tea caddy	coffee pot	high chair	slop basin	buck basket
tea chest	comb brush	ink bottle	soupspoon	budgerigar
tea cloth	container	ink holder	spin-drier	butter dish
tea plate	corkscrew	inventory	spin-dryer	cabbage net
tea table	crumb tray	jack towel	sponge bag	calefactor
teaspoon	cullender	jewel case	sprinkler	candelabra
trencher	cushionet	kitchener	stair rods	canterbury
triptych	dartboard	lampshade	stamp case	cat hammock
tweezers	davenport	lampstand	steel wool	ceiling fan
umbrella	deckchair	lazy Susan	stopwatch	chandelier
vestiary	devonport	letterbox	string box	chessboard
vestuary	directory	lightbulb	sugar bowl	chiffonier
wall safe	dish clout	loving cup	table bell	chopsticks
wardrobe	dish cover	marquetry	table hook	clamp irons
watch key	dishcloth	master key	table lamp	clothes peg
water can	dog basket	mousetrap	tableware	clothes pin
water jug	dog collar	muffineer	tea kettle	coal bucket
water pot	dog kennel	music book	telephone	coal bunker
water tap	dust brush	nail brush	timepiece	coat hanger

coffee mill
cook's knife
crumb brush
crumb cloth
curtain rod
dandy brush
deep freeze
dishwasher
dog blanket
down pillow
dumb waiter
egg poacher
elbow chair
escritoire
feather bed
fingerbowl
fire basket
fire bucket
fire escape
fire screen
fire shovel
fish basket
fish carver
fish kettle
fish trowel
flesh brush
floorcloth
flour crock
flower bowl
fly catcher
fly swatter
footwarmer
four-poster
garbage can
gas bracket
gas lighter
gramophone
grand piano
hair lotion
hair pomade
humidifier
jardiniere
jelly mould
knife board
lead pencil
letter rack
liquidizer
loose cover
marking ink
milk boiler
music stand
music stool
musical box
napkin ring

needle book
needle case
needlework
nightlight
nutcracker
opera glass
pan scourer
paper stand
paperknife
patio doors
pencil case
peppermill
percolator
Persian mat
Persian rug
pewter dish
photograph
piano stool
pianoforte
pile carpet
pillowcase
pillowslip
pincushion
plate glass
pocketbook
prayerbook
rattan cane
razor strop
rolling pin
rotisserie
saddlebags
salamander
salt cellar
scatter rug
sealing wax
secretaire
shower bath
slow cooker
smoke alarm
soda syphon
spirit lamp
stamp album
stationery
stepladder
strip light
table linen
tablecloth
tablespoon
television
time switch
timekeeper
tobacco jar
toilet roll
toilet seat

toothbrush
toothpaste
truckle bed
trug basket
trundlebed
typewriter
upholstery
vapour bath
video tapes
waffle iron
warming pan
wash basket
wassail cup
watch chain
watchglass
watchguard
watchlight
watchstand
window seat
wine bottle
wine cooler
work basket
wristwatch

11
account book
address book
airing horse
alarm clock
alarm watch
attaché case
baking sheet
basket chair
bed hangings
billiard cue
bolster case
book matches
boot scraper
braising pan
bread grater
butter knife
butter stamp
button stick
candelabrum
candlestick
CD jewel case
centrepiece
chafing dish
cheese board
cheval glass
chiffonnier
clothes hook
clothes line
coal scuttle

coffee table
coir matting
counterpane
curtain hook
curtain rail
curtain ring
despatch box
dining table
dinner plate
dinner table
dispatch box
dog biscuits
door knocker
dredging box
dripping pan
finger glass
firelighter
first aid box
floor polish
flour dredge
foot cushion
footscraper
fountain pen
gaming table
garden chair
hearth brush
knick-knacks
lamp chimney
langesettle
leather case
linen basket
meat chopper
minute glass
minute watch
mosquito net
net curtains
nutcrackers
ormolu clock
paper basket
paperweight
paring knife
picture rail
pipe lighter
pocket flask
pocket knife
porridge pot
portmanteau
primus stove
pudding bowl
pumice stone
reading lamp
roll-top desk
saddle cloth
safety razor

shopping bag
siphon stand
slate pencil
stair carpet
straw pillow
sugar dredge
syphon stand
table napkin
table runner
tape measure
tea canister
thermometer
tin-lined box
tissue paper
tobacco pipe
toilet brush
toilet cover
toilet table
tooth powder
vacuum flask
waffle irons
washing line
washleather
wassail bowl
waste basket
water filter
water heater
watering can
watering pot
window blind
writing desk

12

adhesive tape
antimacassar
bedside light
bedside table
blotting book
bottle opener
breakfast cup
bucking stool
budgie's cage
burglar alarm
camp bedstead
candle sconce
candleholder
carpet beater
carving knife
chaise longue
chesterfield
churchwarden
clothes brush
clothes drier
clothes horse

console table
cottage piano
cup and saucer
dehumidifier
despatch case
dessertspoon
dispatch case
double boiler
dressing case
drinking horn
electric bulb
electric fire
electric iron
electric lamp
extractor fan
fan regulator
field glasses
fire detector
fish strainer
flour dredger
flower basket
folding chair
folding stool
French window
gate-leg table
Gladstone bag
hot cupboard
hot water tank
hubble-bubble
ironing board
ironing table
kitchen range
kitchen table
kneehole desk
knife cleaner
knife machine
looking-glass
loudspeakers
magazine rack
measuring cup
measuring jug
nail scissors
nutmeg grater
opera glasses
packing cloth
packing paper
packing sheet
paraffin lamp
picnic basket
picnic hamper
playing cards
porridge bowl
postage stamp
potato masher

potato peeler
pudding basin
pudding cloth
reading glass
record player
refrigerator
roasting rack
rocking chair
rocking horse
security lock
standard lamp
straw bolster
sweating bath
table lighter
table service
tape recorder
tin-lined case
toasting fork
tobacco pouch
toilette case
Turkey carpet
upright piano
visitors' book
walking staff
walking stick
washing board
water pitcher
Welsh dresser
wicker basket
Windsor chair
wine decanter
writing paper
writing table

13

audio cassette
billiard balls
billiard table
blotting paper
captain's chair
carpet sweeper
chopping block
chopping board
chopping knife
coffee grinder
cribbage board
dressing table
electric clock
electric razor
electric stove
extractor hood
feather pillow
feeding bottle
filing cabinet

folding screen
food processor
lemon squeezer
medicine glass
microwave oven
netting needle
newspaper rack
packing needle
Persian blinds
Persian carpet
petrol lighter
ping-pong table
razor stropper
remote control
satellite dish
saucepan brush
sewing machine
smoke detector
smoothing iron
sounding board
straw mattress
styptic pencil
turnover table
umbrella stand
vacuum cleaner
video cassette
video recorder
visiting cards
wash-hand stand
water softener
window curtain
Witney blanket

14

anglepoise lamp
billiard marker
cassette player
chamber hanging
chest of drawers
cocktail shaker
crockery washer
eiderdown quilt
electric cooker
electric geyser
electric kettle
feather bolster
fuelless cooker
galvanized pail
glove-stretcher
hostess trolley
hot water bottle
kitchen dresser
knife sharpener
meerschaum pipe

mincing machine
pressure cooker
scrubbing brush
tobacco stopper
Venetian blinds
washing machine

15
cassette recorder
electric blanket
feather mattress
garden furniture
gate-legged table
inflatable chair

knitting needles
pestle and mortar
photograph album
photograph frame
pneumatic pillow
TV remote control
vegetable cutter

16
condensation trap
personal computer
satellite decoder

Jewellery

3
gem
pin

4
band
bead
clip
gaud
ouch
ring
stud
torc
unio

5
aglet
badge
beads
bezel
bijou
brait
bugle
cameo
clasp
crown
ivory
jewel
links
nacre
paste
pearl
tiara
union
watch

6
albert
amulet
anklet
armlet
bangle
bauble
brooch
choker
diadem
enamel
fibula
gewgaw
labret
ligure
locket
olivet
pearls
signet
sphere
telesm
tiepin
torque
turkis
wampum

7
annulet
armilla
cat's eye
circlet
chaplet
coronet
crystal
ear stud
earcuff
eardrop

earring
espinel
jewelry
pendant
regalia
ringlet
rivière
sceptre
spangle
trinket

8
aigrette
armillet
bracelet
carcanet
cardiace
claddagh
diamanté
filigree
hawk's-eye
intaglio
necklace
nose ring
nose stud
pectoral
scarf pin
shirt pin
sparkler

9
breast pin
brilliant
carbuncle
cufflinks
girandole
gold tooth

gold watch
jewellery
lavalière
medallion
navel ring
navel stud
paillette
press stud
seed pearl
solitaire
sparklers
starstone
thumbring
trinketry

10
amber beads
black pearl
coral beads
glass beads
hair brooch
puzzle ring
rhinestone
signet ring
tongue stud
watch chain
watchstrap
wristwatch

11
aiguillette
cameo brooch
slave bangle
wedding band
wedding ring

12
bead necklace
eternity ring
gold bracelet
gold earrings
link bracelet
platinum ring

13
chain bracelet
coral necklace
mother-of-pearl
mourning ring
paste necklace
pearl necklace
precious stone
solitaire ring
string of beads

14
engagement ring
fraternity ring
friendship band
mourning brooch
string of pearls

15
crystal necklace
diamond bracelet
diamond necklace
diamond earrings

16
costume jewellery
diamanté necklace
diamanté bracelet
diamanté earrings
twinset and pearls

LAW AND GOVERNMENT

Legal Terms

2
JP
KC
QC

3
act
aka
bar
DPP
fee
IOU
law
rob
sue
use

4
abet
ACAS
bail
bars
Bill
case
dock
fair
fine
gaol
jail
jury
lien
m'lud
oath
plea
quit
rape
rent
riot
seal
silk
stay
suit
tort
will
writ

5
alias
alibi

alien
arson
award
bench
cause
clerk
costs
court
crime
false
forge
fraud
guilt
in rem
judge
juror
legal
libel
order
PACE
penal
plead
poach
police
prize
proof
quash
right
rules
steal
trial
trust
usher
usury
valid

6
access
action
affirm
appeal
arrest
attorn
bailee
bailor
bigamy
breach
camera
charge

commit
deceit
de jure
disbar
duress
elegit
equity
escrow
estate
felony
fiscal
forger
guilty
Hilary
incest
injury
insult
junior
legacy
malice
master
motion
murder
pardon
parole
piracy
police
prison
puisne
remand
repeal
set-off
surety
surtax

7
accused
alimony
assault
assizes
bailiff
battery
bequest
Borstal
bribery
capital
case law
caution
circuit

codicil
consent
control
convict
coroner
counsel
cruelty
custody
damages
de facto
defence
divorce
ex parte
faculty
forgery
garnish
hanging
harming
hearsay
illegal
impeach
inquest
justice
land tax
larceny
lawless
lawsuit
licence
neglect
non suit
offence
penalty
perjury
poll tax
precept
probate
proving
querent
release
reserve
Riot Act
robbery
servant
service
sheriff
sine die
slander
statute
summary

summons
suspect
treason
trustee
verdict
warrant
witness

8
absolute
abstract
act of god
act of law
advocate
attorney
barratry
birching
bottomry
brawling
burglary
canon law
chancery
civil law
coercion
contract
covenant
criminal
deed poll
disorder
distress
drafting
entailed
estoppel
eviction
evidence
executor
felo de se
fidelity
forensic
guardian
homicide
in camera
indecent
judgment
judicial
law agent
law lords
legal aid
licensee

litigant
majority
mandamus
murderer
novation
nuisance
perjuror
petition
pleading
preamble
prisoner
receiver
recorder
reprieve
Salic law
sedition
sentence
Shops Act
stealing
subpoena
sui juris
testator
trespass
tribunal
Truck Act
true bill
unlawful
validity

9
abduction
accessory
acquittal
ademption
agreement
allotment
annulment
attainder
barrister
blackmail
bona fides
cestui que
champerty
code of law
collusion
common law
copyright
defendant
de son tort

deviation
discharge
dismissal
distraint
embracery
endowment
equitable
execution
executory
extortion
fee simple
Gaming Act
good faith
grand jury
guarantee
guarantor
high court
income tax
indemnity
innocence
intestacy
intestate
judiciary
land court
licensing
litigious
loitering
mala fides
mandatory
murderous
not guilty
not proven
Old Bailey
plaintiff
precatory
precedent
privilege
probation
procedure
refresher
registrar
remission
restraint
servitude
solicitor
statutory
sub judice
summing-up
surrender
testament
testimony

10
alienation

appearance
assessment
assignment
attachment
attornment
bankruptcy
common pleas
common riot
confession
connivance
conspiracy
corruption
decree nisi
deed of gift
defamation
disclaimer
enticement
estate duty
executrix
eye witness
finance act
forfeiture
fraudulent
gaming acts
government
Green Paper
gun licence
hard labour
high treason
illegality
impediment
in chambers
indictment
injunction
inter vivos
judicature
King's Bench
land tenure
law sitting
Law Society
legitimacy
limitation
liquor laws
litigation
magistrate
misconduct
misprision
negligence
next friend
parliament
Poor Law Act
post mortem
prize court
procurator

prosecutor
respondent
revocation
separation
settlement
tortfeasor
trespasser
ultra vires
White Paper

11
advancement
affiliation
appointment
arbitration
arrangement
assize court
association
attestation
civil wrongs
composition
concealment
condonation
conge d'elire
county court
criminal law
death duties
debtors' acts
deportation
dissolution
disturbance
enabling act
enforcement
engrossment
examination
extenuating
extradition
fair comment
fieri facias
foreclosure
impeachment
infanticide
issue of writ
king's pardon
maintenance
market overt
mayor's court
obstruction
prerogative
prosecution
Queen's Bench
regulations
requisition
restitution

root of title
royal assent
sheriff's act
stamp duties
stipendiary
subornation
suicide pact
third degree
trespassing
Vagrancy Act
vesting deed

12
adjudication
bona vacantia
case of thorns
causa proxima
caution money
caveat emptor
charter party
Companies Act
compensation
constabulary
conveyancing
co-respondent
crime and tort
cross examine
crown witness
death penalty
disaffection
embezzlement
encroachment
express trust
ferae naturae
grand assizes
guardianship
Habeas Corpus
imprisonment
infringement
inherent vice
interpleader
intimidation
joint tenancy
king's proctor
land transfer
Lord Advocate
lord of appeal
manslaughter
mensa et thoro
misbehaviour
misdemeanour
misdirection
oral evidence
pendente lite

prescription
privy council
prostitution
Queen's Pardon
ratification
royal charter
royal warrant
sheriff clerk
supreme court
taxing master
testamentary

13
administrator
age of marriage
ancient lights
apportionment
appropriation
burden of proof
charging order
common assault
consideration
court of appeal
Court of Arches
criminal libel
damage feasant
ejection order
ejusdem generis
Ground Game Act
hereditaments
housebreaking
illegal action
interlocutory
judge advocate
justification
law of property

letters patent
lord president
nolle prosequi
parliamentary
petty sessions
public trustee
quantum meruit
recognizances
right of appeal
search warrant
simple larceny
statute barred
treasure trove
trial by combat
trial by ordeal
Witchcraft Act

14
act of indemnity
administration
Admiralty Court
choses in action
common nuisance
common sergeant
companies court
concealed fraud
conjugal rights
county judgment
court of justice
criminal appeal
default summons
false pretences
identification
identity parade
local authority

lord chancellor
naturalization
penal servitude
Queen's evidence
Queen's pleasure
right to silence
Sale of Goods Act
second division
special licence
wrongful arrest

15
act of bankruptcy
Act of Parliament
Act of Settlement
attorney-general
autrefois acquit
benefit of clergy
charitable trust
commercial court
commissary court
compound a felony
compound larceny
consistory court
contempt of court
double jeopardy
emergency powers
latent ambiguity
local government
marital coercion
marriage licence
official secrets
oyer and terminer
power of attorney
quarter sessions

Parliament and Politics

2	gag	**4**	noes	Whig	draft	paper
MP	IRA	ayes	oath	whip	edict	party
PM	law	bill	OPEC	writ	elect	Provo
PR	MEP	chad	pact		enact	purge
UN	opt	coup	pass	**5**	forum	rally
	PFI	DORA	peer	agent	house	right
3	PLO	Duma	poll	amend	issue	SEATO
act	red	gain	rump	boule	junta	sit-in
bar	sit	left	seat	bylaw	legal	tithe
CBI	SDP	lord	spin	chads	lobby	valid
CIA	SNP	mace	Tory	chair	Lords	voter
EEC	tax	NATO	veto	clerk	Nazis	
FBI	TUC	Nazi	vote	count	order	

Law and Government

6

agenda
assent
backer
ballot
budget
caucus
clause
colony
Commie
Cortes
decree
divide
enosis
Fabian
Fuhrer
govern
heckle
Labour
leader
Lib Dem
Maoism
Maoist
member
motion
nation
Nazism
oppose
picket
policy
putsch
quorum
recess
record
reform
report
ruling
satrap
secede
second
senate
speech
strike
summon
tariff
teller
tyrant

7

adjourn
Al Fatah
anarchy
barrack
borough

boycott
cabinet
canvass
censure
chamber
closure
cold war
Comecon
Commons
commune
corn law
council
deficit
detente
dissent
elector
embargo
fascism
fascist
federal
finance
gallery
Hansard
heckler
hot line
impeach
Knesset
lock out
liberal
mandate
Marxism
Marxist
neutral
New Left
opening
outvote
pairing
passage
politic
poll tax
poor law
premier
primary
prolong
propose
radical
reading
recount
re-elect
re-enact
senator
session
speaker
statute

toryism
tribune
tyranny
vacancy
Zionism
Zionist

8

apartheid
assembly
autarchy
autocrat
Black Rod
Blairite
blockade
caudillo
chairman
Chiltern
commissar
commoner
Congress
corn laws
democrat
dictator
dissolve
division
dominion
ecclesia
election
elective
feminism
feminist
free vote
hardline
home rule
hustings
left-wing
majority
minister
ministry
minority
monopoly
national
New Right
official
oligarch
politics
prorogue
republic
rollback
safe seat
schedule
suffrage
Treasury

triumvir
unionism
unionist
whiggery
woolsack

9

amendment
anarchism
autocracy
ballot box
bicameral
Bundestag
coalition
Cominform
Comintern
committee
communism
communist
democracy
deterrent
electoral
exchequer
first lord
legislate
New Labour
oligarchy
oligopoly
ombudsman
party line
politburo
president
red guards
Reichstag
right-wing
sanctions
secretary
shire-moot
show trial
socialism
socialist
Stalinism
Stalinist
Taoiseach
terrorism
Watergate

10

aristocrat
block grant
by-election
capitalism
chancellor
collective

conference
devolution
filibuster
finance act
government
guillotine
invalidate
lower house
monarchism
Monday Club
opposition
parliament
Plaid Cymru
plebiscite
psephology
radicalism
referendum
republican
resolution
revolution
scrutineer
sitting day
spin doctor
Third Reich
Third World
trade union
Trotskyism
Trotskyite
unicameral
upper house
Warsaw Pact
White House
white paper

11

adjournment
aristocracy
back-bencher
ballot paper
bye-election
casting vote
coexistence
congressman
constituent
containment
co-operative
demarcation
dissolution
divine right
enfranchise
finance bill
Hitler Youth
impeachment
imperialist

independent
legislation
legislative
legislature
McCarthyism
nationalist
package deal
party leader
prerogative
private bill
reactionary
revisionism
revisionist
statute book
suffragette
syndicalism
syndicalist
Tammany Hall
Westminster
Witenagemot
yeoman usher

12
commissioner

Common Market
Commonwealth
conservatism
Conservative
constituency
constitution
dictatorship
domino theory
federal union
House of Lords
house of peers
invalidation
lord advocate
lord chairman
madam speaker
privy council
reading clerk
snap division
ways and means
welfare state

13
demonstration
deputy speaker

division lobby
disengagement
free trade area
home secretary
international
lord president
lord privy seal
mister speaker
prime minister
rotten borough
shadow cabinet
single chamber
three-line whip
trade unionist
United Nations
vote of censure

14
constitutional
deputy chairman
deputy premier
deputy sergeant
gerrymandering
House of Commons

lord chancellor
representative
sergeant-at-arms
social democrat

15
attorney-general
cabinet minister
clerk of the house
general election
Marxist-Leninist
minister of state
people's republic
personality cult
totalitarianism

16
electoral college

18
Houses of
    Parliament

MEASUREMENTS, TIMES AND DATES

Coins and Currency

2
as

3
bit
cob
dam
ecu
far
fin
lac
lat
leu
lev
mag
mil
mna
oof
ore
pie
red
ree
rei
sen
sho
sol
sou
tin
won
yen
zac
zuz

4
anna
baht
beka
biga
buck
cent
daum
dawm
dime
doit
duro
euro
joey

kick
kran
kyat
lakh
lira
lire
mail
mark
merk
mina
mite
obol
para
peag
peak
peso
pice
rand
real
rial
riel
ryal
taka
unik
yuan
zack

5
agora
angel
asper
aurei
belga
betso
boole
chiao
colon
conto
copec
crore
crown
daric
dinar
ducat
eagle
franc
groat

haler
koban
kopek
krona
krone
liard
libra
litas
livre
locho
louis
medio
mohar
mohur
noble
obang
ochre
oncer
paolo
pence
pengo
penny
plack
pound
rhino
ruble
rupee
sceat
scudi
scudo
semis
soldi
soldo
stica
styca
sucre
sycee
tical
ticcy
tizzy
toman
uncia
unite
zloty

6
amania

aureus
balboa
baubee
bawbee
bezant
bodole
condor
copang
copeck
couter
deaner
decime
denier
dirham
dirhem
doblon
dollar
escudo
forint
fuorte
gourde
guinea
gulden
heller
kobang
kopeck
lepton
markka
nickel
obolus
pagoda
pagode
peseta
rosser
rouble
rupiah
sceatt
sequin
shekel
souran
stater
stiver
talari
talent
tester
teston
thaler

tickey
tizzie
tomaun
valuta
zechin

7
angelot
bolivar
carolus
centava
centavo
centime
cordoba
crusado
denarii
drachma
guilder
jacobus
lempira
manilla
milreis
moidore
ngusang
pfennig
piastre
pistole
quarter
ringgit
sextans
stooter
testoon
testril
thrymsa
unicorn

8
ambrosin
denarius
didrachm
doubloon
ducatoon
farthing
florence
groschen
imperial
johannes

kreutzer
louis d'or
maravedi
megabuck
napoleon
picayune
portague
quadrans
quetzale
sesterce
stotinka

9
boliviano
cuartillo
didrachma
dupondius
gold broad
gold noble
gold penny
lilang-eni
pistareen
rixdollar
rose-noble
schilling
sestertii
sovereign
spur royal
yellow boy

10
broad piece
crown piece
easterling
emalangeni
first brass
gold stater
quadrussis
reichsmark
sestertium
silverling
stour-royal
tripondius
venezolano

11
Briton crown

Deutschmark	**12**	**13**	Hong Kong dollar
double crown	antoninianus	quarter dollar	king's shilling
double eagle	Deutsche Mark	quarter florin	quarter guilder
george noble	double sequin	quarter laurel	two-guinea piece
guinea piece	quarter noble	twopenny piece	
silver penny	silver-stater		**15**
spade guinea	tribute penny	**14**	five-guinea piece
tetradrachm	two-pound coin	barbadoes penny	two-guilder piece

Time, Dates, Festivals, Seasons, etc.

(H.) = Hindu; (I.) = Islam; (J.) = Jewish; (R.) = Roman

2	Lent	jiffy	decade	Tishri (J.)
Ab (J.)	morn	Kalpa (H.)	Diwali (H.)	ultimo
AD	noon	largo	Easter	Veader (J.)
a.m.	now	later	faster	vernal
Av (J.)	once	month	feriae	vesper
BC	slow	never	ferial	weekly
CE	soon	night	fiesta	whilom
Id (I.)	span	Nisan (J.)	future	whilst
NS	term	nones	heyday	winter
OS	then	of old	hiemal	yearly
p.m.	tick	often	hourly	
	time	Pesch (J.)	Julian	**7**
3	utas	Purim (J.)	Kislev (J.)	allegro
age	week	quick	Lammas	almanac
ago	when	Rajab (I.)	Lenaea	ancient
BCE	Xmas	reign	May Day	andante
BST	year	Sivan (J.)	memory	antique
day	yore	spell	mensal	bedtime
Eid (I.)	Yuga (H.)	Tebet (J.)	midday	betimes
eon	Yule	teens	minute	by and by
era		tempo	moment	Calends (R.)
GMT	**5**	Tevet (J.)	morrow	century
oft	adays	times	o'clock	chiliad
	after	Tisri (J.)	payday	Chisleu (J.)
4	again	today	period	dawning
Abib (J.)	alway	trice	Pesach (J.)	daytime
Adar (J.)	bells	until	presto	diurnal
aeon	clock	watch	rhythm	dog days
ages	cycle	while	rubato	epochal
date	daily		season	equinox
dawn	dated	**6**	second	estival
Elul (J.)	early	adagio	Sha'ban (I.)	eternal
ever	Ellul (J.)	annual	Shebat (J.)	etesian
fast	epact	autumn	Shevat (J.)	evening
Holi (H.)	epoch	Bairam (I.)	spring	fast day
hour	Fasti (R.)	before	summer	fete day
Ides (R.)	feast	betime	sunset	half-day
Iyar (J.)	first	brumal	Tammuz (J.)	Hanukah (J.)
last	flash	curfew	Tebeth (J.)	harvest
late	horal	day off	termly	Heshvan (J.)

Measurements, Times and Dates

high day | Day | Ramadhan (I.) | hodiernal | biennially
hock day | biennial | right now | honeymoon | bimestrial
holiday | bimensal | seasonal | hourglass | centennial
holy day | birthday | seed time | indiction | chiliastic
instant | calendar | semester | lean years | chronogram
interim | carnival | se'nnight | Low Sunday | days of yore
jubilee | Cheshvan (J.) | sidereal | lunar year | Dhul-Hijjah (I.)
Lady Day | day by day | slow time | lunch time | dinner time
lay days | daybreak | sometime | mad moment | Easter term
lustrum | dead slow | speedily | Mardi Gras | Ember weeks
mid-Lent | Dhul-Qi'Da (I.) | Stone Age | market day | estivation
midweek | Dionysia | timeless | Martinmas | fence month
morning | doomsday | tomorrow | matutinal | fiscal year
new moon | duration | twilight | menstrual | Good Friday
nightly | eggtimer | untimely | midsummer | hebdomadal
noonday | Epiphany | up to date | midwinter | Hilary term
proximo | estivate | vacation | nightfall | Homecoming
quartan | eternity | whenever | night-time | isochronal
quarter | eventide | Yuletide | novitiate | lunar cycle
quintan | everyday | zero hour | octennial | lunar month
Ramadan | festival | | overnight | Lupercalia
(I.) | forenoon | **9** | peacetime | Michaelmas
regency | futurist | Adar Shani (J.) | Pentecost | Middle Ages
rent day | futurity | afternoon | postponed | millennium
sabbath | gloaming | afterward | premature | natalitial
Shawwal | half-past | All Hallow | quarterly | Palm Sunday
(I.) | half term | andantino | quick time | quarter day
sundial | half time | antedated | quotidian | Quirinalia
sundown | half year | antelucan | recurrent | ritardando
sunrise | Hannukkah | antiquity | return day | Saturnalia
tax year | (J.) | bimonthly | sexennial | septennial
tea time | hibernal | Boxing Day | speech day | sexagesima
tertian | high noon | Candlemas | sunrising | Shrovetide
Thammuz | Hogmanay | centenary | Thermidor | solar month
(J.) | holidays | Chanukkah | timepiece | sowing time
time gun | Holy Week | (J.) | times past | springtime
timeous | interval | Christmas | timetable | summer term
tonight | Labor Day | civil year | triennial | summertime
triduan | leap year | decennary | trimester | synchronal
undated | Lord's day | decennial | whole time | Theban year
wartime | mealtime | diurnally | yesterday | time signal
weekday | midnight | diuturnal | yestereve | timekeeper
weekend | Muharram (I.) | Easter Day | Yom Kippur | time server
whilere | natal day | Ember days | (J.) | triverbial
workday | noontide | Ember fast | | Twelfth Day
Xmas Day | noon time | Ember tide | **10** | vespertine
yestern | nowadays | Ember week | All Hallows | watch night
| nundinal | feast days | allargando | wedding day
8 | oft-times | fortnight | allegretto | Whit Sunday
aestival | overtime | fruit time | antecedent | wintertime
antecede | Passover (J.) | Halloween | antemosaic | working day
antedate | periodic | happy hour | before time | yesteryear
anterior | postpone | hard times | beforehand | Yom Hashoah
ANZAC | punctual | hereafter | behind time | (J.)

184

11
accelerando
All Fools' Day
All Souls' Day
anniversary
antecedence
antemundane
antenuptial
antepaschal
Anthesteria
bacchanalia
Bank Holiday
Bastille Day
bicentenary
Black Monday
Chalk Sunday
chronograph
chronometer
closing time
Columbus Day
Dominion Day
fortnightly
half holiday
harvest home
harvest time
hebdomadary
holiday time
Ides of March
interregnum
isochronism
isochronous
jubilee year
leisure time
millenarian
Nagasaki Day
New Year's Day
New Year's Eve
Passion Week
prehistoric
present time
punctuality
quadrennial
quartz clock
quartz watch
Rabi' Ul-Awwal (I.)
Rabi' U-Thani (I.)
seeding time
settling day
synchronize

synchronism
synchronous
twelvemonth
Waitangi Day
Whitsuntide
yesternight

12
All Saints' Day
ante meridiem
antediluvial
antediluvian
Ascension Day
Ash Wednesday
asynchronous
betrothal day
bicentennial
Black Tuesday
Bloody Sunday
carbon dating
Christmas Day
Christmas Eve
donkey's years
duodecennial
Easter Sunday
Embering days
emergent year
hebdomatical
Hiroshima Day
Judgement Day
Midsummer Day
Midsummer Eve
platonic year
Plough Monday
post-diluvial
post-diluvian
post meridiem
postponement
quadragesima
quinquennial
red letter day
Rogation days
Rogation Week
Rosh Hashanah (J.)
sidereal year
standard time
synchronized
tercentenary
Thanksgiving

time contract
tricentenary
tropical year
Twelfth Night

13
All Hallowmass
All Hallowtide
April Fools' Day
Assumption Day
breakfast time
calendar month
Childermas Day
Christmastide
Christmastime
Corpus Christi
golden jubilee
golden wedding
Gregorian year
holiday season
Jamada Al-Awwal (I.)
Jamada Al-Thani (I.)
lunisolar year
Michaelmas Day
once upon a time
Orangeman's Day
Shrove Tuesday
silver wedding
synchronicity
Trinity Sunday
Valentine's Day

14
Christmas Night
Day of Atonement (J.)
Maundy Thursday
Michaelmas term
prehistoric age
sabbatical year
synodical month
Walpurgis Night

15
biological clock
early closing day
Independence Day
synchronization
Thanksgiving Day

Weights and Measures

(c.) = coal; (elec.) = electricity; (f.) = fish; (liq.) = liquids; (mus.) = music;
(pap.) = paper; (pub.) = publishing; (s.) = silk or cotton; (w.) = wool;
(w.y.) = worsted yarn

2
A4 (pap.)
as
cm
el
em (pub.)
en (pub.)
kg
km
lb
li
mu
os
oz
pt (pub.)
SI
to

3
ASA
aam
amp (elec.)
are
BSI
BTU
cab
cor
cwt
DIN
day
dwt
ell
erg
fen
fou
hin
kat
keg
kin
kor
lac
lea (s.)
log
mho (elec.)
mil
mow
nit
niu

ohm (elec.)
oka
oke
pic
pica (pub.)
pin
piu
pot (pap.)
rad
rai
rem
rod
sen
sho
sun
tan
tod (w.)
tog
ton
tot
tun (liq.)
vat (liq.)
wah
wey (w.)

4
acre
area
bale
bath
bind (f.)
boll
butt (liq.)
cade (f.)
case
cask (liq.)
cent (mus.)
ch'ih
chop
comb
cord
coss
cran (f.)
darg
demy (pap.)
drah
dram
drop

drum
dyne
epha
feet
foot
funt
gill
gram
half
hand (horses)
hank (w.y.)
hath
heml
hide
hour
inch
keel (c.)
kela
kilo
knot
koss
lakh
last (f. and w.)
link
maze (f.)
mile
mina
moio
mudd
muid
nail
natr
oket
omer
onza
paal
pace
pack
palm
paur
peck
phon
phot
pike
pint
pipe (liq.)
pole
polt

pood
post (pap.)
pund
raik
ream (pap.)
reed
reel (s.)
rood
rope
rotl
sack (c.w.)
sawk
seah
seam
seer
sone
span
step
tael
tare
tola
tone (mus.)
torr
tret
troy
ts'un
unit
vara
volt (elec.)
warp (f.)
watt (elec.)
week
wrap (w.y.)
yard
year

5
almud
anker
ardeb
bahar
barge (c.)
baril
barre
bidon (liq.)
bigha
brace
breve (mus.)

cable
candy
caneh
canna
carat
catty
cawny
chain
chang
cheki
chien
cloff
clove
coomb
count (w.y.)
crore
crown (pap.)
cubic
cubit
cusec
cycle
danda
ephah
farad
fermi
galon
gauge
gerah
grain
gross
henry
hertz (elec.)
homer
joule
kaneh
katti
kileh
leash
legua
liang
libra
ligne
lippy
litre
livre
masha
maund
mease

metre
minim (liq. and mus.)
month
neper
obole
ocque
okieh
ounce
pally
pearl
pecul
perch
picul
piede
plumb
point (pub.)
poise
pound
proof
pugil
purse
qirat
quart
quire (pap.)
quota
royal (pap.)
sajen
shaku
sheet (pap.)
shock
sicca
skein (s.)
space (pub.)
stere
stone
stoup (liq.)
terce (liq.)
tesla
therm
tithe
toise
token (pap.)
tonne
trone
truss
tsubo
ungul
vedro
verst
weber

6
ampere (elec.)

aroura
arpent
arroba
arshin
assize
bandle
barrel
batman
bundle
bushel
calory
candie
cantar
casing (pap.)
cental
chatak
chopin (liq.)
cottah
cuarta
decare
denier
djerib
double
drachm
endaze
fanega
fathom
feddan
firkin
firlot
fother
gallon (liq.)
gramme
kantar
kelvin
kentle
league
libbra
megohm (elec.)
metric
micron
minute
modius
moiety
morgen
newton
noggin
obolus
octant
octave
octavo
oxgang
parsec
pascal

pocket
(hops)
pottle (liq.)
quarto
(pap.)
quaver
(mus.)
rotolo
sajene
schene
second
shekel
shtoff
staten
suttle
talent
thrave
thread (s.)
tierce (liq.)
visham
weight
yojana

7
acreage
boiling
braccio
caldron (c.)
calorie
Celsius
centner
century
chalder
chittak
coulomb
(elec.)
dangali
deciare
decibel
diopter
drachma
ellwand
furlong
gilbert
gravity
half-aum
half-ton
hectare
koonkee
leaguer
maximum
measure
megaerg
megaton

mileage
millier
minimum
minimus
modicum
outsize
pailful
per cent
poundal
quantar
quantum
quartan
quarter
quinary
quinhl
rontgen
rottolo
sarplar (w.)
scruple
seamile
spindle (s.)
stadium
stature
stremma
ternary
ternion
tonnage
virgate
x-height (pub.)

8
alqueire
angstrom
caroteel
centiare
centibar
chaldron (c.)
chaudron (c.)
chetvert
crotchet (mus.)
cubic ton
decagram
decigram
distance
division
elephant (pap.)
foolscap (pap.)
footrule
freezing
graviton
half hour
half inch
half mile
hogshead (liq.)

imperial
infinity
kassabah
kilodyne
kilogram
kilowatt
(elec.)
kincatty
metrical
mutchkin
(liq.)
parasang
plateful
puncheon
(liq.)
quadrant
quantity
roentgen
semitone
(mus.)
serplath
ship-load (c.)
short ton
spoonful
toll dish
tonelada
yardland
yardwand
zolotnik

9
altimetry
amplitude
areometry
bisegment
cuartilla
cubic foot
cubic inch
cubic yard
decalitre
decametre
decilitre
decimetre
decistere
dekalitre
dekametre
dimension
foot-pound
half ounce
half pound
hectogram
Irish mile
isometric
kilocycle

kilohertz (elec.)
kilolitre
kilometre
large sack (c.)
light year
line space (pub.)
long dozen
megacycle
megahertz (elec.)
metric ton
milestone
milligram
nanometre
net weight
quadruple
quarterly
quintuple
Scots mile
sea league
semibreve (mus.)
text white (pub.)
yardstick

10
barleycorn
barrelbulk
centesimal
centigrade
centilitre
centimetre
centistere
cubic metre
dead-weight
decagramme
decigramme
dessiatine
dessyatine
double-demy (pap.)
double-post (pap.)
dry measure
Fahrenheit
fluid ounce

hectolitre
hectometre
kilogramme
lunar month
microfarad (elec.)
millesimal
millilitre
millimetre
millionary
quadrantal
semiquaver (mus.)
square foot
square inch
square mile
square yard
super-royal (pap.)
tripartite
tron weight
troy weight

11
avoirdupois
baker's dozen
centigramme
day's journey
double-crown (pap.)
double-royal (pap.)
equibalance
equidistant
fluid drachm
half a league
hand-breadth
heavyweight
hectogramme
imperial-cap (pap.)
long hundred (eggs and f.)
long measure
milligramme
pennyweight
shipping ton
short weight
square metre

thermal unit
trone weight
wine measure
yard measure

12
auncel weight
bantam-weight
boiling point
cable's length
cubic measure
great hundred
hair's breadth
half-quartern
lines per inch (pub.)
measured mile
nautical mile
printer's ream (pap.)
Reaumur scale

13
calendar month
featherweight
freezing point
hundredweight
inside measure
linear measure
medicine glass
square measure

14
character space (pub.)
cubic decimetre
demisemiquaver (mus.)
double-foolscap (pap.)
double-imperial (pap.)

15
cubic centimetre
square decimetre

MEDICINE

The Human Body

BONES

3
jaw
rib

4
ulna

5
anvil
costa
femur
ilium
incus
pubis
skull
spine
talus
tibis
vomer

6
carpal

carpus
coccyx
cuboid
fibula
hallux
hammer
pelvis
rachis
radius
sacrum
stapes
tarsal
tarsus

7
cranium
hip bone
humerus
ischium
jawbone
kneecap
kneenap

malleus
mastoid
maxilla
patella
phalanx
scapula
sternum
stirrup

8
backbone
clavicle
heel bone
mandible
scaphoid
vertebra

9
anklebone
calcancus
cheekbone
funny bone

hyoid bone
maxillary
nasal bone
phalanges
thighbone
wristbone

10
astragalus
breastbone
cannon bone
collarbone
haunch bone
metacarpal
metacarpus
metatarsal
metatarsus

11
ethmoid bone
floating rib
frontal bone

12
parietal bone
spinal column
temporal bone

13
occipital bone
sesamoid bones
shoulder blade
zygomatic bone

14
innominate bone

15
vertebral column

MUSCLES

5
psoas
teres

6
biceps
rectus
soleus
vastus

7
deltoid
gluteus

iliacus
triceps

8
anconeus
masseter
opponens
pectoral
peroneus
platysma
postural
rhomboid
scalenus

serratus
skeletal
tibialis

9
depressor
iliopsoas
mylohyoid
obturator
popliteus
quadratus
sartorius
sphincter

supinator
trapezius
voluntary

10
brachialis
buccinator
epicranius
hyoglossus
quadriceps
stylohyoid
temporalis

11
orbicularis
sternohyoid

12
styloglossus

13
gastrocnemius
sternomastoid

MAJOR ARTERIES AND VEINS

5
aorta
iliac
renal
ulnar

6
radial
tibial

7
carotid
femoral
hepatic
jugular

8
brachial
cephalic
thoracic

9
pulmonary

10
innominate

mesenteric
subclavian
suprarenal

13
hepatic
portal

189

GLANDS

5
liver
sweat

6
buccal
pineal
tarsal
thymus

7
adrenal
Cowper's
gastric
mammary
parotid
thyroid

8
Brunner's
ductless
exocrine
pancreas
prostate
salivary

9
endocrine
meibomian
pituitary
sebaceous

10
Bartholin's

sublingual
suprarenal
vestibular

11
Lieberkühn's
parathyroid

12
submaxillary

13
bulbourethral
submandibular

THE EAR

5
anvil
helix
incus
pinna

6
concha
hammer
stapes
tragus

7
cochlea

eardrum
malleus
mastoid
saccule
stirrup
utricle

8
inner ear
ossicles

9
endolymph
labyrinth

middle ear
perilymph

10
oval window
scala media

11
round window

12
organ of Corti
scala tympani

13
auditory nerve
receptor cells
tunnel of corti

14
eustachian tube
fenestra ovalis
scala vestibuli

15
basilar
  membrane

fenestra rotunda
stapedius muscle
vestibular nerve

16 *and over*
membrane of reissner
  (18)
semicircular canal
  (17)
tectorial membrane
  (17)
tympanic membrane
  (16)

THE EYE

3
rod

4
cone
iris
lens

5
fovea
pupil

6
cornea
retina

sclera

7
eyelash

8
choroids

9
blind spot

10
optic nerve
yellow spot

11
ciliary body
conjunctiva

12 *and over*
aqueous humour
  (13)

hyaloid canal (12)
lacrimal gland
  (13)
meibomian gland
  (14)
vitreous humour
  (14)

Medical Fields

7
anatomy
myology
otology
urology

8
cytology
eugenics
nosology
oncology
serology

9
aetiology
andrology

audiology
histrology
necrology
neurology
orthotics
osteology
pathology
pleoptics
radiology
rhinology

10
cardiology
embryology
geriatrics
immunology

morphology
nephrology
obstetrics
orthoptics
proctology
psychology
semeiology
teratology

11
dermatology
gerontology
gynaecology
haematology
laryngology
logopaedics

paediatrics
radiography
stomatology

12
cytogenetics
epidemiology
orthopaedics
pharmacology
radiobiology
therapeutics
traumatology

13
endocrinology
ophthalmology

psychometrics

14
otolaryngology
symptomatology

15
neurophysiology
psychopathology

16
gastroenterology
psychogeriatrics

Illnesses and Injuries

2
ME
MS
TB
VD

3
cut
flu
RSI
STD

4
ache
acne
AIDS
burn
cyst
pain
rash
stye

5
caries
cramp
croup
ebola
graze
lupus
mumps
piles
polio
scald
shock
spasm
stone
ulcer

6
angina
asthma
bruise
cancer
dengue
eczema
hernia
herpes
labour
nausea
otitis
plague
rabies

scurvy
sprain
strain
stroke
thrush
typhus

7
abscess
allergy
anaemia
anthrax
earache
bulimia
choking
cholera
colitis
fistula
flutter
giardia
gumboil
itching
leprosy
lockjaw
lumbago
malaria
measles
mycosis
obesity
relapse
rickets
rubella
rupture
scabies
seizure
tetanus
vertigo

8
abrasion
anorexia
backache
beri-beri
bleeding
botulism
bruising
calculus
cold sore
cystitis
dementia
diabetes
embolism

epilepsy
fracture
gangrene
glaucoma
grand mal
headache
impetigo
jaundice
mastitis
migraine
neuritis
neurosis
orchitis
paranoia
petit mal
pleurisy
ringworm
sciatica
scrofula
shingles
sickness
smallpox
syphilis
tapeworm
tinnitus
toxaemia
trachoma
vitiligo
vomiting
wheezing

9
addiction
agoraphobia
arthritis
bilharzia
cirrhosis
chlamydia
diarrhoea
dizziness
dysentery
emphysema
enteritis
halitosis
gallstone
heartburn
hepatitis
impotence
influenza
leukaemia
nephritis
paralysis

pneumonia
poisoning
psoriasis
psychosis
sclerosis

10
alcoholism
Alzheimer's
asbestosis
bronchitis
chickenpox
common cold
diphtheria
depression
gingivitis
gonorrhoea
laceration
laryngitis
Lassa fever
meningitis
rheumatism
sore throat
thrombosis

11
emaciation
farmer's lung
haemophilia
haemorrhage
haemorrhoid
heart attack
hydrophobia
hypothermia
infertility
miscarriage
pharyngitis
prickly heat
slipped disc
strep throat
tonsillitis
yellow fever

12
athlete's foot
constipation
fibrillation
heart disease
hypochondria
hypertension
incontinence
inflammation

malnutrition
osteoporosis
Parkinsonism
sandfly fever
scarlet fever
thalassaemia
tuberculosis
typhoid fever
writer's cramp

13
bubonic plague
cardiac arrest
Crohn's disease
electric shock
elephantiasis
German measles
hypoglycaemia
leishmaniasis
leptospirosis
poliomyelitis
schizophrenia
whooping cough

14
angina pectoris
blood poisoning
Bright's disease
claustrophobia
conjunctivitis
cystic fibrosis
hyperglycaemia
Kaposi's sarcoma
river blindness
simple fracture

15
gastroenteritis
Hodgkin's disease
morning sickness

16 and over
altitude sickness
(16)
compound fracture
(16)
first-degree burn
(16)
greenstick fracture
(18)
Huntington's chorea
(17)

legionnaire's disease (19)
multiple sclerosis (17)
muscular dystrophy (17)

nervous breakdown (16)
Parkinson's disease (17)
second-degree burn (16)

sickle-cell anaemia (17)
third-degree burn (15)

Medication

4
dopa

5
aloes
jalap
l-dopa
opium
senna

6
heroin
prozac
Viagra

7
aconite
aspirin
bromide
cascara
chloral
codeine
doxepin
emetine
heparin
hirudin
insulin
menthol
mogadon
mustine
pulvule
quinine
sotalol
suramin
tylocin

8
antabuse
barbital
colcynth
colistin
diazepam
ethotoin
glucagon
hyoscine
laetrile
levodopa

mannitol
morphine
naproxen
neomycin
oxazepam
pimozide
subtilin
urethane
viomycin
warfarin

9
aloxiprin
amiloride
awapetine
barbitone
beclamide
benzhexol
biperiden
bisacodyl
bisulphan
buphenine
carbachol
carbromal
castor oil
clemizole
clonidine
clopamide
cortisone
cyclizine
digitalis
digitoxin
dithranol
Epsom salt
etoglucid
frusemide
gallamine
glymidine
iprindole
isoniazid
kanamycin
lorazepam
meclozine
megestrol
melphalan
mepacrine
mestranol

metformin
methadone
mianserin
mycomycin
nadrolone
nialamide
nicotinyl
nifuratel
nux vomica
oestrogen
oxacillin
pethidine
phenazone
phenetoin
polymixin
primidone
promazine
proquanil
pyocyanin
quinidine
rifamycin
rimiterol
stanolone
sulthiame
triclofos
troxidone
vanomycin

10
alprenolol
amantadine
ampicillin
antazoline
basitracin
benorylate
candicidin
carbomycin
cephalexin
clofibrate
clonazepam
clorindole
colchincine
cytarabine
dicoumarol
dipenzepin
disulfiram
erythritol

ethambutol
ethinamate
ethynodiol
fenoprofen
flurazepam
gentamycin
ichthammol
isoxuprine
ketoprofen
lincomycin
meperidine
mepyramine
methyldopa
metoprolol
nitrazapam
novobiocin
oxprenadol
oxypertine
papaverine
penicillin
phenacetin
piperazine
prednisone
propanolol
resorcinol
salbutamol
strychnine

11
alka seltzer
allopurinol
amodiaquine
amphetamine
amyl nitrate
apomorphine
bethanidine
capreomycin
carbimazole
cycloserine
deserpidine
diamorphine
doxorubicin
doxycycline
ethisterone
hydroxyurea
hydroxyzine
hyoscyamine

idoxuridine
ipecacuanha
mathimazole
methicillin
methoxamine
mithramycin
naphazoline
nikethamide
paracetamol
paromomycin
progestogen
terbutaline
theobromine
thymoxamine
tyrothrycin
vasopressin
vincristine

12
amphotericin
bromo seltzer
chlorambucil
chlorbutanol
chlorhexadol
debrisoquine
dichlorophen
erythromycin
fluoxuridine
Glauber's salt
guanethidine
indomethacin
isoprenaline
oxolinic acid
piperidolate
prednisolone
pyrazinamide
Rochelle salt
seltzer water
streptomycin
tetracycline
trimeprazine
valproic acid

13
aminophylline
amitriptyline
betamethasone

butobarbitone
carbenicillin
cephaloglycin
cephalosporin
chloromezanone
co-trimoxazole
dexamethasone
diathiazinine
dihydralazine
diprophylline
glibenclamide
hexobarbitone
methanderione
methylene blue
mitrobronitol
nalidixic acid
penicillamine
phenothiazine
phenylephrine

protriptylene
salicylic acid
spectinomycin
sulphadiazine
triamcinolone

14
amylobarbitone
beclomethasone
bendrofluazide
benzodiazepine
chloral hydrate
chlorcyclizine
chlorothiazide
chlorpropamide
chlorthalidone
cyclobarbitone
cyclopentamine
dexamphetamine

dextromoramide
diethylpropion
dihydrocodeine
dimethisterone
ethacrynic acid
glutethimidine
heptabarbitone
hydrocortisone
liquid paraffin
methoserpidine
milk of magnesia
paramethadione
pentobarbitone
phenethicillin
seidlitz powder
sodium sulphate
sulphacetamide
xylometazoline

15
chloramphenicol
chlormethiazole
methylcellulose
nitrogen mustard
oxytetracycline
phenolphthalein
thyrocalcitonin
trifluoperazine

16
benzyl penicillin
cyclophosphamide
dextromethorphan
lithium carbonate
paraformaldehyde
phenoxybenzamine
tetrahydrozoline

Therapies, including Complementary Therapies

4
EMDR
TENS
yoga

5
reiki

6
tai chi

7
massage
Rolfing
shiatsu

9
ayurvedic
iridology
herbalism

10
apitherapy

art therapy
autogenics
Gerson cure
homeopathy
osteopathy
sex therapy

11
acupressure
acupuncture
homoeopathy
kinesiology
naturopathy
panchakarma
play therapy
reflexology

12
aromatherapy
chiropractic
drama therapy
group therapy
hydrotherapy

hypnotherapy
light therapy
magnotherapy
music therapy
ozone therapy
shock therapy
sleep therapy

13
balneotherapy
colour therapy
family therapy
primal therapy
psychotherapy

14
Bowen technique
crystal therapy
electrotherapy
gestalt therapy
mechanotherapy
release therapy

15
aversion therapy
Rogerian therapy

16 *and over*
Alexander technique (18)
behaviour therapy (16)
cognitive therapy (16)
confrontation therapy (20)
electroconvulsive therapy (24)
electroshock therapy (19)
humanistic therapy (17)
meta-aromatherapy (16)
occupational therapy (19)
recreational therapy (19)
regression therapy (17)
relaxation therapy (17)

PEOPLES, LANGUAGES AND NATIONALITIES

2	Celt	Nuba	Blood	Kazak	Shilh
Ga	Chad	Nuer	Bulom	Khasi	Shona
Wa	Copt	Nupe	Bussi	Khmer	Sinic
Wu	Cree	Nyao	Caddo	Kiowa	Sioux
	Crow	Pali	Campa	Kissi	Sotho
3	Dane	Pedi	Carib	Kongo	Swazi
Edo	Dari	Pict	Chaga	Lamba	Swede
Ewe	Dyak	Pima	Chewa	Lango	Swiss
Fon	Efik	Pole	Chimu	Latin	Tajik
Fox	Erse	Russ	Chopi	Lenge	Tamil
Fur	Fang	Sauk	Creek	Lipan	Tembu
Gur	Finn	Scot	Croat	Lomwe	Temne
Hun	Fula	Sena	Cuban	Lulua	Teton
Ibo	Garo	Serb	Cymry	Lunda	Tigre
Ido	Gaul	Shan	Czech	Malay	Tonga
Ijo	Ge'ez	Sikh	Dayak	Mande	Tussi
Ila	Gogo	Slav	Dinka	Maori	Tutsi
Iru	Gond	Sobo	Dogon	Masai	Uzbek
Jew	Goth	Susu	Doric	Mende	Venda
Kru	Grig	Teso	Dutch	Miami	Wappo
Kui	Guro	Thai	Dyold	Moqui	Welsh
Kwa	Haya	Tswa	Dyula	Mossi	Wolof
Lao	Hehe	Turk	Fante	Munda	Xhosa
Luo	Hima	Urdu	Frank	Nahua	Yaqui
Mon	Hopi	Wend	Galla	Nandi	Yuchi
Shi	Hupa	Yako	Ganda	Naron	Yunca
Suk	Hutu	Yuma	Gbari	Ngala	Yupik
Tiv	Igbo	Zend	Gipsy	Ngoni	Zande
Twi	Iowa	Zulu	Gissi	Nguni	
Ute	Jute	Zuni	Gondi	Nguru	
Vai	Kelt		Grebo	Nkore	**6**
Yao	Kurd	**5**	Greek	Norse	Abnaki
	Lala	Acoli	Gypsy	Nyong	Acholi
4	Lapp	Afars	Hadza	Nyoro	Aeolic
Agni	Lari	Aleut	Haida	Omaha	Afghan
Akan	Lett	Anuak	Hausa	Oriya	Altaic
Ambo	Loma	Aryan	Hindi	Osage	Angoni
Arab	Lozi	Asian	Huron	Oscan	Apache
Avar	Luba	Attic	Idoma	Parsi	Arabic
Baga	Mali	Aztec	Incas	Punic	Arawak
Bali	Mano	Bamum	Indic	Pygmy	Argive
Beja	Manx	Bantu	Iraqi	Riffs	Aymara
Bena	Maya	Bassa	Irish	Roman	Aztecs
Bete	Meru	Batak	Kadai	Ronga	Bakota
Bini	Moki	Baule	Kafir	Rundi	Balega
Bisa	Moor	Bemba	Kamba	Sango	Baltic
Bodo	Moxu	Benga	Kamla	Saudi	Baoule
Boer	Naga	Berta	Kansa	Saxon	Basque
Bubi	Nama	Bhili	Karen	Scots	Basuto
					Bateke

Bayaka
Berber
Biloxi
Bokmal
Brahui
Breton
Briton
Bulgar
Caribs
Cayuga
Celtic
Chagga
Chokwe
Cocopa
Coptic
Creole
Cymric
Dakota
Danish
Dogrib
Dorian
Eskimo
Fijian
French
Fulani
Gaelic
Gallic
Gascon
German
Gothic
Hebrew
Herero
Ibibio
Indian
Inupik
Ionian
Italic
Jewish
Judaic
Kabyle
Kaffir
Kanuri
Kichai
Kikuyu
Korean
Kpelle
Kpessi
Kurukh
Libyan
Lumbwa
Luvale
Manchu
Mandan
Micmac

Mixtec
Mohave
Mohawk
Mongol
Murozi
Navaho
Ndonga
Nepali
Ngbaka
Ngombe
Ngwato
Nootka
Norman
Nsenga
Nubian
Nyanja
Ojibwa
Oneida
Ostiak
Ostman
Ottawa
Paiute
Papuan
Parian
Parsee
Pashto
Patois
Pawnee
Pequot
Pericu
Piegan
Polish
Pueblo
Pushto
Pushtu
Quakaw
Rajput
Rolong
Romaic
Romany
Rwanda
Ryukyu
Sabine
Salish
Sambaa
Samoan
Santee
Sarcee
Seneca
Senufo
Serere
Sindhi
Slavic
Slovak

Somali
Soviet
Sukuma
Syriac
Syrian
Telegu
Telugu
Teuton
Theban
Thonga
Tlokwa
Toltec
Tongan
Trojan
Tsonga
Tswana
Tuareg
Tungus
Turkic
Tuscan
Veddah
Viking
Votyak
Warega
Warrau
Yankee
Yemeni
Yoruba
Zenaga

7
Abenaki
Acadian
African
Amerind
Amharic
Angolan
Arabian
Aramaic
Aramean
Arapaho
Araucan
Arikara
Armoric
Ashanti
Asiatic
Avestan
Baganda
Bagirmi
Bakweii
Balanta
Balochi
Bambara
Bangala

Bapende
Barotse
Barundi
Basonge
Batonka
Batutsi
Bedouin
Belgian
Bengali
Berbers
Bisayan
British
Bunduka
Burmese
Bushmen
Catalan
Catawba
Chechen
Chilcal
Chilean
Chinese
Chinook
Choctaw
Cornish
Cypriot
Dagomba
Dalicad
English
Finnish
Flemish
Frisian
Gaulish
Griquas
Guarani
Haitian
Hamitic
Hebraic
Hessian
Hidatsa
Hittite
Iberian
Ilocano
Iranian
Israeli
Italian
Karanga
Khoisan
Kirghiz
Kurdish
Kuwaiti
Laotian
Lappish
Latvian
Lingala

Lombard
Lugbara
Maduran
Mahican
Malinke
Maltese
Mandyak
Mapuche
Marathi
Mashona
Mexican
Mohegan
Mohican
Moorish
Mordvin
Morisco
Mozareb
Mulatto
Nahuatl
Namaqua
Natchez
Nauruan
Ndebele
Ngbandi
Nilotes
Nilotic
Nynorsk
Ojibway
Orejone
Ottoman
Pahlavi
Palaung
Persian
Prakrit
Punjabi
Quechua
Romance
Russian
Rwandan
Samburu
Samiote
Samoyed
Sandawe
Santali
Semitic
Serbian
Serrano
Shawnee
Shilluk
Siamese
Slovene
Songhai
Spanish
Spartan

Stonies	Dutchman	Nigerian	Cambodian	Uruguayan
Swahili	Egyptian	Nuba-Fula	Cantonese	Winnebago
Swedish	Estonian	Nyamwesi	Caucasian	
Tagalog	Ethiopic	Old Norse	Ceylonese	**10**
Tibetan	Etruscan	Old Saxon	Chari-Nile	Aboriginal
Tigrina	Eurasian	Onondaga	Cheremiss	Abyssinian
Tlingit	Frankish	Parthian	Chickasaw	Anglo-Saxon
Tonkawa	Gallican	Pelasgic	Chipewyan	Araucanian
Turkana	Garnbian	Peruvian	Chippeway	Assiniboin
Turkish	Georgian	Phrygian	Cimmerian	Athabascan
Ugandan	Germanic	Powhatan	Colombian	Australian
Umbrian	Ghanaian	Prussian	Congolese	Autochthon
Umbundu	Gujarati	Quichuan	Dravidian	Babylonian
Venetic	Gujerati	Romanian	Esperanto	Bathlaping
Walloon	Guyanese	Romansch	Esquimaux	Bella Coola
Watutsi	Hawaiian	Rumanian	Ethiopian	Circassian
Wichita	Hellenic	Sanskrit	Frenchman	Cornishman
Wyandot	Helvetic	Scotsman	Hanseatic	Costa Rican
Yiddish	Honduran	Scottish	Hibernian	Dutchwoman
Zairese	Illinois	Seminole	Hottentot	Ecuadorian
Zambian	Illyrian	Shoshoni	Hungarian	Englishman
	Irishman	Shushwap	Icelander	Finno-Ugric
8	Iroquois	Sicilian	Icelandic	Florentine
Abderite	Japanese	Slavonic	Israelite	Guatemalan
Aguaruna	Javanese	Spaniard	Jordanian	High German
Akkadian	Kashmiri	Sudanese	Kabardian	Hindustani
Albanian	Kickapoo	Sumerian	Kannarese	Hottentots
Algerian	Kimbundu	Tallensi	Karankawa	Indonesian
American	Kingwana	Teutonic	Kgalagedi	Irishwoman
Andorran	Kipsigis	Tunisian	Low German	Israelitic
Antiguan	Kootenay	Turanian	Malaysian	Karamojong
Assyrian	Kuki-Chin	Turkomen	Mauritian	Leni-Lenape
Austrian	Kukuruku	Vandalic	Menominee	Lithuanian
Bahamian	Kwakiutl	Visigoth	Mongolian	Melanesian
Balinese	Kwanyama	Welshman	Nepaulese	Mingrelian
Bavarian	Lebanese		Norwegian	Minnetaree
Bergdama	Liberian	**9**	Ostrogoth	Monegasque
Bermudan	Mahratti	Abkhasian	Pakistani	Montagnais
Bohemian	Makassar	Aborigine	Penobscot	Neapolitan
Bolivian	Malagasy	Afrikaans	Provencal	Nicaraguan
Bushongo	Malawian	Afrikaner	Rhodesian	Nicobarese
Cambrian	Mamprusi	Algonkian	Roumanian	Old English
Canadian	Mandarin	Algonquin	Samaritan	Panamanian
Chaldaic	Mandingo	Anatolian	Sardinian	Paraguayan
Chaldean	Mandinka	Apalachee	Sere Mundu	Patagonian
Chamorro	Matabele	Arrnenian	Sinhalese	Philippine
Cherokee	Memphian	Ashochimi	Sri Lankan	Philistine
Cheyenne	Menomini	Assarnese	Sundanese	Phoenician
Comanche	Moroccan	Barbadian	Taiwanese	Polynesian
Corsican	Moru-Madi	Bengalese	Tanzanian	Pomeranian
Cushitic	Muskogee	Blackfeet	Tocharian	Portuguese
Cyrenaic	Negritos	Brazilian	Tuscarora	Rajasthani
Delaware	Nepalese	Bulgarian	Ukrainian	Scotswoman
Delphian	Nez Perce	Byzantine	Ulotrichi	Senegalese

Serbo-Croat
Shoshonean
Venezuelan
Vietnamese
Welshwoman

11
Afro-Asiatic
Argentinian
Azerbaijani

Bangarwanda
Bangladeshi
Belorussian
Frenchwoman
Greenlander
Mauretanian
Narraganset
Palestinian
Scots Gaelic
Sino-Tibetan

Susquehanna
Trinidadian

12
Byelorussian
Cornishwoman
Englishwoman
Indo-European
Lunda-Bajokwe
Moru-Mangbetu

New Zealander
Plattdeutsch
Scandinavian
Tirlbeto-Burman

13
Middle English
Passamaquoddy
Pidgin English
Queen's English

PLANTS

Cereals, Rice, etc.

3
far
oca
rye
zea

4
bere
bran
corn
dari
dohl
dura
gram
malt
meal
oats

rice
sago
teff

5
bajra
bajri
durra
durum
emmer
ervum
fundi
grain
grist
grout
maize
mummy

paddy
pulse
rivet
spelt
straw
typha
wheat

6
barley
darnel
dhurra
farina
hominy
mealie
meslin
millet

muesli
nocake
raggee
shorts

7
cassava
corncob
rokeage
sorghum
tapioca
zea mays

8
mangcorn
seed corn
semolina

9
arrowroot
buckwheat
garavance
middlings
pearl rice
pot barley
seed grain
sweet corn

10
barleycorn
barleymeal
Guinea
corn
Indian
corn

11
pearl barley
pearl millet
spring wheat
summer
wheat
turkey wheat
winter
wheat

12
German
millet
Indian millet
mountain rice
Scotch barley
winter barley

Flowers

3
ins
lei
may

4
aloe
arum
balm
flag
ixia
lily
musk
pink
rabi
rose
sego
weld

5
agave
aspic
aster
briar
broom
canna
daisy
flora
gorse

gowan
henna
lilac
lotus
lupin
ox-eye
oxlip
pansy
peony
petal
phlox
poker
poppy
sepal
sisal
stock
tansy
thyme
tulip
viola
yucca
yulan

6
acacia
acaena
alpine
alsike
arnica

azalea
balsam
bellis
bennet
borage
bryony
cactus
camass
clover
coleus
cosmos
cotton
cowpea
crocus
dahlia
darnel
fennel
iberis
kochia
lupine
madder
mallow
mimosa
myrtle
nenne
nettle
opulus
orchid
oxalis

petrea
rocket
salvia
scilla
sesame
squill
sundew
teasel
thrift
tulipa
violet
wattle
yarrow
zinnia

7
aconite
aloysia
alyssum
anemone
begonia
blossom
bouquet
bugloss
burdock
campion
catmint
chaplet
chicory

clarkia
cowslip
cup rose
day lily
deutzia
dittany
dog rose
festoon
freesia
fuchsia
gentian
gerbera
gladdon
guarana
heather
hemlock
honesty
hyacine
jacinth
jasmine
jonquil
kingcup
lantana
linaria
lobelia
lupinus
marybud
may lily
melissa

milfoil
nigella
nosegay
opuntia
papaver
petunia
primula
rambler
rampion
roselle
sea-pink
spiraea
syringa
tea rose
thistle
timothy
ursinia
verbena
vervain
witloof

8
abutilon
acanthus
ageratum
agrimony
amaranth
angelica
arum lily

asphodel	toadflax	pimpernel	poinsettia	horn-of-plenty
auricula	tuberose	polygonum	polianthus	Iceland poppy
bedstraw	turnsole	pyrethrum	potentilla	Jacob's ladder
bluebell	valerian	saxifrage	ranunculus	lady's slipper
buddleia	veronica	speedwell	snapdragon	morning glory
camellia	viscaria	spikenard	sweet briar	none-so-pretty
capsicum	wild rose	sunflower	touch-me-not	old man's beard
catchfly	wisteria	tiger lily	wallflower	orange flower
clematis	woodbine	torch lily	white poppy	pasque flower
cockspur	xanthium	tormentil	wind flower	pheasant's ego
crowfoot		verbascum		rhododendron
cyclamen	**9**	water flag	**11**	snow in summer
daffodil	Aaron's rod	water lily	antirrhinum	Solomon's seal
dianthus	amaryllis	wolf's bane	bittersweet	sweet William
dropwort	aquilegia		blood flower	virgin's bower
erigeron	arrowroot	**10**	cabbage rose	
eucharis	buttercup	agapanthus	calceolaria	**13**
feverfew	calendula	amaranthus	convolvulus	alpine flowers
foxglove	campanula	aspidistra	cotoneaster	blanket flower
gardenia	candytuft	belladonna	everlasting	bleeding heart
geranium	carnation	bell flower	fig marigold	bougainvillea
gladiola	celandine	busy lizzie	forget-me-not	Bristol flower
gloriosa	cherry pie	calliopsis	gillyflower	cherry blossom
gloxinia	China rose	China aster	globeflower	Christmas rose
harebell	cineraria	cinquefoil	guelder rose	chrysanthemum
haresear	clove pink	citronella	honey-flower	creeping jenny
hepatica	cockscomb	coquelicot	honeysuckle	crown imperial
hibiscus	coltsfoot	cornflower	kidney vetch	grape hyacinth
hyacinth	columbine	corn violet	lady's mantle	huntsman's horn
japonica	composite	cranesbill	leopard lily	marsh marigold
laburnum	coreopsis	crow flower	London pride	orange blossom
larkspur	corn poppy	damask rose	loosestrife	passion flower
lavatera	cymbidium	delphinium	love-in-a-mist	rose of Jericho
lavender	dandelion	Easter lily	meadowsweet	sweet calabash
lent lily	digitalis	fritillary	Nancy pretty	traveller's joy
magnolia	dog violet	gaillardia	pepper elder	trumpet flower
marigold	dove's foot	goatsbeard	poppy mallow	water hyacinth
moss rose	edelweiss	golden drop	ragged robin	winter aconite
musk rose	eglantine	granadilla	rambler rose	
noisette	eyebright	gypsophila	red-hot poker	**14**
nymphaea	forsythia	heart's-ease	sea lavender	Canterbury bell
oleander	gladiolus	helianthus	spear flower	cardinal flower
phacetia	goldenrod	heliotrope	strawflower	lords and ladies
phormium	hellebore	immortelle	sweet rocket	love-in-idleness
plumbago	hollyhock	lady's smock	sweet sultan	shepherd's purse
pond lily	hydrangea	marguerite	tiger flower	
primrose	impatiens	mayblossom	wild flowers	**15**
rock rose	jessamine	mignonette	wood anemone	Christmas
samphire	lotus lily	nasturtium		flower
scabious	mayflower	nightshade	**12**	lily of the valley
skullcap	monkshood	orange lily	apple blossom	Michaelmas
snowdrop	moon daisy	ox-eye daisy	autumn crocus	daisy
stapella	narcissus	pennyroyal	cuckoo flower	star of
sweet pea	patchouli	periwinkle	heather bells	Bethlehem

Fruit

3
Cox
fig
haw
hip
nut
uva

4
akee
crab
date
gage
kaki
kiwi
lime
mare
mast
pear
plum
rasp
sloe
ugli

5
abhal
agava
agave
apple
arnot
betel
cubeb
drupe
grape
grout
guava
lemon
mango
melon
merry
morel
olive
papaw
peach
pecan
prune
ribes
rubus

6
almond
banana

cherry
citron
citrus
cobnut
damson
durian
elk nut
ginger
linden
loquat
lychee
medlar
muscat
nutmeg
orange
papaya
pawpaw
peanut
pignut
pippin
pomelo
punica
quince
raisin
rennet
russet
samara
sharon
walnut
zapote

7
apricot
avocado
bramble
buckeye
bullace
cassava
cedrate
cheston
coconut
codling
corinth
currant
deal nut
dessert
dogwood
filbert
genipap
golding
hautboy
hog-plum

kumquat
malmsey
mayduke
mineola
morello
pumpkin
rhubarb
rosehip
satsuma
soursop
sultana
tangelo
wilding

8
allspice
bayberry
beechnut
bergamot
betelnut
bilberry
breadnut
buckmast
burgamot
calabash
cat's head
chestnut
coquilla
cream nut
date plum
dogberry
earthnut
figapple
fox grape
hazelnut
honeydew
ivory nut
japonica
mandarin
may apple
minneola
mulberry
muscatel
musk pear
oleaster
pearmain
plantain
prunello
quandong
rambutan
shaddock
sweeting

tamarind
tayberry
Valencia
whitsour
windfall

9
apple john
beechmast
blueberry
brazil nut
buck's horn
butternut
carmelite
cherimoya
corozo nut
crab apple
cranberry
damascene
greengage
groundnut
hindberry
king apple
love apple
mirabelle
monkey nut
muscadine
musk apple
musk melon
nectarine
nonpareil
oxycoccus
persimmon
pineapple
pistachio
rambostan
raspberry
star apple
tamarinds
tangerine
victorine
Worcester

10
bird cherry
blackberry
blackheart
breadfruit
cantaloupe
charentais
clementine
clingstone

cream fruit
damask plum
elderberry
florentine
gooseberry
granadilla
grapefruit
Indian date
loganberry
Madeira nut
mangosteen
marking nut
orange musk
pome citron
queen apple
redcurrant
redstreak
sorbapple
stone fruit
strawberry
watermelon
wild cherry
winter pear

11
anchovy pear
bitter apple
blood orange
boysenberry
candleberry
China orange
chokecherry
French berry
granny smith
huckleberry
leathercoat
monkey bread
myrtle berry
navel orange
pomegranate
pompelmoose
quarrington
russet apple
scuppernong
sharon fruit
winter apple

12
bitter almond
blackcurrant
chaumontelle
Chester grape

chocolate nut
cochineal fig
cooking apple
custard apple
passion fruit
pistachio nut
serviceberry
Victoria plum
white currant

whortleberry
winter cherry
winter citron

13 *and over*
alligator pear (13)
Barbados cherry (14)
Blenheim orange (14)
Cape gooseberry (14)

Catherine pear (13)
conference pear (14)
cornelian cherry (16)
golden delicious (15)
mandarin orange (14)
morello cherry (13)
preserved fruit (14)
Seville orange (13)

Herbs and Spices

3
bay
rue

4
balm
dill
mace
mint
rape
sage
woad

5
anise
basil
chive
clary
clove
cress
cumin
grass
myrrh
senna
tansy
thyme

6
bennet
betony

borage
capers
catnip
chilli
chives
cloves
endive
fennel
garlic
ginger
hyssop
isatis
lovage
nutmeg
orpine
pepper
savory
sesame
sorrel

7
aconite
burdock
caraway
catmint
cayenne
chervil
chicory
comfrey
dittany

gentian
henbane
juniper
lettuce
milfoil
mustard
oregano
paprika
parsley
pimento
rampion
saffron
spignel
succory
tabasco
vanilla

8
agrimony
allspice
angelica
camomile
cardamom
cardamon
cinnamon
feverfew
hog's bean
lavender
lungwort
marigold

marjoram
origanum
rosemary
samphire
tarragon
turmeric
wormwood

9
baneberry
bear's foot
chamomile
chickweed
clary sage
coriander
eyebright
fenugreek
goose foot
groundsel
hellebore
horehound
lemon balm
liquorice
sea fennel
spearmint
tormentil

10
asafoetida
hyoscyamus

lemon thyme
motherwort
penny royal
peppermint
pulmonaria
watercress
willow herb

11
dragon's head
hedge hyssop
horseradish
pot marigold
pot marjoram
sweet rocket
swine's cress
winter green

12 *and over*
adder's tongue (12)
chrysanthemum (13)
Florence fennel (14)
medicinal herb (13)
mournful widow
  (13)
southernwood (12)
summer savory (12)
sweet marjoram
  (13)
winter savory (12)

Miscellaneous Plants

3
box
cos
hop
ivy
oat
oca
pea
rue
rye
tea
yam
zea

4
alfa
aloe
arum
balm
bean
beet
bent
cane
cole
corn
crab
dill
diss
dock
fern
flag
gale
hemp
herb
holm
ilex
iris
jute
kale
kali
leek
ling
mint
moss
musk
nard
peat
pipi
race
rape
reed
rhea

rice
root
rush
sage
sago
sloe
spud
star
tare
taro
thea
tree
tutu
ulex
vine
wald
weed
woad
wort

5
agave
algae
anise
aspic
aster
bhang
brake
briar
broom
bugle
cacao
calla
clary
clove
couch
cress
cumin
cycad
daisy
durra
erica
fungi
furze
gorse
gourd
grass
henna
holly
kunai
liana
lotus

lupin
maize
medic
morel
olive
osier
oxlip
paddy
phlox
poker
radix
rheum
rubia
savoy
sedge
senna
shrub
sisal
stole
sumac
swede
tansy
thorn
thyme
urena
vetch
vicia
viola
vitis
wheat
withy
wrack
yerba
yucca
yupon
zamia

6
acorus
amomum
annual
arabis
arbute
azalea
bamboo
barley
batata
bennet
betony
borage
bryony
burnet

cactus
cassia
catnip
cicely
cissus
cistus
clover
cockle
conium
cosmos
cotton
cowage
croton
daphne
darnel
dodder
eddoes
endive
eryngo
fat hen
fennel
ferula
fescue
fungus
fustet
galium
garlic
gromil
henbit
hervea
hyssop
iberis
indigo
jujube
kalmia
kiekie
lichen
locust
lolium
loofah
lupine
madder
maguey
mallow
manioc
marram
millet
mimosa
myrtle
nettle
nubbin
oil nut

orchid
oxalis
pampas
peanut
pepper
potato
privet
protea
quinoa
radish
raggee
rattan
redtop
rocket
sabine
scilla
sesame
smilax
sorrel
spurge
squall
squash
sundew
teasel
thrift
urtica
viscum
wicker
yarrow

7
absinth
aconite
all-good
all-heal
althaea
aquatic
arbutus
barilla
begonia
bistort
bogbean
bracken
bramble
bugloss
bulrush
burdock
bur-reed
calamus
calypso
campion
caraway

cassada
cassava
catmint
chicory
clarkia
clot-bur
columba
comfrey
cowbane
cow-itch
cowslip
cow weed
creeper
cudbear
cudweed
cup moss
dittany
dogbane
dog's rue
ear-wort
elatine
epacris
esparto
eugenia
felwort
festuca
ficaria
figwort
foxtail
frogbit
fumaria
funaria
genista
gentian
gerbera
ginseng
gutwort
heather
hemlock
henbane
herbage
honesty
hop bind
hop vine
humulus
ipomaea
jasmine
Jew's ear
jonquil
juniper
karatas
lobelia

lucerne	amphigen	duckweed	oleander	wall-wort
lychnis	angelica	dumb cane	oleaster	wartwort
mahonica	anthemis	earth nut	peat moss	water-poa
matweed	asphodel	earth pea	phormium	wild oats
monocot	banewort	eglatere	pilewort	wild rose
mullein	barberry	epiphyte	pink root	wind seed
mustard	bearbind	erigeron	plantlet	with-wine
nonsuch	bear's ear	erisimum	plantule	woodbine
opuntia	bellwort	euonymus	plumbago	woodruff
panicum	berberis	finochio	polygala	woodsage
papyrus	berberry	fireweed	pond weed	wormwood
parelle	bignonia	flaxweed	prunella	xanthium
parsley	bilberry	fleabane	puffball	zingiber
primula	bindweed	flixweed	purslane	
pumpkin	bogberry	foalfoot	putchock	**9**
quamash	bogwhort	foxglove	red algae	abrotanum
quassia	boxthorn	fumitory	rib grass	aerophyte
ragwort	brassica	galangal	roccella	amaryllis
rambler	bullweed	garcinia	rock rose	arbor-vine
rampion	camomile	girasole	rosebush	artemisia
rhubarb	cannabis	gloxinia	rosemary	artichoke
robinia	capsicum	glumales	rye grass	asclepias
saffron	catchfly	glumella	sainfoin	balsamine
salsify	cat's tail	glyceria	saltwort	basil weed
salsola	centaury	goutweed	seedling	bean caper
sanicle	cerealia	gratiola	sengreen	bearberry
sarcina	charlock	gromwell	septfoil	bent grass
senecio	chayroot	harebell	shamrock	bird's foot
seringa	cinchona	hare's ear	skull-cap	bloodroot
solanum	cinnamon	hartwort	soapwort	blue algae
soybean	cleavers	hawkweed	sourdock	briar root
spiraea	clematis	hawthorn	sow bread	brooklime
sporule	clubmoss	hibiscus	stapelia	brookmint
statice	cocculus	ice plant	starwort	brookweed
syringa	cockspur	knapweed	sun plant	broomcorn
thistle	cockweed	lacebark	sweetsop	broomrape
tobacco	coleseed	laceleaf	tamarack	butterbur
trefoil	cornflag	larkspur	tamarisk	candytuft
truffle	cornrose	lavender	tara fern	canebrake
uncaria	costmary	lungwort	tarragon	cardamine
vanilla	cowberry	lustwort	tea plant	carrageen
verbena	cowgrass	male fern	tickweed	caryopsis
vervain	cow-wheat	mandrake	tremella	celandine
vetiver	crow silk	mangrove	tuberose	chamomile
waratah	danewort	marjoram	turk's cap	chaparral
zedoary	dewberry	mat grass	turmeric	chaya root
zizania	diandria	may bloom	turnsole	cherry bay
	dog briar	milkweed	valerian	chickweed
8	dog grass	monocarp	veratrum	china root
acanthus	dog's bane	moonseed	veronica	choke weed
adiantum	dolichos	mushroom	viburnum	cineraria
agrimony	downweed	myosotis	victoria	club grass
air plant	dropwort	nonesuch	wait-a-bit	coal plant
amaranth	duckmeat	nut grass	wallmoss	cockscomb

203

cock's head	honeywort	sweet root	diadelphia	rest harrow
colchicum	horehound	sweet rush	dog's fennel	rhein berry
colocynth	horsefoot	sweet wood	dog's poison	rhinanthus
colt's foot	horsetail	sweet wort	dog's tongue	rose acacia
columbine	hypericum	taraxacum	dracontium	rose mallow
coral wort	Indian fig	thorn-bush	entophytes	salicornia
coriander	jessamine	toadstool	eriocaulon	saprophyte
corn poppy	Job's tears	tonka bean	eupatorium	setterwort
corn salad	kite's foot	toothwort	fimble hemp	shave grass
cotyledon	knee holly	tormentil	friar's cowl	silver weed
cramp bark	knot grass	trifolium	fritillary	sneezewort
crowberry	lady's muck	umbilicus	furrow weed	sow thistle
cuckoo bud	lark's heel	villarsia	gaultheria	Spanish nut
culver key	liquorice	wall cress	globe daisy	speargrass
decagynia	liverwort	waterlath	globularia	spleenwort
decandria	meadow rue	waterwort	goatsbeard	stonebreak
desert rod	milk vetch	wax myrtle	goosegrass	stork's bill
digitalis	mistletoe	whitecrop	granadilla	sweet briar
digitaria	monk's hood	widow wail	grass wrack	swine bread
dittander	moschatel	wolf's bane	gymnosperm	swinegrass
dockcress	mousetail	wolf's claw	heartsease	swordgrass
doob grass	nepenthes	wormgrass	helianthus	tiger's foot
duck's foot	patchouli	woundwort	herb robert	touch-me-not
duck's meat	pellitory	xanthosia	herds grass	tragacanth
dulcamara	pimpernel		honey stalk	Venus's comb
dyer's weed	poison ivy	**10**	Indian corn	wall pepper
eglantine	poison oak	Adam-and-	Indian reed	water plant
equisetum	pyracanth	Eve	Indian shot	way thistle
euphorbia	pyrethrum	adder grass	Jew's mallow	whitethorn
euphrasia	rafflesia	agrostemma	kidneywort	wild indigo
evergreen	red clover	alabastrus	king's spear	willow herb
evolvulus	red pepper	amaranthus	knapbottle	willow weed
eyebright	rocambole	angiosperm	lycopodium	witch hazel
fenugreek	rock cress	arbor vitae	maidenhair	wolf's peach
fever root	safflower	belladonna	manila hemp	wood sorrel
feverwort	saxifrage	bitterwort	may blossom	yellow-root
forsythia	smartweed	brome grass	mock orange	yellow-wort
gelanthus	snakeroot	brown algae	mock privet	
germander	snakeweed	butterbush	muscardine	**11**
glasswort	snowberry	butterweed	nasturtium	bear's breech
golden cup	soap plant	candelilla	nightshade	bishop's weed
goldenrod	socotrine	cascarilla	nipplewort	blackbonnet
goose corn	spearmint	cinquefoil	panic grass	bottle gourd
goosefoot	spearwort	cloudberry	passiflora	brank ursine
grapewort	speedwell	corncockle	pennyroyal	calceolaria
grasspoly	spikenard	corn rocket	pentstemon	calcyanthus
greenweed	spirogyra	cotton rose	peppermint	canary grass
ground ivy	spoonwort	cottonweed	pepperwort	chanterelle
groundnut	stonecrop	couch grass	periwinkle	coffee plant
groundsel	sugar beet	cow parsley	poker plant	convolvulus
hair grass	sugar cane	crake berry	potentilla	corn parsley
hellebore	sun spurge	crotalaria	pyracantha	cotton grass
hoarhound	sweet flag	cuckoopint	race ginger	cotton plant
holly fern	sweet john	devil's club	ranunculus	crest marine

cuckoo's meat
dame's violet
dog's cabbage
dog's mercury
dragon's head
Dragon's wort
Dutch clover
erythronium
everlasting
fescue grass
fig marigold
finger grass
fuller's weed
giant cactus
giant fennel
greendragon
guelder rose
hart's tongue
hob thistle
honeysuckle
humble plant
Iceland moss
Indian berry
Indian cress
indigo plant
kidney vetch
lattice leaf
laurustinus
London pride
marram grass
marsh mallow
meadow-sweet
milk thistle
millet grass
moon trefoil
moving plant
oyster plant
pelargonium
pepper grass
poison sumac
prickly pear
ribbon grass
ripple grass
scurvy grass
sempervivum
serpentaria
snail clover
snail flower

sparrow wort
stagger bush
star thistle
swallow-wort
sweet cicely
sweet cistus
sweet potato
swine's cress
thorough wax
tinkar's root
tonquin bean
tussac grass
viper's grass
water radish
water violet
white clover
white darnel
winter berry
winter bloom
winter cress
wintergreen
wood anemone
xanthoxylum
zygophyllum

12
adder's tongue
aerial plants
bladderwrack
buffalo grass
Christ's thorn
compass plant
corn marigold
cow's lungwort
custard apple
deadly carrot
dragon's blood
echinocactus
erythroxylon
feather grass
fennel flower
fool's parsley
German millet
globe thistle
hempagrimony
hound's tongue
Indian millet
Indian turnip

mangel wurzel
melon thistle
palma christi
pickerel weed
pitcher plant
quaking grass
reindeer moss
rhododendron
sarsaparilla
snail trefoil
Solomon's seal
southern wood
Spanish broom
Spanish grass
sparrow grass
spear thistle
strangleweed
swine thistle
timothy grass
tobacco plant
torch thistle
Venus flytrap
vinegar plant
virgin's bower
water hemlock
water parsnip
water pitcher
water soldier
white campion
whitlow grass
whortleberry
wild Williams
winter cherry
yellow rattle

13
crown imperial
dog's-tail grass
elephant grass
elephant's foot
flowering fern
flowering rush
globe amaranth
golden thistle
Indian tobacco
meadow saffron
raspberry bush
Scotch thistle

spike lavender
summer cypress
sweet marjoram
traveller's joy
Venus's fly trap
vervain mallow
viper's bugloss
wall pennywort
water calamint
water crowfoot
water hyacinth
wayfaring tree

14
blackberry bush
blue couch grass
carline thistle
distaff thistle
fuller's thistle
giant groundsel
golden lungwort
golden mouse-ear
gooseberry bush
lords and ladies
mountain sorrel
prince's feather
sensitive plant
shepherd's pouch
shepherd's purse
shepherd's staff
snake's-head iris
Spanish bayonet
starch hyacinth
treacle mustard
wood nightshade

15
golden saxifrage
Italian rye grass
shepherd's needle
Venus's navelwort
virginia creeper
woody nightshade

16
deadly nightshade

Trees, Shrubs and Bushes

2	doob	butea	sumac	kittul	blossom
bo	holm	cacao	taxus	kumbuk	blue gum
ti	hura	carob	thorn	laurel	boxwood
	ilex	cedar	tilia	lignum	buckeye
3	kina	china	trunk	linden	cabbage
asa	kiri	clove	tsuga	locust	camphor
ash	lana	copse	tulip	macoya	canella
bay	leaf	coral	walan	mallee	catalpa
bel	lime	dwarf	yucca	mastic	coconut
box	lote	ebony	yulan	medlar	conifer
elm	milk	elder	zamia	mimosa	coquito
fig	mowa	fagus		myrtle	cork oak
fir	nipa	fruit	**6**	nettle	cowtree
gum	palm	glade	acacia	nutmeg	cypress
haw	pear	glory	almond	orange	daddock
hip	pine	grass	aralia	papaya	dogwood
hop	pipe	grove	arbute	pawpaw	dottard
ita	plum	guava	balata	pepper	duramen
ivy	pole	hazel	balsam	poplar	durmast
may	rata	henna	bamboo	privet	elk wood
nut	rimu	holly	banana	quince	elm tree
oak	roan	Judas	banyan	redbud	fan palm
sal	root	karri	baobab	red fir	fig tree
sap	rose	kauri	bog oak	red gum	fir cone
tea	sloe	kunai	bonsai	rubber	fir tree
tod	sorb	larch	bo-tree	sallow	foliage
yew	teak	lemon	bottle	salvia	fuchsia
	teil	lilac	branch	sapota	gum tree
4	twig	macaw	brazil	sappan	heather
acer	ulex	mango	buriti	she oak	hemlock
akee	vine	maple	butter	sissoo	hickory
aloe		myall	button	sorrel	holm oak
amla	**5**	nyssa	carapa	spruce	jasmine
arar	abele	oaken	cashew	sylvan	juniper
arum	Abies	olive	catkin	tallow	king gum
atap	acorn	osier	caudex	timber	kumquat
bael	agave	palas	cedrat	tupelo	logwood
balm	agila	papaw	cerris	veneer	mugwort
bark	alder	peach	cerrus	vinery	nut pine
bass	amber	pecan	cherry	walnut	oak tree
bead	anise	picea	citron	wattle	oil palm
beam	anona	pinon	coffee	willow	orchard
bhel	apple	plane	cornel	yampon	palmyra
bito	arbor	plank	daphne		pollard
bixa	areca	quina	deodar	**7**	quillai
bole	Argan	roble	emblic	ambatch	red pine
cork	aspen	roots	fustic	aniseed	redwood
dali	assai	rowan	ginkgo	Arbutus	rosebay
dari	balsa	salal	gomuti	ash tree	sandbox
date	beech	sally	illipe	avocado	sapling
deal	birch	sapan	jarrah	banksia	sapwood
dhak	bunya	smoke	jujube	bay tree	sequoia

service
shallon
silk oak
snow gum
soursop
spindle
spiraea
tanghin
teatree
varnish
wallaba
wax palm
wax tree

8

alburnum
allspice
ash grove
barberry
bass wood
bayberry
beam tree
beachnut
berberis
bergamot
black gum
box elder
calabash
camellia
chestnut
cinchona
coco palm
coco tree
cork tree
coolabah
crab tree
date palm
eucalypt
fraxinus
gardenia
giant gum
guaiacum
hardbeam
hawthorn
holly oak
hornbeam
ironbark
ironwood
jack tree
jack wood
japonica
kingwood
laburnum
lacebark

lavender
lima wood
long jack
magnolia
mahogany
mangrove
manna-ash
milk tree
mulberry
musk wood
oleaster
oleander
palmetto
palm tree
pandanus
pear tree
pinaster
pine cone
pine tree
pistacia
pockwood
quillaia
raintree
red cedar
red maple
rosemary
rosewood
royal oak
sago palm
saltbush
scrub oak
seedling
silky oak
sugar gum
swamp oak
sweet bay
sweet gum
sycamore
tamarind
tamarisk
toon wood
viburnum
white ash
white fir
white gum
white oak
wisteria
witch elm
wormwood

9

ailanthus
algarroba
aloes wood

alpine fir
angophora
araucaria
balsam fir
bearberry
blackwood
brown pine
buckthorn
butternut
carob tree
china tree
coral tree
crab apple
deciduous
euphorbia
evergreen
flame tree
forest oak
forsythia
fruit tree
grapevine
greenwood
ground ash
ground oak
hackberry
ivory palm
jacaranda
Judas tree
kokrawood
lance wood
mangroves
mistletoe
paper bark
persimmon
pistachio
plane tree
poison ivy
quickbeam
rowan tree
sapodilla
sassafras
satinwood
Scotch elm
Scotch fir
screw pine
shade tree
shell bark
silver fir
snake wood
sour gourd
stone pine
sweetwood
thorn tree
touch-wood

tulip tree
whitebeam
white pine
whitewood
yacca wood
zebra wood

10

almond tree
arbor vitae
bird cherry
blackthorn
blue spruce
brazilwood
breadfruit
bunya-bunya
burra-murra
butter tree
coastal tea
coniferous
cotton tree
cottonwood
Douglas fir
dragon tree
eucalyptus
fiddle wood
flooded gum
frangipani
garlic pear
green-heart
holly berry
Indian date
japati palm
Joshua tree
kunai grass
letter wood
mangosteen
orange-ball
orange wood
pagoda tree
paper birch
pine needle
poinsettia
prickly ash
quercitron
raffia palm
rubber tree
sandalwood
Scotch pine
silk-cotton
silver-bell
sneeze-wood
Spanish fir
strawberry

sugar-maple
swamp maple
tall wattle
weeping ash
white cedar
white thorn
wild cherry
witch hazel
yellow-wood

11

Algerian fir
bean trefoil
black walnut
black wattle
black willow
bottlebrush
cabbage palm
camphor tree
cedar wattle
coconut palm
cotoneaster
copper beech
cypress pine
dawn redwood
elaeocarpus
golden chain
guelder rose
hoary poplar
honey locust
Japan laurel
jumping bean
leper wattle
lignum vitae
mountain ash
pencil cedar
phoenix palm
phyllanthus
pomegranate
quicken tree
red-iron bark
red mahogany
silver birch
slippery elm
spindle tree
talipot palm
white poplar
white spruce
white willow

12

almond willow
Benjamin tree
betel nut palm

cherry laurel
creosote bush
crow's foot elm
cucumber tree
custard apple
flowering ash
golden wattle
horse chestnut
incense cedar
monkey puzzle
Norway spruce

silver-wattle
snowball tree
Spanish cedar
swamp cypress
tree of heaven
umbrella palm
virgin's bower
weeping birch
white cypress
winter cherry

13 *and over*
bird's-eye maple
  (13)
bougainvillea (13)
Cedar of Lebanon
  (14)
Christmas tree (13)
dog-wood wattle
  (13)
horse chestnut (13)
Japanese cedar (13)

Japanese maple (13)
Jerusalem cherry
  (15)
partridge wood (13)
Spanish chestnut
  (15)
sunshine wattle (14)
trembling poplar
  (15)
wayfaring tree (13)
weeping willow (13)

Vegetables

3
oca
pea
soy
yam

4
bean
beet
cole
corn
kale
leek
lima
neep
okra
peas
sage
soya
spud

5
caper
chard
chick
chili
chive
colza
cress
fitch
gourd
maize
mooli
onion
pease
pulse

savoy
swede

6
carrot
celery
endive
fennel
garlic
greens
lentil
marrow
murphy
nettle
orache
porret
potato
radish
sprout
squash
tomato
turnip

7
cabbage
cardoon
chicory
frijole
gherkin
haricot
hotspur
lettuce
mustard
parsley
parsnip
pea bean

peppers
pimento
pumpkin
salsify
seakale
shallot
skirret
spinach
sprouts

8
allspice
beetroot
borecole
broccoli
capsicum
celeriac
chickpea
cucumber
eggplant
eschalot
kohlrabi
lima bean
mung bean
mushroom
plantain
scallion
soyabean
zucchini

9
artichoke
asparagus
aubergine
broad bean
calabrese

courgette
curly kale
dandelion
green peas
horsebean
mangetout
marrowfat
puy lentil
red pepper
split peas
sweetcorn
turban top
turnip top

10
adzuki bean
beet radish
cos lettuce
cow parsnip
French bean
kidney bean
King Edward
red cabbage
runner bean
turnip tops
watercress
Welsh onion

11
bean sprouts
brown lentil
cauliflower
French beans
green pepper
haricot bean
horseradish

ratatouille
scarlet bean
spinach beet
sweet potato
water radish
water rocket

12
bamboo shoots
chat potatoes
corn on the cob
giant shallot
savoy cabbage
Spanish onion
spring onions
spring greens
white cabbage

13 *and over*
broccoli sprouts (15)
Brussels sprouts
  (15)
continental lentil
  (17)
globe artichoke (14)
horse cucumber (13)
Jerusalem
  artichoke (18)
ladies' fingers (13)
marrowfat peas (13)
purple broccoli (14)
scarlet runner (13)
spring cabbage (13)
tankard turnip (13)
vegetable marrow
  (15)

RELIGION, MYTHOLOGY AND DIVINATION

Arthurian Legend

3
Kay

4
Mark
Wart

5
Grail

6
Arthur
Avalon
Elaine
Gawain
Iseult
Isolde
Merlin

7
Camelot
Galahad
Mordred
Tristan

8
Bedivere

Lancelot
Percival
Tristram

9
Excalibur
Guinevere
Holy Grail

10
Fisher King
(the)
King Arthur
Round Table

11
Morgan le
Fay

13
Lady of the Lake (the)

14
Uther Pendragon

15
Sword in the Stone
(the)

Biblical Characters

3
Dan
Eli
Eve
Gad
God
Gog
Ham
Job
Lot

4
Abel
Adam
Ahab
Amos
Baal
Boaz
Cain
Esau
Jehu
Joab
John
Jude
Leah
Levi
Luke
Magi
(the)
Mark
Mary
Moab

Noah
Paul
Ruth
Saul
Shem

5
Aaron
Annas
Asher
Caleb
Cyrus
Dagon
David
Demas
Devil
(the)
Enoch
Hagar
Herod
Hiram
Hosea
Isaac
Jacob
James
Jesse
Jesus
Jonah
Judah
Judas
Laban
Magog

Moses
Naomi
Peter
Sarah
Satan
Silas
Simon
Titus

6
Andrew
Balaam
Christ
Daniel
Darius
Elijah
Elisha
Esther
Gideon
Haggai
Isaiah
Jahweh
Jairus
Joseph
Joshua
Josiah
Judith
Martha
Miriam
Naboth
Nathan
Philip

Pilate
Rachel
Reuben
Salome
Samson
Samuel
Simeon
Thomas
Yahweh

7
Abraham
Absalom
Ananias
Delilah
Ephraim
Ezekiel
Gabriel
Japheth
Jehovah
Jezebel
Lazarus
Lucifer
Malachi
Matthew
Meshach
Michael
Obadiah
Pharaoh
Raphael
Rebecca
Solomon

Stephen
Timothy
Zebedee
Zebulun

8
Abednego
Barabbas
Barnabas
Benjamin
Caiaphas
Habakkuk
Hezekiah
Issachar
Jeremiah
Jeroboam
Jonathan
Matthias
Mordecai
Naphtali
Nehemiah
Shadrach
Zedekiah

9
Bathsheba
Beelzebub
Nathaniel
Nicodemus
Thaddaeus
Zacchaeus
Zechariah

10
Belshazzar
Methuselah
Simon Magus
Theophilus

11
Bartholomew

12
Herod Agrippa
Herod Antipas
Queen of Sheba
(the)

13
Herod the Great
(13)
Judas Iscariot (13)
Mary Magdalene
(13)

14 and over
John the Baptist
(14)
Joseph of
Arimathea (17)
Nebuchadnezzar
(14)
Pontius Pilate (13)
Simon of Cyrene
(13)

Books of the Bible

Ap. = Apocrypha; NT = New Testament; OT = Old Testament

3
Job (OT)

4
Amos (OT)
Ezra (OT)
Joel (OT)
John (NT)
Jude (NT)
Luke (NT)
Mark (NT)
Ruth (OT)

5
Hosea (OT)
James (NT)
Jonah (OT)
Kings (OT)
Micah (OT)
Nahum (OT)
Peter (NT)
Titus (NT)
Tobit (Ap.)

6
Baruch (Ap.)
Daniel (OT)
Esdras (Ap.)
Esther (OT, Ap.)
Exodus (OT)
Haggai (OT)
Isaiah (OT)
Joshua (OT)
Judges (OT)
Judith (Ap.)
Psalms (OT)
Romans (OT)
Samuel (OT)
Sirach (Ap.)

7
Ezekiel (OT)
Genesis (OT)
Hebrews (NT)
Malachi (OT)
Matthew (NT)
Numbers (OT)
Obadiah (OT)
Susanna (Ap.)

Timothy (NT)

8
Habakkuk (OT)
Jeremiah (OT)
Nehemiah (OT)
Philemon (NT)
Proverbs (OT)

9
Ephesians (NT)
Galatians (NT)
Leviticus (OT)
Maccabees (Ap.)
Zechariah (OT)
Zephaniah (OT)

10
Chronicles (OT)
Colossians (NT)
Revelation (NT)

11
Corinthians (NT)
Deuteronomy (OT)

Philippians (NT)

12
Ecclesiastes (OT)
Lamentations (OT)

13
Song of Solomon (OT)
Thessalonians (NT)

14 and over
Acts (of the Apostles)
(17) (NT)
Bel and the Dragon (15)
(Ap.)
Ecclesiasticus (14) (Ap.)
Epistle of Jeremy (15)
(Ap.)
Song of the Three Holy
Children (26) (Ap.)
The Prayer of
Manasseh (19) (Ap.)
The Wisdom of Solomon
(18) (Ap.)

Celtic Mythology

3
Anu
Bel
Mab

4
Badb
Bran
Brid
Dana
Danu
Llyr
Math
Nudd

Ogma
Yule

5
Dagda
Epona
Macha
Maeve
Niamh
Nuada
Oisin
Pwyll
Sidhe
Sulis

6
Badhbh
Brigit
Fingal
Imbolc
Ogmios
Oimelc

7
Belinus
Beltane
Branwen
Pryderi
Samhain

8
Ceridwen
Ligmasad
Mathonwy
Morrigan (the)
Rhiannon
Rosmerta
Tir na n'Og

10
Angus mac Og
Cuchulainn
Mabinogion (the)

11
Finn mac Cool

12
Land of the Young

13
Mother Goddess

14
Herne the Hunter
Tuatha Dé Danaan

Classical Mythology

Gk = Greek only; R. = Roman only

2	Irus	Cilix	manes	Aeneid
Ge	Itys	Circe	Maron	Aeolus
Io	Jove (R.)	Creon	Medea	Aerope
	Juno (R.)	Crete	Medon	Aethra
3	Kore	Cupid (R.)	melia	Agenor
Ate	Leda	Damon	Metis	Aletes
Bel	Leto	Danaë	Midas	Aloeus
Bia	Luna (R.)	devas	Mimas	Althea
Deo (Gk)	Maia (Gk)	Diana (R.)	Minos	Amazon
Dis (R.)	Mars (R.)	Dione	Muses	Amycus
Eos (Gk)	moly	Dirce	naiad	Antion
Ida	Mors (R.)	Dolon	Niobe	Aphaea
Ino	Muse	Doris	Nisus	Apollo
Ker	Nike (Gk)	dryad	nymph	Aquilo
lar (R.)	Opis	Edoni	Notus	Asopus
Nix (Gk)	Otus	Epeus	oread	Athena (Gk)
Nox (R.)	Rhea (Gk)	Fates	Orion	Athene (Gk)
Nyx (Gk)	Rome	Fauna (R.)	Paean	Athens
Ops (R.)	Styx	Flora (R.)	Pales (R.)	Atreus
Pan (Gk)	Tros	Gorge	Paris	Augeas
Pax (R.)	Troy	Hades (Gk)	Perse	Aurora (R.)
Sol (R.)	Upis	Harpy	Picus (R.)	Balius
	Zeus (Gk)	Helen	Pluto (R.)	Baucis
4		Helle	Poeas	Boreas
Abas	**5**	Herse	Priam	Byblis
Ajax	Actor	Horae	Remus	Byblus
Amor (R.)	aegis	Hydra	satyr	Cabiri
Ares (Gk)	Aegle	Hylas	Sibyl	Cadmus
Argo	Agave	Hymen	Sinis	Calais
Auge	Alope	Iasus	Sinon	Canens
Bias	Amata	Idmon	Siren	Castor
Ceto	Ampyx	Iliad	Syren	Caunus
Ceyx	Arete	Ilium	Talus	Celeus
Core	Argos	Ionia	Terra (R.)	Charis
Dido	Argus	Iphis	Theia	Charon
Echo	Arion	Irene	Thoas	Chione
Enyo (Gk)	Asius	Iulus	Thyia	Chiron
Eros (Gk)	Atlas	Ixion	Titan	Chthon
Fata (R.)	Attis	Janus (R.)	Venus (R.)	Clytie
Faun	Belus	Jason	Vesta (R.)	Codrus
Fury	Beroe	Ladon	Zetes	Consus (R.)
Gaea (Gk)	Butes	Laius		Cratos
Gaia (Gk)	Cacus	Lamus	**6**	Creusa
Hebe	Calus	lares (R.)	Acamus	Cronus (Gk)
Hera (Gk)	Canis	lases (R.)	Adonis	Cybele (R.)
Hero	Capra	Lethe	Aeacus	Cycnus
Idas	Capys	Liber (R.)	Aeëtes	Cyrene
Ilus	Ceres (R.)	Linus	Aegeus	Danaus
Iole	Cetus	Lotis	Aegina	Daphne
Iris	Chaos	Lycus	Aeneas	Delphi

Dryope
Egeria (R.)
Elatus
Erebus
Euneus
Europa
Evadne
Evenus
Faunus (R.)
Furies
genius (R.)
Geryon
Gorgon
Graces
Graeae
Haemon
Hecabe
Hecate
Hector
Hecuba
Helice
Helios (Gk)
Hellen
Hermes (Gk)
Hestia (Gk)
Hyades
Hygeia
Hyllus
Hypnos (Gk)
Iasion
Icarus
Iolaus
Ismene
Italus
Ithaca
Latona (R.)
Lucina (R.)
Lycaon
maenad
meliae
Medusa
Megara
Memnon
Mentor
Merops
Mestra
Minyas
Moerae (Gk)
Moirae (Gk)
Mopsus
Mygdon
naiads
Neleus
Nereid

Nereus
Nessus
Nestor
nymphs
Oenone
Oeonus
Ogyges
Ogygia
Ogygus
Oileus
Olenus
Ophion
oracle
orphic
Orthus
Oxylus
Pallas
Parcae (R.)
Peleus
Pelias
Pelops
Peneus
Perdix
Pheres
Pholus
Phylas
Plutus (Gk)
Pollux
Pomona (R.)
Procne
Psyche
Pyrrha
Pythia
Python
Rhesus
Rhodes
Saturn (R.)
Scylla
Selene (Gk)
Semele
Semnai
Simois
Sirens
Sirius
Somnus (R.)
Sphinx
Syrinx
Talaus
Tellus (R.)
Tereus
Tethys
Teucer
Theano
Thebes

Themis
Thetis
Thisbe
Thyone
Titans
Tityus
Triton
Typhon
Ulixes
Uranus (Gk)
Vulcan (R.)
Xuthus
Zethus

7

Acastus
Acestes
Achaeus
Achates
Acheron
Actaeon
Admetus
Aepytus
Aesacus
Alcmene
Alcyone
Alpheus
Amazons
Amphion
Ampycus
Amymone
Amyntor
Ancaeus
Antaeus
Antenor
Antiope
Arachne
Arcadia
Ariadne
Artemis (Gk)
Asteria
Athamas
Autonoe
Avernus
Bacchae
Bacchus
Belenos
Bellona (R.)
Bona Dea (R.)
Briseis
Bromius
Busiris
Caeneus
Calchas

Calypso
Camenae (R.)
Camilla
Canthus
Cecrops
centaur
Cepheus
Cheiron
Chimera
Chloris
Chryses
Cinyras
Clymene
Cocytus
Copreus
Coresus
Coronus
Curetes
Cyclops
Dactyls
Daphnis
Demeter (Gk)
Echemus
Echidna
Electra
Elicius
Elpenor
Elysian
Elysium
Epaphus
Epigoni
Erigone
Erinyes
Eumaeus
Eumelus
Eurytus
evil eye
Fortuna (R.)
Galatea
Gelanor
Glaucus
Gordius
Gorgons
Gratiae (R.)
Gryphon
Harpies
Helenus
Hesione
Hilaira
Iacchus
Iapetus
Icarius
Iobates
Jocasta

Jupiter (R.)
Laertes
Laocoon
Laodice
Latinus
Leander
Lynceus
Macaria
Machaon
maenads
Mercury (R.)
Minerva (R.)
Mithras (R.)
Nemesis
Nephele
Neptune (R.)
Nereids
Nycteus
Oceanus (Gk)
Oedipus
Ogygian
Olympia
Olympus
Omphale
oracles
Orestes
Ormenus
Orpheus
Orphism
Orthrus
Pandion
Pandora
Pegasus
penates (R.)
Perseis
Perseus
Phegeus
Phemius
Phineus
Phoebus
Phoenix
Phorcus
Phrixus
Pierian
Pleiads
Pleione
Priapus
Procles
Procris
Proetus
Proteus
Pylades
Pyramus
Pyrrhus

Romulus
Silenus
Stentor
Telamon
Temenus
Thaumas
Theonoe
Theseus
Triopas
Troilus
Ulysses
vestals (R.)
Virbius (R.)
Xanthus

8

Absyrtus
Acheloüs
Achilles
Acrisius
Adrastia
Adrastus
Aegimius
Aegyptus
Agamedes
Aglauros
Agraulus
Alcestis
Alcimede
Alcinous
Alcmaeon
ambrosia
Anchises
Anticlea
Antigone
Antiphus
Aphareus
Apsyrtus
Arcesius
Arethusa
Argonaut
Arimaspi
Ascanius
Asterion
Asterius
Astraeus
Astyanax
Atalanta
Avernian
Bebryces
caduceus
Caeculus
Callisto
Carmenta

(R.)
Carthage
Cephalus
Cerberus
Cercopes
Chalybes
Charites
Chimaera
Chryseis
Cretheus
Cylopes
Daedalus
Damocles
Dardanus
Deianira
Delphyne
Diomedes
Dionysus (Gk)
Dioscuri
Endymion
Enyalius
Epicasta
Eriphyle
Eteocles
Eumolpus
Euphemus
Euryclea
Eurydice
Eurynome
Ganymede
Harmonia
Heliades
Heracles
Hercules
Hermione
Hyperion
Iphicles
Juventas (R.)
Labdacus
Lampetie
Laodamas
Laodamia
Laomedon
Lapithae
Lupercus (R.)
Maeander
Marpessa
Megareus
Melampus
Meleager
Menelaus
Minotaur
Morpheus (R.)
Mulciber (R.)

Myrtilus
Nausicaa
Oceanids
Odysseus
Oenomaus
Olympian
Opheltes
Palaemon
Pandarus
Panopeus
Panthous
paradise
Pasiphae
Pelasgus
Penelope
Pentheus
Periphas
Phaethon
Philemon
Philomel
Phlegyas
Pierides
Pittheus
Pleiades
Podarces
Polyxena
Porthaon
Poseidon (Gk)
Psamathe
Quirinus (R.)
Sarpedon
Schedius
Silvanus (R.)
Sisyphus
Tantalus
Tartarus
Tecmessa
Telephus
Thamyris
Thanatos (Gk)
Theogony
Thyestes
Tiresias
Titaness
Tithonus
Victoria (R.)
Zephyrus

9

Aegisthus
Agamemnon
Alcathous
Alcyoneus
Androgeus

Andromeda
Aphrodite (Gk)
Argonauts
Aristaeus
Asclepius
Assaracus
Autolycus
Automeden
Aventinus
Bacchante
Carmentis (R.)
Cassandra
Chalcodon
Charybdis
Chthonius
Deiphobus
Demophoon
Deucalion
di penates (R.)
Enceladus
Ephialtes
Eumenides
Eurybates
Eurypylus
Eurysaces
Faustulus (R.)
hamadrya
Hippolyte
Hypsipyle
Idomeneus
Iphigenia
Iphimedia
Melanippe
Melanthus
Menoeceus
Menoetius
Metaneira
Mnemosyne
Narcissus
Nyctimene
Oceanides
Palamedes
Palladium
Pandareos
Pandrosos
Parnassus
Patroclus
Philammon
Philomela
Phoroneus
Polydamas
Polydorus
Polynices
Pygmalion

Salmoneus
Scamander
sibylline
Sthenelus
Strophius
Teiresias
Telchines
Telegonus
Thersites
Tisamenus
Trojan War
Vertumnus (R.)

10

Aetholides
Amphictyon
Amphitrite
Amphitryon
Andromache
Antilochus
Archemoros
Callirrhoe
Cassiopeia
cornucopia
Corybantes
Cyparissus
Delphinius
Eileithyia
Epimetheus
Erechtheus
Erymanthus
Gorgophone
Hephaestus (Gk)
Hesperides
Hippocrene
Hippodamia
Hippolytus
Hippothous
Lifthrasir
Melanippus
Melantheus
Melanthius
Menestheus
Nausithous
Parnassian
Persephone (Gk)
Phlegethon
Polydectes
Polydeuces
Polymestor
Polyphemus
Porphyrion
Procrustes
Prometheus

Proserpine (R.)	**11**	**12**	**14**
Rhea Silvia (R.)	Aesculapius (R.)	Clytemnestra	Elysian Fields
Samothrace	Arimaspians	Golden Fleece (the)	(the)
Scamandrus	Bellerophon	Rhadamanthys	Hermaphroditus
Talthybius	Britomartis	vestal virgin	
Telemachus	Gordian knot		**15**
Tlepolemus	Helen of Troy	**13**	Sword of Damocles
Trophonius	Lotus-eaters	Hundred-handed	(the)
Vortumnnus (R.)	Semnai Theai	Mother Goddess	

DIVINATION

CHINESE ZODIAC SIGNS

buffalo (7)	dragon (6)	horse (5)	pig (5)	rat (3)	snake (5)
dog (4)	goat (4)	monkey (6)	rabbit (6)	rooster (7)	tiger (5)

SIGNS OF THE ZODIAC

Aquarius (8) (the water carrier)	Libra (5) (the scales)
Aries (5) (the ram)	Pisces (6) (the fish)
Cancer (6) (the crab)	Sagittarius (11) (the archer)
Capricorn (9) (the goat)	Scorpio (7) (the scorpion)
Gemini (6) (the twins)	Taurus (6) (the bull)
Leo (3) (the lion)	Virgo (5) (the virgin)

DIVINATION METHODS

4
dice

5
omens
runes
Tarot

6
I-Ching
itches
sortes

7
candles
dowsing
scrying

8
dominoes

9
ceromancy (wax)
geomancy (patterns
   in the earth)
palmistry
tea leaves

10
cartomancy
hippomancy (horses)
lithomancy (gems)
numerology
Tarot cards

11
ailuromancy (cats)
bibliomancy (books,
   especially the Bible)
clairvoyance
crystal ball
lychnomancy
   (candles)

12
arachnomancy (spiders)
lampadomancy (lamps)
superstition
tasseography (tea leaves)

13
catoptromancy (mirrors)

14
crystallomancy (crystal
   ball gazing)
sortes Biblicae

THE TAROT

3	Death	Swords	Strength	11
Sun (the)	Devil (the)			Major Arcana
	Disks	7	9	Minor Arcana
4	Lovers (the)	Chariot (the)	Hanged Man (the)	
Cups	Tower (the)	Emperor (the)	Pentacles	12
Fool (the)	Wands	Empress (the)		Blasted Tower
Moon (the)	World (the)	Juggler (the)	10	(the)
Pope (the)		Justice	Heirophant (the)	
Star (the)	6		High Priest (the)	13
	Batons	8	House of God	High Priestess
5	Papess (the)	Magician (the)	(the)	(the)
Coins	Staves	Judgment	Temperance	

Egyptian Mythology

2	4	5	6	7	9
Ma	Amon	Ament	Amon-Ra	Behdety	Harakhtes
Nu	Amun	Ammon	Anquet	Khepera	Harmakhis
Ra	ankh	Anhur	Anubis	Renenet	Harsaphes
	Apis	Horus	Bastet	Sakhmet	Harsiesis
3	Aten	Khnum	Hathor	Sekhmet	Mertseger
Bes	Bast	Neith	Khepri	Taueret	Renenunet
Geb	Hapi	Pasht	Khonsi		
Min	Isis	Sebek	Khunum	8	
Mut	Ma'at	Seker	Osiris	Haroeris	
Nun	Ptah	Thoth	Renpet	Meshkent	
Nut	Sati		Selket	Nephthys	
Set	Seth		Tefnut		
Shu	Shai		Upuaut		

Faiths and their Followers

3	deism	Muslim	animist	8	Hinduism
Jew	deist	Parsee	ascetic	Agnostic	humanism
Zen	Druid	Quaker	atheism	Anglican	humanist
	Hindu	Sabian	atheist	Arianism	idolater
4	Islam	Shaker	Baha'ism	Arminian	idolatry
Copt	pagan	Shiite	Baptist	Buddhism	Lutheran
Jain	Parsi	Shinto	Gnostic	Buddhist	Mahayana
Shia	Saiva	Sufism	Jainism	Catholic	Mazdaism
Sufi	Sunna	Taoism	Judaism	ditheism	Moravian
Sikh	Sunni	Taoist	Lollard	ditheist	Mazdaist
Toc H	Wicca	voodoo	macumba	Donatism	Orthodox
	witch	Wahabi	Puritan	Donatist	paganism
5		Wiccan	Sikhism	Druidess	Puseyism
Amish	6		Wahhabi	Druidism	Puseyite
Arian	Mormon	7	warlock	Erastian	santeria
Baha'i	Moslem	animism		Hasidism	Satanism

215

Satanist
Tantrism
Wahabism
Wesleyan

9
Adventism
Adventist
Calvinism
Calvinism
Christian
Huguenot
Jansenism
Jansenist
Low Church
Methodist
Methodism
Mormonism
Nestorian
pantheism
pantheist
Parseeism
Sabianism
shamanism
Shintoism
theosophy
Theravada
tritheism
tritheist
Unitarian
Vaishnava
Wahhabism
Waldenses

10
Albigenses
Anabaptism
Anabaptist
asceticism
Brahmanism
evangelism
Free Church
Gnosticism
gymnosophy
High Church
idolatress
Lollardism
Manichaean
Mohammedan
monotheism
monotheist
polytheism
polytheist

Protestant
Puritanism
sun worship
theosopher
Tractarian
Waldensian

11
Agnosticism
Albigensian
Anglicanism
Arminianism
Broad Church
Catholicism
Christianity
creationism
creationist
Erastianism
fire worship
Hare Krishna
Lutheranism
Plymouthism
Rastafarian
Scientology
spiritualism
spiritualist
Wesleyanism
Zen Buddhism
Zoroastrian

12
Confucianism
Coptic Church
devil worship
gymnosophist
High Anglican
Low Churchman
Nestorianism
Presbyterian
Salvationism
Salvationist
theosophist
Trinitarian
Unitarianism

13
Anglo-Catholic
Baptist Church
Church in Wales
Eastern Church
Greek Orthodox
High Churchman
Manichaeanism

Mohammedanism
Nonconformism
Nonconformist
Protestantism
Reform Judaism
Roman Catholic
Salvation Army
Scientologist
sun worshipper
Tractarianism

14
fire worshipper
fundamentalism
fundamentalist
Orthodox Church
Oxford Movement
Pentecostalism
Pentecostalist
Rastafarianism
Trinitarianism
Zoroastrianism

15 *and over*
ancestor worship (15)
Anglo-Catholicism (16)
Christadelphian (15)
Christian Science (16)
Christian Scientist (18)
Churches of Christ (16)
Church of England (15)
Church of Jesus Christ of Latter-Day
    Saints (36)
Church of Scotland (16)
Congregationalism (17)
Congregationalist (17)
devil worshipper (15)
Dutch Reformed Church (19)
Episcopal Church (15)
Episcopalianism (15)
Free Church of Scotland (20)
Jehovah's Witness (15)
Jehovah's Witnesses (17)
Orthodox Judaism (15)
Plymouth Brethren (16)
Presbyterianism (15)
Roman Catholicism (16)
Roman Catholic Church (19)
Russian Orthodox (15)
Seventh Day Adventism (19)
Seventh Day Adventist (19)
Society of Friends (16)
United Reformed Church (20)

Hindu Mythology and Belief

3
Uma

4
Agni
Bana
deva
Devi
Kali
Kama
Ketu
Mara
Maya
puja
Rama
Sita
Siva
Soma
Teli
Veda
Yama
yoga

5
Aditi
asura
Durga
Ganga
Gauri
Indra
Kalki
karma
Kurma
Laxmi
Mitra
Nandi
prana
Radha
Rudra
Saiva
Sakti
Shiva
Sudra
Surya
Ushas
Vedas

6
ahimsa
ashram
Avatar
Brahma
Buddha
chakra
dharma
Ganesa
Ganesh
Garuda
Matsya
moksha
Natraj
Puchan
Purana
Shakti
Skanda
Vamana
Varaha
Varuna
Vishnu
Yaksha

7
Avatars
Brahman
Brahmin
chakras
darshan
Ganesha
Hanuman
Harijan
Krishna
Lakshmi
Narayan
Parvati
Rig Veda
Rukmani
Savitar
Vaisya

8
Balarama
Bhairavi
Ganapati
Narayana
Narsingh
Nataraja
Ramayana (the)
Shaivism
Shaivite
Tvashtar

9
Kartikeya
Kshatriya
kundalini
Narashina
Prajapati
Sarasvati
Saraswati
Vaishnava
Vajrayana

10
Jagannatha
Juggernaut
Kartikkaya
Narasingha
Prajapatis
Satyabhama
Upanishads (the)

11
Mahabaharata (the)
Ramachandra

12
Bhagavad Gita (the)

13
reincarnation

Nine Muses

Calliope (9)
Clio (4)
Erato (5)
Euterpe (7)
Melpomene (9)
Polyhymnnia (11)
Terpsichore (11)
Thalia (6)
Urania (6)

Nine Virtues

charity (7)
faith (5)
fortitude (9)
hope (4)
justice (7)
love (4)
modesty (7)
prudence (8)
temperance (10)

Norse Mythology

3
Ask
Bor
Hel
Hod
Ran
Sif
Tiw
Tyr
Ull

4
Buri
Garm
Gerd
Loki
Odin
Surt
Thor
Ymir

5
Aegir
Aesir
Alcis
Bragi
Donar
Embla
Freya
Freyr
Frigg
Hoder
Idunn
Jotun
Mimir
Nanna
Njord
Norns
Orcus
Sigyn
Vanir
Vidar
Woden
Wotan

6
Asgard
Balder
Fafnir
Fenrir
Freyja
Frigga
Gefion
Hermod
Hoenir
Kvasir
Weland

7
Alfheim
Audumla
Bifrost
Gungnir
Heimdal
Midgard
Muspell
Nerthus
Wayland
Weiland

217

8	Ragnarok	Brunhilde	**10**	**11**
Brynhild	Sleipnir	Jotunheim	Jörmungand	Skidbladnir
Draupnir	Valhalla	Mannaheim	Muspelheim	Svartalheim
Fjorgynn	Vanaheim	Siegfried	Nehallenia	
Heimdall		Valkyries	Nidavellir	**12**
Mjollnir	**9**	Yggdrasil		Wayland Smith (the)
Niflheim	Aurgelmir			World Serpent

Other Mythical Creatures, People (including Deities) and Places

3	gnome	seraph	**8**	**10**
elf	golem	sphinx	Apollyon	changeling
fay	hodag	spirit	Atlantis	chupacabra
imp	lamia	sprite	basilisk	cockatrice
nix	nymph	Utopia	bogeyman	Grim Reaper (the)
roc	pisky	wraith	cherubim	hippogriff
	pixie	zombie	demoness	Jabberwock
4	Santa		devilkin	leprechaun
Baal	Satan	**7**	El Dorado	Little John
Eden	satyr	banshee	gargoyle	little folk
faun	shade	Beowulf	Gilgames	Maid Marian
jinn	spook	Bigfoot	good folk	salamander
ogre	sylph	bogyman	Lyonesse	Santa Claus
peri	troll	brownie	phantasm	sea serpent
pixy		centaur	seraphim	selkie folk
Puck	**6**	erl-king	spriggan	Tooth Fairy (the)
yeti	Azazel	gremlin	succubus	Wonderland
	Baalim	griffin	werewolf	
5	bunyip	Grendel		**11 and over**
alfar	cherub	Grimnir	**9**	Abominable Snowman (the)
angel	daemon	gryphon	archangel	(17)
Ariel	dragon	incubus	archfiend	Cloud Cuckoo Land (15)
bogie	dybbuk	knocker	Ashtoreth	doppelgänger (12)
bucca	faerie	Lorelei	Beelzebub	Easter Bunny (11)
demon	goblin	Lucifer	cailleach	Father Christmas (15)
devil	Ishtar	manitou	elemental	Flying Dutchman (the) (14)
djinn	kelpie	mermaid	Davy Jones	Jabberwocky (11)
dwarf	kobold	Old Nick	fairyland	Jersey Devil (the) (11)
elves	kraken	phantom	Friar Tuck	little people (12)
faery	Lilith	phoenix	Gilgamesh	Loch Ness Monster (the)
fairy	Mammon	Sandman	hobgoblin	(15)
fetch	merman	(the)	Robin Hood	Never-Never Land (14)
fiend	Moloch	sylphid	Sasquatch	poltergeist (11)
genie	Nessie	Titania	Shangri-La	Robin Goodfellow (15)
genii	Oberon	unicorn	white lady	Sheela-na-gig (11)
ghost	ogress	vampire	wood nymph	Spring-Heeled Jack (16)
ghoul	piskie			
giant	selkie			

Religious and Ecclesiastical Terms

3	hymn	Bible	Omega	chapel	lector	Romish
alb	icon	bless	pahul	cherub	lesson	rosary
ark	idol	bodhi	papal	chrism	Levite	rubric
ave	ikon.	canon	Pasch	Christ	litany	sacred
BVM	Imam	carol	piety	church	living	Saddhu
God	INRI	chant	pious	clergy	manger	santon
haj	ka'ba	chela	prior	cleric	mantle	schism
Jah	kara	choir	psalm	collar	mantra	scribe
law	kesh	cotta	Purim	curacy	Marian	seraph
lay	kirk	credo	rabbi	curate	martyr	sermon
nun	lama	creed	relic	deacon	matins	server
pew	Lent	cross	saint	deadly	Maundy	sexton
pie	Mass	culpa	salat	decade	Medina	shaman
pyx	monk	curia	Sarum	decani	missal	sharia
RIP	nave	deity	Satan	devout	mortal	shrine
see	N. or M.	demon	selah	dharma	mosaic	shrive
sin	oath	devil	stole	divine	mosque	sinful
vow	pall	dirge	Sudra	dossal	mullah	sinner
yin	pope	dogma	Sunna	Easter	mystic	sister
	pray	elder	synod	Elohim	nimbus	spirit
4	puja	ephod	taboo	Essene	novena	stalls
abbé	rite	exalt	terce	father	novice	Sunday
alms	rood	faith	Torah	Fatima	nuncio	suttee
amen	sawm	fakir	tract	ferial	oblate	tablet
apse	sect	flock	vedic	friary	occult	Talmud
bell	sext	friar	vicar	gloria	office	te deum
bris	soul	glory	vigil	Gospel	ordain	temple
Cana	Sura	godly	zakat	gradin	orders	tierce
cant	text	grace	zazen	grotto	orison	tippet
cell	veil	habit	Zohar	guimpe	pagoda	Tophet
cope	vows	hafiz		hallow	palmer	trance
cowl	Word	halal	**6**	heaven	papacy	triune
cult	(the)	hijab	abbacy	Hebrew	papist	unholy
cure	Xmas	Hijra	abbess	Hegira	parish	venial
dean	yang	image	Advent	Hejira	parson	verger
Ebor	yoga	Jesus	amulet	heresy	pascal	vestry
eruv	zend	jihad	anoint	hermit	pastor	virgin
evil	Zion	Kaaba	anthem	homily	popery	vision
ewer		Koran	ascend	hymnal	praise	votive
Fall	**5**	laity	ascent	intone	prayer	wimple
(the)	abbey	lauds	ashram	Jahweh	preach	Yahweh
fast	abbot	limbo	armlet	Jesuit	priest	
font	abyss	logos	Assisi	Jewish	primus	**7**
guni	agape	manse	beadle	Judaic	priory	acolyte
hadj	aisle	matin	Belial	kachha	proper	Ahriman
hajj	Allah	Mazda	bishop	kakkar	psalms	Alcoran
halo	Alpha	Mecca	Brahma	kangha	pulpit	Alkoran
harp	altar	mercy	Buddha	kirpan	rector	alms bag
hell	amice	mitre	burial	kosher	repent	ampulla
holy	angel	mohel	candle	latria	reveal	angelic
hood	banns	myrrh	cantor	lavabo	ritual	angelus
host	beads	nones	censer	layman	rochet	apostle

219

baptism	gradine	piscina	**8**	dalmatic	Kabbalah
baptist	hassock	pontiff	ablution	deaconry	lay clerk
baptize	heathen	poverty	affinity	devilish	Lazarist
beatify	heretic	prayers	agnus dei	devotion	libation
believe	hexapla	prebend	alleluia	diaconal	Lord's Day
bigotry	holy day	prelate	All Souls	dies irae	lych gate
biretta	Holy See	primacy	almighty	diocesan	Mass book
blessed	holy war	primate	altar boy	disciple	mea culpa
brother	hosanna	profane	anathema	divinity	meditate
Calvary	hymnary	prophet	anointed	doctrine	minister
cassock	hymnody	psalter	antiphon	doxology	ministry
chalice	impiety	raiment	antipope	Ember Day	minorite
chancel	impious	Ramadan	apostasy	Emmanuel	miserere
chaplet	incense	rebirth	apostate	enthrone	Mohammed
chapter	infidel	recluse	auto-da-fé	epiphany	monachal
charity	introit	rectory	ave maria	episcopy	monastic
chrisom	Jehovah	rejoice	basilica	eternity	mozzetta
cloister	Judaize	requiem	beatific	ethereal	mujtahid
Cluniac	justify	reredos	believer	Eusebian	nativity
collect	kenosis	retable	benifice	evensong	Nazarene
confirm	Lady Day	retreat	berretta	evermore	Nazareth
convent	Lateran	Sabbath	biblical	evildoer	neophyte
convert	lectern	sainted	blessing	exegesis	obituary
Creator	liturgy	saintly	bless you	exegetic	oblation
crosier	Lourdes	sanctum	brethren	exequies	offering
crozier	Low Mass	sanctus	breviary	exorcism	orthodox
crucify	Lucifer	satanic	canonize	exorcist	pantheon
crusade	madonna	saviour	canticle	exorcize	pardoner
deanery	mandala	secular	Capuchin	faithful	Passover
decanal	maniple	service	cardinal	frontlet	pastoral
defrock	mastaba	Shabbat	catacomb	God's acre	pericope
dervish	mattins	shahada	celibacy	Golgotha	Peshitta
diocese	menorah	shariah	celibate	gurdwara	pharisee
diptych	Messiah	shariat	cemetery	Hail Mary	pontifex
Elohist	mezuzah	Shaitan	cenobite	hallowed	preacher
epistle	mid-Lent	Shastra	cenotaph	heavenly	predella
epitaph	minaret	soutane	ceremony	hecatomb	prie-dieu
eternal	minster	steeple	chastity	hell fire	priestly
exegete	miracle	stipend	chasuble	hierarch	prioress
fanatic	mission	sub-dean	cherubic	hieratic	prophecy
fasting	muezzin	synodal	cherubim	High Mass	prophesy
frontal	narthex	tantric	choirboy	hinayana	psalmist
funeral	nirvana	tempter	chrismal	holiness	psalmody
Galilee	nocturn	tonsure	christen	holy city	psaltery
gaudete	nunnery	trinity	ciborium	Holy Land	quietism
Gehenna	Opus Dei	unction	clerical	holy name	quietist
gentile	oratory	Vatican	compline	Holy Week	rabbinic
Gideons	ordinal	vespers	conclave	Holy Writ	Ramadhan
glorify	orphrey	Vulgate	covenant	Holy Year	redeemer
goddess	Our Lady	wee free	creation	hymn book	religion
godhead	paschal	worship	credence	Immanuel	response
godless	passion	Xmas day	crucifer	immortal	revealed
godlike	penance	Yahwist	crucifix	infernal	reverend
good man	pilgrim		Crusader	Jubilate	reverent

rogation
sacristy
Sadducee
sanctify
sanctity
scapular
Sephardi
seraphic
seraphim
sidesman
skullcap
summoner
superior
surplice
swastika
Tenebrae
theodicy
theology
theogony
thurible
thurifer
transept
triptych
unbelief
venerate
versicle
vestment
viaticum
vicarage
vocation
ziggurat

9
ablutions
adoration
alleluiah
allelujah
All Saints
altar rail
Amaterasu
anchorite
anointing
antiphony
Apocrypha
apostolic
archangel
archfiend
Ascension
Ashkenazi
atonement
Ayatollah
baptismal
baptistry
beatitude

Beelzebub
Bethlehem
Bible Belt
bishopric
bismillah
Black Mass
blasphemy
born-again
Candlemas
canonical
Carmelite
catechism
catechist
catechize
cathedral
celebrant
celebrate
celestial
chorister
Christmas
churching
churchman
clergyman
cloistered
coenobite
communion
confessor
converted
Cordelier
cremation
Dalai Lama
(the)
dalmatica
damnation
deaconess
deadly sin
Decalogue
dedicated
Dei Gratia
desecrate
devotions
diaconate
dissenter
doctrinal
dog collar
Dominican
Easter day
Ember
Days
encyclical
episcopal
eucharist
firmament
genuflect

godliness
gospeller
graveyard
Gregorian
hagiology
Halloween
hereafter
(the)
hermitage
heterodox
Hexateuch
hierogram
hierology
high altar
Holy Ghost
holy table
holy water
hymnodist
hymnology
incumbent
induction
interdict
interment
Jerusalem
joss stick
Lamb of God
justified
Lammas Day
last rites
Latin Mass
laudation
layperson
lay reader
Lazarists
Low Sunday
Mariology
martyrdom
moderator
monastery
mortal sin
Mosaic law
mysticism
novitiate
obedience
obeisance
obsequies
offertory
officiant
officiate
orthodoxy
papal bull
Paraclete
patriarch
Pentecost

plainsong
postulant
prayer mat
prayer rug
preaching
precentor
presbyter
priestess
profanity
psalm book
prothesis
purgatory
Quicunque
reliquary
religious
repentant
reverence
righteous
rural dean
sacrament
sacrarium
sacrifice
sacrilege
sacristan
salvation
sanctuary
Sanhedrin
scripture
sepulchre
solemnize
spiritual
stability
suffragan
suffrages
synagogue
synodical
synoptics
synoptist
teleology
Testament
theocracy
theomachy
theophany
unworldly
venerable
venial sin
vestments
visionary

10
absolution
abstinence
Ahura Mazda
All Hallows

altar bread
altar cloth
altar front
altarpiece
altar steps
altar table
antichrist
apocalypse
archbishop
archdeacon
archimagus
archpriest
armageddon
assumption
baptistery
bar mitzvah
bat mitzvah
Beatitudes
benedicite
Bernardine
bible study
black friar
Buddhistic
canonicals
Carthusian
catechumen
ceremonial
clerestory
Church Army
church bell
churchgoer
churchyard
circumcise
Cistercian
confession
consecrate
consistory
dedication
devotional
Dominicans
Eastertide
ecumenical
Ember Weeks
episcopacy
episcopate
evangelism
evangelist
evangelize
evil spirit
exaltation
fellowship
free chapel
Gethsemane
god-fearing

Good Friday
hephteuch
heterodoxy
hierocracy
hierophant
high priest
Holy Family
Holy Father
Holy Orders
holy roller
Holy Spirit
house of God
iconoclasm
iconoclast
immaculate
impanation
indulgence
infallible
inner light
invocation
irreverent
lady chapel
Last Supper
lay brother
Lord's Table
magnificat
mariolatry
Mark of Cain
meditation
ministrant
misericord
missionary
mujtahidün
monstrance
omnipotent
omniscient
ophiolatry
ordination
Palm Sunday
Pentateuch
pharisaism
possession
pilgrimage
prayer book
prebendary
presbytery
priesthood
prophetess
rabbinical
rectorship
redemption
repentance
revelation
rock temple

rood screen
Sabbath day
sacerdotal
sacrosanct
sanctified
sanctifier
schismatic
scriptural
Scriptures
secularism
secularist
septuagint
Sexagesima
Shrovetide
shibboleth
soothsayer
tabernacle
temptation
39 articles
theologian
Tridentine
unbaptized
unbeliever
veneration
visitation
white friar
Whit Sunday
worshipper
Zend-Avesta

11
age of reason
All Souls' Day
altar screen
antiphonary
apotheosize
archdiocese
arches court
Benedictine
benediction
benedictory
bitter herbs
blasphemous
bodhisattva
chrismation
Christendom
christening
church house
churchwoman
closed order
commination
comminatory
Common Grace
communicant

contemplate
convocation
crematorium
crucifixion
Curia Romana
deification
desecration
Diet of Worms
divine light
divine right
doxological
ecclesiarch
ecclesiology
eschatology
established
eternal life
evangelical
everlasting
freethinker
Geneva Bible
genuflection
Granth Sahib
graven image
hagiography
hierography
Holy Trinity
hymnography
hymnologist
iconography
immortality
incarnation
inquisition
intercessor
irreligious
irreverence
Judgment Day
kirk session
lay preacher
Lion of Judah
Lord's prayer
Lord's Supper
miracle play
Nicene Creed
omnipotence
omnipresent
omniscience
original sin
parishioner
passing bell
passion play
Passion Week
paternoster
patron saint
Pearly Gates

pharisaical
pontificate
prayer beads
prayer wheel
priestcraft
procession
proselytism
proselytize
Reformation
religionary
religionism
religionist
religiosity
reservation
ritualistic
rosary beads
sacramental
Sacred Heart
sacring bell
sanctus bell
take the veil
unchristian
unrighteous
Whitsuntide

12
All Saints' Day
annunciation
altar frontal
archdeaconry
Ascension Day
Ash Wednesday
Augustinians
Benedictines
Bible Society
canonization
chapel of ease
Christmas Day
Christmas Eve
church living
church parade
church school
churchwarden
circumcision
confessional
confirmation
congregation
consecration
consistorial
disestablish
dispensation
Easter Sunday
ecclesiastic
ecclesiology

enthronement
episcopalian
evangelicism
false prophet
frankincense
general synod
Good Shepherd
holy of holies
hot gospeller
hymnographer
inner sanctum
intercession
interdiction
Kingdom of God
Last Judgment
New Testament
nunc dimittis
obedientiary
Old Testament
omnipresence
purification
Quadragesima
reconsecrate
red letter day
Resurrection
Rogation Days
Rogation Week
Second Advent
Second Coming
Septuagesima
Sunday school
thanksiving
Tower of Babel
transmigrate
vicar general

13
All Hallows Eve
antichristian
Apostles' Creed
archbishopric
archdeaconate
beatification

bidding prayer
burial service
burnt offering
canonical hour
church service
confessionary
contemplative
convocational
Corpus Christi
excommunicate
glorification
holy communion
holy innocents
incense burner
infallibility
justification
miracle worker
mission church
moral majority
paschal candle
prayer meeting
proselytizing
Quinquagesima
reincarnation
sacerdotalism
sanctuary lamp
scripturalist
Shrove Tuesday
Synod of Whitby
televangelism
televangelist
Trinity Sunday
unconsecrated
unevangelical
Vicar of Christ
way of the cross

14
antiscriptural
black letter day
church assembly
church planting
communion table

Dead Sea Scrolls
ecclesiastical
ecclesiologist
extreme unction
Gregorian chant
Maundy Thursday
Mother Superior
predestination
reconsecration
redemptionists
Rogation Sunday
sanctification
sign of the cross
Society of Jesus
transmigration
total immersion

15 *and over*
Alternative Service Book (22)
Ark of the Covenant (16)
Athanasian Creed (15)
Book of Common Prayer (18)
cardinal virtues (15)
Counter-Reformation (18)
dark night of the soul (18)
excommunication (15)
Five Pillars of Islam (18)
Four Horsemen of the Apocalypse (27)
harvest festival (15)
Immaculate Conception (20)
infernal regions (15)
Mothering Sunday (15)
revealed religion (16)
sanctum sanctorum (16)
Sermon on the Mount (16)
Stations of the Cross (18)
suffragan bishop (15)
Synoptic Gospels (15)
Ten Commandments (15)
transfiguration (15)
transubstantiation (18)
unleavened bread (15)

Seven against Thebes

Adrastus (8)
Amphiaraus (10)
Capaneus (8)
Hipomedon (9)
Parthenopaeus (13)
Polynices (9)
Tydeus (6)

Seven Deadly Sins

anger (5)
covetousness (12)
envy (4)
gluttony (8)
lust (4)
pride (5)
sloth (5)

Three Fates

Atropos (7)
Clotho (6)
Lachesis (8)

Three Furies

Alecto (6)
Megaera (7)
Tisiphone (9)

Three Gorgons

Eurayale (8)
Medusa (6)
Stheno (6)

Three Graces

Aglaia (6)
Euphrosyne (10)
Thalia (6)

Three Harpies

Aello (6)
Celaeno/Podargo (7)
Ocypete (7)

Three Seasons

Dike (4) (justice)
Eirine (6) (peace)
Eunomia (7) (order)

Twelve Labours of Hercules

1 Kill the Nemean lion
2 Kill the Hydra
3 Capture the Cerynitian Hind
4 Capture the boar of Erymanthus
5 Clean out the Augean stables
6 Kill the birds of Lake Stymphalos
7 Capture the Cretan bull
8 Bring back the horses of Diomedes
9 Obtain the girdle of Hippolyte
10 Bring back the cattle of Geryon
11 Bring back the golden apples of the Hesperides
12 Bring back Cerberus from the underworld

SCIENCE AND TECHNOLOGY

Agriculture

3
awn
bin
cob
cod
cow
cub
dig
ear
ewe
far
feu
hay
hep
hip
hoe
hog
ket
kex
kid
kip
lea
moo
mow
pig
pip
ram
ret
rye
sow
ted
teg
tup
vag
vat
zea

4
akee
aril
avel
bale
barn
bawn
beam
beef
bent
bere
bigg

boon
bran
bull
byre
calf
cart
clay
corn
cote
crop
culm
curb
drey
dung
farm
foal
gait
galt
gape
harl
haum
herd
hind
hink
holt
hops
hull
husk
kine
lamb
lime
loam
lyme
malm
mare
marl
meal
milk
neat
neep
nide
nout
nowt
oast
oats
odal
paco
peat
pest

pone
quey
rabi
rake
rape
resp
rime
root
roup
runn
rust
ryot
sand
scab
seed
sere
shaw
silo
skep
skug
slob
sock
soil
soya
span
stot
teff
toft
tope
tore
udal
vale
vega
weed
wold
yean
zebu

5
ammon
aphid
araba
baler
beans
bhyle
biddy
borax
bosky
bothy

braxy
briza
calve
carse
cavie
chaff
churn
clevy
closh
couch
croft
crone
crops
dairy
ditch
drill
drove
durra
ergot
ervum
farcy
fruit
fungi
gavel
gebur
glume
grain
grass
graze
guano
halfa
hards
haugh
haulm
hedge
hilum
hoove
horse
humus
kulak
lande
llano
lobby
maize
mower
mummy
ovine
plant
ranch

rumen
sewel
sheep
sheth
shoat
shuck
spelt
spuds
staig
stall
stead
stich
stipa
stock
straw
swill
tilth
tiver
tuber
veldt
vimen
vives
vomer
wagon
wheat
withe
withy
worms
yield

6
aerato
angora
animal
arable
arista
barley
basset
beeves
binder
bosket
bottle
butter
carney
cattle
cereal
clover
colter
corral

cowman
cratch
cutter
digger
disbud
dobbin
drover
earing
eatage
ecurie
enspan
fallow
farina
farmer
fodder
forage
furrow
gargol
garran
gaucho
gimmer
gluten
grains
grange
harrow
heifer
hogget
hogsty
hopper
huller
incult
inning
inspan
intine
jument
linhay
llanos
malkin
manger
manure
mealie
merino
milium
millet
milsey
mowing
nubbin
padnag
pampas

piglet
pigsty
plough
podzol
polder
porker
potato
punner
raggee
rancho
hreaper
roller
runrig
sheave
silage
socage
sowans
sowing
spruit
stable
steppe
stover
tanist
tomand
travis
trough
turnip
turves
warble
weevil

7
acidity
alfalfa
anthrax
avenage
binding
boscage
budding
bulchin
bullock
buttery
cabbage
calving
combine
compost
copland
cornage
coulter

cowherd
cowshed
demesne
digging
dipping
docking
drought
droving
eanling
erosion
farming
fee-tail
foaling
foldage
foot rot
forcing
fox trap
gadsman
granger
grazing
hallier
harvest
hay cart
hay rick
hedging
herding
hogcote
hop pole
hunkers
implant
infield
innings
kidling
lambing
laniary
layland
leasowe
lucerne
maizena
marlite
milk can
milking
misyoke
morling
multure
murrain

novalia
organic
nursery
pabular
paddock
panicum
pannage
pasture
peonage
piggery
pinetum
pinfold
polders
popcorn
poultry
prairie
praties
predial
provine
pruning
pulping
pummace
radicel
raking
rancher
reaping
rearing
retting
rhizome
rokeage
rundale
rustler
ryotwar
sickled
slanket
spancel
stacker
station
stooker
stubble
stuckle
subsidy
subsoil
swinery
tantony
tascall

tax cart
threave
thwaite
tillage
tilling
tractor
trammel
trekker
trotter
udaller
vaquero
vitular
wagoner
windrow
yardman

8
agronomy
branding
breeding
clipping
cropping
ditching
drainage
elevator
ensilage
farmyard
forestry
gleaning
grafting
hayfield
haymaker
haystack
haywagon
hopfield
kohlrabi
landgirl
loosebox
milkcart
pedigree
pig swill
plougher
rootcrop
rotation
set aside
shearing

sheep dip
vineyard
watering
wireworrn

9
agrimotor
agroville
allotment
cornfield
dairy farm
dairymaid
disc drill
fertility
fungicide
gathering
grassland
harrowing
harvester
haymaking
horserake
husbandry
implement
incubator
livestock
pasturage
penthouse
phosphate
pig trough
ploughing
rice field
screening
separator
shorthorn
sugar beet
sugar cane
swineherd
thrashing
threshing
trenching
winnowing

10
agronomist
battery hen
cattle cake

cultivator
fertilizer
harvesting
husbandman
irrigation
mould board
plantation
rounding up
self-binder
transplant
weedkiller
wheatfield

11
agriculture
cake crusher
chaff cutter
chicken farm
crude plough
cultivation
fertilizing
germination
insecticide
motor plough
pastureland
poultry farm
reclamation
stock taking
water trough
weed control

12
agribusiness
agricultural
feeding stock
fermentation
horticulture
insemination
market garden
smallholding
swathe turner
turnip cutter

Astronomy

ASTEROIDS

4	Hebe	**5**	Vesta	**6**	Pallas	**8**
Eros	Juno	Ceres		Icarus		Hyperion

ASTRONOMICAL TERMS

3
orb
Sol
sun

4
belt
nova
star

5
comet
epact
epoch
error
flare
giant
label
lunar
nadir
orbit
phase
solar
space
stars
umbra

6
Apollo
astral
aurora
binary
Corona
domify
galaxy
gnomon
lunary
meteor
nebula
octile
parsec
planet
pulsar
quasar
radius
sphere
sun-dog
syzygy
vector
vertex
Viking
zenith

zodiac

7
apogean
big bang
cepheid
cluster
eclipse
equinox
gibbous
mock sun
nebulae
nebular
new moon
perigee
radiant
sextile
spectra
sputnik
stellar
sunspot
transit

8
aerolite
aerolith
almagest
altitude
aphelion
asterism
asteroid
draconic
ecliptic
epicycle
Explorer
full moon
latitude
meridian
Milky Way
occulted
parallax
parhelia
penumbra
perigean
quadrant
quadrate
quartile
quintile
red giant
sidereal
solstice
spectrum

spheroid
starless
systemic
universe
Van Allen
Vanguard
variable
zodiacal

9
aerolitic
arc-en-ciel
ascendant
ascension
astrology
astronomy
black hole
celestial
cosmogony
cosmology
Curtation
draconian
elevation
ephemeris
epicyclic
firmament
hour angle
light year
longitude
magnitude
meteorite
meteoroid
Minuteman
North Star
parhelian
planetary
planetoid
Ptolemaic
reflector
refractor
satellite
solar wind
star-gazer
starlight
sublunary
supernova
telescope
trioctile
uranology
Via Lactea

10

aberration
apparition
astrologer
astrometer
astronomer
astronomic
atmosphere
brightness
cometarium
Copernican
cosmic rays
Crab nebula
depression
discoverer
double star
earthshine
elongation
exaltation
extra-solar
hour circle
lunar cycle
lunar month
lunar probe
opposition
outer space
perihelion
precession
prominence
refraction
retrograde
siderolite
star-gazing
supergiant
terminator
trajectory
uranoscopy
white dwarf

11
astrography
blazing star
conjunction
declination
falling star
giant planet
last quarter
metemptosis
meteorolite
minor planet
neutron star
occultation
photosphere

observatory
planetarium
solar system
spectrology
terrestrial
uranography

12
astronautics
astronomical
astrophysics
chromosphere
doppler shift
eccentricity
event horizon
first quarter
Halley's comet
intermundane
interstellar
lunar eclipse
lunar rainbow
Saturn's rings
shooting star
sidereal time
solar eclipse
spectroscope
spiral galaxy
Van Allen Belt
variable star

13
constellation
meteorography
sidereal clock
Wolf-Rayet star
zodiacal light

14
annular eclipse
Aurora Borealis
interplanetary
radio astronomy
radio telescope
right ascension
summer solstice
transit of Venus
vertical circle
winter solstice
zenith distance

15
armillary sphere

Aurora Australis
celestial sphere
Fraunhofer lines
meteoric showers

16
Alphonsine tables
astronomical unit
Magellanic Clouds

CONSTELLATIONS AND GROUPS OF STARS

(P) = popular name for a constellation

3
Ara
Cup (P)
Leo
Ram (P)

4
Apus
Argo
Bull (P)
Crab (P)
Crow (P)
Crux
Grus
Hare (P)
Lion (P)
Lynx (P)
Lyra
Lyre (P)
Pavo
Swan (P)
Vela
Wolf (P)

5
Aries
Arrow (P)
Cetus
Crane (P)
Draco
Eagle (P)
Hydra
Indus
Lepus
Libra
Lupus
Mensa
Musca
Norma
Orion
Pyxis
Tucan (P)
Twins (P)

Virgo

6
Antlia
Aquila
Archer (P)
Auriga
Boötes
Caelum
Cancer
Carina
Corvus
Crater
Cygnus
Dipper (P)
Dorado
Dragon (P)
Fishes (P)
Fornax
Gemini
Hydrus
Indian (P)
Lizard (P)
Octans

5
Aries
Octant (P)
Persei
Pictor
Pisces
Plough
Puppis
Scales (P)
Scutum
Square (P)
Taurus
Tucana
Virgin (P)
Volans

7
Centaur (P)
Cepheus
Columba
Dolphin (P)

Furnace (P)
Giraffe (P)
Lacerta
Peacock (P)
Pegasus
Perseus
Phoenix (P)
Pleiads
Sagitta
Scorpio
Sea goat (P)
Serpens
Serpent (P)
Sextans
Unicorn (P)

8
Aquarius
Circinus
Equuleus
Eridanus
Great Dog (P)
Hercules (P)
Leo Minor
Pleiades
Scorpion (P)
Scorpius
Sculptor
Ship Argo (P)
Triangle (P)

9
Andromeda (P)
Centaurus
Chameleon
Compasses (P)
Delphinus
Great Bear (P)
Little Dog (P)
Monoceros

Noah's Dove (P)
Ophiuchus
Ploughman (P)
Reticulum
Swordfish (P)
Telescope (P)
Ursa Major
Ursa Minor
Vulpecula

10
Atlantides
Canis Major
Canis Minor
Cassiopeia (P)
Charioteer (P)
Flying Fish (P)
Greyhounds (P)
Horologium
Little Bear (P)
Little Lion (P)
Microscope (P)
Piscis Aust.
Sea Monster (P)
Triangulum
Watersnake (P)

11
Capricornus
Hunter Orion (P)
Little Horse (P)
Sagittarius
Southern Fly (P)
Telescopium
Water-bearer (P)

Winged Horse (P)

12
Charles's Wain
Flying dragon (P)
Microscopium
Southern Fish (P)

13
Berenice's Hair (P)
Canes Venatici
Coma Berenices
Crux Australis
Northern Crown (P)
Painter's Easel (P)
River Eridanus (P)
Serpentbearer (P)
Southern Cross (P)
Southern Crown (P)

14
Bird of Paradise (P)
Camelopardalis
Corona Borealis
Musca Australis
Sculptor's Tools (P)

15
Corona Australis
Piscis Australis
Sculptor's Chisel

PLANETS AND SATELLITES

2	5	Spica	Phobos	7	8	11
Io	Ariel	Titan	Phoebe	Iapetus	Callisto	Evening Star
	Dione	Venus	Saturn	Jupiter	Ganymede	Morning Star
4	Earth		Tethys	Mercury	Hesperus	
Mars	Mimas	6	Triton	Neptune		
Moon	Pluto	Deimos	Uranus	Titania	9	
Rhea	Regel	Europa		Umbriel	Enceladus	
	Rigel	Oberon				

STARS

4	6	7	Proxima	Centauri	Bellatrix
Mira	Altair	Antares	Regulus	Denebola	Fomalhaut
Vega	Castor	Canopus		Kapteyn's	
	Crucis	Capella	8	Lodestar	10
5	Pollux	Dog Star	Achernar	Pole Star	Betelgeuse
Algol	Shaula	Lalande	Alpherat		
Deneb	Sirius	Polaris	Arcturus	9	13
Hamal		Procyon	Barnard's	Aldebaran	Alpha Centauri

Biology, Botany and Zoology

3
ADH, ADP, ATP, bud, CNS, cud, DNA, ear, egg, eye, FAD, fin, gel, gum, gut, IAA, jaw, lip, NAD, ova, pod, rib, RNA, rod, sap, sex

4
anal, anus, apex, axon, bark, bile, bird, body, bone, bulb, burr, cell, claw, cone, cork, corm, cyst, food, foot, gall, gene, germ, gill, hair, hand, head, hoof, host, iris, leaf, lens, life, limb, lung, milk, NADH, NADP, neck, node, ovum, pith, pome, pore, root, salt, seed, skin, stem, tail, urea, vein, wilt, wing, wood, yolk

5
aorta, aster, auxin, berry, birth, blood, bract, brain, calyx, cilia, class, cline, clone, colon, cutin, cycad, cycle, death, digit, drupe, druse, fauna, femur, fibre, flora, fruit, genus, gland, gonad, graft, heart, humus, hymen, ileum, imago, larva, latex, liver, lymph, molar, mouth, mucus, NADPH, nasal, nasty, nerve, order, organ, ovary, ovule, penis, petal, phage, plant, pubic, pubis, pupil, ramus, resin, scale, semen, sense, sepal, shell, shoot, sinus, skull, smell, sperm, spine, spore, stoma, style, sweat, taste, thigh, tibia, touch, trunk, tuber, urine, vagus, villi, virus, whorl, wrist, xylem

6
achene, aerobe, albino, allele, amnion, animal, annual, anther, artery, atrium, biceps, biotic, botany, branch, caecum, canine, carpal, carpel, caudal, chitin, climax, cloaca, coccyx, cocoon, coelum, cornea, cortex, dermis, embryo, enamel, energy, enzyme, facial, faeces, family

fibril	stigma	ecdysis	tap root	feedback
fibrin	stolon	ecology	tetanus	flagella
fibula	sucker	elastin	thallus	flatworm
floral	tactic	enteron	thyroid	follicle
flower	tannin	epigeal	trachea	ganglion
foetus	telome	gastric	triceps	genetics
forest	tendon	genital	tropism	genitals
floral	testis	gizzard	urethra	genotype
fusion	thorax	habitat	vacuole	germ cell
gamete	tissue	haploid	viscera	holdfast
gemmae	tongue	hearing	vitamin	homodont
genome	ureter	hepatic	zoology	hypogeal
girdle	uterus	hormone		inner ear
growth	vagina	humerus	**8**	lamellae
gullet	vessel	incisor	abductor	lenticel
hybrid	vision	insulin	abscisin	life span
hyphae	zygote	isogamy	acrosome	ligament
joints		jejunum	adductor	mast cell
labial	**7**	keratin	aeration	maxillae
labium	abdomen	lacteal	alkaloid	membrane
lamina	adenine	linkage	allogamy	mesoderm
larynx	adrenal	mammary	alveolus	midbrain
leaves	aerobic	medulla	amoeboid	moulting
lignin	albumen	meiosis	anaerobe	movement
mammal	anatomy	mitosis	antibody	muscular
mantle	annulus	myotome	appendix	mutation
marrow	antenna	nectary	auditory	mycelium
mucous	antigen	nostril	autogamy	nerve net
muscle	asexual	nucleus	bacteria	nucellus
mutant	atavism	oogonia	biennial	ontogeny
nectar	auricle	organic	bile duct	pancreas
neural	biology	osmosis	biomorph	papillae
neuron	biotope	oviduct	bisexual	parasite
oocyte	bipolar	petiole	blastula	pectoral
oogamy	bladder	pharynx	brachial	perianth
palate	bronchi	pigment	carapace	perineum
pectin	cambium	pinnate	carotene	placenta
pelvic	capsule	plastid	cellular	plankton
pelvis	cardiac	plumule	cell wall	polarity
phlegm	carotid	protein	cerebral	polysome
phylum	cell sap	pyloric	cerebrum	pregnant
pistil	chalaza	radicle	chordate	prop root
plasma	chiasma	rhachis	clavicle	protozoa
pollen	cochlea	rhizoid	cleavage	receptor
purine	conifer	rhizome	clitoris	ribosome
radius	corolla	root cap	coenzyme	root hair
rectum	cranial	species	collagen	ruminant
retina	cranium	spindle	cytology	sclereid
runner	creeper	sternum	dendrite	seedling
sacrum	culture	stomach	duodenum	skeleton
sexual	cuticle	stomata	ectoderm	spiracle
spinal	cutting	synapse	efferent	syncarpy
spleen	diploid	systole	egestion	taxonomy
stamen	dormant	tapetum	endoderm	tegument

tentacle
thalamus
tracheid
tympanum
vascular
vertebra
virology
zoospore

9
adrenalin
allantois
amino acid
anabolism
anaerobic
anisogamy
antennule
appendage
arteriole
autonomic
basal body
branchial
branching
capillary
carnivore
cartilage
cellulose
centriole
chiasmata
chromatid
chromatin
chrysalis
commensal
corpuscle
cytoplasm
Darwinism
diaphragm
digestion
dominance
dura mater
dysploidy
ecosystem
ectoplasm
endocrine
endoplasm
epidermis
evolution
excretion
excretory
exodermis
fertilize
forebrain
germinate
gestation

gynaecium
haemocoel
halophyte
herbivore
hindbrain
histology
ingestion
inhibitor
internode
intestine
life cycle
life forms
megaspore
micropyle
middle ear
migration
mutagenic
nephridia
nerve cell
notochord
nucleolus
olfactory
oogenesis
operculum
optic lobe
organelle
oxidation
pacemaker
perennial
pericycle
phagocyte
phellogen
phylogeny
pituitary
proboscis
pulmonary
recessive
reticulum
retractor
sclerotic
sebaceous
secretion
secretory
selection
sieve cell
sieve tube
sporangia
Sporogony
stone cell
substrate
succulent
symbiosis
tricuspid
umbilical

unisexual
ventricle
xerophyte

10
acoelomate
actomyosin
alimentary
androecium
antheridia
anticlinal
aortic arch
apical cell
archegonia
autecology
biological
blastocoel
blastocyst
blastoderm
blastopore
bronchiole
catabolism
centrosome
cerebenum
chemotaxis
chromosome
coleoptile
copulation
dehiscence
dermatogen
entomology
epiglottis
epithelium
fibrinogen
generation
geotropism
glomerulus
grey matter
guard cells
herbaceous
hereditary
homocercal
homozygous
hygrophyte
hypophysis
incubation
inhibition
integument
interferon
Krebs cycle
Lamarckism
leaf sheath
leucoplast
locomotion

lymphocyte
metabolism
morphology
mother cell
negentropy
nerve fibre
neural tube
nitrifying
nucleotide
oesophagus
omnivorous
osteoclast
parasitism
parenchyma
pathogenic
periosteum
phelloderm
phototaxis
physiology
pineal body
polyploidy
population
prokaryote
prothallus
protoplasm
pyramidine
saprophyte
sarcolemma
schizogony
sieve plate
sporophyte
strophiole
subspecies
succession
synecology
vegetation
vegetative
vertebrate
viviparity

11
aestivation
allelomorph
antibiotics
archenteron
autotrophic
autotropism
carbon cycle
carboxylase
carnivorous
chlorophyll
chloroplast
collenchyma
competition

conjugation
deamination
dessication
endothelium
environment
erythrocyte
exoskeleton
facultative
gall bladder
gametophyte
genetic code
germination
Golgi bodies
haemocyanin
haemoglobin
heterospory
hibernation
homeostatis
inheritance
loop of Henle
monoculture
muscle fibre
nematoblast
nucleic acid
orientation
parturition
pericardium
pinocytosis
plasmolysis
polar bodies
pollination
polypeptide
pseudopodia
respiration
somatic cell
spermatozoa
sub-cellular
triploblast
white matter
zooplankton

12
archesporium
back-crossing
bacteriology
biochemistry
buccal cavity
central canal
denitrifying
diploblastic
distribution
ectoparasite
endoparasite
endoskeleton

fermentation
flexor muscle
gastrulation
heliotropism
heterocercal
heterogamete
heterozygous
hypothalamus
invagination
invertebrate
mammary gland
medullary ray
microbiology
mitochondria
myelin sheath
nerve impulse
phospholipid
phototropism
red blood cell

reductionism
reproduction
sclerenchyma
smooth muscle
spermatozoid

13
accommodation
bacteriophage
bicuspid valve
binary fission
cephalization
chemoreceptor
decomposition
erector muscle
extracellular
Fallopian tube
fertilization
hermaphrodite

homoiothermic
insectivorous
intracellular
marine biology
mitochondrion
morphogenesis
multinucleate
ovoviviparity
palisade cells
parthenocarpy
photoreceptor
phytoplankton
plasmodesmah
proprioceptor
striped muscle
thermotropism
thigmotropism
translocation
transpiration

14
Brunner's glands
chemosynthesis
extensor muscle
Haversian canal
osmoregulation
oxyhaemoglobin
photoperiodism
photosynthesis
polysaccharide
vascular bundle

15
multiple fission
parthenogenesis

Chemical Elements

actinium (Ac)
aluminium (Al)
americium (Am)
antimony (Sb)
argon (Ar)
arsenic (As)
astatine (At)
barium (Ba)
berkelium (Bk)
beryllium (Be)
bismuth (Bi)
bohrium (Bh)
boron (B)
bromine (Br)
cadmium (Cd)
caesium (Cs)
calcium (Ca)
californium (Cf)
carbon (C)
cerium (Ce)
chlorine (Cl)
chromium (Cr)
cobalt (Co)
columbium (Cb)
copper (Cu)
curium (Cm)
dubnium (Db)

dysprosium (Dy)
einsteinium (Es)
erbium (Er)
europium (Eu)
fermium (Fm)
fluorine (F)
francium (Fr)
gadolinium (Gd)
gallium (Ga)
germanium (Ge)
gold (Au)
hafnium (Hf)
helium (He)
holmium (Ho)
hydrogen (H)
indium (In)
iodine (I)
iridium (Ir)
iron (Fe)
krypton (Kr)
lanthanum (La)
lawrencium (Lr)
lead (Pb)
lithium (Li)
lutetium (Lu)
magnesium (Mg)
manganese (Mn)

mendelevium (Md)
mercury (Hg)
molybdenum (Mo)
neodymium (Nd)
neon (Ne)
neptunium (Np)
nickel (Ni)
niobium (Nb)
nitrogen (N)
nobelium (No)
osmium (Os)
oxygen (O)
palladium (Pd)
phosphorus (P)
platinum (Pt)
plutonium (Pu)
polonium (Po)
potassium (K)
praseodymium (Pr)
promethium (Pm)
protactinium (Pa)
radium (Ra)
radon (Rn)
rhenium (Re)
rhodium (Rh)
rubidium (Rb)
ruthenium (Ru)

samarium (Sm)
scandium (Sc)
selenium (Se)
silicon (Si)
silver (Ag)
sodium (Na)
strontium (Sr)
sulphur (S)
tantalum (Ta)
technetium (Tc)
tellurium (Te)
terbium (Tb)
thallium (Tl)
thorium (Th)
thulium (Tm)
tin (Sn)
titanium (Ti)
tungsten (W)
uranium (U)
vanadium (V)
xenon (Xe)
ytterbium (Yb)
yttrium (Y)
zinc (Zn)
zirconium (Zr)

Chemistry

2
mu
pH

3
DNA
EMF
fat
gas
ion
oil
ore
pKa
PVC
RNA
sol
TCP
TNT

4
acid
atom
base
bond
cell
clay
coal
coke
keto
lime
meta
mica
mole
neon
rust
salt
slag
soda
spin

5
aldol
alkyl
alloy
amide
amine
amino
anion
anode
argon
azote
basic

beryl
borax
brass
chalk
ester
ether
ethyl
freon
glass
group
ionic
lipid
lysol
metal
model
monad
nylon
oxide
ozone
phase
radon
redox
resin
roast
solid
steel
sugar
vinyl

6
acetal
acetic
acetyl
acidic
adduct
aerate
alkali
alkane
alkene
alkyne
amatol
ammine
atomic
barium
bleach
borane
borate
bronze
buffer
butane
casein
cerium

chrome
dipole
dry ice
energy
enzyme
ethane
ferric
galena
gangue
gypsum
halide
iodide
iodine
iodite
iodize
isomer
liquid
litmus
methyl
octane
olefin
period
pewter
phenol
phenyl
potash
proton
quartz
raceme
reduce
refine
retort
ribose
silica
sinter
solute
starch
sterol
tannin
teepol
teflon
thymol

7
acetate
acetone
acidity
aerosol
alchemy
alcohol
alumina
amalgam

ammonal
ammonia
analyse
aniline
anodize
antacid
aspirin
bauxite
benzene
bismuth
bonding
bromate
bromide
calomel
camphor
carbide
cathode
chemist
chloric
cocaine
codeine
cyanate
cyanide
diamond
dioxide
ebonite
element
entropy
ferment
fermium
ferrate
ferrous
formate
gallium
gelatin
glucose
halogen
hydrate
hydride
isotope
menthol
methane
mineral
neutral
neutron
nitrate
nitride
nitrite
nucleon
orbital
organic
osmosis

osmotic
oxidant
oxidize
peptide
perspex
plastic
polymer
propane
protein
pyrites
quantum
quinine
reagent
soda ash
soluble
solvent
spectra
sucrose
titrate
toluene
tritium
valence
valency
veronal
vitamin
vitriol

8
actinide
aldehyde
alkaline
ammonium
analysis
antimony
aromatic
asbestos
atropine
Bessemer
caffeine
carbolic
carbonic
carbonyl
catalyst
charcoal
chemical
chlorate
chloride
chromate
chromite
cinchona
corundum
covalent

cryolite
cyanogen
diatomic
diborane
didymium
disilane
dissolve
electron
emission
enthalpy
ethylene
fluoride
formalin
fructose
glucinum
glycerol
graphite
half-life
hematite
hydrated
hydroxyl
ideal gas
inert gas
iodoform
kerosene
kinetics
litharge
magnesia
manganin
marsh gas
masunum
methanol
molecule
morphine
nichrome
nicotine
noble gas
non-metal
particle
periodic
peroxide
phosgene
reactant
reaction
refining
rock salt
saturate
silicane
silicate
solution
spectrum
suboxide

sulphate
sulphide
sulphite
test tube
unit cell
unstable
water gas

9

acetylene
acylation
alchemist
alcoholic
aliphatic
allotropy
aluminate
amino acid
anhydrous
apparatus
aqua regia
bell metal
brimstone
carbonate
carbonium
catalysis
cellulose
chemistry
chokedamp
corrosion
diazonium
digitalin
duralumin
galvanize
haematite
histamine
homolysis
hydration
hydroxide
indicator
inorganic
insoluble
isomerism
limestone
limewater
magnetite
manganese
metalloid
molecular
monatomic
nitration
oxidation

palladium
permalloy
petroleum
phosphate
phosphide
polar bond
polyester
polythene
polyvinyl
quicklime
rare gases
reductant
reduction
resonance
semi-metal
stability
sulphuric
synthesis
synthetic
titration
vulcanite

10

acetic acid
allotropes
analytical
bimetallic
bond energy
bond length
catenation
chalybeate
chemically
chloroform
dative bond
double bond
electronic
exothermic
flotation
formic acid
free energy
heavy water
hydrolysis
isocyanide
laboratory
lactic acid
lanthanide
latent heat
mass number
molybdenum
natural gas
neutralize

nitric acid
nucleotide
oxalic acid
phosphorus
polymerize
saccharide
solubility
transition

11

acetylation
benzoic acid
bicarbonate
cholesterol
crystallize
dehydration
electrolyte
elimination
endothermic
equilibrium
free radical
ground state
hydrocarbon
litmus paper
naphthalene
non-metallic
paraldehyde
pitchblende
polystyrene
precipitate
prussic acid
quicksilver
radioactive
ribonucleic
sublimation
substituent
tautomerism

12

acetaldehyde
alkali metals
alkyl halides
atomic number
atomic weight
blast furnace
carbohydrate
carbonic acid
chlorination
condensation
covalent bond
deliquescent

diamagnetism
disaccharide
displacement
dissociation
distillation
electrolysis
fermentation
formaldehyde
German silver
Haber process
halogenation
hydrochloric
hydrogen bond
permanganate
Prince's metal
rate constant
sulphonamide
tartaric acid

13

carbon dioxide
chain reaction
giant molecule
lattice energy
molecular mass
periodic table
petrochemical
precipitation
radioactivity
reaction order
semiconductor
sulphuric acid

14 *and over*

Born-Haber cycle (14)
carbon monoxide (14)
carboxylic acid (14)
decarbonization (15)
deoxyribonucleic (16)
electrochemical (15)
ferro-manganese (14)
Grignard reagent (15)
monosaccharide (14)
organo-metallic (14)
oxidizing agent (14)
phosphor bronze (14)
photosynthesis (14)
polysaccharide (14)
reaction profile (15)
saponification (14)
trinitrotoluene (15)

Computers and the Internet

2	ISA	CMOS	scan	MS-DOS	newbie
AI	ISP	code	SCSI	octal	online
IT	JPG	copy	SGML	opt-in	output
OS	key	CTRL	site	parse	packet
PC	LAN	data	SMTP	paste	PASCAL
WP	LCD	disc	sort	pixel	portal
	LED	disk	spam	proxy	QWERTY
3	LOL	down	SRAM	queue	reboot
AGP	MMX	drag	surf	query	record
Alt	NAP	DRAM	SVGA	reset	return
ATM	net	drop	TIFF	route	router
BAK	NIC	dump	type	SDRAM	screen
BAT	OCR	echo	unit	shell	script
bay	OLE	edit	UNIX	shout	server
bit	PAL	exit	user	slave	sign on
BMP	pad	feed	VESA	store	source
BPS	PCI	file	VRAM	tower	spider
bug	PDF	font	VRML	trash	subnet
bus	PIC	hack	WORM	video	syntax
CAB	PIF	head	WRAM	virus	telnet
CAD	PIN	home			thread
CAM	POP	host	**5**	**6**	upload
CGA	PPM	HTML	ABEND	access	usenet
CGI	PSU	HTTP	alias	analog	user ID
com	PUB	icon	ASCII	anorak	visits
CPU	RAM	ISDN	ATAPI	applet	window
CRT	ROM	ISOC	BASIC	archie	
Cut	RSI	Java	cache	back up	**7**
DAC	RTF	JPEG	CD ROM	banner	acronym
DAT	Sig	Kbps	click	binary	ActiveX
DLL	SYS	link	clone	bitmap	archive
DNS	Tab	load	COAST	boot up	booting
DOS	Tag	LOGO	COBOL	cookie	browser
DPI	URL	loop	CORAL	cursor	chip set
DTP	USB	MAPI	crash	decode	circuit
DVD	VDU	menu	debug	dot.com	clip art
EGA	VGA	MIDI	drive	delete	command
end	WAV	MIME	email	driver	compile
ESC	WPM	move	enter	DVD ROM	com port
EXE	WWW	MPEG	field	escape	corrupt
FAQ	XML	node	flame	folder	default
FAT	Y2K	ODBC	frame	format	density
fax	Zip	ODMA	index	gopher	digital
FPU		page	input	hacker	DirectX
FTP	**4**	path	key in	indent	dynamic
hit	ADSL	perl	LINUX	kermit	EDO RAM
hub	ANSI	ping	log in	kernel	emulate
ICQ	BIOS	port	log on	laptop	execute
IDE	boot	POST	macro	log off	gateway
INI	byte	quit	micro	log out	graphic
IRC	chip	RAID	modem	memory	hot zone
IRQ	CIFS	save	mouse	Mosaic	imaging

235

install
integer
kilobit
mailbox
megabit
menu bar
monitor
network
offline
PCI bus
pentium
pointer
printer
proggie
program
readout
recover
restore
scanner
spammer
storage
toolbar
utility
website
web page
windows
WYSIWYG

8

activate
arrow key
baud rate
boot disk
bookmark
bus mouse
capacity
caps lock
chat room
cold boot
databank
database
databits
diskette
document
download
emulator
ethernet
extranet
Facsimile
fax modem
file type
firewall
firmware
flash ram

flat file
function
game port
gigabyte
hard disc
hard disk
hardware
home page
hotspots
image map
internet
internic
intranet
joystick
keyboard
kilobyte
livewire
local bus
megabyte
notebook
password
print out
protocol
real time
recovery
scalable
shift key
shortcut
shutdown
software
space bar
spooling
swapfile
terabyte
terminal
timed out
topology
truetype
truncate
typeface
veronica
warm boot
wildcard
word wrap
zip drive

9

back plane
backspace
bandwidth
batch file
cartridge
character
clipboard

dialog box
directory
disk cache
disk drive
dot matrix
e-commerce
emoticons
fat client
favourite
floptical
flowchart
groupware
hard drive
highlight
hyperlink
hypertext
interface
IP address
mail merge
mainframe
megahertz
microchip
menu driven
news group
overwrite
partition
processor
Real Audio
shareware
shift key
shockwave
signature
snail mail
soundcard
uninstall
video card
virus scan
webmaster
word break

10

base memory
clock speed
control key
controller
daisy chain
decryption
domain name
encryption
ergonomics
file format
file server
floppy disk
frame relay

hypermedia
impression
JavaScript
mirror site
multimedia
nanosecond
numeric pad
page layout
paintbrush
peripheral
power cable
programmer
resolution
screen name
serial port
subroutine
system disk
voice modem
web browser
whiteboard
winchester
wraparound

11

animated GIF
aspect ratio
beta version
cache memory
close button
compression
coprocessor
cut and paste
diagnostics
display unit
drag and drop
edutainment
fibre optics
function key
gopherspace
hexadecimal
input device
interactive
IRQ conflict
machine code
mailing list
motherboard
nettiquette
plug and play
power supply
programming
replication
ribbon cable
ring network
silicon chip

smart system
spreadsheet
time sharing
unformatted
visual basic
workstation

12

active window
Anonymous
 FTP
boolean logic
circuit board
client server
CPU memory
 bus
default value
device driver
graphics card
host computer
housekeeping
laser printer
multitasking
output device
parallel port
primary cache
response time
screen filter
search engine
serial access
shell account
splash screen
subdirectory
user friendly
World Wide
 Web

13

compatibility
context switch
digital camera
expansion card
expansion slot
file extension
microcomputer
millennium
 bug
printer driver
root directory
semi-conductor
shrink
 wrapped
virtual
 memory

word processor

14
computer dating
data protection
expanded memory
extended memory
file conversion
instruction set
microprocessor
page impression
push technology
Rich Text Format
secondary cache
systems analyst
teleconference

temporary files
version control
word processing

15
defragmentation
high density disk
machine language
operating system
systems analysis
upper memory area
video conference

16 *and over*
anti-virus software (17)

artificial intelligence (22)
central processing unit (21)
command interpreter (18)
computer literacy (16)
control character (16)
conventional memory (18)
data transfer rate (16)
desktop publishing (17)
dial up connection (16)
digital video disk (16)
direct cable connection (21)
electronic commerce (18)
general protection fault (22)
high capacity disk (16)
personal computer (16)

Engineering

See also **Tools and Instruments.**

3	axle	pipe	weld	helix	rough	X-rays
ace	beam	plan	wire	hinge	rusty	
amp	belt	plug	work	hoist	screw	**6**
BHP	bolt	pump	worm	ingot	shaft	analog
bit	burr	rack		input	short	aerial
cam	byte	rail	**5**	jenny	shunt	anneal
cog	cast	reel	alloy	jewel	slack	barrel
dam	cone	road	anode	joint	slide	bit-end
EMF	cowl	rope	blast	joist	sling	blower
erg	flaw	rung	braze	keyed	smelt	bobbin
fan	flux	rust	cable	laser	spoke	boiler
fit	fuel	shop	chair	level	spool	bridge
gab	fuse	skid	chase	lever	spout	buffer
hob	gear	slag	civil	maser	stamp	burner
hub	glue	slue	clamp	miner	steam	camber
IHP	hasp	stay	cleat	model	still	clutch
ion	hook	stop	compo	motor	strap	cotter
key	hose	sump	crane	mould	strut	couple
lag	jack	tamp	crank	oakum	swage	cradle
nut	kiln	tank	crate	oiler	taper	cut-out
ohm	lens	test	deuce	pedal	tewel	damper
oil	lift	tire	dowel	pivot	tools	derail
ram	link	tool	drill	plant	tooth	duplex
rig	lock	tram	drive	power	T-rail	dynamo
RPM	loom	tube	elbow	press	train	energy
sag	main	turn	felly	pylon	valve	engine
tap	mill	tyre	flows	quern	video	fitter
tie	mine	unit	flume	radar	waste	flange
UHF	nail	vane	flush	radio	wedge	funnel
VHF	nave	vent	force	relay	wharf	geyser
	oily	void	gauge	resin	wheel	girder
4	pawl	volt	grace	rigid	wiper	gutter
arch	pile	weir	H-beam	rivet	works	hinged

intake	tinned	furnace	suction	cryotron
jigger	toggle	fuse box	sump pit	cylinder
kibble	torque	gas trap	support	Davy lamp
lacing	tripod	gearing	syringe	dead lift
ladder	tubing	gimbals	tamping	declutch
lamina	tunnel	hydrant	tension	draw gear
latten	uncoil	inertia	test bay	draw link
magnet	vacuum	jointer	testing	edge rail
milled	washer	journal	thimble	electric
mining	welded	lagging	tie beam	elevator
moment	welder	lockage	tilting	engineer
monkey		lock-nut	tin mine	enginery
nipple	**7**	machine	tinning	fan blast
nozzle	adapter	magneto	torsion	feed pipe
oil can	air duct	manhole	tracing	feed pump
oil gas	airfoil	mill cog	tramcar	fireclay
output	air pipe	mill dam	tramway	fireplug
petrol	air pump	milling	treadle	flywheel
pinion	air tube	monitor	trolley	fracture
piston	air trap	moulded	turbine	friction
pulley	artisan	moulder	turning	fuse clip
rarefy	battery	mud hole	unscrew	galvanic
repair	bearing	mud sill	viaduct	gas gauge
retard	belting	nuclear	voltage	gas mains
rigger	booster	Ohm's law	voltaic	gas works
rocket	bracket	oil fuel	welding	gland nut
roller	car tyre	oil lamp	wet dock	governor
rotary	caisson	oil pump	wringer	gradient
rundle	casting	pattern	wrought	hardware
saw pit	cathode	pig iron		hot blast
sheave	chamfer	pinhole	**8**	hot press
siding	chimney	pontoon	a-centric	ignition
sleeve	cistern	program	air brake	injector
sluice	clacker	pug mill	air valve	ink stone
smithy	column	rag bolt	annealed	insulate
socket	conduit	railway	aqueduct	ironwork
solder	cuffing	ratchet	axletree	irrigate
spigot	derrick	reactor	balancer	Jacquard
static	digital	refract	ball cock	joint box
stoker	drawbar	riveter	bevelled	junk ring
strain	drawing	road bed	bridging	klystron
stress	dry dock	roadway	camshaft	laminate
strike	dry pile	sawmill	cam wheel	land roll
sucker	dynamic	seawall	cassette	leverage
switch	exciter	shackle	castings	limekiln
swivel	exhaust	shuttle	cast iron	linotype
system	eyebolt	sleeper	chauffer	lock gate
tackle	factory	smelter	cog wheel	lock sill
tappet	ferrule	soup pan	compound	lock weir
temper	firebox	spindle	computer	loop line
tender	forging	stamper	concrete	lynch pin
thrust	founder	stand-by	corn mill	magnetic
tie bar	foundry	statics	coupling	main line
tie rod	fulcrum	stopper	cradling	mechanic

mill pond	throttle	dynamical	mechanics	tin lining
mill race	tide mill	earthwork	mechanism	tin mining
momentum	tile kiln	eccentric	mechanist	train road
monorail	time ball	electrify	mechanize	transform
monotype	tinplate	electrode	mild steel	trunk line
moulding	tractile	escalator	millstone	tunnel pit
movement	traction	female die	mine shaft	turntable
mud valve	tractive	fire brick	mud sluice	twin cable
oilstone	train oil	fish joint	nodal line	unscrewed
oil store	tram rail	fishplate	nose piece	vibration
oil stove	turbojet	floodgate	off-spring	vulcanite
operator	turnpike	fog signal	oil engine	vulcanize
ozonizer	tympanum	foot valve	oil geyser	waste weir
pendulum	uncoiled	force pump	perforate	watermark
penstock	unsolder	framework	petrol can	water tank
pile shoe	velocity	funicular	piston rod	well drain
platform	water gas	galvanism	pneumatic	whip graft
polarity	windmill	galvanist	polarizer	white heat
pressure	wind pump	galvanize	porous pot	winepress
pump gear	wire-draw	gas engine	power loom	wire gauze
pump hood	wireless	gas fitter	programme	wire wheel
purchase	wood mill	gas geyser	propeller	worm wheel
radiator	workable	gas holder	prototype	X-ray plant
rag wheel	workshop	gasometer	pump break	
rail road		gas retort	pump spear	**10**
recharge	**9**	gearwheel	pump stock	accelerate
refinery	acoustics	horse mill	radiation	air machine
register	air engine	hydraulic	rectifier	alarm gauge
repairer	air filter	hydrostat	reflector	alternator
rheostat	air vessel	idle wheel	regulator	automation
rigidity	amplifier	induction	repairing	automobile
ring bolt	artificer	inductive	reparable	bevel wheel
shearing	baseplate	inertness	reservoir	broad gauge
silk mill	bevel gear	injection	resultant	cantilever
skew arch	brakedrum	insertion	rheomotor	caseharden
smelting	brakepipe	insulated	road metal	centigrade
soft iron	brick kiln	insulator	roughcast	clack valve
software	blue light	ironsmith	sandpaper	coach screw
spinnery	blueprint	ironworks	shop board	combustion
split pin	cast steel	jet engine	shunt coil	crankshaft
stamping	chain belt	knife edge	slide rule	crown wheel
standard	chain pump	laminated	smack mill	dead weight
starling	clockwork	Lewis bolt	soldering	derailment
stone pit	condenser	Leyden jar	spring box	dielectric
stopcock	conductor	limelight	spur wheel	discharger
strength	cotter pin	lubricant	stanchion	disc wheels
stuffing	craftsman	lubricate	steam pipe	dish wheels
tail race	crosshead	machinery	stiffener	diving bell
tapering	cyclotron	machinist	stock lock	donkey pump
telotype	datum-line	magnetist	stoke hole	drawbridge
tempered	dead level	magnetize	structure	earth plate
template	diaphragm	male screw	superheat	economizer
terminal	disc brake	man engine	telephone	efficiency
textbook	disk brake	master key	tempering	electrical

electronic
embankment
emery cloth
emery paper
emery wheel
engine room
escapement
fire escape
flange rail
fluid drive
footbridge
fuse holder
galvanized
gas turbine
glass paper
goods train
goods truck
grid system
guillotine
hair spring
heart wheel
horsepower
hydrophore
Indian fire
inflexible
instrument
insulating
insulation
iron heater
irrigation
isodynamic
laboratory
lamination
leaf bridge
lock paddle
locomotive
lubricator
macadamize
magnetizer
male thread
mechanical
nodal point
paper cable
percolator
petrol tank
piledriver
pneumatics
powder mill
powerhouse
power-plant
programmer
pulverizer
pump handle
refraction

rejointing
resistance
revolution
rubber-wire
safety-lamp
scoop-wheel
self-acting
skew bridge
smokestack
soap boiler
socket pipe
socket pole
solid state
stationary
steam gauge
stiffening
streamline
structural
swing wheel
swivel hook
telegraphy
telescopic
television
temper heat
thermopile
thermostat
toll bridge
torque tube
transients
transistor
tunnelling
unsoldered
voltaic arc
voltaplast
water crane
water power
watertight
water tower
waterwheel
waterwings
waterworks
wave motion
well boring
windtunnel
wiped joint

11

accelerator
accumulator
aerodynamics
air fountain
anelectrode
atomic clock
bell founder

bell foundry
block system
Bramah
 press
brush wheels
cable laying
candlepower
carburettor
compression
computation
contrivance
coupling box
coupling pin
damask steel
diamagnetic
driving band
driving belt
dynamometer
edge railway
electrician
electricity
electric jar
electrolyse
electrolyte
electronics
endless belt
engineering
exhaust pipe
female screw
frame bridge
gas governor
graving dock
helical gear
incinerator
inking table
iron filings
iron founder
iron foundry
laminations
latten-brass
lock chamber
low pressure
lubrication
machine tool
maintenance
manilla rope
manufactory
mono-railway
narrow gauge
oil purifier
oil strainer
perforation
piledriving
pilot engine

power factor
rack railway
rarefaction
reconstruct
retardation
revolutions
rolling mill
rubber cable
safety valve
searchlight
service pipe
skeleton key
socket joint
steam boiler
steam engine
steam
 hammer
stuffing box
suction pipe
suction pump
summit level
superheater
swing bridge
switchboard
synchronism
synchronize
synchrotron
tappet valve
toggle joint
transformer
transmitter
trundle head
tube railway
underground
uninsulated
voltaic pile
vulcanizing
warping bank
water cement
water engine
water furrow
water hammer
water supply
welding heat
wind furnace
wire drawing
wire grading
workmanship
wrought iron

12

acceleration
anti-friction
arterial road

artesian well
assembly line
balance
 wheel
belt fastener
blast furnace
block machine
block signals
canalization
chain reactor
coaxial cable
counterpoise
danger signal
diamagnetism
diesel engine
differential
disc coupling
disintegrate
donkey engine
double acting
driving shaft
driving wheel
dry-core cable
eccentric
 rod
electric bulb
electric fire
electric fuse
electric iron
electric wire
electrolysis
electromotor
endless screw
engine driver
exhaust valve
female thread
flexible wire
floating dock
flying bridge
flying pinion
founder's dust
founder's sand
gas condenser
gas container
gas regulator
hanging valve
high pressure
hydraulic ram
hydrodynamic
inking roller
installation
jewel bearing
lubrifaction
machine tools

magnetomotor
make-and-break
manilla paper
marine boiler
marine engine
master spring
mini-computer
negative pole
non-conductor
nuclear power
oxy-acetylene
palification
pattern maker
petrol engine
petrol filter
plummer block
polarization
pressure pump
pyro-electric
radiator muff
ratchet wheel
Reaumur scale
rolling press
rolling stock
service cable
short circuit
shunt winding
single acting
sleeve button
slitting mill
solar battery
specific heat
spinning mill
stamping mill
steam heating
steam turbine
steam whistle
suction valve
synchronized
terminal post
thermocouple
toothed wheel
transmission
unmechanical
water battery
water turbine
wheel-and-axle
wheel cutting
working model

13
buffing spring
civil engineer
compound-wound
control theory
Cornish boiler
Cornish engine
counterweight
direct current
draught engine
drummond light
eccentric gear
electric cable
electric clock
electric fluid
electric light
electric motor
electric stove
electrifiable
electromagnet
engine-turning
expansion gear
flexible cable
floodlighting
fluid flywheel
friction balls
friction cones
inflexibility
injection cock
insulated wire
kinetic energy
lifting bridge
liquid starter
lubrification
magnetic fluid
magnetization
movement maker
non-conducting
overshot wheel
pneumatic tyre
pontoon bridge
pressure gauge
printing press
rack-and-pinion
roller bearing
series winding
shock absorber
standard gauge
telegraph line
telegraph pole

telegraph wire
telephone line
telephone wire
thermo current
throttle valve
thrust bearing
water drainage
wave mechanics
whirling table
X-ray apparatus

14
analog computer
blowing machine
contra rotation
diesel electric
discharge valve
discharging rod
disintegration
eccentric strap
eccentric wheel
electric cooker
electric cut-out
electric kettle
electrodynamic
electrostatics
electrothermic
explosive rivet
floating bridge
friction clutch
friction wheels
galvanized iron
hydraulic press
insulated cable
lubricating oil
magnetic needle
multi-core cable
nuclear reactor
petrol strainer
plaster of Paris
pneumatic drill
portable engine
reconstructlon
resino-electric
resultant force
shellac varnish
shunt regulator
thermo-electric
three-core cable
traction engine

universal joint
vitreo electric
voltaic battery
washing
    machine
wave telegraphy

15
brake
    horsepower
block signalling
Centigrade
    scale
concentric cable
digital computer
electric battery
electric circuit
electric current
electric machine
electrification
electrochemical
electrodynamics
electrokinetics
electromagnetic
electronegative
electronic brain
electropositive
expansion engine
Fahrenheit scale
friction rollers
galvanic battery
hydraulic cement
insulating paper
irrigation canal
linotype machine
machine
    language
magnetic battery
magneto-electric
ohmic resistance
perpetual
    motion
pressure
    machine
railway engineer
smelting furnace
specific gravity
spigot-and-socket
tensile strength
water-tube boiler

Mathematics

2
Ln
p.c.
pi

3
add
arc
cos
log
set
sin
tan

4
area
axes
axis
base
cone
cube
edge
face
line
loci
math
mean
plus
ring
root
sine
term
unit
zero

5
acute
angle
chord
conic
cosec
cotan
cubic
curve
equal
focal
focus
force
graph
group
index
lemma

limit
locus
maths
minus
plane
point
power
probe
proof
radii
range
ratio
slope
solid

6
centre
choice
circle
conics
conoid
convex
cosine
cuboid
degree
divide
domain
equals
factor
height
matrix
maxima
median
minima
minute
modulo
moment
motion
normal
number
oblate
oblong
obtuse
period
radial
radian
radius
random
scalar
secant
sector
series

sphere
square
subset
vector
vertex
volume

7
algebra
average
cissoid
complex
concave
conical
cycloid
decagon
divisor
ellipse
evolute
hexagon
indices
inverse
mapping
maximum
minimum
modulus
nonzero
numeral
oblique
octagon
percent
polygon
produce
problem
pyramid
rhombic
rhombus
scalene
section
segment
subtend
surface
tangent
theorem
trapeze
unitary

8
abscissa
addition
analysis
binomial

bisector
calculus
centroid
circular
codomain
constant
converse
cosecant
cube root
cuboidal
cylinder
diagonal
diameter
dihedral
distance
division
elliptic
equation
friction
frustrum
function
geometer
geometry
gradient
helicoid
heptagon
identity
infinity
integers
integral
involute
matrices
meridian
momentum
multiply
negative
new maths
operator
ordinate
osculate
parabola
parallel
pentagon
positive
quadrant
quartile
quotient
rational
rhomboid
rotation
sequence
spheroid

subtract
symmetry
triangle
trigonal
variable
velocity

9
amplitude
asymptote
Cartesian
chi-square
corollary
cotangent
directrix
dodecagon
ellipsoid
expansion
factorize
frequency
geometric
half-angle
hexagonal
hyperbola
identical
imaginary
increment
induction
inflexion
intersect
isosceles
logarithm
Napierian
numerator
numerical
octagonal
parabolic
parameter
perimeter
polygonal
polyhedra
primitive
quadratic
rectangle
remainder
resultant
spherical
trapezium
trapezoid

10
arithmetic

concentric
continuity
decahedron
derivative
dimensions
epicycloid
equivalent
expression
hyperbolic
hypotenuse
hypothesis
irrational
kinematics
multiplier
octahedron
orthogonal
osculation
paraboloid
percentage
polyhedral
polyhedron
polynomial
proportion
regression
right
angle
semicircle
square
root
statistics
stochastic
tangential
unit
vector

11
approximate
associative
coefficient
combination
commutative
coordinates
denominator
determinant
eigenvector
equiangular
equilateral
equilibrium
exponential
geometrical
hyperboloid
icosahedron

integration	**12**	**13**	**14**		
isomorphism	acceleration	approximation	arithmetic mean		
orthocentre	conic section	circumference	complex numbers		
permutation	differential	geometric mean	convexo-concave		
probability	dodecahedron	linear algebra	multiplication		
progression	eccentricity	parallelogram	natural numbers		
real numbers	harmonic mean	perpendicular	transformation		
rectangular	intersection	plane geometry			
rectilinear	least squares	power function	**15**		
right-angled	number theory	quadrilateral	binomial theorem		
subtraction	semicircular	right bisector	differentiation		
symmetrical	straight line	solid geometry	rational numbers		
tetrahedron	substitution				
translation	trigonometry				

Physics

2	wave	weber	battery	spectra	overtone
a.c.	work		beta ray	statics	particle
d.c.	X-ray	**6**	calorie	thermal	pendulum
		ampere	candela	torsion	polaroid
3	**5**	atomic	cathode	voltage	positive
bar	anode	baryon	Celsius	voltaic	positron
bel	curie	camera	circuit		pressure
EMF	cycle	charge	coulomb	**8**	rest mass
erg	diode	corona	crystal	adhesion	roentgen
gas	earth	dipole	current	aerofoil	solenoid
lux	farad	energy	damping	antinode	spectrum
mev	field	fusion	decibel	beat note	velocity
ohm	fluid	impact	density	betatron	
rpm	focus	isobar	dry cell	brownian	**9**
UHF	force	kelvin	elastic	cohesion	acoustics
VHF	image	lepton	element	duo-diode	adiabatic
	joule	liquid	entropy	dynamics	amplifier
4	laser	magnet	fission	electric	amplitude
atom	lever	moment	gaseous	electron	antimeson
cell	light	motion	gravity	emission	barometer
dyne	lumen	newton	hyperon	free fall	black body
dux	maser	optics	impulse	friction	bolometer
foci	meson	period	inertia	graviton	capacitor
halo	motor	photon	machine	half-life	coherence
heat	phase	plasma	maxwell	infra-red	condenser
lens	pitch	proton	neutron	isogonic	conductor
mach	power	quanta	nuclear	kilowatt	cyclotron
mass	prism	torque	nucleon	kinetics	electrode
node	radar	triode	nucleus	klystron	frequency
pile	radio	vacuum	nuclide	magnetic	gamma rays
pole	shell	vector	optical	magneton	generator
rays	solid	weight	orbital	molecule	gyroscope
spin	sonic		pi-meson	momentum	harmonics
tube	sound	**7**	quantum	negative	impedance
volt	speed	ammeter	reactor	negatron	induction
watt	valve	aneroid	rontgen	neutrino	insulator

isoclinic
Leyden jar
magnetism
magnetron
manometer
mechanics
plutonium
potential
radiation
radio wave
real image
rectifier
resonance
spark coil
vibration
viscosity
voltmeter

10

aberration
absorption
achromatic
antilepton
antimatter
antiproton
atomic bomb
atomic mass
ballistics
binoculars
cathode ray
Centigrade
conduction
convection
cosmic rays
dielectric
dispersion
electrical
Fahrenheit
heavy water
horsepower
inductance
ionization

kinematics
latent heat
microscope
omega meson
oscillator
precession
reflection
refraction
relativity
resistance
ripple tank
scattering
shunt-wound
supersonic
thermionic
thermopile
transistor
vacuum tube
wavelength

11

accelerator
band spectra
capacitance
capillarity
centrifugal
centripetal
compression
conductance
declination
diffraction
electricity
falling body
focal length
gravitation
hypercharge
newton-metre
oscillation
positronium
radioactive
resistivity
restitution

series wound
solar energy
spectrogram
statcoulomb
synchrotron
temperature
transformer
transuranic

12

acceleration
angstrom unit
antiparticle
atomic number
atomic weight
beta particle
centre of mass
cloud chamber
conductivity
critical mass
diamagnetism
eccentricity
electrolysis
electroscope
interference
kilowatt-hour
oscilloscope
permittivity
polarization
spectrograph
wave equation

13

alpha particle
bubble chamber
chain reaction
critical angle
discharge tube
elastic impact
electric field
electric motor
electric power

electromagnet
electromotive
electron shell
electrostatic
Geiger counter
gravitational
induction coil
kinetic energy
magnetic field
magnetic poles
paramagnetism
photoelectric
quantum number
quantum theory
radioactivity
rectification
scintillation
semiconductor
standing waves
thermal capacity
transmutation

14

electric energy
electrostatics
ferromagnetism
nuclear reactor
thermodynamics
thermoelectric

15

centre of gravity
electric current
electrification
electromagnetic
Planck's constant
potential energy
specific gravity

16

terminal velocity
Wheatstone bridge

Sciences

5
logic

6
augury
botany
conics
optics

7
algebra
anatomy
biology
cookery
ecology
farming
finance
geodesy
geogony
geology
gunnery
history
hygiene
myology
orology
otology
pandect
phonics
physics
poetics
science
statics
surgery
tanning
trivium
weaving
zoology
zootomy

8
aerology
agronomy
analysis
atmology
barology
bio-assay
biometry
breeding
bryology
calculus
commerce
cytology

dairying
dosology
dynamics
ethology
etiology
eugenics
forestry
genetics
geometry
glyptics
horology
kinetics
medicine
mycology
nosology
ontology
penology
pharmacy
politics
pomology
posology
rheology
rhetoric
sinology
sitology
spherics
taxonomy
tidology
tocology
topology
typology
virology
zymology

9
acoustics
aerometry
aetiology
agriology
aitology
allopathy
altimetry
anemology
annealing
areometry
astronomy
audiology
barometry
biometrics
bleaching
cartology
chemistry

chiropody
chorology
cosmology
dentistry
dietetics
diplomacy
economics
embalming
emetology
engraving
ethnology
gardening
geography
gnomonics
harmonics
histology
horometry
husbandry
hydrology
hygrology
hymnology
ichnology
lithology
mammalogy
mechanics
micrology
neurology
ophiology
orography
osteology
otography
pathology
petrology
philology
phonetics
phonology
phytogeny
phytology
phytotomy
radiology
sitiology
sociology
surveying
taxidermy
telephony
uranology
zoography

10
actinology
aerography
aesthetics

apiculture
archaeology
arithmetic
ballistics
bathymetry
biophysics
cardiology
catoptrics
cell biology
chromatics
clinometry
conchology
craniology
demography
dendrology
docimology
Egyptology
embryology
energetics
entomology
entomotomy
enzymology
eudiometry
gastrology
geophysics
homeopathy
hydraulics
hydrometry
hydropathy
hygrometry
hypsometry
immunology
kinematics
lexicology
metallurgy
microscopy
morphology
nematology
nephrology
nosography
obstetrics
odontology
oneirology
organology
osteopathy
pedagogics
phlebology
photometry
phrenology
physiology
planimetry
pneumatics

potamology
psychiatry
psychology
relativity
seismology
selenology
semeiology
somatology
spasmology
spermology
splenology
splenotomy
statistics
technology
telegraphy
teratology
topography
toxicology
trepanning
typography

11
aeronautics
aerostatics
agriculture
anemography
arachnology
archaeology
arteriology
arteriotomy
campanology
carcinology
cartography
chondrology
chronometry
climatology
cosmography
craniometry
criminology
cupellation
cybernetics
dermatology
dermography
desmography
diacoustics
electricity
electronics
engineering
entozoology
ethnography
foundations
games theory

geomedicine
gynaecology
haematology
heliography
homoeopathy
hydrography
hyetography
ichthyology
ichthyotomy
lichenology
linguistics
mathematics
methodology
micrography
myodynamics
neurography
ornithology
osteography
paediatrics
paleography
petrography
photography
phytography
probability
prophylaxis
pteridology
radiography
sericulture
skeletology
spectrology
stereometry
stereoscopy
stethoscopy
stratigraphy
thanatology
uranography
ventilation
watchmaking

12
aerodynamics

amphibiology
anthropology
architecture
astrophysics
atomic theory
auscultation
biochemistry
biogeography
brachygraphy
chronography
cometography
cytogenetics
econometrics
electropathy
epidemiology
epirrheology
floriculture
geochemistry
horticulture
hydrostatics
lexicography
lymphography
microbiology
neuroanatomy
neurobiology
number theory
oceanography
orthalmology
organography
ornithoscopy
palaeography
pharmacology
physiography
pisciculture
pneumatology
protozoology
seismography
silviculture
spectroscopy
spermatology
stratigraphy

sylviculture
syndesmology
synosteology
trigonometry
zoophytology

13
anthropometry
arboriculture
arteriography
bioenergetics
cephalography
chondrography
chrematistics
climatography
combinatorics
crustaceology
endocrinology
geochronology
geomorphology
helminthology
hydrodynamics
hydrokinetics
ichthyography
land measuring
land surveying
lichenography
linear algebra
marine biology
matrix algebra
meteorography
palaeontology
pharmaceutics
psychophysics
psychotherapy
quantum theory
saccharometry
sedimentology
splanchnology
stoichiometry
wave mechanics

zoophysiology

14
architectonics
bioclimatology
chromatography
cinematography
electrobiology
electrostatics
fluid mechanics
hippopathology
hydrophytology
macroeconomics
microeconomics
natural history
natural science
parapsychology
photogrammetry
phytopathology
psychonosology
radiochemistry
symptomatology
syndesmography
thermodynamics

15
computer science
crystallography
electrodynamics
electrokinetics
material science
neurophysiology
psychopathology
thermochemistry

Tools and Instruments

See also **Engineering.**

2	rule	knife	bow-saw	pliers	capstan
PC	sock	laser	brayer	plough	catling
	spud	lathe	broach	pontee	cautery
3	tool	level	burton	pooler	chamfer
awl	trug	lever	camera	rammer	chip-axe
axe	tube	maser	chaser	rasper	chopper
bit	vice	mower	chisel	reaper	cleaver
die	whim	parer	colter	riddle	compass
dog		peavy	crevet	ripsaw	couloir
fan	**5**	plane	cruset	rubber	coulter
gad	agate	plumb	dibber	sander	counter
gin	anvil	preen	dibble	saw set	crampon
hod	auger	prise	doffer	screen	crisper
hoe	basil	probe	dredge	scythe	crowbar
jig	beele	prong	driver	segger	cuvette
loy	bench	punch	dynamo	shears	derrick
saw	besom	quern	fanner	shovel	diamond
zax	betty	quoin	faucet	sickle	divider
	bevel	ratch	ferret	sifter	dog belt
4	blade	razor	filter	skewer	doubler
adze	borer	relay	flange	sledge	drudger
bill	brace	sarse	folder	slicer	fistuca
bore	burin	scale	funnel	square	forceps
burr	chuck	screw	gasket	stadda	fretsaw
cart	churn	sieve	gimlet	stiddy	fruggin
celt	clamp	spade	graver	stithy	gradine
crab	clams	spike	hackle	strike	grainer
dial	clasp	spile	hammer	tackle	grapnel
file	clock	spill	harrow	tenter	grub axe
fork	cleat	style	jagger	tester	hacksaw
frow	cramp	swage	jigger	trepan	handsaw
gage	crane	temse	jig saw	trocar	hatchel
grid	croom	tommy	ladder	trowel	hatchet
hink	croze	toner	lancet	tubber	hay fork
hook	cupel	tongs	laptop	turrel	jointer
jack	dolly	tromp	lister	wimble	mandrel
last	drill	trone	mallet	wrench	mattock
lens	flail	U-tube	megger		nippers
loom	flang	valve	mortar	**7**	nut hook
mall	fleam	wedge	muller	aerator	pH meter
maul	flume	winch	nozzle	ammeter	pickaxe
mule	forge		octant	aneroid	piercer
nail	gauge	**6**	octile	balance	pincers
peel	gavel	abacus	orrery	bandsaw	plummet
pick	gouge	barrow	oliver	bearing	pole axe
pike	hoist	beetle	pallet	bellows	pounder
plow	incus	bender	pencil	binocle	pricker
pole	jacks	blower	pestle	boaster	quadrat
rake	jemmy	bodkin	pitsaw	bradawl	salt-pan
rasp	Jimmy	borcer	planer	caltrop	scalpel

scauper	crucible	stiletto	cutter bar	optometer
scraper	detector	strickle	dog clutch	pedometer
screwer	diagraph	tenon saw	draw knife	periscope
scriber	die stock	throstle	draw-plate	pitch fork
seed lop	dowel bit	tooth key	dynameter	plane iron
sextant	drill bow	tweezers	dynometer	planisher
snubber	edge tool	twist bit	eidograph	plumbline
spaddle	filatory	udometer	engiscope	plumbrule
spanner	fire kiln	watercan	eriometer	polygraph
spittle	flame gun	water ram	excavator	polyscope
sprayer	flax comb	waywiser	excitatory	pyrometer
strocal	gas meter	weed hook	eyeleteer	rain gauge
sundial	gavelock	windlass	fillister	rectifier
tenoner	gee cramp	windmill	fining pot	retractor
thimble	glass pot	wireless	flow meter	rheometer
trestle	handloom	zootrope	fork chuck	rheoscope
triblet	handmill		garoscope	rheotrope
T-square	hand vice	**9**	gasometer	rotameter
turbine	hay knife	acoumeter	gas pliers	saccarium
twibill	horologe	aeolipile	generator	scarifier
twister	horse hoe	aerometer	graduator	screwjack
vernier	iriscope	altimeter	gyroscope	scribe awl
wet bulb	lapstone	altometer	hammer axe	set-square
whip saw	lead mill	ambulator	handbrace	shearlegs
whittle	manostat	antimeter	handscrew	sheep hook
woolder	mitre box	apparatus	handspike	shot gauge
	molegrip	arcograph	heliostat	slide rule
8	muck rake	areometer	hodometer	sonometer
analyser	nut screw	astrolabe	holing axe	steelyard
bark mill	odometer	atmometer	holometer	sugar mill
bar shear	ohm meter	auriscalp	hour glass	tasimeter
beakiron	oilstone	auxometer	hummeller	telegraph
bench peg	otoscope	backstaff	implement	telephone
bill hook	paint pad	barograph	jackknife	telescope
biograph	panel saw	barometer	jackplane	televisor
bioscope	picklock	baroscope	jackscrew	tellurion
bistoury	pinchers	baseplate	lace frame	tide gauge
bloomary	plumb bob	belt punch	lawnmower	tin opener
blowlamp	polisher	bench hook	lithotome	trebucket
blowpipe	power saw	bolt auger	logometer	try square
boathook	prong hoe	boot crimp	lucimeter	turf spade
bootjack	puncheon	canker bit	magnifier	turn bench
boot last	quadrant	cannipers	manometer	turnscrew
boot tree	reap hook	can opener	marigraph	voltmeter
bowdrill	receiver	centrebit	megaphone	watermill
bull nose	recorder	clepsydra	megascope	wattmeter
butteris	rheostat	compasses	metronome	wind gauge
calender	saw wrest	condenser	microtome	zoeotrope
calipers	scissors	corkscrew	microtron	
canthook	scuffler	cornmeter	nail punch	**10**
centre bit	shoehorn	cosmolabe	nilometer	acetimeter
chopness	slate axe	cotton gin	nut wrench	acidimeter
computer	solenoid	cramp iron	oleometer	altazimuth
crow mill	spy glass	curry comb	optigraph	anemograph

anemometer
anemoscope
angioscope
anglemeter
astrometer
astroscope
audiometer
audiophone
balling-gun
binoculars
bush harrow
calculator
calorifier
chiroplast
churn staff
claspknife
clawhammer
clinometer
cold chisel
collimator
crane's bill
cross staff
cryophorus
cultivator
cyanometer
cyclograph
declinator
dray plough
drift bolts
drillpress
drillstock
drosometer
duplicator
ear trumpet
elaeometer
elaiometer
emery wheel
endiometer
field glass
fire engine
fire escape
firing iron
goniometer
gravimeter
grindstone
heliograph
heliometer
helioscope
heliotrope
hydrometer
hydrophore
hydroscope
hyetograph
hyetometer

hygrometer
hygroscope
instrument
lactometer
lactoscope
litrameter
macrometer
masonry bit
masticator
metrograph
micrometer
microphone
microscope
mitre block
motor mower
mould board
multimeter
multiplier
nail drawer
night glass
nitrometer
noctograph
ombrometer
operameter
ozonometer
paintbrush
pantograph
pantometer
pelvimeter
pentagraph
perforator
phonograph
phonoscope
photometer
photophone
piezometer
pipe wrench
plane table
planimeter
pleximeter
pole finder
protractor
pulsimeter
radiometer
respirator
safety lamp
screw press
sleek stone
snowplough
spirometer
spokeshave
steam gauge
steam press
stepladder

tachometer
teinoscope
tenterhook
theodolite
thermostat
thumbscrew
thumbstall
tilt hammer
transistor
tribometer
trip hammer
tuning fork
turf cutter
turnbuckle
typewriter
viscometer
voltameter
water clock
watercrane
water gauge
waterlevel
water meter
water poise
wheel brace

11

actinography
actinometer
aleurometer
alkalimeter
atmidometer
beam compass
breast drill
calorimeter
cardiograph
chaff cutter
chain blocks
chain wrench
cheese press
chlorometer
chlorograph
chronometer
chronometer
chronoscope
cigar cutter
clog almanac
comptometer
conchometer
cosmosphere
countersink
craniometer
crazing mill
crisping pin
crosscut saw

dendrometer
depth finder
diagnometer
drill barrow
drill harrow
drill plough
dynamometer
eccaleobion
eclipsareon
elatrometer
fanning mill
graphometer
grubbing hoe
helvehammer
indigometer
jagging iron
locatograph
machine tool
magnetophon
monkey block
odontograph
optical lens
paint roller
plantascope
ploughshare
pluviameter
pluviometer
pointed awl
poking stick
polarimeter
polariscope
polemoscope
pruning hook
pseudoscope
rabbet plane
range finder
reaping-hook
salinometer
sawing stool
screwdriver
seismograph
seismometer
seismoscope
sideroscope
single-edged
skim coulter
sliding rule
snatch block
spherograph
spherometer
spirit level
squaring rod
steam hammer
stereometer

stereoscope
stethometer
stethoscope
stone hammer
straw cutter
strike block
stubble rake
sward cutter
swingplough
tape measure
teleprinter
thaumatrope
thermometer
thermoscope
torsiograph
transformer
transmitter
turfing iron
two-foot rule
warping hook
warping post
weeding fork
weeding hook
wheelbarrow
zymosimeter

12

aethrioscope
alcoholmeter
arithmometer
assay balance
averruncator
barking irons
belt adjuster
blanchimeter
bow compasses
brace-and-bits
branding iron
breastplough
burning glass
camera lucida
caulking tool
centrolinead
chondrometer
control valve
counter gauge
cradle scythe
cramping iron
crimping iron
crisping iron
curling tongs
declinometer
drill grubber
driving shaft

driving wheel
ductilimeter
electrometer
electrophone
electroscope
ellipsograph
elliptograph
emery grinder
endosmometer
enorthotrope
evaporometer
field glasses
flour dresser
galactometer
galvanometer
galvanoscope
glass furnace
harmometer
hat stretcher
hydraulic ram
inclinometer
kaleidoscope
laryngoscope
machine ruler
magnetograph
magnetometer
mandrel lathe
marline spike
measuregraph
microcoustic
monkey wrench
night glasses
opera glasses
oscillograph
otacousticon
perambulator
pruning knife
psychrometer
pulley blocks
reading glass

running block
scarificator
scribing iron
sledge hammer
sliding bevel
sliding scale
socket chisel
spectrometer
spectroscope
speed counter
sphygmometer
stone breaker
straightedge
straightener
swingle knife
thermocouple
touch needles
trench plough
tuning hammer
turfing spade
turning lathe
tympanometer
water bellows
weather glass
weeding tongs
zenith sector

13
alcoholimeter
alcoholometer
bubble chamber
burning mirror
butcher's broom
camera obscura
chopping block
chopping knife
chromatometer
cylinder press
diaphonometer
dipleidoscope

dipping needle
electric drill
electric mixer
electrophorus
esthesiometer
Geiger counter
grappling-iron
hydraulic jack
mowing machine
packing needle
parallel ruler
pneumatometer
potientiometer
pressure gauge
probe scissors
pyrheliometer
reflectometer
refractometer
saccharometer
scribing block
sewing machine
sidereal clock
soldering bolt
soldering iron
sowing machine
spinning jenny
spinning wheel
spring balance
stocking frame
subsoil plough
sympiesometer
three-foot rule
two-hole pliers
watt-hour meter
weeding chisel

14
aesthesiometer
air thermometer
blowing machine

carding machine
circumferentor
desk calculator
dinactinometer
draining engine
draining plough
geothermometer
hydrobarometer
interferometer
manifold writer
ophthalmoscope
pneumatic drill
radio telescope
reaping machine
shepherd's crook
smoothing plane
sonic altimeter
swingling knife
three-metre rule
thrusting screw
weeding forceps
wire micrometer

15
carpenter's bench
chemical balance
crimping machine
digital computer
dredging machine
drilling machine
envelope machine
entrenching tool
magnifying glass
mariner's compass
pestle and mortar
pump screwdriver
solar microscope
weighing machine
whitworth thread

SPORTS, GAMES AND HOBBIES

Dance

3
act
bop
fan
hay
hop
jig
pas
set
tap

4
ball
clog
hula
jive
jota
juke
kola
loop
pogo
polk
polo
reel
step
turn
vira

5
bebop
caper
conga
cueca
dansa
disco
fling
galop
Irish
limbo
loure
mambo
pavan
polka
rondo
round
rumba

samba
stomp
tango
twist
valse
waltz

6
ballet
bolero
boogie
boston
cancan
cha-cha
chasse
corant
do-si-do
gallop
lavolt
masque
minuet
morisk
morris
pavane
redowa
reigen
retire
rhumba
rondel
shimmy
stroll
trance
valeta
watusi

7
beguine
carioca
ceilidh
chicken
classic
farruca
footing
foxtrot
gavotte
hoedown

knees-up
lambada
lamento
lancers
la volta
llorona
maypole
mazurka
measure
morisco
old-time
one-step
planxty
polacca
rondeau
sardana
shuffle
tandava
two-step
ziganka

8
assemble
attitude
ballroom
boogaloo
cabriole
cake walk
chaconne
cotillon
courante
danseuse
excuse-me
fan dance
fandango
flamenco
galliard
habanera
hand jive
hornpipe
hula-hula
hunt ball
Lindy hop
madisona
merengue
moonwalk

murciana
pachanga
tap dance
tea dance
waltzing

9
allemande
arabesque
barn dance
bossa nova
cha-cha-cha
clog dance
cotillion
ecossaise
eightsome
farandole
folk dance
gallopade
jitterbug
Kathakali
pas de deux
paso doble
passepied
pirouette
polonaise
poussette
promenade
quadrille
quickstep
rock 'n' roll
sevillana
slow waltz

10
belly dance
boston reel
break dance
charleston
Furry dance
gay Gordons
hokey-cokey
locomotion
saltarello
seguidilla
snake dance

strathspey
sword dance
tarantella
torch dance
turkey-trot
walkaround

11
black bottom
bumps-a-daisy
circle dance
dinner dance
folk dancing
Lambeth walk
line dancing
morris dance
pas de basque
rock and roll
schottische
square dance
varsovienne

12
belly dancing
danse macabre
funky chicken
maypole dance
skater's waltz
Virginia reel

13 *and over*
ballroom dance (13)
Boston two-step (13)
Circassian circle (16)
country dancing (14)
eightsome reel (13)
Highland fling (13)
light fantastic (14)
military two-step (15)
St Bernard's waltz (15)
Scottish dancing (15)
Sir Roger de Coverley (18)
strip the willow (14)
Viennese waltz (13)

Sports, Games and Hobbies

3	draw	team	fives	spurt	falcon	quoits
ace	epée	toss	fluke	stalk	finish	rabbit
art	faro	tote	glaze	start	fluker	racing
bat	foil	trap	halma	stump	flying	racket
bet	fore	trey	hobby	stunt	gambit	raffia
bob	foul	trip	joker	swing	gamble	raffle
bow	gala	trot	joust	tarot	gammon	rattle
box	game	turf	kayle	throw	gillie	recite
bye	goal	vint	kendo	touch	gobang	record
cue	golf	vole	knave	track	go-kart	revoke
cup	grab	volt	lasso	train	googly	riddle
dan	hunt	walk	links	trial	gully	riding
die	I-spy	whip	lists	trump	gymnic	rowing
fun	jack	wide	loser	vault	hammer	rubber
gym	jazz	xyst	lotto	veney	hazard	rugger
jog	judo	yoga	lucky	wager	header	runner
lap	king	yo-yo	match	whist	hiking	savate
l.b.w.	knar		monte	yacht	hockey	scorer
lie	knur	**5**	mount		hoopla	second
lob	love	amuse	music	**6**	hunter	see-saw
mat	ludo	arena	ombre	aikido	hurdle	shinny
oar	luge	baign	opera	archer	jetton	shinty
out	main	bails	pace	ballet	jigger	single
par	mate	bandy	pacer	banker	jigsaw	skater
peg	meet	basto	party	basset	jockey	skiing
put	mime	batik	piste	battue	karate	slalom
rod	miss	bingo	pitch	bewits	kicker	slider
run	mora	bogey	point	bowler	knight	soccer
set	odds	boule	poker	bowman	kung-fu	soiree
ski	pace	bowls	prize	boxing	lariat	squash
tag	pawn	boxer	queen	bridge	leg-bye	stroke
taw	play	caddy	quits	caddie	loader	stumps
tee	polo	capot	racer	casino	lobber	T'ai chi
tie	pool	cards	reins	cinema	manege	tarots
top	punt	chase	relay	cinque	marker	tennis
toy	quiz	cheat	revel	clumps	mashie	tierce
try	race	chess	rider	cobnut	masque	tip-cat
win	ride	clubs	rifle	cockal	maying	toss-up
won	ring	craps	rodeo	cockal	no-ball	travel
	rink	dance	roque	course	not-out	trophy
4	ruff	darts	rugby	cratts	outing	umpire
arts	shot	Derby	rummy	crambo	outrun	unfair
bait	sice	deuce	samba	crease	pacing	venery
ball	side	dicer	score	cup tie	paddle	victor
bias	skip	diver	skate	dealer	pelota	vigaro
bite	slam	dormy	skier	defeat	piquet	wicket
boat	slip	drama	slice	discus	pistol	winner
brag	snap	drawn	slide	diving	player	xystos
club	solo	drive	slosh	domino	poetry	yorker
crib	spar	dummy	spade	driver	punter	
dice	suit	extra	spoon	dyeing	putter	**7**
dive	swim	field	sport	ecarte	puzzle	agonism
				euchre		

agonist	fielder	play day	whip top	goal line
allonge	fishery	playing	winning	golf ball
amateur	fishing	play off	wrestle	golf club
ambs-ace	fluking	pontoon	writing	gymkhana
ames-ace	forward	pottery		handball
angling	fowling	potting	**8**	handicap
archery	fox hunt	primero	all-fours	harriers
athlete	gambler	pub quiz	antiques	high jump
auction	glasses	pushpin	applique	hurdling
average	glazing	putting	aquatics	jiujitsu
bathing	gliding	rackets	baccarat	jousting
batsman	golf bag	rambler	baseball	juggling
batting	gunning	reading	biathlon	knitting
beagles	gymnast	referee	bost race	korfball
benefit	hawking	regatta	boundary	lacrosse
bezique	hunting	reversi	canoeing	leapfrog
bicycle	hurling	ringtaw	carnival	long jump
boating	innings	rinking	carolina	long stop
bone ace	javelin	roadhog	catapult	love game
bowling	jogging	running	ceramics	lucky dip
bran-pie	jujitsu	sailing	champion	marathon
bruiser	jumping	saltant	charades	may games
canasta	keep fit	scooter	cheating	meditate
carving	lamping	scoring	chessmen	Monopoly
cassino	last lap	scratch	climbing	motoring
century	leaping	sculler	commerce	movement
charade	loggats	sea trip	contract	napoleon
checker	lottery	shuffle	counters	natation
chicane	love all	singing	coursing	ninepins
codille	love set	singles	cribbage	olympiad
collage	low bell	skating	cup final	olympics
concert	macrame	ski jump	dead heat	out-field
contest	mahjong	sliding	deck golf	outsider
cookery	marbles	snooker	dominoes	painting
cooking	maypole	St Leger	doublets	palestra
cooncan	misdeal	stadium	drag-hunt	pall-mall
cricket	montant	starter	draughts	patience
crochet	mosaics	sub-aqua	duelling	petanque
croquet	netball	surfing	eurythme	ping-pong
curling	niblick	tatting	eventing	pinochle
cycling	oarsman	tilting	exercise	pole jump
cyclist	oarsmen	tinchel	face card	pony race
dancing	off-side	tombola	fair play	printing
decider	old-maid	top spin	falconry	proverbs
diabolo	origami	tourney	fielding	pugilism
dice-box	outdoor	trained	flat race	pugilist
discard	outride	trainer	football	pyramids
doddart	pageant	trapeze	foot race	quatorze
doubles	pallone	vaulter	forfeits	racquets
drawing	pastime	wagerer	fox chase	rambling
dribble	pat ball	walking	full back	roulette
driving	pharaoh	wargame	gambling	rounders
etching	picquet	weaving	game laws	sack race
fencing	pitcher	weights	gin rummy	Scrabble

sculling
shooting
sing-song
skipping
skittles
sledding
softball
somerset
spadille
sparring
sporting
stalking
stumping
swimming
teamwork
teetotum
third-man
tiny golf
toboggan
training
tray-trip
trial run
tricycle
trotting
tumbling
turf club
twitcher
umpiring
vaulting
vauntlay
walkover
wall-game
woodwork
yachting

9

advantage
adventure
agonistes
agonistic
amusement
archeress
athletics
Aunt Sally
babyhouse
badminton
bagatelle
ball games
bandalore
bicycling
bilboquet
billiards
blackjack
bob cherry

breakdown
broad jump
bull board
bull feast
bullfight
camelling
challenge
checkmate
cherry pit
chicanery
clock golf
close time
cockfight
cockmatch
conqueror
court card
crazy golf
cricketer
cup winner
decathlon
deck games
decoy duck
dirt track
dog racing
drawn game
dumbbells
embrocado
engraving
entertain
equitancy
fairy tale
fancy ball
ferreting
fish spear
frivolity
gardening
gate money
goal posts
golf clubs
grand slam
gymnasium
gymnastic
hatha yoga
hopscotch
horseplay
horserace
ice hockey
joy riding
lampadist
lob bowler
make merry
marooning
marquetry
megaphone

merrimake
merriment
merriness
motorboat
newmarket
night club
nine holes
novelette
overmatch
pacemaker
pageantry
palestric
palmistry
parcheesi
pedalling
philately
plaything
pole vault
potholing
prize ring
programme
promenade
quadrille
racehorse
racestand
reception
relay race
repasture
revelment
revel rout
river trip
rolly poly
scorching
scorecard
scrapbook
sculpture
showplace
shrimping
ski runner
skylarker
sleighing
smock race
solitaire
spectacle
sportsman
springing
square-leg
stalemate
stool ball
stopwatch
storybook
stroke oar
summerset
symposiac

symposium
tablegame
tabletalk
test match
tie dyeing
tip and run
torch race
touch line
trap stick
trial game
trial race
trump card
untrained
victoress
vingt-et-un
wandering
water jump
water polo
whipper-in
whirligig
whistling
woodcraft
wrestling
yacht race
yachtsman

10

acrobatics
agonistics
agonothete
backgammon
ballooning
basketball
bat fowling
battledoor
battledore
bear garden
blind harry
challenger
chessboard
collecting
competitor
conundrums
cover-point
cricket bat
cup-and-ball
deck quoits
deck tennis
derby sweep
dog walking
doll's house
dumb crambo
eel fishing
embroidery

enamelling
equitation
fancy dress
fast bowler
feathering
feuilleton
field games
fishing net
fishing rod
fisticuffs
fives court
flat racing
flop-dragon
fly-fishing
fox-hunting
goalkeeper
goalkicker
grandstand
greasy pole
groundbait
gymnastics
handspring
handy-dandy
hippodrome
hobby horse
hockey ball
hockey club
hotcockles
hucklebone
humming-top
hunting box
hurdle race
ice dancing
ice sailing
ice skating
kettle pin
lace making
lampadrome
landing net
lansquenet
lawn tennis
ledger line
lob bowling
masquerade
meditation
midget golf
Monte Carlo
needlework
opposition
palestrian
pancratist
pancratium
paper chase
pentathlon

philopoena
pony racing
pot hunting
prison base
prize fight
put-and-take
racecourse
raceground
recreation
relaxation
riding pony
riding whip
rollicking
rotary club
roundabout
rowing club
saturnalia
scoreboard
scratch man
sea bathing
shovepenny
shuffle cap
silk screen
skateboard
ski running
skylarking
slow bowler
snapdragon
somersault
spillikins
stirrup cup
strokesman
surf riding
sweepstake
switchback
table bowls
tap dancing
tarantella
tauromachy
team spirit
television
tennis ball
thimblerig
tomfoolery
tournament
travelling
trial match
trick track
tricycling
trivia quiz
troumadame
victorious
volley ball
vulnerable

weighing-in
whirlabout
word making
working out

11
agonistical
athleticism
bear baiting
birdwatcher
bull baiting
bumblepuppy
calligraphy
chariot race
chess player
competition
competitive
county match
cricket ball
croquet ball
deck cricket
Derby winner
dicing house
disportment
diving board
fast bowling
field sports
fishing line
five hundred
flaconnade
fleet-footed
fluking-iron
folk dancers
free fishery
garden party
general post
grand circle
grass skiing
gymnasiarch
hang gliding
happy family
heavyweight
hide-and-seek
high jumping
high pitched
hill walking
hockey stick
horse racing
horse riding
hunt counter
hunting horn
ice yachting
indian club
inter county

lawn bowling
lightweight
lithography
long jumping
magic square
make-believe
masquerader
merrymaking
minute watch
oarsmanship
open-air life
picnic party
pillow fight
pole jumping
prawning net
prize giving
prizewinner
promenading
protagonist
public stand
regatta card
riding horse
river sports
rouge-et-noir
rough riding
sand sailing
schottische
scuba diving
shovel board
show jumping
shuttlecock
sightseeing
single stick
skating club
skating rink
skittle pool
slot machine
slow bowling
snowballing
soap bubbles
span-counter
spelling bee
springboard
stirrup lamp
stonewaller
summersault
sweepstakes
sword player
table tennis
tale telling
tennis court
tent pegging
theatre-goer
tobogganing

top-spinning
totalisator
toxophilite
trap-and-ball
trick riding
trolmydames
trout stream
uncontested
unexercised
water skiing
whipping-top
wild fowling
windsurfing
winning crew
winning side
winning team
wood cutting
world record
yacht racing

12
bantamweight
billiard ball
birdwatching
bobsleighing
bowling alley
brass rubbing
bullfighting
butterfly net
calisthenics
championship
club swinging
cockfighting
competitress
consequences
cricket match
curling stone
deer stalking
draughtboard
drinking bout
field glasses
figure skater
first-nighter
flower making
glass blowing
googly bowler
hoodman-blind
horsemanship
housewarming
hunting horse
huntsmanship
jigsaw puzzle
losing hazard
magic lantern

marathon race
marking board
medicine ball
merry-go-round
miss milligan
mixed bathing
mixed doubles
nimble footed
novel reading
obstacle race
Olympic games
opera glasses
parallel bars
parlour games
pitch and putt
pitch-and-toss
pleasure trip
point-to-point
pole vaulting
professional
prize fighter
prize-winning
pyrotechnics
Pythian games
racing stable
rock climbing
roller skater
rope climbing
rope splnning
rope throwing
sailboarding
sand yachting
scotch hopper
shrimping net
skipping rope
skittle alley
span farthing
speed skating
starting post
state lottery
steeplechase
step aerobics

stilt walking
stirrup strap
storytelling
swimming gala
table croquet
table turning
tennis player
tennis racket
theatre-going
thoroughbred
tiddley-winks
tittle-tattle
wicket keeper
winning horse
winter sports

13
alectoromachy
alectryomachy
aquatic sports
auction bridge
ballad singing
blind man's buff
bubble blowing
camera obscura
Christmas tree
chuck farthing
cribbage board
cricket ground
cricket stumps
croquet mallet
deck billiards
divertisement
double or quits
entertainment
featherweight
figure skating
fishing tackle
googly-bowling
Grand National
ground-angling
hare-and-hounds

horizontal bar
international
jigsaw puzzles
jollification
kiss-in-the-ring
machine junket
model yachting
motor cruising
musical chairs
Olympian games
parlour tricks
pillion riding
prisoner's base
prize fighting
record breaker
roller skating
roulette table
speed merchant
spirit rapping
sportsmanship
squash rackets
stalking horse
starting point
steeplechaser
sword fighting
ten-pin bowling
track and field
vantage ground
vaulting horse
victor ludorum
weightlifting
whippet racing
wicket keeping
winning hazard

14
all-in wrestling
billiard marker
billiard player
bladder angling
children's party
coin collecting

contract bridge
discus throwing
divertissement
double patience
downhill skiing
driving licence
ducks-and-drakes
hunt the slipper
hunt the thimble
long-arm balance
mountaineering
record breaking
rubicon bezique
shove-halfpenny
steeplechasing
Trivial Pursuit
weight training

15
ballroom dancing
cinderella dance
consolation race
creative writing
cross-country running
cross-country skiing
crossword puzzle
crown green bowls
dirt-track racing
greyhound racing
javelin throwing
king-of-the-castle
National Lottery
public enclosure
short-arm balance
stamp collecting
talking pictures
three-legged race
unsportsmanlike
youth hostelling

TRADE, COMMERCE AND PROFESSIONS

Business, Commerce and Economics

2	bull	mint	brand	quota	bounce	in cash
A1	bust	nett	bribe	quote	bounty	income
CA	call	note	buyer	rally	bourse	in debt
EU	cash	OPEC	buy in	rates	branch	indent
FT	cess	owed	buy up	remit	broker	insure
	chip	paid	by-law	repay	bubble	jobber
3	City	PAYE	cargo	rider	budget	job lot
bid	(the)	poll	cheap	score	burden	labour
buy	coin	pool	check	scrip	buying	ledger
COD	cost	post	chips	share	buy out	lender
cut	deal	PSBR	clear	shark	by-laws	liable
Dow	dear	puff	clerk	short	cartel	liquid
DTI	debt	punt	costs	sight	cheque	Lloyd's
dun	deed	ramp	cover	slump	change	lock-up
ECU	dole	rate	crash	stock	charge	margin
EEC	dues	real	cycle	talon	client	market
EMU	dump	rent	debit	taxes	corner	mark-up
fee	duty	ring	draft	tight	coupon	mature
f.o.b.	earn	risk	entry	tithe	credit	merger
GDP	easy	sale	ex cap.	token	crisis	minute
GNP	EFTA	scot	ex div.	trade	cum. div.	mutual
IMF	euro	sell	float	trend	dealer	nem. con.
job	even	sink	folio	trust	deal in	Nikkei
lot	fine	sold	funds	usury	debtor	notice
Ltd	firm	spot	gilts	value	defray	office
net	fisc	stag	goods	wages	demand	on call
owe	free	tare	gross	worth	dicker	on cost
par	FTSE	term	hedge	yield	docket	option
pay	fund	turn	House		dot.com	one-off
PIN	gain	vend	index	**6**	drawee	outbid
plc	GATT	wage	issue	accept	drawer	outlay
rig	gild		lease	accrue	equity	outlet
sum	gilt	**5**	limit	advice	estate	output
tax	giro	agent	money	agency	excise	packet
tip	glut	angel	notes	amount	expend	parity
VAT	gold	asset	offer	assets	export	pay day
WTO	good	at par	order	assign	factor	paying
	hire	audit	owing	at cost	figure	pay-off
4	idle	award	panic	avails	fiscal	pay out
back	lend	batch	paper	bailee	freeze	pledge
bail	levy	bid up	payee	bailor	go down	plunge
bank	lien	block	payer	banker	growth	policy
bear	loan	board	plant	barter	hammer	profit
bill	long	bonds	pound	bearer	holder	public
bond	loss	bonus	price	borrow	honour	punter
boom	mart	books	proxy	bought	import	quango

257

quorum		expense	pre-empt	amortize	employer
racket	**7**	exploit	premium	antedate	emporium
rating	account	exports	prepaid	appraise	endorsee
realty	actuary	ex works	pricing	assignee	endorser
rebate	advance	factory	product	assigner	entrepot
recoup	allonge	failure	profits	auditing	equities
redeem	annuity	fall due	promote	back bond	estimate
refund	arrears	finance	pro rata	bailment	evaluate
remedy	at sight	flutter	pyramid	bank bill	exchange
rental	auction	forward	realize	bankbook	expenses
report	auditor	freight	receipt	bank giro	exporter
resale	average	funding	reissue	bank loan	ex gratia
retail	backing	futures	renewal	banknote	ex rights
return	bad debt	gearing	reserve	bank rate	feedback
salary	balance	haulage	returns	bankrupt	finances
sample	banking	hedging	revenue	barratry	flat rate
save	bank run	holding	rigging	basic pay	goodwill
up	bargain	imports	royalty	below par	gratuity
saving	bidding	imprest	salvage	berthage	hallmark
sell in	bonanza	indorse	selling	blue chip	hammered
sell up	bullion	inflate	sell-out	book debt	hard cash
set off	buy back	in funds	service	borrower	hard sell
settle	buydown	insured	sold out	bottomry	importer
shares	cambist	interim	solvent	business	increase
shorts	capital	invoice	squeeze	buying in	indebted
silver	cashier	jobbers	stipend	carriage	industry
simony	ceiling	jobbing	storage	cashbook	interest
specie	certify	killing	subsidy	cash down	in the red
spiral	chamber	lay days	surplus	cash flow	investor
spread	charter	leasing	swindle	cash sale	lame duck
staple	company	lending	takings	clearing	manifest
stocks	consols	limited	tax-free	commerce	mark down
strike	convert	lockout	tonnage	consumer	markings
supply	crossed	lottery	trade in	contango	maturing
surety	customs	lump sum	trading	contract	maturity
surtax	cut-rate	manager	traffic	creditor	merchant
tariff	damages	mint par	trustee	credit to	monetary
taxman	day book	minutes	utility	cum bonus	monetize
teller	dealing	name day	vending	currency	monopoly
tender	declare	nest egg	venture	customer	mortgage
ticket	default	net gain	war bond	cut-price	net price
trader	deficit	no funds	war loan	dealings	novation
unload	deflate	nomimal	warrant	defrayed	on credit
unpaid	deposit	on offer	way bill	delivery	on demand
usance	douceur	on order	write up	director	on strike
usurer	draw out	package	year end	disburse	operator
valuta	dumping	partner		discount	ordinary
vendor	duopoly	payable	**8**	dividend	overhead
vendue	economy	pay cash	above par	Dow Jones	overtime
volume	embargo	payment	acceptor	drawings	par value
wampan	endorse	payroll	accounts	dry goods	passbook
wealth	engross	pay slip	act of God	earnings	poundage
wind	entrust	pension	after tax	embezzle	price cut
up	ex bonus	per cent	agiotage	employee	price war

proceeds
producer
property
purchase
receipts
receiver
recovery
reinvest
reserves
retailer
retainer
scarcity
schedule
security
shipment
sinecure
solvency
spending
spot cash
sterling
straddle
supertax
swindler
takeover
taxation
tax dodge
tax haven
taxpayer
trade gap
transfer
Treasury
turnover
undercut
unquoted
variable
wage rate
warranty
windfall
write off

9

actuarial
ad valorem
aggregate
allotment
allowance
annuitant
ante-dated
anti-trust
appraisal
appraiser
arbitrage
arrearage
assurance

averaging
bank stock
bilateral
blank bill
book value
bordereau
borrowing
brokerage
by-product
call money
call price
carry over
certified
chartered
clearance
commodity
cost price
cum rights
debenture
debit card
debit note
deck cargo
deduction
defaulter
deflation
demurrage
depletion
depositor
dishonour
easy money
easy terms
economics
economies
economist
economize
emolument
endowment
exchequer
executive
extortion
face value
fair price
fair trade
fiat money
fiduciary
financial
financier
fine paper
firm offer
firm price
first call
first cost
flotation
franchise

free trade
fully paid
garnishee
gilt-edged
globalism
going rate
guarantee
guarantor
hard money
import tax
in arrears
incentive
income tax
indemnify
indemnity
indenture
inflation
insolvent
insurance
inventory
leasehold
liability
liquidate
liquidity
list price
long-dated
mail order
marketing
middleman
mortgagee
mortgagor
near money
negotiate
net income
order book
outgoings
overdraft
overdrawn
overheads
packaging
paymaster
pecuniary
petty cash
piecework
PIN number
portfolio
post-dated
preferred
price list
price rise
prime cost
principal
privatize
profiteer

promotion
purchaser
put option
quittance
quotation
ratepayer
ready cash
recession
redundant
reflation
reimburse
repayable
repayment
resources
restraint
reversion
royalties
sell short
shift work
short bill
shortfall
short time
sideline
sight bill
slush fund
speculate
spot price
stamp duty
statement
stock list
stockpile
subscribe
subsidize
surcharge
syndicate
tax return
ticket day
trade fair
trademark
trade name
tradesman
treasurer
undersell
unit trust
utilities
valuation
vendition
viability
wage claim
warehouse
wealth tax
wholesale
winding up
work force

work sheet
work study
World Bank

10

acceptance
accountant
account day
accounting
accumulate
active bond
adjustment
advice note
appreciate
assessment
assignment
attachment
auctioneer
automation
average out
bank credit
bank return
bankruptcy
bear market
bearer bond
bill broker
bill of sale
block grant
bondholder
bonus issue
bonus share
bookkeeper
bucket shop
bulk buying
bull market
calculator
call option
capitalism
capitalist
capitalize
capitation
chain store
chequebook
closed shop
collateral
colporteur
commercial
commission
compensate
competitor
consortium
conversion
credit bank
credit card

credit note
credit slip
cumulative
defalcator
del credere
depreciate
depression
deregulate
direct cost
dirty money
drawn bonds
elasticity
employment
encumbered
engrossing
evaluation
excise duty
ex dividend
first offer
fiscal year
fixed costs
fixed price
fixed trust
free market
floor price
forwarding
free market
funded debt
gross value
ground rent
growth area
honorarium
import duty
income bond
indexation
industrial
insolvency
instalment
in the black
investment
joint stock
lighterage
liquidator
living wage
long period
loss leader
management
marked down
marketable
mass market
mercantile
monetarism
monetarist
money order

monopolize
moratorium
negotiable
non-payment
no par value
note of hand
obligation
open cheque
open credit
opening bid
open market
open policy
option rate
overcharge
paper money
pawnbroker
percentage
plough back
pre-emption
preference
prepayment
price index
production
profitable
profits tax
prospector
prospectus
prosperity
prosperous
provide for
purchasing
pure profit
pyramiding
quarter day
ready money
real estate
real income
recompense
redeemable
redemption
redundancy
remittance
remunerate
rock bottom
sales force
scrip issue
second-hand
securities
selling out
settlement
serial bond
share index
short bonds
short-dated

sole agency
speculator
statistics
stockpiles
stock split
subscriber
tax evasion
ticker tape
tight money
trade cycle
trade price
trade union
ultra vires
underwrite
unemployed
upset price
wage freeze
Wall Street
wholesaler
working day
work to rule
written off

11
account book
accountancy
acquittance
advance note
advertising
arbitration
asking price
auction ring
auction sale
average bond
bank account
bank balance
bank of issue
bear squeeze
beneficiary
big business
bill of entry
billionaire
bimetallism
black market
blank cheque
bonded goods
bonus scheme
bookkeeping
budget price
businessman
capital gain
cash account
central bank
certificate

circulation
commitments
commodities
common stock
competition
competitive
consignment
consumption
convergence
co-operative
corporation
counterfeit
cum dividend
customs duty
days of grace
death duties
demand curve
demand draft
demutualize
deposit rate
deposit slip
devaluation
discounting
dishonoured
distributor
dividend tax
double-entry
down
  payment
endorsement
expenditure
fixed assets
fixed charge
fixed income
fluctuation
foreclosure
free on board
freight note
Gresham's
  Law
gross income
high finance
hypothecate
income stock
indirect tax
industrials
issuing bank
job analysis
joint return
labour force
legal tender
liquidation
loan capital
manufacture

market overt
market price
mass-produce
merchandise
middle price
millionaire
minimum
  wage
money lender
money
  market
money supply
nationalize
negotiation
net interest
net receipts
open account
option price
outstanding
overpayment
overtrading
package deal
partnership
pay on
  demand
point of sale
postal order
poverty line
premium
  bond
price fixing
price freeze
property tax
purchase tax
Queer Street
raw material
realization
reinsurance
reserve bank
restructure
revaluation
rights issue
risk capital
safe deposit
sales ledger
savings bank
sell forward
selling day
shareholder
single-entry
sinking fund
small trader
sold forward
speculation

stagflation
stakeholder
stockbroker
stockjobber
stock market
stockpiling
stocktaking
subsistence
supermarket
syndicalism
take-home pay
takeover bid
time deposit
transaction
undercharge
undervalued
underwriter
with profits

12

above the line
account payee
ad valorem tax
amalgamation
amortization
appreciation
assembly line
balance sheet
banker's draft
banker's order
bargain price
below the line
bilateralism
bill of lading
board meeting
Board of Trade
bond creditor
bonded stores
bottomry bond
branch office
bridging loan
buyer's market
callable bond
capital gains
capital goods
capital stock
carrying over
carry over day
cash and carry
caveat emptor
charter party
clearing bank
closing price
common market

compensation
consumer goods
contract note
cost of living
credit rating
current price
current ratio
customs union
deflationary
denomination
depreciation
deregulation
differential
direct labour
disbursement
discount rate
disinflation
distribution
Dutch auction
earned income
embezzlement
econometrics
economy drive
entrepreneur
exchange rate
export credit
first refusal
fiscal policy
fixed capital
floating debt
frozen assets
going concern
gold standard
hard currency
hire purchase
indirect cost
inflationary
interest rate
invoice clerk
irredeemable
joint account
keep accounts
labour market
laissez-faire
life interest
liquid assets
manufacturer
marginal cost
mass-produced
maturity date
mercantilism
merchant bank
mixed economy
monetization

money changer
national bank
national debt
nearest offer
nominal price
nominal value
official list
opening price
overcapacity
pay as you earn
pay in advance
paying-in-slip
policy holder
present worth
price ceiling
price control
price current
price rigging
productivity
profiteering
profit margin
profit motive
profit taking
public sector
rate of growth
raw materials
receivership
redeployment
remuneration
remunerative
reserve price
rig the market
rising prices
running costs
sale or return
sales manager
salesmanship
severance pay
share capital
shareholding
share options
sliding scale
social credit
soft currency
specie points
statistician
sterling area
stock in trade
stockjobbery
stockjobbing
surplus value
tax avoidance
tax collector
tax exemption

terms of trade
tiger economy
trade balance
trade deficit
trading stamp
transfer deed
treasury bill
treasury bond
treasury note
trial balance
trustee stock
underwriting
unemployment
valued policy
welfare state
works council

13

acceptilation
allotment note
appropriation
articled clerk
average clause
backwardation
bank statement
blank transfer
bullion market
business cycle
clearing house
contract curve
credit account
credit control
credit squeeze
crossed cheque
current assets
discount house
dividend yield
dollar premium
Dow-Jones index
exchequer bill
financial year
free trade area
free trade zone
futures market
globalization
gross receipts
guarantee fund
incomes policy
interim report
issued capital
livery company
Lombard Street
long-dated bill
making-up price

non-cumulative
not negotiable
ordinary share
outside broker
overhead price
paid-up capital
par of exchange
participating
premium income
private sector
privatization
profitability
profit sharing
public company
quota sampling
rateable value
restructuring
sales forecast
settlement day
share transfer
silent partner
specification
Stock Exchange
switch selling
taxable income
trade discount
value added tax
vendor's shares
wasting assets
wheeler-dealer
works councils

14
account current
advance freight
apprenticeship
balance of trade
bearer security
bill of exchange
blocked account
break-even point
bureau de change
capital account
capital gearing
capitalization
consumer credit
convertibility
corporation tax
current account

current balance
debenture stock
decimalization
deferred rebate
deferred shares
deposit account
discount market
economic growth
featherbedding
Federal Reserve
fiduciary issue
finance company
floating charge
founders' shares
fringe benefits
full employment
garnishee order
general average
general manager
half-commission
holder for value
holding company
hyperinflation
infrastructure
inscribed stock
invisible trade
joint stock bank
letter of credit
limited company
liquidity ratio
Lloyd's Register
loan conversion
macroeconomics
managing agents
market research
microeconomics
monthly account
mortgage broker
new issue market
nominal capital
option dealings
ordinary shares
oversubscribed
preferred stock
progress chaser
promissory note
quality control
random sampling
rate of exchange

rate of interest
receiving order
revenue account
short-term gains
social security
superannuation
surrender value
trading account
uberrimae fidei
unearned income
working capital

15
average adjuster
bonded warehouse
building society
capital employed
commission agent
consignment note
dividend warrant
entrepreneurial
exchange control
ex-gratia payment
foreign exchange
golden handshake
interim dividend
investment trust
labour-intensive
liquidity ratios
marine insurance
multilateralism
nationalization
non-contributory
political science
preference bonds
preference share
preferred shares
preference stock
public ownership
public relations
purchasing power
rationalization
redemption yield
reducing balance
secured creditor
sleeping partner
sterling balance
unissued capital

Professions, Occupations, Trades, etc.

2
GP
MO
PA
PM

3
doc
don
pro
rep
spy
vet

4
alma
ayah
bard
boss
char
chef
cook
crew
diva
dyer
gang
grip
hack
hand
head
herd
lead
maid
mate
mime
page
peon
poet
seer
serf
temp
tout
ward

5
actor
ad-man
agent
baker
bosun
caddy
clerk
clown
coach
comic
crier
curer
daily
envoy
extra
fakir
fence
filer
flier
gipsy
gluer
groom
guard
guide
gypsy
hirer
hiver
leech
mason
medic
miner
navvy
nurse
oiler
owler
pilot
piper
plyer
quack
rabbi
rater
reeve
scout
sewer
shoer
smith
sower
staff
sweep
tamer
tiler
tuner
tutor
usher
valet

6
airman
archer
artist
aurist
author
bagman
bailer
balker
banker
barber
bargee
barker
barman
batman
bearer
binder
bookie
bowman
brewer
broker
bugler
bursar
busker
butler
cabbie
cabman
calker
canner
carter
carver
casual
censor
clergy
cleric
codist
coiner
comber
coolie
cooper
copper
co-star
cowboy
cowman
critic
cutler
cutter
dancer
dealer
digger
docker
doctor
dowser
draper
drawer
driver
drover
editor
factor
farmer
feller
fisher
fitter
flayer
forger
fowler
framer
fuller
gaffer
ganger
gaoler
gaucho
gauger
geisha
gigolo
gilder
gillie
glazer
glover
graver
grocer
guider
gunman
gunner
harper
hatter
hawker
healer
heaver
hodman
hooper
horner
hosier
hunter
intern
issuer
jailer
jobber
jockey
joiner
jurist
keeper
lackey
lander
lascar
lawyer
lector
lender
loader
logman
lumper
marker
master
matron
medico
mender
menial
mentor
mercer
milker
miller
minter
monger
mummer
mystic
nailer
notary
oboist
oilman
orator
ostler
packer
parson
pastor
pavier
pedant
pedlar
penman
picker
pieman
pirate
pitman
plater
player
porter
potboy
potter
priest
pruner
purser
querry
ragman
ranger
ratter
reader
reaper
reaver
rector
regent
relief
renter
rigger
ringer
robber
roofer
rooter
sacker
sailor
salter
salvor
sapper
sawyer
scribe
sealer
seaman
seizor
seller
server
setter
sexton
signer
singer
skivvy
slater
slaver
sleuth
snarer
socman
sorter
souter
spicer
squire
stager
stoker
storer
tabler
tailor
tamper
tanner
tasker
taster
teller
tester
tiller
tinker
tinner
toller
touter
tracer
trader
tubman
turner
tycoon
typist
usurer
vacher
valuer
vamper
vassal
vendor
verger
verser
viewer
waiter
walker
waller
warden
warder
warper
washer
weaver
weeder
welder
whaler
worker
wright
writer

7
abacist
acolyte
acrobat
actress
actuary
almoner
analyst
Arabist
arbiter
artisan
artiste
assayer
assizer
assurer
auditor
aviator
awarder
bailiff
bandman
barmaid
bellboy
bellhop
birdman
blaster

blender	dustman	mangler	skinner	arborist	embalmer
boatman	farrier	marbler	skipper	armourer	emissary
bookman	fiddler	marcher	slipper	armorist	engineer
bottler	fireman	mariner	smelter	arrestor	engraver
bouncer	flesher	marshal	socager	assessor	enroller
breeder	florist	masseur	soldier	attorney	essayist
brigand	flunkey	matador	soloist	bagpiper	examiner
builder	flutist	mealman	spencer	bandsman	exorcist
butcher	footboy	midwife	spinner	bargeman	explorer
callboy	footman	milkman	spotter	bearherd	exporter
cambist	foreman	monitor	stainer	bedesman	factotum
carrier	founder	newsboy	stamper	bedmaker	falconer
caseman	friseur	oculist	stapler	bit-maker	farmhand
cashier	frogman	officer	steward	bleacher	ferryman
caterer	furrier	orderly	surgeon	boatsman	figurant
caulker	gateman	packman	swabber	bondmaid	film star
cellist	girdler	pageboy	sweeper	bondsman	finisher
chanter	glazier	painter	taborer	botanist	flautist
chapman	gleaner	palmist	tallier	bowmaker	fletcher
chemist	gleeman	peddler	tapster	boxmaker	fodderer
cleaner	glosser	pianist	teacher	brewster	forester
clicker	grafter	picador	tipster	broacher	forgeman
clippie	granger	planner	tracker	cabin boy	fugleman
coalman	grantee	planter	trainer	cellarer	gangster
cobbler	grantor	pleader	trapper	ceramist	gardener
cockler	grazier	plumber	trawler	chandler	gavelman
collier	grinder	poacher	trimmer	choirboy	glassman
co-pilot	gymnast	pop star	trucker	claqueur	goatherd
copyist	hackler	postboy	trustee	clothier	governor
coroner	harpist	postman	tumbler	coachman	guardian
corsair	haulier	presser	turnkey	codifier	gunsmith
counsel	helotry	printer	vintner	collator	hammerer
courier	herbist	puddler	violist	comedian	handmaid
cowherd	herdman	rancher	wagoner	compiler	handyman
cowpoke	heritor	realtor	warrior	composer	hatmaker
crofter	hogherd	refiner	webster	conjurer	haymaker
cropper	hostler	riveter	weigher	conveyor	headsman
curator	indexer	roadman	wheeler	courtier	helmsman
currier	inlayer	roaster	whetter	cow-leech	henchman
danseur	ironist	rustler	wireman	coxswain	herdsman
dentist	janitor	sacrist	woodman	croupier	hireling
dietist	juggler	saddler	woolman	cutpurse	histrion
ditcher	junkman	sampler	workman	dairyman	home help
diviner	juryman	samurai	wrapper	danseuse	hotelier
dominie	keelman	scourer		deckhand	houseboy
doorman	knacker	scraper	**8**	defender	huckster
dragman	knitter	servant	adscript	designer	huntsman
drapier	laceman	sharper	aeronaut	director	importer
drawboy	linkboy	shearer	algerine	dog-leech	improver
drayman	linkman	shipper	analyzer	domestic	ink maker
dredger	lombard	showman	aphorist	doughboy	inventor
dresser	mailman	shunter	apiarist	dragoman	japanner
drogman	maltman	silkman	apron-	druggist	jet pilot
drummer	manager	simpler	man	educator	jeweller

jongleur	pressman	supplier	barrister	daily help
labourer	probator	surveyor	barrow boy	dairymaid
landgirl	procurer	swindler	beefeater	decorator
landlady	promoter	tabourer	beekeeper	desk clerk
landlord	prompter	tallyman	biologist	detective
lapidary	provider	taverner	boatswain	dietitian
larcener	psalmist	teamster	bodyguard	dispenser
larderer	publican	thatcher	boilerman	dissector
leadsman	pugilist	thespian	bondslave	distiller
lecturer	purveyor	thresher	bondwoman	draftsman
linesman	quarrier	tin miner	bookmaker	dramatist
lumberer	raftsman	tinsmith	bootblack	drawlatch
magician	ranchero	torturer	bootmaker	drum major
magister	rapperee	toymaker	buccaneer	drum maker
maltster	receiver	truckman	burnisher	drysalter
masseuse	recorder	turncock	bus driver	ecologist
measurer	relessor	turnspit	cab driver	enameller
mechanic	repairer	tutoress	cafe owner	engineman
melodist	reporter	unionist	cameraman	engrosser
mercator	resetter	valuator	car driver	errand boy
merchant	restorer	vintager	caretaker	estimator
metal-man	retailer	virtuoso	carpenter	examinant
milkmaid	retainer	vocalist	casemaker	excavator
millhand	reviewer	waitress	catechist	excerptor
milliner	romancer	wardress	cellarman	exchanger
minister	rugmaker	warrener	chanteuse	exciseman
minstrel	rumourer	watchman	charwoman	executive
modeller	salesman	waterman	chauffeur	eye doctor
muleteer	satirist	wet nurse	cheapjack	fabricant
muralist	sawbones	whaleman	chorister	fashioner
musician	scullion	wigmaker	clarifier	felt maker
novelist	sculptor	winnower	clergyman	figurante
onion-man	seamster	wrestler	clinician	film actor
operator	seedsman		clogmaker	film extra
optician	sempster	**9**	coalminer	film maker
ordainer	servitor	alchemist	coalowner	financier
ordinand	shearman	alluminor	collector	fire eater
organist	shepherd	anatomist	colourist	fish curer
outrider	shipmate	annotator	columnist	fisherman
overseer	shopgirl	announcer	comprador	flag maker
pargeter	showgirl	arborator	concierge	freelance
penmaker	sidesman	architect	conductor	freighter
perfumer	sketcher	archivist	conserver	fruiterer
peterman	smuggler	art critic	cosmonaut	furbisher
pewterer	spearman	art dealer	cost clerk	furnisher
picaroon	speed cop	artificer	costumier	galvanist
pinmaker	spurrier	art master	courtesan	gas fitter
plougher	starcher	astronaut	couturier	gazetteer
polisher	stitcher	attendant	cowfeeder	gem cutter
portress	stockman	authoress	cowkeeper	geologist
postiler	storeman	auxiliary	cracksman	gluemaker
potmaker	stripper	balladeer	craftsman	goldsmith
preacher	strummer	ballerina	crayonist	gondolier
prefacer	stuntman	bank agent	cymbalist	gospeller

governess	man-at-arms	privateer	tentmaker	astrologer
guardsman	mannequin	professor	test pilot	astronomer
guitarist	mechanist	profilist	therapist	auctioneer
harlequin	medallist	provedore	theurgist	audit clerk
harmonist	memoirist	publicist	timberman	balloonist
harpooner	mercenary	publisher	toolsmith	ballplayer
harvester	mesmerist	pulpiteer	town clerk	bandmaster
Hellenist	messenger	puppeteer	town crier	bassoonist
herbalist	metallist	qualifier	tradesman	beadswoman
herbarian	metrician	quarryman	tragedian	beautician
herborist	middleman	racketeer	treasurer	bell ringer
hired hand	mill owner	railmaker	trepanner	bibliopole
hired help	mortician	recruiter	tributary	billposter
Hispanist	musketeer	reformist	trumpeter	biochemist
historian	myologist	rehearser	tympanist	biographer
homeopath	navigator	ribbonman	usherette	blacksmith
hop picker	neologian	roadmaker	varnisher	bladesmith
hosteller	neologist	ropemaker	versifier	blockmaker
housemaid	newsagent	roundsman	vetturino	bluejacket
housewife	nursemaid	sacristan	vexillary	bombardier
hygienist	odd job man	safemaker	violinist	bondswoman
hypnotist	office boy	sailmaker	volcanist	bonesetter
ingrafter	operative	scenarist	voltigeur	bookbinder
innkeeper	ordinator	schoolman	wadsetter	bookkeeper
inscriber	osteopath	scientist	warranter	bookseller
inspector	otologist	scrivener	washerman	bootlegger
intendant	outfitter	scytheman	waxworker	bricklayer
ironsmith	paralegal	secretary	webmaster	brickmaker
itinerant	paramedic	ship owner	whipper-in	brushmaker
jack-smith	paymaster	ship's mate	whitester	bureaucrat
kennel man	pedagogue	shoeblack	winemaker	caravaneer
lacemaker	performer	shoemaker	wood reeve	cartoonist
lacquerer	physician	sightsman	workwoman	cartwright
lady's maid	physicist	signalman	zookeeper	cash keeper
lampooner	pitsawyer	sinologue	zoologist	cat breeder
land agent	planisher	soapmaker	zootomist	ceramicist
landreeve	plasterer	solicitor		chair maker
larcenist	ploughboy	sonneteer	**10**	chargehand
launderer	ploughman	stableboy	able seaman	charioteer
laundress	pluralist	stable lad	accomptant	chorus girl
legionary	poetaster	stableman	accoucheur	chronicler
librarian	pointsman	stagehand	accountant	circuiteer
linotyper	policeman	stationer	acolothist	claim agent
lion tamer	pop artist	steersman	advertiser	clapper boy
liveryman	portrayer	stevedore	aerologist	classicist
loan agent	portreeve	subeditor	agronomist	clockmaker
loan shark	postilion	succentor	air hostess	clog dancer
locksmith	postwoman	swineherd	air steward	cloth maker
log roller	poulterer	switchman	algebraist	coachmaker
lumberman	precentor	swordsman	amanuensis	coal backer
machinist	preceptor	syndicate	apothecary	coalheaver
magnetist	predicant	tablemaid	apprentice	coastguard
majordomo	prelector	tactician	arbitrator	collocutor
male model	priestess	tap dancer	art teacher	colloquist

colporteur	geographer	negotiator	schoolmarm	troubadour
comedienne	glossarist	newscaster	scrutineer	typesetter
compositor	glue boiler	news editor	sculptress	undertaker
compounder	gold beater	newsreader	sea captain	veterinary
concordist	gold washer	newsvendor	seamstress	victualler
consultant	governante	nosologist	second mate	vivandiere
contractor	grammarian	nurseryman	seminarist	voice coach
controller	gunslinger	obituarist	serving man	wainwright
copyholder	hall porter	oil painter	ship broker	watchmaker
copywriter	handmaiden	orchardist	ship holder	waterguard
cordwainer	harvestman	overlooker	shipmaster	weather man
counsellor	hatcheller	panegyrist	shipwright	wharfinger
cultivator	head porter	park keeper	shopfitter	whitesmith
customs man	head waiter	park ranger	shopkeeper	wholesaler
cytologist	hierophant	park warden	signwriter	winegrower
delineator	highwayman	pasquilant	silentiary	wine waiter
directress	homoeopath	pastry cook	silk mercer	wireworker
disc jockey	horn player	pathfinder	silk weaver	woodcarver
discounter	horologist	pawnbroker	sinologist	woodcutter
dishwasher	house agent	pearl diver	skirmisher	woodmonger
dispatcher	huckstress	pedicurist	slop seller	woodworker
distrainer	husbandman	peltmonger	soap boiler	wool carder
dockmaster	inoculator	penologist	specialist	wool comber
dog breeder	institutor	perruquier	staff nurse	wool driver
dog trainer	instructor	pharmacist	steersmate	wool sorter
doorkeeper	ironmonger	philologer	stewardess	wool trader
dramaturge	ironworker	piano tuner	stipulator	wool winder
dressmaker	journalist	pickpocket	stock taker	yardmaster
drummer boy	journeyman	platelayer	stone borer	zinc worker
dry cleaner	knackerman	playwright	stonemason	zoographer
emblazoner	land worker	politician	strategist	zymologist
enamellist	laundryman	postillion	street ward	
ephemerist	law officer	postmaster	supervisor	**11**
epitaphist	legislator	prescriber	surcharger	accompanist
evangelist	librettist	prima donna	swan keeper	acoustician
fellmonger	lighterman	private eye	symphonist	adjudicator
file cutter	lime burner	procurator	tally clerk	allopathist
film critic	linotypist	programmer	taskmaster	antiquarian
film editor	liquidator	proprietor	taxi driver	apple grower
fire worker	lobsterman	prospector	tea blender	army officer
fishmonger	lock keeper	protractor	tea planter	arquebusier
flight crew	lumberjack	puncturist	technician	artillerist
flowergirl	magistrate	pyrologist	technocrat	art mistress
folk dancer	manageress	quizmaster	theologian	audiologist
folk singer	manicurist	railwayman	threnodist	audiotypist
forecaster	manservant	rat catcher	timekeeper	auscultator
frame maker	matchmaker	recitalist	tractarian	bank cashier
freebooter	medical man	researcher	traffic cop	bank
fund raiser	militiaman	ringmaster	trafficker	manager
gamekeeper	millwright	roadmender	tram driver	bargemaster
game warden	mineralist	ropedancer	transactor	basketmaker
gear cutter	missionary	roughrider	translator	batti-wallah
geisha girl	naturalist	safe blower	trawlerman	battologist
geneticist	nautch girl	saleswoman	treasuress	beachcomber

bell-founder	executioner	lifeboatman	portraitist	telephonist
bill-sticker	face painter	lightkeeper	preceptress	ticket agent
bird-catcher	facilitator	linen draper	print seller	toastmaster
bird-watcher	factory hand	lithologist	probationer	tobacconist
boatbuilder	faith healer	lorry driver	promulgator	tooth drawer
body servant	field worker	madrigalist	proofreader	topographer
boilermaker	figure maker	maidservant	property	torch bearer
boilersmith	filing clerk	mammalogist	man	town planner
bondservant	finestiller	master baker	proprietrix	toxophilite
broadcaster	firefighter	medicine man	questionary	transcriber
bullfighter	fire insurer	memorialist	radiologist	transporter
businessman	fourbisseur	merchantman	rag merchant	travel agent
candlemaker	fruit picker	metal worker	representer	tree surgeon
car salesman	funambulist	miniaturist	rhetorician	typographer
chair mender	galley slave	money broker	roadsweeper	underbearer
chalk cutter	genealogist	money-lender	safebreaker	underletter
chambermaid	ghost writer	monographer	sandwich	underwriter
chiffonnier	glass blower	mule spinner	man	upholsterer
chirologist	glass cutter	music critic	Sanscritist	vine dresser
chiromancer	glass worker	music master	saxophonist	waiting maid
chiropodist	gravedigger	myographist	scoutmaster	washerwoman
choirmaster	greengrocer	mysteriarch	scrapdealer	wax chandler
chronologer	haberdasher	mythologist	scrip holder	weather girl
clock setter	hagiologist	necrologist	secret agent	wheel cutter
cloth worker	hairdresser	necromancer	seditionary	wheelwright
condisciple	hairstylist	needlewoman	servant girl	whitewasher
condottiere	hedge priest	neurologist	serving maid	witchdoctor
conductress	hierologist	neurotomist	sharebroker	woolstapler
confederate	histologist	night porter	sheep farmer	xylophonist
congressman	horse doctor	night sister	shepherdess	zoographist
consecrator	horse jockey	nightworker	shipbreaker	
constituent	horse trader	nomenclator	shipbuilder	**12**
conveyancer	hospitaller	numismatist	ship's master	accordionist
co-ordinator	hotel keeper	office staff	shop steward	actor-manager
coppersmith	housekeeper	onion seller	silk thrower	air stewardess
cosmogonist	housemaster	opera singer	silversmith	ambulanceman
cosmologist	housemother	ophiologist	slaughterer	anaesthetist
crane driver	hymnologist	orientalist	smallholder	artilleryman
cub reporter	illuminator	orthopedist	sociologist	bagpipe maker
cypher clerk	illusionist	osteologist	stage driver	ballet dancer
delivery man	illustrator	pamphleteer	stage player	ballet master
demographer	infantryman	panel beater	stakeholder	bellows maker
dispensator	interpreter	pantomimist	steeplejack	bibliologist
double agent	interviewer	paperhanger	stipendiary	bibliopegist
draftswoman	iron founder	parlourmaid	stockbroker	booking clerk
draughtsman	ivory carver	pathologist	stockjobber	bus conductor
duty officer	ivory turner	pearlfisher	stonecutter	cabinet maker
electrician	ivory worker	petrologist	storekeeper	calligrapher
emblematist	kennelmaid	pettifogger	stripteaser	caricaturist
embroiderer	kitchenmaid	philologist	sundriesman	cardiologist
entertainer	land steward	philosopher	system	carpet fitter
estate agent	laundrymaid	phytologist	maker	cartographer
ethnologist	leading lady	phonologist	taxidermist	cerographist
etymologist	ledger clerk	polyphonist	telegrapher	cheesemonger

chief cashier
chimney sweep
chiropractor
chronologist
churchwarden
circuit rider
civil servant
clarinettist
clerk of works
cloth shearer
coach builder
coleopterist
commissioner
conchologist
confectioner
corn chandler
cosmographer
costermonger
crafts master
craniologist
cryptogamist
deep-sea diver
demonologist
demonstrator
dendrologist
dramaturgist
ecclesiastic
Egyptologist
elecutionist
engine driver
entomologist
entomotomist
entrepreneur
escapologist
ethnographer
experimenter
farm labourer
film director
film producer
first officer
flying doctor
footplateman
geometrician
geriatrician
glass grinder
glossologist
greasemonkey
guild brother
hagiographer
haliographer
harness maker
horse breaker
horse courser
horse knacker

hotel manager
house steward
house surgeon
hydrographer
hydropathist
hypothecator
immunologist
instructress
invoice clerk
joint trustee
jurisconsult
king's counsel
knife grinder
knife thrower
land surveyor
lath-splitter
lexicologist
lithographer
longshoreman
loss adjuster
lumber dealer
maitre d'hotel
make-up artist
manual worker
manufacturer
mass producer
meat salesman
metallurgist
mezzo-soprano
microscopist
mineralogist
money changer
monographist
mosaic artist
mosaic worker
music teacher
mythographer
newspaperman
nutritionist
obstetrician
office junior
orchestrator
organ builder
organ grinder
orthodontist
orthographer
ovariotomist
paper stainer
pattern maker
pediatrician
phonographer
photographer
phrenologist
physiologist

plant manager
ploughwright
plumber's mate
postmistress
practitioner
press officer
prestigiator
prison warder
prize fighter
professional
propagandist
proprietress
psychiatrist
psychologist
publicity man
puppet player
pyrotechnist
quarry master
racing driver
radiographer
receptionist
restaurateur
riding master
right-hand man
rubber grader
sales manager
scene painter
scene shifter
schoolmaster
screenwriter
scriptwriter
scullery maid
seed merchant
seismologist
sharecropper
sharpshooter
ship chandler
shoe repairer
silver beater
slaughterman
snake charmer
social worker
soil mechanic
special agent
speechwriter
spice blender
sportscaster
sportswriter
stage manager
statistician
stenographer
stonebreaker
stonedresser
stonesquarer

street trader
sugar refiner
tax collector
tax inspector
technologist
telegraphist
test engineer
therapeutist
toll gatherer
toxicologist
transplanter
trichologist
undermanager
veterinarian
waiting woman
warehouseman
water diviner
weather woman
wine merchant
wood engraver
works manager

13

administrator
agriculturist
antique dealer
arachnologist
archaeologist
arithmetician
articled clerk
Assyriologist
barber surgeon
bibliographer
calico printer
campanologist
chartographer
chirographist
choreographer
chronographer
civil engineer
clearstarcher
coffee planter
cometographer
contortionist
cotton spinner
counterfeiter
cryptographer
deipnosophist
dermatologist
diagnostician
diamond cutter
draughtswoman
drawing master
dress designer

drill sergeant
electroplater
electrotypist
emigrationist
entozoologist
epigrammatist
estate manager
fencing master
fortune-teller
freight broker
galvanologist
gastriloquist
glossographer
glyphographer
ground bailiff
gynaecologist
harbour master
hieroglyphist
horse-milliner
ichthyologist
industrialist
intelligencer
letter founder
lexicographer
maid-of-all-work
master builder
master mariner
mathematician
meteorologist
metoposcopist
music mistress
night watchman
office manager
ornithologist
orthographist
paediatrician
park attendant
pattern cutter
periodicalist
pharmaceutist
physiognomist
physiographer
poultry farmer
privateersman
process server
psalmographer
psychoanalyst
pteridologist
public speaker
Queen's Counsel
racing tipster
revolutionary
riding teacher
sailing master

schoolteacher
science master
security guard
shop assistant
silk throwster
station master
stenographist
stereoscopist
stethoscopist
street sweeper
subcontractor
superintendent
supernumerary
systems analyst
thaumaturgist
thimble rigger
toll collector
trade unionist
tramcar driver
tram conductor
ventriloquist
violoncellist
window cleaner
window dresser
writing master

14

administratrix
anthropologist
autobiographer
bacteriologist
ballet mistress
billiard player
chamber counsel
chimney
    sweeper
citizen-soldier
classics master
colour sergeant
commissionaire
customs officer
discount broker
drawing teacher
ecclesiologist
educationalist
encyclopaedist
exchange broker
garden designer
grammaticaster
handicraftsman
heresiographer
horse whisperer
horticulturist
house decorator

house furnisher
language master
leather dresser
manual labourer
market gardener
medical officer
merchant tailor
miscellanarian
money scrivener
mother superior
painter-stainer
pharmacologist
pneumatologist
psalmographist
reception clerk
representative
riding mistress
sales assistant
schoolmistress
science teacher
ship's carpenter
siderographist
spectacle maker
store detective
spectroscopist
superintendent
systems analyst
tallow chandler
watercolourist
weather prophet

15

arboriculturist
assistant master
Bow Street runner
classics teacher
cosmetic surgeon
crossing sweeper
crustaceologist
dancing mistress
diamond
    merchant
domestic servant
drawing mistress
flight attendant
forwarding agent
funeral director
gentleman farmer
hackney
    coachman
heart specialist
helminthologist
hierogrammatist
historiographer

instrumentalist
insurance broker
jack-of-all-trades
language teacher
musical director
numismatologist
ophthalmologist
palaeontologist
physiotherapist
platform speaker
portrait painter
programme seller
provision dealer
psychotherapist
railway engineer
resurrectionist
science mistress
scripture reader
sleeping partner
stretcher bearer
ticket collector
tightrope walker
tonsorial artist

16 and over
bilingual secretary
    (18)
classics mistress
    (16)
interior designer
    (16)
landscape
    architect
    (18)
landscape
    gardener
    (17)
language mistress
    (16)
lighthouse keeper
    (16)
master of
    foxhounds
    (17)
quantity surveyor
    (16)
veterinary
    surgeon
    (17)
weather forecaster
    (17)

TRANSPORT

Air and Space Travel

3	5		7	8	9
ace	aloft	cut out	aileron	aerodyne	aerodrome
air	apron	de-icer	air base	aerofoil	aeroplane
fin	blimp	elevon	aircrew	aeronaut	afterburn
gap	cabin	flight	airdrop	aerostat	air intake
jet	cargo	floats	air flow	airborne	air pocket
mig	chock	flying	air foil	aircraft	airworthy
Mir	chord	galley	air lane	air brake	altimeter
pod	cleat	gas-bag	airlift	airfield	
rev	crash	glider	airline	airframe	
rib	crate	hangar	airmiss	air force	
UFO	ditch	hijack	airport	airliner	
yaw	drift	intake	air raid	airplane	
	drone	jetlag	airship	air route	
4	flaps	launch	airsick	airscrew	
APEX	flier	module	aviator	airspace	
bank	float	octane	azimuth	airspeed	
bump	frame	piston	bale out	airstrip	
buzz	glide	ramjet	ballast	altitude	
crew	jumbo	refuel	balloon	anhedral	
dive	pilot	rocket	biplane	anti-icer	
dock	pitch	rudder	birdman	approach	
drag	plane	runway	blister	autogiro	
flap	pylon	yawing	bomb	aviation	
fuel	radar		bay	aviatrix	
hull	range	**7**	capsule	backwash	
kite	rev up	aileron	ceiling	ballonet	
knot	slots	air base	cellule	barostat	
land	stall	aircrew	charter	black box	
lane	strut	airdrop	chassis	blast off	
lift	stunt	air flow	chopper	buoyancy	
loop	valve	air foil	clipper	clearway	
mach		air lane	cockpit	Concorde	
MRCA	**6**	airlift	compass	corridor	
NASA	aerial	airline	contact	cruising	
nose	airbus	airmiss	co-pilot	decalage	
prop	air dam	airport	cowling	dihedral	
roll	airman	air raid	descent	drip-flap	
slip	airway	airship	ejector	drop-tank	
span	Apollo	airsick	fairing	elevator	
spin	basket	aviator	fighter	envelope	
STOL	beacon	azimuth	flyover	flat spin	
tail	bomber	bale out	flypast	fuel pipe	
taxi	camber	ballast	freight	fuselage	
trim	canopy	balloon	gliding	grounded	
veer	cruise	biplane	gondola	gull wing	
VTOL		birdman	helibus	gyrodyne	
wind		blister	jet pipe	gyrostat	
wing		bomb	jump jet	headwind	
york		bay	landing	heliport	
zoom			lift-off	hijacker	
			Mae	in-flight	
			West	jet pilot	
			nacelle	jet plane	
			nose-cap	joystick	
			on board	jumbo jet	
			pancake	longeron	
			payload	long-haul	
			re-entry	moonshot	
			retract	near miss	
			ripcord	non-rigid	
			shuttle	nose down	
			skyjack	nose-cone	
			spinner	nosedive	
			sputnik	pitching	
			tail fin	radiator	
			take-off	seaplane	
			taxiing	sideslip	
			Trident	spaceman	
			trimtab	squadron	
			Tristar	stopover	
			twinjet	streamer	
			winglet	subsonic	
			wingtip	tail skid	
				tail unit	
				tailwind	
				terminal	
				throttle	
				triplane	
				turbofan	
				turbojet	
				twin-tail	
				volplane	
				warplane	
				wind cone	
				windmill	
				windsock	
				wing flap	
				Zeppelin	

amphibian
astrodome
astronaut
autopilot
cabin crew
caravelle
carlingue
club class
coleopter
cosmonaut
countdown
crash-land
crow's-foot
cyclogiro
delta-wing
dirigible
empennage
freighter
fuel gauge
gyroplane
jet bomber
jetlagged
launch pad
launching
lift wires
longerons
low-flying
Machmeter
microlite
monocoque
monoplane
moon buggy
navigator
overshoot
parachute
power dive
propeller
rotaplane
rudder bar
sailplane
satellite
semi-rigid
short-haul
skywriter
spacecrew

spaceship
spacesuit
spacewalk
stability
stratojet
swing wing
tailplane
taxiplane
test pilot
touch down
turboprop
twin-screw
wind gauge

10
aerobatics
aero-engine
aeronautic
aerostatic
air balloon
air control
air defence
air hostess
air service
air steward
air support
air traffic
anemometer
ballooning
balloonist
barrel roll
bird strike
cantilever
cargo plane
Challenger
dive bomber
flight deck
flight path
flight plan
flying boat
fuel intake
ground crew
gyrocopter
hang glider
helicopter

hydroplane
jet fighter
landing run
mach
  number
multiplane
outer space
oxygen mask
pilot plane
robot plane
rudder post
slipstream
solo flight
space probe
spacecraft
splashdown
stabilizer
stewardess
supersonic
test flight
turbulence
V-formation

11
aeronautics
aerostatics
afterburner
air corridor
airsickness
air terminal
air umbrella
blind flying
combat plane
ejector seat
flying speed
free balloon
ground speed
heat barrier
heavy
  bomber
interceptor
landing deck
landing gear
leading-edge
loop the loop

moon landing
mooring mast
ornithopter
parachutist
pressurized
retractable
retro-rocket
sesquiplane
slotted wing
soft landing
space centre
space flight
space rocket
space travel
stabilizers
stunt flying
twin-engined
vapour trail
victory roll

12
airfreighter
air-sea rescue
arrester gear
beacon lights
belly landing
control tower
crash landing
ejection seat
economy class
fighter pilot
flying circus
flying saucer
gliding angle
hedgehopping
jet-propelled
landing light
landing speed
landing wires
launching pad
maiden flight
manned rocket
night fighter
pilot balloon
pressure suit

pursuit plane
radar scanner
radial engine
sound barrier
space capsule
space shuttle
space station
space vehicle

13
airworthiness
business class
charter flight
control column
convertiplane
cruising speed
fighter bomber
forced landing
ground control
head-up
  display
in-line engines
radiolocation
shock absorber
undercarriage

14
automatic pilot
engine
  mounting
escape velocity
heavier-than-
  air
holding pattern
lighter-than-air
looping the loop
space traveller
weightlessness

15
aircraft carrier
decompression
flight attendant
semi-
  retractable

Cars and Driving

2
AA
c.c.
GT
h.p.
RV

3
bus
cam
can
cap
car
cog
fan
fit
HGV
hub
JCB
jet
key
lap
lug
map
MOT
nut
oil
pin
pit
RAC
rev
rim
rod
run
ton
top
van

4
axle
belt
body
bolt
boot
boss
bulb
bush
clip
coil
cowl
dash
disc

door
dray
drum
duck
flat
fuse
gage
gate
gear
hood
hoot
horn
idle
jack
lane
lock
nail
park
pink
plug
pump
road
roll
rope
seat
skid
sump
tail
tank
test
tire
tour
tube
TWOC
tyre
veer
wing

5
apron
bezel
brake
cable
chain
chart
choke
clamp
coupé
cover
crank
cut in
drive

float
frame
gauge
grill
joint
knock
lay-by
level
lever
model
motor
on tow
pedal
rally
rev up
rivet
rotor
route
scale
screw
sedan
shaft
shift
spark
speed
spoke
sprag
stall
start
stick
ton up
tools
tread
U-turn
valve
wheel
wiper
works
yield

6
adjust
air bag
big end
bonnet
bumper
bypass
camber
car tax
charge
clutch
con rod

cut out
dazzle
de-icer
de luxe
detour
dickey
dimmer
divert
driver
dynamo
engine
fender
fitter
flange
funnel
garage
gasket
grease
handle
hot rod
hubcap
idling
klaxon
louvre
mascot
milage
mirror
octane
oilcan
one-way
petrol
pile-up
pinion
pintle
piston
saloon
signal
spokes
spring
swerve
switch
tappet
timing
torque
towbar
winker

7
air hose
airlock
axle box
battery

bearing
blinker
blowout
bollard
build-up
bus lane
bus stop
carpark
carport
cat's eye
chassis
contact
control
cooling
dipping
drive-in
driving
exhaust
fanbelt
flasher
flyover
gearbox
give way
goggles
gudgeon
hardtop
highway
hot-wire
joyride
kingpin
L driver
L plates
licence
linkage
locknut
log book
luggage
magneto
map-case
mileage
misfire
missing
mixture
muffler
no entry
non-skid
off-ramp
oil-feed
parking
pillion
pinking
pull out

reverse
roadhog
roadmap
roadtax
rolling
run into
seizing
skidpan
spindle
springs
starter
sun roof
tax disc
test run
toolkit
top gear
touring
towrope
traffic
trailer
viaduct
warning
wingnut

8
air brake
air inlet
airtight
armature
arterial
Autobahn
back seat
backfire
body shop
bodywork
brakerod
camshaft
cat's eyes
clearway
coasting
converge
coupling
crankpin
cruising
cul-de-sac
cylinder
declutch
delivery
dipstick
driveway
fast lane
fastback

feed pipe	skid mark	diversion	switch off	mileometer
feed pump	skidding	drum brake	T junction	motorcycle
flat tyre	slip road	estate car	tail light	off-roading
flywheel	slow down	filler cap	tail wheel	overtaking
foglight	slow lane	footbrake	taximeter	panel beater
footpump	solenoid	framework	test drive	petrol pump
freezing	speed gun	free-wheel	third gear	petrol tank
friction	speeding	front axle	tire lever	piston ring
fuelpipe	squad car	front seat	trunk road	private car
fuel tank	stock car	fuel gauge	two-seater	radial tire
garaging	tail gate	gear lever	tyre lever	radial tyre
gasoline	tail skid	gearshift	underpass	rear mirror
gradient	tailpipe	generator	underseal	rev counter
gridlock	taxi rank	Grand Prix	wheel base	right of way
guide-rod	throttle	grease box	wheel spin	roadworthy
handpump	tire pump	grease gun		roundabout
ignition	track rod	guarantee	**10**	rumble seat
inlet cam	two-speed	handbrake	access road	safety belt
jerrycan	tyre pump	headlight	adjustment	side mirror
joyrider		hit-and-run	alternator	signalling
jump lead	**9**	indicator	amber light	spare wheel
jump seat	air filter	inner tube	anti-dazzle	speed limit
knocking	alignment	joyriding	antifreeze	streamline
manifold	anti-glare	insurance	bevel wheel	suspension
motoring	autoroute	limousine	bottom gear	tachograph
motorway	back wheel	lubricate	box spanner	tachometer
mudguard	ball-valve	monocoque	brake light	third-party
nearside	batteries	motor show	brake pedal	three-speed
odometer	brake drum	motorbike	brakeblock	toll bridge
oil gauge	brakeshoe	motorcade	broken down	touring car
oncoming	breakdown	nipple key	car licence	traffic cop
open road	bump start	oil filter	combustion	traffic jam
overhaul	bus driver	overdrive	commutator	two-wheeler
overpass	cab driver	overrider	crankshaft	upholstery
overtake	car driver	passenger	crossroads	ventilator
overturn	chain-link	patrol car	dickey seat	wheelbrace
pavement	chauffeur	petrol can	drive shaft	windscreen
prowl car	clearance	piston rod	dry battery	windshield
puncture	coachwork	point duty	endorsement	wing mirror
radiator	concourse	police car	fifth wheel	
rattling	condenser	racing car	fluid drive	**11**
rear axle	cotter pin	radial tyre	four-seater	accelerator
rear lamp	crank axle	rear light	front wheel	accessories
ring road	crankcase	reflector	gear casing	accumulator
road rage	crossroad	revving up	gear change	blind corner
road sign	cutting in	road sense	green light	brake-lining
road test	dashboard	road works	gudgeon pin	built-up area
roadside	dashlight	saloon car	headlights	carburetter
roof rack	death seat	sidelight	horsepower	carriageway
rush hour	deathtrap	spare tire	inlet valve	clutch pedal
shoulder	defroster	spare tyre	insulation	compression
side road	dipswitch	speed trap	lighting up	convertible
sideslip	dirt track	sports car	low-tension	crash helmet
silencer	disc brake	stoplight	lubricator	decarbonize

de-luxe model
distributor
driving test
endorsement
exhaust pipe
exhaust port
feeler gauge
front lights
highway code
ignition key
interrupter
lorry driver
lubrication
luggage rack
median strip
motor spirit
needle valve
number plate
oil pressure
overhauling
overheating
over-revving
owner-driver
petrol gauge
power brakes
pre-ignition
racing model
radiator cap
request stop
reverse gear
reverse turn
screen wiper
self-starter
sliding roof
speed camera
speedometer
splashboard
sports model
streamlined
sunshine roof
synchromesh

thermometer
through road
trafficator
vacuum brake
weighbridge
wheel wobble

12
acceleration
approach road
arterial road
ball bearings
clutchspring
coachbuilder
countershaft
crash barrier
cylinder head
diesel engine
differential
double-decker
driving chain
driving shaft
exhaust valve
float chamber
freewheeling
fuel injection
gear changing
hard shoulder
lock-up garage
miles per hour
motorcyclist
parking light
parking meter
parking place
petrol filter
pillion rider
racing driver
ratchet wheel
registration
repair outfit
road junction

running board
single-decker
sparking plug
starter motor
steering gear
steering lock
transmission
two-speed gear
warning light

13
admission pipe
Belisha beacon
breakdown
  gang
chain adjuster
connecting rod
cooling system
courtesy light
cruise control
driving mirror
fluid flywheel
handbrake turn
hydraulic jack
induction pipe
inspection pit
licence holder
no-claims
  bonus
pillion riding
pneumatic tyre
power steering
pressure-gauge
rack-and-pinion
roller-bearing
servo-assisted
shock absorber
shooting brake
speed merchant
starting motor
steering wheel

traffic signal

14
adjusting screw
circuit breaker
compression tap
contact breaker
double-declutch
driving licence
exhaust-cam axle
filling station
four-wheel drive
friction clutch
grease injector
lighting-up time
lubricating oll
luggage carrier
miles per gallon
propeller shaft
rear-wheel drive
reclining seats
reversing lights
service station
side impact bars
starting handle
steering column
third-party risk
three-point turn
three-speed gear
universal joint

15 and over
carriage builder (15)
central reservation
  (18)
dual carriageway (15)
front-wheel drive (15)
instrument panel (15)
insurance policy (15)
seating capacity (15)
windscreen wiper (15)

Ships, Boats and Sailing

2	ark	CIF	fid	hoy	oar	sea	tub	bale
AB	arm	cog	FOB	jaw	ply	set	tug	bark
A1	bac	con	fog	jib	ram	SOS	way	beam
RM	bay	cot	fox	lee	RIB	sub	yaw	beat
RN	bow	cox	gig	log	rig	tar		bend
	box	ebb	guy	man	rum	TBD	**4**	boat
3	cat	eye	HMS	MFV	run	top	ahoy	boom
aft	cay	fay	hog	nut	sag	tow	back	bows

brig	last	taut	bosun	hound	sheer	batten
bunk	lead	tend	botel	jetty	sheet	bawley
bunt	line	tide	bower	kayak	shelf	beacon
buoy	list	tilt	bowse	kedge	shell	becket
buss	load	toss	boyer	ketch	shoal	billow
calk	loof	trim	brace	kevel	shore	bireme
calm	luff	trip	brail	lay-to	siren	bonnet
club	lute	veer	briny	lay up	skeet	boomer
comb	mast	waft	cabin	leach	skiff	bridge
cott	mess	wake	cable	leaky	sling	bug-eye
crew	mine	wapp	cadet	leech	sloop	bumkin
deck	mole	warp	canoe	ligan	smack	bunker
dhow	moor	wave	caper	liner	sound	burton
dive	neap	wear	cargo	lobby	spars	caique
dock	oars	west	casco	lurch	sprit	cablet
dory	pair	whip	caulk	metal	stack	canvas
down	peak	wind	chain	misty	steer	careen
duck	pier	wing	chart	mouse	stern	carina
DUKW	pink	yard	check	naval	storm	carvel
east	pole	yarn	chock	north	surge	comber
eddy	poop	yawl	clamp	oakum	swell	convoy
fall	port		cleat	ocean	swing	cooper
fend	prow	**5**	coble	order	thole	course
flag	punt	aback	craft	oiler	tidal	crayer
flow	quay	abaft	crank	orlop	tramp	crotch
foam	raft	abeam	cuddy	panch	trice	cruise
fore	rail	afore	dandy	P-boat	truck	cutter
foul	rake	afoul	davit	pilot	truss	debark
four	rank	after	depth	pitch	U-boat	decker
furl	rate	ahead	diver	prahu	waist	dinghy
gaff	ride	ahull	douse	prick	watch	diving
gale	RNLI	aloft	downs	prize	weigh	dogger
gang	roll	apeak	dowse	prore	wharf	double
gear	rope	aport	draft	prove	wheel	dragon
girt	RORO	atrip	drift	Q-ship	whiff	driver
grab	rove	avast	E-boat	radar	winch	droger
grog	rung	aviso	eight	radio	wreck	dromon
hank	saic	balsa	entry	range	xebec	dugout
hard	sail	barca	ferry	razee	yacht	embark
haul	scud	barge	fifie	refit		engine
haze	seam	batel	flake	rhumb	**6**	ensign
hazy	ship	beach	fleet	right	aboard	escort
head	sink	belay	float	ropes	adrift	fathom
helm	skeg	belee	fluke	rower	afloat	fender
hold	skid	below	gauge	royal	anchor	fo'c'sle
hove	slip	berth	grave	R-boat	argosy	for'ard
hulk	slue	bibbs	gusty	sabot	armada	fother
hull	snub	bight	hands	saiok	ashore	funnel
jack	spar	bilge	hatch	sally	astern	furled
junk	stay	bilts	haven	salve	aweigh	galeas
keel	stem	bitts	hawse	salvo	awning	galiot
knot	swab	blirt	hitch	sands	balker	galley
koff	swig	block	hoist	screw	banker	gasket
land	tack	board	horse	scull	barque	gromet

gunnel	piracy	tosher	carline	felucca	Jack Tar
halser	pirate	towage	carling	fin keel	jib boom
hawser	piston	trough	carrack	fishery	jibstay
hooker	pooped	unbend	carrier	flotsam	keelage
hopper	poppet	unbitt	cast off	flotson	keelson
hounds	PT boat	uncoil	cat hole	flyboat	landing
hove-to	puffer	undock	catboat	fogbank	lanyard
inship	pulwar	unfurl	catfall	foghorn	lashing
jetsam	puteli	unlade	cathead	foretop	lastage
jigger	raider	unload	cat's paw	forward	latches
kedger	randan	unmoor	channel	founder	leaking
kumpit	rating	unship	charter	four-oar	lee-gage
lading	ratlin	vessel	claw off	freight	lee side
land ho	reefed	voyage	clinker	freshen	lee tide
lateen	reefer	wafter	clipper	freshet	leeward
launch	rigged	whaler	coaling	frigate	lighter
lay-off	rigger	wherry	coaming	frogman	listing
leeway	rocket		coaster	futtock	loading
limber	rudder	**7**	cockler	galleon	logbook
Lloyd's	sailor	aground	cockpit	galliot	logline
locker	saique	airboat	collier	gangway	logreel
lugger	saloon	almadie	compass	gimbals	lookout
manned	salute	athwart	conning	go about	luffing
marina	salvor	backing	coracle	go below	lugsail
marine	sampan	bale out	cordage	gondola	maintop
marker	sculls	ballast	corsair	grapnel	man-o'-war
maroon	Seacat	beached	counter	grating	mariner
marque	sealer	bearing	crabber	graving	marines
masted	seaman	beating	cresset	grommet	marline
masula	seaway	bilboes	cringle	gudgeon	marling
mayday	settee	blister	cruiser	gunboat	matelot
mid-sea	sheets	boarder	currach	gun deck	minisub
mizzen	shroud	bobstay	cyclone	gunnage	monitor
moored	signal	bollard	deadeye	gun port	moorage
mutiny	sinker	boomkin	deep-sea	gunroom	mooring
nautic	sinnet	bowline	degauss	gunship	mudhook
neaped	slaver	bow wave	dismast	gunwale	muletta
needle	spider	boxhaul	dockage	guy rope	oarsman
nuggar	splice	bracing	dog vane	half pay	oceanic
nugger	squall	breaker	dolphin	halyard	offward
offing	square	budgero	drabler	harbour	old salt
on deck	stocks	bulwark	draught	harpoon	on board
oomiak	stormy	bumboat	dredger	haul off	outport
outfit	strake	bunkage	drifter	head off	oversea
packet	strand	buntine	drogher	head sea	painter
paddle	stream	bunting	dromond	headway	pair-oar
patrol	tackle	buoyage	dry dock	heave to	pearler
pay off	tanker	caboose	dunnage	hog boat	pennant
pay out	tartan	calking	ease off	horizon	permagy
pedalo	tender	can buoy	ebb tide	iceberg	pinnace
pennon	thwart	capsize	eel punt	ice boat	piragua
Pharos	tiller	capstan	embargo	ice-floe	pirogue
pillow	timber	captain	eye bolt	inboard	polacca
pintle	toggle	caravel	fairway	inshore	polacre

pontoon	tacking	bargeman	fife rail	land ahoy
pooping	tackled	barnacle	faltboat	landfall
port-bar	tackler	beam ends	fireboat	landmark
quayage	tactics	bearings	fireship	landsman
rafting	tartane	becalmed	flag rank	landward
rations	tempest	berthage	flagship	land wind
ratline	thimble	berthing	flatboat	larboard
reefing	tonkong	bilander	floating	lead line
reeming	tonnage	binnacle	flotilla	leeboard
ride out	top deck	boat deck	fogbound	lee shore
rigging	top mast	boathook	foot rope	lifebelt
rollers	topping	bolt rope	forefoot	lifeboat
rolling	topsail	bowsprit	foremast	lifebuoy
rope end	topside	broach to	forepeak	lifeline
rowboat	tornado	bulkhead	foresail	load line
rowlock	torpedo	bull's eye	foreship	loblolly
rundown	tow boat	bulwarks	forestay	logboard
sailing	towline	buntline	forewind	longboat
salvage	towpath	car ferry	free port	long haul
scupper	towrope	castaway	gaffsail	longship
scuttle	transom	caulking	galleass	low water
seacard	trawler	chandler	galliass	magazine
seafolk	trireme	claw away	gallivat	mailboat
sea haar	trysail	club-haul	go aboard	mainboom
sea lane	tugboat	coalship	go ashore	main deck
sea legs	typhoon	coasting	half-deck	mainmast
seamark	unladen	cockboat	halliard	mainsail
sea ooze	unsling	corocole	hatchway	mainstay
sea room	unslung	corvette	head into	mainyard
seasick	vedette	crossing	headfast	make sail
sea sled	veering	crowfoot	headsail	man-of-war
seaward	waftage	cruising	headwind	maritime
set sail	ward off	cutwater	helmless	martinet
sextant	warping	dahabeah	helmsman	masthead
shallop	warship	dahabiya	high seas	mastless
shelves	wavelet	dead slow	high tide	messmate
shipper	waveson	deadwood	hoogarts	midships
shipway	wet dock	deckhand	hornpipe	monohull
shoaler	wrecked	derelict	hoveller	moorings
shrouds	wrecker	disembay	hull-down	moulinet
sickbay	yardarm	ditty-bag	icebound	mutineer
sinking		ditty-box	icefield	mutinous
skipper	**8**	dockyard	ice yacht	nauscopy
skysail	anchored	dogwatch	Indiaman	nautical
slipway	anteport	doldrums	ironclad	navigate
spanker	aplustre	doubling	iron-sick	neap tide
spencer	approach	downhaul	jackstay	netlayer
spy boat	armament	drifting	jeffison	ordnance
squally	at anchor	driftway	jet-boat	outboard
stand-by	aweather	easterly	johnboat	overrake
steamer	backstay	eastward	jury mast	overseas
steward	backwash	east wind	keelboat	paravane
stopper	baghalak	eight-oar	keelhaul	periplus
stowage	barbette	even keel	keel over	picaroon

pierhead	streamer	beaconage	freighter	orlop deck
pilotage	stunsail	below deck	frigatoon	outrigger
plimsoll	submerge	bilge keel	funny boat	overboard
poop deck	surfboat	bilge pump	gangboard	parbuckle
porthole	tackling	blue peter	gangplank	periscope
portside	tafferel	boardable	gather way	peter boat
post boat	taffrail	boat drill	gin palace	pilot boat
pratique	thole pin	broadside	groundage	pilot ship
pump room	tilt boat	bomb ketch	guard boat	powerboat
put about	timoneer	bucentaur	guard ship	press-gang
quadrant	tranship	bunkering	half-hitch	privateer
quarters	traverse	cable ship	hard aport	prize crew
reef knot	trimaran	canal boat	herringer	prize ship
re-embark	unbuoyed	captaincy	high water	promenade
ride easy	uncoiled	careenage	hoist sail	quicksand
ride hard	under way	cargo boat	holystone	recharter
roadster	underset	catamaran	horse boat	reckoning
runabout	unfurled	chartered	houseboat	red ensign
sailboat	vanguard	chartroom	house flag	reef point
sail loft	wall knot	close haul	houseline	refitment
sail room	wardroom	coastwise	hurricane	revictual
sail yard	waterbus	companion	hydrofoil	rhumb line
salvable	waterman	container	jack block	river boat
salvager	water rot	corposant	jack staff	roadstead
sandbank	waterway	crocodile	jack stays	rockbound
scudding	waveworm	crossjack	jollyboat	RORO ferry
schooner	well boat	crosstree	kentledge	rotor ship
seaborne	well deck	crosswind	land ahead	royal mast
sea chest	west wind	crow's nest	lightship	Royal Navy
seafarer	westerly	Davy Jones	lobscouse	rum-runner
seagoing	westward	dead water	lower deck	sailboard
shallows	windlass	deck cargo	maelstrom	sailcloth
shark net	wind-rode	demurrage	mainbrace	sand yacht
sheer off	windsail	departure	mainsheet	seafaring
ship ahoy	windward	depot ship	manoeuvre	sea letter
shipmate	woodskin	destroyer	midstream	seaworthy
shipment	woolding	disanchor	minefield	semaphore
ship oars	wreckage	discharge	minelayer	sheer-hulk
shipping	yachting	disembark	minute gun	sheething
showboat		doggerman	mizenmast	shipboard
skipjack	**9**	dogshores	mizzentop	shipowner
smuggler	about ship	dress ship	moonraker	ship's crew
sounding	admiralty	drift sail	motorboat	shipshape
spyglass	affreight	driftwood	multihull	shipwreck
squadron	afterdeck	Elmo's fire	naumachia	shoreward
stand off	air funnel	ephemeris	navicular	sick berth
standard	all aboard	false keel	navigable	sidelight
staysail	alongside	ferryboat	navigator	sight land
steerage	amidships	fire drill	neptunian	slave dhow
sternage	anchorage	fire float	north wind	south wind
sternway	anchoring	floodmark	northerly	southerly
steam tug	back stays	flood tide	northward	southward
stowaway	bargepole	flying jib	ocean lane	sou'wester
stranded	barnacles	foreshore	oil tanker	speedboat

spindrift
spinnaker
spritsail
stanchion
starboard
stateroom
steamboat
steamship
steersman
sternfast
sternmost
sternpost
stokehold
storeship
storm-beat
stormsail
stormstay
stretcher
submarine
swampboat
tarpaulin
telescope
tide table
tophamper
trade wind
transport
troopship
tunny boat
twin-screw
two-decker
unballast
uncharted
unharbour
unlighted
unsounded
upper deck
vaporetto
waterline
water sail
whaleback
whaleboat
wheelboat

10
A1 at Lloyd's
aboard ship
advice boat
after-guard
after-hatch
after-sails
alongshore
anchor buoy
anchor hold
anchorable

astarboard
ballasting
banana boat
barge yacht
barkentine
battleship
batten down
Bermuda rig
bilgewater
blue ensign
bluejacket
bomb vessel
bootlegger
breakwater
breastfast
bridge deck
brigantine
cargo space
cast anchor
casting net
cattleboat
catch a crab
chain cable
chain ferry
chain plate
charthouse
coal bunker
cockleboat
corkjacket
cross-piece
crosstrees
deadlights
Deal lugger
degaussing
diving bell
diving suit
dockmaster
downstream
drop anchor
drop astern
embarkment
engine room
escutcheon
fathomless
fiddlehead
figurehead
flying boat
four-master
fore-and-aft
forecastle
forge ahead
freightage
freshwater
frostbound

full-rigged
gaff-rigged
harbourage
heavy-laden
high and dry
hollow mast
hovercraft
hydroplane
icebreaker
inflatable
jigger mast
Jolly Roger
jury rudder
jury-rigged
knockabout
landlocked
landlubber
lateen sail
lateen yard
lay a course
liberty man
lifejacket
lighterage
lighthouse
lookout man
loxodromic
manoeuvres
marine soap
marker buoy
martingale
middle deck
midshipman
mizzenmast
mizzensail
mizzenstay
monkey boat
motor yacht
narrowboat
navigating
navigation
night watch
nuclear sub
ocean-going
ocean liner
ore carrier
orthodromy
oyster crab
packet boat
paddleboat
parcelling
patrol boat
picket boat
pilothouse
pipe aboard

pirate ship
port of call
powder room
prize court
prize-money
quadrireme
quarantine
raking fire
reduce sail
rendezvous
repair ship
rescue boat
reshipment
rivercraft
rope ladder
round house
royal barge
rudder post
rudderless
Samson post
school ship
seamanlike
seamanship
ship broker
shipmaster
shipwright
signalling
skyscraper
slack water
sloop-of-war
small craft
spring tide
square sail
stanchions
stay tackle
stern-board
stern-frame
sternsheet
submariner
supercargo
supply ship
survey ship
tabernacle
take in sail
tally clerk
target ship
tea clipper
tidal basin
tidal river
tiller rope
topgallant
turret ship
unfathomed
unfordable

upperworks
victualler
Viking ship
water-borne
watercraft
waterspout
watertight
wheelhouse
windjammer
wring-staff

11
abandon ship
barquentine
beachcomber
belaying pin
bulk carrier
capital ship
captainship
centreboard
chafing gear
chasse-marée
close-hauled
cockleshell
compass card
compass rose
contact mine
debarkation
depth charge
dismastment
dock charges
dreadnought
echo-sounder
embarkation
escape hatch
factory ship
fishing boat
foam-crested
fore-topmast
fore-topsail
galley foist
gallows tops
get under way
go alongside
graving dock
ground swell
harbour dues
harness cask
hug the shore
hydroglider
keelhauling
landing deck
lifeboatman
liberty ship

light vessel
loblolly-boy
loxodromics
maintopmast
maintopsail
make headway
marine store
marlinspike
mess steward
middle watch
mizzen course
merchantman
minesweeper
monkey block
motor launch
motor vessel
mystery ship
naval rating
naval vessel
orthodromic
overfreight
paddle wheel
pilot cutter
port charges
port of entry
press-of-sail
prize vessel
quarterdeck
quinquereme
racing shell
range-finder
reconnoitre
riding light
Rob-Roy canoe
sailing date
sailing ship
Samson's post
sardine boat
searchlight
seasickness
sheet anchor
shipbreaker
ship's doctor
ship's papers
sliding keel
slave trader
snatchblock
sounding rod
south-wester
spanking boom
spring a leak
standing off
station bill
steam launch

steam vessel
steerage way
stern chaser
sternsheets
storm signal
submersible
supertanker
three-decker
three-masted
three-master
thwartships
tidal waters
torpedo boat
torpedo tube
unballasted
unchartered
under canvas
under-masted
unnavigable
unnavigated
unsheltered
unsoundable
victual ship
waistcloths
waterlogged
weatherdeck
weather gage
weathermost
weather roll
weather side
weigh anchor
white ensign

12
air-sea rescue
between decks
bill of lading
breeches buoy
cabin cruiser
cable's length
canvas length
caulking iron
change course
coasting boat
coasting ship
collision mat
companionway
conning tower
counter-brace
despatch boat
displacement
double-banked
double-braced
double-manned

East Indiaman
equinoctials
ferry steamer
fishing smack
floating dock
forestaysail
futtock plate
ground tackle
hard-aweather
heavy cruiser
jack-o'-lantern
jacob's ladder
landing barge
landing craft
lateen-rigged
light cruiser
longshoreman
low water mark
magnetic mine
maiden voyage
man overboard
marine boiler
marine engine
marlinespike
measured mile
merchant ship
minesweeping
mosquito boat
motor drifter
motor trawler
naval command
navigability
orthodromics
outmanoeuvre
outward-bound
Plimsoll line
Plimsoll mark
privateering
pirate cutter
pleasure boat
police launch
pontoon crane
recommission
ride at anchor
river gunboat
sculling boat
ship chandler
shipping line
ship's husband
slack in stays
square-rigged
square-rigger
starboard bow
steam gondola

stern-wheeler
stream anchor
studding sail
survey vessel
Thames bawley
tourist class
training ship
transhipment
tramp steamer
Trinity House
troop carrier
undercurrent
unfathomable
war insurance
weather cloth
weatherboard
weatherbound
weatherglass
weatherproof
westerly wind
will-o'-the-wisp

13
affreightment
battlecruiser
Bermuda cutter
Canadian canoe
cat-o'-nine-tails
close quarters
compass signal
container ship
dead reckoning
deck passenger
double-sculler
fishing tackle
floating light
four-oared boat
grappling iron
high water mark
hovelling boat
hurricane deck
life preserver
mizzen ngging
motor lifeboat
naval dockyard
naval ordnance
navigableness
northeast wind
northerly wind
northwest wind
order of battle
paddle steamer
passenger boat
passenger ship

re-embarkation	**14**	powder magazine	cable-laying ship
revenue cutter	circumnavigate	prevailing wind	cable-repair ship
royal dockyard	coasting vessel	running rigging	circumnavigable
sailing vessel	compass bearing	schooner-rigged	command of the
ship of the line	despatch cutter	screw propeller	sea
weather report	disembarkation	seaplane tender	companion
ship's chandler	eight-oared boat	ship's carpenter	ladder
southeast wind	electric launch	swivel rowlocks	marine insurance
southerly wind	flotilla leader	topgallant mast	mariner's
southwest wind	futtock shrouds	torpedo gunboat	compass
spilling lines	hard-astarboard	Yorkshire coble	operation orders
starboard beam	letter of marque		submarine
starboard side	Lloyd's Register	**15**	chaser
steering wheel	mushroom anchor	Admiralty Office	topsail schooner
trading vessel	naval architect	aircraft carrier	victualling yard

Vehicles

2	Lada	moped	hearse	**7**	pedicab
BR	limo	motor	herdic	autobus	pedrail
MG	LNER	plane	hot rod	autocar	Peugeot
RV	loco	pulka	Jaguar	balloon	phaeton
VW	luge	ratha	jalopy	bicycle	Porsche
	mini	sedan	jampan	britzka	post bus
3	pram	sulky	jigger	caboose	pullman
BMW	skis	tonga	jitney	cacolet	railbus
bus	sled	train	Lancia	caravan	railcar
cab	tank	trike	landau	caravel	scooter
car	taxi	truck	limber	cariole	sidecar
dan	tram	wagon	litter	caroche	taxicab
fly	trap		Morris	chariot	tilbury
gig	tube	**6**	Nissan	chopper	tipcart
GWR	van	banger	oxcart	crawler	tonneau
HGV	wain	barrow	pochay	Daimler	tractor
JCB	whim	beetle	pulkha	dogcart	trailer
jet		berlin	random	droshky	tramcar
LMS	**5**	bowser	saloon	Ferrier	trishaw
rig	artic	calash	skibob	fourgon	Triumph
	bandy	camion	Skidoo	gritter	trolley
4	bogey	camper	sledge	growler	trundle
Audi	bogie	chaise	sleigh	gyrocar	tumbrel
auto	brake	dennet	Snocat	hackery	tumbril
biga	brett	digger	spider	hackney	turnout
bike	buggy	dodgem	surrey	hardtop	vis-à-vis
cart	caddy	doolie	tandem	haywain	voiture
drag	chair	drosky	tender	helibus	
dray	coach	engine	tourer	kibitka	**8**
duck	coupe	estate	Toyota	mail car	barouche
ekka	crate	fiacre	troika	mail-van	bendibus
Fiat	cycle	gharry	waggon	minibus	brakevan
Ford	dilly	gingle	weasel	minicab	britzska
heap	float	go-cart	wheels	minicar	brougham
jeep	lorry	hansom		omnibus	cablecar

Cadillac
Cape cart
carriage
carriole
carryall
carrycot
clarence
curricle
cycle car
dragster
dustcart
equipage
fastback
fly coach
golfcart
goods van
handcart
ice yacht
jetliner
jump seat
mail cart
milk cart
motorbus
motorcar
old crock
pushcart
quad bike
quadriga
rally car
rickshaw
roadster
rockaway
runabout
scout car
sociable
stanhope
steam car
stock car
tarantas
toboggan
tricycle
unicycle
Vauxhall
victoria
wagon-lit

9
ambulance
amphibian
applecart

automatic
baby buggy
bandwagon
bath chair
boat train
bobsleigh
box wagon
bubble car
buckboard
bulldozer
bumper car
cabriolet
cattle car
charabanc
diligence
dining car
dodgem car
dormobile
dune buggy
estate car
Gladstone
guard's van
half-track
hansom cab
hatchback
ice skates
Land Rover
landaulet
limousine
low-loader
mail coach
mail train
milk float
milk train
monocycle
motorbike
motorcade
moving van
muletrain
palanquin
post chaise
prison van
racing car
rocket car
saloon car
sand yacht
scrambler
skimobile
sports car
streetcar

stretcher
tarantass
tin lizzie
wagonette
water cart

10
automobile
beach buggy
Black Maria
boneshaker
chapel cart
convertible
conveyance
donkey cart
fire engine
four-by-four
four-in-hand
glass coach
goods train
goods truck
hackney cab
hand barrow
hobbyhorse
hovercraft
invalid cab
jinricksha
juggernaut
knockabout
locomotive
mobile home
motor lorry
motorcoach
motorcycle
paddy wagon
pony engine
post-chaise
pullman car
Range Rover
roadroller
Rolls Royce
sedan chair
smoking car
snowmobile
snowplough
spacecraft
spring cart
stagecoach
state coach
swamp buggy

timwhiskey
tip-up lorry
touring car
tramway car
trolley bus
trolley car
velocipede
voiturette
waggonette
war chariot
wheelchair

11
armoured car
brewer's dray
bullock cart
caterpillar
delivery van
fire balloon
four-wheeler
goods waggon
gun-carriage
horse litter
jaunting car
landaulette
magic carpet
mail phaeton
Morris Minor
quadricycle
sleeping car
state landau
steam engine
steamroller
stretch limo
three-in-hand
transporter
trolleybus
waggon train
wheelbarrow

12
autorickshaw
baby carriage
breakdown van
coach-and-four
coach-and-pair
express train
furniture van
hackney coach
invalid chair

luggage train
motor scooter
pantechnicon
perambulator
railway train
three-wheeler
watering cart

13
ambulance
   cart
electric truck
forklift truck
governess cart
mourning
   coach
penny farthing
people carrier
spider phaeton
state carriage
steam carriage
wheel carriage

14
ambulance
   wagon
bathing
   machine
Conestoga
   wagon
luggage trailer
off-road
   vehicle
traction engine

15 *and over*
hackney
   carriage (15)
invalid
   carriage (15)
prairie
   schooner
   (15)
railway
   carriage (15)
recreational
   vehicle (19)

WARFARE

Armour and Weapons

3	bilbo	couter	**7**	oil bomb	corselet
ABM	birch	cudgel	arblast	panoply	crossbow
arm	blade	cuisse	assegal	Patriot	culettes
axe	bolas	dagger	ataghan	Polaris	damaskin
bow	CS gas	device	bar-shot	poleaxe	dynamite
dag	fusée	dragon	basinet	poniard	eel spear
gas	fusil	dumdum	bayonet	quarrel	elf arrow
gun	grape	espada	bazooka	rabinet	enforcer
pig	H-bomb	Exocet	besagew	roundel	falchion
ram	hobit	gorget	big guns	sabaton	falconet
Uzi	jerid	greave	brasset	shotgun	field gun
wad	knife	hanger	breaths	side-arm	firearms
	kukri	helmet	Bren gun	sjambok	fireball
4	lance	homing	buckler	Skybolt	firebomb
ammo	lasso	jezail	calibre	Sten gun	firelock
arms	lathi	lariat	carbine	tear gas	fireship
ball	Luger	lassoo	car bomb	torpedo	gadlings
bill	Maxim	lorica	chamber	Trident	garrotte
bolt	panga	mailed	chopper	trigger	gas shell
bomb	pouch	Mauser	cordite	vamplet	gauntlet
butt	rifle	mortar	couteau	ventail	gavelock
cane	sabre	musket	cuirass	warhead	gisarme
club	salvo	muzzle	curtana	wind gun	gunsight
Colt	shaft	napalm	curtein		half-pike
cosh	shell	Panzer	cutlass	**8**	hand-pike
dart	sight	pellet	djerrid	amusette	haquebut
dirk	skull	petard	dualine	arbalest	hardware
épée	sling	pistol	dudgeon	armalite	heavy gun
flak	spear	poleyn	elf-bolt	arquebus	howitzer
foil	staff	pom-pom	espadon	atom bomb	jazerant
gaff	stave	powder	firearm	attaghan	land mine
goad	stick	primer	fire-pot	balister	launcher
helm	sword	quiver	gas mask	ballista	Lewis gun
ICBM	targe	ramrod	greaves	bascinet	magazine
jack	tawse	rapier	grenade	basilisk	Maxim gun
kris	visor	ray gun	gunshot	birdbolt	naval gun
mace		recoil	halberd	blowpipe	ordnance
mail	**6**	Semtex	handgun	bludgeon	palstaff
mine	ack-ack	shield	harpoon	broad-axe	paravane
pike	airgun	sights	hatchet	Browning	partisan
Scud	armlet	stylet	holster	burganet	pauldron
shot	armour	swivel	javelin	burgonet	petronel
slug	barrel	target	longbow	buzz bomb	phosgene
tank	basnet	tasset	lyddite	canister	pipe bomb
	bodkin	umbril	machete	carabine	pistolet
5	bonnet	weapon	megaton	case shot	plastron
A-bomb	buffer	Webley	missile	catapult	pyroxyle
aegis	bullet	zipgun	murrion	chausses	revolver
arrow	cannon		nuclear	claymore	ricochet

ringmail
scabbard
scimitar
scorpion
shrapnel
siege gun
skean-dhu
spadroon
spontoon
steam gun
stiletto
time fuse
tomahawk
Tommy gun
truncheon
umbrière
vambrace
vamplate
weaponry
whiz-bang

9

ack-ack gun
arquebuse
arrowhead
artillery
automatic
aventaile
backpiece
ballistic
bastinado
battleaxe
Big Bertha
blackjack
Blue Water
boar spear
Bofors gun
bomb chest
bombshell
boomerang
booby trap
Brown Bess
cannonade
cartouche
cartridge
chain mail
defoliant
demi-lance
Derringer
deterrent
detonator
doodlebug
equalizer
fish spear

flintlock
garde-bras
gelignite
grapeshot
guncotton
gunpowder
hand-staff
headpiece
heelpiece
lance rest
launch pad
long-range
matchlock
Mills bomb
Minuteman
munitions
musketoon
needle gun
poison gas
pourpoint
powder keg
quaker gun
saltpetre
slingshot
small arms
small bore
smoke bomb
spring gun
starshell
stinkbomb
sword cane
truncheon
turret gun
volley gun
ward staff
xyloidine
zumbooruk

10

ammunition
arcubalist
assault gun
atomic bomb
battery gun
blind shell
Blue Streak
body armour
bowie knife
brigandine
broad arrow
broadsword
burrel shot
cannonball
cannon shot

cataphract
coat of mail
demi-cannon
field-piece
flick knife
flying bomb
Gatling gun
grainstaff
harquebuse
knobkerrie
lambrequin
Lee-Enfield
letter bomb
limpet mine
machine gun
Minie rifle
mustard gas
napalm bomb
nightstick
parcel bomb
petrol bomb
powder horn
projectile
pyroxyline
rocket ball
shillelagh
short-range
Sidewinder
six-shooter
sticky bomb
sword stick
touchpaper
Winchester

11

Agent Orange
anti-tank gun
armoured car
basket sword
blockbuster
blunderbuss
bow and arrow
breastplate
chlorine gas
cluster bomb
contact mine
depth charge
elephant gun
gun carriage
hair trigger
hand grenade
hawk missile
kalashnikov
Lochaber axe

mine thrower
morning star
mountain gun
neutron bomb
powder chest
powder flask
safety catch
scale armour
Scud missile
smart weapon
Thompson gun
water cannon

12

acoustic mine
Armstrong gun
battering ram
boarding pike
breech loader
cartridge box
cavalry sword
conventional
dumdum bullet
flame-thrower
fowling piece
hydrogen bomb
Lancaster gun
landing craft
launching pad
magnetic mine
Mills grenade
mitrailleuse
muzzle loader
poisoned dart
quarterstaff
rocket mortar
suit of armour
tracer bullet
trench mortar
wheel-lock dag

13

ball cartridge
brass knuckles
cartridge case
cruise missile
guided missile
high-explosive
knuckleduster
magazine rifle
mortar carbine
percussion cap
poisoned arrow
scalping knife

semi-automatic
shrapnel shell
submachine gun
submarine mine
thermonuclear

14
armour-piercing
blank cartridge
duelling pistol
incendiary bomb
nitroglycerine
nuclear weapons
rocket launcher

sawn-off shotgun
smallbore rifle

15 *and over*
air-to-air missile (15)
anti-aircraft-gun (15)
antipersonnel mine (17)
ballistic missile (16)
bolt action rifle (15)
bulletproof vest (15)
double-barrelled (15)
double-edged sword (16)
fragmentation bomb (17)
heat-seeking missile (18)

intercontinental ballistic
  missile (32)
light machine gun (15)
missile launcher (15)
Molotov cocktail (15)
plastic explosive (16)
sawed-off shotgun (15)
single-barrelled (15)
surface-to-air missile
  (19)
surface-to-surface
  missile (23)
thermonuclear weapon
  (19)

Battles and Sieges

4
Alma (the)
Ebro (the)
Jena
Loos
Mons
Nile (the)
Zama

5
Alamo (the)
Boyne (the)
Bulge (the)
Crécy
Issus
Liège
Malta
Marne (the)
Paris (siege
  of)
Rhine (the)
Sedan
Somme (the)
Ypres

6
Actium
Arbela
Arnhem
Atbara (the)
Cannae
Lutzen
Midway
Naseby
Pinkie
Sadowa

Shiloh
Tobruk
Verdun
Wagram

7
Alamein
Antwerp
Britain
Cambrai
Colenso
Corunna
Dresden
Flodden
Iwo Jima
Jutland
Leipzig
Lemberg
Lepanto
Marengo
Megiddo
Orléans (siege
  of)
Plassey
St Lucia
Salamis

8
Antietam
Ardennes
Atlantic (the)
Blenheim
Culloden
Edgehill
Fontenoy
Hastings

Mafeking (siege
  of)
Marathon
Omdurman
Philippi
Poitiers
Saratoga
Spion Kop
Stirling
Waterloo

9
Agincourt
Balaclava
Bay of Pigs (the)
Chaeronea
El Alamein
Gallipoli
Kimberley (siege
  of)
Ladysmith (siege
  of)
Leyte Gulf
Pharsalus
Ramillies
Sedgemoor
Solferino
Stormberg
Trafalgar
Vicksburg

10
Adrianople
Austerlitz
Brandywine
Bunker Hill

Camperdown
Cold Harbor
Copenhagen
Gettysburg
Goose Green
Gravelotte
Imjin River
Malplaquet
Paardeburg
River Plate (the)
Sevastopol (siege
  of)
Stalingrad
Tannenberg
Tel-el-Kebir
Wilderness

11
Bannockburn
Guadalcanal
Halidon Hill
Hohenlinden
Marston Moor
Pearl Harbor
Port Stanley
Prestonpans
Thermopylae
Wounded Knee

12 *and over*
Bloemfontein (12)
Bosworth Field (13)
Fredericksburg (14)
Little Bighorn (12)
Magersfontein (13)
Passchendaele (13)

Military and Warfare Terminology

2	kepi	array	range	bunker	legion	stripe
RN	kill	baton	ranks	castle	maquis	stroke
	levy	beret	rebel	charge	marker	subdue
3	line	beset	recce	cohort	mining	supply
arm	loot	blast	relay	colour	mobile	target
DMZ	mess	blitz	repel	column	muster	tattoo
dud	mine	booty	rifle	combat	mutiny	thrust
foe	moat	busby	round	convoy	occupy	treaty
gas	NATO	cadre	route	cordon	oppose	trench
gun	navy	cells	sally	curfew	orders	trophy
HMS	park	clean	salvo	debris	outfit	turret
jam	PIAT	corps	scale	decamp	parade	unhurt
kit	plan	cover	seize	defeat	parley	vallum
man	post	craft	shako	defect	parole	valour
map	push	decoy	shell	defend	patrol	victor
MIA	raid	demob	shift	deploy	permit	volley
RAF	rake	depot	shock	desert	pocket	walled
sap	ramp	ditch	shoot	detach	pursue	war cry
USA	rank	draft	siege	detail	puttee	
USN	rape	dress	smart	disarm	raider	**7**
USS	raze	drill	snipe	dog tag	ransom	advance
van	rear	enemy	sonar	donjon	rapine	airdrop
war	rout	enrol	sonic	dugout	rappel	airlift
	ruse	equip	squad	embark	ration	air raid
4	sack	feint	staff	embody	ravage	alcazar
ally	shot	field	stand	engage	rebuff	archery
arms	sink	fight	storm	Enigma	recoil	armoury
army	slay	flank	strap	enlist	redcap	arsenal
AWOL	spot	flare	track	enmity	relais	assault
band	spur	fleet	troop	ensign	relief	baldric
bang	take	foray	truce	escape	report	baggage
base	tank	front	wound	escarp	resist	barrack
bear	taps	group		escort	retake	barrage
belt	tent	guard	**6**	firing	retire	bastion
berm	tilt	guide	ack-ack	flight	review	battery
camp	trap	harry	action	forces	riddle	besiege
D-day	unit	Jerry	allies	forted	rioter	bivouac
draw	USAF	jihad	all out	gabion	roster	body bag
duck	wage	khaki	ambush	glacis	saddle	bombard
duel	ward	leave	animus	guards	salute	bomb bay
duty	wing	lines	armada	guidon	sconce	bombing
fife	yomp	march	armour	harass	sensor	bomblet
file	zero	medal	assail	hawhaw	signal	brigade
fire	zone	melee	at ease	helmet	sign up	bulwark
flag		mufti	attack	impact	sniper	canteen
flak	**5**	onset	backup	impale	sortie	carrier
foot	abort	parry	bailey	inroad	spoils	cashier
fort	agent	peace	banner	invade	square	cavalry
fray	alert	power	battle	invest	stores	charger
halt	annex	prime	billet	inwall	strafe	chevron
host	armed	radar	blow up	killed	strife	citadel
jeep	armor	rally	breech	kitbag	strike	cold war

colours	jump jet	standby	civil war	lay waste
command	Kremlin	subvert	collapse	lodgment
company	landing	support	conflict	loophole
conchie	lookout	tactics	conquest	Mameluke
conquer	looting	trailer	corvette	mantelet
counter	lunette	traitor	decimate	marching
courage	maniple	treason	decisive	mark time
cruiser	mantlet	triumph	defector	martello
crusade	march on	unarmed	defender	massacre
curtain	Marines	uniform	demilune	militant
debouch	martial	valiant	despatch	military
defence	megaton	vanfoss	detonate	mobilize
defiant	militia	victory	disarray	movement
degrade	missing	wage war	dispatch	Mulberry
destroy	mission	ward off	dive-bomb	musketry
détente	neutral	warfare	division	mutineer
disband	nuclear	war game	dogfight	mutinous
dismiss	on guard	warlike	drumfire	near miss
dungeon	outpost	warlord	duelling	on parade
echelon	outwork	warpath	earth bag	open fire
envelop	overrun	war song	embattle	opponent
epaulet	paladin	warworn	embodied	ordnance
evacuee	parados	windage	enceinte	outflank
fallout	parapet	wounded	enfilade	outguard
fanfare	pass out		entrench	overcome
fatigue	patriot	**8**	escalate	overkill
fend off	pennant	accoutre	evacuate	pacifist
fighter	phalanx	activate	eyes left	palisade
flanker	pillbox	advanced	fencible	paradrop
fortify	platoon	airborne	field day	parallel
fortlet	postern	aircraft	fighting	partisan
forward	priming	air force	flagpole	password
foxhole	protect	alliance	flagpost	pavilion
frigate	pursuit	armament	flotilla	pay corps
gallery	quarter	armorial	fortress	prisoner
gas mask	rampage	armoured	furlough	quarters
germ war	rampart	arms race	garrison	quisling
go to war	rations	Army List	gauntlet	radio fix
guérite	ravages	attacker	gonfalon	railhead
gunboat	ravelin	baldrick	guerilla	ramparts
gunfire	Red Army	barbette	hang fire	rear line
gunnery	redoubt	barbican	hill fort	rearward
gunroom	refugee	barracks	hold fire	re-embark
gunship	regular	bartizan	infantry	regiment
gunshot	repulse	bawdrick	informer	reprisal
harness	reserve	bearskin	invasion	reveille
Harrier	retreat	blockade	janizary	ricochet
holster	reverse	bomb site	jingoism	rifle pit
holy war	salient	buttress	kamikaze	roll call
hostage	sandbag	campaign	knapsack	sabotage
hostile	section	casemate	Land Army	saboteur
invader	service	cenotaph	Landwehr	saluting
jamming	sinking	casualty	last post	scramble
jankers	sniping	chivalry	lay siege	security

sentry-go	alarm post	embattled	overpower	Wehrmacht
services (the)	armistice	encompass	overthrow	white flag
shabrack	army corps	encounter	overwhelm	
shelling	artillery	enemy camp	packdrill	**10**
shooting	assailant	enemy fire	parachute	active duty
shot hole	atomic war	enrolment	patriotic	active list
skirmish	attention	epaulette	phoney war	Air Command
soldiery	attrition	equipment	pressgang	air defence
squadron	ballistic	espionage	projector	amphibious
stalward	banderole	eyes front	protector	annexation
stampede	bandolier	eyes right	rearguard	annihilate
standard	banquette	field army	rebellion	antagonism
star fort	barricade	firepower	reconquer	Armageddon
stave off	battalion	flagstaff	red ensign	armed truce
stockade	battle cry	flash burn	reinforce	attackable
stoppage	beachhead	forage cap	rencontre	ballistics
storming	beleaguer	fortalice	revetment	barbed wire
straddle	bellicose	front line	Royal Navy	battle flag
strafing	bloodshed	fusillade	safe haven	battle hymn
strategy	body count	gallantry	safe house	battle line
strength	bombed-out	gas attack	sally port	battlement
struggle	bombproof	gladiator	sea battle	battleship
supplies	bombs	guardroom	semaphore	blitzkrieg
support	away	guerrilla	sentry box	blockhouse
surprise	bombshell	gun battle	shellfire	bombing run
surround	bombsight	gun turret	slaughter	breastwork
sword arm	bomb	haversack	slope arms	bridgehead
tactical	squad	heavy fire	slow march	bugle corps
total war	bugle call	home front	stack arms	call to arms
training	camouflet	Home Guard	stand fast	camel corps
transfer	cannonade	hostility	stand fire	camouflage
traverse	captaincy	incursion	strategic	campaigner
trenches	cashiered	insurgent	submarine	cantonment
turbojet	cavalcade	invalided	surrender	capitulate
turncoat	ceasefire	irregular	sword knot	chauvinism
unallied	challenge	janissary	task force	checkpoint
unharmed	chevalier	land force	terrorism	combat zone
uprising	cold steel	Landsturm	terrorist	commandeer
vanguard	colonelcy	legionary	trainband	commisslon
vanquish	combatant	lifeguard	transport	decampment
vigilant	combative	logistics	treachery	declare war
war crime	conqueror	loopholed	tricolour	defendable
war dance	conscript	Luftwaffe	troopship	defensible
war grave	crack shot	manoeuvre	under fire	demobilize
warhorse	crossfire	march-past	unguarded	deployment
weaponry	crow's foot	megadeath	uniformed	despatches
yeomanry	defection	mercenary	uninjured	detachment
world war	defensive	militancy	unopposed	detonation
zero hour	desertion	minefield	unscathed	direct fire
	destroyer	mujahedin	unsheathe	dispatches
9	devastate	objective	vigilance	dive-bomber
aggressor	discharge	offensive	war effort	divisional
air attack	disengage	onslaught	War Office	dragonnade
air strike	earthwork	operation	watchword	drawbridge

Warfare

duty roster
embankment
encampment
engagement
engarrison
enlistment
entrenched
epauletted
escalation
evacuation
expedition
firing line
flying camp
Foot Guards
garrisoned
glasshouse
ground fire
guardhouse
hand-to-hand
heliograh
inspection
insurgency
investment
invincible
jingoistic
lay siege to
Life Guards
light horse
limited war
line of fire
manoeuvres
martial law
militiaman
militarism
muster book
muster roll
need to know
nerve agent
neutralize
night watch
no man's land
nuclear war
occupation
operations
over the top
patriotism
patrolling
point blank
portcullis
prison camp
projectile
propaganda
protection
provision

quick march
raking fire
reconquest
recruiting
regimental
rencounter
rendezvous
resistance
revolution
rifle corps
rifle range
route march
rules of war
sabretache
sentry duty
sentry post
shellproof
shell shock
siege train
signal fire
signalling
slit trench
soldiering
stand guard
state of war
stronghold
subjection
subsection
submission
subversion
superpower
surrounded
sword fight
take up arms
terreplein
trajectory
trench foot
undefended
under siege
unsheathed
victorious
vulnerable
war council
war machine
watchtower

11
area bombing
armed combat
armed forces
at the double
barrack room
battledress
battlefield

battlegroup
battle order
battle royal
besiegement
bombardment
bulletproof
castellated
change sides
collaborate
conquerable
countermine
defenceless
declaration
devastation
disarmament
disbandment
dive-bombing
draft dodger
dress parade
ejector seat
embarkation
emplacement
envelopment
fatigue duty
fifth column
firing party
firing squad
flying corps
flying party
forced march
friend or foe
germ warfare
gun carriage
Horse Guards
hostilities
impregnable
indefensive
machicolate
Maginot line
Marine Corps
minesweeper
peacekeeper
peace treaty
platoon fire
postern gate
present arms
put to flight
rangefinder
rank and file
reconnoitre
recruitment
regular army
requisition
running fire

safe-conduct
searchlight
shock troops
shoot to kill
siege warfare
smokescreen
stand at ease
state of siege
stray bullet
supply depot
take by storm
thin red line
unconquered
underground
unprotected
war criminal
war memorial
white ensign

12
advance guard
annihilation
anti-aircraft
armour-plated
Bailey bridge
battleground
battlemented
beat a retreat
bomb disposal
bush fighting
cannon fodder
chauvinistic
capitulation
civil defence
collaborator
commissariat
commissioned
conscription
council of war
countermarch
counterscarp
court-martial
covering fire
decommission
draft dodging
ejection seat
fatigue party
field kitchen
flying column
forward march
friendly fire
garrison town
go over the top
ground troops

guerrilla war
headquarters
hollow square
indefensible
intelligence
invulnerable
landing craft
landing party
Light Brigade
light cavalry
line of battle
machicolated
march against
medical corps
militaristic
mine detector
mobilization
non-combatant
outmanoeuvre
paramilitary
peacekeeping
pioneer corps
raiding party
religious war
retrenchment
rocket attack
Royal Marines
Royal Signals
shell-shocked
shock tactics
shoulder arms
shoulder belt
siege warfare
signal rocket
surveillance
theatre of war
unvanquished
white feather
who goes there

13
accoutrements
advanced guard
armed services
barrack square
battle cruiser

battle fatigue
carpet bombing
carrier pigeon
circumvallate
collaboration
combat fatigue
counterattack
counterstroke
expeditionary
fatigue parade
field of battle
fighting force
flying colours
fortification
guard of honour
invincibility
King's shilling
light infantry
machicolation
martello tower
mounted police
mushroom
  cloud
order of battle
ordnance depot
pitched battle
point of impact
pontoon bridge
rallying point
re-embarkation
regular troops
reinforcement
Royal Air Force
running battle
shoulder strap
special forces
splinterproof
storming parry
strategically
suicide bomber
swordsmanship
trench warfare
unarmed
  combat
unconquerable
Victoria Cross

war department

14
air raid shelter
ammunition dump
auxiliary force
barrage balloon
blockade runner
demobilization
fifth columnist
fortifications
general reserve
mechanized army
military police
nuclear warfare
pincer movement
Pyrrhic victory
reconnaissance
reinforcements
Royal Artillery
Royal Engineers
Royal Tank Corps
security forces
standing orders
supreme command
volunteer force
walking wounded
war of attrition
winter quarters

15
aircraft carrier
casualty station
clearing station
discharge papers
displaced person
dressing station
ethnic cleansing
guerilla warfare
invulnerability
married quarters
military academy
military college
military funeral
military honours
mounted infantry

non-commissioned
observation post
point-blank range

16
collateral damage
counteroffensive
passing-out parade
peacekeeping force
precision bombing
preemptive attack
preemptive strike
war establishment

17 *and over*
biological warfare
  (17)
concentration camp
  (17)
conscientious
  objector (21)
demilitarized zone
  (17)
expeditionary force
  (18)
helicopter gunship
  (17)
post-traumatic
  stress disorder
  (27)
recruiting sergeant
  (18)
rules of engagement
  (17)
soldier of fortune
  (16)
Special Air Service
  (17)
Special Boat Service
  (18)
special operations
  (17)
stand to attention
  (16)

Military Ranks and Personnel

AIR FORCE

3
ace

4
WAAF

5
major (US)
pilot

6
airman (US)
fitter
rigger

7
aviator
captain (US)
colonel (US)
general (US)

8
corporal
mechanic
observer
sergeant

9
air gunner
bomb aimer
navigator

10
air marshal
bombardier
nose gunner
rear gunner
tail gunner
technician

11
aircraftman
belly gunner

bomber pilot

12
air commodore
aircraftsman
fighter pilot
group captain
major general (US)
pilot officer

13
aircraftwoman
flying officer
staff sergeant (US)
wing commander

14
aircraftswoman
air vice-marshal
master sergeant (US)
squadron leader

warrant officer

15
air chief marshal
first lieutenant (US)

16 *and over*
brigadier general (16) (US)
flight lieutenant (16)
general of the air force (20) (US)
lieutenant colonel (17) (US)
lieutenant general (17) (US)
marshal of the Royal Air Force (25)
second lieutenant (16) (US)
technical sergeant (17) (US)

ARMY AND MARINES

2
CO
GI

3
ADC
CSM
NCO
RSM
vet

4
cook
para
peon

5
Anzac
cadet
major
miner
rebel
scout
sepoy

Tommy
uhlan

6
archer
batman
bomber
bowman
bugler
cornet
driver
ensign
Ghurka
gunner
hussar
lancer
marine
ranger
ranker
rookie
sapper
sentry
troops
yeoman

Zouave

7
captain
colonel
Chindit
Cossack
draftee
dragoon
drummer
general
hoplite
janizar
jemadar
marshal
officer
orderly
pikeman
pioneer
private
recruit
redcoat
regular
reserve

samurai
soldier
subadar
trooper
vedette
veteran
warrior

8
adjutant
armourer
bandsman
cavalier
chaplain
commando
corporal
crusader
deserter
doughboy
engineer
fencible
fugelman
fusilier
havildar

marksman
messmate
muleteer
rifleman
risaldar
sentinel
sergeant
serjeant
spearman

9
beefeater
berserker
brigadier
cannoneer
centurion
combatant
commander
conductor
conscript
desert rat
drum major
estafette
field rank

grenadier
guardsman
lifeguard
musketeer
paymaster
pipe major
signaller
signalman
subaltern
tactician
trumpeter
volunteer

10
aide-de-camp
bandmaster
bombardier
carabineer
cavalryman
commandant
cuirassier
drummer boy
halberdier
instructor

lansquenet
lieutenant
militiaman
other ranks
paratroops
serviceman
strategist

11
auxiliaries
bashi-bazook
bersaglieri
condottiere
crack troops
crossbowman
enlisted man
foot soldier
infantryman
legionnaire
Landsknecht
parachutist
paratrooper
rangefinder

Territorial
Tommy Atkins

12
armour bearer
artilleryman
brigade major
ensign bearer
field marshal
field officer
horse soldier
major general
master gunner
officer cadet
staff officer
storm trooper
trumpet major

13
army commander
barrack master
dispatch rider
drill sergeant

lance corporal
lifeguardsman
machine gunner
prisoner of war
quartermaster
sergeant major
staff corporal
staff sergeant

14
citizen soldier
colonel-in-chief
colour sergeant
liaison officer
master sergeant
medical officer
orderly officer
provost marshal
second corporal
signals officer
standard
  bearer
warrant officer

15
adjutant-general
corporal-of-horse
first lieutenant (US)
gentleman-at-arms
gunnery sergeant (US)
honorary colonel
household troops
lance bombardier
orderly corporal
orderly sergeant
ordnance officer
provost sergeant

16
brigadier general
general of the army
  (US)
second lieutenant

17
lieutenant colonel
lieutenant general

NAVY

4
cook
Easy
mate
Wren

5
bosun
cadet
diver

6
cooper
ensign
lascar
marine
master
purser
rating
reefer
seaman
stoker
yeoman

7
admiral

armorer
captain
deckboy
fireman
jack tar
lookout
matelot
messman
recruit
shipman
skipper
steward
surgeon

8
armourer
cabin boy
chaplain
coxswain
engineer
flag rank
helmsman
leadsman
messmate
motorman
ship's boy

winchman

9
artificer
boatswain
captain RN
commander
commodore
cook's mate
donkeyman
engineman
navigator
paymaster
powder boy
sailmaker
ship's cook
signalman
tugmaster

10
able
  seaman
apprentice
coastguard
gun captain
instructor

lieutenant
midshipman
shipmaster
ship's baker
shipwright
torpedoman
wardmaster

11
chief stoker
electrician
extra master
flag captain
flag officer
gunner's mate
leading wren
master's mate
port admiral
port officer
post captain
rear admiral
vice admiral
watchkeeper

12
cabin steward

chief officer
chief skipper
chief steward
first officer
fleet admiral
  (US)
master-at-arms
master gunner
petty officer
powder monkey
schoolmaster
second master
senior purser
ship's surgeon
supply rating
telegraphist
third officer

13
armourer's
  mate
captain's clerk
chief armourer
chief engineer
fourth officer
harbourmaster

leading seaman
leading stoker
radio operator
sailing master
seaman recruit (US)
second officer
signal officer
sub-lieutenant
third engineer
torpedo gunner

14
boatswain's mate
flag-lieutenant
fourth engineer
leading steward
ordinary seaman
rating observer
second engineer
ship's carpenter
unknown soldier

warrant officer

15 *and over*
admiral of the fleet (17)
boarding officer (15)
chief petty officer (17)
first lieutenant (15)
lieutenant-commander (19)
seaman apprentice (16) (US)

Wars and Revolutions

7
Boer War
Gulf War

8
Crusades

9
Korean War
Opium Wars
Punic Wars
Six Day War
Trojan War

10
Balkan Wars

Crimean War
Gallic Wars
Mexican War
Vietnam War

11
Iran-Iraq War

12 *and over*
American Civil War (16)
American Revolution (18)
American War of Independence
  (25)
Arab-Israeli Wars (15)
Boxer Rebellion (14)
English Civil War (13)

Falklands War (12)
First World War (13)
French Revolution (16)
Hundred Years' War (15)
Indian Uprising (14)
Irish Civil War (13)
Mexican Revolution (17)
Napoleonic Wars (14)
Peninsular War (13)
Russian Revolution (17)
Second World War (14)
Spanish Civil War (15)
Thirty Years' War (14)
War of the Pacific (15)
Wars of the Roses (14)
Yom Kippur War (12)

MISCELLANEOUS

Arabic Alphabet

2	ra	**3**	jim	mim	sin	**4**	**5**
ba	ta	ayn	kaf	nun	tha	alif	ghayn
fa	ya	dad	kha	qaf	waw	dhai	
ha	za	dai	lam	sad	zay	shin	

Collective Terms

3
gam (of whales)
mob (of kangaroos)
nye (of pheasants)
pod (of whales or peas)
rag (of colts)
run (of poultry)
set (of various articles)

4
army (of frogs)
bale (of turtles)
bevy (of larks, quails, swans)
bury (of rabbits)
cast (of hawks)
cete (of badgers)
dole (of doves)
dout (of wild cats)
down (of hares)
dule (of doves)
erst (of bees)
fall (of woodcock)
gang (of elk)
herd (of buffalo, cattle, cranes, deer, donkeys, elephants, giraffes, goats, horses, oxen, pigs)
hive (of bees)
host (of angels, sparrows)
husk (of hares)
knob (of pochards, teal, toads, widgeon)
knot (of toads)
leap (of leopards)
lepe (of leopards)
mute (of hounds)
nest (of mice, rabbits, wasps)
nide (of pheasants)

pace (of asses)
pack (of dogs, grouse, hounds, wolves)
peal (of bells)
rope (of onions, pearls)
rout (of wolves)
rush (of pochards)
safe (of ducks)
sawt (of lions)
sord (of mallards, wild fowl)
span (of mules)
stud (of mares)
sute (of mallards, wild fowl)
trip (of goats)
turn (of turtles)
walk (of snipe)
wing (of plovers)
wisp (of snipe)
yoke (of oxen)
zeal (of zebras)

5
batch (of bread and various)
bench (of bishops, magistrates)
blast (of hunters)
bloat (of hippopotami)
blush (of boys)
brace (of ducks, partridges, etc.)
brood (of hens)
bunch (of flowers, grapes, teal, widgeon)
caste (of bread)
charm (of goldfinches)
cloud (of gnats)
covey (of partridges)
crash (of rhinos)

doylt (of tame swine)
drift (of swine)
drove (of cattle)
fleet (of cars, ships)
flock (of geese, pigeons, sheep)
flush (of mallards)
grist (of bees)
leash (of bucks, hounds)
plump (of wild fowl)
posse (of police)
pride (of lions)
sedge (of bitterns, herons)
shoal (of fish)
siege (of herons)
skein (of geese)
skulk (of foxes)
sloth (of bears)
smack (of jellyfish)
squad (of beaters, soldiers)
stalk (of foresters)
swarm (of bees and other insects)
tribe (of goats)
troop (of boy scouts, Brownies, cavalry, kangaroos, lions, monkeys)
watch (of nightingales)
wedge (of swans)

6
ambush (of tigers)
barren (of mules)
budget (of papers)
bundle (of asparagus, firewood, and various)
clutch (of eggs, hens)

colony (of ants, gulls, rats)
covert (of coots)
desert (of lapwings)
family (of otters)
flight (of aeroplanes, doves, dunlins, pigeons)
gaggle (of geese)
galaxy (of beauties)
harras (of horses)
kennel (of dogs)
kindle (of kittens)
labour (of moles)
litter (of cubs, kittens, pigs, pups)
melody (of harpers)
murder (of crows)
muster (of peacocks, soldiers)
parade (of elephants)
parcel (of penguins)
rafter (of turkeys)
school (of dolphin, porpoises, whales)
sleuth (of bears)
spring (of teal)
string (of pearls, racehorses)

troupe (of actors, dancers, minstrels)
warren (of rabbits)

7
battery (of guns)
bouquet (of flowers)
clamour (of rooks)
clouder, clowder (of cats)
cluster (of grapes, stars)
company (of actors, capitalists, widgeon)
descent (of woodpeckers)
dopping (of sheldrakes)
draught (of butlers)
fluther (of jellyfish)
rookery (of rooks)
sounder (of pigs)

8
building (of rooks)
busyness (of ferrets)
paddling (of ducks)
richesse (of martens)
singular (of boars)

9
badelynge (of ducks)
cowardice (of curs)
morbidity (of majors)
mustering (of storks)
obstinacy (of buffalos)
sachemdom (North American Indians)
shrubbery (of shrubs)
subtiltie (of sergeants)
syndicate (of capitalists)
tittering (of magpies)

10
chattering (of choughs)
exaltation (of larks)
observance (of hermits)
parliament (of owls)
shrewdness (of apes)
simplicity (of subalterns)
unkindness (of ravens)

11 *and over*
congregation (of birds, worshippers) (12)
murmuration (of starlings) (11)
pandemonium (of parrots) (11)

Colours

3	iris	black	ochre	burnet	pastel	biscuit
aal	jade	brown	olive	castor	pearly	caldron
aba	lake	camel	ombre	cerise	pirned	caramel
dun	lark	capri	peach	cherry	purple	carmine
jet	navy	cocoa	prune	chroma	rachel	chamois
red	noir	coral	rouge	citron	raisin	corbeau
tan	onyx	cream	sepia	claret	reseda	crimson
	opad	cymar	shade	copper	russet	emerald
4	pied	delft	taupe	dorado	salmon	filbert
bleu	pink	flesh	topaz	flaxen	shrimp	fuchsia
blue	plum	green	umber	garnet	silver	heather
bois	puce	hazel	white	golden	titian	ingénue
bure	rose	henna		indigo	violet	jacinth
cuir	ruby	ivory	**6**	jasper	yellow	jonquil
drab	sand	jaune	acajou	madder	zircon	lacquer
ebon	shot	jewel	alesan	maroon		lavande
ecru	vert	khaki	argent	matara	**7**	magenta
gold		lemon	auburn	motley	anamite	mottled
grey	**5**	loden	bistre	orange	apricot	mustard
gris	amber	maize	blonde	orchid	ardoise	nacarat
hopi	beige	mauve	bronze	oyster	aureate	natural

neutral	eggshell	dutch blue	oxford blue	Castilian red
old rose	gun metal	flesh pink	petrol blue	celadon green
pearled	hazelnut	green-blue	polychrome	hunter's green
platina	hyacinth	harlequin	powder blue	hyacinth blue
saffron	larkspur	leaf green	terracotta	logwood brown
scarlet	lavender	lime green	zenith blue	midnight blue
sea blue	mahogany	moonstone		overseas blue
sky blue	mole grey	moss green	**11**	sapphire blue
tea rose	mulberry	nile green	bottle green	solferino red
thistle	navy blue	olive drab	burnt almond	tyrian purple
tile red	pea green	parchment	cardinal red	verdant green
tilleul	pistache	pearl grey	clair de lune	
tussore	poppy red	raspberry	forest green	**13**
violine	primrose	royal blue	gobelin blue	bishop's purple
	sapphire	tangerine	horizon blue	bishop's violet
8	sea green	tomato red	hunter's pink	Cambridge blue
absinthe	shagreen	turkey red	lapis lazuli	mother-of-pearl
alizarin	spectrum	turquoise	lemon yellow	pepper-and-salt
amaranth	viridian	verdigris	lipstick red	tortoiseshell
aurulent		vermilion	parrot green	
baby blue	**9**	wally blue	peacock blue	**14**
baby pink	alice blue		pomegranate	periwinkle
bordeaux	aubergine	**10**	smoked pearl	blue
burgundy	azure blue	aquamarine	solid colour	pistachio green
capucine	blue-green	bois de rose	ultramarine	
chaldera	cadet blue	café au lait	versicolour	**15**
chestnut	cadet grey	castor grey	walnut brown	Caledonian
ciel blue	carnation	cobalt blue	yellow ochre	brown
cinnamon	carnelian	congo brown		chartreuse green
crevette	champagne	ensign blue	**12**	
cyclamen	chocolate	liver brown	ball park blue	**16**
eau de nil	cochineal	marina blue	canary yellow	chartreuse
eggplant	delph blue	marine blue	carrot colour	yellow

French Revolutionary Calendar

6
Nivôse (snow, Dec.)

7
Floreal (blossom, April)
Ventôse (wind, Feb.)

8
Brumaire (fog, Oct.)

Fervidor (heat, July)
Frimaire (sleet, Nov.)
Germinal (seed, March)
Messidor (harvest, June)
Pluviôse (rain, Jan.)
Prairial (pasture, May)

9
Fructidor (fruit, Aug.)

Thermidor (heat, July)

11
Vendémiarire (vintage,
Sept.)

Greek Alphabet

2	xi	eta	tau	iota	**5**	kappa	**6**	**7**
mu		phi		zeta	alpha	omega	lambda	epsilon
nu	**3**	psi	**4**		delta	sigma		omicron
pi	chi	rho	beta		gamma	theta		upsilon

Hebrew Alphabet

2	**3**		**4**			**5**		**6**	
		Nun		Heth	Shin		Lamed		Tzaddi
He	Ain	Tau	Ayin	Kaph	Teth	Aleph	Schin	Daleth	
Pe	Jod	Yod	Beth	Koph	Vain	Cheth	Zayin	Samech	
	Mem		Caph	Resh	Zade	Gimel		Samekh	

Heraldry

2	gules	herald	gyronny	heraldic	escutcheon
or	gutté	impale	impaled	indented	fleur-de-lis
	gyron	mascle	leopard	insignia	fleur-de-lys
3	harpy	mullet	lozenge	invected	honourable
bar	label	naiant	lozengy	Lyon King	impalement
	motto	nebulé	martlet	mantling	King of Arms
4	pheon	Norroy	nombril	naissant	knighthood
arms	rebus	pallet	passant	opinicus	lambrequin
bend	sable	raguly	phoenix	ordinary	pursuivant
boar	scarp	rustre	potenty	sanguine	quartering
coue	torse	sejant	purpure	seahorse	quatrefoil
enty	**6**	shield	quarter	sinister	supporters
fess	argent	vested	rampant	standard	surmounted
flag	armour	voided	rayonny	tincture	
fret	armory	volant	roundel	tressure	**11**
helm	at gaze	vorant	salient	trippant	achievement
lion	baston	wivern	saltant		bar sinister
Lyon	bezant	wyvern	saltire	**9**	Clarencieux
orle	billet	**7**	scallop	abatement	compartment
pale	blazon	adorsed	sea lion	banderole	countervair
pall	border	adossed	sexfoil	blazoning	cross-fleury
paly	canton	annulet	slipped	combatant	dimidiation
pean	charge	armoury	statant	displayed	engrailment
pile	checky	attired	tierced	embattled	grant of arms
rose	chequy	bearing	trefoil	engrailed	marshalling
semé	couped	bendlet	unicorn	erminites	
urdé	coward	bordure	urinant	hatchment	**12 and over**
vair	dexter	cadency	**8**	lionceaux	bend sinister (12)
vert	dragon	chevron	addorsed	lioncelle	bendy-sinister (13)
5	emblem	courant	antelope	Lyon-Court	counterchanged
armed	erased	croslet	billetté	regardant	(14)
azure	ensign	dolphin	blazonry	scutcheon	counter-paled (12)
badge	ermine	dormant	caboched	spur-rowel	counter-passant
barry	falcon	endorse	caboshed	**10**	(14)
baton	fecial	engrail	chaperon	blue mantle	cross-crosslet (13)
bendy	fillet	ermines	couchant	camelopard	emblazonment
chief	flanch	estoile	crescent	cinquefoil	(12)
crest	fleury	flanche	dancetty	Clarenceux	escutcheoned {12)
cross	fretty	fretted	emblazon	coat of arms	heraldic emblem
eagle	fylfot	gardant	erminois	cockatrice	(14)
erect	garter	gironny	flanched	difference	inescutcheon (12)
fesse	ground	greaves	gonfalon	emblazonry	Lyon King at
field	helmet	griffin	hauriant	escalloped	Arms (14)
					unscutcheoned (13)

Jewish Year

2	4	Iyar	Nisan	6	Tishri	7
Ab	Abib		Sivan	Kislev	Vendar	Heshvan (7)
	Adar	5	Tebet	Shabat		
	Elul	Iyyar	Tisri	Tammus		

Miscellaneous People

2	pal	dean	lass	swot	blood	envoy
BA	pet	dear	liar	tart	board	exile
DD	PhD	doer	loon	team	booby	extra
Gl	pig	doge	lord	them	boyar	fakir
MA	rat	doll	lout	thug	bride	felon
ma	she	dolt	lush	tike	broad	fence
me	sir	doxy	male	toff	brute	fiend
MP	son	drip	mama	tool	bully	fifer
Mr	sot	duce	mate	tory	cadet	firer
pa	spy	duck	mess	tsar	cheat	flier
us	tar	dude	mime	twin	chief	flirt
we	tot	duke	minx	twit	child	flock
ye	wag	dupe	miss	tyke	choir	fogey
	wit	earl	mite	tyro	chuff	fraud
3	yob	emir	mome	user	chump	freak
ace	you	folk	monk	vamp	churl	friar
aga		fool	muff	waif	clown	gamin
ass	**4**	funk	mute	ward	count	gaper
bey	aide	gang	mutt	ward	crank	gazer
BSc	ally	gawk	ogre	wean	creep	giant
cad	amma	girl	page	whig	crone	GI Joe
cid	aunt	goer	papa	wife	crony	gipsy
dab	babe	gull	peer	wino	crook	giver
dad	baby	haji	peon	yogi	crowd	goose
deb	band	head	pimp		cynic	grass
don	bard	heel	pope	**5**	dandy	groom
elf	bear	heir	prig	adept	darky	guest
fag	beau	herd	punk	agent	decoy	guide
fop	bird	hero	rake	aider	deist	hater
gun	boor	hick	roue	airer	devil	heavy
guy	bore	hobo	rube	alien	diver	hewer
hag	boss	host	runt	ameer	donna	hider
ham	brat	idol	sage	angel	donor	hiker
imp	buck	imam	salt	aunty	doter	hippy
kid	bull	jack	scab	bairn	doyen	hussy
kin	cadi	jade	seer	baron	dozer	idiot
lad	chap	jill	self	beast	droll	idler
man	chum	jilt	serf	bedel	drone	in-law
men	clan	jury	shah	begum	dummy	issue
mob	colt	khan	silk	being	dunce	joker
Mrs	cove	king	sire	belle	duper	Judas
mug	crew	kith	slut	bigot	dwarf	judge
mum	curé	Kiwi	snob	biter	eater	junta
nun	czar	lady	soak	black	elder	juror
oaf	dame	lama	star	blade	enemy	knave

laird	proxy	thief	bigwig	double	gunman
laity	prude	title	bishop	dragon	gunner
leper	pryer	toady	blonde	drawee	gusher
liege	puker	tommy	bomber	drawer	halter
limey	pupil	toper	boozer	driver	harlot
local	puppy	tramp	bowler	drudge	healer
locum	pygmy	trier	bursar	ducker	hearer
loser	quack	troop	busker	duenna	heater
lover	queen	twins	buster	duffer	heaver
madam	queer	uncle	cadger	dynast	hector
mahdi	rabbi	urger	caesar	egoist	hedger
maker	racer	vegan	caliph	envier	helper
mamma	rajah	vexer	caller	eraser	herald
mater	raker	vicar	camper	escort	hermit
mayor	raver	vixen	cantor	eunuch	hinter
mimic	rebel	voter	captor	expert	hippie
minor	reeve	wazir	carper	fabler	hitman
miser	rider	wench	carver	family	hoaxer
moron	rival	whore	casual	father	holder
mouse	rogue	widow	censor	fawner	hooter
mover	rough	wight	chaser	feeler	hopper
mower	rover	witch	childe	fellow	howler
mufti	rower	women	client	female	hoyden
mummy	ruler	wooer	clique	fencer	huffer
muser	sahib	yahoo	coaxer	Fenian	humbug
nabob	saint	yobbo	codger	fiance	hummer
nanny	saver	yokel	cohort	fibber	hunter
nawab	scamp	youth	consul	filler	hurler
niece	scion		coolie	finder	hussar
ninny	scold	**6**	copier	foiler	hymner
noble	scout	abaser	co-star	forcer	iceman
noddy	screw	abuser	cotter	friend	infant
nomad	shark	adored	cousin	Fuhrer	inmate
nymph	sheik	adorer	coward	gaffer	ironer
ogler	shrew	albino	craven	gagger	jeerer
owner	silly	allies	creole	gainer	jerker
pacer	siren	alumna	cretin	gasbag	jester
pacha	skier	amazon	curate	gauger	Jesuit
padre	snail	ambler	damsel	geezer	jet set
pagan	sneak	angler	dancer	genius	jilter
party	sorry	au pair	darner	gentry	jogger
pasha	sower	auntie	dauber	getter	jolter
pater	spark	backer	debtor	gigolo	jumper
patsy	sport	bailie	defier	gillie	junior
payee	squaw	bandit	delver	glider	junker
payer	staff	barfly	denier	godson	junkie
peach	stoic	batman	deputy	golfer	kaiser
piler	stray	beadle	despot	gossip	keeper
pin-up	swain	beater	digger	granny	keeper
piper	swell	beauty	dimwit	grazer	kicker
porer	synod	beldam	dipper	groper	kidder
poser	taker	better	dodger	grouch	killer
posse	tenor	bibber	doodle	grower	kisser
prior	thane	bidder	dotard	gulper	knight

knower	mortal	Pommie	rusher	stager	warder
lacker	mother	poseur	rustic	starer	warmer
lagger	mugger	poster	sadist	stayer	warner
lancer	mulier	pourer	sailor	stooge	washer
lander	mullah	pouter	savage	sucker	waster
lapper	mummer	prater	savant	suitor	wearer
lasher	myself	prayer	sbirro	sultan	weeder
lassie	nagger	pretor	scaler	tacker	weeper
layman	nation	preyer	scorer	talker	whiner
leader	native	primus	scouse	tartar	wincer
leaper	needer	prince	scrimp	tasker	winder
leaser	nephew	prover	second	taster	winker
leaver	nipper	public	seeker	tatler	winner
lecher	nitwit	puffer	seizer	tearer	wisher
legate	nobody	puller	selves	teaser	wizard
lender	nodder	pumper	senate	teller	worker
lessee	noodle	pundit	sender	tenant	worthy
lessor	notary	punter	senior	Teuton	wretch
letter	novice	puppet	sentry	theist	writer
lifter	nudist	purger	sexton	throng	yapper
lisper	nuncio	purist	shadow	tilter	yeoman
lister	ogress	pusher	shaker	toiler	yonker
loafer	old boy	quaker	shaman	tomboy	zealot
lobber	old lag	quoter	sharer	tooter	zombie
lodger	old man	rabble	shaver	tosser	
looker	opener	racist	sheikh	truant	**7**
loonie	oracle	ragtag	sheila	tutrix	abetter
looter	orator	raider	shogun	tyrant	acceder
lurker	orphan	railer	shover	umpire	accuser
madcap	outlaw	rammer	shower	umpire	adapter
madman	pandit	ranger	shrimp	undoer	admirer
maiden	panter	ranter	sigher	uniter	adviser
maniac	papist	rapist	sinner	urchin	aircrew
marine	parent	rascal	sipper	vamper	alcalde
marker	pariah	rating	sirdar	vandal	also-ran
martyr	parter	reader	sister	varlet	alumnus
masher	patron	reaper	sitter	vendee	amateur
masker	pauper	rector	skater	vendor	amorosa
master	pawner	regent	slayer	verger	amoroso
matron	pedant	rhymer	slicer	vestal	anybody
medium	pedlar	ringer	slider	vestry	apostle
melter	peeler	rinser	sloven	victim	ascetic
member	peeper	rioter	smiler	victor	assizer
menial	pelter	ripper	smiter	viewer	assumer
mentor	penman	risker	smoker	Viking	atheist
midget	penpal	roamer	snarer	virago	athlete
mikado	person	roarer	sniper	virgin	attaché
minion	piecer	rocker	snorer	vizier	avenger
missis	pigeon	Romany	soaker	votary	averter
missus	pinner	rookie	solver	voyeur	babbler
mister	placer	rotter	sparer	wafter	bailiff
mocker	player	rouser	spouse	walker	ballboy
monkey	police	rubber	square	wanton	baronet
moppet	poller	runner	squire	warden	bastard

Miscellaneous

batsman	convict	drifter	floater	heroine	knocker
beatnik	copycat	driller	flouter	hidalgo	know-all
bedmate	co-rival	drinker	foister	hipster	laggard
bedouin	coroner	drowner	fondler	hitcher	laugher
beldame	Cossack	dualist	forager	hoarder	leaguer
bellman	council	duchess	founder	hobbler	learner
beloved	counter	dueller	freeman	hoodlum	legatee
bencher	courser	dullard	frisker	hostage	liberal
best man	courter	dweller	frowner	hostess	limiter
bigshot	coxcomb	edifier	Fuehrer	hothead	loather
blabber	crawler	egghead	fumbler	huddler	lobcock
blender	creator	egotist	gabbler	humbler	lookout
boarder	creeper	ejector	gallant	hurrier	lowbrow
boaster	cringer	elector	gambler	husband	lunatic
boggler	cripple	elegist	garbler	hustler	maestro
bookman	croaker	emperor	general	hymnist	magnate
bouncer	crooner	empress	gentile	imagist	mahatma
bounder	crusher	emptier	GI bride	imbiber	majesty
breeder	cry baby	enactor	giggler	impeder	mangler
brother	cuckold	endower	glutton	imposer	manikin
brownie	culprit	endurer	gobbler	imputer	mankind
bucolic	curator	engager	gourmet	inciter	marcher
buffoon	cyclist	enjoyer	grandam	inducer	marplot
bumpkin	czarina	enticer	grandee	infanta	marquis
bungler	dabbler	entrant	grandma	infante	marshal
burgess	dallier	epicure	grantee	infidel	meddler
burgher	dangler	equerry	granter	ingrate	menacer
bushman	darling	erecter	grantor	injurer	mestizo
bustler	dastard	eremite	grasper	insured	milksop
cacique	dauphin	escapee	groupie	insurer	mingler
cackler	dawdler	escaper	grouser	invader	minikin
caitiff	debaser	esquire	growler	invalid	misdoer
captain	debater	exactor	grown-up	inviter	mobster
captive	defacer	exalter	grudger	invoker	modiste
casuist	defamer	exciter	grunter	jackass	monarch
caveman	defiler	exegete	guesser	jack tar	monitor
changer	defunct	exposer	guzzler	jacobin	moulder
chanter	deluder	failure	gymnast	jangler	mounter
Charlie	denizen	fair sex	habitué	jemadar	mourner
charmer	derider	fall guy	haggler	Jezebel	mouther
cheater	desirer	fanatic	half-wit	Joe Soap	mudlark
checker	devisee	fancier	handler	jostler	muezzin
citizen	deviser	fascist	hangman	juggler	mugwump
climber	devotee	fathead	has-been	jumbler	mulatto
clipper	diarist	faulter	hatcher	juryman	mumbler
clubman	dibbler	feaster	haunter	justice	nettler
cockney	diehard	fiancee	head boy	khalifa	nibbler
cognate	divider	fidalgo	headman	killjoy	niggard
colleen	diviner	fiddler	heathen	kindler	niggler
colonel	doubter	fielder	heckler	kindred	nominee
compere	dowager	filcher	heiress	kinglet	notable
comrade	dragoon	flapper	hellhag	kingpin	oarsman
consort	dreader	flasher	hellion	kinsman	obligee
convert	dreamer	fleecer	heretic	kneeler	obliger

oddball	provost	scholar	speller	thumper	wastrel
offerer	prowler	scoffer	spender	tickler	watcher
officer	puncher	scolder	spiller	tiddler	waterer
old fogy	punster	scorner	spitter	tippler	waverer
old girl	puritan	scraper	sponger	toaster	weigher
old maid	pursuer	scrooge	sponsor	toddler	welcher
old salt	puzzler	sculler	spotter	tomfool	wencher
opposer	quaffer	sea-lord	sprayer	toppler	whipper
orderer	queller	seceder	spurner	tosspot	whisker
outcast	querent	securer	spurrer	tourist	widower
Oxonian	querist	seducer	stabber	trainee	wielder
paddler	questor	seminar	stand-by	trainer	windbag
paladin	quitter	senator	stand-in	traitor	wise guy
papoose	radical	service	starlet	treader	witling
paragon	rambler	settler	starter	treater	witness
partner	ravener	shammer	stealer	tribune	wolf cub
parvenu	reacher	sharper	stepson	tricker	worrier
patcher	realist	shedder	steward	trifler	wounder
patient	rebuker	sheriff	sticker	tripper	wrapper
patriot	reciter	shifter	stiller	trollop	wrecker
peasant	recluse	shooter	stinger	trooper	wrester
peruser	redhead	shopper	stinker	trouper	wringer
pervert	redskin	shouter	stinter	trudger	yielder
piercer	reducer	show-off	stirrer	trustee	Zionist
pilgrim	referee	shyster	stooper	truster	
pincher	refugee	sibling	stopper	tsarina	**8**
pioneer	refuser	signior	strayer	tumbler	abdicant
plaiter	refuter	skimmer	striker	twirler	abductor
planner	regular	skipper	striver	twister	absentee
playboy	relater	skulker	stroker	upstart	academic
pleader	remover	slacker	student	usurper	accepter
pleaser	renewer	slammer	stylist	utopian	achiever
plodder	replier	slasher	subadar	utterer	adherent
plotter	rescuer	sleeper	sub-dean	vacuist	adjutant
plucker	reserve	slinger	subduer	vagrant	adulator
plunger	retaker	smasher	subject	vampire	advocate
pontiff	retinue	snapper	suicide	vaulter	aesthete
pounder	reverer	snarler	sultana	vaunter	agitator
praetor	reviver	sniffer	supremo	veteran	agnostic
praiser	rhymist	snipper	suspect	viceroy	alarmist
pranker	riddler	snoozer	swagman	villain	alderman
prefect	roadhog	snorter	swearer	villein	allottee
prelate	royalty	snuffer	sweeper	visitor	allotter
premier	ruffian	society	swiller	vouchee	alter ego
presser	ruffler	soloist	swimmer	voucher	altruist
pricker	rumbler	someone	swinger	voyager	ancestor
primate	runaway	soother	tarrier	vulture	antihero
prinker	rustler	sophist	tattler	waddler	antipope
private	saluter	soprano	taunter	wagerer	apostate
proctor	saviour	spaniel	templar	waltzer	appeaser
prodigy	scalder	spanker	tempter	want-wit	appellee
progeny	scalper	spanner	thinker	war baby	appellor
prophet	sceptic	speaker	thriver	warbler	approver
protegé	schemer	speeder	thrower	warlock	archduke

arranger	chairman	detector	examiner	hastener
arsonist	champion	devourer	exceeder	hazarder
aspirant	chaperon	dictator	exceptor	head girl
assassin	chaplain	diffuser	executor	headsman
assembly	children	digester	expiator	hectorer
assertor	chuckler	diner-out	expirant	hedonist
assignee	cicerone	diplomat	exploder	helpmate
assignor	cicerone	director	explorer	helpmeet
assuager	civilian	dirty dog	exponent	hierarch
attacker	claimant	disciple	extender	highbrow
attestor	clansman	disgrace	extoller	highness
audience	cofferer	disponee	fatalist	hijacker
autocrat	cognizee	disponer	favourer	hinderer
bachelor	cognizor	disposer	feminist	homebody
balancer	colonial	disputer	ferreter	homicide
ballgirl	colonist	ditheist	figurant	honourer
bankrupt	combiner	diverter	finalist	hooligan
banterer	commando	divorcee	finisher	horseman
baritone	commoner	divulger	flaunter	huckster
baroness	commuter	do-gooder	flincher	humanist
beanpole	complier	dogsbody	folk hero	humorist
beginner	consumer	douanier	follower	humpback
beguiler	convener	drencher	fomenter	idealist
believer	conveyer	dribbler	foregoer	idolater
bellower	coquette	drunkard	foreseer	idolizer
bestower	co-regent	duellist	forgiver	imaginer
betrayer	corporal	duettist	franklin	imbecile
big noise	cottager	dukeling	freedman	imitator
bigamist	courtier	dyslexic	freshman	immortal
blackleg	co-worker	effector	front man	impairer
blazoner	crackpot	elegiast	fugitive	imparter
blighter	creditor	elevator	fusilier	impeller
bluecoat	criminal	embracer	futurist	implorer
bohemian	crusader	emeritus	gadabout	impostor
bookworm	customer	emigrant	galloper	improver
borderer	czarevna	emissary	gamester	impugner
borrower	dalesman	emulator	gaolbird	inceptor
boy scout	daughter	enforcer	garroter	indicter
braggart	deaf-mute	enhancer	gatherer	indigene
brethren	debutant	enjoiner	giantess	inductee
brunette	deceased	enlarger	godchild	inductor
burgrave	deceiver	enquirer	go-getter	indulger
busybody	defector	enricher	goodwife	inferior
cabalist	defender	enslaver	gourmand	inflamer
callgirl	deferrer	ensnarer	graduate	informer
cannibal	delegate	eschewer	grandson	initiate
canoeist	democrat	espouser	grumbler	innocent
cardinal	depriver	esteemer	guardian	inquirer
carouser	derelict	eulogist	habitant	insister
castaway	deserter	everyman	hanger-on	inspirer
caudillo	deserver	everyone	harasser	insulter
caviller	despiser	evildoer	hardener	intended
celibate	detainee	evocator	harridan	intender
cenobite	detainer	examinee	harrower	intimate

intruder	man-hater	offender	promiser	resolver
investor	mannikin	official	promoter	resorter
islander	marauder	old-timer	proposer	restorer
jabberer	margrave	old woman	protegée	retarder
jackaroo	marksman	oligarch	provisor	retorter
Jacobite	marquess	onlooker	provoker	returner
jailbird	marquise	operator	punisher	revealer
jingoist	martinet	opponent	purifier	reveller
John Bull	martinet	optimist	quadroon	revenger
joy-rider	May Queen	outsider	quaestor	revolter
juvenile	mayoress	overlord	quaverer	rewarder
kingling	mediator	overseer	quencher	riffraff
kinsfolk	merryman	pacifier	quibbler	rifleman
lady love	messmate	pacifist	Quisling	romancer
ladyship	mimicker	palatine	ransomer	romantic
lame duck	minister	paleface	ratifier	rotarian
lamenter	mislayer	pamperer	ravisher	royalist
latinist	mistress	panderer	reasoner	ruralist
launcher	modalist	paramour	rebutter	saboteur
laureate	modifier	parasite	recaptor	satanist
lawgiver	molester	pardoner	receiver	scrawler
lawmaker	monsieur	parodist	reckoner	scuffler
lay clerk	moon calf	partaker	recoiler	seafarer
lay elder	moonling	partisan	recorder	searcher
layabout	moralist	passer-by	recorder	seconder
layer-out	motorist	patentee	recreant	seigneur
laywoman	murderer	penitent	redeemer	selector
legalist	murmurer	perjurer	reformer	sentinel
levanter	mutineer	pesterer	refunder	sergeant
leveller	mutterer	pharisee	regicide	shrieker
libellee	namesake	pilferer	rejecter	shrimper
libeller	narrator	pillager	rejoicer	shrinker
licenser	narrower	placeman	relapser	shuffler
liegeman	naturist	playgoer	relation	sidekick
life peer	neophyte	playmate	releasee	sidesman
linesman	nepotist	plebeian	releaser	simperer
lingerer	neurotic	poisoner	reliever	skeleton
linguist	new broom	polluter	remarker	sketcher
listener	newcomer	poltroon	reminder	slattern
literati	nihilist	ponderer	remitter	slowpoke
litigant	nobility	pontifex	renderer	slugabed
live wire	nobleman	popinjay	renegade	sluggard
logician	nuisance	populace	repealer	slyboots
loiterer	numberer	prattler	repeater	small fry
lordling	numskull	preparer	repeller	snatcher
lordship	nursling	presager	reporter	snuffler
loyalist	objector	presbyte	reprover	sodomite
luminary	obscurer	presumer	repulser	solitary
lyricist	observer	princess	resenter	somebody
maharaja	obtainer	prisoner	reserver	songster
maligner	obtruder	prodigal	resident	son-in-law
manciple	occupant	producer	resident	sorcerer
mandarin	occupier	profaner	resigner	spinster
mandarin	octoroon	promisee	resister	splitter

Miscellaneous

spreader	truckler	affirmant	charlatan	debauchee
springer	truelove	aggressor	charterer	debutante
sprinter	tsarevna	alcoholic	chatterer	declaimer
squaller	turncoat	anarchist	chevalier	declarant
squasher	twaddler	annuitant	chieftain	defaulter
squatter	twitcher	apologist	chiseller	defeatist
squeaker	two-timer	appellant	Christian	defendant
squealer	underdog	applauder	clatterer	defrauder
squeezer	unionist	applicant	clientele	deliverer
squinter	upholder	appraiser	coadjutor	demagogue
squireen	vagabond	archdruid	coalition	demandant
squirter	vanguard	archenemy	colleague	demi-monde
stancher	venturer	arriviste	collector	dependant
stickler	verifier	assailant	collegian	depositor
stinkard	vilifier	associate	combatant	desperado
stitcher	villager	augmenter	comforter	despoiler
stowaway	violator	authority	commander	destroyer
stranger	viscount	automaton	commander	detractor
stripper	visitant	backbiter	committee	dignitary
stroller	wallower	banqueter	commodore	disburser
strutter	wanderer	barbarian	communist	discerner
stumbler	war bride	bargainer	community	discloser
suborner	wayfarer	battleaxe	companion	disgracer
suckling	waylayer	bedfellow	concubine	disguiser
sufferer	waymaker	bedlamite	confessor	dispeller
summoner	weakener	beggarman	confidant	disperser
superior	weanling	bel esprit	conformer	displayer
superman	welcomer	biblicist	Confucian	disprover
supposer	wheedler	bicyclist	conqueror	disputant
surmiser	whistler	blockhead	conscript	dissenter
survivor	whitener	bluebeard	consenter	dissident
suzerain	whizz-kid	blunderer	consignee	disturber
sybarite	wiseacre	blusterer	consignor	divinator
tacksman	wonderer	bodyguard	constable	dogmatist
tallyman	wrangler	bolsterer	contemner	dolly bird
tartuffe	wrestler	bon vivant	contender	dominator
taxpayer	wriggler	bourgeois	contralto	do-nothing
teddy boy	yeomanry	boyfriend	contriver	driveller
teenager	yodeller	brigadier	converter	drum major
telltale	yokemate	bystander	co-patriot	dyspeptic
testator	yourself	cabin crew	cordelier	early bird
theorist	zemindar	candidate	corrector	earthling
thrasher		canvasser	corrupter	eccentric
threader	**9**	card sharp	court fool	Edwardian
thruster	aborigine	careerist	cover girl	electress
thwarter	absconder	castellan	crack shot	emendator
tightwad	abstainer	catchpole	cricketer	enchanter
top brass	academist	celebrant	crookback	encomiast
torturer	accessory	celebrity	cupbearer	energizer
townsman	acclaimer	cellarist	custodian	energumen
traducer	addressee	centurion	cut-throat	enfeebler
trampler	addresser	chain gang	Dalai Lama	engrosser
trembler	adulterer	chantress	daredevil	enlivener
triplets	adversary	character	dark horse	entangler

entourage	godmother	inveigher	moralizer	pilgarlic
entreater	grand duke	inveigler	mortgagee	pinchfist
epileptic	grandpapa	Jack Ketch	mortgagor	pin-up girl
epistoler	grandsire	jay-walker	Mrs Grundy	plaintiff
evacuator	gratifier	jitterbug	multitude	platonist
everybody	great-aunt	job hunter	muscleman	plunderer
exciseman	greenhorn	job seeker	mutilator	plutocrat
executive	grenadier	jobsworth	mythmaker	plutonist
executrix	greybeard	joint heir	Narcissus	poetaster
exhibitor	groveller	journeyer	neglecter	policeman
ex-officer	guerrilla	justifier	neighbour	portioner
exploiter	guest star	kidnapper	Neptunian	possessor
expositor	guinea pig	kinswoman	next of kin	postponer
expounder	half-caste	know-it-all	nominator	postulant
exquisite	haranguer	lackbrain	nonentity	potentate
extractor	harbinger	ladies' man	non-smoker	pot-hunter
extravert	harbourer	landowner	nourisher	precentor
extremist	harnesser	lawmonger	novitiate	precursor
extrovert	hearkener	lay reader	nullifier	predicant
falsifier	hellhound	lazybones	numbskull	predictor
family man	highflier	libellant	occultist	preferrer
favourite	hillbilly	liberator	offspring	prelatist
fetishist	household	libertine	ombudsman	presbyter
fire eater	housewife	lifeguard	oppressor	presentee
first-born	hunchback	lionheart	Orangeman	presenter
flatterer	hypocrite	lip-reader	organizer	preserver
forebears	ignoramus	liturgist	other half	president
foreigner	immigrant	liveryman	ourselves	pretender
forfeiter	immolator	lord mayor	pacemaker	pretender
forgetter	impeacher	lost sheep	palaverer	preventer
formalist	inamorata	loudmouth	panellist	principal
fort major	inamorato	lowlander	paralytic	proceeder
fortifier	increaser	magnifico	parricide	proconsul
forwarder	incumbent	magnifier	part-owner	profferer
fossicker	incurable	maharajah	passenger	profiteer
foster son	indicator	majordomo	patriarch	projector
foundling	indweller	makepeace	patrician	prolonger
foxhunter	inebriate	mammonist	patricide	promissor
fratricide	inflicter	mannerist	patroness	promulger
free agent	informant	masochist	peasantry	proselyte
freelance	infractor	matriarch	peculator	prosodist
free-liver	infringer	matricide	penfriend	protector
freemason	inheritor	meanderer	pen-pusher	protester
fulfiller	initiator	medallist	pensioner	protruder
furtherer	innovator	messieurs	perceiver	purchaser
gainsayer	in-patient	metrician	perfecter	purloiner
garnisher	inscriber	middle man	performer	rabbinist
garrotter	insolvent	miscreant	permitter	racketeer
gathering	inspector	mitigator	personage	raconteur
gentleman	instiller	mixed-race	personnel	rainmaker
girl guide	insurgent	moderator	persuader	ransacker
girl scout	intestate	modernist	perturber	rapturist
go-between	intriguer	modulator	perverter	ratepayer
godfather	introvert	moonraker	pessimist	recipient

Miscellaneous

recoverer
rectifier
redresser
registrar
regulator
rehearser
reinsurer
renouncer
renovator
represser
reprobate
requester
respecter
rhymester
ridiculer
ritualist
roisterer
Romanizer
roughneck
routinist
rubrician
ruminator
Samaritan
Sassenach
satellite
satisfier
Saturnist
saunterer
scapegoat
scarecrow
scavenger
scholiast
schoolboy
scoundrel
scrambler
scratcher
scribbler
sea lawyer
secretary
sectarian
separator
serenader
sermonist
shaveling
shortener
shoveller
sightseer
simpleton
skindiver
skinflint
skylarker
slanderer
slobberer
slowcoach

slumberer
smatterer
sniveller
socialist
socialite
sojourner
solicitor
solitaire
son-of-a-gun
sophister
sophomore
sovereign
spectator
spokesman
sportsman
sprinkler
sputterer
squabbler
stammerer
star pupil
stargazer
statesman
stigmatic
straggler
strangler
stretcher
stripling
strongman
struggler
stutterer
subaltern
submitter
subverter
succeeder
successor
succourer
suggester
sultaness
suppliant
supporter
surfeiter
susceptor
suspecter
sustainer
swaggerer
swallower
sycophant
symbolist
syncopist
tactician
Talmudist
temptress
termagant
terminist

terrorist
testifier
theorizer
thunderer
tormentor
town clerk
town crier
townsfolk
traveller
traverser
treasurer
trepanner
tribesman
trickster
underling
valentine
venerator
verbalist
versifier
vestryman
Victorian
vigilante
visionary
volunteer
vulcanist
warmonger
wassailer
whipper-in
whosoever
womanizer
womankind
womenfolk
worldling
wrongdoer
xenophobe
yachtsman
young lady
youngling
youngster

10
aboriginal
absolutist
accomplice
admonisher
adulteress
adventurer
aficionado
aide-de-
    camp
alcoranist
allegorist
ambassador
ambidexter

ancestress
anecdotist
anglophile
anglophobe
anglophone
Anglo-Saxon
antagonist
antecedent
antecessor
antecursor
archbishop
aristocrat
assemblage
babe-in-arms
babysitter
bamboozler
basket case
beautifier
benefactor
bergmaster
better half
big brother
blackamoor
blackguard
black sheep
blasphemer
bobbysoxer
bogtrotter
bootlicker
borstal boy
bridegroom
bridesmaid
bureaucrat
bush ranger
campaigner
capitalist
caravanner
card player
carabineer
catechumen
cavalryman
centralist
chancellor
changeling
chatterbox
chauvinist
cheesecake
churchgoer
Cinderella
clodhopper
cloisterer
cloistress
coadjutant
coadjutrix

cohabitant
commandant
competitor
complainer
confessant
confidante
considerer
contendent
contestant
controller
co-operator
copyholder
corregidor
councillor
councilman
counsellor
countryman
covenanter
crackbrain
cringeling
crosspatch
crown agent
curmudgeon
czarevitch
daggle-tail
dauphiness
daydreamer
day-tripper
declaimant
delegation
delinquent
demoiselle
depositary
deprecator
depredator
deputation
descendant
dilettante
diminisher
directress
discharger
discoverer
disparager
dissembler
distracter
dock master
dogmatizer
dominicide
doorkeeper
dramatizer
drug addict
drug dealer
drug pusher
dunderhead

Dutch uncle	fund-raiser	lawbreaker	opium eater	questioner
early riser	gastronome	lay brother	opposition	ragamuffin
elaborator	gentlefolk	left-winger	originator	recidivist
electorate	girlfriend	legislator	out-patient	reclaimant
elucidator	glacialist	legitimist	overrunner	recognizer
emboldener	glitterati	licentiate	overturner	recognitor
empiricist	goalkeeper	lieutenant	painstaker	reconciler
empoisoner	gold-digger	literalist	pall-bearer	reimburser
encourager	goodfellow	loggerhead	panegyrist	relinquent
encroacher	grand juror	lotus-eater	paper tiger	rememberer
engenderer	grandchild	lower class	paraphrast	reproacher
Englishman	grandmamma	machinator	parliament	reprobater
enigmatist	grandniece	magistrate	past master	reproducer
enthusiast	grand-uncle	magnetizer	patronizer	republican
enumerator	grass widow	maiden aunt	peacemaker	repudiator
enunciator	great-uncle	maiden lady	pedestrian	restrainer
epitaphist	half-sister	malefactor	Peeping Tom	restricter
epitomizer	harmonizer	malingerer	pensionary	retributer
equestrian	hatchet man	manoeuvrer	persecutor	reverencer
eternalist	headhunter	man of straw	persifleur	revivalist
evangelist	headmaster	married man	personator	rhapsodist
excellency	heresiarch	marshaller	petitioner	ringleader
exhortator	her indoors	mastermind	phenomenon	ringmaster
expatiator	high priest	matchmaker	philistine	sacrificer
explicator	highlander	mayor-elect	plagiarist	scrapegrace
expurgator	hitch-hiker	merrymaker	polo player	schematist
extenuator	human being	methuselah	polygamist	schismatic
extirpator	iconoclast	middlebrow	polyhistor	scrutineer
eye witness	identifier	midshipman	polytheist	sea captain
fabricator	ideologist	militarist	population	secularist
factionist	idolatress	mindreader	positivist	sensualist
fagot-voter	impenitent	ministrant	postmaster	separatist
fashionist	importuner	mint-master	pragmatist	sermonizer
federalist	imprisoner	misogamist	preadamite	seventh son
fire master	incendiary	misogynist	proclaimer	shoplifter
fire-raiser	individual	monarchist	procreator	sinecurist
flagellant	inhabitant	moneyed man	procurator	smart aleck
flourisher	inquisitor	monogamist	profligate	snuff taker
fly-by-night	inquisitor	monologist	progenitor	solemnizer
footballer	insinuator	monomaniac	prohibiter	solicitant
footlicker	instigator	monopolist	prolocutor	son and heir
forefather	institutor	monotheist	promenader	songstress
foreleader	interferer	mountebank	pronouncer	soothsayer
foremother	interloper	mouthpiece	propagator	speculator
forerunner	interposer	namby-pamby	prophesier	spoilsport
forswearer	intervener	ne'er-do-well	propounder	squanderer
fraternity	introducer	neutralist	proprietor	starveling
free spirit	jackadandy	nincompoop	proscriber	stepfather
free trader	jackanapes	noblewoman	prosecutor	stepmother
freeholder	kith and kin	nominalist	prostitute	stepsister
freelancer	lady-killer	obstructer	proveditor	stimulator
frequenter	landholder	occasioner	psychopath	stipulator
fuddy-duddy	landlubber	old soldier	pulverizer	strategist
fund-holder	languisher	opinionist	quarreller	street arab

Miscellaneous

strokesman
subscriber
substitute
subtractor
sugar daddy
supplanter
supplicant
suppressor
surmounter
suscipient
sweetheart
sworn enemy
syllogizer
syncopater
syncretist
synonymist
tale bearer
tale teller
tantalizer
taskmaster
tea drinker
televiewer
temporizer
tenderfoot
tenderling
textualist
textuarist
themselves
thickskull
third party
threatener
timeserver
time-waster
tithing-man
tramontane
transferee
transferer
transmuter
trespasser
troglodyte
troubadour
tub-thumper
tweedledee
tweedledum
tuft-hunter
unbeliever
undertaker
unemployed
upper class
upper crust
utopianist
vacillator
vanquished
vanquisher

Vaticanist
vegetarian
vice-consul
vicegerent
vice-master
vice-regent
vindicator
voluptuary
wallflower
well-wisher
whomsoever
widow-maker
wine-bibber
wirepuller
withdrawer
withholder
woman-hater
worshipper
yoke-fellow
young blood
yourselves

11
abbreviator
abecedarian
academician
accompanist
accumulator
adventuress
animal lover
archduchess
aristocracy
aristocracy
assay-master
association
bandy player
beauty queen
belligerent
beneficiary
Bible reader
bibliolater
bibliophile
bird's-nester
birdwatcher
blackmailer
bloodsucker
blue-eyed boy
blunderhead
bourgeoisie
breadwinner
brotherhood
burgomaster
calumniator
cave dweller

centenarian
chamberlain
chance-comer
cheerleader
cheese parer
chucklehead
clairvoyant
coalitioner
cognoscenti
co-inheritor
commentator
complainant
comptroller
condisciple
confamiliar
confiscator
conjecturer
connoisseur
conspirator
constituent
continuator
contributor
co-ordinator
corporation
court jester
cross-bearer
crossbowman
crown lawyer
crown prince
deliberator
denunciator
depopulator
depreciator
devotionist
dilapidator
diluvialist
diplomatist
dipsomaniac
directorate
discipliner
discourager
dishonourer
dissentient
distributor
doctrinaire
domestician
double agent
draggle-tail
dram drinker
drug peddler
eager beaver
earl-marshal
electioneer
emancipator

embellisher
embroiderer
enchantress
encounterer
endeavourer
enlightener
enlisted man
entertainer
epigenesist
epistolizer
equilibrist
equivocator
establisher
euphemerist
exaggerator
exasperater
executioner
father-in-law
fault-finder
femme fatale
fifth column
fighting man
fire-starter
fire-watcher
first cousin
flag officer
flat dweller
foot soldier
forestaller
foster child
francophile
francophobe
francophone
freethinker
functionary
galley slave
gallows bird
gatecrasher
gentlefolks
gentlewoman
ginger group
glue sniffer
goddaughter
grandfather
grand master
grandmother
grandnephew
grandparent
grand vizier
gull catcher
guttersnipe
half-brother
hard drinker
harum-scarum

helping hand
high society
hobbledehoy
homo sapiens
hyperbolist
hypercritic
imperialist
inaugurator
infantryman
interceptor
intercessor
internuncio
interrupter
interviewer
intimidator
joint tenant
knucklehead
leaseholder
libertarian
lickspittle
lilliputian
litterateur
living image
lord provost
lower orders
lycanthrope
manipulator
marchioness
marrying man
masquerader
materialist
matinee idol
maxim-monger
merry Andrew
metaphorist
middle class
millenarian
millionaire
misanthrope
misbeliever
misinformer
monopolizer
moonlighter
mother-in-law
mountaineer
Mrs Malaprop
name-dropper
nationalist
necessarian
neutralizer
night-walker
nondescript
non-resident
nosey parker

opportunist
owner-driver
pacificator
panicmonger
papal legate
papal nuncio
parishioner
participant
peace-broker
pearly queen
peripatetic
perpetrator
personality
phenomenist
philatelist
philosopher
physicalist
policewoman
pound-keeper
predecessor
prince royal
prize-winner
probabilist
probationer
prodigal son
proletarian
proletariat
promulgator
propitiator
protagonist
protectress
protestator
protocolist
protonotary
puisne judge
Punchinello
punctualist
purgatorian
queen mother
questionist
rank and file
rapscallion
rationalist
reactionary
recommender
recompenser
religionist
replenisher
reprehender
resuscitant
reversioner
right-winger
Rosicrucian
royal family

rugby player
sabbatarian
sacrilegist
sans-culotte
scaremonger
school board
scoutmaster
scripturist
scrutinizer
search party
shareholder
simple Simon
singularist
sister-in-law
sleepwalker
speculatist
speechmaker
speed skater
spendthrift
squirearchy
stakeholder
stepbrother
stockholder
stonewaller
stool pigeon
story-teller
street child
stump orator
subordinate
suffragette
surrenderee
surrenderer
sword-bearer
sword player
sworn friend
sympathizer
systematist
tautologist
tax assessor
tax gatherer
teetotaller
teleologist
telepathist
thanksgiver
theosophist
time-pleaser
Tommy Atkins
torch-bearer
town council
town dweller
transsexual
trencherman
trend setter
undersigned

undervaluer
undesirable
vestry clerk
viscountess
Walter Mitty
war criminal
wastethrift
weathercock
wreckmaster

12
abolitionist
acquaintance
advance party
agent-general
ambassadress
antediluvian
anticourtier
appropriator
artful dodger
asylum seeker
awkward squad
bachelor girl
backwoodsman
benefactress
bible-thumper
bibliomaniac
blood brother
bluestocking
bottle-washer
brother-in-law
bounty hunter
chief justice
chief mourner
chief of staff
church member
churchwarden
civil servant
civil service
coalitionist
collaborator
Colonel Blimp
commiserator
commissioner
committee man
communicator
complimenter
conservative
consignatory
conquistador
constabulary
contemplator
contemporary
controverter

Miscellaneous

convalescent
conventicler
conventioner
convivialist
co-respondent
corporealist
cosmopolitan
crown-equerry
demimondaine
demonstrator
determinator
dialectician
disciplinant
discommender
discontinuer
disenchanter
disorganizer
dispossessor
disseminator
doppelganger
double-dealer
eavesdropper
educationist
elocutionist
encumbrancer
enfranchiser
entrepreneur
exclusionist
excursionist
exhibitioner
experimenter
expostulator
ex-serviceman
extemporizer
extensionist
exterminator
featherbrain
field officer
filibusterer
foster father
foster mother
foster parent
foster sister
foundationer
gastronomist
gesticulator
globe-trotter
grey eminence
guest speaker
hair-splitter
headmistress
headshrinker
heir apparent
holidaymaker

humanitarian
impersonator
impoverisher
inspectorate
intellectual
intercipient
interlocutor
intermeddler
intermediary
interpolator
interrogator
investigator
irregularist
kleptomaniac
knight errant
landed gentry
leading light
legacy hunter
letter writer
longshoreman
lord temporal
lounge lizard
mademoiselle
maid of honour
man-about-town
married woman
marrying kind
master-singer
melancholist
mezzo-soprano
misconstruer
misinformant
morris dancer
natural child
near relation
neoplatonist
noctambulist
nonagenarian
non-combatant
notary public
nouveau riche
obscurantist
octogenarian
office bearer
old gentleman
parish priest
peace-breaker
peace officer
peregrinator
persona grata
philosophist
pillion rider
poet laureate
poor relation

postgraduate
precipitator
prevaricator
primogenitor
proprietress
proselytizer
public figure
queen-consort
queen-dowager
queen-regnant
recriminator
redemptioner
relinquisher
remembrancer
remonstrator
residentiary
resolutioner
resuscitator
roller blader
roller skater
rolling stone
salvationist
scatterbrain
schoolfellow
second cousin
second fiddle
sequestrator
sexagenarian
sheriff clerk
single mother
single parent
single person
sole occupant
somnambulist
somniloquist
spiritualist
staff officer
stepdaughter
stormtrooper
straightener
street urchin
stuffed shirt
sub-committee
subpurchaser
Sunday driver
swashbuckler
sworn enemies
systematizer
tax collector
tennis player
testificator
transgressor
transmigrant
transvestite

troublemaker
truce-breaker
truncheoneer
ugly customer
ugly duckling
undermanager
universalist
velocipedist
versificator
village idiot
vicar-general
water bailiff
way passenger
wicket keeper
wool gatherer
working class

13

adminiculator
administrator
anagrammatist
Anglo-American
annexationist
anthropophagi
antisocialist
apothegmatist
archpresbyter
archtreasurer
army commander
barrack master
bibliophilist
blood relation
borough master
castle-builder
chamber-fellow
comprovincial
conceptualist
concessionist
consul-general
conventionist
co-religionist
correspondent
count palatine
county council
daughter-in-law
deck passenger
devotionalist
discriminator
distinguisher
district judge
éminence grise
exhibitionist
experimentist
fashion-monger

first offender
foot passenger
fortune-hunter
foster brother
fresh-air fiend
generalissimo
granddaughter
grand-seigneur
hard bargainer
high churchman
high constable
high priestess
hypochondriac
identical twins
Job's comforter
judge-advocate
laughing stock
life-annuitant
lord spiritual
machiavellian
millennialist
miracle worker
misanthropist
mischief-maker
mounted police
nonconformist
parliamentary
paterfamilias
perfectionist
philhellenist
philosophizer
predestinator
prime minister
Prince of Wales
Princess Royal
protectionist
proverbialist
public trustee
reprobationer
revolutionary

sadomasochist
social climber
sophisticator
speed merchant
spindleshanks
spiritualizer
state criminal
state prisoner
strike-breaker
tranquillizer
transmigrator
undergraduate
understrapper
vice-president
young offender

14

antiaristocrat
archchancellor
armchair critic
auditor-general
billiard player
chief constable
colour sergeant
corpuscularian
crown solicitor
destructionist
disciplinarian
dowager duchess
gentleman-usher
high court judge
fifth columnist
foster daughter
galactophagist
good-for-nothing
ichthyophagist
indifferentist
king's messenger
latitudinarian
lord chancellor

lord lieutenant
lord of the manor
man in the street
medical officer
ministerialist
misinterpreter
obstructionist
paragrammatist
parochial board
philanthropist
political agent
procrastinator
prognosticator
progressionist
prohibitionist
promise-breaker
provost-marshal
quadragenarian
quodlibetarian
requisitionist
restorationist
sabbath-breaker
sacramentarian
sensationalist
sentimentalist
septuagenarian
skittles player
smooth operator
squandermaniac
stamp collector
superior person
ultramontanist
valetudinarian
vice-chancellor
waifs and strays
weather prophet
whippersnapper

15

advocate-general

archchamberlain
astronomer royal
attorney general
autograph hunter
cabinet minister
chargé d'affaires
circumnavigator
constitutionist
conversationist
district officer
election auditor
emancipationist
experimentalist
fellow traveller
governor-general
heir presumptive
insurrectionary
insurrectionist
intellectualist
messenger-at-arms
parliamentarian
persona non grata
plenipotentiary
privy councillor
queen's messenger
sheriff's officer
shrinking violet
suffragan bishop
supernaturalist
surveyor-general
Tom, Dick and
  Harry
vice-chamberlain

16

pillion passenger

17

chattering classes
confirmed bachelor

Names for Boys

2	Lou	Cain	Jake	Rory	Bjorn	Duane	Inigo
Al	Loz	Carl	Jean	Ross	Blake	Dylan	Isaac
Cy	Mac	Cary	Jeff	Rudy	Bobby	Earle	Jacky
Ed	Mat	Chad	Jess	Ryan	Boris	Eddie	Jacob
Jo	Max	Chas	Jock	Saul	Brent	Edgar	Jaime
Oz	Mel	Clem	Joel	Sean	Brett	Edwin	Jamal
Si	Nat	Cole	Joey	Seth	Brian	Edwyn	James
	Ned	Curt	John	Siôn	Bruce	Eldon	Jamie
3	Nye	Dave	José	Stan	Bruno	Elias	Jared
Abe	Pat	Davy	Josh	Theo	Bryan	Ellis	Jason
Alf	Pip	Dean	Juan	Toby	Bunny	Eliot	Jerry
Ali	Rab	Dewi	Jude	Todd	Byron	Elmer	Jesse
Art	Ray	Dick	Karl	Tony	Cahal	Elroy	Jimmy
Asa	Reg	Dirk	Keir	Trev	Caleb	Elton	Johan
Baz	Rex	Doug	Kent	Walt	Calum	Elvis	Jonah
Ben	Rob	Drew	Kirk	Wilf	Carew	Elwyn	Jonas
Bob	Rod	Duke	Kurt	Will	Carlo	Emile	Jules
Dai	Ron	Earl	Kyle	Wynn	Carol	Emlyn	Keanu
Dan	Roy	Eddy	Lars	Yves	Cecil	Enoch	Keith
Del	Sam	Eden	Leon	Zack	Chaim	Ernie	Kenny
Den	Sid	Emil	Liam		Chris	Ernst	Kerry
Des	Sim	Eoin	Llew	**5**	Chuck	Errol	Kevin
Don	Stu	Eric	Luke	Aaron	Clare	Evans	Klaus
Eli	Syd	Eryl	Lyle	Abdul	Claud	Ewart	Kumar
Ern	Tam	Esau	Marc	Abram	Claus	Felix	Larry
Gaz	Ted	Esra	Mark	Adolf	Cliff	Floyd	Leigh
Gil	Tel	Euan	Matt	Ahmed	Clint	Frank	Lenny
Gus	Tim	Evan	Merv	Aidan	Clive	Franz	Leroy
Guy	Tom	Ewan	Mick	Aiden	Clyde	Fritz	Lewis
Hal	Vic	Ewen	Mike	Alban	Colin	Garry	Linus
Huw	Viv	Eyre	Milo	Alfie	Conan	Gavin	Lloyd
Ian		Ezra	Neal	Algie	Conor	Geoff	Louie
Ike	**4**	Finn	Neil	Allan	Corin	Gerry	Louis
Ira	Abel	Fred	Nick	Allen	Cosmo	Giles	Lucas
Ivo	Adam	Gary	Noah	Alvin	Craig	Glenn	Luigi
Jay	Alan	Gene	Noel	Amand	Cyril	Glynn	Lyall
Jem	Alec	Glen	Olaf	André	Cyrus	Grant	Meyer
Jim	Aled	Glyn	Omar	Angel	Damon	Gregg	Micky
Job	Alex	Greg	Otis	Angus	Danny	Griff	Miles
Joe	Algy	Gwyn	Otto	Anton	Darcy	Guido	Monty
Jon	Ally	Hank	Owen	Anwar	David	Harry	Moses
Kay	Alun	Hans	Ozzy	Arnie	Davie	Harun	Mungo
Ken	Amos	Herb	Page	Aubyn	Denis	Hasan	Murdo
Kim	Andy	Huey	Paul	Barry	Denny	Haydn	Myles
Kit	Bart	Hugh	Penn	Barty	Denys	Heinz	Neddy
Lal	Beau	Hugo	Pete	Basil	Derek	Henri	Niall
Lee	Bede	Iain	Phil	Benji	Derry	Henry	Nicol
Len	Bert	Ifor	Ravi	Benny	Dicky	Hiram	Nigel
Leo	Bill	Ivan	René	Berty	Diego	Humph	Ollie
Les	Bryn	Ivor	Rhys	Bevan	Digby	Hyram	Orson
Lew	Buck	Jack	Rick	Bevis	Dipak	Hywel	Oscar
Lex	Burt	Jago	Rolf	Billy	Donny	Idris	Pablo

Paddy	**6**	Dougie	Hughie	Nevill	Vernon
Paolo	Adolph	Dudley	Hunter	Ninian	Victor
Paton	Adrian	Duggie	Irvine	Norman	Vivian
Pedro	Albert	Duncan	Israel	Norris	Vyvyan
Percy	Alexei	Dustin	Jackie	Norton	Wallis
Perry	Alfred	Dwight	Jarvis	Oliver	Walter
Peter	Andrés	Eamonn	Jasper	Osbert	Warren
Piers	Andrew	Edmond	Jeremy	Oswald	Wesley
Ralph	Anselm	Edmund	Jerome	Padrig	Willie
Ramón	Antony	Edward	Jethro	Pelham	Xavier
Randy	Archie	Egbert	Jockie	Philip	Yehudi
Raoul	Armand	Eldred	Johann	Pierre	
Ricky	Arnold	Elliot	Johnny	Powell	**7**
Roald	Arthur	Ernest	Jordan	Prince	Abraham
Robin	Ashley	Eugene	Joseph	Rabbie	Ainslie
Roddy	Aubrey	Evelyn	Joshua	Rafael	Alberto
Roger	Austin	Fabian	Josiah	Rajesh	Alfonso
Rolfe	Aylwin	Faisal	Julian	Ramesh	Alister
Rollo	Barney	Fergus	Julius	Ramsay	Amadeus
Romeo	Bernie	Finbar	Justin	Randle	Ambrose
Rowan	Bertie	Fintan	Kelvin	Ranulf	Anatole
Royce	Brodie	Forbes	Kester	Reggie	Andreas
Rufus	Callum	Freddy	Kieran	Reuben	Aneurin
Sacha	Calvin	Gareth	Kirwan	Rhodri	Anthony
Sammy	Carlos	Gaston	Laurie	Richie	Antoine
Sandy	Caspar	George	Lennie	Robbie	Antonio
Scott	Cathal	Gerald	Leslie	Robert	Auberon
Serge	Cedric	Gerard	Lester	Rodger	Auguste
Shane	Cennyd	Gideon	Lionel	Rodney	Balfour
Shaun	Cesare	Giulio	Lucian	Roland	Barnaby
Silas	Cieran	Gordon	Ludwig	Ronald	Barnard
Simon	Claude	Graeme	Luther	Ronnie	Bernard
Spike	Connor	Graham	Magnus	Rowley	Bertram
Steve	Conrad	Gregor	Marcel	Rudolf	Beverly
Sunil	Conway	Grevis	Marcus	Rupert	Brandon
Taffy	Curran	Gunter	Marius	Samson	Brendan
Tariq	Dafydd	Gussie	Marlon	Samuel	Brynmore
Teddy	Dallas	Gustav	Martin	Seamus	Calvert
Terry	Damian	Gwilym	Marvin	Selwyn	Cameron
Timmy	Damien	Hamish	Melvin	Seumas	Caradoc
Titus	Daniel	Harold	Merlin	Shamus	Carlyon
Tobin	Darren	Haroun	Mervyn	Sidney	Charles
Tommy	Daveth	Harris	Mickie	Simeon	Charlie
Ulric	Declan	Harvey	Miguel	Steven	Chester
Uriah	Delroy	Hassan	Milton	Stevie	Clayton
Vince	Dennis	Hayden	Morgan	St John	Clement
Wally	Denzil	Haydon	Morris	Stuart	Clinton
Wayne	Dermot	Hector	Morvyn	Sydney	Compton
Willy	Derren	Herbie	Mostyn	Teddie	Connell
Wolfe	Derric	Herman	Murray	Thomas	Crispin
Wyatt	Dickie	Hilary	Nathan	Tobias	Derrick
Wylie	Donald	Horace	Neddie	Trefor	Desmond
Wynne	Donnie	Howard	Nelson	Trevor	Diarmud
	Dougal	Hubert	Nevile	Tyrone	Diggory

Dominic
Donovan
Douglas
Dunstan
Edouard
Emanuel
Emilius
Ephraim
Etienne
Eustace
Everard
Feargal
FitzRoy
Francis
Frankie
Freddie
Georgie
Geraint
Gervais
Gervase
Gilbert
Gilmour
Godfrey
Goronwy
Grahame
Gregory
Gunther
Gustave
Gwillym
Herbert
Hermann
Hilaire
Horatio
Humphry
Hussain
Hussein
Ibrahim
Ishmael
Isidore
Jackson
Jacques
Jeffrey
Jocelyn
Johnnie
Kenrick
Kenneth
Krishna
Lachlan
Lambert

Leonard
Leopold
Lindsay
Lindsey
Ludovic
Malachi
Malcolm
Matthew
Maurice
Maxwell
Merrill
Michael
Montagu
Murdoch
Neville
Nicolas
Orlando
Orville
Osborne
Padraic
Patrick
Phillip
Phineas
Quentin
Quintin
Randall
Ranulph
Raphael
Raymond
Raymund
Richard
Rowland
Rudolph
Rudyard
Russell
Seymour
Sheldon
Sigmund
Solomon
Spencer
Spenser
Stanley
Stephen
Stewart
Terence
Timothy
Tristan
Umberto
Vaughan

Vincent
Wallace
Wilfred
Wilfrid
Wilhelm
William
Winston
Zachary
Zebedee

8
Abdullah
Adolphus
Alasdair
Alastair
Algernon
Alisdair
Alistair
Aloysius
Alphonse
Alphonso
Aristide
Augustus
Barnabas
Beaumont
Benedict
Benjamin
Bertrand
Beverley
Campbell
Clarence
Clements
Clifford
Courtney
Crawford
Cuthbert
Diarmaid
Dominick
Ebenezer
Emmanuel
Ethelred
François
Franklin
Frederic
Geoffrey
Giovanni
Giuseppe
Greville
Griffith

Gustavus
Hannibal
Harrison
Havelock
Horatius
Humphrey
Ignatius
Immanuel
Jeremiah
Jonathan
Jonathon
Kimberly
Kingsley
Lancelot
Laurence
Lawrence
Llewelyn
Llywelyn
Ludovick
Marshall
Matthias
Meredith
Mohammed
Montague
Mordecai
Mortimer
Nicholas
Perceval
Percival
Rafferty
Randolph
Randulph
Reginald
Roderick
Ruairidh
Ruaraidh
Sinclair
Stafford
Thaddeus
Theobald
Theodore
Trelawny
Tristram
Vladimir

9
Alejandro
Alexander
Alexandre

Alphonsus
Archibald
Aristotle
Augustine
Christian
Cornelius
Courtenay
Courteney
Ferdinand
Francisco
Frederick
Glanville
Jefferson
Kimberley
Launcelot
Llewellyn
Mackenzie
Marmaduke
Nathaniel
Peregrine
Rodríguez
Salvatore
Sebastian
Siegfried
Stanislas
Sylvester
Thaddaeus
Valentine
Zachariah

10 and over
Alessandro (10)
Barrington (10)
Bartholomew (11)
Caractacus (10)
Carmichael (10)
Christopher (11)
Constantine (11)
Maximilian (10)
Montgomery (10)
Sacheverel (10)
Stanislaus (10)
Theophilus (10)
Washington (10)
Willoughby (10)

Names for Girls

2	Pru	Gaby	Nora	Caryl	Irene	Nadia
Bo	Rae	Gail	Olga	Cathy	Janet	Nancy
Di	Ros	Gert	Oona	Celia	Janey	Naomi
Jo	Sal	Gill	Page	Chloe	Janie	Nelly
Mo	Sue	Gina	Rena	Chris	Jayne	Nerys
Vi	Uma	Gita	Rene	Cindy	Jenny	Netta
	Una	Gwen	Rita	Cissy	Jessy	Niamh
3	Val	Hope	Rosa	Clara	Josie	Nicky
Ada	Viv	Ilse	Rose	Clare	Joyce	Niobe
Amy	Win	Inez	Rosy	Coral	Julia	Norah
Ann	Zoë	Inge	Ruby	Daisy	Julie	Norma
Ava		Iona	Ruth	Debra	Karen	Olive
Bea	**4**	Iris	Sara	Delia	Kathy	Olwen
Bel	Abby	Irma	Sian	Della	Katie	Oprah
Bet	Aimi	Isla	Sita	Diana	Kelly	Pansy
Cat	Alba	Jane	Suky	Diane	Kensa	Patsy
Con	Alex	Jean	Susy	Dilys	Kerry	Patty
Deb	Ally	Jess	Tess	Dinah	Kitty	Paula
Dee	Alma	Jill	Tina	Dolly	Kylie	Pearl
Dot	Anna	Joan	Toni	Donna	Laila	Peggy
Ena	Anne	Joni	Vera	Doris	Laura	Penny
Eva	Avis	Jude	Vita	Edina	Leigh	Petra
Eve	Babs	Judy	Zara	Edith	Leila	Pilar
Fay	Beck	June	Zena	Elena	Letty	Pippa
Flo	Bess	Kate		Elise	Libby	Polly
Gay	Beth	Kath	**5**	Eliza	Lizzy	Poppy
Hat	Cara	Katy	Adela	Ellen	Lorna	Raven
Ida	Cath	Kaye	Adele	Ellie	Lotte	Rhoda
Ina	Cely	Lara	Aggie	Elsie	Lotty	Rhona
Ivy	Cher	Leah	Agnes	Emily	Lucia	Robin
Jan	Cleo	Lena	Ailsa	Erica	Lucie	Robyn
Jen	Cora	Lila	Alice	Ethel	Lydia	Rosie
Joy	Dana	Lily	Amber	Ettie	Lynda	Rowan
Kay	Dawn	Lisa	Anäis	Ethne	Mabel	Sadie
Kim	Dido	Liza	Angie	Faith	Madge	Sally
Kit	Dora	Lois	Anita	Fanny	Maeve	Sandy
Lee	Edie	Lola	Annie	Fiona	Magda	Sarah
Liz	Edna	Lucy	April	Fleur	Máire	Senga
Lou	Ella	Lulu	Avril	Flora	Màiri	Shona
Lyn	Elsa	Lynn	Aysha	Freda	Mandy	Sonia
Mae	Else	Mary	Barbi	Gemma	Margo	Stacy
Mai	Emma	Maud	Becky	Grace	Maria	Susan
May	Emmy	Maya	Bella	Greta	Marie	Susie
Meg	Enid	Mimi	Belle	Hazel	Maude	Sybil
Mel	Eryl	Moll	Beryl	Heidi	Mavis	Tammy
Mia	Esmé	Mona	Bessy	Helen	Megan	Tanya
Nan	Etta	Myra	Betsy	Helga	Merle	Terry
Pam	Etty	Nell	Betty	Henny	Mitzi	Tessa
Pat	Evie	Nena	Biddy	Hetty	Moira	Tilda
Peg	Faye	Nina	Bunty	Hilda	Molly	Thora
Pia	Fifi	Noel	Carla	Holly	Morag	Tracy
Pip	Fran	Nita	Carol	Honor	Moyra	Trudy

Miscellaneous

Valda
Venus
Vicki
Vicky
Viola
Wanda
Wendy
Zelda

6

Agatha
Aileen
Alexia
Alicia
Alison
Althea
Amanda
Amelia
Andrea
Angela
Anneka
Anthea
Astrid
Audrey
Aurora
Ayesha
Beatty
Bethan
Bertha
Bessie
Bianca
Billie
Blythe
Bobbie
Brenda
Bridie
Brigid
Bryony
Carmel
Carmen
Carole
Carrie
Cecile
Cecily
Charis
Cherie
Cherry
Cheryl
Cicely
Cissie
Claire
Connie
Cybill
Daphne

Davina
Debbie
Delyth
Denise
Dervla
Dionne
Dorcas
Doreen
Dottie
Dulcie
Eartha
Edwina
Eileen
Eithne
Elaine
Eloise
Elvira
Esther
Eunice
Evadne
Evelyn
Fallon
Fatima
Finola
Gaynor
Gertie
Gladys
Glenda
Glenys
Gloria
Glynis
Gracie
Gudrun
Hannah
Hattie
Hayley
Helena
Helene
Hester
Hilary
Honour
Ianthe
Imelda
Imogen
Ingrid
Isabel
Iseult
Ishbel
Isobel
Isolde
Jackie
Jamila
Janice
Jemima

Jessie
Joanna
Joanne
Joleen
Jordan
Judith
Juliet
Keisha
Kizzie
Kirsty
Laurel
Lauren
Lesley
Leslie
Lilian
Lizzie
Lolita
Lottie
Louisa
Louise
Maggie
Maisie
Marcis
Margot
Marian
Marion
Martha
Maxine
Millie
Minnie
Miriam
Muriel
Myrtle
Nadine
Nellie
Nessie
Nettie
Nicola
Nicole
Noreen
Olivia
Oonagh
Paloma
Pamela
Pattie
Petula
Phoebe
Rachel
Rhonda
Robina
Roisin
Rosina
Rowena
Roxana

Sabina
Sabine
Sandra
Saskia
Selina
Serena
Sharon
Sheena
Sheila
Sheryl
Simone
Sinéad
Sophia
Sophie
Sorcha
Stacey
Stella
Sylvia
Tamara
Tamsin
Teresa
Thelma
Tracey
Tricia
Trixie
Ulrica
Ursula
Verity
Violet
Vivian
Vivien
Vyvyen
Willow
Winnie
Winona
Wynona
Yvette
Yvonne

7

Abigail
Adeline
Allison
Annabel
Annette
Antonia
Anushka
Ariadne
Augusta
Babette
Barbara
Beatrix
Belinda
Bernice

Bethany
Beverly
Blanche
Blodwen
Bridget
Bronwen
Caitlin
Camilla
Candice
Carmela
Carolyn
Cecilia
Chantal
Charity
Chelsea
Clarice
Claudia
Colette
Colleen
Corinne
Cynthia
Darlene
Deborah
Deirdre
Demelza
Désirée
Dolores
Dorothy
Eleanor
Elspeth
Estelle
Eugenie
Eveline
Fenella
Florrie
Flossie
Frances
Frankie
Georgia
Gillian
Gwyneth
Harriet
Heather
Isadora
Isidora
Jacinta
Janette
Jasmine
Jeannie
Jessica
Jocasta
Jocelyn
Johanna
Josette

Juliana
Juanita
Justine
Kathryn
Katrina
Kerensa
Kirstie
Latisha
Lavinia
Leonora
Letitia
Lillian
Loretta
Lucille
Lucinda
Madonna
Mairead
Marilyn
Marjory
Marlene
Martina
Martina
Matilda
Maureen
Melanie
Melissa
Mildred
Miranda
Myfanwy
Nanette
Natalia
Natalie
Natasha
Nigella
Octavia
Pandora
Parvati
Pauline
Phyllis
Queenie
Rachael
Rebecca
Roberta
Rosalie
Rosetta
Roxanne
Sabrina
Shelagh
Shirley
Siobhán
Susanna
Susanne
Suzanne
Tabitha

Tatiana	Dorothea	Mercedes	**9**	Millicent
Theresa	Drusilla	Michaela	Alexandra	Philomena
Therèse	Eleanora	Michelle	Anastasia	Pierrette
Tiffany	Emmeline	Mireille	Annabelle	Priscilla
Valerie	Felicity	Morwenna	Bathsheba	Stephanie
Vanessa	Florence	Ottoline	Cassandra	Thomasina
Yolanda	Francine	Patience	Catherine	Valentine
Zenobia	Georgina	Patricia	Celestine	
	Germaine	Paulette	Charlotte	**10**
8	Gertrude	Penelope	Christina	Bernadette
Adelaide	Gervaise	Philippa	Christine	Blodeuwedd
Adrienne	Griselda	Primrose	Claudette	Christabel
Angelica	Hermione	Prudence	Constance	Christiana
Angharad	Hortense	Prunella	Elisabeth	Christobel
Arabella	Isabella	Rhiannon	Elizabeth	Clementine
Beatrice	Iseabail	Rosalind	Esmeralda	Ermyntrude
Berenice	Jeanette	Rosamond	Francesca	Evangeline
Beverley	Jennifer	Rosamund	Frederica	Fredericka
Caroline	Julianna	Roseanne	Gabrielle	Gwendolene
Cathleen	Juliette	Rosemary	Genevieve	Gwendoline
Catriona	Kathleen	Samantha	Georgiana	Hildegarde
Ceridwen	Kimberly	Sapphire	Geraldine	Jacqueline
Charlene	Laetitia	Tallulah	Guinevere	Margherita
Chrissie	Lakeishe	Theodora	Gwendolen	Marguerite
Clarissa	Lorraine	Tomasina	Henrietta	Petronella
Consuelo	Lucretia	Veronica	Josephine	Wilhelmina
Cordelia	Marcelle	Victoria	Katharine	
Cornelia	Margaret	Violetta	Katherine	
Courtney	Marianne	Virginia	Kimberley	
Danielle	Marjorie	Vivienne	Madeleine	
Dominique	Mathilda	Winifred	Margarita	

NATO Phonetic Alphabet

4	Papa	Bravo	Tango	Victor	Foxtrot
Echo	X-ray	Delta		Whisky	Uniform
Golf	Zulu	Hotel	**6**	Yankee	
Kilo		India	Juliet		**8**
Lima	**5**	Oscar	Quebec	**7**	November
Mike	Alpha	Romeo	Sierra	Charlie	

Palindromes

3	eke	non	tut	noon	minim	pull-up
aga	ere	nun	wow	otto	put-up	redder
aha	eve	oho		peep	radar	
ama	ewe	oxo	**4**	poop	refer	**7 and over**
ana	eye	pap	abba	sees	rotor	Able was I ere I
bab	gag	pep	anna	toot	sagas	saw Elba (19)
bib	gig	pip	boob		sexes	deified (7)
bob	gog	pop	deed	**5**	shahs	Malayalam (9)
bub	hah	pup	dood	alula	solos	reifier (7)
dad	huh	s.o.s.	ecce	civic	tenet	repaper (7)
did	mam	tat	keek	kayak		reviver (7)
dod	mum	tit	kook	level	**6**	rotator (7)
dud	nan	tot	ma'am	madam	marram	

Seven Sages

Bias (4)
Chilon (6)
Cleobonlos (10)

Periander (9)
Pittacus (8)

Solon (5)
Thales (6)